THE FOOD BOOK

THE FOOD BOOK

Written by Isabel Moore for the Food Foundation

Published by BBC Worldwide Ltd
80 Wood Lane
London W12 0TT

First published 2002

All contributor photographs were supplied by the Food Foundation, with the exception of that of Prue Leith p9, which has been reproduced by permission of Matthew Leighton Photography. Food photograhs on pages 6, 7, 8 and 9 were supplied by UK Channel Management Ltd.

ISBN 0 563 48848 4

Commissioning Editor: Vivien Bowler
Project Editor: Sarah Emsley
Copy-editor: Norma MacMillan
Design Manager: Sarah Ponder
Designer: Peter Coombs
Production Controller: Kenneth McKay

Set in Helvetica Neue
Printed and bound in Great Britain by The Bath Press
Cover printed by Belmont Press, Northampton

Notes on cross references: references to other entries that may provide wider or more general information, as well as components of entries that may benefit from further explanation and terms that may be unfamiliar to some readers, have been **emboldened** to direct readers to relevant additional information. Readers should use the index to locate the page numbers of these cross references.

Acknowledgements

The Publishers would like to thank Antonio Carluccio, Anton Edelmann, Matthew Fort, Sophie Grigson, Ken Hom, Prue Leith, Giorgio Locatelli, Orlando Murrin, Nick Nairn, Gary Rhodes, Jancis Robinson, Rick Stein and Antony Worrall Thompson for their contributions. Thanks also to Ian Jesnick and Bridget Bottomley from the Food Foundation, and Nick Thorogood, Gareth Williams and Jean Egbunike from UK Food Television for their help and support in the preparation and marketing of this book.

Contents

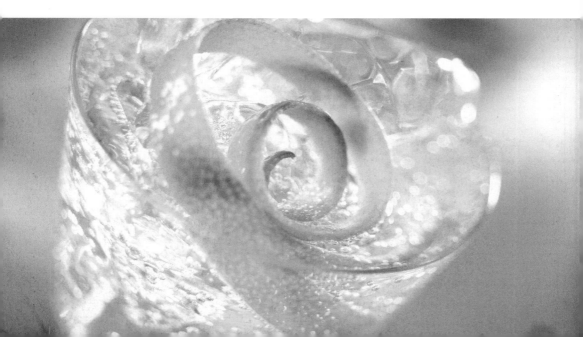

Foreword

Like many people, I learned to cook from the wisdom and ways of my mother, as indeed she had learned from her mother. The secrets of the kitchen were written down and treasured in a stained and greasy small, grey notebook with the single word 'Recipes' embossed on the front. No one can make rice pudding like my mother, nor roast potatoes with such a perfect crust and fluffy middle. Such simple gastronomic treats fuelled my passion for food. As a teenager, I started making cakes (cheap and much appreciated birthday presents), and by the time I was a media student I had learned the seductive power of a skilfully cooked candlelit meal.

Nearly all my working life has been spent in television (after a brief stint in the cookware department of Selfridges) and, when it comes to winning combinations, television and food mix perfectly. From the informative and educational era of Marguerite Patten, to the ground-breaking (and often oddly coloured) world of Fanny Cradock, right up to the style-setting programmes of Jamie Oliver and Nigella Lawson, people enjoy eating with their eyes – watching food on TV.

So I was delighted to be given the opportunity in 2001 to launch a food channel with one simple, clear vision – to celebrate fantastic food. UK Food is the UK's only dedicated food channel; it has a passion for food and prides itself on making mouthwatering television. Shortly after it was set up, we were asked to be involved with this book, which seemed entirely appropriate. To produce fantastic food you need to know how to choose the right ingredients, and hopefully within these pages you will find all the information you need – on everything from vegetables to rice, dairy products to herbs, and cakes to drinks.

I also have a personal interest in being connected with The Food Book, as I am both the channel editor of UK Food and a trustee of The Food Foundation. I love food and like to spend my weekends in the kitchen trying out new flavour combinations or following the recipes in my favourite cookbooks. I hope this book, like our UK Food channel, will not only entertain and inform you but also inspire you to do the same.

Nick Thorogood.

Channel Editor, UK Food Television

Introduction

Prue Leith

The Food Foundation trustees have seen this project grow over three years from a big, ambitious idea to a big, ambitious book. It answers a genuine need, as any cookery teacher, home cook, food journalist, food producer, retailer, researcher or chef will quickly discover.

Isabel Moore has done a painstaking and scholarly job. There have been food anthologies before, but few as comprehensive and up to date as this one. It is a reference work of real interest and authority, covering almost every aspect of food and drink, from almond to yoghurt. This might make it all sound rather worthy. In fact, it is a riveting read, and not just for the dedicated foodie. Many people are passionate about food, and of course this book is for them. But it is also, we hope, for the many more who are only mildly interested in the subject. You could hardly read an entry in The Food Book without becoming first intrigued, then absorbed and finally fascinated.

As befits a project with The Food Foundation's backing, introductions to each section have been contributed by top food writers and chefs. There's the talented Giorgio Locatelli on pasta, rice and grains, the Savoy's Anton Edelmann on dairy foods, the inimitable Rick Stein on fish, and the hugely knowledgeable Sophie Grigson on vegetables and pulses. Orlando Murrin is inspirational about fruit, while Gary Rhodes rhapsodises on the pleasures of baking and Antony Worrall Thompson lets his sweet tooth get the better of him on confectionery. We also have Antonio Carluccio on nuts, seeds and oils, Ken Hom on the role of herbs and spices in the kitchen and Nick Nairn on sauces and condiments. Jancis Robinson's well-known passion for wine is wisely tempered with advice to drink lots of water, while Matthew Fort's introduction to the section on meat unconsciously sums up the whole purpose of this book. He says, 'The more you know, the better you'll eat. The better you eat, the happier you'll be.'

Prue Leith O.B.E.

Grains, Rice & Pasta

Grains, rice and pasta are the essentials of good cooking. They are extremely versatile and provide the perfect starting point for a never-ending variety of dishes.

Coming from northern Italy, I grew up with pasta and rice as my staple diet and I am passionate about using them in my cooking. These and other grains make a tasty, nutritious, healthy and economical base for all sorts of different meals, all year round. They are easy to cook with and to store. You can use them to create any type of dish for any occasion, from a quick snack for one, to something to keep the kids happy, to a special meal for family or friends. Unlike vegetables, meat and fish, they become an integral part of the meal, helping to

...grains make a tasty, nutritious, healthy and economical base for all sorts of different meals...
Giorgio Locatelli

create a fusion of flavours, textures and aromas.

But there is more to these staples than their ability to act as a superb base for other foods. Rice is the most widely used ingredient in the world, and pasta has become increasingly popular throughout Europe and beyond. The more you use them, the more you will appreciate the variety and potential of pasta, rice and other grains.

The information in this section will help you understand all the different types of grains, rice and pasta. I hope this knowledge will encourage you to widen your repertoire and inspire you to get into the kitchen and start cooking.

barley

Barley (*Hordeum vulgare*) is a grass that probably originated in the Middle East or northern Africa but will grow almost anywhere providing the climate is cool to temperate; major producers are Russia, Germany and North America. It looks rather like wheat, grows to about 1m in height, and has a head or ear consisting of a central spike with rows of often bearded **grains** on either side – most modern varieties have three grains per side (six-rowed barley), although some are two-rowed. Only about 10 percent of the crop is used as food, with the remainder destined for animal fodder and for brewing and distilling.

To make barley fit for human consumption, first the inedible husk is removed, then the grain is processed into various forms, including hulled barley, a 'whole grain' that is basically only cleaned and dried before being sold; yellowish pot barley, which has some (but not all) of its **bran** layers removed; pearl barley, where both the bran layers and germ are discarded and the remaining grain is then polished into fine, medium or coarse creamy granules, or sometimes milled into a fine meal or **flour**; and barley flakes, made from grains that are steamed and rolled in the same way as **oats**. Some varieties are also germinated, dried and roasted to create malt, which is used in brewing and to flavour breads, cakes and breakfast cereals like cornflakes.

using it Hulled and pot barley need to be soaked for 3–4 hours before being cooked; pearl barley does not require soaking and can be added directly to dishes, provided they contain enough liquid. Basic cooking involves only liquid and the grains, in proportions of about four parts liquid to one part grain, plus seasoning. To cook, stir the soaked or unsoaked barley into the boiling liquid and bring back to the boil, then reduce the heat, cover and simmer for about 1 hour or until the grains are tender, stirring occasionally.

Hulled, pot and pearl barley can all be served in the same way as **rice** and **couscous**, or added in small quantities to stews and stuffings to bulk them out. The major cooking use now, however, is as a soup ingredient; pearl barley in particular is added to many vegetable and meat-based soups and is a classic ingredient in Scotch broth. Toasted barley flakes are also sometimes used to thicken soups and stews or in baking. Barley flour is only used occasionally in western cultures, mostly to make bread (since it is low in gluten, it is normally used in conjunction with wheat flour) – but in other parts of the world it's much more popular. In Tibet, for instance, barley is toasted and then ground into a flour known as *tsampa*, which is the basis of (among other things) a porridge made with tea and yak butter.

word origin Barley comes from the Old English *baerlic*, which is probably related to a similar Norse word for the grain. A 'barley mow' was once a stack of barley, although nowadays it's more likely to be the name of a pub. Barley water (see **fruit drinks**) and barley sugar are so named because originally their chief flavouring was pearl barley.

did you know?

• Barley was probably the first wild grain to be cultivated by humans – we know it was being used in what is now Syria about 10,000 years ago, and there are also early signs of it in Ethiopia. It was the staple grain of the ancient world, the basic ingredient in those two necessities of everyday life, bread and beer. By 2000BC, in Babylon, it seems that beer was considered the more important of the two since almost half the barley crop was being used for brewing. By Greek and Roman times, barley was beginning to lose out to wheat in breadmaking, although the Romans did still feed it to their gladiators, who were colloquially known as *hordearii* or barley-eaters.

bran

This is the outer edible part of **grains**, separate thin skins or layers that cover the endosperm (the starchy heart of the grain that is usually milled to make flour) and germ (the embryo of the new plant that's embedded in the endosperm). Most grains are processed to remove the bran layers and germ from the endosperm, but those described as 'wholegrains' will still have most, if not all, their bran intact.

using it The bran removed from the rest of the grain is sometimes sold as a separate product, but it's mostly available as part of something else – in wholegrains, wholemeal flours and instant breakfast cereals, for example. As a separate product, bran can be eaten raw or cooked: a spoonful or two of raw bran can be sprinkled over more or less anything to add crunch and fibre. It can also be used to bulk out and thicken stuffings, soups and stews or added to baked goods, especially muffins and biscuits.

word origin Bran comes from the Old French *bren*.

> ### did you know?
>
> • The bran contains much of a grain's fibre as well as important vitamins, minerals and oil. When eaten regularly, particularly in the form of wholegrains and wholegrain products, bran can help to prevent constipation and lower the risk of diseases such as diverticulitis and bowel cancer.

breakfast cereals

These are processed **grain** products that usually also include ingredients like dried fruit, nuts and (especially) sugar to flavour and sweeten them. They fall into two rough categories: instant cereals, which are prepared grains that only need to be mixed with milk to be eaten, for example **cornflakes** and **muesli**; and cooked cereals like **porridge**, which are cooked for varying lengths of time (never long) before being eaten.

Most cooked cereals are **oat**-based, but instant ones can be made from any grain – wheat, rice and maize are the most popular – and some are a mixture of two or more. Wheat-only cereals include shredded wheat, which is made by softening grains, then processing them between rollers until they form long strands which are formed into 'cakes' and baked dry. Most rice cereals are based on rice that's 'puffed', either by heating the grains to expand them in a very hot, pressurized cylinder (when the pressure is released, the rice puffs up and explodes out of it) or by puffing them in special ovens. Some maize-based cereals are puffed too, but the classic is still cornflakes.

using them As the name suggests, breakfast cereals are primarily served at the start of the day, usually with milk and sometimes with the addition of fresh fruit, nuts or other ingredients like honey or desiccated coconut, but most also make good snack foods. Some cereals are used occasionally in other ways too: sprinkled over desserts to provide extra crunch or added to baked goods.

> ### did you know?
>
> • Many instant cereals were invented as part of a religion-based, vegetarian health movement in the United States in the 19th century. The first packaged breakfast cereal was called 'granula' and had to be soaked overnight to make it digestible, unlike its modern successor, granola, which is like a toasted muesli. Other early cereals included 'granose', a wheat-based version of cornflakes produced by Dr John Harvey Kellogg, and shredded wheat, invented by Henry Perky, a Denver lawyer with chronic indigestion.
> • Alexander Anderson, a biochemist from Minnesota, is the father of modern puffed cereals. He hit on the prototype of the pressure cylinder that makes them puff by packing his grains (originally rice) into an old

cannon left over from the Spanish-American War and then exploding them from it. His puffed rice first saw the light of day as a popcorn-type snack at the 1904 St Louis World Fair, and in spectacular fashion: the new product was shot out of eight bronze cannons over the heads of its target audience.

buckwheat

Although thought of as a cereal **grain**, buckwheat is really an annual plant from the same family as rhubarb. It is native to central Asia, but now grows in temperate areas around the world; major producers include Russia, Poland, North America and Australia. Common buckwheat (*Fagopyrum esculentum*), as the name suggests, is the most widely cultivated species; others include perennial buckwheat (*Fagopyrum cymosum*) and tartary buckwheat (*Fagopyrum tartaricum*).

The buckwheat plant grows to nearly 1m in height, can produce two or three crops a year and is cultivated for its small, dark triangular seeds which are technically dry fruits. Like grain seeds, those of buckwheat are mostly made up of starch and so are treated in much the same way: crushed first to remove the outer hulls and then processed or milled, depending on the product being made. When the hulled seeds, or 'groats' (either whole or cracked), are roasted they are often called kasha. The groats are also milled into flour.

using it This is a minor 'grain' outside eastern Europe, so buckwheat products tend to be found only in larger supermarkets and healthfood shops. Kasha, which has a nutty, slightly bitter taste, makes a good substitute for **rice** or **bulghur wheat**. To cook kasha, simmer it in double its volume of liquid for 8–15 minutes or until tender. Buckwheat flour is used in Russia to make blinis, in Brittany to make a special type of crêpe (see **pancake**) and in Italy to create gnocchi. If mixed with wheat flour (buckwheat flour is gluten-free), it can be made into strong-tasting, yeasted breads. Commercially, buckwheat flour is used to make soba noodles.

word origin Buckwheat is so called because of the seeds' resemblance to those of the beech tree, from the Dutch *boecweite*, meaning 'beechwheat'.

did you know?

• Buckwheat was probably first cultivated in China and relatively late, around the 5th century AD. About 200 years later it had certainly spread to Japan and India, but doesn't seem to have reached Europe until the 15th century, travelling via the Middle East, if its French and Italian names are anything to go by (both translate as 'saracen corn').

bulghur wheat

Also called bulgur or burghul, this is whole grains of **wheat** that have been steamed, dried and crushed to remove some of their bran before being cracked into small golden-brown granules. Although a cracked wheat, bulghur wheat is not the same as the product sold as cracked wheat – the latter isn't steamed before being dried and crushed.

using it Bulghur wheat needs to be rehydrated before being eaten and there are two ways to do this. If using in a cold dish, simply cover with boiling water (three parts water to one part grains) and leave to soak for up to 1 hour; drain well. If serving hot, add to boiling water or stock (in the same proportions of grain to liquid) and simmer for 10–15 minutes.

Bulghur can be used instead of **rice** in pilaffs and similar dishes or as a substitute for **couscous**, and it makes a good accompaniment for spicy stews and curries. It can also be added to stuffings for poultry and vegetables. The classic Lebanese salad, tabbouleh, consists of bulghur wheat, tomato, onion, parsley, mint, oil and lemon juice.

word origin Bulghur is Turkish and means 'bruised grain'.

• This is a staple grain in parts of the Balkans and Middle East, where it has been eaten for thousands of years. In Syria, it's pounded to a paste with flavoured minced lamb, then used as a coating for cooked meat mixtures to make the national dish, kibbeh.

cornflakes

This is an instant **breakfast cereal** made from **maize**. To make cornflakes, the maize kernels are milled into grits, which are steamed in giant pressure cookers and then flavoured with malt extract; after this the malted grits are dried and tumble-roasted to bring out their flavour; finally, they are flattened into their familiar shape by heavy rollers and 'tempered' to even out the moisture content.

using them Most cornflakes are drenched in milk and eaten for breakfast, but the malty taste can be enjoyed in cooking too: crushed and sprinkled over soft vegetable and fish casseroles and potato-topped pies to add crunch; scattered over scoops of ice-cream (then served with hot chocolate or jam sauce); or used to add flavour to biscuits and sweets.

• Dr John Harvey Kellogg was a Seventh Day Adventist who ran a sanatorium in Battle Creek, Michigan during the latter part of the 19th century. Unfortunately, most of his patients found the meatless diet on offer there to be monotonous, so he and his wife were continually trying to come up with interesting ways to serve their staple grains and nuts. They launched their first flaked cereal in 1895; it was wheat-based and was made by cooking wheat berries and then flattening them until they were dry. By the early years of the 20th century the flakes were being made from maize, and cornflakes were born.
• While J H and his wife were inventing cereals,

J H's brother Will (W K) turned out to be a genius at selling them. He set up the Battle Creek Toasted Corn Flake Company in 1906 and, to distinguish it from all the other similar products being made by companies in Battle Creek at the time (there were 42 of them), all the Kellogg flakes came with W K's signature on the packet to confirm they were genuine. Today the company (renamed the Kellogg Company in 1922) is a global one, manufacturing in 19 countries around the world and with annual sales of around $9 billion.

cornflour

A finely ground starch obtained from **maize**, cornflour is made by softening whole maize kernels in a weak acid solution, then coarsely grinding them to get rid of the **bran** layers and germ (the embryo of the new plant). What remains is then 'washed' to remove any non-starchy elements before it is dried and ground further into a powder.

using it Cornflour's main use is as a thickening agent in both sweet and savoury cooking. It will lump easily if added directly to hot liquid, so is normally first blended to a paste with a little liquid ('slaked') before being stirred into the dish to be thickened. Cornflour is also a good coating for fish or meat to be stir-fried, and combined with liquid and flavourings it makes a light tempura batter for deep-fried food.

word origin Cornflour was invented in the United States. It acquired the first part of its name because the grain used to make it (maize) was called corn by early settlers – in British English 'corn' was once used to describe the major grain crop of an area, regardless of what the crop actually was. The 'flour' part is a variation of the word 'flower', because the meal ground from grain was considered to be the most valuable part of it, just as the flower is the most important part of a plant. In the US today, the term cornstarch is more commonly used.

• Most baking powder contains cornflour because without it the other ingredients – an acid such as cream of tartar and an alkali (nearly always bicarbonate of soda) – make an unstable mixture. If it came into contact with any liquid, even just moisture in the kitchen, it could spontaneously activate and release its carbon dioxide gas (which is what raises breads and cakes). The cornflour prevents this from happening.

COUSCOUS

This is a small granular pasta normally made from **wheat**, although occasional versions are made from **barley** or **millet**. The traditional way to make couscous grains is to sprinkle **semolina** and flour with cold salted water and to hand-roll in sweeping movements that bind the mixture into tiny flour-coated granules. Commercially, the same ingredients are processed mechanically into granules, which are then steamed and dried.

The name couscous is also given to a stew cooked with and served over the pasta. Most of the stews are meat-based, lamb or chicken being the most popular. Harissa, a fiery sauce made from red chillies, garlic, fresh coriander, caraway and salt, is sometimes stirred into the stew and nearly always accompanies it.

using it Couscous grains range in size from minute to (relatively speaking) reasonably large, and in type from the traditional to the quick-cooking; there are even boil-in-the-bag and exotically flavoured versions available now. Traditional couscous needs pre-soaking and is time-consuming to cook – usually being steamed over the stew it is to accompany – but most readily available versions are much quicker and simpler. Using roughly their volume of boiling water, they can either be soaked or simmered and need just 10–15 minutes before they are rehydrated.

Couscous can be used in the same way as **rice** or **bulghur wheat**, not just as an accompaniment, but also as the basis of main dishes like pilaff. There are a number of good ways to serve couscous: add mixed mushrooms cooked with a little chilli and crème fraîche just before serving hot; flavour with cinnamon sticks, cardamom pods and cumin seeds during cooking, then toss with raisins, slivered almonds and chopped pistachios before serving with barbecued meat or spicy sausage; or rehydrate the couscous and cool, then mix with prawns, chopped tomatoes, peppers and red onion in a spicy **vinaigrette**. In North Africa, it is occasionally sweetened and spiced with cinnamon, and served as a sweet dish with milk or yoghurt.

word origin Both grains and dish were introduced into the rest of Europe by the French about 400 years ago; the name is French, coming from the Arabic *kaskasa,* meaning 'to pound'.

• Couscous is both the staple grain and the national dish of several North African countries, especially Morocco, Tunisia and Algeria, and is also found in areas like Senegal. It dates back to at least the 13th century.

dumplings

In Europe and the English-speaking world, a dumpling is usually a ball of dough cooked by boiling or steaming (the type described here). Oriental dumplings are more akin to filled pasta (see **noodles**).

Dumplings can be savoury or sweet, large or small, yeast-risen or not, and while most are based on flour, vegetables such as potato and pumpkin, beef suet and stale bread are also used. Most are filled or flavoured – herbs, saffron and minced liver are popular additions to savoury mixtures, while fruit, honey and spices are often included in sweet ones. In England, central Europe and Germany, dumplings are usually golfball-sized, but the special Italian ones called gnocchi are daintier, rarely much larger than a thumbnail. Gnocchi may be based on a mixture of **semolina**, potato and wheat flours, or made from flours such as wheat and **buckwheat** alone, and traditional flavourings include mashed pumpkin, spinach, ricotta and herbs.

using them Dumplings can be cooked directly in a meat or vegetable stew or soup, by adding them for the last 20 minutes or so of the cooking time. Or they can be simmered separately in liquid (stock for savoury dumplings; fruit juice, sugar syrup or light custard for sweet ones). Gnocchi are boiled in the same way as filled **pasta**, and served in the same way too, usually with a simple sauce (see **pasta sauces**). Sweet fruit dumplings are also sometimes baked rather than boiled (see **apple**).

Savoury dumplings were traditionally a thrifty cook's way of using up leftover bread or dough, and they helped main-course soups and meat dishes to go further. They are still served in this way rather than as a dish in their own right. Sweet dumplings normally have an accompanying sauce such as custard, cream or fruit coulis.

word origin Dumpling dates back to the 17th century (although the dish itself is much older) and comes from the word *dump*, meaning the 'consistency of dough'.

did you know?

- In England, dumplings are particularly associated with the county of Norfolk, and Mrs Beeton's basic recipe (raised bread dough shaped into small 'eggs' and cooked in boiling water) is called Norfolk dumplings. She serves them with gravy as a savoury dish and with jam, treacle or a mixture of butter and sugar for a sweet one.

flour

This is a finely ground meal obtained by milling **grains**. Any grain can be used and all the major ones are, but in the western world 'flour' without further qualification normally means **wheat** flour. Starchy plants like potato, buckwheat, chickpea and chestnut are all also ground into flours.

Flours are defined by whether they contain **bran** and germ or not, by their colour and by the type of grains milled to make them. Wholemeal, for instance, is a brown wheat flour that contains the whole of the grain (wholemeal-type flours milled from other grains are called wholegrain). Brown or wheatmeal flour usually contains about 85 percent of the grain, but can also be a blend of wholemeal and white flours, or a refined flour with some bran and germ added back in. White flour is milled only from the starchy endosperm of the grain, with none of the bran and germ. Whether wholemeal, brown or white, flour can be plain (without raising agents) or self-raising (with raising agents added to it), or it can be strong (sometimes labelled 'bread' flour) if it is milled from a hard variety of wheat that is high in gluten. Granary, which is made from a mixture of wheatmeal flour and malted wheatflakes, and Hovis, white wheat flour mixed with cooked wheatgerm, are both proprietary brands of flour.

There are two main stages in modern roller milling, the process that creates refined white flour: the first stage is to separate the whole wheat grains into their major parts (the bran, germ and endosperm) and then to discard the first two; the second stage is to process the endosperm (which contains all the grain's starch) to make a flour. Stage one is accomplished by cleaning the grains and moistening them before passing them through a series of grooved 'break' rollers that sheer off the bran layers and extract the germ; the bran and germ are then mechanically sifted out from the endosperm.

At the end of stage one the endosperm is processed into a coarse meal, which is called **semolina**. In stage two, the semolina is ground between multiple giant steel 'reduction' rollers until it becomes a fine meal, almost a powder. Since the bran and germ are the most nutritious parts of the wheat grain and these are removed, it is required by law to have synthetic vitamins and minerals added back into the resulting white flour.

Traditionally white flour was 'aged' for a month or so before being used, partly to improve its baking qualities (the gluten content becomes stronger as it 'settles' and thus makes more elastic doughs) and partly because oxygen in the air whitened its colour slightly (it's yellowish when it emerges from milling). Modern refined white flour is often treated with ascorbic acid (vitamin C) to obtain the same effects.

Most white flours are now milled using the factory process described above, but some flours are produced in a more traditional way, by being ground between millstones. These stoneground flours are made by cleaning whole grains, pulverizing them between two giant circular, grooved stones and then 'bolting' or sieving them through mesh until they become a fine meal. Stoneground flours are usually coarser and heavier than factory-milled flours.

using it Baking is the major use for flour, and different types are recommended for different forms of baking. Strong flour is preferred for yeast baking since it contains more gluten-forming proteins than soft-wheat flours – it is gluten that makes yeast doughs elastic and helps breads to rise. Plain and self-raising flours, which contain more starch and less gluten than strong flour, are better for cakes and biscuits, where the aim is for a light crumbly texture, and for most pastries. Breads, cakes and pastry can be made from wholemeal or brown flour alone, but they will be quite heavy in texture. For this reason, a mixture of wholemeal and white flours is often used.

Flour isn't only used in baking, Ii's a major ingredient in other dishes too, such as dumplings, pasta and batters for pancakes, Yorkshire pudding and so on. It is also used to thicken sauces, gravies and stews, and as a coating for fish fillets, chicken joints and meats that are to be fried.

word origin From medieval times on, the name was *flower*, because the meal ground from grain was considered to be the most valuable part of it, just as the flower is the most important part of a plant; the spelling was amended to flour a century or so ago.

The central role that flour has always played in daily life means that elements of the flourmaking process have become part of our language. For example, 'separating the wheat from the chaff', literally meaning to separate the usable part of the grain from the rest, is now used metaphorically to mean distinguishing between the parts of value and those with none. 'It's all grist to his mill', meaning he will use everything available to him, has its origins in flour processing too – grist is the name given to the blend of grains poured into the millstones to be ground. Millstones themselves are heavy objects, so to have 'a millstone round your neck' is obviously to be hugely burdened.

did you know?

• The first flours were probably made by crushing grains in something similar to a crude mortar with a pestle, and the results must have been dusty and coarse, more like grits than the fine flour we use today. Improvements came about gradually, until the invention of the 'quern' around 500BC. This was an ingenious arrangement of two grooved round stones set one on top of the other; the lower stone was stationary while the upper one was attached to a pivot that allowed it to rotate. The grain was poured into a hole in the centre of the stacked stones and handles attached to the pivot were turned so that the upper stone could revolve and grind the grain. Later refinements included the 'hour-glass' mill, which could be much larger. In this the lower stone was still stationary, but on top of it was a large hour-glass shape made up of an upper hollow stone funnel for the grain and a lower enclosed cone that pulverized the grain as the stone turned.

• It was women, slaves, animals and other unfortunates who operated early millstones but there was a limit to what they could push, so gradually other means of propulsion were harnessed. The Romans were the first to use water power, where large wheels. at first horizontal in the water then vertical, were geared up to the stones. By the 11th century, windmills appeared. Modern stone mills are much more sophisticated than anything that has gone before, of course, but they are recognizably descended from these earlier efforts.

• Wholemeal and wholegrain flours are now more highly prized than white ones but until recently the opposite was true, and the whiter and finer the flour, the more desirable and expensive it was. In medieval times, *pandemain* or *manchet*, made from wheat flour that had been sifted two or three times, was the best bread and was eaten only by the rich and powerful. Lesser folk had to make do with *maslin*, baked from a mixture of wheat and rye flours, while the poor were more likely to have dark, heavy barley or oat bread, or mixed barley and rye.

grains

These are the edible part of various cultivated grasses of the *Gramineae* family of plants, such as **barley**, **maize**, **millet**, **oats**, **rice**, **rye**, **wheat** and sorghum. The word grain is also used to describe the processed seeds of other plants like **buckwheat** and **wild rice**, which are used in the same way.

Grains (also called berries, groats or kernels, depending on the individual plant) are technically fruits, the reproductive part of the plant. They form in heads called 'ears' (if they are arranged in rows around a central stalk) or in 'panicles' (if they are small branchlets sprouting from the main stalk that end in 'spikelets', which are the small flower clusters that normally develop into grains). Some, like barley, oats and rice, are covered by an inedible husk that has to be removed

before the grain can be processed, but otherwise all of them have essentially the same structure. On the outside are several thin layers or skins (the **bran**), which store oils, minerals, most of the B vitamins and 20 percent of the proteins (all these nutrients are lost when the grains are refined). Inside are the endosperm, the largest part of the grain, which contains mostly carbohydrate in the form of starch and varying amounts of protein; and the germ or embryo of the new plant, which is located at the base of the grain and provides protein, some B vitamins, vitamin E and essential oil.

All grains can be grown conventionally or organically, and to get from plant to plate, they are processed in various ways. Some are simply cleaned, dried and sold as 'wholegrains', but most are separated into their major parts. The bran and germ are hived off to be used separately (sometimes as animal fodder), and the endosperm is milled into flour, refined into pearls and polished (mostly barley and rice), or flaked, rolled or puffed to make breakfast cereals.

using them Grains are a staple part of home cooking. Whole or flaked grains need to be rehydrated either by soaking or cooking, and quantities and proportions vary depending on the grain (see individual entries for specific information). All refined grains will keep well in a cool dry place for up to a year. Those that contain the germ (wholegrain or wholemeal products and some breakfast cereals, for instance) are more perishable because the germ includes oil that can become rancid; these will keep for about six months.

Grains are also used in virtually every area of commercial food and drink production, most notably to make pasta, bread, breakfast cereals, drinks like beer, whisky and vodka and, indirectly, meat and dairy products, since they provide the basis of most animal feed.

word origin Plants that produce grains are called cereal plants, from the Latin *cerealis* which is derived from Ceres, the Roman goddess of agricullture. The word grain itself is Middle English, borrowed from Old French and ultimately derived from the Latin *granum,* meaning 'seed'.

did you know?

- Most cereal plants started out as wild grasses or weeds, and two – barley and wheat – were among the first plants to be cultivated by humans to ensure a regular crop. This simple act revolutionized how people lived: before this they were mostly nomadic hunter-gatherers, but now they had to stay put to tend the crop and be there when the grains matured. This led to settled communities of people, the first villages. Even the first attempts at writing and arithmetic can be traced back to cereal production – the earliest known examples of both are records of grain transactions.

- Although some grains are now grown all round the world, most continents (and parts of continents) have their traditional dominant staples – wheat, rye and oats in Europe (the last two primarily in northern areas), maize and wheat in the Americas, rice in Asia, and millet and sorghum in Africa. Their importance to the local diet varies from continent to continent too: grains still make up about 80 percent of the calories consumed in China and not much less than that in the Indian subcontinent and parts of Africa, but they account for much less than this in western societies. However, we eat them indirectly by consuming meat and dairy products.

- Grains are not 'complete' foods in terms of protein, being deficient in one or more essential amino acids, mainly lysine, which is usually obtained from animal foods and pulses. To get the most from grains in a diet where meat is rarely or never eaten, therefore, they need to be combined with pulses to maintain a healthy balance. This is something the peoples of Mexico (beans and maize) and the Indian subcontinent (lentils and rice) have been doing by instinct for thousands of years.

- Quinoa, which is a pseudo-grain (botanically the fruit of an annual herb related to spinach and beetroot), has been grown in Andean South America since ancient Incan times. It is still an important food in South America, where it is often milled into flour for tortillas and other baked goods. In the United Kingdom it is mainly sold as processed golden grains, which need to be rinsed until the water runs clear before cooking, and then simmered in roughly double their volume of liquid for about 15 minutes. Quinoa can be used in the same way as couscous, bulghur wheat or rice.

lasagne

Lasagne is both broad, flat, rectangular sheets of pasta and the baked dish that incorporates them. The sheets are made in the same way as any other **pasta**, usually from durum wheat **semolina** and water or eggs, and are available plain or flavoured, normally *verdi* (with the addition of spinach, which colours the pasta green). There is also a wholemeal version.

The dish lasagne is made by layering the pasta sheets in an ovenproof container with a cooked meat or vegetable filling and (usually, but not always) a sauce plus cheeses such as grated Parmesan, and then baking until a golden crust forms on top. For a classic Italian lasagne the filling would probably be a meat *ragu* like Bolognese and the sauce a type of **béchamel**, but there are many variations. Other meat- or fish-based fillings include cooked meatballs or chopped browned spicy sausages, prawns or cooked smoked fish. Vegetable fillings can range from sliced tomatoes or browned aubergine slices to blanched spinach blended with ricotta and pine nuts. Tomato sauce could be used instead of béchamel, and shredded or sliced mozzarella substituted for grated Parmesan or used in addition to it.

using it Fresh lasagne sheets need to be part-cooked before being used. Drop them, a few sheets at a time, into plenty of boiling salted water and cook for 10–60 seconds or until softened, then plunge into cold water to stop them from cooking further. Semi-fresh and dried lasagne will have cooking instructions on the packet; some dried sheets can be used without pre-cooking.

word origin   Lasagne is Italian and plural, the singular being *lasagna*, which is how the dish is often spelled in the United States. The modern Italian word comes from the Latin *lasanum*, which meant either a cooking or chamber pot (perhaps an example of the ancient Roman sense of humour – it could have been cooked in the former and expelled into the latter).

did you know?

• Ancient Romans added cooked dough strips called *lagani* to meat and bean dishes and these may have been an ancestor of modern lasagne. Recognizable versions of both the modern dish and pasta sheets were definitely around by medieval times, and not only in Italy: a 15th-century English cookery manuscript features a recipe for *Losyns*, thin sheets of dough that should 'drye harde and seethe in broth' before being layered with cheese and baked until done.

maize

Also known as corn, maize (*Zea mays*) is an annual grass that originated in Central America but is now grown primarily in the United States, Brazil, China and India. The plant can reach epic proportions in cereal plant terms – more than 3m in height – and gives a whole new meaning to the words 'fast-growing' since under ideal conditions it can increase by 11cm in 24 hours. The solid stalk supports a roughly 50cm-long ear, whose long modified leaves (known as shucks) protect roughly 1000 individual **grains** (called kernels) that are arranged in clinging rows around a central 'cob'.

The five major varieties of maize produce kernels ranging in colour from white through the most usual yellow, to red, blue, black and even variegated. Dent corn has large, starchy grains with a dimple (or dent) in the crown, made when the endosperm of the grain collapses slightly during drying. Mostly used as animal feed or for industrial products, dent corn accounts for nearly 75 percent of world production and is the type grown most widely throughout the 'cornbelt' states of the midwestern United States. Flint corn has small kernels with a hard outer skin and is now grown mostly in South America and southern Europe. Flour corn, the type most often used for human food, has large, soft starchy kernels that grind easily; some varieties produce blue-coloured grains which are made into novelty tortillas or corn chips. The small hard-skinned kernels of **popcorn** have just the right proportion of moisture to starch so that they will 'pop' when heated. **Sweetcorn**, which has tender yellow or white kernels, contains a gene that delays the conversion of its plant sugar into starch (thus keeping it sweet).

Sweetcorn is eaten fresh as a vegetable, but the other varieties are processed into various forms. For hominy, maize kernels are first boiled with lime, ash or other alkaloid solutions to loosen the hulls and partly cook them, then the hulls are washed away and the germ usually removed before what remains is cleaned and dried or canned. Dried hominy may be coarsely ground to make grits or finely milled to make *masa harina*, the flour used for corn tortillas. Maize kernels are also dry-milled, usually by being tempered and degermed, to make cornmeal or polenta; finely milled to make cornflour; or steamed, dried, flavoured and rolled to make cornflakes.

using it   Hominy can be added to stews, casseroles and soups to bulk them out, or cooked to serve as a side dish. Hominy grits can be cooked like cornmeal or **polenta** by simmering in boiling water or milk until very thick, then serving as it is or cooled, cut into squares and fried. Cornmeal is widely used all over North America in stuffings, toppings for pies, fritters and, especially, breads and muffins.

These direct uses are only the start, however. About three-quarters of the maize crop is used for other things, almost every thing, in fact: the food industry makes it into syrup, cooking oil and margarine, and adds it to baby food, ketchup, pickles and almost anything else that needs thickening; the drinks industry uses it to create alcohol (whisky and the South American beer made from chewed maize kernels called *chicha*) and to colour soft drinks; agriculture feeds it more or less non-stop to animals (which means there's maize in most dairy foods and meats); other businesses use it to make soap, toothpaste, industrial solvents, adhesives, and a coating for cardboard and other paper and plastics; and it is even used in folk art to create dollies and pipes.

word origin Maize is derived from the Spanish *maiz*, courtesy of Christopher Columbus who, in the West Indies in 1492, probably became the first European to come across it; in the local Haitian language the grain was *mahiz*, meaning 'stuff of life'.

The word 'corn' literally means 'grain or seed' and has the same origin as 'grain': the Indo-European *grnom*, a 'worn-down particle', which turned up in a more recognizable form in the Latin *granum*. In the British English sense, however, corn is simply the major grain crop of an area (this is the way it's used in the Bible), which is why early colonists in the New World called maize – the major native crop they found – corn. Indian corn was an alternative name given to it around the same time, although this is now used mostly to describe decorative variegated types of maize.

• Maize was part of the staple diet of all the great native cultures of the Americas, and archaeological remains found in what is now Mexico show it was being grown there around 5500 years ago. The mystery isn't so much when it was first farmed as how: most other grains were initially cultivated from wild grasses that self-seeded, but maize has always needed human help to reproduce. One possible close

relative has appeared during the last 30 years, however, a plant called *teosinte* (*Zea mexicana*), which still grows in the wild in Mexico and which can self-seed. It's possible that this plant crossbred with another as yet unknown one in antiquity to provide the plant we now know.

• The growing, planting and reaping of maize occupied a central part in most people's lives, so early American cultures worshipped it: the Pueblo peoples performed special corn dances every August to appease the corn gods; the Mayas built time around the different stages of its cultivation; and the Aztecs topped them all by using human sacrifice to keep the gods happy and the grain growing.

• Once the Spaniards introduced maize into Europe, the Venetians (who controlled trade with the Middle East and Asia) quickly spread it eastwards, and it had reached China by 1516. Magellan took maize seeds with him on his round-the-world voyage in 1519 and planted them as he went, and the Portuguese took it to Africa where it was used to buy slaves. It proved so easy and quick to grow there that 'mealie' (from the Portuguese *milho grosso*) is still a staple grain of the central and southern parts of the continent.

• All grains are deficient in the essential amino acid lysine, but maize contains less than the others; unlike them, it also lacks tryptophan and has niacin in an unusable form. Too much reliance on maize alone, therefore, can lead to deficiency diseases like pellagra, which is still common in parts of Africa. Early American cultures compensated for these deficits by boiling maize with a little lime or ash (which released the niacin) before using it to make flour, and by eating the resulting breads and porridges with beans, tomatoes and fish, all of which supply the missing amino acids and vitamins.

millet

This fast-growing grass flourishes mainly in hotter, dry regions around the world. Major producers include India, Nigeria and China, where millet is grown primarily as a food crop and, to a lesser extent, parts of the United States and central Europe, where it's now mostly cultivated as fodder and birdseed. The plant can grow to about 2m in height, although most varieties are about half this size. Each one is topped with a large panicle or seedhead containing many tiny edible **grains** that are processed to be sold as granules, flakes or flour.

There are four main species: common millet (*Panicum miliaceum*), which originated in the Middle East and is now cultivated mostly in northern China and cooler regions of India; finger millet (*Eleusine coracana*), which comes from eastern Africa, and is still grown there and in tropical parts of India; pearl or cattail millet (*Pennisetum typhoideum*), native to Africa and cultivated in hot dry regions of Africa and India; and foxtail millet (*Setaria italica*), which is grown in central and southern Europe, the United States and Japan.

using it Millet granules and flakes need to be rehydrated and cooked before use. To do this, add up to double their volume of boiling salted water and simmer for about 40 minutes, when they should have absorbed the water. Fluff up the grains, stir through some oil or butter if liked, and serve.

In parts of Asia and Africa, millet is a staple grain, made into porridges and bread (Indian roti bread is traditionally made from finger millet), but in Europe and the rest of the western world it is used only occasionally in cooking and to brew beer. It can make a change from commoner grains, however; for example substituted for **rice**, **bulghur wheat** or – especially – **couscous** in recipes. The strong, slightly bitter taste means it would also make a good accompaniment for spicy curries, and it can be used to bulk out soups (especially those containing sweetish vegetables like parsnips and carrots) and meat pies. Millet flour has no gluten-forming proteins, so it is sometimes used to make breads and biscuits suitable for coeliacs (people with gluten intolerance).

word origin Millet is French and comes from the Latin *milium*, the word for the grain.

did you know?

• Millet was being cultivated in both Africa and China at least 5000 years ago and was one of the most important grains in antiquity, grown by most of the early civilizations. Two species (common and foxtail millet) were among the five 'sacred' staple grains of ancient China. It reached Europe about 2000BC.

muesli

Muesli is a high-fibre instant **breakfast cereal** made from **grains**, dried fruit and nuts which is usually mixed with cold milk before eating. Ingredients vary from manufacturer to manufacturer, but all include dried grain flakes (a mixture of barley, oats and wheat is one popular combination but some have more exotic ingredients like popped buckwheat and amaranth), dried fruits such as sultanas, raisins, banana slices and dates, nuts like brazils and hazels, and sometimes seeds as well. Most commercial muesli is artificially sweetened although some 'natural' ones aren't.

using it Muesli can be made at home by blending together toasted or untoasted grain flakes with a selection of the other ingredients noted above, in any proportion that takes your fancy. And a basic recipe can be varied more or less indefinitely: use only one type of grain; add or substitute other dried fruits or nuts like prunes and dried apricots, pistachios or walnuts; and soften with fruit juice or purée and crème fraîche instead of milk. Chopped fresh fruit like apples, bananas or berries also tastes good stirred in just before serving.

A basic muesli mixture, commercial or home-made, can also be used in other ways: beat it with softened butter and use as a crumble topping, particularly for sweet fruit crumbles; soften it slightly with cream or crème fraîche, then stir through vanilla ice-cream or yoghurt as a dessert; sprinkle over gingerbread or similar teabreads as a topping; or use to flavour biscuits.

word origin The name is Swiss-German and means a 'mixture of pulpy food'.

• Muesli was the brainchild of Max Bircher-Benner, who ran a health clinic in Zurich towards the end of the 19th century (about the time that John Harvey Kellogg was running *his* in Battle Creek, Michigan; see **cornflakes**). Bircher-Benner advocated a vegetarian, mostly raw, diet based on vegetables, grains, fruit and nuts, and his first muesli was made from raw oats that had been soaked overnight in milk, grated fresh apple, lemon juice and honey. Commercial muesli was introduced into Britain during the 1920s, although it didn't become widely available until about 40 years after that and only left the fanatical fringe of breakfast health foods 10 years or so ago.

noodles

In western Europe and the English-speaking world, noodle is the collective name given to oriental pasta (the type described here). In parts of eastern and central Europe, particularly Germany, however, it is also used to describe a long ribbonlike **pasta**.

Unlike Italian pasta, oriental noodles come in only a few different shapes and sizes, but they are made from many different types of **flour**. Rice and wheat flours are the most commonly used, but buckwheat, bean (soya, chickpea and mung) and even potato flours are also popular. Chinese versions include wheat noodles, often enriched with egg, which come in varying widths and usually in compacted nests; wonton wrappers, round or square sheets made from wheat flour and usually enriched with egg, and the similar but thinner spring roll wrappers; rice noodles, made from rice flour and water, which can be very fine vermicelli or wider and flat, when they are called rice sticks; cellophane noodles, also called transparent or bean thread noodles, which are translucent vermicelli made from mung bean flour; and crispy noodles, short, flat translucent yellow ribbons made from potato

flour. Japanese noodles include soba, thin, light brown strings made from buckwheat flour; udon, almost translucent, thickish wheat noodles; and somen, thin vermicelli made from wheat flour dough that's coated in vegetable oil before being extruded into strands. There are also noodles from South-east Asia, including paper-thin rice paper wrappers made from rice flour.

using them Dried Chinese noodles are usually soaked or boiled before being stir-fried or deep-fried; occasionally they are steamed. A classic way to serve noodles in China and South-east Asia is in soup and for this they are not soaked first, but are stirred straight into the rest of the ingredients and cooked for a few minutes. Noodles are also frequently added to stir-fries in China (chow and other 'mein' dishes; *chow mein* means fried wheat noodles in Chinese), which is how we often eat them in western countries too. Wonton, spring roll and rice paper wrappers, available fresh or frozen from Chinese stores, can be stuffed in the same way as **ravioli** and simmered or steamed, although since they are usually larger than ravioli they need to be cooked for a little longer. Stuffed steamed wonton 'dumplings' are an integral part of Chinese dim sum, the array of little dishes served in tea houses and restaurants all day.

To cook dried Japanese noodles, add to boiling water and cook, stirring occasionally, until tender: somen will cook quickly, in about 3–5 minutes; soba needs 5–7 minutes and udon 10–12 minutes.

In Japan, noodles are served as light snack meals called *kake* or *mori* – the former is noodles with soup, the latter noodles with a dipping sauce. Nearly every type is served in special broths called *kakejiru*, which can range from the simple (dashi or stock, mirin and soy sauce plus a few flavourings like ginger) to the elaborate (all of the above and more, with a selection of tempura-type deep-fried seafood on top). Dipping sauces are always served cold regardless of whether the noodles are hot or cold. They are made from roughly the same ingredients as a basic broth; soba and somen noodles are often served chilled in this way, and usually with a selection of flavourings, vegetables, **tofu** or seaweed such as nori added.

word origin Noodle comes from the German *nudeln,* meaning pasta.

did you know?

• Pasta may have originated in China and it was certainly being manufactured commercially there by the time of the Han Dynasty in AD100. Early noodles were made from rice in the south, where it was primarily grown, and from millet in the north, although later barley and especially wheat superseded millet.
• The Chinese took noodles with them wherever they went in Asia and in particular to Thailand, Indonesia, Vietnam and the Philippines, all of which adopted and adapted them to their own tastes. They even introduced them to Japan: dumpling-like ancestors of the oldest Japanese noodle, udon, first appeared there in the 8th century, and the name is an adaptation of the original Japanese word for noodles, *konton,* which in turn was a local corruption of *wonton.* There are some noodles in the Indian subcontinent too (*sev,* which are made from chickpea or *besan* flour, are a popular snack food), but they are much less common there than in other parts of Asia.

oats

According to Dr Johnson who enlisted them in his war of attrition against the Scots, oats are 'A grain, which in England is generally given to horses but in Scotland supports the people'. Horticulturally, however, *Avena sativa* is an annual grass that flourishes in cool, wet northern climates and grows to about 1.25m in height; each stalk is topped by a large loose panicle that produces a series of small **grains** that range in colour from white through red to grey or even black. In human food terms, oats are a minor grain: about 95 percent of the world crop is used as animal fodder and the remainder is enjoyed mostly in small pockets of northern European popularity, such as Scotland, Wales and Scandinavia. Leading producers include Russia (the largest), the United States, Poland and Germany.

The outer inedible husks stick closely to the grains or groats, so oats are cleaned, dried and then husked after harvesting. Only after this are the groats processed for sale. To make pinhead oatmeal, the husked groats are fed through perforated cylinders and then mechanically cut; for rolled oats, pinheads are steamed and then rolled out to varying degrees of flatness (the flatter they are, the more quickly they will cook); and coarse or fine oatmeal and flour are obtained by milling the whole groats. Instant rolled oats are cooked and dried before being rolled very thinly. Oat bran is occasionally separated out from the rest of the kernel and sold separately.

using them Most processed oats need to be rehydrated and cooked before being eaten, normally by being simmered in liquid for 20–30 minutes; manufacturers usually give guidelines on the packet.

Pinhead oats are only used occasionally now, probably because they require more cooking than other types. Most rolled oat products are sold as hot breakfast cereals or mixed with other grains to produce instant ones like muesli. Porridge is the classic oats-only hot breakfast dish, made by cooking the oats in boiling water or milk; brose is the *Braveheart* version of this, the oats being stirred into boiling water and then eaten immediately, uncooked.

Rolled oats can also be used in other ways: blend with softened butter and flavourings to provide a topping for savoury or sweet crumble mixtures or pies; add to stuffings, stews, pâtés and soups to bulk them out (they are used commercially in this way in sausage, black pudding and haggis); and coat slices of meat or fish such as herring to be pan-fried. Oats are occasionally used to make desserts too, the classic one being cranachan or crowdie, a mixture of toasted oat flakes, stiffly whipped double cream, honey and a spoonful or two of Drambuie or malt whisky, topped with fresh raspberries; atholl brose is more or less the same thing with more whisky and no raspberries.

Oatmeal is widely used in baking, most importantly to make oatcakes, flat savoury biscuits that are perfect with cheese. It is also used in several sweet biscuits and muffins. Oats have negligible amounts of gluten-forming proteins (which help yeast doughs to rise), so although oat flour is sometimes used to make bread, it is normally mixed with wheat flour which contains plenty of gluten.

word origin Oat comes from the Old English *ate*, a word that seems to have come from nowhere to describe the grain. To 'sow wild oats', meaning to enjoy committing (many) youthful excesses, *did* come from somewhere: the principle that it was a terrible idea to sow 'bad' (wild oats) when 'good' (other cultivated grains) were available.

did you know?

• Oats started out as a barley and wheatfield weed, and weren't deliberately cultivated until around 2000 years ago. They were not hugely popular with the Romans, who tended to think of them as a sort of diseased wheat and, although they used oats as animal fodder and for medicinal purposes, they considered anyone who actually ate them to be barbarian. Despite this, or perhaps because of it, they introduced oat cultivation into Britain. Oats were eaten all over the British Isles as a sort of gruel or porridge until around the 17th century, when their popularity began to fade in England.

pasta

This is a flour and water dough particularly associated with Italy which is cut, stamped or extruded into various shapes and then dried before cooking, normally in boiling water. Pasta can be made from any type of **flour** (some is produced from **maize**, for example), but over 95 percent of commercial pasta is made from durum wheat **semolina**, the milled flour of the hardest-grained, least starchy species of **wheat**. The high gluten-forming protein content of durum wheat semolina enables dough made from it to retain its shape and to dry out efficiently without cracking. Most pasta is plain, produced from just white flour and water, but some is made from wholemeal flour and some is enriched by substituting egg for water. Other types are coloured by adding spinach juice (for green pasta), beetroot or tomato juice (red) or squid ink (black), or they may be flavoured with herbs, pepper, chilli, dried mushroom and so on.

Nearly all pasta is now made commercially by machine, even the initial mixing and kneading of the ingredients to make an elastic dough. What happens after this depends on the type of pasta it will become: the dough can be forced through perforated slits (ribbon pasta), extruded through tiny or larger round perforations (spaghetti) or through special perforations containing steel pins (macaroni), rolled out into thin sheets (lasagne), filled and cut into individual stuffed shapes (ravioli), or stamped or moulded into different shapes (such as conchiglie). The resulting pasta is normally then dried by being exposed to carefully regulated, hot humid air for varying amounts of time; some better-quality pasta can be dried for up to a day and a half before it reaches the correct texture.

Pasta is only rarely made at home these days and then usually with a pasta-making machine. Since durum wheat semolina is only rarely obtainable for home cooks, most home-made pasta is made with strong plain flour plus eggs – ordinary wheat flour is starchier than durum wheat semolina, and the addition of eggs helps to prevent the dough from breaking as it's rolled and shaped. To make machine pasta, the dough is first divided into small portions. With the rollers at their widest setting, each portion is passed through the machine five or six times. When the sheet of dough feels elastic, the rollers are gradually narrowed, with the dough being fed through until it reaches the appropriate degree of thinness. For stuffed pasta, the dough is now ready to be cut and shaped; for flat ribbon pasta, it should be dried out for 5 minutes before being fed through the cutting blades.

There are hundreds of different pasta shapes, including cannelloni (large hollow tubes), conchiglie (shells), farfalle (supposedly like butterflies, but in reality looking like bows), fettuccine (the Roman version of Bolognese tagliatelle – narrow flat ribbons), fusilli (corkscrews), linguine (like thin spaghetti), macaroni (the original classic hollow pasta tubes that range in size from tiny to large), pappardelle (long flat ribbons similar to fettuccine but broader), penne (small, straight macaroni-like pasta cut on the diagonal), rigatoni (ridged small macaronis), trofie (small squiggles made mostly in the northern part of Italy around Genoa), vermicelli (the thinnest stranded pasta of all) and ziti (largish smooth macaroni tubes that originated in southern Italy). See also **lasagne**, **ravioli** and **spaghetti**.

using it Apart from the different varieties available, there are also three types of pasta on offer: fresh (usually home-made), commercial fresh (actually semi-fresh) and dried. Fresh pasta is very perishable and needs to be eaten on the day it is made, although it freezes well; only good Italian delicatessens and the food halls of one or two large department stores offer properly fresh commercially made pasta in this the United Kingdom. Semi-fresh is the pre-packed pasta sold as fresh in supermarkets and some delicatessens – it keeps for about two weeks; nearly all the major types of pasta, like penne, lasagne, spaghetti, tagliatelle and fusilli, are now available in this form. Dried pasta is sold everywhere and keeps for a year or so in a cool dry place.

In Italy, thin vermicelli and very small pasta shapes are added to soups (called *pasta in brodo*), to cook in the liquid with the other ingredients. Most pasta, however, is cooked on its own in lots of boiling salted water, the time depending on the size, shape and type of pasta. Pasta that is to be incorporated in a baked dish (*pasta al forno* in Italy) is also usually cooked first in boiling water. Most manufacturers give cooking instructions on the packet, although to be sure the pasta is *al dente* (firm to the bite, the ideal texture), you should start testing a minute or so before the suggested time is up. Boiled pasta is always served (dressed) with at least a few other ingredients which are added after it is cooked; it should be served as soon as possible after being drained, since it will continue to cook in its own heat, and shapes will start to stick together if left for any length of time. Dressing ingredients can range from the basic to the elaborate (see **pasta sauces**).

In Italy pasta is served as a separate course (*pasta asciutta*) preceding a meat or fish dish, but elsewhere it is normally eaten in larger quantities as a main course.

word origin Pasta is Italian, meaning 'dough' or 'paste', and is relatively recent even there. In medieval times the word *macaroni* was often used generally to mean any kind of pasta rather than referring to specific tubular types, and this was the word used in England too when pasta dishes were first recorded here; macaroni comes from a Greek word meaning 'barley food'. Pasta as a general English description only dates back half a century, when different types of pasta began to be widely available.

As a general rule, any pasta with 'ini' at the end of it (macheroncini, for instance) means a narrower or smaller version of the main type (macheroni or macaroni in this case).

Those with 'oni' at the end (conchiglioni, for example) will be larger than the standard type, and some small tubes like penne can be rigati (ridged) or lisci (smooth). Otherwise, most modern pastas are named for some physical aspect or other, usually their shape, occasionally their colour. Hence lumache (which is shaped like a snail shell), orecchiette (which means little ears), paglia e fieno (straw and hay, a reference to the yellow and green colours of the two pastas that form it) and penne (quill). It's perhaps less easy, however, to see where linguine (little tongues) and the delicious chewy strozzapreti (priest stranglers) came from!

did you know?

• It's a fairly safe bet that the *idea* of pasta has been around almost since unleavened bread was invented, since it's made from more or less the same dough. Not surprisingly, one school of thought (an Italian one) believes pasta originated in Italy, and there is an Etruscan wall painting dating from around the 4th century BC that, with a bit of imagination and goodwill, could show pasta-making equipment, including a surprisingly modern-looking ridged cutting wheel that might have been used to shape the dough. If it is dough-making equipment, however, there's no indication of how it was cooked and eaten. Classical Romans did have pasta-like strips of dough called *lagani*, which they may have inherited from the Greeks, but again we have no record of how they were cooked.
• Meanwhile, there was pasta in other parts of the world too, most notably in the Far East where the Chinese were manufacturing noodles commercially by about AD100. Less than a millennium later they were common in parts of the Middle East, and we know these ones were boiled in much the same way as modern pasta. From the Middle East to eastern Italy, and particularly Venice, is not very far, so pasta, or the modern idea of it, may well have been introduced to Italy in this way. Another possibility is that the Arabs brought it to Europe as they conquered and settled from the 8th century on – Sicily is the site of the first recorded sighting of pasta in Europe and was part of the Arab empire at one time. However and wherever it

started, the one thing historians are now agreed on is that pasta was not brought back to Italy by Marco Polo when he returned from China in 1295; dried (i.e. commercially made) pasta was quite common in various parts of the country at least 20–30 years before this time.

pasta sauces

Pasta sauces have much the same function as salad dressings: they are there to add extra taste and texture to the main ingredient, in this case **pasta**.

There are hundreds of different combinations used to dress pasta, some of them so basic they hardly merit the description sauce. The simplest are instant mixtures of a few ingredients that are stirred through the pasta in quantities and proportions to suit personal taste. Popular ones include olive oil and crushed garlic warmed just until the garlic colours; chopped chillies softened in olive oil, then tossed with the pasta and some grated Parmesan; cubed mozzarella or gorgonzola cheese heated with a little milk until beginning to melt – grated Parmesan and chopped walnuts could be added too; chopped tomatoes warmed in olive oil until they begin to lose their shape, then mixed with chopped black olives and, optionally, shredded mozzarella; double cream and butter heated until smooth and thick, then added to the pasta with grated Parmesan (this is the classic Alfredo sauce for fettuccine); and pesto sauce, a rich mixture of pounded fresh basil, garlic, pine nuts, grated Parmesan and olive oil.

Other sauces require only slightly more preparation and cooking, and proportions are again mostly down to personal taste. These include carbonara (cooked pancetta or bacon pieces tossed through hot pasta with a mixture of uncooked beaten eggs and grated cheese – the pasta 'cooks' the eggs lightly); amatriciana (chopped pancetta or bacon and onion cooked in olive oil with fresh tomatoes and, sometimes, a little chilli, served with grated pecorino cheese); clam or mussel (small fresh clams or mussels steamed open with a little white wine, herbs and crushed garlic); mushroom (cultivated and wild mushrooms cooked in butter or olive oil, with or without crème fraîche and nutmeg); and lemon (thick cream, butter and lemon zest and juice warmed until smooth).

Some classic sauces usually take longer to cook, but most are straightforward and could be prepared in quantity so that part could be frozen to be used as an instant sauce later. These include fresh tomato; roasted vegetable (chopped vegetables sprinkled with olive oil and cooked in the oven until soft, then tossed with a little more oil plus balsamic vinegar and chopped herbs); puttanesca (tomatoes, garlic, black olives, capers, anchovies and, usually, chilli cooked together until smooth); spicy sausage or meatballs (simmered in tomato sauce); and ragu, the Italian word for a rich meat sauce, the most famous of which is Bolognese (minced beef, chicken livers and vegetables simmered slowly with white wine and tomatoes).

using them Most home-made pasta sauces are ridiculously easy to make, but if you prefer you can use one that is ready-made. Most of these taste better if they are 'doctored' before being served – the addition of fresh herbs, a few drops of wine, a crushed garlic clove, tomato purée, cream, shredded or cubed cheese, mushrooms or peas can cheer them up no end. Grated cheese (freshly grated Parmigiano-Reggiano for preference) is served with nearly all pasta dishes except those with fish-based sauces.

The quantity of sauce to pasta is to some degree personal preference, but there should be a good balance between the two and the pasta should be coated rather than drowned: more is often less in this context. The type of pasta to serve with individual sauces is also mostly a matter of personal preference, but there are some general guidelines: smooth long pastas like spaghetti and linguine go well with nearly everything but are particularly good with tomato and creamy smooth sauces, while stubbier and hollow pastas like penne, macaroni and conchiglie go well with those with 'bits' in them, like meat and chunky fish sauces. Filled pastas are often served with a simple sauce too (see **ravioli**).

Some pasta like macaroni can be served baked as well as boiled, and others like lasagne are rarely cooked in any other way. And some of the sauces described above, particularly longer-cooking ones like tomato and ragu, are often cooked with these pastas too, as is **béchamel sauce** with or without cheese, the latter being the standard accompaniment for baked macaroni in Britain.

word origin Some individual sauces have interesting backgrounds and names. There really was an Alfredo, for instance, and he invented his delicious cholesterol nightmare in his restaurant in Rome. Amatriciana is named after the small town it comes from, Amatrice in Lazio near Rome. *Puttanesca* means 'sluttish', and was given to this particular sauce allegedly because it was a favourite work-break snack for Roman prostitutes; the hotter they liked it, the livelier they were reputed to be.

polenta

This is both an Italian cornmeal ground from **maize** kernels and the porridge-like dish made from it. Polenta meal can vary from coarse to fine and is normally yellow, although some types are white or creamy-coloured. Cooked in the traditional way, polenta meal is simmered and stirred for 30–40 minutes until thick – and the cook is exhausted. It can be served hot at this point (when it is often called 'wet' polenta); or it can be left to cool and set in a flat dish, then later cut into small rectangles or slices and fried quickly on both sides until a light crust is formed, or grilled until the surfaces are mottled.

using it Most polenta meal on sale in the United Kingdom is the quick-cook type, which cuts out a lot of the effort that used to go into cooking it; one or two manufacturers go even further, offering thick rolls of pre-cooked polenta that need only to be sliced to the required size and fried or grilled.

Wet polenta on its own can be stodgy, so other ingredients are usually added to improve the taste. Flavourings can be simple, such as generous quantities of butter and/or freshly grated Parmesan and lots of black pepper; or more elaborate, like freshly made tomato sauce, cooked mixed mushrooms with crème fraîche or mascarpone, or chopped chicken livers cooked with sliced onions and red peppers then stirred through with grated Parmesan. Fried or grilled polenta slices can be sprinkled with grated Parmesan or topped with slices of mozzarella and then heated until the cheese begins to melt, or used like **lasagne** in a layered baked dish.

Wet polenta makes a good accompaniment for meat, especially stews, spicy sausages and small roasted birds like quail or partridge. Fried or grilled polenta slices are a traditional Venetian accompaniment to cuttlefish, fried fish and calf's liver, but could also be served with steaks or chops.

word origin Polenta is Italian and comes from the Latin *polenta,* meaning 'hulled or crushed grain', particularly crushed barley.

did you know?

• Polenta is a speciality of northern Italy, and in particular Friuli, the province behind Udine and Venice that stretches towards the Yugoslavian border, where maize is still grown. Polenta has been made from maize since shortly after it first became available during the late 15th and early 16th centuries (courtesy of the Spaniards who brought it back from Central America and the Venetians who traded it around Europe). Before this it was ground from chestnuts, and something similar may have been produced from barley in antiquity, if the origin of the name is anything to go by.

popcorn

This is a special type of **maize** (*Zea mays* var. *everta*), with **grains** or kernels that 'pop' when exposed to high heat. In appearance, fresh popcorn kernels look similar to those of sweetcorn, and are grown and harvested in the same way. Unpopped kernels can vary in colour (although most are yellow), but all popped ones are either white or yellow.

Each popcorn kernel is made up of a small central core of moisture inside a starchy endosperm (the largest part of the grain), which in turn is enclosed by a horny outer skin. It pops because of its unique proportion of moisture to starch and its harder-than-usual outer casing. When a kernel is exposed to high heat, the moisture at its centre vaporizes and expands, and in doing so puts so much pressure on the starch surrounding it that it puffs up and eventually explodes (with an audible pop) through the hard skin, allowing the vapour to escape.

using it To make popcorn on a conventional cooker, heat butter or oil until very hot in a popcorn maker or heavy pan, then spread the kernels over the bottom, cover the pan tightly and shake it slightly from time to time – when the pops are about two seconds apart the popcorn is ready. Alternatively, you can cook special popcorn pouches in a microwave.

Some popcorn comes already flavoured, but both sweet and savoury flavours can be added at home. Toss freshly made popcorn with herbs and melted butter, with melted butter and salt, with grated cheese or with chilli; or with maple syrup, honey or desiccated coconut for a sweet finish.

word origin In the United States, where modern popcorn comes from, the original name described the action – popped corn – but had been shortened to the current word by the mid-19th century.

• Popcorn is all-American in more ways than one might think: 5000-year-old popcorn remains have been found in what is now New Mexico in the United States; a Zapotec funeral urn shows that it was known in Central America around 1700 years ago; and tombs in modern-day Peru in South America have yielded 1000-year-old grains of popcorn so well preserved they would probably still pop.

• Modern popcorn dates back about 200 years and only really took off commercially in 19th-century America with the invention of a machine that could pop large quantities at any one time. It never looked back, even during the Depression in the 1920s, and was the snack of choice when cinemas began to be popular; popcorn went into a decline when film attendance did during the 1950s, but later became a favourite with television viewers too. Each American is now thought to get through about 68 quarts of the stuff a year (that's about 65 litres).

porridge

Porridge can be a general description (for a mush made from **grains** or pulses), or a specific one (in the United Kingdom, it is a mush of ground or rolled **oats** particularly associated with Scotland). The general type of porridge is found all around the world: in Tibet, it is *tsampa*, made from toasted barley flour, salted tea and yak butter; in parts of Africa it is made from millet or mealie, a kind of **maize** meal; and closer to home in Italy, it is maize-based and known as **polenta**. British porridge is made from fine, medium or coarse oatmeal, or sometimes from rolled oats. The classic Scottish method is to stir the meal into already boiling salted water (about 500ml water will cook roughly 75g oatmeal), then to simmer for 20–30 minutes, stirring occasionally. It's eaten hot, sometimes with extra salt and a little hot milk.

using it Most supermarket porridges are quick-cooking so the cooking time is reduced to just a few minutes, and they are usually stirred into just-boiling milk or a mixture of milk and single cream or water. Sugar or golden syrup is added to taste rather than the traditional salt.

Porridge is normally eaten as a warming **breakfast cereal**, but it can also be served as a substantial pudding: cook with single or whipping cream and plenty of brown sugar, then refrigerate until cold. Before serving top with fresh raspberries and stiffly whipped cream, or stir through some sultanas, slivered almonds and crème fraîche.

word origin Porridge goes back to the 16th century when it first emerged as a corruption of *pottage*, the all-purpose boiled dish typically made from grains or pulses that nearly everyone ate most of the time. Pottage in its turn comes from the Old French *potage*, which meant more or less anything cooked in a pot.

• Cooking grains or pulses in boiling water to soften them and make them easier to digest is nearly as old as civilization, and pottages have been a staple food all around the world since earliest times. The Egyptians and Greeks normally made theirs from barley, classical Roman peasants had millet pottages that were sometimes mixed with pulses like lentils, while early Americans north and south made theirs from maize. Frumenty, the name for a refined porridge of wheat usually simmered in flavoured milk, was even eaten by kings, if a scene in the Bayeux Tapestry is anything to go by. Many pottages were made from dried peas, ancestors of today's pease pudding.

• In Britain during medieval times pottages could be made from any grain or vegetable; everyone ate them, although the rich made theirs from expensive cereals like wheat and served them as an accompaniment to game, while the poor made theirs from cheaper barley or dried legumes and ate them as a complete meal. Up until a few hundred years ago, pottages could be eaten for breakfast, lunch *and* dinner, sometimes on the same day.

ravioli

The most famous type of filled **pasta**, ravioli is shaped like a small square envelope. Stuffings are usually pre-cooked or made from ingredients that need little or no cooking, and range from traditional ones such as ricotta and cooked spinach or chopped chicken livers and Bolognese sauce, to newer combinations like goat's cheese and smoked salmon or roasted peppers and chilli.

Although ravioli is the most famous stuffed pasta, there are many others, including agnolotti, small crescent-shaped packages that usually contain meat; cappelletti, which are shaped like small hats (the literal meaning of the word); tortellini, small ring shapes that originated in Bologna; and the confusingly similar in sound tortelloni, which are larger than tortellini and square in shape.

using it Filled pastas are sold fresh or semi-fresh and are cooked like other pastas, in plenty of boiling salted water. The cooking time is 3–8 minutes – they're usually ready when they float to the surface. They should be drained and served as quickly as possible, usually with grated cheese and a simple sauce of some kind: olive oil and chopped chilli or garlic, for instance, a knob or two of butter or a tomato sauce.

word origin Ravioli is thought to have originated in Genoa. The name comes from *rabiole*, a local dialect word meaning 'bits and pieces', probably an indication that it evolved as a good way of using up leftovers.

did you know?

• Ravioli is one of the oldest pastas we know about and there are records of several versions of it in both Italy and England during the 14th century. In Italy, one of the original fillings consisted of mashed pork, eggs, grated cheese and herbs, while an English recipe for '*rauioles*' was meatless, a mixture of grated cheese, butter, egg and saffron.

rice

Rice (*Oryza sativa*) is a grass that probably began life in central Asia. Although originally a dry-land plant, it has now developed into a mostly semi-aquatic one. It flourishes best in moist tropical climates (about 90 percent of the world crop is grown in the Asian monsoon belt), but also does well in warm temperate ones like that of California. Rice, in fact, is grown in over a hundred countries around the world and is the staple grain of more than half the world's population. Chief producers tend to be major users like China, India, Bangladesh, Indonesia and Thailand, although significant amounts are also grown in Italy, Australia and parts of Africa; the United States, which grows less than 2 percent of world supply, nevertheless accounts for over 60 percent of exported rice. Despite its name, **wild rice** is only distantly related to rice.

Rice plants can grow to almost 5m high although the average is half that; each plant has a main stalk and some subsidiary ones called 'tillers', which are topped by a panicle of flowers or 'spikelets' that produce creamy, red, blue or purple **grains**. Some rice is still grown on dry land, but most is produced in water: in naturally rain-fed fields; in areas prone to seasonal flooding (like deltas); and, especially, in paddies, which are terraced fields enclosed by special dykes and created in such a way that they can be flooded and drained as the plants grow. It takes 3–6 months to produce rice, but paddies can support at least two crops a year and don't need to be 'rested' before being resown. Production in much of the world is manual – planted, back-breakingly tended and then harvested by hand and dried, before being threshed (the process that removes the grains from the stalks) – but in western countries, especially the United States, everything that can be is mechanized: the fields are prepared by laser beams, seeds are mostly planted by aircraft, and special combine harvesters built to move through mud gather and thresh the ripened plant.

Processing rice is time-consuming and complicated, even when done mechanically. The first stage is to remove the husk to get at the edible part of the grain; after this, some rice is simply dried and sold as brown or 'wholegrain' rice. Most rice, however, is milled by being 'rasped' mechanically to remove most of the **bran** layers and the germ, then often 'polished' by a wirebrush machine to remove the aleurone layer as well (this thin skin between the bran layers and endosperm contains fat, which can limit the keeping qualities of the rice). The processing removes vitamins and minerals from the rice, so some are therefore added back as a coating on the grain.

Although there are nearly 8000 varieties of rice that have been used at some point as food, nowadays there are only three main commercial categories, divided according to shape: long-grain, which has thin grains that are about four times longer than they are wide, and which remains dry and separate when cooked; medium-grain, which has slightly fatter grains that are twice as long as they are wide, is tender when cooked, but becomes sticky as it cools; and short-grain, which has grains that are almost round in shape, and stays moist and sometimes sticky when cooked.

The way rice is processed also identifies it. For brown rice only the outer husk is removed, which means it retains all the nutritious bran and germ. White rice is husked and then milled (as above) to remove either the germ and outer layers of bran only (unpolished rice) or all of the germ and bran including the aleurone layer (polished rice), the whitest type. Parboiled rice is cleaned, soaked and steamed, then dried before being milled. This treatment enables some of the vitamins and minerals from the bran layers to be transferred into the endosperm so that they aren't lost during milling, and also helps the aleurone layer to stick to the endosperm and remain in the finished rice. As a result, parboiled rice is more nutritious than other white rices. Pre-cooked rice is husked and milled, then cooked before being heat-dried. White rice is also occasionally processed into flakes (in much the same way as **oats**), steamed in vacuums so that it 'puffs' (see **breakfast cereals**), or milled into a fine flour.

Some rice is identified by where it comes from (or came from). Basmati, for instance, is the collective name for a group of very slim, long-grain rices only grown in northern India and Pakistan. From South-east Asia comes slightly sticky, long-grain fragrant Thai or jasmine rice. Another long-grain rice is Carolina, so-called because it was originally grown in South Carolina, although it now more often comes from Texas, California or Arkansas. Camargue is a red-brown long-grain rice grown in the Camargue region of south-western France, which is similar to brown rice in flavour. See also **risotto**.

using it There is an enormous number of different rices on offer, ranging from conventional to boil-in-the-bag or ready-flavoured. All of them need to be cooked before being eaten and nearly all manufacturers give detailed instructions on the packet. Some rices, in particular basmati, need to be rinsed in several changes of water before cooking, to remove some of the starch so that the grains don't stick together when they are cooked. Most, however, don't require this and, in fact, it would wash away the nutrient coating on refined rices. Manufacturers' instructions should say whether rinsing is recommended or not.

Savoury rice is often used as an accompaniment to oriental meals, either plain or with simple flavourings like egg strips or slivered nuts and spices; it can also be added to stuffings, pie fillings and croquettes, and form the basis of main-course salads.

In a swathe of countries stretching from southern Europe to the Indian subcontinent, rice isn't just served as an accompaniment to or as an ingredient in other food, but as the main event, the basis of some of the great classic dishes of the world. The original inspiration was probably Middle Eastern pilaff, a dish of perfectly separate rice grains cooked with elaborate flavourings such as meat, vegetables and spices. Further east, this became Persian *pulow*, which then travelled with the Moghuls to India, where it became the basis of pulao – rice delicately seasoned with fruit and nuts and often served with creamy kormas. Pilaff went west too, and in particular to the southern part of Spain where it eventually reappeared as paella, in which ingredients such as chicken, chorizo sausage, seafood, tomatoes and various vegetables are cooked in olive oil with rice, saffron and pimento (see **paprika**), traditionally in an open shallow pan called a *paellera*.

Any short-grain rice can be made into a pudding, not just what is sold as pudding rice. One way to make a good rice pudding is to simmer the rice in milk (normally roughly double its volume) for about 15 minutes, then combine it with sugar, spices, butter and eggs before baking for about 45 minutes until thick. A rice pudding can be served hot or cold, on its own or with stewed fruit. For a fancier finish, stir in some slivered almonds, crystallized fruits and spices, then pour into a wet mould and chill until cold and firm. It should be turned out for serving.

Rice is used extensively by the food industry to make baby food, breakfast cereals, oriental noodles and rice vinegar, among other things. It's also the basis for several alcoholic drinks including sake, a type of beer made from rice that has been fermented twice and is part of Japanese religion as well as of Japanese life (Shinto has several sake gods and sacred sake is used in its rituals in much the same way as wine is during Christian ones.)

word origin Rice comes from the Greek *oruza*, which may in its turn have come from early Sanskrit. 'Paddy', the irrigated field where most rice is grown, comes from Malay and means 'rice grown in deep water'. Basmati, still grown in the foothills of the Himalayas as it has been for thousands of years, means 'fragrant'.

did you know?

• The first evidence of rice cultivation was in southern China and northern Thailand about 5500 years ago, although indications are that it probably spread there from the Indian subcontinent. Wherever it started, cultivation spread gradually westwards through Persia and from there to the rest of the Middle East and northern Africa. Rice was known to both the Greeks and the Romans, but they don't seem to have eaten it. It was probably the Arabs who really introduced rice into Europe as they conquered and settled from the 8th century AD on – they grew it in southern Spain and possibly in Sicily too.

• Rice was established in North America only in the late 1680s (when a ship captain from Madagascar is supposed to have given some 'golde seed rice' to a planter in South Carolina). Cultivation was concentrated in large plantations tended by slaves from western Africa, who were often skilled in planting and growing rice because a red-grained minor species (*Oryza glaberrima*) originated there. The native species is still grown in parts of Africa, but Asian *sativa* types, imported by slave traders and settlers and preferred by them, are now more widespread.

• Throwing rice at newlyweds is common in western cultures, but it's actually eastern in origin – rice was a symbol of fertility for Hindus and was scattered over a happy pair on their wedding day as a blessing on their marriage and a hope that it would be fruitful.

risotto

This is both a type of nutty short-grain **rice** grown in Italy and the dish made from it. The different varieties of risotto rice are graded by size into *superfino* (large), *fino* (medium) and *semifino* (short and stubby) and include Arborio, the commonest type and a superfino; Carnaroli, considered to produce the best risotto and also a superfino; and Vialone nano, a semifino.

A classic risotto dish can be soupy and creamy or drier and stickier, depending on preference and which part of Italy the recipe comes from (a soupy risotto is the Venetian style, the drier version is preferred in Lombardy). Risotto is made by stirring the uncooked rice into melted butter or oil and cooking it for a minute or so before adding the liquid, a bit at a time, stirring very frequently. As each batch of liquid is absorbed, more is added – the rice should never be drowned by the liquid. Quantities of liquid to rice vary slightly from type to type and from manufacturer to manufacturer, as do timings, but as a general guide about a litre of liquid will be needed for 250g rice, and it will take 20–25 minutes to cook. The best way to judge if the risotto is ready is to extricate a few grains and taste them – they should be *al dente*, firm to the bite like pasta. The risotto is finished by what is called *mantecare* in Italy: stirring in butter and (usually) grated Parmesan to taste.

using it Risotto rice always has flavourings added to it during cooking and more may be stirred in at the end. These may include chopped vegetables (particularly onion and garlic), herbs, saffron threads (the soaking water should be added too), cubed mozzarella or gorgonzola, rehydrated dried porcini and their liquid and/or sliced fresh mushrooms, chopped and skinned fresh tomatoes, and finely chopped seafood, poultry or meat – in fact, almost anything and everything, at least in theory.

Classic risottos include alla milanese (onion, saffron and chopped beef marrow); nero (chopped cuttlefish or squid and their ink); alla marinara (various seafood, usually prawns, clams or mussels in their shell and chopped squid); and primavera (literally spring vegetables, which could include some or all of onion, broccoli, courgettes and perhaps artichoke hearts). The most famous of all is risi e bisi, rice cooked with bacon or pancetta, chopped onion and small green peas, which in medieval times was ceremoniously eaten by the Doge on April 25 each year to mark the special day of Venice's patron saint, St Mark (which, rather handily, also marked the start of the fresh pea season).

word origin Risotto is Italian and means 'little rice'.

did you know?

• There were small pockets of rice production in the Po Valley in northern Italy from about the 10th century on, but it wasn't until six centuries after this that various irrigation projects began to make large-scale cultivation feasible. Nowadays Italy is a major European producer, and in some northern parts of the country risotto is as popular as pasta for the *I primi*, the course that precedes the meat or fish in formal Italian meals.

rye

Rye (*Secale cereale*) is an annual grass that flourishes in harsh northern climates and poor soil. It is grown mostly in northern central Europe (Russia and the Ukraine together produce about half the world crop) and in North America, particularly Canada and the Dakotas. Only about 10 percent of the crop ends up as food, most of the rest being mixed with other grains as animal fodder or bedding, or made into **whisky** (particularly in Canada) and **vodka** (particularly in eastern Europe). Rye is also used by various industries as packing materials and to make paper and mats.

Rye can reach almost 2m in height and its

stalks are crowned with thin bearded ears or spikes made up of two rows of long, narrow darkish **grains**. The plant can sometimes be the unfortunate host to ergot, a poison caused by *Claviceps purpurea,* a horny blackish fungus that can form and grow in place of seeds on several types of cereal plant, but prefers rye. Not surprisingly then, rye grains are always thoroughly cleaned and dried to remove any ergot before the husks are removed and the grains processed for sale. Some is made into cracked rye or grits by being cracked into several pieces, or rolled into flakes like **oats**, but normally rye grains are milled into flour, which can be light or dark.

using it Like all dried grains, rye grits and flakes need to be rehydrated and cooked before being eaten. They taste better if they are lightly toasted in a little butter before being simmered in roughly double their volume of water for 15–20 minutes. Use them in the same ways as **rice** or **millet**, or as a breakfast cereal.

Rye flour is popular for breadmaking because, like wheat, it contains the gluten-forming proteins that make raised bread light and airy. In this case, however, they are weaker, so loaves made from rye flour alone (like German pumpernickel) tend to be dense, heavy and quite flat. The most usual combination is to make 'rye' bread from a mixture of rye and wheat flours so that the finished product will have a texture similar to wheat-only bread. Many rye breads are leavened with a sourdough starter (see **bread**) rather than conventional yeast.

word origin Rye has Slavic/Germanic origins: the Russian word for the grain is *roz* and the German one *roggen*.

• Rye is native to central Asia, where it started out as a wheatfield weed. It reached Europe by about 2000BC,

although it wasn't cultivated until about a thousand years later. As a northern grain, it became popular with all the northern European cultures, but was considered unpleasant by the Romans who couldn't understand why anybody would want to cultivate it, never mind eat it. It was introduced into England by the Anglo-Saxons and remained more widely grown here than wheat until medieval times.

• In the Middle Ages ergot was often milled with grains of rye, and eating bread containing it caused frequent epidemics of severe illness and death. The symptoms were gruesome – usually a progressive gangrene that ended by the affected limb turning black and dropping off, and the victim presumably dying. Other symptoms involved twitching fits, hallucinations and mental derangement. Surprisingly, however, in modern times ergot has turned out to have medicinal value – it is now made into drugs used to prevent haemorrhaging after childbirth and to relieve migraines. Modern research also uncovered the fact that ergot contains lysergic acid, and yet more research eventually turned up a variant of the acid that became the 1960s designer drug, LSD.

semolina

This is both a floury meal milled from **grains** and, in the United Kingdom, an old-fashioned milk pudding made from the meal. Most semolina meal is made from durum **wheat** and is produced during the process of making **flour**: grooved 'break' rollers sheer off the bran layers and extract the germ from the whole grains, then what remains (the endosperm, now reduced to minute particles) is put through a series of sifters to rid it of any lurking bran and germ; the resulting meal is semolina. The pudding is made from coarser grades of meal.

using it Semolina meal isn't as widely available as it once was, but some supermarkets and most healthfood shops stock coarser varieties as 'pudding' semolina, and occasionally also have finer meals as part of speciality flour sections. Although in Britain (if used at all) it's mostly turned into pudding in the same way as **rice**, semolina can actually be used like any other flour or **cornflour**: as a thickener for sauces, fruit purées, stews or soups, or mixed with wheat flour to give an interesting texture to cakes and biscuits.

The food industry worldwide now uses more semolina than home cooks. In Asia, fried sweetened semolina is the basis of a type of halva, a sweet snack/dessert containing sultanas and nuts. In Europe and North Africa, semolina is the basis of couscous, gnocchi (see **dumpling**) and, most importantly, most commercial pasta.

word origin Semolina comes ultimately from the Latin *simila,* meaning 'fine flour', and first appeared in English about 250 years ago.

did you know?

• In the United Kingdom, semolina is remembered chiefly by an older generation marked for life by its frequent appearance at school dinners, but in Victorian times it was valued and used much more imaginatively than it has been since. Mrs Beeton, for instance, gives several recipes in her *Book of Household Management.* She made a savoury pudding from semolina, milk, grated cheese, butter, mustard and cayenne pepper, and used semolina to flavour and thicken soufflés and coat croquettes as well. Her sweet recipes included a standard milk pudding and a moulded semolina milk jelly set with gelatine.

spaghetti

This thin, round stranded **pasta** is now so popular it accounts for over half of all pasta eaten annually around the world. It is made in the same way as any other type, but rarely at home, since shaping it by hand is enormously difficult. Commercially, shaping is done by machine – the pasta dough is forced through special perforated plates that extrude it into long, narrow or not-so-narrow strings.

Although spaghetti is by far the most common stranded pasta, there are a few others, including bucatini (broad, long and hollow-tubed), linguine (slightly thinner than standard spaghetti) and spaghettini (an especially thin spaghetti).

using it Spaghetti is occasionally available fresh or semi-fresh, but most is sold dried. It also comes in various flavours and colours, and in different lengths that could be described as long or longer.

Spaghetti is cooked in the same way as other types of pasta, and manufacturers normally give detailed instructions on their packaging. The strands should all be added to the water at once, preferably unbroken, and the best way to do this is to put them into the pan diagonally, then gradually push them down into the water as they soften. Give them a good stir round to be sure the strands are separate.

Like other pasta, spaghetti is 'dressed' with a sauce, and nearly all of those listed under **pasta sauces** will complement it well. Eating spaghetti, particularly in public, can worry some people, but it's simple enough: all you need to do is twirl some strands around your fork (a dessert spoon will help position them) and eat; the main trick is not to put too much pasta onto the fork in the first place.

word origin Spaghetti is Italian, from the word *spago,* meaning 'strand' or 'string' – the literal translation would be 'thin strings'. Our fondness for spaghetti has meant that the word is now used in other ways too, most notably in 'spaghetti junction' (a bewildering network of roads all converging together at different levels) and 'spaghetti western' (a cheap cowboy film made by Italians and shot originally in Italy, although most later ones were actually filmed in Spain).

did you know?

• Spaghetti is a fairly modern pasta. The first record of it didn't appear until nearly midway through the 19th century, and it only became feasible commercially about half a century later with the invention of machines that could extrude the strings easily.

wheat

A grass plant that originated in the Middle East, wheat now grows in temperate climates around the world, particularly in North America, eastern Europe and China. The wheat plant can reach about 1.5m in height, and is topped by a spike or ear consisting of layers of 'spikelets', small clusters of flowers, most of which develop into tufted or untufted white, yellow, red or even purple **grains** when fertilized.

There are over 40,000 varieties, many of them hybrids, and about 30 species, including: common wheat (*Triticum aestivum*), sometimes called bread wheat, which accounts for most of world production and is the one normally used as human food; durum wheat (*Triticum durum*), the hardest-grained type, which is generally milled into a coarse meal called **semolina**; spelt (*Triticum speltum*), one of the earliest species and now mostly milled into a speciality flour or processed into small brown grains that are used in the same way as **rice**, especially in Germany and eastern Europe; and emmer (*Triticum dicoccum*), another ancient species, now mostly used as animal fodder.

Wheat needs to be processed to be usable and the first steps (separating the grain from the plant and the husk, or 'lemma', from the grain) are now carried out instantly by the combine harvester that gathers the crop. The remaining grain is then treated in various ways depending on how it's to be used. Most is dried and milled into flour, but wheat can also be dried and sold as whole-wheat grains or 'berries', roughly cracked into small pieces to become cracked or kibbled wheat, steamed in addition to this to become **bulghur wheat**, rolled in the same way as **oats** to make wheat flakes, or shredded or puffed to become instant breakfast cereals. During the milling process, the outer **bran** layers and germ (the embryo of the plant) are usually removed from the rest of the grain (the starchy part that's ground to make flour) and used as animal fodder or sold separately as wheatbran or wheatgerm. Most durum wheat semolina is made into pasta, but some is mixed with flour to become **couscous**.

using it Most wheat products are widely available, many in pre-cooked or quick-cook versions. Wholewheat grains, which can be used in the same way as brown rice, need the longest cooking. Simmer them in three times their volume of liquid for 60–90 minutes (the pre-cooked version is, of course, much quicker to cook). Cracked wheat needs about 30 minutes cooking and bulghur wheat even less.

Wheat is now the most widely grown cereal plant in the world, and the reason isn't hard to find – it is the basis of baked goods, most pasta and many breakfast cereals. Flour milled from wheat makes better cakes, pastry and bread than any other grain. It is, in fact, essential to make light-textured yeast-raised bread, because although the endosperms of most grains contain gluten-forming proteins, they are strong enough in only two (wheat and **rye**) to create a dough elastic enough to expand under pressure without breaking. As a result of this, flours milled from other grains that are to be made into this type of bread are usually mixed with wheat flour to improve their gluten content.

Other industries use the wheat plant in various ways too: stems are dried to make straw or fertilizer; wheatstarch is added to some adhesives; and alcohol distilled from wheat is used as a fuel and to make synthetic rubber.

word origin White wheat flour has been prized throughout history, at least partly for its fine colour, which instantly conferred status because it was more expensive to produce than other, cruder darker flours. The name for the grain reflects this, coming from the Old English *hwaete*, which is related to a similar German word meaning 'white'.

• Apart from barley, wheat is the oldest cultivated grain in the world, possibly descended at least partly from wild einkorn (*Triticum monococcum*), which is still grown in parts of eastern Europe and northern Africa, and from wild emmer. Wheat grains and primitive farming equipment dating back to about 8000BC have been found in modern-day Syria and we know it was grown in early Egypt; it reached ancient Britain around 3500BC.

• The Greeks and Romans both used wheat to make bread, and the latter were impressed enough by both the quality and quantity grown in Britain to export it to other parts of their empire. Production slumped after the Romans left, and later invaders (mostly Anglo-Saxons) preferred rye, but by medieval times its fortunes had revived, although it was so expensive only the rich could afford bread made from wheat alone.

• Wheat didn't reach the New World until Christopher Columbus took it on his second voyage to Central America in 1493. French settlers introduced it into Canada about 150 years later, and a few years after that early English colonists tried growing it in Virginia and New England, although without much success. By the mid-19th century, however, it was being planted in the North American 'breadbasket' states that now produce over 80 percent of world exports.

wild rice

Wild rice (*Zizania palustris*) is not a true **grain**, but the seeds of an aquatic grass that originated in the Great Lakes area of North America; about 75 percent of world supply still comes from this region. The plant can grow to nearly 3m in height and is topped with a loose panicle arranged in small branchlets whose flowers mature into the long slender grains. Despite being called 'wild' rice, most is now cultivated in paddies and mechanically harvested. Once gathered, the grains are cleaned and cured for a few days before being roasted to develop flavour and make the husks easier to remove. Then they are cleaned again and milled. It takes almost 1.5kg of unhusked wild rice to make 500g of the finished product.

using it Wild rice can be combined with other ingredients like vegetables and slivered nuts to make a stuffing for peppers, courgettes or poultry; used as the basis for pilaffs or salads; or served as an accompaniment for spicy sausages or roast duck and game birds. It is often sold mixed with long-grain rice. To cook wild rice alone, first rinse it well under cold running water, then simmer in water, in a covered pan, for 20–30 minutes or until tender. It almost quadruples in volume after cooking, so although it's expensive it goes quite far.

word origin Despite the name, this plant is only distantly related to rice and no longer really deserves the 'wild' part. The Native American name for it was *manomin*, meaning 'good berry', an acknowledgment of its status as an important, nutritious winter staple.

• The story of wild rice reads like something out of Mark Twain or Longfellow: battles were fought between tribes like the Sioux and Chippewa for control of the best lakes, since possession of the grain could make the difference between life and death during long, freezing winters. The month of harvest (September) was called the Wild Rice Moon. Native Americans harvested wild rice by what was called the canoe-and-flail method: a team of two went out in a canoe on the shallow lakes where the plants grew and, while one propelled the boat through the reeds, the other pulled the tops of the plants down and beat out the grains into the boat with a stick. In some protected parts of the Great Lakes these traditional methods still survive.

Dairy Foods

Dairy foods have always been part of our staple diet and are invaluable when preparing good food. I happen to think that we produce the best cream and milk in the world in the United Kingdom, and today we also have an extensive range of delicious cheeses and butters from around the world to choose from.

Some people are wary of including too many dairy products in their diet, and I can understand this. On the plus side, though, foods such as milk, cheese and yoghurt provide some excellent nutritional benefits. Whatever your concerns about health, there is nothing like the real thing. I believe it is better to use dairy products in moderation than to replace them with inferior substitutes. A little can make an enormous difference. Good-quality dairy products add depth and

Good-quality dairy products add depth and intensity of flavour to all sorts of dishes.
Anton Edelmann

intensity of flavour to all sorts of dishes. You can use them in sweet and savoury dishes, sauces, soups and baking, and ice-creams and drinks.

In this section you will find lots of interesting facts about dairy foods. As a trustee of The Food Foundation, I am delighted that this book has been written, as I have always believed that the more you know about what goes into your body, the better your decisions will be about what you choose to eat and cook.

And the more I think about it, it occurs to me that a chef could add even more information, expertise and ideas about the use of dairy foods in cooking – but perhaps that's another book that needs to be written!

blue cheese

Blue cheese can be made from goat's, ewe's or cow's milk, be pasteurized or unpasteurized, range from soft to firm in texture and be matured or ripened for anything from a few weeks to about 18 months. It is made in the same way as most other **cheese**: first a bacterial culture, then rennet are added to milk so that it will separate into solid curds and liquid whey; then the curds are concentrated by draining off more whey. During the production process, however, blue cheeses are also injected with a mould, either *Penicillium roqueforti* or *Penicillium glaucum*, to give them blue (or occasionally green) 'veins'. The point at which the mould is added depends on the type of blue cheese being made: with some it's at the start of the process, with others it's just before the cheese is 'formed' or shaped, or just after. At the ripening stage, the cheese is usually pierced with long needles so that oxygen can circulate through it and allow the moulds to do their work.

There are three blue cheeses regarded as among the finest of all cheeses: gorgonzola, made in Lombardy in Italy from cow's milk, is washed in a brine solution during ripening to help it develop its tart flavour; Roquefort, made from unpasteurized ewe's milk around the village of Roquefort-sur-Soulzon in the Aveyron in southern France, is matured in special caves nearby; and Stilton, considered to be the best of the English blue cheeses, is made from pasteurized cow's milk and has a thick greyish-brown brushed crust. Of the many other blue cheeses, dolcelatte is the brand name of a mild, factory-made gorgonzola; cashel blue is a creamy white-coloured cheese made from cow's milk in County Tipperary in Eire; and blue vinney is a semi-firm cheese traditionally made in Dorset.

using it Good-quality blue cheese can be served by itself as a separate course or as part of a selection for such a course. In the United Kingdom Stilton is still occasionally handed round after dinner with port – on formal occasions it used to be served as a whole round, with a long-handled scoop to spoon out the cheese.

Most blue cheeses can be used in cooking: mashed into mayonnaise to make blue cheese dressing, for instance; cut into cubes and stirred into **risottos**, particularly with spinach and sliced mushrooms, or melted over a low heat with the same ingredients and used as a pasta sauce; blended with crème fraîche and chopped walnuts as a first-course stuffing for pear halves or crêpes; or beaten with butter to make a garnish for steaks and chops.

word origin The names of individual cheeses tend to reflect their origin, and some are much younger than the cheeses themselves. Gorgonzola, for instance, is named after a village near Milan where the cheese was first made, but until about a hundred years ago it was known as *stracchino*, literally a 'tired' cheese, because it was made from the milk of cows that had just made their long autumn trek to warmer southern pastures.

did you know?

• Some blue cheeses are ancient, others modern. Roquefort and gorgonzola are among the oldest: the former was known to the Romans, while the latter can be traced back to the 9th century and may be even older than that. Shropshire blue, on the other hand, was only created during the 20th century (in Scotland, despite the name), as was Danish blue, a factory cheese made from pasteurized and homogenised cow's milk.
• Stilton has been around since at least the 18th century and is named after a village in the Midlands where the cheese was first sold, although it has never actually been made there – it originated in the nearby village of Quenby. It's now produced in the surrounding area in Nottinghamshire, Leicestershire

and Derbyshire and is protected by a special Association of Stilton Cheesemakers. According to the 18th-century novelist Daniel Defoe, it was once ripened rather more than modern palates would probably care for: he claimed it was served so thickly covered with maggots that a spoon was provided to eat them with.

Brie

This is a round flat **cheese** with a mottled downy rind and soft melting interior. It is made in the usual way by adding a bacterial culture and then rennet to pasteurized or unpasteurized cow's milk to create curds. But for Brie, once the curds have formed they are removed from the liquid whey and spooned directly into special perforated shallow rings without being cut up; the whey remaining in the curds is then allowed to drain off without pressing. The thick edible crust is created by spreading *Penicillium camemberti* or *Penicillium candidum* mould over the surfaces of the cheese at the beginning of the ripening period, and allowing it to work gradually from the outside into the centre. Camembert, a similar rind cheese that originated in Normandy, is made from the same mould and in the same way.

Although it's French in origin, Brie, or approximations of it, are now made around the world, in factories as well as artisanally. The two best ones, Brie de Meaux and Brie de Melun, however, are still made in the traditional way in France and are now protected by the cheese equivalent of *appellation contrôlée* status; the former is ripened for about a month, while the latter is either sold 'fresh' or ripened for two months.

using it At its best, Brie should look plump and feel soft yet resilient when pressed. Smell is important too, and a good Brie will have a rich, almost nutty aroma and taste – underripe ones can smell (and taste) slightly soapy. A traditionally made Brie is superb on its own or with bread or biscuits to complement it, and any Brie would make a good sandwich or vol-au-vent filling,

ploughman's lunch or salad ingredient. It's even cooked occasionally: cut into small pieces, dipped in beaten egg, coated in breadcrumbs and deep-fried is one possibility; cut thinly and layered into a summer vegetable casserole another.

word origin The name comes from the area of origin, in the Île de France around Paris. The two classic Bries are also named after the areas in which they are made: Meaux, a small town to the north-east of Paris, and Melun, which is located south of the city.

did you know?

Brie is one of the older French cheeses (it may date back to the 8th century) and has always been considered one of the finest, a reputation confirmed in 1815 during treaty negotiations that took place after the Battle of Waterloo. All the nations represented submitted national cheeses as part of an impromptu competition during a formal dinner. Talleyrand, the French representative, offered a perfect Brie de Meaux and the contest was over.

butter

If **cream** is beaten violently for long enough it will eventually lose most of its liquid and solidify into a thick spread – butter. In the western world nearly all butter is made from cow's milk cream, although a curiosity-value quantity is produced using goat's milk; in other parts of the world, however, and particularly in Asia and parts of Africa, the milk of ewes, yaks, water buffaloes and even donkeys is used. The word also occasionally describes a mashed paste made from nuts like peanuts and the fat produced during the chocolate-making process.

Ironically, butter imitations like **margarine** are actually less simple to produce than the real thing. Modern commercial butter is made by adding a bacterial culture to the cream skimmed off from milk so that some of its lactose (sugar) turns into lactic acid, which gives the finished product its unique taste. It is then churned (agitated by paddles) until the solid fats begin to separate out from the rest of the mixture (this is 'buttermilk', the equivalent of whey in cheesemaking). As churning continues, the fat globules coalesce into lumps and more buttermilk is drained off until the lumps eventually become one thick mass, which is finally 'washed' in water to remove as much buttermilk as possible. Salt is also usually added to the mixture (it can be up to 2 percent of the total), which helps to preserve it as well as contributing flavour. The finished product is made up of 80 percent fat, 16–18 percent water (depending on whether it's salted or not) and 2 percent milk solids.

using it In most northern European and English-speaking countries, butter is primarily used as a spread for bread and as a cooking fat. It has a low smoke point (see **oils**), so when using it for frying care must be taken not to overheat it, which will impart a burnt taste. The solution is either to clarify it (see later) or use it with an oil like sunflower or olive that has a higher smoke point, but even so neither is suitable for deep-frying, where temperatures have to be high for the cooking method to be effective.

In savoury cooking, butter is part of a classic roux, the mixture of melted butter and flour that forms the basis of French sauces like béchamel, and of beurre manié, or kneaded butter, the paste of butter and flour stirred into soups, stews and other dishes to thicken them at the end of cooking. Butter is one of the main ingredients in hot sauces like hollandaise, and a knob or two will enrich almost any dish it's added to, either just before the end of cooking for dishes like omelette, scrambled eggs, **risotto** or **polenta**, or just before serving for boiled potatoes and other plainly cooked vegetables. It can also be used to make flavoured butters (blended with ingredients such as parsley, garlic and lemon zest), to

garnish fried or grilled meat or fish.

All the best baked items include liberal quantities of butter – classic sponges, shortbread and croissants are just three – and it is also used to make melt-in-the mouth pastry, including classic shortcrust and puff. In desserts and confectionery, butter enriches many sweets and sauces like toffee.

Butter should be stored, covered, in the refrigerator between uses and will keep for 3–4 weeks. Clarified butter and ghee, where the non-fat elements (water and milk solids) are removed so that the butter doesn't burn so easily, keep better than ordinary types, for about two months.

word origin Butter comes from the Greek *bouturon,* meaning 'cow's cheese'. The texture is smooth, which could be the origin of 'to butter (up)' someone, to try to get on their good side, normally by flattering them.

did you know?

• Credit for the discovery of butter is generally given to the earliest farmers of the Middle East, who seem to have been highly adaptable when it came to dairy foods (see **cheese** and **yoghurt**). The probability is that at some point milk was left around for so long that it solidified into something akin to butter, and (on the principle of waste not, want not) uses were found for it anyway.
• Early southern Europeans like the Greeks and Romans didn't use butter to cook with and rarely ate it on bread; in fact, during classical times in that part of the world butter was a medicine rather than a food, something spread over cuts and bruises to make them heal more quickly and prevent them from stinging. During medieval times the rich taste of butter and other dairy foods was forbidden during Lent, although wealthy northern Christians could buy themselves special dispensations that allowed them to ignore the ban.
• Buttermilk, traditionally the liquid left after butter is churned from cream, is now made commercially by adding a bacterial culture to skimmed milk. The mildly sour taste is particularly useful in baking, especially for making biscuits, soda breads and scones.

Cheddar

This is a hard, yellow English **cheese** made from pasteurized or occasionally unpasteurized cow's milk. After the usual bacterial culture and rennet cause the milk to separate into solid curds and liquid whey, a special technique called 'cheddaring' is used to concentrate the curds. First they are milled and heated to form a soft mass which is cut into slabs that are stacked on top of each other to press out the remaining whey. Then the curds are milled again, salted, moulded into shape and ripened. The cheddaring method is used to make other, similar hard cheeses such as Gloucester, too.

Before ripening, traditional Cheddar is wrapped in bandages to encourage the bacteria in the cheese to do their job and to provide a strong brownish rind; industrially made versions are usually ripened in blocks wrapped in plastic. Cheddar can be ripened or matured for anything from three months (as is the case with most industrially made cheese) up to 18 months (for traditionally made Cheddars).

using it Cheddar is perfect for a cheese board, for serving with bread (the addition of pickle turns it into a ploughman's lunch) or as a snack with fruit, particularly apple. In chunks, slices or shreds, any type could be the centrepiece of a main-course salad.

Cheddar is widely used in cooking. Grated, it can be stirred into béchamel sauce to spoon over white fish fillets, cauliflower and other vegetables; it can be packed into baked potatoes; mixed into pastry for meat or other savoury pies; used to flavour cheese straws and scones; and sprinkled over any dish to be *gratiné* (heated under the grill until the cheese topping has melted and is turning brown). It has a particular affinity with eggs, so is added to **soufflés** and omelettes, and is also made into a thick sauce with ale and mustard or Worcestershire sauce to be spread over toast and grilled until bubbling for Welsh rarebit.

word origin Cheddar comes from the village of the same name in Somerset, where the cheese was first made.

● Cheddar is a medieval cheese – first records of it date back to about 1500 – so it's a relative newcomer compared to its rival Cheshire, which may go back to Roman times. Although West Country Cheddars are the classic ones, Cheddar-style cheese is now made in other parts of England, and in Scotland, Ireland and Wales too. In fact, this is one of the most widely produced cheeses in the world, made pretty much everywhere that the British have settled, including North America, South Africa, Australia and New Zealand.

cheese

Cheese is a dairy product made from milk that has coagulated into solid lumps or curds. Technically, it can come from the milk of any mammal, but is produced commercially mainly from that of cows, goats, ewes and water buffaloes. The milk can be pasteurized or unpasteurized, organic or not, full cream or skimmed. Around 100 litres are needed to make about 5kg of cheese.

No one knows how many different cheeses there are in the world, but an educated guess suggests several thousand at least, around 700–800 of them in France alone. And there is a bewildering number of different types: cheese can be tiny or huge (from less than 25g to upwards of 120kg), tall or flat, and round, square, log- or even heart-shaped; it can also be fresh or ripened (matured), natural or processed, white, yellow, orange or red, veined or not, rinded or not. Cheese was probably born to be eaten with wine and, like wine, the relatively straightforward process of making it can result in an end product with a dazzling variety of complex tastes and textures.

There are three basic stages in cheesemaking and many variations within them. Broadly speaking, the first is to curdle and coagulate the milk in a controlled way so that the casein proteins it contains separate out from the liquid whey into solid lumps or curds. The next is to remove the whey and concentrate the curds so that the final cheese can reach the desired degree of softness or firmness. The last stage (which not all cheeses go through) is to 'ripen' or mature it until the final taste and texture are achieved.

Most modern cheese (and all fresh cheese) is made from milk that has been pasteurized, a heat process that kills nearly all the bacteria the milk contains and helps to keep it fresh for longer. The curdling and coagulation process, therefore, begins by adding special lactic-acid-producing bacterial cultures to the warmed milk to turn the lactose (milk sugar) it contains into lactic acid (milk can't coagulate until it is acidic) and create weak curds. Cultures are added to the milk whether it's pasteurized or not, since they help control the rate at which the lactose sours into lactic acid. Some simple cheeses like **cottage cheese** are made from milk that has only been soured to the desired degree in this way; for most, however, rennet (an enzyme extracted from the stomach of unweaned calves or, increasingly now, a commercially produced version) is also added and it's this that separates the milk into stronger curds and liquid whey. Plant extracts or a substance extracted from yeast mould is used instead of rennet to make vegetarian cheese. The mixture is then left in warm to hot temperatures until the curds have gelled into a large mass. The deep yellow or orange colour of many hard cheeses comes from dye, usually synthetic or processed from annatto seeds, and this is added to the milk at this stage too, either with the bacterial culture or with the rennet.

There are various ways of draining off the whey and concentrating the curds, depending on the type of cheese being made. For some soft cheeses, the curds are simply removed from the whey and ladled into special 'forms', which are perforated moulds that also firm and shape the curds. For most other cheeses, the curds are cut up in various ways or milled into very small grains to release more whey, then heated so that they re-form into a solid mass. Some undergo further draining by being 'cheddared' (see **Cheddar**); some denser cheeses like Gruyère are heated at very high temperatures after being cut up initially so that their 'grains' become harder and drier; and a few like **mozzarella** are shredded, immersed in very hot water and then kneaded into long malleable strands. Salt is added to some cheeses at this stage, which gets rid of yet more whey and also delays the onset of bacterial activity. Some 'fresh' cheese is now ready for sale, but most others have to be ripened. For them, the next stage is to be packed into perforated moulds and pressed to concentrate the curds and remove yet more whey; the amount of pressure exerted varies, with softer, moister cheeses receiving very little and denser, harder ones getting more.

Cheese can be ripened or matured for anything between two weeks and several years. The ripening is done in controlled environments, usually cool and moist for softer cheeses and cool and slightly drier for harder ones. Those cheeses not salted at an earlier stage are salted now and in various ways – some are immersed in brine while others have salt rubbed over their surfaces. Cheeses like Cheddar are wrapped in bandages or a plastic coating to protect their surface during ripening. Those like **Brie** are matured from the outside in by being covered at this stage with a surface mould, while **blue cheese** is ripened in the opposite direction, from the inside out, by being injected with special moulds.

Although cheese can be difficult to categorize, there are recognized groupings, like soft, fresh cheese (cottage cheese, **cream cheese** and **ricotta**), **blue cheese** and goat's cheese (which can vary from soft and fresh to hard and mature). Other types include hard cheeses such as **Parmesan**, which can be made in a number of ways, but which are always matured for at least a few months; semi-soft rinded cheeses, including classics like Camembert, which are always quite flat; and semi-hard unrinded cheeses, such as Gouda and Gruyère, which are cooked at high temperatures before being pressed. The unique holes in Gruyère and Emmenthal cheese are created by a special extra bacterial strain, *Propionibacterium shermani*, added to their starter culture; during ripening, it emits large amounts of carbon dioxide that eventually disappear, leaving the distinctive craters behind.

Processed cheese is made differently from natural cheese: several types of already-made cheese (usually a mixture of fresh and mature) are blended together with milk solids, flavourings, stabilizers and so on, then pasteurized. Cheese spread is made in roughly the same way except that its softer texture means it is allowed to retain more moisture, and a stabilizing vegetable gum is added to the mixture to make it spreadable.

using it   Fresh cheeses are quite perishable, so they should be stored in the refrigerator and used within a week or so of purchase. Ripened or matured cheese keeps better, and how long it will last depends on the condition of the cheese when bought. Newly purchased mature cheese should be stored in protective wrapping, and in the refrigerator if it's hot, but removed to room temperature at least 30 minutes before being served. In cooler weather most firm cheeses can be kept at dry room temperature, and surface-ripened cheeses like Brie nearly always mature better when stored in this way.

Good-quality cheese can be eaten as a course on its own. In the United Kingdom, this is traditionally at the end of a meal, usually accompanied by bread or biscuits and sometimes celery or grapes, but in France the cheese course is served between the main course and dessert, often with green salad. In Italy, cheese would normally be eaten *instead* of dessert rather than before or after, admittedly by those who have already survived antipasta or pasta followed by a main course and vegetables. In Germany, Holland and Scandinavia, slices of cheeses like Gouda and Münster are served with cooked ham for breakfast as well as at other times of the day.

Cheese is widely used as an ingredient. Most types can be used uncooked in a sandwich filling, as a topping or as a salad ingredient. When using cheese in cooking, the golden rules are simple: heat it slowly rather than quickly, and add it towards the end of cooking, to prevent it becoming stringy. Mixing cheese with flour (to make pastry, for instance) avoids this since the starchiness of the flour protects the cheese during the baking process. Mixing it with wine (as in fondue) also works because the alcohol keeps the cheese below boiling point.

word origin   Cheese comes from the Latin *caseus*. The ancient Romans were keen cheesemakers and carried both their techniques and word with them as they conquered and settled their empire – hence German *käse* and Spanish *queso,* as well as English *cheese*.

did you know?

• No one knows how old cheese is, but it was probably discovered by accident and not long after animals like sheep and goats were domesticated, around 11,000 and 9500 years ago respectively. The likelihood is that it was first made in the Middle East, perhaps from milk that had been stored in a 'bag' made from the stomach of calves (which contains rennet). However it happened, it didn't take long for people to appreciate its practicability as well as its taste, since it kept much better than the milk it came from.

• All the ancient civilizations made cheese: trace remains have been found in an Egyptian tomb dating back to about 3000BC, while Homer's pre-classical Greek heroes appear to have been nurtured on something that could be a distant ancestor of modern feta. Although the first cheeses were simple fresh ones, the process soon became more sophisticated: by the second century BC, the Romans were using rennet to control the type of curds they created, and about 200 years after that they were moulding and pressing curds to extract more whey and thus make firmer cheeses.

• During the Middle Ages, cheese was eaten as a 'white meat' during the many meatless days imposed by the medieval Christian calendar, although it was banned along with other dairy foods during Lent. Cheesemaking skills were refined in the great feudal houses and monasteries of the time and some modern cheeses can trace their origins to these latter institutions – English Wensleydale, for instance, was first made by the monks at Jervaulx Abbey in Yorkshire.

cottage cheese

Although this simple **cheese** can be made in the same way as most other cheeses, by adding rennet to milk so that it will coagulate, it's usually produced simply by adding a bacterial culture to skimmed milk to curdle it into weak curds and whey. Either way, once the curds have formed, they are cut up and warmed in the whey until the mixture reaches the desired consistency (normally separate grains of curd are still visible), then washed and rinsed a few times to remove more whey before being packed for sale.

Some farmhouse-type cottage cheese is sold as curd cheese, which is made in the same way as cottage cheese except that the curds are processed in the whey until the texture is smooth and lump-free. Fromage frais is the French equivalent of this, and quark is the German version of fromage frais. All of these are available with varying fat contents. Cottage-type cheeses can taste bland, so flavourings like pineapple, salmon or chives are often added to the basic mixture to enhance its appeal.

using it One of the original reasons for the popularity of cottage cheese was that it was easy to spread and could be used instead of butter on bread, although it's rarely used in this way now. Its chief virtue is probably that most varieties are low in fat (and therefore calories).

Cottage cheese can be a handy salad item, either with savoury ingredients like tomato and cucumber, or fruits such as peaches and berries. Curd cheese is excellent in cheesecakes. Fromage frais and quark can be served as lower-fat alternatives to cream with puddings and desserts and can also be used in cooking, either to add creamy richness to savoury dishes or in fillings for cakes.

word origin The first cottage cheeses were made at home simply by ladling the curds into a bag and draining out as much whey as possible, probably the reason it was originally called 'cottager's cheese'. Now the name gives a suitably rustic feel to what is essentially an industrially made cheese. Quark is the German word for curd.

cream

Fat globules make up about 4 percent of unhomogenized **milk** and since they are lighter than the rest of it (which is mostly water), they eventually rise to the surface: cream at its simplest. The traditional method of making cream was based on this. Milk was poured into large shallow pans and set aside overnight or longer (the longer it was left, within reason, the thicker the top became); at the end of this period, the top layer (the cream) was skimmed off and used. Nowadays, the process is mechanized and the fat is spun from the rest of the milk in a centrifuge until it reaches the right consistency, then it is pasteurized to kill off any bacteria that may have formed. Like milk, commercial cream is now nearly always made from cow's milk.

The longer milk is centrifuged, the thicker the cream becomes and the more fat globules it will contain. Cream is sold according to its fat content: half cream (which is half milk and half cream) contains 12 percent fat, single cream has 18–19 percent, whipping cream has 35–39 percent and double cream is spun for long enough to acquire 48 percent fat. Clotted cream, the speciality of south-western England, has a whopping 55–63 percent fat. It is made by heating or scalding the milk at very high temperatures, then leaving it to cool slowly before the cream is skimmed off. The unique taste of **soured cream** and crème fraîche is achieved by adding a bacterial culture to milk (see separate entry).

using it Most creams will keep for 3–5 days in the refrigerator; clotted cream lasts longer, for 7–14 days.

The great advantage cream has over milk (apart from its richer taste) is that its consistency and quantity can change – it becomes markedly thicker and can expand in volume by as much as 50 percent by being beaten. The more fat it contains, the more stiffly cream will whip, although it needs to contain a minimum of 35 percent fat to thicken properly (single cream, therefore, is not suitable for whipping). The whipping should start off slowly and build up gradually until the cream reaches the required thickness. Whipping should then stop, because if it is beaten too long cream can turn into something akin to butter.

Whether it's whipped or simply used as is, there is very little that isn't improved by being served with cream or having cream added to it. Cream is served as an accompaniment to many puddings and desserts. It may also be part of the dessert itself: in mousses and cold **soufflés**, as a layer in trifles or as a filling for meringues, cheesecakes and charlottes. It is used widely in baking too, and stiffly whipped cream is piped like icing to decorate cakes, used to sandwich cake layers together, and as a filling for pastries like choux buns. In savoury cooking a few spoonfuls of cream add extra richness to

sauces like **béchamel**; improve the texture of **risottos** and meat- or tomato-based pasta sauces; and enrich puréed soups and dips.

word origin Cream comes from the Old French *cresme*, which is derived from the Greek *chriein*, meaning 'to anoint' (the same root as Christ, the 'anointed' Son of God). The rich good taste and the fact that cream traditionally rose to the top of the milk have given us, among other phrases, 'the cream …' (the best or top) and 'to cream off' (to take the best bits).

did you know?

- The flavour of cream, like that of milk, can vary according to the breed of cow it comes from and the diet it's fed. Most British creams are made industrially from the milk of many farms, often from different areas, and so tend to be fairly bland. In France, however, creams (including crème fraîche) produced at Isigny-Sainte-Mère in Normandy have a distinctive flavour. They are made only from milk from controlled sources and are protected by the equivalent of *appellation contrôlée* status, something always indicated on the label.

cream cheese

Initially, cream cheese was made by simply allowing **cream** to solidify naturally. Nowadays, however, most is produced by adding a special bacterial culture to a mixture of cow's cream and milk, then leaving the mixture until it reaches the correct texture before pasteurizing it.

There are many different types of cream cheese. Familiar brand-name and supermarket 'soft cheeses' are available in full-fat and reduced-fat versions, but some French cream cheeses take the first part of their name seriously and are made with extra cream; the result is delicious but a saturated-fat nightmare – the so-called 'triple-cream' cheese Brillat-Savarin, for example, weighs in at about 70 percent fat or more. Another rich 'cheese' is ultrasmooth mascarpone, with 46 percent fat (it's not really a cheese as it is normally made by adding lemon juice or citric acid to cream rather than a bacterial culture).

using it Most cream cheeses are fresh (only one or two of the French double or triple creams are matured) and are therefore quite perishable. The factory-produced soft cheeses contain stabilizers and preservatives that enable them to be kept in the refrigerator for several months.

How cream cheeses are used depends on the individual type. Soft cheeses, for instance, are used almost exclusively as a spread for bread or sandwiches or in baking, particularly to make cheesecake. Mascarpone is normally used in cooking too: it's a traditional ingredient in tiramisu and gives a sweet edge and richness to pasta sauces. The French double- and triple-cream cheeses are normally served as part of a cheese course.

word origin All these cheeses contain some cream, hence the first part of the name; the second part comes from the Latin word for cheese, *caseus*.

did you know?

• Until relatively recently, cream cheese was made at home without either baterial cultures or citric acid. The Victorian Mrs Beeton, for instance, made it by tying double cream into a clean wet cloth and hanging it in a cool place for about 7 days to let the liquid drain out. After this, it was transferred to a mould already lined with muslin and kept under slight pressure for 2–3 days, turning a few times each day, until it reached the right consistency.

egg

Many creatures produce eggs, but only those of the odd reptile, some birds and most fowl are eaten by humans. And of these, although the eggs of ducks, geese, ostriches and quail are all available commercially, about 95 percent come from chickens (the subject of this entry).

First and foremost, eggs are an efficient method of reproduction, designed not only to house the fertilized or unfertilized germ or seed of the bird, but also to nourish and protect it from bacteria and other hazards until a chick hatches. Each one consists of four main parts: the yolk, which contains the germ; the surrounding white or albumen, which provides many of the proteins a fertilized germ will need; layers of fibrous membrane just inside the shell, which protect it against bacteria; and, finally, a porous shell, which encloses and protects all of the other parts and allows oxygen to enter the egg and carbon dioxide to leave it. The shell makes up about 10 percent of the weight of an average egg, the yolk accounts for another 30 percent (about half of which is fat and protein) and the balance is accounted for by the white, which is about 90 percent water and 10 percent protein.

Producing eggs is big business. Over 80 percent of those sold in the United Kingdom come from battery – or intensively-reared – chickens, where the birds (about 30–100,000 of them at times) are kept in tiers of cages in large sheds and are fed a grain-based diet that can include fish meal, soya, animal proteins and antibiotics. A typical battery hen lays close to 300 eggs in a year. Double-yolk eggs occur occasionally when a hen produces two yolks at the same time and, until recently, they were passed onto the food processing trade as something of an aberration; now they are sometimes marketed as a novelty. Unless identified to the contrary, double-yolk eggs come from battery hens. Farm-assured eggs, which usually carry the Little Red Tractor logo, come from farms that are individually vetted for compliance with animal husbandry and welfare standards; these hens are also intensively farmed. Barn or perchery eggs are from hens raised indoors in large sheds in conditions somewhat less crowded than battery farming, although their diet is roughly the same. Four-grain eggs come from hens fed a more natural grain-based diet that contains no animal protein; otherwise conditions are the same as in the barn system. Free-range eggs can either be produced from hens with the same indoor space as barn hens, but with at least some access to outside space, or from those that genuinely spend most of their time outdoors and in addition have good-quality indoor space. Organic eggs can also come from hens living in varying conditions – the best are in small flocks with free access to the outdoors and live in much less crowded conditions; all organic poultry has feed that is organically based and does not contain antibiotics.

The majority of eggs sold in Great Britain have brown or white shells, although pale blue, greenish-blue, pink, speckled and other shells are increasingly being seen. The colour has no bearing on either taste or nutritional value, but is just due to the breed of hen. Yolks can also vary in colour, from pale yellow to a much deeper shade. This used to be solely attributable to diet, paler yolks denoting a wheat-based diet, darker yellow indicating one based on maize; nowadays, however, many yolks are dyed a uniform yellow by adding colouring to the hens' feed. Eggs are graded before being packed by 'candling' them – screening them electronically in front of a light source so that any imperfections like blood spots on the yolk can be detected through the shell. Those that have no imperfections are graded A and sold in supermarkets and other shops according to size; those with a lower grading are used commercially in baking and other processed foods.

using it Most eggs will keep for up to three weeks, stored in the refrigerator in their box. The freshness of eggs has a bearing on how they can be used in cooking (very fresh eggs are best for poaching and frying, while for hard-boiling it's better to use eggs 1–2 weeks old). There is a simple way to test freshness. Put the egg in a bowl of cold water: if it lies horizontally on the bottom, it's very fresh; if it begins to point upwards, it's at least a week old; if it stands vertically, it is stale and should be thrown out.

There are many basic ways to cook eggs. To boil, use eggs at room temperature if possible. Put the egg into a pan of barely simmering water, bring back to a simmer and cook to taste: depending on type and size, allow 3–4 minutes for soft yolks, 5 minutes for medium and 8–10 minutes for hard (quail's eggs will take 2–3 minutes less than this; duck eggs will take a minute or so longer and goose eggs 4–5 minutes longer). To poach, if the eggs are not very fresh, add a few drops of vinegar to a wide pan of simmering water. Crack open the egg and slide it in, then cook for 4–5 minutes. To fry, crack the egg into a pan containing hot oil or melted butter and cook for 4–6 minutes. To scramble, lightly beat two or three eggs together, with a few spoonfuls of milk or cream and some seasoning, then cook gently in melted butter, stirring to 'scramble', until softly set. Fresh herbs or other flavourings can be added during cooking and a knob of butter stirred in just before the end. See also **omelette** and **soufflé**.

Eggs are a major ingredient in many dishes, and may be used whole or separated into yolk and white, to take advantage of their individual qualities. For example, both whole beaten eggs and egg yolks are added to mixtures to thicken and to make them set, as in custard. Egg whites, whisked until stiff, are folded into soufflé mixtures to lighten them and increase volume, and are turned into meringues. Beaten eggs also have adhesive qualities and so are used to moisten food such as fish fillets and meat escalopes before coating with crumbs.

Eggs are added to pasta dough to enrich it and add colour, and are an integral ingredient in pancake batter. They are part of nearly all cake and biscuit recipes and are in most richer breads and pastries too. They are used widely in puddings and desserts as well, in particular being an integral part of ice-cream.

Eggs are a first-class protein food; they supply all the essential amino acids and contain many essential vitamins and minerals. Because the yolk is high in dietary cholesterol, there have been concerns about how many eggs we eat; however, the intake of foods high in saturated fats has more effect on blood cholesterol levels (and on increasing the risk of heart disease) than cholesterol intake through foods such as eggs. Eggs are also famous (or infamous) for harbouring bacteria that cause food poisoning – salmonella bacteria, for instance, used to be common among hens and were also present in their eggs. As a safety precaution, therefore, many laying hens (all those producing Lion-marked eggs, for instance) are now vaccinated against salmonella. Nevertheless, the FSA advise that raw eggs (uncooked) and dishes made from them may pose a health risk. Boiled, poached, fried or scrambled eggs may be eaten softly cooked, but vulnerable groups such as the elderly, pregnant women and young children should have eggs cooked until they are firm.

word origin Egg was borrowed from Old Norse about 700 years ago, but the origins are much older than that, going back to ancient Indo-European roots that are related to various words for 'bird'. The many phrases built around eggs reflect both their fragility and core position in our diet, hence 'don't put all your eggs in one basket' (don't put all your assets in one place) or 'to walk on eggs' (to tiptoe gingerly).

• Our earliest ancestors probably ate birds' eggs when they could find them, and all civilizations from the

Egyptians on have used them in cooking. It was probably their reproductive function that initially made them a symbol of fertility and hope to pre-Christian and early Christian peoples, something still celebrated in the giving and decorating of eggs at Easter.

• Which *did* come first, the chicken or the egg? Obviously we can't have one without the other, but there were eggs in the world long before there were chickens. In fact, the first crude eggs evolved in the oceans about a billion years ago as a method of reproduction when creatures became multi-celled rather than simple organisms. It took much longer (another three-quarters of a billion years) for reptiles to evolve shells so that their eggs could survive on land, and birds were producing eggs with shells around 100 million years after that. Chickens, on the other hand, are a much more recent development on the evolutionary scale, being domesticated from Indian jungle fowl about 4000 years ago.

ice-cream

This is a frozen dish normally made from cream, milk, eggs, sugar and flavouring. Nearly all ice-creams are sweet, with flavourings such as vanilla, chocolate, coffee and fruit, but they can also be made with savoury ingredients such as tomato, avocado or even crab. Most sweet ice-cream is based on a **custard** blended with whipped cream, although there are lighter versions made with sweetened fruit purée and cream.

Ice-cream can be made at home, at its simplest in ice trays in the freezer, or, for a better texture, in a special ice-cream maker. These can range from old-fashioned hand-cranked churns that rely on a supply of salt and crushed ice (and much elbow grease) to, more usually nowadays, an electric machine that agitates the mixture during freezing to incorporate some air into it and keep it smooth.

Good-quality commercial ice-cream is usually made using natural ingredients and incorporating just enough air to make it spoonable and to prevent ice crystals from forming. Many cheaper ones, however, have only a nodding acquaintance with the cream, milk and egg base of the traditional dish, substituting instead skimmed milk powder, vegetable fats, emulsifiers and large amounts of sugar and artificial sweeteners; much greater quantities of air are also incorporated, which makes the finished result more spoonable but dilutes its taste.

using it   Ice-cream keeps indefinitely in the freezer but it needs to be softened, either in the refrigerator or at room temperature, before it is served. Most commercial ice-creams can be spooned within about 10 minutes of being removed from the freezer, whereas home-made ice-cream can take a bit longer to soften.

Ice-cream is the classic 'instant' dessert. It tastes fine on its own, in a single flavour or a mixture, but is mostly served as an accompaniment to other desserts – pies, cakes, baked or steamed puddings and crêpes all taste better served with a scoop or two. Occasionally it becomes a major ingredient in a dessert, such as in Baked Alaska (see **meringue**). But the glory of ice-cream is the sundae, where it is combined with fresh fruit, nuts, whipped cream, and chocolate and other sweet sauces. Among the classic sundaes are banana split, traditionally served in a long narrow dish, in which a halved banana is topped with scoops of differently flavoured ice-cream and covered with chocolate sauce; and knickerbocker glory, a layered concoction of vanilla ice-cream, fresh fruit slices and a scoop of different flavoured ice-cream, which is topped with whipped cream and crowned with a cherry.

word origin   Old-fashioned ice-cream churns nestled in crushed ice that gradually made the mixture colder and colder as the paddles were agitated, hence the first part of the name. The second part is indirectly derived from the Greek *chriein,* 'to anoint'.

• The first references to something that sounds vaguely like ice-cream didn't occur until about the 1st century BC in China. They may not have been to modern taste, based as they were on a mixture of buffalo's milk, flour and camphor, a bitter crystalline substance obtained from a relative of the laurel tree. By the end of the 13th century, knowledge of cooling techniques had arrived in Italy, introduced (depending on who you believe) by Marco Polo or by Arabs from northern Africa and Sicily. Iced dishes and drinks became all the rage, so by the time the Italian Catherine de' Medici arrived in France during the 16th century to marry the French king Henry II she was accompanied by an army of cooks, including several who were expert in creating iced desserts. A century later, a French chef employed by the British king, Charles I, was making these desserts from a mixture of cream and eggs.

• The modern partner of portable ice-cream, the cone, was invented at the beginning of the 20th century, probably by a Syrian wafflemaker named Ernest Hamwi, working in the United States. His stand at the 1904 St Louis World Fair was next to that of an ice-cream seller, and at one point the latter ran out of dishes in which to serve his ice-cream. Hamwi is supposed to have saved the day by rolling up his waffles so that they could act as instant containers.

• Ice-cream isn't just a western phenomenon – there's a long tradition of ice-cream-making in the Indian subcontinent too. Their version, called kulfi, is made by simmering milk until it has reduced by about two-thirds, and infusing it with flavourings like cardamom, almonds, pistachios and rosewater before cooling and freezing until it becomes solid.

meringue

Meringue is both a mixture of stiffly whisked egg whites and sugar and an airy, crisp cake made from such a mixture. There are three different types of meringue mixture. Simple meringue (sometimes called *meringue suisse*) is the easiest and is made by gradually adding caster sugar to whisked egg whites (about 50g sugar to each white) and continuing to whisk until very stiff; you should be able to turn the bowl upside down without the mixture dropping out. *Meringue italienne* is made by whisking egg whites until they are stiff, then gradually adding a hot sugar syrup and continuing to whisk until the mixture is glossy and stiff. 'Cooked' meringue (or *meringue cuite*) is made by whisking egg whites with sifted icing sugar (about 50g per white) in a bowl set over simmering water until the mixture is very stiff.

Meringue cakes are normally made by piping or moulding the mixture into mounds, shells or other shapes on a lined baking sheet, then baking, or more accurately 'drying out', in a very cool oven. The meringue should be the palest gold when cooked.

using it The three types of meringue are almost interchangeable, although simple meringue is the one likely to be used at home. It provides the topping for lemon meringue pie and is shaped into baked meringue shells to be sandwiched together with whipped cream. It's also often used to create two modern classics: Pavlova, a baked meringue 'nest' filled with whipped cream and fresh fruit, and Baked Alaska, which consists of a thin sponge base topped with ice-cream that is completely covered with meringue, then baked briefly in a very hot oven until the meringue coating turns golden. Both *meringue italienne* and cooked meringue are used by professional bakers as the basis of *petits fours* and for decorative meringue baskets, among many other things.

Flavourings and colourings can be added to meringue mixtures, including grated orange zest, coffee essence, vanilla extract, ground nuts like hazelnuts or pistachios, spices such as cinnamon or nutmeg, and spirits like rum or brandy.

word origin Meringue is French and has been around in English since at least the beginning of the 18th century. There are various exotic tales about its origin, the best

(and least likely) claiming that it comes from the Polish *marzynka* and was created by a chef of king Stanislaus of Poland. (The king is supposed to have passed the recipe onto his daughter, who in turn passed it on to the French queen Marie Antoinette, a famous lover and possible maker of meringues.) A more prosaic (and more likely) explanation is that it was named after the German town of Mehringhen, where a Swiss chef named Gasparini invented it. Pavlova, claimed by both Australia and New Zealand, was created (and named) to celebrate a performance of *Swan Lake* by the Russian ballerina Anna Pavlova.

did you know?

• The idea that makes Baked Alaska work (that whisked egg whites are poor conductors of heat, so the heat of the oven won't penetrate to the ice-cream during cooking) is generally credited to an 18th century American adventurer and scientist named Count Rumford. The Count was born plain Benjamin Thompson in Massachusetts and during a colourful career was (among other things) a British spy during the American War of Independence and designer of the English Gardens in Munich; his title was courtesy of the Holy Roman Empire.

milk

This is the first food we taste, the stuff created by nature so that a female mammal can nurture her young. Although all pregnant mammals produce milk, only that of a few – cows, goats and occasionally sheep and water buffaloes – is commercially processed to be consumed by humans or used to make dairy products such as **butter**, **cream**, **cheese** and **yoghurt**. Over 90 percent of our milk comes from cows. Cow's milk contains protein, fat and carbohydrate (as lactose) and is an excellent source of calcium and vitamin B2, but it is low in iron and vitamins D and E.

The quality and taste of milk, like that of meat, is affected by many things, including the type of animal it comes from, its breed, what it eats and even when it's milked. Most of our milk is obtained from special breeds of intensively farmed cattle, like Holsteins and Friesians, or a cross between the two. Although most of these spend some time outdoors during summer, in winter they are normally tethered indoors with little space and fed a high-protein diet based on grains, soya and fish meal to increase their yield. Milk certified as organic by the Soil Association, the most stringent of the British certifying organizations, comes from cows that are part of smaller herds, which spend a fair amount of time outside at pasture and are fed a grass-based diet that is at least 80 percent organic.

After milk is taken from the cow, it is usually pasteurized – heated by various methods at various temperatures (all under boiling point) and for varying lengths of time, then cooled rapidly to kill off harmful bacteria and increase its keeping qualities. Most milk is also homogenized, that is, pressured through small nozzles so that the fat globules break down into smaller particles distributed more evenly throughout the milk; this prevents the fat or 'cream' rising to the top and further improves the keeping qualities. All cartoned and most bottled milk is now homogenized as well as pasteurized.

Contrary to rumour, there isn't that much fat in full-fat milk, only about 3–6 percent, depending on the breed of cow the milk comes from (Holsteins and Friesians are at the lower end of this scale, traditional breeds like Jersey and Guernsey towards the upper end). Despite this, a lot of milk is skimmed in a centrifuge to remove more or less all of its fat (skimmed milk contains around 0.3 percent), or semi-skimmed so that the final fat content is about 1.75 percent. Removing the fat from milk does not appreciably alter the vitamin and mineral content, except for the fat-soluble vitamins A and D. However, since milk is not a major source of these vitamins in our diet, the advantage of cutting

down on saturated fat outweighs any loss of nutrients. (Note, though, that because young children rely heavily on milk for their energy requirements, only full-fat milk should be given to children until they are two years old. After this time, semi-skimmed milk can be given if the child is eating and growing well; skimmed milk should not be used for children under five.)

Milk can be heated at very high temperatures for a second or two, then chilled quickly to create UHT (ultra-heat-treated) milk, or heated at similar temperatures for longer to become sterilized milk. Full-fat and skimmed milk are also sometimes concentrated until they have lost just over half their liquid, to become evaporated milk, which is homogenized and stabilized before being sterilized in its container (the heat it's subjected to at the sterilization stage creates its unique, slightly nutty 'cooked' taste); for condensed milk, which is similar although very sweet, the addition of various sugars means it doesn't have to be sterilized. Some milk, nearly always skimmed, is also dried to a powder.

using it Milk is drunk by itself hot or cold, added to tea, coffee and cocoa, and is a staple ingredient in most western kitchens. To use it hot or warm it should be heated carefully, preferably over low or medium heat rather than high, and covered rather than open, or at least stirred constantly to prevent a skin from developing on the top. In savoury cooking, it's used to poach white or smoked fish fillets, supplies the liquid in sauces like **béchamel**, thins out puréed soups and, in small quantities, is stirred into cooked potatoes to help them mash effectively and into beaten eggs to make them go further and lighten their taste. In sweet dishes, milk is the liquid component in custard, is added to batters for pancakes and used to make milk shakes. And it would be difficult to bake without using milk, a basic ingredient in many biscuit, cake, pastry and scone recipes.

Evaporated and condensed milk play their part in cooking too, particularly in sweet dishes. The former can be substituted for fresh milk in some recipes, added to fruit salads and pies instead of cream, or used to make an instant dessert by being stirred into jelly cubes with equal quantities of boiling water to dilute them, then left to set. Condensed milk is mostly used in sweet-making, particularly for toffee and fudge.

Commercially, milk – especially skimmed milk powder – is widely used in manufacturing other dairy products like cheese, cream, ice-cream and yoghurt, as well as in more unlikely savoury products like sausages and ready-made fish pies.

Fresh milk keeps in the refrigerator for 3–6 days; UHT and sterilized milk can be stored in a cool dry place for several months, although they should be kept in the refrigerator once opened and used up within a few days. Evaporated and condensed milks will keep in the same way as any other canned product. Unopened dried milk powder keeps indefinitely in a cool dry place, but once it has been rehydrated it should be treated in the same way as fresh milk.

word origin The origins of milk are very ancient, probably from an Indo-European source meaning 'to wipe' or 'stroke', a tender description of the traditional act of pulling on cows' udders in order to release their milk. Milk has always been fundamental to well-being; hence to possess the 'milk of human kindness' means to be full of compassion and fine feelings; and the recognition that milk was necessary to any *quality* of life led to its being used in the Bible as a metaphor for the Promised Land, a 'land flowing with milk and honey'.

did you know?

• All mammals spend the first part of their life drinking only their mother's milk or an approximation of it, but humans are unique in that they also drink and use the milk of other mammals. No one knows when this began, but the likelihood is that it happened fairly quickly after the animals themselves began to be domesticated (sheep were the first, about 11,000 years ago). By around 7000 years ago, cave paintings suggest that animals were not only being milked by humans, but that milk was being used to make cheese too.

• Our consumption of milk is unique in another respect: we continue to use it long after we've been weaned onto solid food. Or at least some of us do; drinking milk and using it to make other dairy products is mostly a western phenomenon, and many Asians and Africans (among others) are lactose-intolerant; that is they lose the ability to digest the sugar in milk as they grow to adulthood. Until recently it was assumed that this was a deficiency and that the 'normal' human state was to be lactose-tolerant, but recent research has confirmed the reverse is true, and that western peoples have probably genetically evolved themselves over thousands of years so that their adult bodies can absorb milk sugar. Lactose-intolerant people can, in fact, sometimes consume dairy foods like yoghurt and soured cream where lactic-acid-producing bacteria are added to milk to turn the lactose or sugar into lactic acid.

• For most of its existence, milk was obtained in the usual way, by manually manipulating the udders of the cow to release the liquid. Yields were low and even an expert milker could only manage about six animals an hour. The invention of the first milking machines in 1894 changed all that, and modern ones can now milk 100 cows in the same length of time. In terms of purity, while country dwellers may have enjoyed fresh clean milk straight from the cow, by the 18th century most other people had access only to dirty, diluted versions of the real thing, which often helped to spread disease. Pasteurization, something now routinely carried out on 99 percent of milk, first began in the early years of the 20th century, both to raise the general quality of the product and to stop the spread of tuberculosis and other diseases.

mozzarella

A soft, fresh egg-shaped Italian cheese, mozzarella is made either from cow's milk or from that of water buffaloes. It is a spun or *pasta filata* cheese. After a bacterial culture and then rennet is added to the milk to coagulate it into solid curds and liquid whey, the curds are concentrated, first by being cut to release more whey and then by being immersed in hot water to soften so that they can be 'kneaded' or spun out to form long elastic strands. When the proper consistency is reached, small pieces are moulded into shape before being plunged into cold water to help them maintain their shape; they are salted and packed (usually in whey) for sale.

There are several different types. *Mozzarella di bufala* is the original cheese, made only in Italy from buffalo's milk. Softer and less rubbery than other versions, it's always packed in whey. Ordinary oval-shaped mozzarella is made from cow's milk and is sometimes called *fior di latte.* It is mostly made in Italy and it is stored in whey or brine. Block mozzarella is mostly made in Denmark and the United States (although some is made in Italy) and is sold dry; it's only really suitable for cooking. Others that are occasionally available include tiny mini-mozzarellas called bocconcini, which are made from cow's milk and stored in whey, and smoked mozzarella, a largish oval cheese made from cow's milk in Italy and the United States, which is smoked over burning wood.

using it Being a fresh cheese, mozzarella is perishable and should be kept in the refrigerator. Once the package has been opened, any remaining cheese should be stored in a bowl of water (or the reserved whey) in the refrigerator and used within a day or so.

Mozzarella is rarely eaten as part of a special cheese course (although a good buffalo mozzarella would be fine for this), but is widely used with other ingredients. It makes a popular first-course salad with sliced tomatoes, avocado and fresh basil, for instance, and a good sandwich filling, particularly with tomato and Parma ham or crumbled bacon. An Italian classic is

mozzarella in carrozza, a mozzarella sandwich dipped into beaten egg and flour, then deep-fried until golden. Mozzarella is also an integral part of a good pizza and a 'layer' in traditional lasagne, as well as a component of many sauces for pasta.

word origin Mozzarella means 'little slice' in Italian, a reference to the way it's made, by shredding the curd mixture.

did you know?

There have been water buffaloes in the southern part of Italy almost since Roman times, and cheese made from their milk dates back to about the 15th century. The best buffalo mozzarella still comes from the southern part of the country, from an area to the south of Naples, and was originally made from unpasteurized milk.

omelette

A savoury or sweet dish made from beaten eggs, classic standard omelettes can be plain (without a filling or topping) or filled, and rolled up, folded into a semi-circle or cooked into a flat round 'cake'. Soufflé omelettes are made slightly differently, by separating out the egg whites and whisking until stiff before folding into the yolk mixture. These omlettes can be cooked both on top of the stove and in the oven, but usually finish cooking under the grill. Fillings and flavourings are limited only by the cook's imagination. Popular ones include grated cheese, herbs, mushrooms, sliced peppers, chopped ham and chopped potato for savoury omelettes, and jam, puréed fruit and honey for sweet ones.

To make a classic French omelette, cook the beaten seasoned eggs (about three per person) gently in melted butter in a small heavy pan until almost set, stirring only enough to let uncooked egg run onto the pan, then roll up or fold over and slide out onto a plate. Add any filling as the eggs are setting or just before rolling up the omelette. For a flat omelette, ingredients such as chopped onions and other vegetables may be cooked in the pan before the eggs are added. A few omelettes are cooked on both sides rather than just one, something that may hark back to the original dish.

using it Savoury omelettes are usually served as a light meal, but could also be cut up and used as a sandwich filling or garnish for rice dishes. Sweet omelettes are served as a dessert.

word origin Omelette is French and derived from the Latin *lamella,* meaning 'thin metal plate'. It first appeared in English around the 16th century, although the dish was known before this.

did you know?

• Omelettes are very old – we know that thick egg 'cakes' were around during Roman times, and that they may have been Arab in origin. The modern Middle Eastern/North African eggah, Spanish tortilla (a flat, heavy omelette and not to be confused with Mexican bread) and Italian frittata are probably all descended from this ancient version. Light fluffy French omelettes go back to medieval times.

Parmesan

In English-speaking countries, the word Parmesan is still sometimes used generally to describe Italian cow's milk cheeses of the *grana* family, whose identifying features include graininess and an extremely hard texture. The best of the *granas*, and the one the English name comes from, is Parmigiano-Reggiano, a yellow cheese that is so hard it's normally split open into irregular pieces with a special wide-bladed instrument, rather than being sliced in the usual way with a knife or wire. (Other *granas* include grana padano, which is made near Parmigiano-Reggiano in the Po Valley in northern Italy; a similar sheep's milk cheese used in the same way as the *granas* is pecorino romano, which is made primarily in the Lazio region around Rome.)

True Parmigiano-Reggiano is made from unpasteurized milk in the same way as most other **cheese**: first a bacterial culture and then rennet are added to the milk so that it will coagulate into solid curds and liquid whey, after which the curds are cut into very small grains to release more whey and then 'cooked' or heated so that the grains fall to the bottom of the heating container and form a solid mass. This mass is lightly pressed into moulds, then brined and ripened for between eighteen months and four years. All genuine Parmigiano-Reggiano cheese is branded by having the name stamped on the crust before the cheese is brined.

using it The most widely available 'Parmesan cheese' is sold pre-grated in tubs. It is, in fact, a mixture of several different types of hard, unidentified cheese that may or may not include *granas*, and it has very little taste. Commercial fresh grated or fresh shaved Parmesan is now also sold in small tubs and is usually Parmigiano-Reggiano; this keeps for anything from a few days to two months in the refrigerator. Most supermarkets now also sell packaged wedges of Parmigiano-Reggiano, grana padano or pecorino romano, all of which will keep for a few weeks.

The best way to buy Parmesan is in a solid hunk prised from a fresh drum of Parmigiano-Reggiano. It should be a good yellow colour, slightly crumbly in texture and moist and salty to taste; any that's whitening around the edges and dry should be avoided. To protect it, the cheese should be wrapped in several layers of foil and stored in the refrigerator. Shave or grate it as near to being used as possible, since it loses flavour quickly once it's been taken from the block.

A hunk of fresh moist Parmigiano-Reggiano tastes wonderful served with olives, salami and fruit like figs and pears.

But its true calling is as a near-perfect cooking cheese, since it melts when it comes into contact with heat rather than becoming rubbery or stringy. Grated Parmesan is an ingredient in classic Italian sauces like pesto and carbonara, as well as being sprinkled over nearly all pasta dishes, **risottos**, many soups and gratin dishes. Shaved Parmesan is a fashionable addition to salads and antipasto.

word origin   The name Parmesan comes from the region of origin, the valley of the river Po around the city of Parma.

did you know?

- Parmigiano-Reggiano was already established in Italy by the 13th century, and an imaginary mountain grated from it is lovingly described in Boccaccio's *Decameron*, written a hundred years or so later. It's still made artisanally rather than in a factory and only in five specially designated areas in the region, protected by law in much the same way as a good wine.

ricotta

This soft, creamy Italian cheese used to be made solely from the whey left over when curds formed during the making of cheeses like **Parmesan** and provolone. Nowadays, however, it's more likely to be made from whole or skimmed cow's or even ewe's milk.

Traditional ricotta was (and still is) possible because whey contains enough proteins to enable it to form into a soft mass with a little help. Making it, therefore, begins in the same way as for most other **cheese** by adding first a bacterial culture, then rennet to milk to separate the curds from the whey. The curds are then heated or 'cooked' to concentrate them so that they can be made into a hard cheese, and the whey is drained off. Some previously curdled whey or commercial coagulant is now added to the drained-off whey and the mixture heated or 'cooked' again until it forms soft curds. These are then pressed lightly to extract

some more liquid before being sold as a fresh unripened cheese, or drained more thoroughly into a firmer shape, which is dried before being sold.

using it   Ricotta is widely used in both savoury and sweet cooking. For savoury dishes, the great affiliation is with pasta – it 'layers' those cooked in the oven, like lasagne, fills those that are stuffed, like ravioli, and can be combined with other ingredients such as bacon and peas to make simple stovetop sauces for pasta shapes. It also makes a good stuffing base for vegetables like peppers or baked potato. In sweet cooking, ricotta can be sprinkled with brown sugar and/or marsala (or with rum, sugar and a little finely ground coffee powder) and served as a simple dessert, but more usually it is an ingredient in other dishes such as Sicilian cassata, with sponge, chocolate and glacé fruit, and cheesecake.

word origin   Ricotta is Italian for 'recooked', a reference to the way the cheese is made.

did you know?

- The first real description of the modern cheese appeared in Italy during the early 15th century, although something similar was made by the ancient Romans.
- The whey left over from Parmesan production has other uses too: some is fed to the pigs that are specially bred to produce **prosciutto.**

soufflé

A light raised dish made from separated **eggs**, a soufflé can be sweet or savoury. Nearly all savoury soufflés are baked, but sweet soufflés can be cooked or uncooked. The basic mixture is usually flavoured with already cooked or easily cooked ingredients, in savoury soufflés these can range from grated cheese (Cheddar or Parmesan, for instance),chopped ham, chopped vegetables like asparagus or broccoli, to fish such as cooked salmon or crab; sweet soufflés can be flavoured with spirits (brandy, Grand Marnier and rum), coffee, chocolate, citrus zest and juice, and fruit purées.

Hot savoury soufflés are traditionally made by beating a chosen flavouring into thick **béchamel sauce**, then blending in egg yolks and, finally, stiffly whisked egg whites. For sweet baked soufflés the base is usually a thick pastry cream rather than béchamel. The mixture is baked in a greased, straight-sided soufflé dish until dramatically risen. It used to be thought that opening the oven door during cooking would cause the soufflé to collapse, but this is not likely (although draughts should be avoided). The important thing is to serve the soufflé as soon as it is ready.

For cold soufflés, the base is normally a sauce such as béchamel, **custard** or sabayon (egg yolks and caster sugar whisked in a bowl set over a pan of hot water until thick and light). The flavouring is added with softened gelatine and, when the mixture is on the point of setting, stiffly whisked egg whites and whipped cream are folded in. The mixture is set in a soufflé dish fitted with a paper collar, so that when the collar is removed the dessert has the appearance of having risen in the oven like a hot soufflé.

using it Savoury soufflés can be served as first or main courses, while sweet ones make elegant desserts.

word origin Soufflé is French and means 'puffed up'.

soured cream

This is a slightly thickened single **cream** whose lactose (sugar) has been converted into lactic acid to give a characteristic 'sour' taste. It's made commercially by adding a special bacterial culture to cream that has been pasteurized and homogenized (see **milk**), then allowing it to ferment. It is re-pasteurized to kill the bacterial activity before being sold.

The French version of soured cream, crème fraîche, is twice as rich and

thicker. A half-fat crème fraîche is also available. Smetana is a mixture of soured cream and skimmed milk that contains 10 percent fat.

using it Most soured creams will keep in the refrigerator for 10–21 days.

The slightly tart, refreshing taste of all soured creams works well in both savoury and sweet dishes. In savoury cooking, they can be stirred into hot and cold soups, sauces, quiche fillings and vegetable purées to enrich them. (If to be cooked, soured cream and smetana should not be boiled, as this will cause them to separate and curdle; being higher in fat, crème fraîche can be boiled.) They also make a good filling for baked potatoes, especially mixed with chopped herbs and garlic. In sweet cooking, they are added to cheesecakes, cakes and biscuits, and they make delicious partners for sweet fruits like pineapple as well as pies and hot puddings such as crumbles.

did you know?

• Soured cream is particularly associated with the cooking of central and eastern Europe, where it has been widely used for centuries. Nearly all the classics from that part of the world, from Russian borscht to Hungarian goulash, either contain it or are served with it. It began to make an appearance in other parts of Europe and English-speaking areas of the world around 30 years ago.

yoghurt

Variously spelled yoghurt, yoghourt and yogurt, this is a thick, fermented (curdled) dairy product made from **milk**. All kinds are used – cow's milk is the most common, but yoghurt is also made from goat's, ewe's and water-buffalo milk – and the milk may be full-fat or skimmed.

To make yoghurt, milk is first boiled to kill off the micro-organisms it contains. Commercially, skimmed milk powder is then usually added to enrich it and stabilizers like gelatine and pectin are stirred in to help it set. When the mixture cools to 45°C, a yoghurt 'culture' is added, normally the bacteria *Lactobacillus bulgaricus* and *Streptococcus thermophilus*. These work by converting part of the lactose (sugar) in the milk into lactic acid (it is this that gives plain yoghurt its slightly tart taste). Once the yoghurt has finished fermenting, which can take anything from 4–6 hours, sweeteners and flavourings such as fruit are added.

For most commercial yoghurt, the bacterial culture is added before the yoghurt is put into pots, but set yoghurts have the bacterial culture added in the pot. Greek yoghurts are made using a slightly different combination of bacterial cultures and they are strained to remove some of the liquid, making them very rich and thick. Bio yoghurts also use a slightly different bacterial culture, usually *Lactobacillus acidophilus* and *Lactobacillus bifidus*, which are thought to be particularly beneficial to the digestive system.

All yoghurt is 'live' – it contains living bacteria – even if it is not labelled as such. The exception is yoghurt that has been processed so it can be stored without refrigeration (the processing kills the bacteria).

using it Most yoghurts keep for around 8–15 days in the refrigerator.

Yoghurt can be eaten for breakfast, as a snack or for dessert, and used instead of cream as an accompaniment for puddings and desserts. Plain yoghurt can also be used instead of **cream**, **soured cream** or crème fraîche in cooking, in both savoury and sweet dishes, although care should be taken when heating it. Mixing in a little cornflour will prevent it from separating.

Yoghurt is widely used in Balkan, Middle Eastern and Asian cooking, particularly Indian. It is the basis of tzatziki and raita, for instance, the flavoured yoghurt-based salads/dips found throughout the area, it is used in marinades, and it is the cooking liquid in dishes such as korma and rogan josh. It also forms the basis of drinks, in particular lassi, which is basically diluted yoghurt either spiced with cumin or sweetened with sugar and sometimes flavoured with rosewater.

word origin All the various spellings for this word in English come from the Turkish name for the product, *yoghurt*, probably because yoghurt was first introduced to the rest of Europe from that part of the world.

did you know?

• Although it has only been around in western Europe and the English-speaking world for 80–90 years, and popular and widely available for much less than that, yoghurt has been eaten by people in other parts of the world for 7000 years or more. No one knows for sure how and where it originated, but the first yoghurt was probably made by accident and in the Middle East. What *is* known is that once they had it, people were quick to realize how valuable it was, and it soon spread westwards to the Balkans and eastwards to Persia, then to other parts of Asia including the Indian subcontinent.

• The first person in western Europe to advocate eating yoghurt was a Russian colleague of the French chemist Louis Pasteur named Ilya Metchnikoff, a Nobel Prize winner in 1908 for his discovery that white cells fight bacterial infection. He observed that many of the inhabitants of Balkan and eastern European countries who ate yoghurt as a staple part of their diet (Bulgarians, for instance) lived to a ripe old age, and leapt to his own conclusions. It might taste good and it might be reasonably healthy (although adding lots of sugar destroys some of the good it might do you), but modern science suggests that yoghurt is not the elixir of life that Metchnikoff thought it to be.

Fish & Seafood

We are at long last becoming aware of the important role that fish and shellfish play in a healthy diet. Much as I still enjoy the occasional pleasures of dishes such as steak and kidney pudding and Lancashire hotpot, these are relics from another age, when British food was all we ate and when we worked much harder physically and needed more calories. These days we're used to being able to buy fresh produce from all over the world, and we know what to do with it. We eat speedier, lighter meals, and fish fits our requirements perfectly. It's light and low in fat. All fish, but particularly oily ones like herring, salmon and mackerel, contain omega-3 fatty acids, which can help reduce the risk

of heart disease and strokes and are thought to be vital for the development of unborn babies. If we all ate seafood three or four

There's nothing more joyful or exhilarating to me than fresh fish simply cooked
Rick Stein

times a week, we'd probably improve our chances of living longer.

Interestingly our taste in fish has changed, partly because of changing availability. Until recently, most people would have listed cod, haddock and plaice as their favourites, or, if they were well off, turbot, salmon and Dover sole. These days, though, you could add hitherto little-known fish such as monkfish, John Dory and sea bass, plus exotic fish like snapper, tuna and swordfish. That goes for shellfish, too. In addition to our own lobster and crabs, we can now eat Balmain bugs from Australia, soft-shell crabs from America and large prawns from Thailand, India and Madagascar.

We are all getting more enthusiastic about fish. A programme made by the BBC, called 'The Nation's Favourite Food', listed fish and seafood in the top ten. For someone who has spent thirty-odd years trying to enthuse the previously rather indifferent population of these islands, surrounded by one of the world's richest fishing grounds, this has come as a very pleasant surprise. Annual consumption has started to rise, we're on the way. As I wrote once, 'There's nothing more joyful or exhilarating to me than fresh fish simply cooked.' I hope that this section inspires you to find out more about fish and become a convert to the pleasures of cooking and eating it.

Rick Stein

anchovy

This is any one of a family of small oily fish related to herring that congregate in warmer waters throughout the world. The major food species, the greenish-blue *Engraulis encrasicolus*, is European in origin, mostly inhabiting the Mediterranean and Black Seas and parts of the eastern Atlantic. It rarely grows to more than about 12cm long. A related species, *Engraulis ringens*, is found off the western coasts of Latin America and is normally processed into fish meal.

Although anchovies are commonly found fresh in southern Europe, nearly everywhere else they are only available cured. Curing is still normally done in the traditional way, by storing the fresh fish in salt for a day or so, then either beheading and gutting them or leaving them whole before washing in brine and 'dry-salting' them (see **fish**); it can take anything from 2–5 months for the salted fish to mature and dry out. Finally, they are cleaned and usually filleted before being canned or bottled, occasionally just in salt but now usually in olive or vegetable oil.

using it Canned or bottled anchovies can be stored indefinitely, but once opened should be kept in the refrigerator and used within a few days. Those preserved in salt need to be rinsed under cold running water or soaked for 30–60 minutes to remove the salt before use.

Fresh anchovies look and taste similar to **sardines** and can be grilled or barbecued in the same way. Cured anchovies are occasionally the main ingredient in dishes, particularly in Mediterranean France and Italy. In France, they are pounded with garlic, herbs and olive oil to make anchoïade, a paste traditionally spread on bread to be toasted in the oven; or mashed with black olives, garlic, capers, lemon juice and olive oil to make tapenade, which is also spread over bread or used to stuff hard-boiled eggs. In Italy, the classic anchovy dish is bagna cauda, a mixture of olive oil, garlic and chopped anchovy fillets that's heated and mashed until it becomes a thick fondue-like sauce for raw vegetables and bread.

For the most part, however, cured anchovies are used in small quantities as a flavouring or garnish. For example, they can be pounded into softened butter with a little lemon juice to make a classic accompaniment for fish, or mashed into a tomato-based pasta sauce, and as a garnish they are a classic part of dishes like pizza and salade niçoise (see **salad**).

Some modern condiments like Worcestershire sauce contain anchovies, and they are also made into anchovy essence, which is used as a flavouring in many ready-made foods, including some unexpected ones like Melton Mowbray pie.

word origin Spain was an early provider of cured anchovies to Britain, and it's from the Spanish *anchova*, meaning 'dry' or 'dry fish', that anchovy comes.

did you know?

• Anchovy has been a popular flavouring ingredient for over 2000 years and both the Greeks and Romans made a condiment from the fermented entrails of fish, including anchovies. Garum or liquamen, as the Romans called the one they made, was probably similar to modern-day fish sauce, and was added to nearly all foods to provide extra flavour and saltiness.

caviar

This is the salted roe, or eggs, of several species of sturgeon, a northern hemisphere fish that is mostly found in the Caspian Sea. It isn't all that difficult to 'make' caviar. Adult female fish are caught before spawning and their eggs (which can make up 10–20 percent of the body weight) removed; these are cleaned and salted before being packed for sale. The more lightly salted, the better – the best grade of caviar is called *malassol*, which means lightly salted in Russian.

Some caviar is pasteurized to preserve it, although this can harden the eggs. Traditionally, Russia and the Caspian states that once formed part of the old Soviet Union, such as Kazakhstan, were the major suppliers of caviar, but within the last few decades Iran has also become an important producer.

There are three types: beluga comes from the largest species of sturgeon (*Huso huso*, which can weigh as much as 850kg) and varies in colour from very light to dark grey; sevruga (*Acipenser stellatus*) is a smaller species with darker, smaller eggs; and oscietra (*Acipenser guldenstaedti*) has eggs that normally range from light to dark brown in colour, but occasionally provides the rarest of all caviars, the yellow 'golden' variety. Of the three, beluga is considered the best but makes up only a tiny part of the market; sevruga is the most widely available and least expensive (although where caviar is concerned this is relative). The damaged eggs of fish caught towards the end of the season are made into salty pressed caviar by being drained to remove about 35 percent of their moisture.

True caviar, even pressed caviar, shouldn't be confused with the cheaper black or red lumpfish roe (*Cyclopterus lumpus*) or the roes of chum **salmon** (*Oncorhynchus keta*), called red caviar.

using it Caviar keeps for a couple of months in the refrigerator; once it has been opened it should be used within 2–4 days. Silver or metallic spoons react with the eggs and spoil the taste, so bone or plastic ones are recommended for eating it.

The classic way to serve the best caviar is on its own as an appetizer over crushed ice – it needs nothing but a spoon; however, it could be accompanied by thin toast and butter or eked out with blinis (Russian **pancakes**) and soured cream or chopped hard-boiled egg and onion.

word origin Despite the fact that caviar is almost synonymous with Russia, the name comes from the Turkish *khavyar*, which could be derived either from the Crimean town of Kaffia, once an important international trading port, or from an earlier Persian word *chav-jar,* meaning 'cake of power'.

did you know?

• Aristotle in ancient Greece knew of caviar and the Chinese were trading it a millennium ago, but it was eaten outside Russia and other Caspian countries only by the rich and powerful and has remained a byword for luxury right up until modern times. Towards the end of the 19th century, its elitist status was confirmed in France when the owner of the fashionable Ritz hotel added it to his menus. A hundred years or so on, that status is perpetuated by cost: 250g of beluga caviar retails at over £1000.

• The flesh of sturgeon can be eaten too, although it runs a poor second to the eggs in popularity stakes. Given the size of most species, the 'meat' is available as thin fillets or steaks, and can be cooked in the same way as **tuna** or veal **escalopes**.

clam

Technically, a clam is any two-shelled **mollusc** that can hinge itself tight shut. Popularly, however, the name is reserved for several specific species found burrowing in cooler shallow coastal waters around the world, ironically including some whose shells gape open slightly. Clams are particularly associated with the eastern seaboard of the United States, although there are also native European and Asian species.

There are two major types of American clam: hard-shell clams and soft-shell clams. Hard-shell clams (*Mercenaria mercenaria*) have round shells and firm flesh, and come in various sizes up to about 12cm. On the East Coast, where they are also called quahog, there are littlenecks, the smallest, then cherrystones, followed by the largest, called chowders. Soft-shell clams, including steamers (*Mya arenaria*) and razor clams, can be as large as the largest hard-shells, although they normally average out at around 6cm; despite their name, they have brittle shells. Both larger hard-shell clams and soft-shells are now also found in some northern parts of Europe.

Elsewhere, the French reserve the word clam for hard-shell types, and call native European varieties by different names, some of which have found their way into English. So palourdes (*Venerupis pullastra*), occasionally called carpet-shells in Britain, are smallish clams with grooved yellowish shells, while praires or Venus clams (*Venus verrucosa*) are warty and wavy-shelled. Razorshells (*Solen marginatus* and others), the other type occasionally available, have long brownish rectangular 'soft' shells that look like old-fashioned straight razors, hence the name. All razorshells gape slightly when raw and, like other soft-shells, are exceptions to the rule that raw open clams should be discarded. In Japan, where clams are a favourite seafood, the most common species is the chestnut-shaped hamaguri (*Meretrix lusoria*).

using it When preparing hard-shell clams, discard any that are open and don't close when tapped (they are dead), then scrub clean and rinse. Soft-shell and razorshell clams need to be kept in water for about a day after buying to get rid of the grit and dirt that often find their way inside the shells.

Small hard-shell clams can be eaten raw, with a squeeze of lemon; open them in the same way as **oysters**. Larger clams are cooked, usually by steaming with flavouring herbs and vegetables until the shells open (any that don't open should be discarded). After steaming they can be left on the half shell and topped with a flavouring mixture before briefly baking or grilling. Soft-shell clams are normally steamed, although they

are also occasionally 'shucked' (removed from their shells), coated in batter and fried.

Canned or bottled clams are more widely available than fresh ones and can be substituted for them in many recipes, including American clam chowder, a thick soup that can be made creamy in New England-style or with tomatoes (Manhattan). Clams are also added to rice dishes such as **risotto** and paella, and made into a sauce for pasta.

word origin Clam comes from the Old English *clamm*, meaning a 'bond' or 'bondage' (the same root as the word clamp), a reference to the way clams hinge themselves shut. Quahog comes from a Native American word meaning 'hard shell'.

• Although clams have been known in Europe since neolithic times, it's the history of the American varieties that is particularly colourful. Native Americans ate them (the all-American clambake was popular long before Europeans arrived) and they were so popular among some tribes they were used to make 'wampum' or bead money.

cod

The cod is a member of the *Gadidae* family of coldwater white **fish**, which also includes coley, haddock, hake and whiting. It can grow to about 1.5m long, although half that size is more usual. It has a large head and a pale lateral line running the length of its body; its colour varies according to habitat, but is normally greyish-green with dappled patches on the back and sides, silver on the underbelly. The flesh is firm and white, and becomes flaky when cooked.

Cod breeds prolifically but has been overfished for so many years now that it is becoming scarcer and more expensive every year, even in traditional habitats like the northern Atlantic (*Gadus morhua*), around Greenland (*Gadus ogac*) and in the northern Pacific (*Gadus macrocephalus*).

using it Fresh cod is available whole or cut into steaks and fillets; the fish is also sold smoked (both fillets and the roe), and occasionally salted. Fresh cod can be cooked by almost any method, from steaming and poaching to frying, grilling, deep-frying and roasting. Whatever method is used, it should not be overcooked as this will make it dry.

Plainly fried, steamed or grilled cod can be served with anything from a squeeze of lemon juice to a traditional sauce such as parsley-flavoured **béchamel**, **hollandaise** or meunière (melted butter and lemon juice). Classic deep-fried battered cod is usually served with chips and tartare sauce or malt vinegar. Cooked cod can also be mixed with vegetables and a thick white sauce, then topped with mashed potato for a fish pie; blended with egg, fresh breadcrumbs and flavourings like coriander, spring onions and ginger, then dipped in a tempura batter and deep-fried for oriental-style croquettes; or mixed with mashed potato and seasonings to make traditional fish cakes.

As smoked cod is cold-smoked (see **smoked fish**), it needs to be cooked before being eaten. It can be added to chowders, poached to be served cold with mayonnaise and boiled potatoes, or used in the Anglo-Indian dish kedgeree, a pilaff-type mixture of smoked fish, basmati rice, hard-boiled eggs and curry powder. Smoked cod's roes (eggs) are the basic ingredient in the Greek dip taramasalata, with milk-soaked breadcrumbs, olive oil, lemon juice and garlic.

Salt cod is dry-salted (see **fish**) until it has lost about one-third of its moisture ('wet' salt cod, the type popular in France and Italy) or until it has lost about two-thirds. This latter is the type usually found in Britain, and also particularly favoured in Spain and Portugal where it's more or less a staple food. Salt cod needs to be rehydrated and desalted before being used, by being soaked in water that is changed several times. The fish is simmered in flavoured liquid for about 10 minutes before being used. The classic salt cod dish is French brandade de morue, a spicy mayonnaise-like paste made by combining cooked salt cod with lots of garlic, olive oil, milk and (sometimes) mashed potatoes; it's usually served with bread as a first course.

word origin A possible root may be the Old English *codd*, meaning 'bag', presumably a reference to the fish's appearance (if it's true). Codswallop, sadly, isn't an angry cod with a powerful right fin, but a mixture of someone's name (Hiram Codd, who invented a type of mineral-water bottle with a stopper) and wallop, an old slang word for beer; it may mean 'rubbish' or 'nonsense' now, but originally codswallop was the name given by dedicated beer drinkers to any mineral water or weak drink.

did you know?

• Three or four hundred years ago cod was one of the most available and cheapest fish in northern Europe and America; there were so many huge shoals off the coast of New England, in fact, that a beautiful cape near Boston was named after it. Cod didn't have a particularly good reputation, however, perhaps because it was usually eaten dried, salted or smoked (probably almost out of its skin) to provide Lenten and Friday food for those too poor to afford something better and unlucky enough to live too far away from a source of fresh fish. Its standing only improved in Victorian times, perhaps because of better availability of the fresh fish as well as the magic partnership with chips.

• Cod has the same nutrients as other white fish, but its liver is especially rich in omega-3 essential fatty acids and the fat-soluble vitamins A and D. Since the liver isn't usually eaten, these nutrients are extracted from it and made into cod liver oil, which is sold as an omega-3/vitamin supplement.

crab

There are about 4500 different species of this **crustacean** around the world. Most are water-based, although a few types scuttle about on land, all of them shedding, or moulting, their outside skeleton or carapace so that they can grow. Crabs have a tiny 'face' (mostly bulging eyes) on the edge of a large round or oval body and their five pairs of limbs – including a heavy pair of pincers – are positioned around their body. The limbs are detachable, a useful trait if one is caught by predators or stuck between rocks, and will eventually grow back during the course of their moults. They range in size from a tiny crab that lives inside oyster shells to a giant Japanese one that measures about 4m wide.

There are many edible varieties, of which the following are the most common. The blue crab (*Callinectes sapidus*) is native to the eastern seaboard of North America, particularly around the coast of Maryland, although it has now been introduced into the Mediterranean. Its flesh is white and meaty. It is considered to be a particular delicacy when eaten in its moulted state as the soft-shell crab. Since the blue crab sheds and regrows its carapace in just over 24 hours, the window of opportunity for soft-shell eating isn't huge, so these days the crabs are caught in advance and kept under observation in special floats until they oblige (in summer, with a peak in June and July). The brownish-red common crab (*Cancer pagurus*) is found along the northern Atlantic coasts of Europe as well as the eastern ones of North America, and is the crab normally available in Britain. The spider crab (*Maia squinado*) is a northern European species particularly popular in France; it's lack of popularity elsewhere may have something to do with its unlovely appearance – it has a warty back and long, thin menacing legs, hence the name – but it has marvellous sweet flesh. The snow crab (*Chionoecetes opilio*) inhabits the deep cold waters of the Atlantic Ocean, and is usually canned or processed rather than sold fresh.

using it Nearly all fresh crabs sold in supermarkets and fishmongers are already cooked. When buying, look for legs tucked up against the body, which means the crab was cooked when still very fresh, a good thing where taste is concerned. Getting at the flesh requires patience and tools – lobster crackers or a small hammer to crack the claws and a skewer to extricate the meat from all the nooks and crannies. Fresh crabmeat is classically served with mayonnaise, or is 'dressed' by arranging the creamy brown and flaky white meat separately in the cleaned shell. Crabmeat can also be used in many other ways, such as in a sandwich filling, to make crabcakes or in a pasta sauce.

Soft-shell crabs are fried or grilled quickly, then usually sauced simply with melted butter or lemon.

word origin Crab comes from the Old German *krabben,* meaning 'to scratch or claw'.

• The meat from a crab makes up just 30–35 percent of its total weight. In the common crab, about two-thirds of this meat is brown. A male or cock crab is usually more expensive than a female or hen because its meat is considered to be better. The gender can be established by checking the flap or tail, which is located under the carapace: if it's broad and roundish the crab is female; thinner and pointy, it's male.

crustacean

Crustaceans are one of the two main types of shellfish (the other is **molluscs**), edible sea creatures with external shells or skeletons. Crustaceans have jointed limbs, no backbones and skeletons that are discarded from time to time so that they can grow (the shells grow back again, larger so that they can enclose the expanded flesh); most also have segmented bodies. They are often described as decapods or ten-legged creatures, the ten 'legs' sometimes being roughly equal in size, and sometimes consisting of one pair of heavy pincers or claws (used to catch food and chop or crush it) and four pairs of long, thin legs. Crustaceans include **crab**, **lobster**, **prawn**, **scampi** and **shrimp**.

using it Crustaceans deteriorate quickly after they die and should therefore be bought live, or cooked and eaten on the day they are bought, depending on the individual type. Traditionally, they were smoked or canned to preserve them (prawns and crab in particular), but most are now frozen, usually minus their shells. Frozen shellfish should never be refrozen after being thawed, and most should be thawed before being cooked.

Cooking crustaceans is straightforward, and while getting to the flesh can pose problems, when you do it is almost without exception sweet and succulent. See individual entries for further information.

word origin Crustacean is a simple description of what it is, coming from the Latin *crusta,* meaning 'shell' or 'rind', the same root as the word crust.

did you know?

• Of the two kinds of shellfish, crustaceans have always been relatively rare, with the possible exception of crab, so for most of history they have been the food of the rich rather than the poor. By the time Marco Polo visited China in the 13th century, this division was already clear. Prawns, for instance, were made into delicate little *dim sum* for the powerful elite, while the more common molluscs, such as oysters and mussels, were offloaded onto the peasants.

• Crustaceans contain a variety of minerals and B vitamins and they are low in saturated fat, although they tend to be high in cholesterol. However, it is

considered more important to have a diet low in saturated fat than to avoid cholesterol-rich foods.

fish

There are thousands of different types of fish in the world (one guesstimate says close to 30,000), although only a few hundred are eaten regularly. Nearly all of them are cold- rather than warm-blooded, and most live in saltwater seas or oceans, although some are found in freshwater rivers, streams and lakes, and a few (primarily **salmon** and eel) migrate from one to the other during their lifetime, usually to spawn. Broadly speaking, fish can be divided into two categories: those with bony skeletons (the vast majority) and those without (cartilaginous fish like **skate** and **shark**, whose skeletons are made up of cartilage rather than bone). Sea creatures such as **molluscs** and **crustaceans** are boneless too, although some have external skeletons.

Bony fish come in all shapes, sizes and colours: there are those with sleek tapered bodies adapted to moving around in open seas, like **herring** and **cod**; a few that are extra-long and almost snake-like in appearance, like eel; and those that float at or near the seabed, called flatfish, that are built for inertia rather than movement. These latter fish have broad, flat oval or round unwieldy bodies that tilt slightly to one or other side, so that both of their eyes gravitate to the upper side – some like **sole** have eyes on the right side of their 'head', while left tilters like **turbot** have theirs on that side of their body. Skin colour varies from light, almost colourless, silver to the brightest of oranges, reds and greens and can be an indication of habitat since it acts as camouflage, among other things: those fish that live in bright warm waters come in rainbow colours, while those from cooler climates tend to reflect their steelier environment.

Living in water poses different challenges to living on land, and the way fish have adapted to meet these challenges has a direct bearing on what we eat. The flesh of fish, like that of animals, is made up of muscle, the bits that enable it to move. Water is buoyant, however, so a fish doesn't need a heavy skeleton to counteract the force of gravity as an animal does on land, and its body therefore has less skeleton and more muscle (flesh). But water is denser than air, so although the fish can use this buoyancy to float around most of the time without using its muscles all that much, when more than this is necessary, it needs muscles that are powerful enough to propel it quickly against the resistance it meets; fish muscle fibres, therefore, are short and come in segments (the natural flakes you can see when cooking it), which contract to shoot it quickly through the water in short bursts. They also have less tough connective tissue than animals to hold their muscle segments together and this also affects what we eat: fish flesh is more tender than that of **meat,** but also more fragile, which is why it can break up during cooking.

How a fish gets from its habitat to ours has changed radically during the past half century. Fishing boats and equipment are now more sophisticated so catches have become much larger, and larger nets have made it more difficult to differentiate between young fish and adult ones. As a result, once seemingly inexhaustible stocks are diminishing at an alarming rate and there are now rigid international quotas governing the quantities of most fish that can be taken from the sea. In addition, many of the traditional areas of supply like the North Sea and the Mediterranean have become so polluted that some pink-fleshed fish are now dyed that colour since their flesh has become grey from pollution. Special laws have also been put into place to protect what are called game or sport fish (marlin is an example of the former, salmon the latter) during the times when they spawn.

One consequence of all this is that fish prices have gone up; another that some fish have begun to be 'farmed', that is bred and raised in special cages to guarantee regular supplies – there are now 1000–1500 such farms around the coasts of the United Kingdom, providing about one in three of the fish we eat, and numbers are rising. **Trout** and salmon are the two most frequently farmed fish, but several others, like **sea bass**, tilapia and turbot are now beginning to be raised in this way too.

using it Fresh fish decays quickly once it leaves water and ideally should be eaten as soon as it's caught, or at least as soon afterwards as is practicable. There are many good ways of checking for freshness: for whole fish, it shouldn't smell particularly 'fishy', the eyes should be bright and clear, the body stiff rather than soft, the gills red rather than brownish, and the skin should be brightly coloured and spring back when pressed. For fillets and steaks, flesh should be firm to the touch and any attached skin clear rather than muddy. Fresh fish should be stored loosely wrapped or in airtight packaging in the refrigerator and most should be used within 1–2 days. Both supermarkets and fishmongers descale, gut and clean fish before selling it, and divide it into steaks or fillets too, if appropriate.

Any fish can be frozen, and nearly all types are now available ready-frozen or commercially frozen, then thawed and sold, something which should be indicated at the point of sale. Fish bought fresh can also be frozen at home, in which case it should be wrapped, stored and used within about two months; it should be thawed thoroughly before being cooked and shouldn't be refrozen uncooked.

Before the advent of freezing, the traditional methods of preserving fish were to smoke it (see **smoked fish**) and to salt it. There are two main methods of salting.

Dry-salting was and still is the method used for most white fish, although it's also the way in which anchovy (an oily fish) is cured. Basically it involves storing the fish in layers of salt until about one-third of their natural liquid has drained out. Cod is the most commonly dry-salted fish these days. For brine-salting, which is used mostly for oily fish like herring, the fish are steeped, whole or filleted, in a flavoured salt and water solution (the brine). Oily fish (again especially herring) is also sometimes preserved by being pickled in a flavoured vinegar mixture.

About 120 years ago another form of preserving was invented: canning. Oily fish lend themselves extremely well to canning, and **tuna**, salmon and **sardines**, in particular, are as popular in this form as they are fresh. The canning liquid varies from fish to fish and from manufacturer to manufacturer, but usually includes brine, oil or a sauce such as tomato.

Although the Japanese sometimes eat fish raw (in sashimi), for nearly everyone else, fish is cooked before being eaten. Culinarily, fish is divided into two main types: oily fish, such as herring, salmon, sardine and tuna, which have firm, fairly dense, rich, flavoured flesh; and white fish, including long tapering types like cod and sea bass as well as flatfish like sole, which have moist, white and delicate flesh.

Whatever cooking method is used, care must be taken not to overcook fish, which would make it dry. There are two ways to check if it is ready. For fish cooked on the bone, use the tip of a knife to gently ease the flesh away from the bone; the flesh should come away without resistance and still be slightly translucent at the bone. For most boneless fish, the flesh should flake apart easily when gently tested with the tip of a knife or fork – the exceptions to this are dense fish such as shark, swordfish and tuna steaks, which are best a bit undercooked. Test them like steak (see **meat**): they should feel just firm and slightly springy when pressed with a finger.

word origin Fish comes from the Old English *fisc*, which is probably related to the Latin for fish, *piscis*. When used in expressions, fish tends to have a negative meaning: 'she's a cold fish' (not showing much emotion), presumably a reference to the fact that fish are cold- rather than warm-blooded; and 'there's something fishy about it' (something 'smells' not quite right), a glimpse into the past when a great deal of smelly (or not very fresh) fish was eaten.

did you know?

• Fish have been swimming in the sea almost since the primordial soup and are one of the oldest forms of life on the planet, predating (among others) amphibians, dinosaurs and mammals, all of which are descended from them, by many millions of years. And they've been part of the human diet, at least for coastal peoples, almost from the beginning. Both the Greeks and Romans were passionate consumers, and some were particularly eager: one Greek gourmet reportedly ate himself to death on fish, while rich Romans were willing to pay the equivalent of hundreds of pounds in today's money for their favourite types.

• The early Christian Church chose a fish as its symbol because the letters of the Greek word for fish (*ichthys*) were also the initial letters in Greek of 'Jesus Christ, Son of God, Saviour'. In the Middle Ages the Church reinforced the link by setting aside Fridays and Lent as special meatless days. The idea was that fish, as mostly cold-blooded creatures, would 'cool' the passions and aid contemplation, as opposed to meat, which came from warm-blooded animals and was therefore considered likely to stir your feelings up, thus making contemplation more difficult. (There was probably a more prosaic reason, too: it was official policy to encourage the development of ports and fishing as a way of guaranteeing a supply of sailors for the navy.)

• All fish are high in protein and a good source of B vitamins. In addition, oily fish contain omega-3 'essential fatty acids' – polyunsaturated fats that can only be supplied by food and which are known to help reduce the risk of heart disease and stroke – and the fat-soluble vitamins A and D. Canned fish such as salmon and sardines, where the bones are eaten, offer an extra source of calcium in the diet.

haddock

The haddock (*Melanogrammus aeglefinus*) is a member of the cod family of **fish** and is found in the same parts of the ocean as cod, notably in the North Atlantic. Greyish-purple or brown in colour, it has a thin dark line down each side and large dark 'thumb' marks behind its head. It's smaller than cod, averaging about 50cm in length and 1.5kg in weight.

using it Although it's occasionally available as a whole fish, haddock is usually sold in fillets, either fresh or smoked. Any recipe for fresh or smoked cod will work equally well with haddock, so it's fried, deep-fried and poached in the same way. Poached fillets are often served with a sauce, and cheese or mushrooms, made by stirring these ingredients into a **béchamel sauce**, complement them well; tartare sauce (see **mayonnaise**) is the standard accompaniment for fried or deep-fried haddock.

Most smoked haddock is cold-smoked (see **smoked fish**) and there are some classic cures. Finnan haddie, for instance, is haddock split down the backbone and then cold-smoked until golden (it started out as whole fish smoked over peat fires in the village of Findon near Aberdeen, hence the name). Arbroath smokies are dry-salted, then tied into pairs by the tail and hot-smoked until a rich dark brown. Cold-smoked haddock must be cooked before eating, but Arbroath smokies simply need warming under the grill or in the oven.

word origin Haddock comes from the Old French for the fish, *hadot*. In modern France smoked haddock is considered better than

fresh and is called *le haddock*; the fresh fish is known by a corruption of its scientific name, *églefin*.

• One favourite explanation for the so-called thumb marks on whole haddock is that they were put there by St Peter when he removed a shekel from the fish's mouth to pay his temple tax. It's legend rather than fact, however, since haddock is a northern saltwater fish that has never been found remotely near the Sea of Galilee.

halibut

The halibut (*Hippoglossus hippoglossus*) is the largest of the flatfish, a greenish-brown monster that can weigh up to 250kg. It is found mostly in northern parts of the Atlantic; a related Pacific species (*Hippoglossus stenolepis*) is slightly daintier, rarely more than about 200kg. The Greenland halibut (*Reinhardtius hippoglossoides*) isn't a true halibut, and has bland flesh that doesn't taste anything like the real thing. Apart from size, the halibut's other claim to fame is that, despite being a bona fide flatfish, it swims upright, like cod or haddock.

using it Given its size, halibut is usually sold as steaks, although smaller **fish**, sometimes called chicken halibut, are also available whole. The flesh is meaty and firm, but tends towards dryness, especially in larger fish. The basic cooking methods for steaks are grilling, frying, braising and poaching. Whole chicken halibut braises well and can also be treated in the same way as whole Dover **sole**.

word origin Halibut comes from the Old English *haly,* meaning 'holy', and *butt* or flatfish. The first part is probably because halibut were one of the fish traditionally eaten on the many meatless days instituted by the medieval church.

herring

Although there is only one major species of herring (*Clupea harengus*), this fish has adapted itself slightly to each of its major habitats in the northern Atlantic, Baltic and North Seas – an Atlantic herring is larger than the others, sometimes reaching 35cm in length (although about 25cm is more common), while its Baltic cousin is less fatty. Wherever it is, herring congregates in gigantic shoals (some are large enough to swamp a middle-sized city). Since it's cheap, plentiful and easy to preserve, it has been a staple food of northern Europe for many hundreds of years.

using it Herring is available fresh, whole or in fillets, as well as smoked, salted and pickled. Basic cooking methods are the same for whole fresh fish and fillets, namely frying, grilling and baking. The classic preparation is to dip the whole fish or fillets in beaten egg, then oatmeal and fry in butter but, like **mackerel**, herring is good with a sharp sauce such as mustard. The soft roes of the male fish, called milts, are good 'devilled' (fried with a little cayenne pepper) on toast.

Herring is probably now more popular preserved than fresh, particularly smoked. **Kipper** is the best-known smoked herring, but there are several other types including bloater, which is briefly salted then hot-smoked until it is straw-coloured; it's usually warmed under a grill or in the oven before being served hot with a knob of butter. Herrings are also salted (see **fish**) – a Dutch and Scandinavian speciality is matjes, young fish preserved in a reddish brine mixture, which are delicious with chopped red onion, beetroot and a dollop of soured cream.

Pickled herring is preserved by being steeped in a flavoured acidic liquid like wine or cider vinegar. The most popular type is rollmops, rolled-up fillets pickled with bay leaf, onion, peppercorns and gherkins. In Scandinavia, a selection of herring dishes, fresh, salted, smoked and pickled, remains a classic part of a smorgasbord.

word origin Herring probably comes from *heri*, meaning 'host' or 'army', an apt description of a shoal of herring. A 'red herring' is now mostly confined to the pages of thrillers, but once upon a time it was the real thing, a fresh herring smoked relentlessly until it was bright red and stiff as a board. It was cheap and kept indefinitely, and so was exported to become the food of slaves on West Indian and American plantations. It had a fairly pungent smell and its current meaning comes from this: red herrings were used in hunting, dragged between the dogs and fox to destroy its scent, thus throwing the dogs off the trail. Bloater is so called because it remains plump (or bloated) after its brief curing; matjes (rather appropriately, as the young fish are caught before their gonads develop) means virgin in both Dutch and Swedish.

● Herrings are modest, but their history is anything but. The Battle of the Herrings was fought in 1429 to prevent 'heryings and other lenten stuffe' from reaching the English army besieging Orleans in France at the time (it didn't work because the English won the battle), and the Hanseatic League, an important association of medieval northern European cities, was created in part to protect herring fishing rights. Herring was so important, in fact, that it became a sort of medieval euro: all the city states issued their own currency, which became confusing for international traders; the herring was uniform in size and weight and found everywhere, and so was used to calculate exchange values.

● Until recently, the tiny silvery whitebait was thought to be a unique species and a special scientific name (*Rogenia*) was assigned to it. Now, however, it is recognized in the United Kingdom as a baby member of the herring family, probably a hybrid of herring itself and sprat (other countries use the same word to identify other tiny fish). Whitebait is usually dipped in batter, deep-fried whole and served with a sprinkling of cayenne pepper.

kipper

This is a mildly cured **herring**, made by splitting a whole fresh fish down the middle, flattening it out and then immersing it briefly in a flavoured salt and water brine; it is then cold-smoked (see **smoked fish**).

using it Kippers are sold fresh smoked or frozen. The deep golden-brown colour of most of them is achieved by dye and, although undyed kippers are much paler, they usually taste better.

During Victorian and Edwardian times kippers were one of the classic British breakfast foods, but now they tend to be eaten only on high days and holidays, often with scrambled or poached eggs. A kipper can be grilled, fried or poached in a jug of boiling water. The best way to eat it is to tackle it skin side up on the plate, which means that the bones won't interfere with enjoyment until the end of the meal. Cooked and flaked kippers can also be stirred into rice or **risotto** dishes, or made into a pâté.

word origin Kipper comes either from the Old English *cypera,* meaning copper (a reference to the colour), or could go back to the fish's origins (see below).

did you know?

• Although herrings have been smoked for many centuries, the kipper as we know it today is a fairly recent invention, and started out life as a smoked salmon – the term 'kipper' was applied to a salmon that had just spawned and was not in good enough condition to sell fresh, and so was smoked. At some point in the 1840s, however, a fish curer from Northumberland began to sell herring 'kippered' in this traditional salmon way and a star was born.

lobster

The powerful pincers and slender 'legs' of this elegant **crustacean** are attached to the upper half of its body, while the lower half or 'tail' is made up of seven armoured sections, the last of which fans out into a sort of propeller. Lobster may look good and taste even better, but it is a vicious predator and – when push comes to shove – will eat its own young or attack other members of its own species, which is why the live ones in restaurant fish tanks often have elastic bands wrapped round their pincers (they also help to protect staff from nasty nips when they have to remove them from the water).

There are various species located around the world, but only three major ones. The American lobster (*Homarus americanus*) is found along the eastern seaboard of North America, from Nova Scotia to the Carolinas, although it's most associated with the state of Maine in the northern United States. Weighing in at an average 1–1.5kg, its shell is dark greenish-blue when raw, but turns red when cooked. The European lobster (*Homarus gammarus*), found in areas as far apart as Scotland and the Mediterranean, is dark blue with some speckles when raw but, like the American version, turns red when cooked. On average it weighs about 750g–1kg. The third species is Norway lobster (*Nephrops norvegicus*) or **scampi**.

using it Lobster is sometimes available fresh cooked in shell, although more frequently as shelled frozen tails or pieces. To deal with a whole lobster, turn it onto its back and split it in half lengthways (a cleaver does this neatly) so you can get at the tail meat. You'll need lobster crackers and a skewer or special fork for the claws.

The simple ways of serving lobster are probably the best for enjoying its sweet flesh: accompanied by melted butter or mayonnaise, or halved then grilled or baked, perhaps with herbs or butter. There are endless fancy sauces and preparations for it too, however, including thermidor, grilled lobster halves served with a mustard-flavoured cheese sauce. It can also be used in a cocktail to be served as a luxurious starter (similar to **prawn**), as a filling for home-made ravioli, as the centrepiece of a main-dish salad, or in a creamy soup called a bisque, where the lobster shell is the basis for the stock.

word origin Lobster comes from the Old English *lopustre*, which is derived from the Latin *locusta* meaning 'crustacean' or 'locust-like'. Boiled lobster isn't just a phrase used to describe the British at the beach: English soldiers used to be called this because they 'turned red' (as lobsters do when they cook) when they donned their redcoat uniforms.

did you know?

• Lobsters have always had the reputation of being food fit for kings, so perhaps it wasn't particularly surprising that a sauce made from them featured highly on one particular special dinner given to honour the French king Louis XIV, who was a great gourmet. When the promised consignment of lobsters failed to arrive, however, the humiliated chef (the greatest of the day, called Vatel) committed suicide.
• The crawfish, also called rock lobster and spiny lobster, is a close cousin to the lobster, and is found in the warm waters of the Mediterranean and Caribbean Seas and in the Pacific Ocean. Its body shape is similar, but without the big claws. Crawfish meat is dense and white, although coarser than that of lobster.

mackerel

This is the name given to a group of oily **fish** that are part of the same family as tuna and distributed more or less all around the world. The common mackerel (*Scomber scombrus*) is the major European species, and swims in huge shoals all over the north Atlantic and the Mediterranean. It is beautiful, with a bluish-green back marked with dark curved bands and a silvery white underbelly, and grows to an average length of around 30cm. Another member of the family is the Spanish mackerel or kingfish, which prefers warmer waters, particularly those of the southern hemisphere; Spanish mackerel tend to be much larger than common mackerel, some species occasionally reaching 1.5m in length.

using it Mackerel is available fresh whole or in fillets, and as hot-smoked fillets (see **smoked fish**). Frying and grilling are the basic methods of cooking the fresh fish, and it is traditionally served with a sharp sauce to 'cut' the oiliness. Gooseberry sauce is the English classic, but one made with rhubarb, mustard or horseradish would work well too. The Japanese combination of grilled mackerel fillets with a dip of soy sauce and crushed chilli also tastes delicious.

Smoked mackerel can be flaked and added to salads (spinach or rocket and potato, for example), **risottos** or scrambled eggs, or puréed with horseradish relish, mustard and soured cream into a pâté.

word origin Mackerel comes from the Old French *maquerel*. It has been used as a slang word for pimp in Britain and France since about the 15th century.

mollusc

Molluscs, one of the two main types of shellfish (the other is crustaceans), are creatures with soft bodies and no backbones. Most have a hard, loose casing that encloses their flesh, either in the form of a two-hinged shell (bivalve) or one shell (univalve), and they can be land-based (such as gastropods like snails) or in the sea (marine). **Clams**, cockles, **mussels**, **oysters** and **scallops** are all marine bivalvular molluscs, while winkles, snails and abalone are univalvular. Some marine molluscs have no shell, although they do have an internal cartilage or bone. They are called cephalopods, from a Greek word meaning 'head footed', an eloquent clue to what they look like with their longish bodies, strange heads and dangly tentacles. Cephalopods include cuttlefish, octopus and **squid**.

using it Like all seafood, molluscs deteriorate quickly after they die, and most should be bought live and preferably cooked and eaten on the day of purchase, or bought frozen. Cephalopods will keep for a day or so, but are also better used sooner rather than later. Frozen molluscs should never be refrozen after being thawed and should be thawed before being cooked. Occasionally some, such as oysters and octopus, are smoked or canned to preserve them.

Shelled molluscs are either eaten raw (oysters and very small clams) or require only minimal cooking, and the flesh, cooked or uncooked, is soft, succulent and surprisingly rich. Cephalopods do require cooking and some larger ones such as octopus need tenderizing beforehand.

word origin Mollusc comes from the middle Latin *molluscus,* which is derived from *mollis,* meaning soft, a reference to the soft, unsegmented flesh.

did you know?

• Dumps, or middens, of mollusc shells have been found in neolithic sites all over coastal Europe, so even our remotest ancestors knew a thing or two about what was good to eat. The ease with which molluscs could be caught (or picked off the seashore in the case of **mussels** and winkles) no doubt contributed to their popularity.
• Molluscs are low in fat and contain B vitamins and a variety of minerals such as iron and selenium.

monkfish

Also known as anglerfish, the extraordinary monkfish (*Lophius piscatorius*) inhabits deep waters from the Mediterranean to the Black Sea, as well as being found in the northern Atlantic. It can be large, growing to around 2m in length, but it is the head (which accounts for more than 50 percent of the body weight) that is unbelievable: huge fleshy lips don't quite conceal what seem to be hundreds of sharp teeth and a large throat. Just behind and on the top of its head are two waving 'fishing rods', the one at the front acting as bait to tempt in unwary prey, the other functioning as a secondary lure in case the first one is bitten off. This set-up is very efficient, and monkfish have been known to swallow fish as long as themselves.

using it Not surprisingly perhaps, the head isn't often displayed on fishmonger's slabs, only the end of the body or tail. The flesh is delicate but meaty, and slightly optimistic comparisons are made with lobster; the only bone is a thick cartilaginous backbone. Frying, barbecuing and grilling are the quick ways to cook monkfish, in fillets removed lengthways from either side of the backbone, or cut into cubes or medallions. The whole tail can also be baked or poached.

word origin The first part of the name comes from the great head, which is alleged to look like a monk's hood. The bendy 'fishing rods' are the origin of the alternative name, anglerfish, since it spends most of its time lurking in mud on the ocean floor, rods alert, waiting for prey to 'angle'.

did you know?

• Under kosher law, only fish that have both fins and scales can be eaten, so monkfish, whose slimy skin is scaleless, is on the forbidden list along with cartilaginous fish like ray and skate, eel, crustaceans and molluscs.

mussel

This is a two-shelled **mollusc** that congregates around many cool to warmish coastlines of the world (although most of those we see in supermarkets and fishmongers are cultivated rather than wild since the latter feed on what they can sift out of coastal, often polluted, waters). There are several species, including the European or blue mussel (*Mytilus edulis*), a small to medium-sized bluish to black-shelled creature native to Europe, but now found all over the northern hemisphere; and the New Zealand green-lipped mussel (*Perna canaliculus*), a Pacific species that is larger than European types.

Cultivating, or 'farming', mussels can take time – 12 months in warmer climates, two years or more in cooler waters. The females spawn in summer, producing about a million 'spats', of which only a small fraction survive to maturity. These attach themselves in clumps, using their 'beards' or byssii, to whatever they can find – most are trained up wooden poles in mud flats or up ropes that are attached to rafts anchored near the shore. Mussel flesh at its best is plump and succulent and can vary in colour from off-white to orange-tinged – the colour is an indication of gender, in fact, since the former is male and the latter female.

using it Fresh mussels are normally sold live, in bags of various weights, although thawed frozen green-lipped mussels are also available individually or cooked on the half-shell. Live mussels should have shiny shells and feel full when handled. Before cooking they need to be cleaned under cold running water and any beards removed; any open or cracked mussels should be discarded. Mussels are always cooked before being eaten, usually by being steamed in a little boiling flavoured liquid until they open (discard any that remain closed). If the steaming is done in wine flavoured with parsley, shallots and garlic, it becomes a classic moules marinière. Mussels can be baked or grilled on the half shell too, in the same way as **clams**.

Steamed open and removed from the shell, mussels can be deep-fried, most usually as part of moules et frites (fried mussels and chips with accompanying mayonnaise), a Belgian speciality now popular all over Europe; mixed with a little of their steaming juice into a wonderful sauce for pasta; or added with other seafoods to rice-based dishes like paella.

word origin Mussel comes from *musculus*, the Latin word for mussel.

• Wild mussels were eaten by our neolithic ancestors and have been farmed since Roman times. The invention of modern myticulture (the name given to their cultivation), however, is generally credited to an Irishman named Patrick Walton who was shipwrecked on the Atlantic coast of France during the 13th century. He slung up nets fixed on poles standing in the water to catch birds to eat; this didn't work particularly well, but he soon noticed that hordes of small mussels were attaching themselves to his poles, and was shrewd enough to realize that by adding more poles he could multiply their numbers considerably and survive. Walton's hurdle system, called *buchots* and streamlined, but not all that much, is still the preferred method of mussel cultivation in France.

oyster

This sought-after two-shelled **mollusc** is now farmed to ensure quality and supply. Producing oysters is a difficult, lengthy business: they start out life as a 'spat' or seed, one of millions of minute blobs that emerge from their parent mollusc, and most spend their first eight or nine months clinging onto old shells, tiles or nets in sea water before being transferred to beds or nets (called basins or parks), situated at the mouth of a river to ensure they grow in a mix of salt and fresh water. In appearance, oysters are round or tear-shaped with a top shell that is larger and flatter than the bottom one, which is cup-shaped and contains the flesh; the flesh is usually silvery or greyish brown.

There are three main types. Native oysters (*Ostrea edulis*), which are northern European in origin, are now farmed, particularly around the coasts of Brittany, Eire and southern England; they have lacy, slightly ridged silvery-grey round shells. American oysters (*Crassostrea virginica*), which come from all along the eastern seaboard of North America, are longer, thinner and larger than natives and often have small barnacles on their shell. Rock or Pacific oysters (*Crassostrea gigas*), which look similar to American oysters, are now widely cultivated in Europe because they only take 2–3 years to reach maturity – native and American oysters take 5–7 years, depending on whether they grow in warmer or cooler waters (the cooler the better, within reason, since although they take longer to grow, the flesh is plumper and more delicious).

Pearl oysters (*Pinctada maxima*) are also edible although they aren't considered to be 'true' oysters. They can be huge (up to 30cm occasionally) with inner shells that turn purple as the oysters mature, and of course there may be a pearl inside, created when a tiny foreign body – usually a grain of sand or minute particle of shell – finds its way inside the shell; the oyster protects itself from the intruder by producing a shiny liquid that hardens around it. *Pinctada maxima* are native to South-east Asia.

using it Oysters are sold live and in their shells, which should be firmly shut or shut tight when touched, and the whole oyster should feel heavy for its size. The old saying that they should be eaten only when there is an 'r' in the month isn't really applicable now, given that they are farmed, but natives at least are at their best during the autumn and

winter months and less good in summer when they reproduce. Oysters should be opened just before being served – held cup side down, with a short broad-bladed knife inserted at the narrower, top or hinge end and slid back and forth sideways until the hinge breaks, then twisted so that the shells come apart; any flesh clinging to the upper shell should be detached before the final twist so that it remains with the juice or liquor in the cup half.

The most common way of serving oysters is raw on the half-shell, with at most an accompanying dip of wine vinegar and chopped shallots or lemon wedges. They are, however, occasionally cooked: in the New Orleans classic oysters Rockefeller, for instance, they are grilled on the half shell with garlic, parsley, celery, breadcrumbs and a splash of Pernod; and in traditional English angels on horseback they are removed from the shells, wrapped in bacon and baked or grilled quickly. Shelled oysters are also occasionally tossed in batter and deep-fried, made into fritters or added to meat pies and stews.

word origin Oyster comes indirectly from the Greek *ostrakon*, meaning 'shell'. The word has also found its way into general English usage, and when Shakespeare wrote that the world is your oyster he meant that there was no end to the opportunities that life could offer (a harking back to the idea that potentially every oyster could yield up a pearl).

did you know?

• There were probably few perks attached to being posted to Britannia if you were a Roman soldier – the weather was lousy and the natives restless – but judging by the number of oyster shells found around the remains of nearly every Roman fort in Britain, the local oysters may well have been one. British oysters may even have been exported back to Rome itself,

perhaps in tanks and smothered in snow and ice to keep them alive until they reached their destination.
• Oysters have a reputation as an aphrodisiac, which may be due to their being a rich source of zinc, a mineral needed for reproduction.

plaice

The plaice (*Pleuronectes platessa*) is an oval-shaped flatfish with a brownish top side marked with bright orange spots. It grows to an average 50cm, and is found all over the northern Atlantic and occasionally in the Mediterranean.

using it Plaice is available throughout the year, whole or filleted. The flesh is best in early spring and quite poor around spawning in early summer. One way to tell if a whole **fish** is fresh or not is to check the spots: if they look faded, the fish has probably been around for a few days.

Poaching, frying and deep-frying are the basic ways of cooking both whole fish and fillets. The flesh is delicate, so care should be taken not to overcook it. It is also somewhat bland in flavour, so benefits from a sauce: cheese, mushroom and even melted butter and lemon all complement it well, as does a delicate oriental dipping sauce made with soy sauce, ginger, spring onion and mirin.

word origin Plaice comes via Old French from the late Latin *platessa,* meaning broad, a reference to its shape.

did you know?

• The American equivalent of plaice is flounder, although the American common flounder (*Pseudopleuronectes americanus*) isn't quite the same fish. To make things more confusing, there is a European flounder (*Platichthys flesus*), found in Atlantic waters from the Baltic to the Mediterranean. It is usually a dextral flatfish like plaice (that is, it has both of its eyes on the right side) but occasionally one turns up with both eyes on the left.

prawn

This is a small **crustacean** that ranges in size from a few centimetres to almost 20cm. It has the standard crustacean equipment of five pairs of 'legs' and a segmented body, but unlike most of the others, a prawn's legs are all roughly the same size and the final body segment tapers into a tail rather than spreading out like a propeller. Shell colour varies according to species, anything from the usual red or translucent to green, blue and even striped, and some are luminescent. The flesh is always firm and white with rosy tints when cooked.

The many different species around the world include common prawn (*Palaemon serratus*), a medium-sized coldwater type found all over European coasts, from Norway to the Mediterranean, whose greyish shell turns red when cooked; deepwater prawn (*Pandalus borealis*), which is pink-red when raw and comes from the cold waters of the North Atlantic; Mediterranean prawn (*Aristeus antennatus*), which is larger than the first two types and has a light red shell when raw; and king tiger prawn (*Penaeus plebejus*) and tiger prawn (*Penaeus esculentus*), both large warmwater species from the Pacific that have brownish and greyish translucent shells respectively when raw. Dublin Bay prawn isn't actually a prawn at all, but a type of small lobster usually known as **scampi**. See also **shrimp**.

using it Prawns are sold fresh or frozen, raw or cooked, in shell or peeled. Although it's better to thaw frozen prawns before using, at a pinch at least smaller ones could be cooked straight from the freezer. Whether raw or already cooked and just being reheated, cooking times should be as brief as possible to prevent prawns from becoming dry and chewy. To peel a prawn, twist off the head and pull off the 'legs', then remove the tail or body shell. The dark vein along the back is edible, but can be removed if you prefer – pull it out with your fingers or the tip of a knife. Keep the shells and heads to make stock.

Large raw prawns are delicious grilled or barbecued in their shells. Small peeled prawns can be added to a stir-fry or a curry sauce, mixed with scrambled eggs, turned into a brilliant soup, or used cold in a salad or as a sandwich filling. Prawns are also an ingredient in several classic sauces for white fish such as *sauce normande*. But the most famous prawn dish is probably prawn cocktail, a 1960s extravaganza of rosy crustaceans and even rosier mayonnaise.

word origin In the Middle Ages the name was *prayne* or *prane*, which gradually evolved into prawn, but the origin is unknown. In the United States, all small crustaceans of this family are called shrimp.

did you know?

• Prawn crackers *do* contain prawns (or should by law). They are made by pounding cooked peeled prawns to a paste, mixing this with tapioca flour, salt and sugar and then cutting the resulting mixture into flower shapes. The shapes are deep-fried in very hot oil to make them swell, and dried in the sun to obtain their final shape and texture.

red mullet

Until a few years ago most northern Europeans were only able to sample this meaty white **fish** in a Greek taverna or southern French bistro because red mullet was considered to be a southern fish. One type, *Mullus barbatus*, is mostly found in the Mediterranean, but the most common red mullet, sometimes called surmullet (*Mullus surmuletus*), is also found in the Atlantic. Red mullets are a bright red colour, and *surmuletus* also has golden-yellow stripes down its length. Mullet averages around 25cm in length, although *surmuletus* can occasionally reach double that.

using it Red mullet appears regularly in both supermarkets and fishmongers now, and it's easy to tell if a whole fish is fresh or not: the colour starts to fade once it is out of the water and the yellow lines on Atlantic mullets start to break up. So the brighter the colour and the more complete the line, if it has one, the fresher the fish. Smaller fish are usually sold whole while larger ones are normally filleted.

Grilling is the best cooking method for both whole fish and fillets. Both could also be braised, particularly with ingredients like black olives, onions, fennel and white wine.

word origin Mullet comes, via Old French, from the Latin *mullus,* meaning 'red mullet'.

did you know?

• Red mullet has always been an important fish in southern Europe, but in ancient Rome it reached the heights of fashion frenzy, with larger fish fetching (in modern-day money) hundreds of pounds. One of the nastiest spectacles of the time involved keeping a red mullet alive in captivity, then watching it die – the colours of the fish changed spectacularly as it did so, which was considered to be an aesthetic treat.
• This fish shouldn't be confused with another, unrelated, family of fish called grey mullet, the most important species of which, *Mugil cephalus*, is found around coastal waters all over the world. Grey mullet (or simply mullet in the United States and Australia) has white, rather muddy flesh, and its chief claim to fame is that taramasalata was traditionally made from its roe.

salmon

There are six species of this member of the northern hemisphere *Salmonidae* family of oily **fish** that also includes trout. In Europe, the most important species is wild Atlantic salmon (*Salmo salar*), which spends most of its life in the Atlantic Ocean from as far north as Scotland, Scandinavia and Canada to as far south as Portugal. An Atlantic salmon can weigh up to 12kg when fully grown and reaches over a metre in length. It has a pinkish tinge to its silvery skin, with black spots on its back that turn reddish-orange when it spawns.

The other salmon species are all found in the Pacific. Sockeye (*Oncorhynchus nerka*), the most important salmon in the United States, grows to about 85cm in length; chinook or king salmon *Oncorhynchus tshawytscha*) is larger, at around 1.5m. Humpback (*Oncorhynchus gorbuscha*) is the smallest of the Pacific group, with soft flesh that is usually canned or smoked; coho (*Oncorhynchus kisutch*), about the same size as sockeye, is also normally canned. The flesh of chum salmon (*Oncorhynchus keta*) is canned or smoked too; and its roes (eggs) are marketed as red **caviar**.

The wild salmon leads a hectic life, spending part of its time in freshwater rivers and part in saltwater oceans or seas. It hatches in fresh water and as it grows is known as a 'parr', the first real stage of its development and the name it keeps until it starts its long swim to the saltwater ocean to become a 'smolt'. It remains in the ocean until it is sexually mature, normally between two and four years old, although one type (called 'grilse') reaches this stage at just over a year old. Whatever its age, the mature fish now starts the long journey back to its native river to spawn, a trip that can be many hundreds of miles. After spawning, known now as 'kelt', the fish either dies or journeys back to the ocean. If it survives (most don't and Pacific salmon never do), it repeats this trip yearly until it dies.

Wild salmon is becoming scarcer and scarcer, mostly due to widespread pollution of the rivers in which it spawns, so nearly all of the salmon we now eat is farmed rather than wild (as many as 1000:1). The new fish are bred in freshwater hatcheries where the parrs remain for 12–18 months before being transferred to their adult lake or estuary cages. Numbers per cubic metre vary from farm to farm, but, compared with the wild fish, farmed salmon live in dense proximity to one another. As a result, this normally very active fish becomes the marine equivalent of a couch potato. Since they have no access to their natural wild food, they are fed a processed diet and antibiotics that help them grow quickly, and strong toxins that control sea lice (which is common among farmed fish). The distinctive pink flesh, which in the wild is the result of a shellfish-based diet, is often achieved in farmed fish with the help of dye.

using it Farming has ensured a regular supply of fresh salmon throughout the year, but wild salmon is a sporting fish and protected by law against being caught outside its season, which runs from about February to September. The flesh of wild salmon is normally very firm whereas that of farmed fish is softer and fattier. It is available fresh as whole fish, joints, steaks or fillets; as hot- or cold-smoked slices (see **smoked fish**); cured, mostly as gravadlax, a Scandinavian dish of fresh salmon fillets marinated in dill, salt, sugar and peppercorns; and canned.

Whole fresh fish and joints are usually baked or poached, then served with sauces such as **hollandaise** (for hot fish) or mayonnaise (for cold). Steaks and fillets can be grilled, fried, baked or poached. Cooked salmon forms the basis of many dishes. A classic is Russian koulibiac (mixed with mushrooms, hard-boiled eggs and rice, then baked in puff pastry).

Smoked salmon is served by itself as a first course or can make a luxurious sandwich filling, be mixed into scrambled eggs, or blended with cream cheese, lemon juice and a little cayenne pepper to make a pâté. Canned salmon is normally served as a sandwich filling, in a salad or used to make a mayonnaise in the same way as tuna.

word origin On its journey back to the river to spawn, wild salmon has to fight its way upstream to get to its spawning ground, and its way of progressing against the currents is to leap out of the water; it is from this action that it gets its name, from the Latin *salire*, 'to leap'.

• Once upon a time, probably during the last Ice Age, some wild salmon in both the Atlantic and Pacific didn't make it to the sea before the rivers in which they spawned froze over. They began, therefore, to emigrate to accessible freshwater lakes instead. Their access to the sea is no longer blocked, but what is now called landlocked salmon (*Salmo salar ouananiche* in the Atlantic and a version of sockeye called 'kokanee' in the Pacific) remain just that, journeying from river to lake as they have done for millennia.

sardine

This is the name given to a group of creatures belonging to the *Clupeidae* family of small oily **fish**, which also includes herring. The most important member, as far as the United Kingdom is concerned, is *Sardina pilchardus*, a pretty fish with silvery skin that rarely grows to more than about 20cm in length. It is found along Atlantic coasts from Norway to Gibraltar. The teenage version is known as sardine and eaten all around the western coasts of Europe, particularly those of Portugal; the adult fish, called pilchard, is more popular in northern Europe and is still found around the southern coasts of England.

Various other types of sardine are found around the globe, including *Sardinella maderensis* or Madeiran sardine, a 25cm-long fish found in the southern Mediterranean and down the western coasts of Africa, and *Sardinops melanosticus*, sometimes called the Japanese pilchard, which is slightly smaller and one of the most popular fish in Japan.

using it Sardines are available fresh and whole, or canned. The best way to cook fresh ones is to grill or barbecue them until the skin is crisp and slightly blackened – it comes away easily at this point, as do most of the bones. They can be fried, too, but other forms of cooking don't really work as the flesh is too oily. Although they are not usually preserved (other than by canning), fresh sardines could be pickled in the same way as rollmops.

This is a fish that is probably nearly as popular canned as fresh, and in fact sardines were the first fish to be canned. They can be stored in oil or brine or, more usually now, in some sort of spicy sauce (tomato and mustard are both common). A simple snack need involve no more than heating the can contents, spreading them over toast and eating the lot, bones and all. Canned sardines can also make a good pasta sauce, an interesting topping for baked potatoes and can be stirred into scrambled eggs.

word origin Sardine probably comes from *Sardo*, the Greek name for the island of Sardinia, once a major sardine-fishing area. The enduring popularity of canned sardines has been immortalized in 'packed like a tin of sardines' (too much squeezed into too small a space).

scallop

This is a bivalvular **mollusc** with a fan-shaped ribbed shell that ranges in colour from cream through pink to brown, depending on the species. The succulent flesh, with its orange 'coral' attached, is reckoned by many to be the sweetest-tasting of all the molluscs.

There are only two major European types. King scallop (*Pecten maximus*), found around Atlantic coasts, particularly those of Scotland, northern France and northern Spain, is quite large (about 12cm in diameter) with one curved and one flat shell. Queen scallop (*Chlamys opercularis*), or queenie, which is found in much the same areas as king scallop, is smaller and both shells are curved. Most scallops, like **oysters**, are hermaphrodites; that is, they are both female and male – in the scallop the coral is the female sexual organ and the white muscle next to the hinge or adductors, the male ones. Although they are sedentary and spend most of their time lurking at the bottom of the sea, scallops can be reasonably mobile when they need to be, moving around by using their adductors to open and close their shells and 'skip' through the water.

using it Scallops are nearly always sold already opened, on the half-shell or completely detached from their shells. The best quality are grey-white in colour – pure white scallops will probably have been soaked in water to plump them up, which affects both texture and taste. Scallops are always cooked before being eaten and are best steamed, baked, sautéed or grilled (threaded onto skewers for easy turning). Cooking time should be only a few minutes, until barely done.

word origin Scallop comes from the Old French *escalope*, meaning 'nutshell'.

did you know?

● The alternative name for king scallop is pilgrim scallop, or coquille Saint Jacques (St James's shell) in French, and thereby hangs a tale. St James is the patron saint of Spain and while disciples were carrying either his body or relics by boat to Compostela in northern Spain, where the cathedral was dedicated to him, they came upon a young man and his horse struggling in the sea. Of course they saved him and converted him to Christianity. When he and his horse eventually returned to dry land, they were both covered with scallop shells. Medieval Christians made pilgrimages to Compostela in much the same way as they did to Canterbury in England and gradually began to wear scallop-shell badges to indicate where they were going and why.

scampi

Scampi is the common British name for Norway lobster (*Nephrops norvegicus*), a smallish species of **crustacean** with a rosy shell and firm-tasting, meaty flesh; it is also called langoustine and Dublin Bay prawn. Scampi are found around the coasts of Europe from as far north as Norway to as far south as northern Africa. Like other lobsters (and unlike prawns), its ten 'legs' are made up of two heavy front pincers or claws and four pairs of thin legs ranged along the upper half of the body, with the final part of its seven armoured segments fanning out into a sort of propeller.

using it Scampi is normally sold cooked, either fresh or frozen. Since in appearance and size it's roughly midway between a large **prawn** and a **lobster**, it can be prepared in the same way as either.

word origin Scampi is the plural of the Italian word for Norway lobster (the singular is *scampo*). It is also used to describe a frozen ready-made dish of breaded processed Norway lobster flesh, which is usually deep-fried or baked and served with tartare sauce.

did you know?

● Crayfish, a first cousin to scampi, is the only edible freshwater shellfish. It has a red, brown or even purple shell, depending on the type, and very sweet flesh. It's a vicious creature that lurks under rocks and can move backwards, a rare accomplishment in the crustacean world. Crayfish is particularly popular in Scandinavia and the southern United States (where it's called crawfish or mudbug).

sea bass

The major European species of sea bass (*Dicentrarchus labrax*) is an elegant, silvery white **fish** that can occasionally grow to as much as a metre in length and is found in the Atlantic and in the Mediterranean and Black Seas. Although it looks beautiful, it is a vicious predator (the southern French name for it is *loup* or wolf), menacing more or less anything smaller than itself that swims in its seas. Relatives include spotted sea bass (*Dicentrarchus punctatus*) and striped bass or striper (*Morone saxatilis*), equally voracious charmers that swim around the eastern Atlantic from southern England to northern Africa and the Pacific and Atlantic coasts of the United States respectively, and the Australian barramundi (*Lates calcarifer*).

using it Sea bass is available whole or in fillets and has delicate but firm flesh and relatively few bones. It can be steamed or otherwise cooked in the same way as **red mullet** or **snapper.** If you are poaching a whole fish, the fishmonger should gut and clean it in the usual way but leave on the scales, which will help to keep the fish in one piece during cooking.

word origin Bass is Middle English, from the German word for the fish, *barse*.

did you know?

• This fish is called sea bass rather than just bass because there are also species of freshwater bass, which flourish in the lakes and rivers of North America and are just as nasty as their seawater relatives. The two major types are identified by the size of their mouth: the smallmouth bass (Micropterus dolomieni) prefers colder northern waters, while the largemouth bass (Micropterus salmoides) prefers warmer, muddier habitats.

sea bream

Bream is one of those words (like **snapper**) that is applied fairly indiscriminately to several different families and species of **fish**, although many of the better-known ones belong to the flattened oval-bodied *Sparidae* family. Many of them are also hermaphrodite, starting off male, thinking better of it, and turning themselves into females as they mature.

All the well-regarded European breams are seawater fish, found mostly in the Mediterranean and eastern Atlantic. They include black bream (*Spondyliosoma cantharus*), which reaches an average 35cm in length, and is blue-grey to black topped with horizontal dark streaks and vertical yellowish ones; common sea bream (*Sparus pagrus*), which occasionally reaches double the size of black bream; dentex (*Dentex dentex*), which deepens in colour as it grows from grey to blue-grey; gilt-head bream (*Sparus aurata*), generally reckoned to have the finest flesh, a silvery fish with golden marks; and ray's bream (*Brama brama*), actually a type of pomfret, although it's usually classified with the breams, and which is brownish grey.

using it Breams are sold whole or in fillets, and are now becoming more widely available thanks to fish farming, particularly around the Mediterranean. The flesh is lean and white but quite bony. They can be treated in the same way as **red mullet** or **snapper**.

word origin Bream comes from the Old French for the fish, *bresme*. Ray's bream is named after the 17th-century naturalist John Ray, who first described it.

did you know?

• Not all breams are seawater fish, although there is only one freshwater type that's occasionally available commercially. *Abramis brama* is a relative of carp, a slightly muddy, bronzy fish with an arched back that occasionally grows to about 75cm in length. It is mostly found in central and northern Europe.

seaweed

There's a lot more than just fish in the sea. Around coastal areas and sometimes now in special farms (particularly in Japan and China) there's also seaweed, fronded algae normally categorized by their colour, which ranges from brownish through red to green or blue-green. Some is sold fresh or semi-dried, but most is dried and then compressed into sheets, ground into powder or turned into types of gum.

There are thousands of species, only a few of which are used as food. Of these the best-known red seaweeds include carrageen or Irish moss (*Chrondus crispus*), which is found on both sides of the Atlantic but, as the alternative name suggests, is particularly associated with Ireland; dulse (*Palmaria palmata*), which grows all around the world; and the *Porphyra* spp., known as nori in Japanese and laver in English. A special gum called agar-agar is also extracted from the red *Eucheuma* spp. Several types of brown seaweed are known as kelp in English, including the *Laminaria* spp., which is made into kombu in Japan. Wakame (*Undaria pinnatifida*) is another type of brown seaweed popular there.

using it The Japanese are particularly enthusiastic seaweed eaters, and kombu, wakame and nori are all part of everyday life there. The first two are soup and stock ingredients (kombu is a basic ingredient in dashi, the Japanese stock used for more or less all soup dishes). Toasted nori sheets are the classic wrapping for sushi and can also be crumbled over raw fish dishes and salads as a garnish.

Of the other edible seaweeds, dried dulse is eaten as a snack food and used as a seasoning; kelps are eaten occasionally too, but are now mostly processed into mineral and vitamin supplements. Laver is sold dried, but the traditional way to prepare it is to boil it for hours into a soft green purée

(known as laverbread). This is served over toast or blended with oatmeal and made into 'cakes', which are fried in bacon fat. The major use of both carrageen and agar-agar is as a gum, which is used as a vegetarian substitute for gelatine (see **jelly**).

word origin The English name for some specific types reflects the fact that seaweeds have always been more popular along the Celtic fringes of Britain than in England: carrageen, for instance, comes from the Irish *carraigin*, meaning 'little rock', presumably a reference to its native habitats, while dulse is derived from the Irish/Scottish Gaelic for the seaweed, *duileasg*.

did you know?

• Vibrant green samphire is another edible maritime plant although it isn't a seaweed. There are two types: marsh samphire (Salicornia europaea), a salty sea vegetable occasionally available at fishmongers, which is traditionally pickled or boiled for about 10 minutes and served with butter; and rock samphire (Crithmum maritimum), generally regarded as the better-tasting of the two, which is related to parsley and fennel. It is also occasionally pickled or boiled as a vegetable.

shark

Sharks are cartilaginous fish (having a skeleton but no bones) with very firm, meaty flesh and scale-less skin. The family includes the spiny dogfish or huss (*Squalus acanthias*), found all over the world in cooler waters but particularly abundant along northern Atlantic and Pacific coasts, and the larger spotted dogfish (*Scyliorhinus stellaris*), common around the Mediterranean and eastern Atlantic. Dogfish grow to 75cm–1.5m long and, depending on the species, can be dappled grey or light brownish-red in colour. The porbeagle or mackerel shark (*Lamna nasus*), which grows to 3m in length, is found in the eastern Atlantic and Mediterranean. It has very fine flesh, which is sometimes smoked.

using it Most fresh shark is sold as steaks and can be cooked in the same ways as **tuna**. Dogfish, however, are usually available as fillets (often described euphemistically as rock salmon), which are normally battered and deep-fried as the fish part of fish and chips.

word origin It isn't altogether clear *why* dogfish are so called, since not by any stretch of the imagination do they resemble dogs. Even the Latin names for the two most common types have doggy connections: *Squalus acanthias* means 'spurdog' and *Scyliorhinus stellaris* is also sometimes called nursehound; to make things even more confusing, some newly spawned dogfish are called 'pups'.

did you know?

• There are over 300 species of shark swimming around in our oceans, ranging from the whale shark, which measures upwards of 15m in length, weighs several tonnes and would scarcely hurt a fly, to the rather more predatory 6m-long great white shark, with its mouthful of large teeth beautifully adapted to shearing and sawing, which attacks everything around it that moves – including people.

shrimp

The words shrimp and **prawn** are now used almost interchangeably to describe the smallest types of **crustacean**, but in the United Kingdom there is technically a difference between those described as prawn and those referred to as shrimp. The latter name is reserved for the very smallest species, the most common of which is the brown or common shrimp (*Crangon crangon*). Despite its name, brown shrimp has a grey shell when raw and only turns brownish when cooked.

using it Brown shrimp is available peeled and cooked, usually frozen, or as part of a dish, such as ready-made potted shrimps, a traditional northern English dish of peeled shrimps preserved in butter. Peeled brown shrimp can be used in the same way as smaller prawns.

word origin Shrimp comes from the Low German *schrempen*, meaning 'to wrinkle'.

did you know?

• In South-east Asia species of very small shrimps similar to brown shrimp are processed into blachan or kapi, strongly-smelling fermented pastes used in the cooking of, respectively, Malaysia and Thailand.

skate

There are nearly a hundred species of this family of cartilaginous **fish**, which lurk near the seabed or burrow into it in cool temperate seas more or less around the world. When they are on the fishmonger's slab, they are all called skate, but while they're in the sea, smaller types tend to be known as ray. Species include common skate (*Raja batis*), which has a smoother skin than most other types; thornback ray (*Raja clavata*), so called because of the numerous spiky spines on its back and considered to have the best flesh; and white ray (*Raja alba*), which also has good flesh.

Skate ranges from dainty (about 70cm long) to massive (around 2.5m), with a long narrow tail and an almost diamond-shaped body, thanks to its flattened pectoral fins known as 'wings'. All skates have thick skin that can be grey-blue, brownish or speckled, and white flesh with an occasional rosy hue. After cooking, the flesh forms delicate 'strings' that scrape away easily from the soft skeleton.

using it You will never see whole skate for sale; in fact, only one part of it, the wings, are widely available, although the 'nob', which is taken from the tail, can occasionally be found. It is one of those rare fish that is better a day or so after it has been removed from the water, mostly because it has a distinctive ammoniac smell when very fresh (see below).

Skate wings are usually fried or poached. The classic accompaniment is black butter, made by melting butter in a small pan until it's a rich brown then stirring in capers, herbs and lemon.

word origin Skate comes via Middle English from the Norse for the fish, *skata*.

did you know?

• Like other cartilaginous fish, skate produces a protective chemical substance called urea when it's alive. This prevents its bodily fluids (which are less salty than the surrounding sea) from leaching out and seawater from penetrating in. When the fish dies, the urea begins to break up, producing ammonia and the characteristic smell. This only lasts for 24–48 hours and in any case disappears once the fish is cooked.

smoked fish

Europeans began to smoke fish millennia ago to preserve them, but nowadays smoking is normally done (much more lightly than it once was) to add flavour and texture. Both oily and white fish are smoked and it's a particularly popular way of flavouring **cod**, **haddock**, **herring**, **mackerel**, **salmon** and **trout**; other fish and seafood, like eel, **oyster**, **prawn** and **tuna**, are sometimes smoked too.

Before the process starts, the raw fish are cured by being steeped in a salt and water brine, or rubbed with a dry mixture of salt, or salt mixed with sugar and other flavourings. They are then smoked in one of two ways. For cold-smoking, the fish are put into special ovens over glowing wood embers at 'cold' temperatures of about 25°C for at least several hours. In hot-smoking, they are suspended over wood fires that can reach

over 90°C; when they reach their optimum heat, the fires are shut down and the fish left to smoke for about 1½ hours. The wood used imparts flavour to the fish, and popular ones include oak and beech.

Cold-smoking produces the traditional silkiness in oily fish like salmon and trout, which can be eaten raw after smoking; cold-smoked white fish such as cod and haddock, however, need to be cooked before eating. Hot-smoked fish, which are cooked in the smoking process, are ready to eat. Mackerel is hot-smoked, as are salmon and trout; the latter look very different from their cold-smoked version, being much thicker and an opaque pink rather than a clear colour. Some fish, particularly kipper, cod and haddock, are traditionally dyed during smoking to give them a strong colour; paler, undyed versions of all of them are also available.

using it Some smoked fish – cold-smoked salmon and trout, for instance – keep in the refrigerator for up to 2–3 weeks, but cold-smoked kipper, cod and haddock should be eaten within a few days of purchase. Hot-smoked fish will keep for 4–6 days.

The classic way to cook smoked white fish fillets like cod and haddock is to poach or 'jug' them: immerse in a bowl of boiling water and leave for about 15 minutes until the flesh becomes opaque; when the fish is cooked through, the bottom skin should peel away quite easily and the fish can then be used as needed.

did you know?

• Meat and poultry can be smoked too. Bacon and sausages may be cold- or hot-smoked. Duck (particularly barbary) and chicken are the most commonly smoked poultry, and both are hot-smoked, which means that they don't need further cooking.

snapper

There are about 185 species of tropical fish called snapper, nearly all of which are found in warmer parts of the Atlantic or in the Indian and Pacific Oceans and called 'red' whether their skin or flesh deserves the description or not. Most reach 75cm–1m in length, range in colour from the famous pink or red through to greenish and even striped, and have slightly forked tails.

The original 'red' snapper is the American snapper (*Lutjanus campechanus*), mostly found around Florida, the Gulf of Mexico and the Caribbean; others include the humpback snapper (*Lutjanus gibbus*), which is native to the Indian and Pacific Oceans, silk snapper (*Lutjanus vivanus*), common off the northern coast of South America, and red emperor (*Lutjanus sebae*), a larger species found around the coasts of Australia and the Seychelles.

using it Although smaller fish are occasionally available whole, most snapper is sold in fillets or steaks. The firm meaty flesh is perfect barbecued or grilled, but can also be baked and fried. Any recipe for **red mullet** would work with snapper.

word origin Snappers have strong jaws, sharp teeth and a tendency to snap the latter together when closing the former; hence their name.

sole

This is the name given to several species of oval flatfish, of which Dover sole (*Solea solea*) is considered to be the best. Found from the North Sea to the Mediterranean, Dover sole is rarely more than about 45cm in length and has dark brownish skin. The only other widely available sole is lemon sole (*Microstomus kitt*), which is actually a member of the *Pleuronectidae* family that includes plaice and turbot and is therefore not a true sole at all. Lemon sole is widely distributed around the coasts of northern Europe, and is slightly larger and lighter in colour than Dover sole, with darkish smudge marks over its top side.

using it Dover sole keeps better than most other fresh fish and many people consider it to be at its best two or three days after being caught (this still means it should be cooked as soon after buying as possible, however, since it will take most of that time to get from fishing boat to shop); lemon sole should be cooked within a day or so of purchase. Both are available whole or in fillets.

Dover sole has superb, firm and meaty yet delicate flesh; lemon sole isn't quite in the same class, but is cheaper and, when fresh, can be very good. The best way to cook both is as simply as possible. Classic sole dishes include paupiettes, made by rolling fillets around various fillings like mushrooms or flavoured butter and poaching until done; and goujons, fillet strips dipped in milk and then flour and deep-fried until browned.

word origin Sole comes from the Latin *Solea,* meaning 'sandal' or 'sole' (of the foot), a reference to the shape of the fish. Dover sole didn't receive its name because the fish was especially good there, but because it was the port that once supplied most of this fish to the London market.

squid

The squid is a cephalopod, a type of **mollusc** with a long torpedo-shaped body supported by a transparent cartilage or 'quill' and triangular fins that are used to propel it about the sea. Its largish head sprouts two very long, thin tentacles and about eight short ones that are used as feeding equipment. Like other cephalopods such as cuttlefish, squid also carries a small sac of blue-black liquid called 'ink' that it squirts at predators to protect itself.

Species of squid are found more or less

around the world, but there are two main food types you are likely to encounter: European squid (*Loligo vulgaris*) is mostly found in coastal waters and called 'calamari' in Greece and 'calamares' in Spain – if you buy squid fresh from the supermarket or from a fishmonger, this is the species you're likely to get; and flying squid (*Illex coindetii*), so called because it sometimes throws itself out of the water as it swims, is usually available frozen. Both types are small in squid terms, reaching an average of 10–15cm in length.

using it   Squid is available fresh and ungutted, or gutted and cleaned, when it will normally have been frozen and then thawed before being put on sale. Gutting isn't difficult to do at home, or you can ask the fishmonger to do it. The popular taverna way of cooking squid is to cut the body into thin rings, dip them and the short tentacles in batter and deep-fry. Squid rings can also be added to a stir-fry, risotto or pasta sauce, or cooked and used in a seafood salad. The body is perfect for stuffing and then baking or poaching.

Squid ink is considered a great delicacy in some parts of the world: it's used commercially to flavour rice or pasta, and at home to create classic southern European dishes like *calamares en sua tinta* (squid in its own ink), where the squid is stewed slowly with its ink and white wine, garlic and herbs.

word origin   The English name goes back to the Middle Ages, but its origins are unknown. The Greek and Spanish words come from the Latin *calamarius,* meaning 'container for ink', a reference to the much-prized blue-black 'blood'.

did you know?

• There have always been rumours of giant squid 'out there' somewhere, lurking at the bottom of the deepest ocean, and reality, for once, has now caught up with myth. A specimen found off the south coast of Australia a year or so ago turned out to be over 4m long, 250kg in weight and from a species no one had ever seen before; it's now residing in a Melbourne museum.

trout

Trout is part of a freshwater family of oily **fish** that also includes salmon. The most important species, which is native to Europe, is *Salmo trutta* and there are two types. Brown trout is a favourite angling fish found only in freshwater rivers and, as its name suggests, is brown in colour, with lots of dark smudges over the top part of its body, including the fins. It can grow to about 50cm and has unremarkable white flesh. Salmon trout (also called sea trout or sewin) is a larger, more adventurous version of brown trout, which starts life in freshwater rivers and then migrates to the saltwater sea, where it can spend several years before returning to its native river to spawn. Salmon trout can reach lengths of over a metre and, like salmon, has light silvery skin with a pinkish tinge and pink flesh, dyed that colour by a diet heavy in shellfish.

The other major species is rainbow trout (*Salmo gairdneri*), a North American freshwater fish with dark silvery skin, dappled fins and a pinkish band down its sides, which has been successfully introduced into the United Kingdom. Like brown trout, wild rainbow trout has a sea-going version, in this case called steelhead trout. Most, however, are farmed and trout farming is big business: special hatcheries obtain eggs from breeding stock, sell them on to 'fingerling' farmers (fingerling being the name for the baby fish), who eventually in their turn supply trout farms, where the fish are kept in ponds, tanks or cages and 'harvested' when they are 300–400g in weight.

using it Rainbow trout is widely obtainable, but salmon trout is available only from time to time, mostly in fishmongers. Brown trout is rarely offered for sale and the easiest way to obtain one is to catch it yourself. Most trout are small, so are usually sold whole, although some larger ones are filleted and sold fresh or smoked (see **smoked fish**).

Brown and rainbow trout are normally cooked whole, and are good grilled, fried or baked. Salmon trout is altogether more delicate than other trout and should be poached or otherwise treated in the same way as salmon. Smoked trout doesn't need to be cooked before being eaten, and can be served in the same way as smoked salmon or with other smoked fish as part of a first course. It also makes a good pâté.

word origin Trout comes via Old English from the Greek *trogein,* meaning 'to gnaw', something this voracious fish enjoys doing to its prey.

did you know?

• Spawning is complicated if you're a wild trout. First the female swims upstream to the chosen area, then turns sideways and, manipulating her tail vigorously, digs out a nest or 'redd', which she then hovers over hopefully. Sure enough, a male trout will turn up and court her by 'dancing' (or quivering) close to her; when the female is ready, she presses herself against the bottom of the redd, the male hovers nearby and, as she releases her eggs, he fertilizes them.

tuna

This group of oily fish are among the heavyweights of the sea, powerful creatures that perpetually crash about oceans all over the world and which can reach lengths of more than 3m. One reason tuna swim so much is that, unlike most other **fish**, they are warm-blooded, and in order to ensure a sufficient supply of oxygen for themselves, they need to move about constantly. Continual exercise develops and darkens muscle tissue, however (the flesh of fish, like that of meat, is simply muscle tissue), so tuna not only have more powerful muscles than most other fish but their flesh has a darker, 'meatier' quality too.

We have access to five main types. Albacore or longfin (*Thunnus alalunga*) is a relative minnow in tuna terms, averaging around 35kg in weight. It has the lightest-coloured meat, which is normally canned. Bigeye (*Thunnus obesus*), obese by name and by nature since it can reach 100kg or more, is also at the pale end of the tuna colour spread and is considered to have excellent flesh. Yellowfin (*Thunnus albacares*), one of the most common species, is rosy pink in colour and provides the fresh or frozen steaks in most supermarkets. Bluefin (*Thunnus thynnus*), the biggest of them all at an average 300–400kg, is found in both the Atlantic and the Pacific and, according to the Japanese, is also the best, the one they traditionally use for sashimi, their raw fish dishes. Skipjack (*Katsuwonus pelamis*), a tropical species that gets its name from its habit of 'skipping' along the surface of the ocean when chasing prey, has light-coloured flesh and is usually canned.

using it Fresh tuna steaks can differ quite drastically in colour, being anything from light salmon-pink to deep blood-red, with many gradations in between; brownish tuna should be avoided, since this can indicate it is starting to lose its freshness. Care should be taken when cooking – like beef steaks, tuna steaks are best served rare or at least underdone, since overcooking can toughen and dry them out. A light salsa (mixtures like puréed grilled peppers, garlic and coriander, or tomato and chilli) or a sauce (fresh tomato and garlic) served alongside will add moisture.

Cooked tuna can be broken into chunks

and used in the same way as canned tuna: as part of a salad (the Italian marriage of tuna with cannellini beans and red onion or the French salade niçoise are just two examples); in a stuffing for vegetables like courgettes or peppers; or mixed with mayonnaise for a sandwich filling. In Italy, tuna mayonnaise is the basis of a classic cold sauce for roast veal.

word origin Tuna comes from *atun*, the Spanish word for the fish.

did you know?

• Port Lincoln in South Australia boasts the world's first tuna farms, special de luxe accommodation for southern versions of the bluefin destined for the Japanese sashimi trade. The pampered inhabitants are caught in large circular nets, then transferred to holding pens where they are fed three times a day on a steady diet of oily fish like anchovies and herrings until they are fat enough to make the grade (this is tuna heaven; wild tuna eat on average only once a week and even then they have to catch their meal first). A single perfect bluefin can fetch up to about £750 in Tokyo.
• Swordfish (*Xiphias gladius*) doesn't *look* anything like tuna – its flesh is white with (at its best) rosy tinges – but it's just as meaty and is cooked in the same ways. Swordfish is found all over the world, although in Europe it's mostly associated with the Mediterranean area. It gets its name from its most prominent asset, a very long, pointed upper jaw perfectly designed to create mayhem among smaller fish that get in its way.

turbot

The turbot (*Psetta maxima*) is a particularly fine-tasting flatfish with a body broader than it is long, and a brownish skin covered with small, dark warty protuberances. Its average weight is 1.5–2kg, although it can occasionally grow to 15–20kg and some smaller ones (chicken turbots) barely reach 750–900g. In the wild, turbot inhabits a vast area stretching from Norway in the north to the Mediterranean in the south, and is now occasionally farmed.

using it Turbot is usually sold as fillets, although chicken turbots are available whole. If at all possible, it should be cooked whole, since the slightly gelatinous bones impart extra taste to the flesh. Whole fish and fillets can be fried, grilled, baked or poached. Any sauce recommended for **sole** can be used for turbot fillets, but **hollandaise** is the classic accompaniment.

word origin Turbot is Old French, but with Scandinavian origins (it's supposedly derived from a local word for thorn, a reference to the knobbly back).

did you know?

• The brill (*Scopthalmus rhombus*) is a European flatfish closely related to turbot and shares its chameleon-like ability to lighten or darken its skin colour (from light yellow to deep brown in this case), depending on environment. The white flesh tastes similar to that of turbot and is used in the same ways.

Meat, Poultry & Game

The history of the United Kingdom is written in its meat. Think of White Park cattle, which can trace their lineage back to prehistoric times; pheasants, which were introduced by the Romans; and the red-legged partridge, brought back by Charles II after he returned from exile in France. Iron Age Britons would have recognized the Soay sheep that still graze here today, while the Gloucester Old Spot pig was developed to meet farming conditions in the 1800s. The Americas gave us the turkey, and we gave them Old Hereford horned cattle, from which all those picturesque longhorn cattle that roam the prairies of the American West are descended.

There are regional associations, too – Welsh Mountain and North Ronaldsay sheep, Sussex chickens and Norfolk Black turkeys, Galloway and Gloucester

Meat – chicken, beef, lamb, pork or game – is at the very heart of our cooking traditions and of our dishes
Matthew Fort

cattle, Berkshire and Tamworth pigs. Each breed was developed in response to local conditions. Then there is the way in which breeds have come and gone as consumer demand, itself the product of other social conditions, has fluctuated. Think of the way in which farmers have been driven to produce leaner and yet leaner animals, in response to recent consumer concerns about health.

For most of us, however, meat is not a history lesson. It is something good to eat, something to be savoured, to be sliced or diced, roasted or grilled, fried or stewed. Meat – chicken, beef, lamb, pork or game – is at the very heart of our cooking traditions and of our dishes. First comes the meat, then the vegetables, and then the gravy and all the other bits and bobs, all reconciled to each other, first through the cooking process and then through the eating.

Most of us eat less meat now than our parents did, and certainly less than our grandparents. That is not necessarily a bad thing – just so long as when we do cook it and eat it, we do so with respect and understanding. The more you know, the better you'll eat. The better you eat, the happier you'll be. So, eat less meat by all means, but eat better meat when you do.

Matthew Fort

bacon

This is a side of pig that has been cured by salting and sometimes smoking. Pigs bred for bacon contain more fat than those raised for fresh **pork**, but otherwise they are reared in the same way and slaughtered at roughly the same age.

Bacon is cured in several different ways: the side can be preserved whole, the legs can be removed and cured separately, or the side can even be butchered first into rolled and boned joints or slices. The process itself also varies from manufacturer to manufacturer and from region to region, although there are two general methods. Dry-curing is the traditional way, where the meat is covered or rubbed down with a curing mixture that includes salts, flavourings and often something sweet like brown sugar, then left for varying lengths of time (up to 10 days isn't uncommon) so that the juices can drain out. Brine-curing is speedier and the one normally used nowadays, especially for mass-produced bacon. Here the meat is either soaked in brine (a salt and water 'pickle' that can include flavourings and sweeteners), or injected with it. After salting, the meat is hung for about a week to mature, and after maturing, it can either be sold as green bacon or it can be smoked (see **meat**).

Different cuts come from different parts of the animal: lean back bacon rashers are sliced from the loin; streaky bacon rashers, which have more fat, come from the belly; steaks are taken from the leg or back and joints from the forehock and collar. Gammon is from the same part of the pig as **ham** (the hind legs) but, unlike ham, comes from an animal where the legs have been cured as part of the side; gammon is sold as joints like slipper, corner or hock, or as steaks, and is used in the same way as bacon.

Although it's most popular in the English-speaking world, types of bacon are produced elsewhere. In Italy, for instance, there are several different versions of pancetta; the most basic one is made from seasoned lean and fat belly of pork, which is rolled up like a **salami** to be cured and nearly always sold unsmoked. In the United Kingdom, pancetta is normally available pre-sliced or chopped into small dice.

using it Good bacon should be reddish-pink in colour and look moist; avoid any that seems hard or dark. Most will keep for 10–14 days in the refrigerator, although once a packet is opened, the remaining slices should be used within 4–5 days.

Basic cooking methods vary from cut to cut. Joints were traditionally boiled, after lengthy soaking to remove excess salt, then often glazed and baked, although most are now sold ready to bake. Rashers and steaks are usually grilled or fried.

Both streaky and back bacon can be chopped and cooked as a flavouring base for hearty casseroles and stews or added to salads, particularly those that include spinach, cos lettuce, radicchio or broad beans. Bacon also works well in a sandwich, with lettuce, tomato and mayonnaise to make a BLT, or with sliced mozzarella, Brie or avocado, and is, of course, the perfect partner for eggs at breakfast time. Streaky rashers will keep the breasts of lean poultry and game birds moist during roasting and are often used as a lining for meat pâtés. Pancetta is the base for many Italian soups and pasta sauces, and is classically mixed with beaten eggs and Parmesan to make carbonara.

word origin Bacon comes from the Old French *bakko*, meaning ham. It was first used in English around the 12th century as an alternative to the Saxon *flitch*, which was more or less the same thing, and for a while the new word described both fresh and cured pork meat before it gradually narrowed into its modern meaning. Gammon also has Old French origins, in this case from *gambe,* meaning 'leg', the part of the animal that gammon comes from.

● Bacon used to be the only meat eaten reasonably regularly by the poor because nearly every peasant family from Anglo-Saxon times on kept a pig, since it could be fed on anything, including scraps from the table. It was normally killed around November or December each year to provide food for the winter, and as much of it as could be was preserved to guarantee some meat for those times to come when fresh meat would be scarce or non-existent. The phrase to 'save his bacon', meaning to prevent someone from being hurt or humiliated, harks back to this: once you'd preserved your bit of pig for the winter, it was important to protect it from scavenging household animals.

● Dunmow in Essex has had a long association with bacon. During the 12th century one of the noble ladies of the region decided to celebrate a happy marriage by offering the 'Dunmow flitch' (a side of bacon) to any couple prepared to go to Dunmow and ceremonially swear they had never fought with their spouse or wished themselves unmarried during the previous year. A flitch was claimed only seven times between the 13th and late 18th centuries, when the custom died out; it was revived during the second half of the 19th century, however, and is now offered every four years. Two couples were awarded their flitch when the ceremony was last held in 2000.

beef

Beef is the meat of domesticated cattle (*Bos taurus*), herbivorous animals raised for their meat or their milk. Most of the beef we eat comes from castrated male cattle (steers) and females (heifers) that are not required for breeding or milk production.

Most cattle are intensively farmed, a system in which calves are moved to special fattening units when they are 4–6 months old, and remain there for the rest of their lives. They are usually kept indoors, although around 30 percent have access to outside grazing, especially during summer. Housed animals are fed on hay, silage, grains like crushed barley or maize, and proteins, which usually include soya and fish meal. (At one point recycled sheep and cattle meat were used too, but BSE and the suspected passing of this to humans, in the form of nvCJD, means this practice has now been banned.) In the most stringent organic systems, calves are weaned from their mothers at about nine weeks old (intensively farmed calves are weaned at about six weeks, and dairy calves are separated from their mothers after a few days and fed on reconstituted milk powder until weaned); the cattle live mostly outside on rotated grazing land, or are housed in well-bedded yards.

There are many breeds and crossbreeds. Those raised for their meat have a good proportion of lean flesh to fat and are sometimes identified at the point of sale. Good-quality British breeds include Aberdeen Angus, Beef Shorthorn and Hereford.

The age at which cattle are slaughtered varies according to breed, weight and to some extent on how they are reared, since grazing animals take longer to reach slaughter weight than those fed on grains and proprietary feeds. It's illegal to sell beef from an animal that is more than 30 months old. After slaughter, the carcass is split into two and theoretically 'hung' (see **meat**), although in reality cheaper cuts for mince and stewing are not, and simply move through the supply chain. The hindquarters, where most of the prime cuts come from, are hung, however, normally for 7–21 days.

How the carcass is divided into joints and cuts varies from country to country, but in the United Kingdom, as a rough rule of thumb, the tenderest, best cuts come from the upper middle to back part of the animal, where the forerib, sirloin, fillet and rump are located; these are made into choice joints or individual cuts such as **steak**. Behind, below and in front of this area the meat is tougher and cheaper. The best cuts here are silverside and topside (sometimes called top round), which come from the backside of the animal; braising steak (or chuck), which comes from the blade (the top area behind the neck); stewing steak, normally from the neck and clod (located just below the neck); and brisket, which comes from below the blade and rib meat on the front half of the animal. Minced beef and offal – the liver, heart and other internal organs and external extremities like the tail – are also eaten (see **kidney**, **liver**, **mince** and **offal**). Some cuts are also cured (see **meat** and **corned beef**).

using it Most beef bought now is young and bright red in colour, and will not have a particularly distinctive taste. Good organic meat, which tends to be older, darker and hung for longer, will have what is the traditional full, richer flavour. White fat suggests that the animal has been reared mostly on grain or proprietary feed; yellowish that it has been raised mostly on grass.

Basic cooking methods vary from cut to cut. Individual prime cuts like steak are grilled or fried, while larger joints such as sirloin or rib are roasted, then served with classic accompaniments which include gravy, **horseradish** relish or sauce, Yorkshire pudding and potatoes roasted in the 'drippings' from the cooking meat. Cheaper lean cuts like topside and occasionally rump are normally pot-roasted or braised. Brisket and silverside are sometimes sold salted and are also occasionally pot-roasted, but the best way to cook them is by long, gentle simmering. Braising and stewing steaks are normally cubed and then stewed or casseroled, although occasionally they are marinated before being cooked (see **venison**). Favourite beef stews include carbonnade, with onions, mustard and beer, topped with French bread slices; and boeuf bourguignonne, with bacon, baby onions, mushrooms and red wine.

There is a large repertoire of dishes for leftover beef too: from the simple, such as roast beef sandwiches, to the more involved, such as cottage pie or hash.

word origin Beef comes from the Latin *bos,* meaning cattle, via the Old Northern French *boef*, and first appeared in English during the 13th century, the gift of the Normans who were enthusiastic beef-eaters. The native English called the animal itself ox, a word still used occasionally to describe less desirable edible parts of it such as the tail and tongue (which were probably all they were allowed to get of it, once the Normans established themselves).

Young beef steers can be lively and sometimes show this by kicking out, the origin of 'beef' meaning to complain or make a nuisance. Yeomen of the Guard have been called beefeaters since around the middle of the 17th century, an indication of their relatively privileged status – the 'eater' part came from the Old English word for servant, but consuming beef implied you were well fed and prosperous.

did you know?

• Modern domesticated cattle are descendants of aurochs (*Bos primigenius*), wild cattle that roamed Europe and Asia towards the end of the last Ice Age, the cattle-like animals depicted in cave paintings. By about 6000 years ago they were being domesticated, worshipped and eaten by the ancient civilizations of the Middle East and the Indus Valley. By 2000 years after that, bulls were being worshipped in Minoan Crete, and King Minos built the world's first labyrinth at Knossos there to house his stepchild, the Minotaur, a monster with the body of a man and the head of a bull; the Minotaur's nourishment included the flesh of seven maidens and seven youths every year.

• No wonder bulls have been worshipped as a symbol of virility and macho power since earliest times. In farms where insemination is done the natural way, the average bull is mated with 30–40 cows a year, but many dairy cows are now artificially inseminated to control breeding, and one sample of bull semen can impregnate 1000 females.

black pudding

Despite the name, this is a type of **sausage**. It includes the blood and fat of an animal, usually pig. Modern British black pudding is made primarily from oatmeal, pig fat and blood, rusk crumbs and grated or chopped onion, and often other ingredients like chopped barley, suet, paprika, marjoram and pennyroyal (a type of mint) as well. Other countries make similar sausages: boudin noir in France, morcilla in Spain and blutwurst in Germany don't normally contain much (if any) cereal but do include chopped onion and sometimes cream too; while an exotic Caribbean version includes pumpkin, sweet potato, spring onions and chillies in addition to pig's blood. White pudding is similar to black pudding except that it's made from 'white' ingredients like fat or suet, eggs, milk and sometimes chicken or rabbit meat rather than blood.

Black pudding is made in much the same way as other sausages, and is boiled after being stuffed; it is sometimes dried before being sold.

using it These puddings need to be cooked before being eaten, and the traditional way to do this is to slice and then grill or fry them for 2–3 minutes per side. Sliced black pudding used to be a staple part of the 'full' cooked breakfast and sometimes still is. Nowadays, however, it's more likely to be served as a lunch or supper dish with ingredients like mashed potatoes and baked beans, bacon slices and apple sauce, or topped with a poached egg. It had something of a modest vogue a few years ago in exotic salads, mixed with items like goat's or feta cheese, salad vegetables and **vinaigrette**.

word origin The name is a literal description of what it is: the ingredients are darkened with pig's blood so that the sausage looks black, and pudding comes, via the French *boudin*, from the Latin *botellus,* meaning 'sausage' – during medieval times a pudding could only be a mixture of savoury ingredients encased in a skin; the sweet dessert meaning of the word only began to appear around the middle of the 16th century.

did you know?

• The Greek poet Homer may have provided the world's first description of a black pudding in *The Odyssey*: he relates how a mixture of animal blood and fat encased in a goat's paunch was roasted by the fire, then presented to the disguised Odysseus when he returned to his palace in Ithaca after his wanderings. The Romans used blood to make sausages too: Apicius, the 1st century AD Roman cookery writer, has a recipe for black pudding made from boiled egg yolks, pine nuts, onions and leeks plus seasonings and blood, which was stuffed into a sausage casing and boiled in flavoured wine. It was the Romans who took the skills of sausage-making all around Europe with them as they conquered and settled.

• Black puddings of one sort or another remained popular all over Europe throughout medieval times and more or less up to the Second World War. Most rural peasants kept a pig or two that would be killed during autumn each year to provide first fresh and then preserved meat for the family through the winter. The more of the animal that could be used the better, so the blood was caught and used to flavour sausages; recipes varied from area to area, although in Britain the best ones were (and still are) reckoned to come from the northern part of England.

chicken

A chicken is a young hen (*Gallus domesticus*), a smallish domesticated fowl with plumage that varies in colour and flamboyance from breed to breed, and which is reared both for its eggs and its meat.

Raising chickens was originally a cottage industry: most were killed late – six months or older was common up until about 40 years ago – and different areas of the country often developed their own identifiable breeds, such as Old Sussex, Scots Grey, Cornish Game and even

Dorking, a type introduced by the Romans whose striking characteristic is that it has five toes (nearly all the others have four). Now chickens are identified by method of production rather than breed, and most are intensively reared (see **poultry**), bred from fast-growing types like Ross or Cob or crossbreeds developed from them, and fed a diet that includes growth promoters to make them grow even faster. Full-size birds are reared until they are about six weeks old, poussins to about four weeks old.

Other production methods take longer and as a result the chickens are more expensive, although the older they are (on the whole), the more distinctive and full their taste. Free-range chickens are raised for between 8 and 11½ weeks depending on whether they are simple, traditional or total free-range birds. Organic birds are also normally reared for at least 11½ weeks.

Most chickens have a wheat-based diet, but corn-fed birds will also be fed maize (corn) – anything from 50 percent or more. They can be intensively reared or free-range. Corn-fed chickens are usually yellow in colour, something sometimes achieved by adding yellow dye to their food rather than by feeding them a surfeit of maize. Poulet de Bresse is a blue-legged French breed, which is identified by a small tag on its leg; Bresse chickens are slow-growing and free-range, with a full flavour.

Poussin, the smallest type of chicken in terms of weight, cannot be more than 750g and averages 400–500g. Full-grown birds can be 1.25–2.75kg.

using it Over 800 million chickens are raised annually in Britain, and they're available whole or in joints – as breasts (bone in or boned, when they are called fillets), legs, thighs and drumsticks (the lower part of the legs). Chicken is also sold as **mince** or as stir-fry strips.

Whatever method is used, chicken must be cooked thoroughly (see poultry). Whole birds can be roasted, stuffed or unstuffed, poached or braised, or split open down the backbone (spatchcocked) and grilled. For roasting, streaky bacon or softened butter may be spread over the breast to keep it moist during cooking; basting from time to time with the pan juices will also help. Braising and poaching can be done in a low oven or on top of the stove. In a classic poule au pot, a whole chicken is stuffed and simmered gently in stock with flavouring vegetables, also the basic cooking method for a comforting chicken soup.

Chicken joints are endlessly versatile. They can be braised or casseroled, cooked in rice-based dishes like paella or **risotto**, coated in batter or spicy breadcrumbs and then fried or deep-fried, sautéed or grilled. Boned breasts (fillets) are particularly convenient: whole they can be poached with a sauce; cubed, they can be grilled as kebabs or tikka; and cut into strips they can be stir-fried. Leftover chicken can be used in just as many ways (see **turkey**) and even the carcass of roasted birds need not be wasted, but can be boiled to make **stock**.

word origin Chicken comes from the Old English *cicen*, which is probably derived from an earlier German word. They've been called other things down the ages too, however, some of them less than flattering – like 'dunghill fowl', the birds kept by most farms for their eggs and which scratched around the farmyard picking up feed where they could.

For such a popular bird, chicken phrases are fairly dismissive. Young chickens are notoriously timid, the origin of 'chicken' meaning cowardly, and the grains normally fed to them are cheap, so 'chicken feed' has come to mean paltry amounts of money. And when they are decapitated, chickens do sometimes move around briefly before collapsing, hence 'running around like a headless chicken' – panicking and therefore not thinking clearly about what you are doing.

did you know?

- Chickens were domesticated from several species of jungle fowl in India about 4000 years ago, probably to ensure a regular supply for cock-fighting, an activity popular throughout the world for millennia and outlawed in the UK only about 150 years ago. From the subcontinent they spread to Greece and Rome, and first arrived in Britain during the 1st century BC. Most early chickens were reared for their eggs, the meat only really being eaten when they could no longer lay. Even so, it was a luxury treat for high days and holy days, and it is only since the Second World War with the advent of intensive farming that chicken has become an inexpensive, everyday meat.
- Jewish mothers have been inextricably associated with chicken for what seems like millennia too, but the links go deeper than making soup. Chicken, in fact, is an integral part of Judaism, being particularly associated with Yom Kippur, the Day of Atonement. It is traditionally served before the fast that marks it, and is also part of *kapparoth*, the ceremony where the ritual slaughterer whirls cocks over the heads of men and hens over those of women, while offering prayers that the sacrificial death of the birds will be acceptable atonements by the community.
- Chickens are unfortunately famous (or infamous) for harbouring bacteria that can cause food poisoning. One of these, salmonella, used to be rampant (in 1979 about 80 percent of British chickens were found to have it), but better hygiene procedures have nearly wiped it out.

corned beef

This is cooked, cured and pressed **beef**. To produce it commercially, the meat is first cooked and then cured by salting, normally by being mechanically injected with a liquid solution that includes flavourings like peppercorns and bay leaf, as well as salts like sodium nitrate and saltpetre (potassium nitrate). The latter give it its characteristic pinkish colour. It is diced and pressed into moulded shapes before being canned or sliced and vacuum-packed for sale. Salt beef, which is cured in a similar way, is made from either silverside or brisket – and the latter is always used for kosher salt beef (silverside can't be classified as kosher since it comes from the hindquarters of the animal).

using it Vacuum-packed corned and salt beef keeps in the refrigerator for up to 10 days, while canned corned beef can be stored indefinitely. Once the packet or can has been opened, the meat should be stored in the refrigerator and eaten within 2–3 days.

Both corned and salt beef are normally sliced and served cold as part of a salad or in a sandwich. They can, however, be used in cooked dishes too: added to mashed potato and shredded cabbage to make a more substantial bubble and squeak, or fried with diced cooked potatoes and onions to make hash; with the addition of chopped beetroot, this becomes a traditional American 'red flannel hash'.

word origin Despite the name, there's no corn or maize in corned meat – the word actually refers to the original way in which the dish was made, when the beef was cured in a brine solution that included very coarse grains (called corns) of salt.

did you know?

- The first recipes for 'corned' beef appeared in England during the 17th century and Mrs Beeton was still making it at home during the mid-1800s. But the real association is with Ireland, where something similar has been eaten since medieval times. From there it spread out to the Americas (most modern commercial corned beef comes from Uruguay or Brazil) and even to several islands in the Pacific where it has become part of the staple diet.

duck

This is a long-beaked, long-necked waterfowl that was domesticated in China about 2000 years ago, although several breeds are still found in the wild. Most European domesticated birds are descended from the black-and-white plumed mallard (*Anas platyrhynchos*), the largest of the available wild species, which is still found in temperate areas all over the northern hemisphere and has now been introduced into Australasia. The only other domesticated species is the barbary or muscovy duck (*Cairina moshata*), a lean musky-flavoured breed that originated in South America.

Some ducks are reared for their eggs, but most are raised for their meat. Like other **poultry**, they can be intensively farmed (as most are), free-range or organic; intensively farmed birds are reared for nine weeks (mallards) or 10–12 (barbary ducks), while free-range and organic birds survive for at least 12 weeks. A few ducks (mostly in France) are raised and force-fed for their liver, called foie gras (see **goose**). Popular breeds of duck include the Aylesbury, a white bird with well-flavoured meat, so named because it was once reared around the Buckinghamshire town; Gressingham, a thick-skinned crossbreed of mallard and domestic duck, with leanish, gamey meat; Norfolk, the standard description for most ducks now since that county is a centre for duck production; Rouen, a French breed with meat that is pink-tinged because it's killed by smothering to preserve the blood in its muscles; and Peking, a breed of duck as well as the classic dish (see below).

The most common wild duck is still the mallard, but one or two smaller ones such as the teal (*Anas crecca*) and wigeon (*Anas penelope*) are also sometimes available during their season, which runs from the beginning of September through to the end of January (or the third week in February if the bird is shot in or above an area below the highwater mark of spring tides). Wild ducks are only rarely hung (see **game**) and then for about a day, and are smaller and leaner than domesticated varieties. They can weigh from about 400g to 2kg, depending on the species; farmed birds range from 2–3.5kg.

using it Farmed ducks are sold whole, as leg portions or as breasts, boned or bone-in; wild ducks are available whole during their season. Whole ducks do not have a lot of meat for their size, which needs to be taken into account when buying. As farmed ducks are very fatty (wild ones are much less so), before cooking the skin on the breast needs to be pricked so that the fat beneath it can run out. Don't discard the fat – it's good to cook with and can be used in the same way as goose fat or made into confit (see **goose**).

Whole birds can be roasted and served with accompaniments such as apple sauce, or à l'orange (with a sauce based on orange liqueur, juice and zest). In Germany and Scandinavia, roast duck is often served with **sauerkraut** (cooked in duck fat) and braised red cabbage (ditto). Wild duck can also be roasted, although being lean it is very good braised. Duck joints, particularly the tougher legs, can be simmered in stews or casseroles. Boned breasts are normally fried, grilled or baked (when they can be served rare), or cut into strips to be stir-fried or used in a *salade tiède* (see **salad**).

word origin Duck comes from the Old English *duce*, which was probably derived from the German *tauchen*, to dip or dive, something the bird does in the wild. Although it's now used to describe anything from a small young bird to a large old one, technically duck refers to a bird over the age of two months; anything younger than this is a duckling.

A 'duck' in cricket is every batsman's nightmare, a score of zero and so called because the figure looks like a duck's egg. A 'lame duck' is someone who is no longer effective (as a real duck in the wild becomes when lamed), while 'dead duck', meaning something with no chance of success, comes from an older expression 'never waste powder on a dead duck', which harks back to the days when ducks were hunted more often than they were farmed.

- The favourite American domesticated duck is called Long Island, and is a direct descendant of the breed known as Peking. And all the Peking and Long Island birds in the United States are descended from three ducks and a drake (a male duck) that arrived in America from China in 1873. The *other* Peking duck is a dish invented in China around the middle of the 19th century. It is made by scalding a duck, bathing the skin in honey and then hanging it up to dry for about 24 hours before roasting until dark red and crisp. Both the skin and the meat are cut into small pieces and served with pancakes, sweet bean or hoisin sauce, and shredded spring onions and cucumber.

escalope

An escalope is a thin slice of boneless **meat** cut from the lean parts of certain animals and poultry, particularly the fillet end of the leg or loin of calves (**veal**), the fillet or tenderloin of pigs (**pork**) and the breast of **turkeys**. The best escalopes are sliced across the grain, the faint pattern of ridges that runs across meat (if they're cut *with* it they can curl up and toughen during cooking).

using it Although they're already thinly sliced, escalopes are normally flattened and stretched still further before being cooked. Slices are usually coated with flour or cornflour to protect them during cooking, then fried, something that shouldn't take more than 2–3 minutes per side. They are often cooked in a sauce such as white or red wine, sliced mushrooms and crème fraîche, or tomatoes, garlic and herbs to keep them moist. In Italy escalopes are called *scaloppine*, and there is a whole repertoire of recipes for them, including topping with or wrapping in prosciutto and fresh sage, then cooking in butter (called saltimbocca); browning quickly, then topping with mozzarella until it melts; or simmering briefly in marsala and finishing with cream. The classic escalope dish, however, is Viennese in origin – Wiener schnitzel ('schnitzel' is German for escalope). For this the escalope is dipped in egg and breadcrumbs, then pan-fried and served with a wedge of lemon. The same dish pops up all over the world with minor variations: in France it is called *escalope panée*; in Italy, *costoletta alla milanese* (although purists use a thin veal chop rather than an escalope); and even in Japan there is a similar dish, called *tonkatsu*, breaded pork escalope that's deep-fried, cut into strips and served with a sauce made from soy sauce, Worcestershire sauce, sake and wasabi, the Japanese horseradish.

word origin Escalope comes from a similar Old French word meaning 'shell', a reference to the shape of the pan in which such meat slices were originally cooked.

frankfurter

This is a thin, soft-textured, smoked **sausage** that is cooked before being eaten. The first frankfurters were made from lean pork and salted bacon fat, but most now have a more complicated set of ingredients including pork and beef trimmings, pig's cheek, tripe and heart, 'binders' like cereal, flour, skimmed milk powder and soya proteins, and seasonings, sweeteners and preservatives such as saltpetre or sodium nitrate, which give the sausage its characteristic pinkish colour.

Early frankfurters were smoked in the traditional way (see **meat**), but modern mass-market ones are made in a continuous process in the same way as other sausages. They are then cased and either sprayed or drenched with liquid smoke before being cooked; the casing is peeled off before the sausages are packaged for sale.

using it Although they're part-cooked before being sold, frankfurters need a final cooking before being eaten, either by simmering them in water for 7–8 minutes or by grilling or frying them for roughly the same length of time.

Natural partners are filling rather than fancy and include **baked beans** and **sauerkraut**.

The most famous frankfurter dish is the sandwich called a hot dog, which was invented in the United States. It couldn't be simpler: a boiled or grilled frankfurter, or 'wienie' (see below), is inserted into a slit-open, soft long roll or bun, and accompanied by (depending on taste) mustard, tomato ketchup, browned sliced onions and special hot-dog relish or pickle. It is served and eaten everywhere, from backyard barbecues to sporting events all over the world.

Other uses for frankfurters include chopping and mixing them with hot potatoes, beetroot, onion and **vinaigrette** to make a warm main-course salad; mixing with onion and baked beans, then topping with a cornbread mixture and baking to make a frankfurter 'pie'; or cooking with chopped red pepper, then mixing with caraway seeds, crème fraîche and olive oil to make a sauce for broad noodles like pappardelle.

word origin   The sausage originated around the city of Frankfurt in Germany, hence the name. It isn't clear how hot dog got *its* name, although one school of thought suggests it could be because of a resemblance between it and a dachshund, the dog with the long low body and very short legs.

did you know?

• Frankfurters were probably invented around the mid-17th century, but in the first years of the 20th century they moved to Vienna in Austria with a sausage butcher from Frankfurt who began to make and sell them as 'wieners' in honour of his new home (the German name for Vienna is *Wien*). And it was as wienies from Austria that they found their spiritual home in the United States. From there, they more or less conquered the rest of the world.

• The most famous hot dog in the world is found at

Nathan's of Coney Island, a beach resort outside New York City. The Nathan in question was Nathan Handwerker, who was a delivery boy to a sausage butcher in Coney Island during the early years of the 20th century. He was egged on by two friends (later to become the early movie stars, Eddie Cantor and Jimmy Durante) to set up in opposition to his old boss and undercut him by selling his sausages for less. He duly opened a nickel (5-cent) hot-dog stand in 1916 and the rest is history. Nathan's frankfurters, incidentally, are kosher, made from beef only, rather than the standard pork or mixed pork and beef – and now cost rather more than a nickel.

game

This is the general word used to describe wild birds and animals (and occasionally fish) that are hunted and killed to be eaten or for sport. In Great Britain there are two types of game: feathered – the ones that fly, basically birds like **pheasant** and **partridge** – and furred, those that are land–based such as deer, from which we get **venison**. Although game is meant by definition to be wild, in practice the stocks of many species are manipulated by one means or another to ensure supply, and some like **quail** and **rabbit** are now more available reared specially for the table than they are as wild animals.

The major game birds and animals, including **duck**, which has both farmed and wild types, are described in individual entries. Other game birds include: red grouse (*Lagopus lagopus*) and black grouse (*Tetrao tetrix*), which are mainly vegetarian birds found in moorlands and forested regions in Scotland and western parts of Great Britain, and which have delicate meat; and ptarmigan (*Lagopus mutus*), which lives mostly in the barren mountains of northern Scotland. Among other game animals is wild boar (*Sus scrofa*), an ancient species of wild pig that was once common in this country; it is now nearly always farmed rather than wild. Its flesh is gamey and strong-tasting, similar to well-hung venison.

Most wild game is protected by law and can only be killed at certain times of the year. The 'season' for feathered game opens on August 12 (known to hunters as the Glorious Twelfth), when grouse and ptarmigan can officially be killed, and ends the following February, the last point at which a partridge, pheasant or wild duck can be dispatched. The only furred game protected in this way is deer. Some game (specifically **pigeon**, quail, rabbit and wild boar) aren't protected because they are considered to be pests or because they are now farmed rather than wild.

With the exception of pigeon, quail, farmed rabbit and often wild duck, game is 'hung' before being sold: if it's a bird it is suspended by the neck on hooks, unskinned, to allow the enzymes in the body to break down and tenderize the flesh. Deer is skinned and 'paunched' (disembowelled) before being hung, while wild rabbit and hare are hung first. Individual animals and birds are hung for different lengths of time, something that depends on personal preference, age of the creature, prevailing weather conditions and, in the case of birds, the state they were in when killed (a badly shot bird will decompose more quickly than a cleanly shot one). The rule of thumb is that the longer (within reason) they are hung, the richer and stronger-tasting the meat will be. Of those described here, grouse is hung on average for 3–4 days and ptarmigan for 3–5 days. After hanging, birds are plucked (i.e. their feathers are removed), then drawn (the head and neck removed, then the innards such as intestines, liver and heart). Furred game is normally jointed before being sold.

using it Fresh wild game is available within its season; frozen is occasionally available during the season and sometimes for a few weeks after it. Farmed game is, of course, more easily obtainable. Young fresh grouse are usually sold with their feet still on and tucked into their body cavity so that prospective buyers can identify the spur, which indicates that the bird is still young (and therefore tender). All game meat can be stored loosely wrapped or in airtight packaging for 2–3 days in the refrigerator, although any **giblets** should be removed immediately you get home and stored separately. Game can be frozen but should be thawed thoroughly, preferably in the refrigerator, before being cooked; it should not be refrozen uncooked.

Young birds (as a rule of thumb those bought before Christmas) are more tender than older ones and are therefore normally roasted, while older ones are braised, casseroled or used as pie fillings or for pâté. Grouse and ptarmigan can be cooked in the same way as pheasant or partridge respectively, and wild boar treated in the same way as venison.

word origin Game comes from the Old English *gamen,* meaning 'amusement' or 'fun'.

did you know?

• It is only comparatively recently that the idea of discriminating between what could be killed and what must be protected has gained credibility throughout the world, and compliance with protection laws is more enthusiastic in some countries than others. One country's protected species isn't necessarily another's, either. In mid-19th century Britain, birds like thrush, lark, heron and swan were still considered 'fair game' (Mrs Beeton has recipes for blackbird pie, roast plover and lark), while in contemporary France many still are: the 1988 English edition of *Larousse Gastronomique* has several recipes for both thrush and lark (political correctness has struck in the 2001 edition and the recipes are omitted, although the entries themselves remain).

giblets

Giblets are the edible inner organs of **poultry** that are removed from the bird when it is 'drawn' or readied for sale – namely, the heart, **liver** and gizzard (part of the stomach).

Most poultry is now sold minus these items; if there, they are usually contained in a plastic bag attached to the legs or placed inside the body cavity.

using them The giblets should be removed from the bird as soon as you get home, stored separately in the refrigerator and used as quickly as possible. As far as using them, there's theory and practice. Theoretically, the liver at least can be cooked separately or at least frozen until you have enough of them to make specific liver dishes, such as a pâté; or all the giblets can be added to a pie filling or casserole. In practice, however, they are either thrown away or (at best) used to make **stock** or **gravy**.

word origin Giblets is Middle English in origin and has been around since about the 15th century. Originally it meant 'inessential parts' or even 'garbage', and was derived from the Old French *gibelet*, a 'game bird stew'.

goose

A goose is a large, migratory water bird with a long neck and webbed feet that is native to Europe and central Asia. Although several wild species are still found in the United Kingdom they cannot legally be sold for their meat – what we buy is the domesticated wild bird reared for the table as **poultry**. Nearly all domesticated geese are descended from the greylag goose (*Anser anser*), a long-beaked bird that nests in the wild in northern areas of Europe, including Scotland.

A few farmed geese are kept for their **eggs**, but most are now reared for their meat, nearly all as free-range birds. The size of the bird will depend on its gender (females reach about two-thirds of the size of males) and the time of year it's killed: baby geese, called goslings, hatch in spring and are reared for at least 16 weeks; but most are reared for much longer for the Christmas trade. September geese will normally be 3–4kg in weight, while Christmas ones can reach 6–8kg or more.

using it Goose is rarely found in supermarkets or even most butchers (although many of the latter will order one for you), and is only available between late summer and the end of the year. It is usually sold fresh, although there's nothing to stop you freezing one at home. Pale fatty skin and a plump breast are the things to look for since they suggest the bird is young and therefore tender.

Most goose is sold whole and the traditional way of cooking is to roast it, basically in the same way as **duck**. Like duck, it doesn't need basting, and so much fat will come out during cooking that you will probably have to spoon it from the pan once or twice. The fat removed from the pan shouldn't be thrown away, as it makes a good general cooking fat, especially for roast potatoes and other vegetables, and can be used for confit (see below). Roast goose is always cooked thoroughly (see **poultry**). Classic accompaniments include gravy, **sauerkraut** (preferably cooked in a little goose fat), braised red cabbage (ditto), apple sauce, sorrel sauce and (if served cold) Cumberland sauce (see **currants**). Older birds are occasionally available as jointed pieces, and any recipe for braised or casseroled **duck** pieces would also work for goose.

In France, goose legs are a traditional ingredient in a cassoulet. The other classic way to prepare them is to cook them in their own fat, then transfer to a storage pot and cover with more goose fat to preserve them. The resulting dish, called confit, lasts for months, and the meat becomes very tender when kept in this way.

word origin Goose comes from the Old English *gos*, which is derived from similar Old German and Old Dutch words. It's used for both male and female birds sold for cooking, although technically a male goose is called a gander.

A whole range of expressions is built around the goose, none of them particularly positive. 'Silly goose' might be said fondly, but still means someone naive and foolish (geese, on the whole, are not reputed to be Mensa material), while 'goose flesh' is skin that pimples up with either cold or fright and is supposed to look like the plucked skin of the bird.

did you know?

* The ancient Egyptians, Greeks and Romans all enjoyed goose. The Romans also declared it sacred to Juno, the wife of their chief god Jupiter, and particularly revered it after the 4th century BC because it was cackling sacred geese that raised the alarm during a failed attack on Rome by the Gauls. In Britain, geese are traditionally associated with Michaelmas Day (September 29), when they were served as the centrepiece of the feast. Those who ate goose then were supposed to enjoy an easy time of it for the rest of the year. Tenants often gave a goose to their landlords at Michaelmas, presumably on the same principle.
* The livers of some geese (and occasional ducks) are hugely enlarged to become **foie gras** (literally 'fat liver' in French). To get them to the usual 675–900g foie-gras weight (duck foie-gras livers average 300–400g), the birds are force-fed enormous amounts of food (normally maize). Although it seems to be the French who eat most of it now, they did not, in fact, invent foie gras. Ancient Egyptians stuffed their geese too and, despite the bird's sacred status, so did classical Romans; they crammed their birds with figs, then steeped the resulting swollen livers in milk and honey to enlarge and flavour them even more.

guinea fowl

There are several species of this domesticated wild bird which is related to the chicken and partridge. The most important is *Numida meleagris*, a handsome bird with light grey speckles on a darker grey plumage, which is native to northern Africa. Guinea fowl can be intensively farmed or free-range (see **poultry**). Free-range birds are reared for at least 11½–13½ weeks, but those that are intensively reared will be younger than this. Average weight is around 1kg and the flesh has a slightly stronger, meatier taste than chicken.

using it Ready-to-cook on supermarket shelves, guinea fowl looks like a small, slightly dark or corn-fed chicken, and can be cooked in the same ways as **chicken** or **pheasant**. Leftover meat can be added to rice-based dishes such as a pilaff or used as a filling for game pie or pâté. The carcass also makes good **stock**.

word origin The name indicates its origins in Guinea, north-western Africa.

did you know?

* Guinea fowl arrived in Europe early and was known to both the Greeks and Romans, who called it Carthage hen in recognition of its geographical origins (the ancient city of Carthage was located in what is now Tunisia). It seems to have gone out of fashion with the fall of Rome, re-emerging around the 14th century as 'Bohemian chicken', allegedly because it was repopularized by gypsies who were sometimes called 'bohemians'.

haggis

This traditional Scottish **sausage** is a relative of **black pudding** and looks like a large hand grenade. It is made from fat, toasted oatmeal, chopped onion, spices and the paunch and pluck of sheep (part of the **offal** of the animal, the former being the stomach lining, which used to be cleaned and used as the casing, the latter a collective word for the heart, liver and lungs – or 'lights' – which are still chopped together and used in the filling). It's made in the same way as other sausages.

using it Most haggis is part-cooked before being sold, but needs to be boiled before it's ready to eat; the amount of time required varies from manufacturer to manufacturer although it is usually 45–90 minutes. The traditional way to serve haggis is to pierce the casing and let the filling mixture spill out onto the plate; classic accompaniments include 'bashed neeps' (mashed swedes) and potatoes. Since it's dense and heavy to taste, some brown sauce or ketchup wouldn't go amiss, either.

word origin Theories abound about where haggis comes from. The close ties between Scotland and France since medieval times supply two of the more plausible ones, that it comes from the French *hachis* meaning 'minced meat', or from a 17th century term for magpie, *haggess* (derived from the Old French for magpie, *agace*). The latter may be more than just fun, since during the Middle Ages the English word magpie donated the second half of its name to make the word *pie*, a mixture of several ingredients enclosed in a casing (in this case pastry), not all that far removed from the concept of haggis.

did you know?

● Although haggis is now the national dish of Scotland, it almost certainly didn't originate there – the most likely inventors were the Romans, enthusiastic sausage-makers who exported their skills to all the countries they conquered and some they didn't. The Roman version would probably have been made from pig's pluck, so was not only adopted by the Scots, but adapted by them to take account of their preference for sheep meat over that of pig, and oats with everything. Until a couple of hundred years ago, direct descendants of the original Roman dish, called hog's

pudding, were quite common in England, especially in south-western parts of the country.
● In Scotland (and anywhere else there are Scots, i.e. virtually everywhere), haggis is ceremoniously served on January 25 each year to commemorate the birthday of the national poet, Robert Burns, possibly the only writer in the world ever to have written an ode about a sausage. His *To a Haggis* is recited during the celebrations, just after the 'great chieftain o' the puddin' race' itself has been bagpiped into the dining room, and the dish is taken with bashed neeps and a large nip or two of malt whisky.

ham

Ham, the cured meat from the upper part of the hind legs of a pig (see **pork**), can be sold uncooked or ready cooked. In the United Kingdom the word nearly always means the latter; for uncooked ham, see **prosciutto**.

Ham legs are removed from the rest of the carcass before curing starts (unlike gammon, which comes from the same part of the pig; gammon legs are cured while still on the side of the animal, see **bacon**). The curing process begins by salting, where the meat is covered with mixtures that nearly always include saltpetre (potassium nitrate) and sodium nitrate, which aid preservation and also give the end product its distinctive pinkish colour. There are two main methods: dry-salting, the traditional way, where salts and other flavourings are spread over the meat and left for varying lengths of time up to several months; and brining, a much speedier process and the one used nowadays for nearly all cooked hams, since the finished product can be ready in as little as 3–4 days. In the brining method, the legs are immersed in flavoured brine or injected with it; boned hams are injected before being boned or after, then also sometimes steeped in brine. Cure flavourings include ingredients like brown sugar, honey or maple syrup as well as various herbs and spices.

Once salting has finished, the ham is steamed, and ham that has been boned is pressed into moulds to shape it – the heat helps to 'set' the mould. Ham to be sold as ready-to-eat is cooked and sometimes smoked (see **meat**) before being packaged for sale.

Specific 'recipes' for ham can vary from this general procedure, depending on their area of origin or the producer. Many, for instance, are still identified by their regional names, including York ham, which is dry-salted, then smoked and matured for several months; Virginia ham, a lean American type that is smoked in hickory and apple wood; jambon de Paris, a mild, unsmoked cooked French ham; and Brunswick ham, a popular German ready-to-eat ham that is lightly smoked over beechwood.

using it Ready-cooked hams are sold sliced and vacuum-packed, sliced fresh from an already cooked joint or canned as boned joints. Vacuum-packed slices will keep in the refrigerator for 10–14 days, while fresh slices or slices from an opened pack should be used within 3–4 days. Canned ham, unopened, keeps indefinitely.

Ready-cooked sliced ham can be used in sandwiches, particularly with coleslaw or mustard, or in a salad. Chopped, it can be added to other ingredients like rice, raisins and chopped shallots to become a stuffing for vegetables like peppers or courgettes; used to fill omelettes; or layered with sliced potatoes, onions and grated cheese, moistened with milk or cream and then baked.

Fresh ham joints can be prepared and glazed in the same way as bacon joints, although dry-salted hams will need to go through a soaking process to remove excess salt before being cooked. Although canned ham joints are already cooked, they can be glazed with mixtures like marmalade or brown sugar and mustard, then baked to serve hot.

word origin Ham dates back to Anglo-Saxon times when it was used to describe the back of the knee (it occasionally still is, in words like hamstring); later it came to mean thigh. It had settled into its modern meaning by about the 17th century. Then – and occasionally now – the word was also applied to cured meat from the same part of other animals, like deer (see **venison**) and wild boar.

kidney

The stomach cavity of all mammals, birds and reptiles contains this pair of brownish jelly-like organs, whose function is to purify the blood by removing waste matter from it. Despite this, the kidneys of several animals are eaten, in particular the multi-lobed ones of calves (veal) and cattle (ox), and the bean-shaped ones of lamb and, occasionally, pig (pork). In cooking terms, kidneys are classified as **offal**.

using it When they are taken out of the animal, kidneys are wrapped in a layer of hard white fat called suet, but this is usually removed before they are offered for sale. To prepare them, the membranes and gristly, central white parts (the cores) are scissored from the meat either before slicing them lengthways in half (veal and ox kidneys) or after (lamb and pork). Kidneys from older animals are more strongly flavoured than those from younger ones, so ox and pork kidneys are usually rinsed in running water, then steeped in milk or water for about an hour to tone them down before they are cooked.

Veal and lamb kidneys are the easiest to prepare, and are good grilled or fried. They are cooked pink since they toughen with overcooking, then often served with a mustard sauce. Lamb kidneys are also part of a traditional English breakfast. Ox and pork kidneys are best chopped and cooked for a long time, so they are usually casseroled, often with other types of meat and strongly flavoured ingredients (as in steak and kidney pudding or pie).

• Although the suet surrounding kidneys is usually removed before the meat is sold, butchers occasionally offer them for sale with the fat still on. Veal kidneys, especially, taste delicious baked 'in their overcoats'. Even if you don't want to do this, the suet could be used instead of oil or butter for frying and especially roasting (it makes spectacular roast potatoes), or grated and used for **pastry** dough.

lamb

This is the meat of a young sheep (*Ovis aries*), defined as one that is marketed within the year of its birth (if it was born after the start of the calendar year) or after the first of October (if it was born during the year before). When the animal is older than this, it's called a hogget, or old-season lamb, until it has its first permanent incisor tooth; after this point the meat becomes mutton, which is tougher, stronger-tasting and darker in colour than lamb and rarely available now. Sheep are farmed primarily for their meat, although their milk is also used commercially to make **cheese** and **yoghurt**.

There are over 70 breeds of sheep in the British Isles, although most meat on sale comes from animals that have been crossbred in a complex system designed to produce lean meat. As a rough rule of thumb, pure breeds are either hill or lowland types, the former being small but hardy and able to survive on fairly bleak terrain for at least part of the year, and the latter growing more quickly to a larger size than hill animals but requiring better-quality grazing land. Most hill ewes (female sheep) are mated with rams (male sheep) from lowland stock

to combine the best of these characteristics, then their lambs in turn are mated with rams from breeds noted for their meat. Although mating is highly managed, the animals themselves are raised fairly naturally, and most feed on grazing land for most of the year, being fed hay and silage (fermented grass) only during winter when grazing can be insufficient. Organic lamb comes from animals that graze on organically cultivated pasturelands.

Very young sucking lambs, which are fed only on their mother's milk and killed before they are weaned, have light-coloured, delicate-tasting meat that is highly prized in continental Europe. They are only rarely available in the United Kingdom. Nearly all lambs in Britain are slaughtered between the ages of 2½–15 months old (the average is 3–6 months), and will have been weaned and grazed before being killed. Lambs raised in salty lowland marshes absorb the salt and iodine in the grass, which gives their flesh a distinctive flavour often identified at point of sale – some Welsh lamb is reared on this type of terrain, as are the French lambs called pré-salé; both are considered great delicacies. Cheap lamb cuts pass through the system after slaughter without being hung, but prime parts of the animal are hung for a minimum of 7 days before being sold (see **meat**).

Cuts vary from country to country. British ones include leg, loin, best end (which comes from between the middle neck and loin and is sometimes called rack of lamb), shank (the lower end of the leg), chops (thick lean ones from the loin or chump), cutlets (thinner chops from the best end or fattier ones from the middle neck), shoulder, breast, and middle neck and scrag. A crown roast is made up from two racks tied together into a ring, bones uppermost and meaty side inwards; a guard of honour is two racks tied together facing each other, meaty side down and the bones pointing inwards to overlap at the top; and noisettes are boneless medallions cut from the centre of the loin fillet. Minced lamb is from cheaper cuts such as breast or neck and scrag. Most of the internal organs of lamb, such as **kidneys**, **liver** and sweetbreads (see **offal**), are also eaten.

using it Lamb is quite seasonal, although thanks to global markets and commercial freezing it's now available throughout the year. It is particularly associated with spring, which is when the first young home-grown lamb from southern parts of the country become available, and continues through summer until autumn. New Zealand and frozen lamb fill any gaps in supply.

Basic cooking methods vary from cut to cut. Prime whole joints like loin and leg (and shoulder, although it's fattier) are normally roasted. Crown roasts are also roasted, with or without a stuffing – the centre can be filled with vegetables, such as peas and carrots, or another mixture before serving. Classic accompaniments for roast lamb include mint sauce or jelly and redcurrant jelly. Onion sauce is also traditional, made by simmering onions in spiced milk until they are very soft, then mixing with fresh breadcrumbs and butter.

Joints are sometimes braised, occasionally after marinating, as in the northern Indian dish raan, where leg of lamb is steeped in a curried yoghurt and ground almond mixture for 48 hours before cooking. Shoulder and leg joints are also often cubed and used to make kebabs or casseroles. Lamb is particularly popular in North Africa, the Middle East and parts of the Indian subcontinent, where it features in many tajines, kormas and birianis. European lamb stews include navarin printanier, in which browned pieces of lamb are cooked slowly with tomatoes, garlic and herbs before young spring vegetables – onions, carrots, turnips and new potatoes – are added.

Chops and cutlets are usually grilled or fried, although they are also sometimes cooked in casseroles like Irish stew (middle neck chops with sliced potatoes, onions, herbs and water or stock). Lamb shanks are usually braised very slowly until the meat is almost falling off the bone, which is how they are cooked in the traditional Greek dish sheftalia. For ways to use minced lamb, see **mince**.

word origin Lamb comes from Old English and probably has Germanic roots.

did you know?

* Sheep will be sheep: they don't get difficult and they tend to be docile and stick together, all of which made them ripe for domestication, something that seems to have first happened in what is now Iraq about 11,000 years ago. They had reached the British Isles by about 4000BC.
* There are none of the taboos that surround pork and beef clinging to lamb – wherever people eat meat, they eat lamb if they can get it. It is particularly associated with celebration and especially those religious celebrations that occur during spring, such as Passover in the Jewish calendar, the Eid festival that marks the last month of the Muslim year, and Easter in the western and Orthodox Christian Churches.

liver

All vertebrates have this organ, which is designed to process food and turn it into substances the body can use, and to neutralize any harmful substances in the blood. The livers of only seven creatures are eaten regularly: four from animals (beef cattle, beef calves, lambs and pigs), which are classified as **offal**, and three from poultry (chickens, ducks and geese), classified as **giblets**. The enlarged and enriched liver of special types of force-fed geese and ducks called foie gras is described separately (see **goose**).

using it Liver from animals is usually sold in slices. Calf's liver is the palest and finest textured, lamb's liver is darker but still fine, and pig's and cattle or ox livers are darker and more coarsely grained than the others. Poultry livers are small and normally come whole as part of the giblets, which are stored in a small bag attached to the legs or in the body cavity of bought birds, although quantities of chicken livers are also sold in tubs or packets.

Liver is always cooked before being eaten, but *how* it's cooked depends on which creature it comes from. Calf's and lamb's liver are usually coated with flour before being fried or grilled; both are often served underdone, and about 3 minutes per side would be enough for an average-size slice of lamb's liver, less than this for thinly sliced calf's liver. Classic partners are lamb's liver with bacon, and calf's liver with fresh sage. For fegato alla Veneziana, calf's liver is cut into strips and cooked with slowly browned onions.

Pig's liver benefits from being soaked for an hour or so in milk to lighten the colour and taste; then it can be cut into thin slices and cooked in the same way as lamb's liver. Alternatively it can be chopped and simmered with wine or stock; added to other meats as part of a stew; or used to make pâté. Ox liver needs long, slow braising or casseroling to tenderize it.

Being small, several poultry livers are needed to make any kind of meal on their own, but in quantity they can be chopped and stir-fried with flavouring vegetables like onion, garlic and peas as a good sauce for pasta or rice; or chopped and fried with some onion, then scrambled with eggs. They can also be used to make a rich pâté.

word origin Liver comes from the Old English *lifer*, which has German origins.

meat

This is the flesh of an animal or bird that is used as food. It includes the flesh of domesticated animals like **lamb**, that of domesticated fowl, or **poultry**, and that of birds or animals that may or may not be wild but are usually protected by law, called **game**. **Offal**, the internal organs and external extremities of domesticated animals, and **giblets**, roughly the same parts of fowl, are also categorized as meat (see separate entries).

Meat is muscle tissue, the bits of an animal or bird that enable it to move. Structurally, it's made up of bundles of individual thin muscle fibres bound together and held in place by sheets of connective tissue, and protected by fat; nutritionally, it contains a mixture of protein, fat and water with the last predominating, although proportions vary from animal to animal and from cut to cut. All of these things help to determine the texture, tenderness and flavour of the meat we buy – as does the age of the creature at slaughter (the younger, the better within reason, although older ones often have more flavour), and where on the body the meat comes from (less-used muscles will be more tender than constantly used ones). Even the condition of the animal or fowl just prior to slaughter is important: the meat of a stressed, exhausted creature will be less tender than that of a calm, well-rested one.

Modern domesticated animals and fowl are nearly always stunned before being slaughtered and their blood is removed by allowing it to 'bleed out' (this protects against spoilage); they are then 'dressed', that is, skinned, and the head, feet and internal organs removed. After this, the carcass of most animals (or sometimes part of the carcass) is hung to 'age' by being suspended on hooks in controlled temperatures and humidity for varying lengths of time to tenderize the flesh and also darken it; beef, lamb and pork meats are all hung, but that of calves (veal) and fowl aren't. (Game is treated differently; see separate entry.) Kosher and halal meat are also treated differently, since Jewish and Muslim religious laws dictate that the animals must be healthy and uninjured when killed and stunning is considered injurious by some religious authorities; many kosher and halal animals are therefore conscious when they are slaughtered.

The way meat from domesticated animals is butchered before being sold varies slightly from country to country, or at least it varies from the United Kingdom to the United States and France, and the variations reflect national preferences in the way it is cooked. British cuts concentrate on obtaining the best joints for roasting and cheaper cuts for stewing, the favourite national ways of cooking meat; Americans, who are particularly fond of steaks and chops, make sure their animals provide a large variety of both; and French cuts dissect the muscles to get boned pieces that can be braised in stock or wine and provide a good variety of meat for grilling and frying. Poultry and game are treated in much the same way in all of these countries.

Before the invention of freezing and canning, meat was preserved in the same way as that of fish, by drying, salting or smoking, or a combination of these. All three are still done today, although more for flavour and texture than for preservation. The oldest method is probably drying and while occasional specific meats like jerky can be cut into strips and either dried in the sun or over a fire, most dried food is now air-dried – South African beef biltong, for instance, is first marinated in a salt and spice mixture, then air-dried and smoked. Drying works by reducing the water content of food to a point where the micro-organisms that cause spoilage can't operate, but it takes time to reach this level and the food meanwhile continues to decay; salting something to be dried helps to speed up the drying process as well as arresting decay, so most dried food is salted before the drying process starts (see **prosciutto** and **salami**). Salting, in fact, with or without drying, is still common and **beef**, **pork** and their many byproducts like **bacon**, **ham** and **sausages** continue to be preserved in this way, either by traditional 'dry-salting' methods or by soaking in or injecting with brine.

Smoking is normally undertaken only after salting has already reduced the moisture content of meat, and creates a 'seal' on the surface that also helps to protect it against spoilage. It is now primarily used to produce bacon, ham and sausages, although poultry is also occasionally smoked. Traditional methods are the same as for **smoked fish**, but mass-produced smoked food is now often produced artificially by using a smoke-flavoured concentrate. Cold-smoked meat (bacon is a good example) needs to be cooked before being eaten; hot-smoked meat, like smoked chicken and some types of sausage, do not because they have already effectively been 'cooked'.

Meat is conventionally seen as a protein food, which is accurate, but lean meat is also a rich source of several essential trace elements, including iron, zinc, copper and selenium, and it contains most B vitamins. One of these is B12, a vitamin found exclusively in foods of animal origin. This is why vegans are advised to take a vitamin B12 supplement or choose foods fortified with vitamin B12, such as breakfast cereals.

using it When buying, the things to look for in cuts of fresh meat are the length of the fibres and the closeness of the grain (the faint 'ridge' pattern made by the bundles of fibres that make up the muscle tissue) – as a rule of thumb, the longer the fibre and the finer the grain, the more tender the meat will be. Connective tissue toughens meat so the less the cut contains, the better. However, even lean cuts should contain some fat, either around the edges as in **steaks** and chops or as tiny flecks, called 'marbling', which are present in individual fibres and between different bundles of fibres of flesh; these are wholly desirable since they help lubricate the meat during cooking.

Most fresh meat will keep for a few days in the refrigerator, loosely wrapped or in airtight packaging, although mince should be used within a day of purchase. Cured meats like bacon and ham last longer (see individual entries). Meat can be frozen, but needs to be thoroughly thawed before cooking, preferably in the refrigerator, and should never be refrozen uncooked. Canned meat can be kept more or less indefinitely in a cool dry place, but once opened should be stored in the refrigerator and used within 3–5 days.

The way fresh meat is cooked varies from animal to animal and from cut to cut, and is described in individual entries, but in general the prime joints are roasted and smaller, individual prime cuts fried or grilled. These can all usually be served rare, medium or well-done. Cheaper cuts are normally stewed or casseroled.

The most accurate way to check if roast meat is cooked is to use a meat thermometer, inserted at the start of cooking or near the end (an instant-read thermometer). This will measure the internal temperature. Individual prime cuts, such as steaks and chops, can be tested for doneness by pressing with a finger. If rare, the meat will feel spongy; if medium, there will be resistance to the touch; if well-done, the meat will feel firm to the touch. After cooking, meat should be left to 'rest' – 5 minutes or so for steaks and 15 minutes for roasts – so that the juices drawn to the surface can be reabsorbed.

word origin Meat comes from an Old English word that meant 'solid' food as opposed to 'liquid' food, i.e. drink (the phrase 'meat and drink to me', as something essential to happiness, is a throwback to this original meaning). It developed its modern meaning around medieval times, when Europeans (or at least rich ones) began to eat quite a lot of it.

• The first hominids seem to have lived mostly on fruit and nuts, but by the time *Homo erectus* came along, meat had been incorporated into the diet. Eating it,

though, was probably hit and miss, depending on what could be caught that was edible, and it wasn't until some animals became domesticated about 11,000 years ago that supplies began to be more reliable.

• Even with domestication, meat, especially beef and veal, was expensive, so by medieval times it had become a symbol of wealth and status, even in Europe where more of it was consumed than anywhere else. The nobility and other powerful classes ate meat regularly, but most other folk made do with a steady diet of gruels and pottages, with meat featuring mostly on special occasions. In England, even the language reflected the great divide: when the Normans (great meat-eaters) arrived they brought with them their words for animal meat. Thus the prime parts of animal flesh were described as *porc* and *boef* to indicate their status (and the origin of those who ate them), while less desirable bits like offal, which were eaten by the natives, and the animals themselves, like pig and ox, which were looked after by them, continued to be described by their Anglo-Saxon names.

• For most of history, domesticated animals and fowl have been reared in conditions close to their natural wild habits, but the Industrial Revolution began a slow change in the developed world, which accelerated in the United Kingdom when the Second World War exposed our vulnerability to being deprived of food imports. The type of intensive farming that is the norm today was developed after this time to increase our self-sufficiency, and was fuelled by a national wish for cheaper, more plentiful meat. Ironically, however, concerns about animal welfare and the safety of intensively-reared meat are now leading to at least a partial return to more traditional farming methods.

• In recent years the fat content of domesticated animals has been reduced by selective breeding methods. Lean red meat is an excellent source of easily absorbed iron, zinc and some B vitamins There is some evidence of a link between red and processed meat consumption and colon cancer. For that reason, the Department of Health has recommended that high consumers of these foods should consider a reduction.

mince

Mince is **meat** that has been finely ground into small strings in a special machine; the word is also used to describe the act of grinding it. The meat is normally from cheaper, fattier cuts, including fat trimmed from prime joints. Minced lamb, pork and turkey are all commercially available, but the most common mince is **beef**. Unlike the others, beef mince comes in several grades ranging from 'ordinary' through 'lean' to 'steak' (which should be rump), and can be from a named breed (Aberdeen Angus beef mince, for instance) or organic.

using it The more white flecks of fat that mince contains, the more 'ordinary' the quality will be; beef steak mince should be a deep colour with only a small proportion of fat flecks. For basic cooking, mince is usually fried until it loses its pinkness (in the case of meat mince) or becomes opaque (in the case of poultry), then simmered with other ingredients including flavourings, vegetables and liquid.

There are many different uses for mince, including pies (cottage or shepherd's), stuffings (for poultry or pasta), sauces (such as Bolognese), meatballs (found in one form or another from Europe through to Asia), and pâtés, a good way to create something special from something modest. Among the many classic dishes are: moussaka (a lamb mince sauce layered with aubergine slices, topped with cheese sauce and baked); chilli con carne (browned beef mince spiced with chilli powder and cumin, simmered with tomatoes and red kidney beans); and Indian kofta (spiced lamb meatballs sometimes bulked out with rice, served with a fragrant sauce). The most popular mince dish, however, is probably the hamburger. At its best, it is made from seasoned steak-quality beef mince alone, although flavourings like grated onion and herbs can be mixed in, and toppings such as cheese, bacon and chilli are sometimes added.

word origin Mince comes from the Latin *minutia,* meaning 'smallness', via the Old French *mincier*.

• In the 1930s Americans called hamburgers 'Wimpy burgers', after a character in the Popeye comic strip. This is, of course, how we first knew them in Britain. But it is the McDonald brothers who are responsible for the massive popularity of the hamburger, having opened a new-style fast-food take-away and drive-in in the 1950s. The McDonald's chain (and other similar operations like Burger King) expanded around the world, taking the burger with them.
• Mincemeat, oddly enough, doesn't contain any mince (it's a mixture of dried fruit, nuts, spices, suet and occasionally brandy, which is mostly now used to fill Christmas pies). During medieval times, however, mincemeat was just that: meat that was minced up, then mixed with spices and probably other ingredients like dried fruit to eke it out, and used as a general filling. The amount of meat in the filling gradually diminished over the years and had more or less disappeared from the mixture by the end of the 17th century; suet, still an ingredient in most modern mincemeat, is the only reminder.

offal

The rough equivalent of **giblets** in poultry, offal is the internal parts and external extremities of animals like cattle, lamb and pig that are removed from the carcass after the animal is slaughtered. Those that are eaten vary from animal to animal, but include the **kidneys**, **liver** and heart of all the animals we cook regularly. In addition, the following are also sometimes found, although more often in butchers' shops than in supermarkets: the sweetbreads (usually the thymus glands, sometimes the pancreatic glands) of lambs and calves; the feet or trotters of calves and pigs; the tongue of cattle and lamb; the tail of mature cattle (oxtail); and tripe, the stomach of ruminants, nearly always cattle. The paunch and pluck of sheep (the former is the stomach lining, the latter a collective way to describe the heart, liver and lungs) are occasionally used together (see **haggis**).

using it Offal, including liver and kidney, is very perishable, so should be stored in the refrigerator and eaten within one day of purchase. It can be frozen, but needs to be thawed before cooking, and should never be refrozen uncooked. It is always cooked, but *how* it is cooked depends on what it is.

Lamb hearts are prepared by removing the tissue and inner tubes in the centre to create a hollow, which is then stuffed to be baked or braised. Both lamb and especially larger ox hearts are also sometimes sliced and fried, usually with other strongly flavoured ingredients, or chopped and stewed slowly. Sweetbreads, which are considered a delicacy, are prepared in several stages: soaked for about 3 hours, then blanched briefly before being pressed between sheets of greaseproof paper for about an hour. Then they can be cooked in various ways, by braising, sautéeing or deep-frying.

Feet or trotters are simmered in stew or stock for a few hours and, as they contain lots of gelatine, the cooking liquid sets to a jelly. Oxtail is normally jointed before simmering slowly as part of a stew or soup until the meat is falling off the bones. Tongue, which is available salted and fresh, needs to be soaked before being cooked: salted tongue overnight and a fresh one for 2–3 hours. It's then simmered in flavoured stock or water until tender after which the skin is stripped off. Tongue is traditionally served cold and thinly sliced as a sandwich filling or as part of a salad.

You either love tripe or hate it, or eat it because it is cheap and filling – this ivory-coloured, slippery-to-the-touch ingredient was once part of the staple diet of poorer families, everywhere that cattle and pigs were raised. Normally it's now bleached and pre-cooked before being sold, so only needs to be boiled for about an hour before being ready to serve. The classic British way to cook tripe is to simmer it in milk with onions, but it can also be cut into strips and fried with onions and a sprinkling of wine vinegar.

word origin Offal comes from the Middle Dutch *afval*, which meant 'bits that fall off', and has been around in English since about the 14th century. At first it was used simply to describe 'waste', but by a century later this had narrowed to more or less its current meaning. In the United States they think offal sounds awful so they call it variety meats.

The offal of deer was once called *umbles*. During medieval times, when the spoils of the hunt were brought back to the manor, the lord and his family got the prime cuts and often ate them sitting on a dais above the ordinary folk, who had to content themselves with the less desirable umbles that were usually baked into a pie – the origin of 'eating humble pie'.

did you know?

• The shin and leg bones of veal calves and mature cattle contain a soft, jelly-like fat called marrow, and marrowbones are also classed as offal. They aren't available in supermarkets, but butchers occasionally have them and could probably be persuaded to chop them into manageable lengths. Marrowbone is now mostly used to enrich stocks and meaty sauces, but the bones used to be served on their own occasionally with long-handled small spoons (necessary to winkle out the marrow) or the marrow was eaten on toast.

• There *should* be a lot of testicles around for sale (another organ classed as offal) since many male calves and lambs bred for their meat are castrated young to make them easier to handle. They are only rarely available, however, and when they are, are usually sold under some euphemism or other: lamb testicles, which look like little white kidneys, are called 'fry' or 'stones' in Britain, and the normally unsqueamish French call them *rognons blancs* (white kidneys).

partridge

There are two main species of this small game bird native to Europe. Grey partridge (*Perdix perdix*) is found all over the United Kingdom, mostly in farming and hedged areas. Both males and females have brownish-grey bodies and greyish-brown legs (hence the name); cocks also have a large dark brown stain on their lower fronts. Red-legged partridge (*Alectoris rufa*) originated in France, but is now also found in south-eastern England; it is larger than grey partridge, with a bluish-brown back, pale blue front with red and brown markings, and red legs.

Partridges are protected by law and can be legally killed only between September 1 and February 1 each year. Like many game birds, they are 'hung' (see **game**), in this case for 3–4 days, depending on how gamey they are required to be. They rarely weigh more than 320g.

using it The classic way to cook a young bird is to roast it, usually covered with either streaky bacon or butter to keep it moist as it cooks. Otherwise it can be cooked in the same way as **pheasant**. Accompaniments include a square of buttered toast (which is sometimes put under the bird for the last 10 minutes of cooking so that the juices can soak into it), gravy and game chips. Very young small partridges are also sometimes spatchcocked (split down the back and flattened out), then grilled. Older partridges, whole or halved, are best braised or casseroled, with wine and carrots and onions, for instance, or on a layer of stock and shredded white or red cabbage with chopped bacon. Cooked meat is also occasionally used as a pie filling or as a basis for pâté.

word origin Partridge comes from the Middle English *partrich*, which in turn is derived from the Old French *pertriz*, the name for the bird.

• The rhyming song *The first day of Christmas* probably originated in France, if it's to be taken literally, since the French red-legged partridge is much more likely to perch on a tree (including pear!) than the native British grey one. Earlier versions of the song were more food-obsessed than the modern: one French version started with the obligatory partridge, but then moved on to turtle doves, wood pigeons, ducks, rabbits, hares, hounds, shorn sheep, horned oxen, turkeys, hams and, finally, 12 small cheeses.

pasty

It used to be said that the devil was afraid to go to Cornwall for fear he would be baked into a pasty, and it does sometimes seem as if nearly everything else probably has been at one time or another. Traditionally, however, this is an oval or semi-circular pastry case filled with meat – any kind of meat depending on availability, including beef, lamb, venison and even bacon – plus one or two vegetables to bulk it out and flavour it. The pastry is normally **shortcrust**, although **puff pastry** is used occasionally. The most famous pasty comes from Cornwall and is classically made from beef or lamb, onion and potato, but there are other versions in other parts of the country, including Scottish bridie, which is filled with shredded beef rump, suet and onions.

using it Pasties have always been filled with what has been around, and this principle can still hold true, so leftover cooked meat is sometimes used rather than raw, chicken or turkey instead of beef or lamb, and a mixture of vegetables and the odd fish too, particularly strongly-flavoured ones like tuna and smoked fish. Exotic spices like saffron (with vegetable-only mixtures) and curry powder or paste (especially with chicken and lamb) can add flavour.

word origin Pasty comes, via Old French, from the Latin *pasta,* meaning 'dough'. When it first arrived in England during the 13th century, a *pastee* was a meat-based pie baked without a dish whose filling had only one ingredient (as opposed to *pie*, where the filling was made up of several or many different ingredients).

• The original pasties weren't for the faint-hearted. Many were great pointed ovals or semicircles that could weigh up to about a kilo and contain a small joint of meat, a whole bird or even (for meatless days) a piece of porpoise rather than diced flesh. Others were a complete meal in themselves: the case was divided into two compartments separated by pastry, one containing the main course, the other filled with sweet ingredients like jam and cooked fruit for dessert.

pâté

This is (usually) a firm savoury 'loaf' made from minced ingredients and flavourings, and cooked in the oven. Traditionally, pâté was made from minced meat like pork, veal, liver or game (or a mixture of these), occasionally even from special ingredients such as foie gras; nowadays, however, fish (normally oily fish like salmon, mackerel and trout) can form the basis of a pâté, as can vegetables. The main ingredients, whatever they are, are bound together with liquid like brandy, wine or egg and are always well seasoned with flavourings such as herbs, salt, peppercorns and garlic.

Pâté can be coarse-textured and solid, when small pieces of the main ingredients will still be recognizable, or delicate and smooth, when the mixture will have been combined into a paste-like texture or 'set' with gelatine or something similar. Meat and vegetable pâtés are always cooked, either in a terrine (a baking dish similar to a loaf pan with a lid) or enclosed in pastry, 'en croûte'. Fish pâtés can be prepared in this way too, but most are now softer, dip-like mixtures made from already-cooked fish or smoked fish that doesn't require cooking, and are whizzed up in a food processor with ingredients like cream cheese, mayonnaise, cream or soured cream.

Some cooked pâtés have fillings and in this case, half the basic mixture is spooned into the baking dish, the chosen filling spread over it, then topped with the remaining mixture. Typical fillings include chopped cooked chicken livers, or vegetable mixtures such as chopped mushrooms.

using it Meat or vegetable pâtés keep in the refrigerator for 3–4 days; ready-made fish ones keep for the same length of time; home-made ones should be eaten within a day.

word origin Pâté is borrowed from medieval French and originally meant a pastry case filled with various ingredients, which could include fish and vegetables as well as meat, and which was served hot or cold; in fact much the same dish as a pie or pasty. Gradually, however, the word came to be applied to the filling itself, whether it was enclosed in pastry or not, and the filling became meat-based rather than anything else.

pheasant

There are two major species of this spectacular creature, the largest of the common game birds. Common pheasant (*Phasianus colchicus*), which originated in what is now Georgia in central Asia, is the smallest of the species found in Europe. The males (or cocks) are larger and showier than the females, with long tails that make up half their total body length and colourful red wattles around their eyes; the smaller females (or hens) tend to be a dull, mottled brown. Golden pheasant (*Chrysolophus pictus*) comes from central China and is larger than the common pheasant. The cock is spectacularly coloured, with a red front and tiger stripes on each side from below the eyes to the top part of the body; the hen is again a dull mottled brown. Both types are found in woodlands, although common pheasant also inhabits open pasturelands near to woods.

Pheasants are protected by law and can only legally be killed between October 1 and February 1 each year. To ensure a steady supply for hunters and the table, however, many are now raised in captivity, then released into the wild at the 'right' time of the year. Like most **game** they are 'hung', for 3–10 days depending on how old the bird is, how gamey it is supposed to be and how cold the weather is. An average bird weighs around 1kg.

using it There will be no indication which species a bird belongs to on the supermarket shelf or butcher's shop, but it should be identified by gender: the hen is considered to be more tender than the cock. Pheasant is available whole, as boned breasts and, occasionally, as jointed pieces.

Younger birds (those available up until Christmas) are usually roasted whole, normally covered with streaky bacon or softened butter to keep them moist during cooking. Accompaniments include gravy and bread sauce, made by stirring fresh breadcrumbs into flavoured hot milk until the mixture is thick, then finishing with a knob of butter. Older birds, being somewhat tougher than young ones, are more often braised or casseroled, whole or jointed. Good flavour partners include walnuts, orange and Madeira; cider, apple and onion; or chestnuts and redcurrant jelly. Pheasant breasts can be cooked in the same way as **chicken** breasts. Older birds or leftover meat can be made into pâté, used as a pie filling or minced for sausages or game 'cakes', and the carcass boiled to make **stock** for soup.

word origin Pheasant is borrowed from the Old French *fesan*, which in turn came from the Greek *phasianos*. Both this and the scientific name for common pheasant have classical connections, being called after the river Phasis in Colchis, an area south of the Caucasus mountains in central Asia. It is here the bird is supposed to have been discovered by Jason and the Argonauts during their quest for the Golden Fleece.

pigeon

There are many species of this sturdy member of the dove family all over the world, the most important one from a culinary point of view being the wood pigeon or ring dove (*Columba palumbus*), a large grey bird with mottled wings. Wood pigeons have been domesticated for many centuries in Britain. The ancestor of all domesticated birds is the wild rock dove (*Columba livia*), now found in its true form only in more remote parts of western Scotland and Ireland, although semi-tame versions congregate in most of the larger cities.

Nearly all pigeons found in shops will be farmed, but there is no 'season' for the wild bird since it is regarded as a pest. Farmed pigeons are only reared for about four weeks, aren't hung and their meat has a bland, mild flavour; wild pigeon meat is denser, darker and more full-flavoured. Pigeon is one of the smaller game birds, weighing on average about 350g.

using it Pigeon is available as whole adult birds, whole squab (young fledglings) or as breasts.

Most whole birds are roasted (if they are younger) or braised (better for older, bigger birds). When roasting, the breast should be covered with streaky bacon or rubbed with softened butter to keep it moist during cooking. Squabs are often spatchcocked (split down the back and flattened), then grilled in the same way as **partridge**.

Pigeon breasts have had a recent vogue as part of 'warm **salads**' (*salades tièdes*). For these the breasts are grilled and served pink. Otherwise, piegon breasts can be browned and then simmered in a sauce, such as white wine and grated orange zest, wild mushrooms and soured cream, or port wine with crushed black grapes. The meat itself could become part of a pie filling, **risotto** or **polenta** dish, or could be minced to make a coarse pâté.

word origin Pigeon comes from the late Latin *Pipio*, a 'bird that coos', via Old French *pijon*, meaning a young bird, and especially a young dove. The 19th-century habit of fixing pigeons to stools as decoys gave rise to the phrase 'stool pigeon', originally something (or someone) that acted as a decoy, but now more commonly used to mean a police informer. 'Pigeonhole' is literally a small slot for mail, or metaphorically a way of categorizing someone rigidly or to delay dealing with something; it comes from the small hole left in dovecots to allow the pigeons to enter and leave.

• Pigeons were first domesticated about 3500 years ago by the Greeks, who built several myths around them. One was about the black pigeons of Dodona, the place where a particularly sacred Oracle to Jupiter was established (oracles were places where the god would advise his followers and foretell the future). The Oracle was set up in Dodona because one black pigeon flew from Thebes in Egypt and landed there, and the god's responses were either cooed by the sacred black pigeons who lived in the area surrounding the site or 'interpreted' by priests from the rustling leaves of the trees that grew around it.

pork

Pork is the fresh meat of pig (*Sus domesticus*), an omnivorous animal descended from wild boar that probably became domesticated about 10,000 years ago. Almost every bit of pork can be used: the meat itself is eaten fresh as pork or cured to make **bacon**, **ham** and various types of **sausage**; the feet or trotters and head are sometimes cooked too, as are the ears, which can be poached, then breaded and deep-fried; the blood is an integral part of **black pudding**; the stomach fat is made into lard; the intestines are cleaned and still sometimes used as casings for sausages; and the skin, or hide, can be made into clothes, bags and furniture coverings.

Three-quarters of all pigs are intensively farmed, and in Great Britain that means they are kept indoors in large sheds with limited individual space, but aren't tethered or crammed into small pens or crates (tethering and penning are still widespread elsewhere in Europe). Farrowing sows – pregnant females about to give birth – *are* still penned to protect the new piglets from being trampled underfoot, however, and the piglets are removed from their mothers when they are 3–4 weeks old. Feed is cereal-based and includes growth promoters and antibiotics.

Over 20 percent of pigs are extensively farmed, that is they live essentially outdoors or have free access to outdoors; these pigs generally live in groups in small shelters or arks, although some have no shelter; feed includes growth promoters and antibiotics. Organic farming makes up the rest. Soil Association-accredited organic pigs live in groups, have good shelter and graze on rotated pasture; piglets are weaned (taken from their mothers) at 8 weeks or older. And the use of farrowing crates, castration, tail docking and teeth cutting – all practised in intensive and in some extensive farming – are not permitted.

Most pigs reared for pork now belong to leaner breeds and are slaughtered at any point between 15 and 31 weeks old (the average is 25–26 weeks); organic pigs and bacon pigs (which are fattier) are reared for about the same amount of time. Sucking pigs, as the name suggests, are young piglets that have only been fed their mother's milk and so have a particularly milky, light flesh; they are killed on average at 3–4 weeks old. Some parts (the leg, for instance) aren't hung before being sold; other parts like the loin are matured for about 7 days or more (see **meat**).

Pork is divided into many cuts, including large pieces such as loin (the upper middle part of the animal), leg, hand and spring (from the shoulder), and fillet or tenderloin (a long, sausage-like cut from the hind part of the loin). Individual pieces are chops (normally from the front or back of the loin or the neck), steaks (usually from the leg) and escalopes and medallions (normally from the fillet). The belly (the lower middle of the animal), a fatty cut, is usually sold as spareribs or sometimes minced. Many of the internal organs and external extremities are also eaten (see **kidney**, **liver** and **offal**).

using it Pork is normally pale pink in colour, although some breeds give almost colourless meat. It should be close-grained and firm, and what fat there is should be of an even thickness and white rather than greyish. Pork should always be cooked thoroughly.

Prime joints like loin and leg are roasted or pot-roasted. To keep leaner joints moist, they can be covered with a crust such as herbs and breadcrumbs or barded with pork fat. Some joints have their own covering of fat, which can be scored and rubbed with salt to produce crackling. Apple sauce is the best-known accompaniment for roast pork, sometimes mixed with other fruits like quince. Chops and steaks are usually grilled, fried or baked. Fillet can be cooked whole (often split and stuffed, then roasted), cut in cubes (for stewing or grilling) or sliced crossways as medallions, which are normally fried.

Pork is to the Chinese what beef is to the Americans and British, and they have hundreds of different ways of cooking it: lean meat can be cut into strips and stir-fried, and joints can be 'red-cooked' (simmered in soy sauce to colour them a dark reddish-brown). Belly and loin are sometimes 'twice-cooked' – first boiled, then cut into thin slices and stir-fried. Spareribs, also much associated with Chinese cookery, are usually marinated in a sticky sweet-and-sour sauce or chilli paste and then baked.

word origin Pork comes from the Latin for the young animal, *porcus*, via the French *porc*, and was first used to describe pig meat in England around the 13th century. A 'porker' is a young pig raised for food, especially fresh meat. The modern word for the animal comes from the first part of the Old English *picbred,* meaning 'acorn', one of pigs' favourite foods.

Pigs are clean, intelligent animals, although you wouldn't think it to look at the phrases associated with them. 'Dirty pig' is actually a contradiction in terms, but means someone who is gross in their habits and appearance. 'This place looks like a pigsty', meaning it looks a terrible mess and said of generations of children's bedrooms, is a definite slander since pigs distinguish neatly (when they have enough space to do so) between those parts of their home where they eat, sleep and perform their necessary functions.

did you know?

• The rich have always eaten pork, but uniquely throughout history pigs also provided many poorer families with some meat too. They are easy to keep, will eat anything including scraps from the table, and most country people and many town dwellers managed to keep one or two. There was a cycle to it all: in Europe, the pig was fattened up until around November or December, then killed, and the fresh meat was eaten (or sold to buy another piglet or two). Everything the family couldn't eat or sell quickly was cured to provide meat over the winter months. This practice still exists in some country areas of Europe, and was found in many more up until the Second World War.

• Although people in most of Europe and parts of Asia have always valued the pig and eaten it as much as they could, there are other parts of the world that have traditionally been more ambivalent about it, and some have even forbidden it as food. In ancient Egypt, for instance, the pig was considered to be unclean and believed to cause leprosy. The Jews may have inherited their distrust of it from the Egyptians, but kosher law now forbids the eating of any pork product (as well as any from rabbit, horse and beasts of prey, and any game killed by gunshot). Muslims also ban it.

poultry

This is fowl domesticated for the table, and includes lean birds such as **chicken**, **guinea fowl** and **turkey** as well as fattier ones like **duck** and **goose**. Poultry can be raised for their **eggs** or their meat, and in one of several ways. Most poultry meat is produced by an intensive rearing process called floor brooding, where the birds are kept in a large shed or barn in controlled temperatures with artificial lighting 23 hours a day; they live on the floor on a litter of wood shavings or chopped straw, are fed automatically and have no access to the outdoors. Each shed will contain many birds, although numbers will vary depending on which type is being reared – an average chicken shed would probably have anything from 10,000–50,000 birds. Poultry reared in this way is killed very young, and the large amount of meat such a system can produce means it can be sold cheaply.

Most intensively reared poultry will be certified as belonging to 'Class A', a British Government grading that guarantees (among other things) that the bird will have a good 'conformation' with a plump well-developed breast and fleshy legs and a thin regular layer of fat on the breast, back and thighs (a thicker layer is permitted for ducks and geese). Many will also carry the Little Red Tractor symbol (British Farm Standard), which confirms they have been reared from traceable stock and have been independenty assessed for compliance with animal husbandry and welfare standards.

Other methods produce more expensive meat since the birds are raised for longer and in better conditions. Free-range can mean any of several things: at the basic level (called simply free-range) the birds live in sheds as in the intensive system, but with fewer of them per square metre. By law they must have continuous access to limited outdoor runs for the latter half of their lives; their diet is therefore, theoretically at least, more varied than that of intensively reared birds and must be 70 percent cereal-based. 'Traditional' free-range birds live in sheds too, but numbers are one fewer per square metre than for ordinary free-range, and the birds also have access to larger outdoor runs; feed is the same as for ordinary free-range birds. Free-range total freedom birds live in sheds in the same conditions as traditional free-range ones, but have access to unlimited outdoor runs.

The description organic can also mean different things, depending on which agency is doing the accrediting. To be certified organic in Britain, a producer must adhere to at least the basic standards set by UKROFS (The UK Register of Organic Food Standards), which interprets EU directives on organic production. All organic birds should have reasonable access to outdoors, be housed in less crowded conditions than intensively-reared birds, and have an organically-based diet that contains no genetically modified material. In the most stringent organic schemes, birds can live in either a fixed shed or mobile accommodation, but in the case of the former there must be fewer birds per square metre than in any other type of rearing, and they must have continuous access to the outdoors after brooding has finished – that is, for the latter two-thirds of their life.

The above categories apply to all poultry to a lesser or greater degree, except for goose which is still basically a free-range niche market in the United Kingdom. Chicken, since it's the most popular type of poultry, is the prototype for the system, but turkeys, guinea fowls and ducks are increasingly categorized in this way too.

using it Most poultry is available throughout the year, although some, especially goose and to some extent turkey, is aimed at the Christmas market and can be less available at other times. Fresh birds will keep in the refrigerator for 2–3 days, but any plastic wrapping should be removed before storing and the bird loosely wrapped; **giblets** should also be removed and stored separately. Poultry can be frozen, but needs to be thawed completely, preferably in the refrigerator, before being used; this can take up to several days in the case of turkeys. Frozen thawed poultry should never be refrozen uncooked.

Poultry is always cooked before being eaten and most must be cooked thoroughly – the exception is duck breasts, which are sometimes served pink. *How* it's cooked depends on the type of bird it is and whether it's whole or in pieces (see separate entries for individual birds). For roast birds, to check the bird is cooked, stick a skewer into the fattest part of the leg; if the juices come out clear, the bird is ready, but if they are still rosy, it needs to be roasted for longer. A more precise way to check if poultry is thoroughly cooked is to use an instant-read thermometer, inserted into the thickest part of the meat at the end of the cooking time, to check the internal temperature. Roasted birds should 'rest' for about 15 minutes before being served.

word origin Poultry comes from the Old French *pouletrie*, which is related to *poulet*, meaning 'young chicken'.

did you know?

• If you've ever wondered why the breast meat of poultry like chicken and turkey is white and the leg meat dark, there is a simple explanation and it has to do with activity and oxygen storage. Muscles that are frequently used need more oxygen than those that aren't and they therefore contain more oxygen-storing pigments called myoglobin in their cells. It is these pigments that make the flesh darker. Chickens and turkeys don't fly so their breasts need less oxygen, but they do stand for long stretches of time, which means that their legs use up more oxygen and so have to store more myoglobin.

• Chicken and turkey, without skin, have the lowest fat content of any domestically reared meat. Most of their fat is in the skin and removing it – before or after cooking – will reduce the fat content by more than half. By contrast, duck and goose contain a substantial amount of fat in proportion to lean meat. All poultry supplies protein as well as a variety of essential minerals such as zinc, iron and selenium, and B vitamins.

prosciutto

Prosciutto is uncooked **ham**, meat from the hind leg of a pig that has been cured and then dried. Like all other types of cured **pork**, prosciutto is cured by salting, either by dry-salting, that is by rubbing salt mixtures over the meat and leaving them on for varying lengths of time, or by brining, where the meat is steeped in a solution of salts and other flavourings and water, or injected with this mixture. Most prosciutto is dry-salted.

The methods by which the ham is cured vary from region to region and from manufacturer to manufacturer. For a typical good-quality prosciutto from Parma in Italy, the 'prosciutto' pig is first fattened on a special diet of grains and whey from **Parmesan** cheese production (whey is the watery part of milk that remains after solid curds form during cheesemaking). After slaughter, the leg is covered with coarse sea salt and left for 30–60 days, turning frequently to make sure the salt penetrates evenly. After being washed to remove the salt, it is aged: initially in well-ventilated windowed rooms for about three months (if weather conditions permit, the windows are opened to expose the ham to the breeze), then for five months or more in dark cellar conditions, where the exposed surfaces of the meat are often coated with special pastes to control the rate of moisture loss (prosciutto legs lose about a quarter of their weight during curing). The quality of the finished product is controlled by government decree and no nitrates such as saltpetre are used in the salting mixture.

Of the other good-quality Italian prosciuttos, the best known is San Daniele, which is made around Friuli near the northern border with Austria and is also quality-controlled by government decree. There the legs are cured without removing the trotters and are piled on top of one another during the curing process so that the salt penetrates deeper into the meat and turns it a darker colour than other types.

Other countries produce good prosciuttos too, particularly France and Spain, and some of these are smoked as well as cured. The most famous French version is jambon de Bayonne, a smoked uncooked ham that originated in the south-western part of the country as its name suggests, although it's now also made elsewhere in France; in Spain, the classics are jamon Serrano, a strong, dark, dry-salted unsmoked ham matured for at least 12 months, mostly in the south-western part of the country, and iberico, made from the small native Iberian pig.

using it Most supermarkets sell prosciutto already cut into thin slices and vacuum-packed, and this keeps for about six weeks or so in a cool place; once opened, any remaining slices should be refrigerated and used within three days. Many delicatessens will have a whole leg of prosciutto and cut it fresh for you to a desired thickness; this should also be kept in the refrigerator and used within 4–6 days.

Prosciutto is ready to eat: as a sandwich filling, as a world-class snack lunch with cheese (particularly a lump of fresh Parmesan) or by itself or with other cured meats like **salami** and mortadella, some lemon and black pepper. It complements fruit well, so is served with several, particularly melon, figs and mango, as a first course. Chopped uncooked prosciutto could also be used in salads: with sliced

mozzarella and tomatoes, with rocket and Parmesan shavings, or with chopped spinach, broad beans and sliced mushrooms. It's equally good as part of cooked dishes: as an instant pasta sauce mixed with olive oil, chopped chilli and grated Parmesan, or in a **risotto** with petits pois, red onion and Parmesan.

word origin Prosciutto is the Italian word for 'ham'; in the United Kingdom, however, it has come to mean uncooked ham sold in very thin slices, usually but not always Italian.

quail

There are about 200 species of this relative of the partridge around the world, the most important of which is the common quail (*Coturnix coturnix*). Native to Europe, this smallest of the game birds is, by bird standards, quite dull-looking, with a mottled brown and white body and dark brown and cream stripes around the head and eyes. Quail is now intensively farmed for the table and there are only a few still left in the wild, mostly in the fields and chalk downlands of southern England. The meat is light and delicate with, as usual, the wild flesh (when this occasionally becomes available) being stronger-tasting than farmed versions. And they really are tiny; the average weight is 150–200g.

using it Since it is now widely farmed, fresh quail is available throughout the year and, given its size, it is only available whole. The traditional way to cook it is to smear it with a little butter or cover with a slice of bacon or two, then roast it. It does have a cavity, of course, but isn't usually stuffed (you'd need a toothpick and unflagging patience to get anything into it). The roast bird is normally served with a sauce, which can vary from gravy to curry.

Other ways to cook it include skewering or spatchcocking (splitting down the back and flattening out), then barbecuing or grilling;

braising with vegetables and wine (good for older birds); or serving with grilled **polenta** in the Italian way. It can also be made into pâté or used as a pie filling.

word origin   Quail comes via Old French from the medieval Latin *coacula*, which was supposed to sound similar to the bird's call.

did you know?

• Quails may be about to boldly go where no quail has gone before – into outer space. As all Trekkies know, it will take more than warp drive to get us out of our planetary system and into far parts of the galaxy: we will need to create our own food as well. Quail chicks have been bred in space laboratory conditions and could be part of outer space cuisine in due course.

rabbit

There are about 30 species of this furry mammal, the most important of which is the European rabbit (*Oryctolagus cuniculus*), a small creature native to the Iberian Peninsula and northern Africa, but now resident in heath and open woodlands all over Europe, Australasia and the Americas. Other types like the cottontail (*Sylvilagus floridanus*) and jack rabbit (*Lepus californicus*) are native to the Americas. The latter is, in fact, a type of hare, although considered to be a rabbit in its native country (hare is a close relative of rabbit).

Most rabbit found on supermarket shelves is intensively farmed in much the same way as **poultry**, although some country butchers still sell wild rabbit, a darker stronger-tasting version of the domesticated one. Wild rabbit is considered to be a pest, so can be hunted throughout the year. It is usually hung for a day or so before being sold. Farmed rabbit is reared to 8–10 weeks old, when it will weigh on average 1.4–2kg; it isn't hung.

using it   Both farmed and wild rabbit are available throughout the year, and sold whole, jointed and sometimes boned and jointed. Farmed rabbit is pale and quite bland in flavour, and doesn't need tenderizing before being used, but wild meat is tougher and will taste better if it's marinated for a few hours before being cooked – marinades can be as simple as vinegar and water or more elaborate, like wine, cider or beer mixed with oil, chopped vegetables and herbs.

Rabbit is normally cooked in pieces as part of a stew or casserole: with white wine, small onions and prunes (a Flemish classic); with mustard and crème fraîche (a French favourite); with chopped apple, cider and even a little Calvados, and some cream swirled in at the end (another popular French dish); or with sweet white wine, a little vinegar, raisins and spices like cinnamon, ginger and cloves (a royal medieval recipe). Jugged rabbit (or hare) is a traditional British recipe: pieces are browned, then cooked slowly in stock; a mixture of its warmed blood, port and redcurrant jelly is stirred in about 10 minutes before the end of cooking (it tastes better than it sounds). Rabbit pieces could also be coated in flour, dipped in egg and spiced breadcrumbs and deep-fried, or otherwise braised or cooked in the same ways as **chicken**.

word origin   Rabbit comes from the Old French *rabotte*, meaning 'young rabbit'. It lends its name to several phrases, most of them negative: the infamous fertility, for instance, has given us 'to breed like rabbits' (have too many children) and 'rabbiting on …' (that is, 'producing' too many words). Even its eating habits haven't escaped: lettuce, a favourite rabbit food, is known as just that, and the description isn't meant to be flattering.

did you know?

• The introduction of rabbits into Britain was one of the odder consequences of the Norman Conquest; they were unknown until the new nobility established special warrens (called conygers) on their estates in the 12th century to guarantee a steady supply of one of their favourite meats (*cony* was the old word for a mature rabbit). Rabbit was particularly useful during the Middle Ages because the flesh of newly born rabbit kittens wasn't considered to be 'meat' and could therefore be eaten on those (many) days during the year when meat was forbidden. Modern wild rabbits are descendants of escapees from these warrens.

• The one thing above all others that rabbits are 'famous' for is their fertility. And they start young: females begin having babies at about four or five months old and have litters of 5–12 kittens at a time (the average is seven) seven or eight times a year, which can add up to nearly 100 a year for a particularly energetic mother. This is one reason why there was a rabbit population explosion during the 20th century that made the human one pale by comparison – in Australia, where it had no natural predators, there were an estimated 300 million rabbits at one point. Something had to give, and myxomatosis, a South American viral disease fatal to rabbits, was what was given to the rabbit populations of Australia and Europe during the 1950s. It decimated them for a few years, but populations have now increased again.

salami

This is the name given to a family of highly spiced cured sausages that originated in Italy but are now made around the world. Salamis can be *crudo*, raw mixtures that include curing salts, which are dried before being sold, or *cotto*, mixtures that are cooked in addition to being cured. The main meat ingredient is normally **pork** (fat plus lean meat) or pork mixed with *vitellone* (young beef). A typical recipe will also include strong seasonings like garlic and peppercorns, and liquid of some kind such as water, wine and even brandy.

Salamis are made in the same way as other sausages. Uncooked ones are usually coarse in texture so that small pieces of meat, fat and prominent seasonings like peppercorns can still be seen in the finished item, while cooked ones are often paste-like. The filling mixtures are poured into casings and the 'ends' tied with string, which for uncooked sausage is traditionally retied several times during the drying process as the sausage shrinks. Some are dried over heat, but most salamis are air-dried by being exposed to cooling breezes for anything from a week or so up to about eight months. During this time the ingredients undergo a type of fermentation, essentially turning the sausage from something perishable into a product that can keep almost indefinitely.

Although salamis are now made in many countries (including France and Spain; see **sausage**), they are still most closely associated with Italy, and classic raw Italian salamis include Fiorentina, a large pork-only coarse sausage; Genovese, made from a mixture of pork and *vitellone*, and studded with white peppercorns; Hungarian, not as the name suggests from Hungary (although the Hungarians make good salami), but an Italian type made from a mixture of pork, beef, paprika, white wine and seasoning; Milano, made from pork, black pepper, garlic and sometimes red or white wine; and peperoni, a small hot sausage made from pork and beef and flavoured with peppers and fennel. Mortadella is the best-known and largest cooked salami, and is classically made from pork, garlic, pepper and salt; it is boiled before being air-dried for a few days.

using it Salami is sold in several ways: as complete sausages called *salamini* (literally, small salami; these tend to be thinner, raw dry types); as ready-sliced and vacuum-packed larger ones (both raw and cooked salamis, particularly in supermarkets); or freshly cut into thin slices from long raw or cooked salamis in delicatessens. All of these keep well: raw complete ones more or less indefinitely, vacuum-packed slices for several weeks in the refrigerator, and opened packets and fresh slices for up to 5–6 days, also in the refrigerator.

Most salamis are good in sandwiches; a

mixture of two or three could be served separately as a first course; and nearly all of them could be part of mixed salads, particularly sturdy potato-based ones. Some, like peperoni and mortadella, are occasionally added to dishes during cooking: the former is often part of pizza toppings and, chopped, could also be stirred into risottos and pasta sauces; the latter is sometimes cubed and added to **risottos** and egg and vegetable dishes, particularly with peas and green beans.

word origin Salami is Italian and plural (the singular form is *salame*). There are at least two possible explanations of where it came from, the straightforward one being that, like sausage (and salad), it comes from the Latin *sal,* meaning salt, a reference to the fact that salami were (and still are) preserved with salting mixtures. But there are also those who believe that it comes from the name of the ancient city of Salamis, which was located in what is now Cyprus. Salamis was occupied by the Romans during classical times, and the Romans were enthusiastic sausage-makers, so this may not be all that fanciful an explanation.

• Mortadella, the most famous *salame cotto*, dates back to at least the 14th century and was once made in monastery kitchens from the still-warm meat of a freshly slaughtered pig. The meat was pounded into paste-like submission with a pestle in a special mortar called *mortaio della carne di maiale* (pork-meat mortar), hastily shortened simply to mortadella and transferred to the mixture created inside it.

sausage

A sausage is a mixture of finely chopped seasoned food normally encased in a skin. Although occasionally made from fish and even from grains, dairy foods and vegetables, the great majority of sausages are made from **meat**. A broad definition would also include

traditional savoury 'puddings' like **black pudding** or **haggis**, where a mixture of finely blended ingredients is spooned, poured or squeezed into a casing of some sort.

The amount of meat in a conventional sausage can vary from about 50 percent to as much as 95 percent, depending on the type, manufacturer and meat being used. Lean pork and fat are the most common basis for meat sausages, but mixtures of pork and beef or pork and veal are common, as are sausages made from beef alone and game meat, especially venison and wild boar; poultry like chicken and duck are also used occasionally. The meat in many mass-produced commercial sausages is often described as 'trimmings', which are the bits left after the butcher has cut the animal into joints. These can include MRM (mechanically recovered meat), which is extracted from the bones after butchering by a mixture of heavy pressure and heat (only the spinal cord of cattle isn't used). Other ingredients include liquid (anything from water to wine and brandy), flavourings and, in the United Kingdom at least, rusk crumbs; most continental European countries don't add fillers of this sort.

Preservatives and the equivalent of the salt, spice and nitrate mixtures used to cure other meats are also added to sausage mixtures – sodium nitrate, in fact, helps to give them their characteristic pinkish colour and also prevents the development of various types of bacteria.

Nearly all sausages are enclosed in a skin or casing. These can be natural, when they are sourced from the intestines of an animal (usually pig or mature cattle) and need to be prepared before being used, or, more commonly now, manufactured from collagen (a protein contained in the skin and connective tissue of animals), plastic or cellulose. On the whole, natural casings are used only for high quality sausages.

To make a commercial sausage, the meat and fat ingredients are mechanically chopped or diced in a large bowl – the blades that do this move so fast and work up such a heat that liquid in the form of ice is often added to the bowl to help bind the mixture, but also to help cool it down – then any other ingredients, including preservatives or curing mixtures, are added and blended in; texture varies from quite coarse, when individual pieces of meat and fat will still be visible in the finished mixture, to an almost slurry-like paste. The mixture is squeezed into the chosen casing after reaching the desired texture, and usually 'nipped' and twisted at intervals to make tubular links. A modern sausage-stuffing machine can 'do' the equivalent of about 2.5km of sausage links in an hour.

Sausages can be grouped into three rough categories. Fresh sausages are ready for sale once they've been put into their casings and 'linked'; they are perishable and need to be cooked before being eaten. These 'wet' sausages include varieties like chipolata, a small, soft all-pork mini-sausage; Cumberland, a coarse-textured pork sausage flavoured with black pepper and sage that comes in a long loop rather than links; and Toulouse, a coarse-textured sausage heavily laced with garlic that's French in origin but now widely available elsewhere. Beyond this is any type of flavoured sausage you can imagine and several you probably can't – hickory-smoked bacon, pork and leek, venison and redcurrant, and beef, mustard and tomato are among a virtually endless list.

Pre-cooked sausages are either part-cooked and smoked in temperature- and humidity-controlled ovens without being dried, or are cooked (normally by boiling) before being air-dried for a few days. Frankfurters belong to the former type, which need to be cooked before being eaten, mortadella to the latter (see **salami**). Raw cured sausages are cased, then dried for anything from a week to eight months, during which they undergo a sort of fermentation

that essentially turns them from something perishable into something that keeps indefinitely. They can then be smoked or left as they are, and either way need no further cooking before being eaten. Classic salami are a good example of this type of sausage.

As well as varying in type, each country has its own sausage traditions and preferences. Sausages are most popular in Europe and those parts of the world colonized by Europeans (although they do exist in other parts of the world), and among Europeans, Germans are the supreme sausage-makers and -eaters. There were roughly 1500 different individual types of German sausages at last count, and they fall into three categories: *brühwurst* (which includes frankfurters), which are usually smoked, then scalded before being sold, and need to be cooked again before being eaten; *rohwurst*, which are similar to salamis, being dried and sometimes smoked before being sold and are ready to eat; and *kochwurst*, which are boiled or steamed to cook them completely before they are sold – liver sausages are the most widely available kochwurst outside Germany.

Other important sausage-making countries include the United Kingdom, France, Spain and Italy. In the United Kingdom, fresh sausages are king and there are only a few other types around, most importantly the saveloy, a smoked sausage similar to frankfurter, made from pork and cereal. In France, fresh sausages are called *saucisse* (Toulouse is the most famous although there are many others); large sausages, fresh or cured, are *saucissons*, and the most popular of these are *saucissons secs*, usually made from pork, peppercorns, red wine and garlic, and roughly the French equivalent of salami. In Spain, there is mostly chorizo, which is (nearly) all things to all people: it can be soft and fresh or hard, dry and cured, smoked or unsmoked, mild or highly spiced, but it always includes pork and pimenton, a type of smoked **paprika**. In Italy, the field is dominated by salami, *crudo* or *cotto*, but there are fresh sausages there too, called *salsiccia*, the most famous of which is the luganega, which is directly descended from a classical Roman recipe, and normally made from pork shoulder, spices and Parmesan cheese.

using it Fresh 'wet' sausages should be stored in the refrigerator and used within 1–2 days of buying, while vacuum-packed semi-fresh ones like frankfurters, haggis and black pudding will keep there for 10–14 days (although once opened they should be eaten within 2–3 days). Dry-cured sausages keep indefinitely in a cool place.

Frying, grilling, barbecuing and baking are the basic ways of cooking fresh sausage. Accompaniments to British-type sausages include chips, egg and baked beans, plus tomato ketchup, brown sauce or sweet pickle. Chipolatas are often baked alongside the Christmas turkey or enclosed in pastry dough to make sausage rolls.

Toulouse and luganegas are often chopped and mixed into a sauce for rice, grains or pasta (they taste particularly good with **polenta** and broad noodles like pappardelle). Any type of chorizo is a classic ingredient in paella; cured chorizo can also be chopped and cooked with scrambled eggs or in omelettes, while fresh ones can be added to highly spiced soups or stews.

word origin Sausage comes via Old Northern French from the Latin *salsus,* meaning 'salted'. 'Banger', an affectionate nickname for fresh sausage, has been around since the early years of the 20th century and is based on the sound sausages make when they are frying. Saveloy has been around for a couple of hundred years and is adapted both in name and recipe from the French *cervelas* sausage (a smoked pre-cooked type now made from a highly spiced mixture of pork, or pork and

beef); *cervelas* in its turn is based on an Italian sausage that was originally sometimes made from pig's brains (*cervello* in Italian).

did you know?

* The Romans were the first great sausage-makers and wherever they went they took their skills with them – they probably introduced sausages into Britain. There was a temporary blip as Europe converted to Christianity, since most early sausages contained blood and Christians frowned on eating it, but they were too convenient a food simply to disappear and while a few types managed to hang onto their blood regardless (black pudding for one), most sausage recipes were adapted to do without it.
* In China, there is a strong sausage-making tradition, and their sausages taste quite different to European ones. They are mostly made from pork, and often better-quality meat than that used for most western ones. This is squeezed into the correct density and coarseness before being mixed with sugar, soy sauce, salt, preservatives and sometimes rice wine. The mixture is stuffed into mostly natural casings and dried over hot coals for up to three days or so, then steamed before being eaten.

steak

When used without qualification, steak means a prime cut of beef, normally (but not always) from the upper hindquarters of the animal. When used *with* qualification, it describes cheaper pieces like stewing beef, less expensive individual cuts of other meats like **pork**, and cross-cut slices from some fish, particularly **cod** and **salmon**.

Like meat in general, beef steak cuts vary from country to country. In the United Kingdom, the most popular types are cut from the best roasting joints like sirloin, rump and fillet, while in France they are châteaubriand, the thick front end of the fillet, which serves two people; tournedos, small thick medallions cut from the fillet; and entrecôte, which is taken from between the ribs of the animal, just behind the shoulder. In the United States, steaks are part of the national culture, so they have many special ones, including porterhouse, cut from the thick end of the loin; club steak, taken from the other, smaller end; and T-bone, which comes from the bit in between and can be huge; sirloins, rib steaks and flanks (thin steaks cut from the stomach just below the loin) are also popular.

using it A good beef steak should be lean and fine-grained but, with the exception of fillet, should still have some fat around it or flecked within it, which helps to keep it moist during cooking. Grilling, barbecuing and frying are the basic cooking methods, although for how long varies wildly from person to person. Possibilities range from the nearly raw (French '*bleu*' or '*saignant*', where the meat is merely flash-fried or seared) to the traditional British affection for steak as old shoe leather. Most steak is now cooked to somewhere between these extremes (see **meat** for checking 'doneness'). Accompaniments include mustard, **horseradish** relish and **béarnaise sauce**; a proper French châteaubriand would probably come with **hollandaise sauce**.

There are endless ways to turn a steak into a fancier dish: to make steak au poivre, for instance, black (or occasionally green) peppercorns are crushed, then pressed into the steak before it's fried, and the dish is 'finished' with brandy and cream; and fillet steaks can be spread with mushroom pâté and enclosed in puff pastry to make individual beef Wellingtons. Steak, particularly rump, is also sometimes cut into strips for dishes like beef Stroganoff, where the strips are cooked with sliced onion and mushrooms, mustard and soured cream.

word origin Steak comes from the Old Norse *steikja*, meaning to 'roast on a spit', and can be traced back to the 15th century. It seems always to have meant prime individual cuts of fried or grilled meat, although initially it was used to describe venison as well as beef.

turkey

The most important species of turkey is *Meleagris gallopavo*, a bird native to Central and North America that looks like a large chicken. It is now domesticated around the world, although a few wild types still linger on in the Americas.

Turkeys are reared in much the same way as **chickens** and other poultry. Intensively farmed turkeys are nearly always crossbred, usually from broad-breasted white-feathered varieties. The males or toms become so large that they are unable to get close enough to the females or hens to mate, so the hens are now fertilized by artificial insemination. Turkeys can also be free-range or organic. At this end of the market there are still one or two traditional breeds noted for their fine flesh, such as the Cambridge bronze. A turkey's weight will depend on gender (toms can be up to 50 percent larger than hens) and the age at which it's killed, which can range from 7–8 weeks to 20 weeks or more for a traditional free-range or organic bird. Whole birds can weigh anything from about 3kg to a monstrous 15kg or more.

using it Traditionally turkeys were bought primarily for celebrations like Christmas and Easter, but smaller birds are now being bred to increase their appeal as year-round food. A fresh whole turkey should be white and firm in texture with soft skin. Apart from being sold whole, turkey is available as prepared stuffed breast joints, as legs, escalopes (sliced boned breast meat) and stir-fry strips.

Whole birds are roasted, stuffed or unstuffed, and streaky bacon or softened butter is normally spread over the breast to keep it moist during cooking; basting from time to time with the pan juices will also help to keep it moist. The breast may need to be covered towards the end of cooking to prevent it from becoming too brown. Roasted turkey is always cooked through (see **poultry**). Accompaniments can be fancy or simple and include gravy, cranberry relish, and garnishes like chipolata sausages or grilled bacon rolls.

Turkey legs can be roasted or braised according to their weight, or the flesh can be removed from the bone, cut up and casseroled in the same way as chicken or **rabbit** pieces. Turkey escalopes are cooked in the same way as any other type (see **escalope**).

A roast turkey is such a large bird that there is nearly always a generous amount of cooked meat remaining after it's served, so there is a whole repertoire of recipes for the leftovers. These include turkey hash, turkey curry, turkey chilli, turkey pilaff and turkey pie; it is also a great sandwich filling, essential in a club sandwich with bacon, tomato and lettuce. The carcass and giblets make good **stock**, which can form the basis of soup – another use for the leftover meat.

word origin Your average 16th-century European couldn't get his or her tongue round the Aztec name for turkey (*uexolotl*), so something more pronounceable had to be found when the bird was introduced from America. The modern word is a shortened version of what they came up with, turkeycock or hen, either because the birds arrived in Europe via 'turkey merchants' (traders who plied the Mediterranean buying and selling merchandise as they went), or because of the general confusion about what the birds actually were – when they first arrived they were thought to be a type of guinea fowl, and guinea fowls were called turkeycocks and turkeyhens because they were imported into Europe via Turkey or 'Muslim' lands. Things were just as muddled in France. When the birds reached there, they were known as *coqs d'Inde* (Indian cocks), probably because of a lingering tendency to describe the Americas as the Spanish Indies. And Indian cocks they stayed, the modern French word *dinde* being a direct descendant of this early description.

• Turkeys were domesticated in what is now Mexico at least 4000 years ago (along with a type of dog similar to the modern chihuahua). By Aztec times they had become a favourite royal food, a tradition adopted by various European royal families after the turkey's introduction during the 1520s. And by the middle of the 16th century, turkeys were popular enough (and accessible enough at least to the nobility and rich middle classes) to be eaten at Christmas, although they wouldn't become the standard Christmas bird in Britain until the 20th century.

veal

This is the meat of young cattle (calves). Veal calves can be reared in any of several ways. In the most intensive method, still practised in parts of Europe but not in the UK, they are removed from their mothers after birth, kept permanently indoors in very small 'crates' and fed on reconstituted milk powder. In Britain only about 4000 calves are raised for veal each year and although conditions can vary, standard rearing methods are more humane. The calves are still removed early from their mothers, but they are then reared in large groups in straw yards with natural lighting. Full free-range and organic calves are kept with their mothers for much longer than in intensive systems (until weaning in the best organic farms, usually around nine weeks) and grazed outdoors.

In the United Kingdom, most veal is 'rosy', from calves that have been weaned onto solids (usually grain for intensively reared animals, pasture for grazed ones) and slaughtered at 16–24 weeks old. In continental Europe, the favourite meat is from milk-fed animals, at best calves fed only their mother's milk and slaughtered at weaning; or, more usually, from intensively reared calves fed on reconstituted milk. Veal isn't hung before being sold. Rosy veal has a stronger, more definite taste than milk-fed veal, which can be delicate to the point of insipidity.

Cuts vary slightly from country to country. British ones include best end (more or less the ribs of the calf behind its shoulder), loin, leg, breast, knuckle or shin (taken from the fore and hind legs), shoulder, and neck and scrag (the bit before the shoulder). **Escalopes** are sliced from the leg or loin of the calf, while chopped pie or stewing veal and **mince** usually come from neck or breast meat. Most of the **offal** of calves is also eaten.

using it Veal is always cooked thoroughly (see **meat** for how to test for 'doneness'). Prime joints like loin, best end and leg are usually roasted. Being very lean, they need to be covered, barded with fat or bacon, or basted during cooking; classic accompaniments include gravy and **caper** sauce. Veal is also pot-roasted and occasionally poached. The classic poached veal dish is vitello tonnato, where it's served cold and thinly sliced with a sauce made from mayonnaise, olive oil, canned tuna, anchovies and capers.

Knuckle or shin of veal isn't widely available, but some butchers will have it and most will order it in. The classic veal shin dish is ossobuco alla Milanese: chopped pieces that are stewed slowly until very tender with onions, celery, carrots, tomatoes and white wine, then finished with a mixture of chopped parsley, garlic and grated lemon zest (known as *gremolada*). Pie or stewing veal can be cooked in the same way as cubed **pork**, in casseroles, pies and stews.

word origin Veal comes, via Old Norman French, from the Latin *vitellus*, a diminutive version of the word for 'calf'.

venison

Venison is the meat of deer, mammals whose males (or stags) have spectacular antlers that they shed each spring. Technically it is the meat of any deer, including caribou, elk and reindeer, but in Great Britain it usually means meat from one of three species: fallow deer (*Dama dama*), which originates in southern Europe and is considered to have the best flesh; red deer (*Cervus elaphus*), the largest of the three and so called because of its dark, rich red summer coat; roe deer (*Capreolus capreolus*), the smallest, which is native to northern Europe and found in various parts of England, Wales and Scotland, but not in Ireland.

Although deer still roam wild in some parts of the country, most are now farmed or kept in controlled herds in special parks. Hunting wild deer is governed by complicated game laws that differ depending on the species involved, whether the deer is male or female, and where it is, and there are different 'close' seasons for England and Wales, Scotland and Eire. The season for male red and fallow deer is May 1 to July 31 in England, Wales and Northern Ireland, March 1 to August 31 in Eire and October 21 to June 30 in Scotland; for females it is from March 1 to October 31 in England, Wales and Northern Ireland, and in Eire and Scotland the dates are the same as for males. Roe deer is different again: the male season is November 1 to March 31 in England and Wales (October 21 to March 31 in Scotland) and the female one is from March 1 to October 31 (April 1 to October 20 in Scotland). Deer are paunched (disembowelled), bled and gutted when killed, then hung for 3–21 days, depending on various factors (see **game**).

Venison is available as large joints like haunch (leg and loin), saddle and loin; as steaks and chops; as medallions (small pieces of fillet); as braising or stewing meat; and as mince and sausages.

using it Farmed venison is available throughout the year, although some supermarkets and butchers don't stock it in late spring or early summer; wild venison is only available during the permitted season. Meat should be rich red in colour, fine-grained and firm in texture, and any fat should be white rather than yellowish (this indicates younger and more tender meat). The meat of the male is supposed to be more tender than the female, although gender is rarely indicated at point of sale, and a lightly hung animal will taste similar to beef. Venison is low in fat and can therefore be quite dry, so it's often marinated before being cooked, or cooked in liquid of some kind (sometimes both). Marinades are often red-wine based, with the addition of ingredients like olive oil, vegetables, and herbs and spices (juniper berries is a favouite spice flavouring).

Prime joints are roasted or pot-roasted. For the former, joints don't have to be marinated (particularly young and milder supermarket meat, which tends to have been hung for only a short time), but they should be rubbed with softened butter or larded with strips of pork fat or streaky bacon (stitched into the meat with a large needle) before being cooked. Venison is at its most tender slightly pink.

Accompaniments for roast venison include poivrade sauce (stock, red wine, wine vinegar and crushed peppercorns), and redcurrant or cranberry jelly; Cumberland sauce (see **currant**) is traditional with cold meat. Venison is also often served with fruit llike apple, pear or Seville orange, either as part of the sauce accompanying it or fried and sliced as a garnish with it. For pot roasting, if joints are marinated – the marinade can be used as the cooking liquid; the meat should be simmered slowly rather than cooked quickly.

Frying and grilling are suitable for steaks, chops and medallions, and they can be served rare, medium or well done. Accompanying sauces include crème fraîche with horseradish, crushed juniper and red wine, or port with lemon juice. Stewing and braising pieces are often marinated before being cooked with the marinade.

word origin Venison comes from the Latin *venatio,* meaning 'hunting' or 'game', via the Old French *veneson*. Originally when the word arrived in England it meant the meat of any furred animal killed by hunting (still its meaning in French); it began to narrow to its modern meaning at the beginning of the 17th century, although it wasn't used exclusively in this sense for a further century or so.

did you know?

• Deer have been killed to provide food for people since prehistoric times, and they have been farmed or their numbers controlled since the days of ancient Egypt. The Normans loved to eat it and they loved hunting it even more, so during the Middle Ages in Britain hunting deer became the sport of the nobility. Great tracts of land were set aside as 'deer parks' to ensure a ready supply of food and sport, some of which still exist. Ordinary people were partial to venison meat too, so the equally noble sport of poaching was probably born about the same time.

Vegetables & Legumes

Just imagine that you are wandering through the best food market you've ever seen. It may be somewhere Mediterranean or Asian, a must-stop site on your holiday itinerary, or closer to home – a summer farmer's market, perhaps, or the indoor market of a busy town, with its heady brew of Caribbean, Indian and Asian stalls as well as the more familiar ones. It's fascinating, isn't it? What is it, though, that looks the most enticing? No doubt about it – it's those wonderful vegetable and fruit stalls. They've got it all: colours so beautiful that only nature could have come up with them; the lustrous gleam of aubergines and peppers against the soft, matt skins of potatoes or carrots; the curves and folds and layers of each and every vegetable.

That's the thing about vegetables – they are just too gorgeous to ignore. Meat, you

That's the thing about vegetables – they are just too gorgeous to ignore.
Sophie Grigson

see, though enticing in some ways, is not exactly photogenic, and is limited in taste and texture. The variety in the vegetable kingdom, on the other hand, is mind-boggling, and the possibilities it provides for the cook are infinite.

So, if you are not already a vegetable enthusiast, or if you fear the thought of dealing with all but the most familiar vegetables, take a fresh look next time you pass the greengrocery section of the supermarket or head out to the smaller shops and markets. Be bold. Try something different, or cook a familiar vegetable in a new way – roasting carrots, for example, with olive oil or whole cloves of garlic in their skins with coarse salt and thyme until very tender and browned. You'll be amazed at the transformation in flavour.

Don't let familiarity breed contempt; don't treat vegetables as an afterthought. Celebrate their beauty, their myriad flavours, their individual textures, and bless the fact that they are also extraordinarily good for you, your family and friends. Yippee!

artichoke

There are two unrelated **vegetables** with this name: the globe artichoke (*Cynara scolymus*), usually simply called artichoke and the one described here, and the **Jerusalem artichoke**, which is discussed in a separate entry. The globe artichoke is a tall member of the thistle family, native to the Mediterranean. It is grown for its large flowerhead, an ingenious arrangement of tightly clinging rows of small purplish to mid-green brittle leaves called bracts that guard a central fibrous 'choke' (actually the undeveloped flowers of the plant) and a 'heart' or bottom. Italy, Spain, France and California are among the major producers.

using it Artichokes have a natural season from about May to September in Europe, but they are sometimes available at other times of the year too. When buying, the head should be trim with tight bracts that squeak when pressed together; slightly gaping and blackening outer bracts mean the artichoke is overripe and will have a large hairy choke. A fresh globe artichoke will keep in the refrigerator for about five days.

Usually only part of the bracts (leaves) and the heart are eaten, although young artichokes – the first of the crop in May – are traditionally consumed whole, bracts, choke and all. For mature heads, snap off the stalk and trim off the top of the head, then cook in boiling water with lemon juice for 20–40 minutes, depending on size; it's ready when an outer leaf can be pulled away easily. Whole young artichokes are boiled, then finished in various ways: for one Roman classic (*alla giudia*) they are halved, then fried in olive oil until crisp.

To eat, remove the leaves one by one, dip the bottom fleshy part into an accompanying sauce, then scrape off the flesh between your teeth; discard the rest of the leaf. Working your way round the outside of the head you will eventually be left with the smaller inner leaves and the hairy choke, all of which should be cut away to expose the meaty heart. This is traditionally eaten with a knife and fork. Classic sauces for globe artichokes include melted butter if served warm, mayonnaise or **vinaigrette** if cold.

Boiled artichokes can be stuffed by removing the hairy choke to create a hollow; stuffing mixtures can range from seafood mayonnaise to a meat or fish mixture that requires a final cooking in the oven. Small hearts, fresh or canned, make an interesting addition to a mixed salad, rice, pizza or pasta dish.

word origin Artichoke comes via Italian from the Arabic for the vegetable, *al-kharsufa*.

did you know?

• Modern artichokes are improved descendants of wild cardoons, small-headed vegetables regarded as a delicacy in ancient Greece and Rome, which are still grown occasionally in parts of Europe. The first globes were developed in Italy during the 15th century, introduced into England during the reign of Henry VIII, and taken to California by Spanish settlers in the 17th century (although they didn't become an important crop there until 200 years later). About 80 percent of the Californian crop is grown around the small town of Castroville, whose other claim to fame is that Marilyn Monroe was crowned Artichoke Queen there in 1948.

asparagus

Native to the Mediterranean and western Asia, asparagus (*Asparagus officinalis*) is grown around the world for its unique shoots or 'spears', which are punctuated and topped by small knobbles (actually tiny leaf-like branches). It takes 2–3 years to produce shoots thick enough to market, and they need to be picked within a six-week period in late spring while they're still edible but not woody, and before foliage appears at the tips. Once they become productive, however, plants can continue producing for 10–20 years. There are two main types. White asparagus is grown under the soil like a root to prevent it from becoming green, and is picked by hand just as or before the tips appear above the ground; it's usually large and mild in flavour. Green asparagus, which can be purple or purple-tipped as well as green, is grown above the ground, and has a more distinctive flavour; it can be harvested manually or mechanically. Spears vary in thickness from emaciated (when they're called 'sprues') to about 4cm.

using it Asparagus is available as complete spears and as 'tips' (the top 5cm or so of the shoot). Spears should be firm, straight and uniformly coloured, and tips should be tight – loose ones indicate an older, less delicate **vegetable**. It will keep in the refrigerator for about three days.

Before cooking, trim off the ends to make the spears a uniform length and to remove any tough, woody parts (spears should ideally be similar in thickness too, so they cook in the same time). There are two ways to cook them. The classic is upright, tied into a bundle, in a covered tall pan, such as a special asparagus steamer, in enough boiling water to come halfway up their length (the idea is that the stalks should boil, while the tips, which are tender and delicate, should steam); cooking time is 6–10 minutes, depending on thickness – test for 'doneness' by piercing a stalk with the tip of a knife. The other, simpler method is to lay them, loose, in a wide pan of boiling water; cooking time is 4–10 minutes. Boiled asparagus is traditionally served with melted butter or **hollandaise** sauce if warm, and **vinaigrette** or mayonnaise if cold. Another delicious way to cook asparagus is by roasting, then 'dressing' with olive oil and shaved Parmesan. Tips and spears cut in pieces can be used in stir-fries.

word origin Asparagus comes indirectly from the Persian *asparag,* meaning 'sprout'. When the vegetable became reasonably popular during the 16th century it was known in English as *sparage*, then *sparagus* and finally *sparrowgrass*, before evolving into the modern word.

did you know?

• Asparagus was a favourite delicacy in the ancient world. The Romans loved it so much they froze it so that they could eat it out of season (relays of fast chariots and runners carried shoots from around Rome, where they were grown, to the Alps, where they could be kept in snow and ice until needed). And emperors with a weakness for asparagus didn't need to forgo its pleasures on tours of far-flung possessions: there was a special fleet on standby to transport choice specimens to wherever they were required. European cultivation seems to have died out after the fall of Rome, although it continued in the Middle East and Mediterranean Africa; it was eventually reintroduced during the Middle Ages.

aubergine

The aubergine (*Solanum melongena*) is a tough perennial plant native to tropical Asia and is a member of the same large family as the tomato, tobacco and deadly nightshade. Major producers include Central America, the West Indies, India and Italy. It is cultivated for its fruit, botanically a giant berry but used as a **vegetable**, which ranges in length from 5–15cm, in shape from oval to round to sausage, and in colour from the usual dark purple to the more occasional white, yellow, light purple or striped. The raw flesh contains many edible seeds and has a spongy consistency that transforms into a greenish-brown, flavourful pulp when cooked.

using it A ripe aubergine should be heavy for its size, with smooth unwrinkled skin; any with soft or brownish blemishes should be avoided. It will keep in the refrigerator for 4–6 days. Aubergine discolours when cut, so should be prepared as near to using as possible.

Until recently, aubergines were sliced or cut and then salted (*dégorgé*) before being cooked, to draw out excess moisture and get rid of a slight bitterness in their taste, but modern, young aubergines no longer need this. Some people still do it, however, so that the aubergines absorb less oil when they are fried (the flesh absorbs huge amounts of it). Aubergines can be cooked in various ways: sliced or chopped, then fried, grilled or baked until nicely browned and tender (this takes 10–20 minutes, according to method); or pierced a few times and then roasted whole in a moderate oven for 15–35 minutes, depending on size. They can also be halved and baked or boiled, then stuffed.

Aubergines are an important ingredient in many Indian dishes, especially vegetable ones, and the basis for *brinjal* chutney (*brinjal* being Hindi for aubergine). In Europe, aubergine is traditionally layered with minced lamb and baked for moussaka; roasted and blitzed with garlic and herbs in dips; and used in summer vegetable stews like ratatouille, with onions, courgettes, peppers and tomatoes.

word origin Aubergine comes via French and Spanish from the Sanskrit *vatingana*, meaning 'anti-fart vegetable'. Some smaller, whiter varieties look vaguely like eggs, which may be why the American name for aubergine is eggplant.

avocado

Although it's normally used as a **vegetable**, the avocado (*Persea americana*) is actually the **fruit** of a tall tree of the laurel family that is native to Central America, where it has been cultivated for over 7000 years. Major modern producers include Israel, Central America, Australia and the United States. The avocado can be smooth-skinned or knobbly, green, purple or even black in colour. It is usually oval in shape, quite like a pear in fact, hence the alternative name of avocado pear. Inside, its flesh is light honey in colour with occasional tinges of green, and buttercream in consistency; there is a large smooth nut or stone in its centre.

using it Good ripe avocados should be slightly soft but firm, especially at the stem end, but not too squashy as this could mean that they will be brown and be inedible inside. Harder avocados will ripen at warm room temperature in 3–5 days. The flesh discolours quickly when exposed to air, so should be sprinkled with lemon juice to keep it creamy once the avocado is cut, or prepared just before serving.

However it is to be used, preparation is simple: halve the avocado lengthways by cutting through the skin to the central stone, then twist the two halves in opposite directions to separate them; the stone should come out easily, leaving a neat cavity for **vinaigrette** dressing or a mayonnaise-based stuffing like crab or prawn. For sliced or chopped avocado, cut the halves into slices, skin and all, then peel off the skin with a knife.

Avocados are normally used raw: chopped in a mixed salad; sliced and served with tomato and mozzarella as a first course; pulped and mixed with crumbled bacon for a sandwich filling; and mashed with citrus juice and seasonings such as chilli into the Mexican dip, guacamole. The puréed flesh can also be mixed with herbs and milk or cream to make a soup. Halved avocados are also occasionally stuffed and baked or grilled.

word origin Avocado comes from the Spanish *aguacate* via Nahuatl, the language of the Aztecs, and *ahuacatl*, which meant 'testicle', perhaps a reference to its shape.

• Although avocados are high in fat (about 20 percent of their edible weight), most of it is monounsaturated. But their fat content makes them high in calories too – an average (150g) avocado checks in at around 300 kcals. For those who might baulk at eating so many calories in one sitting, plastering avocados onto the face, as Aztec and Inca women did, might be a viable option. Beauty masks made from avocado are supposed to help keep the skin smooth and wrinkle-free.

baked beans

The first canned baked beans were produced in 1875 by an American company called Burnham & Morrill, probably for the Maine fishing fleet, and it wasn't until 20 years later that the first Heinz baked beans appeared. Early cans included pork (see below), but it was dropped from the classic recipe during the 1940s because of wartime shortages and never added back in.

using them Eating baked beans cold straight from the can may be one of the first ritual acts of student liberation, but they are actually normally served hot, usually on toast or as part of a cooked breakfast or general fry-up. They also appear in pitta pockets or jacket baked potatoes, with sausage, and as an occasional ingredient in potato-topped pies, rice dishes and vegetable stews.

word origin The canned baked beans so familiar today are a convenient but lesser version of a traditional American dish called Boston baked beans. For this, small white navy or pea beans are soaked and then cooked slowly with a lump of salt pork or bacon, mustard, and molasses and brown sugar to sweeten them. No tomatoes are added.

• Henry John Heinz actually set up shop in 1869 to sell his mother's pickled horseradish (his USP was clear glass jars so that potential customers could see what they were getting). And even by the mid-1890s, when Heinz began to manufacture baked beans, the '57 varieties' was a slogan rather than the size of the product line, a gimmick thought up by Henry John because he liked the sound of the number. Nowadays, Heinz may have nearly 57 versions of baked beans alone, and the total number of their products runs to well over a thousand.

bean

This is a type of **legume** that provides food at virtually every stage of its life, first as a young sprout (e.g. **mung bean**), then as an immature pod (**green bean**) and finally as a mature seed or bean, either fresh (**broad bean**) or dried, when they are more often called pulses, the edible seeds of pod-bearing plants (**lentils** and **peas** are also pulses). There are hundreds of varieties of legumes, belonging to many species and a few genera or families, and most are now cultivated either for their pods or their seeds. *Phaseolus* is the most important family and includes the common bean (*Phaseolus vulgaris*), which can be eaten immature as the French bean or mature as haricot, kidney and other beans; the runner bean (*Phaseolus coccineus*), which is eaten for its pods; and **lima** and butter beans (*Phaseolus limensis*), eaten for their seeds. Other families include *Vigna*, to which mung beans and black-eyed peas belong; *Vicia*, which includes broad beans; and *Glycine*, the most important member of which is the **soya bean**.

The *Phaseolus vulgaris* species includes most of the standard beans used dried or canned. Black beans, which are small and slightly sweet to taste, are sometimes available fresh in the producing countries (Central America and southern parts of the United States), but only dried or canned elsewhere. Haricot, once the general name for any white bean of this type, is now normally used to describe a small off-white oval-shaped bean. Others include the borlotti, a medium Italian speckled bean; cannellini, a largish ivory-coloured kidney bean; flageolet, a tiny French green or white haricot bean, occasionally available fresh as well as dried; kidney, a deep red-coloured bean; pea and navy, a small white bean similar to haricot which is traditionally used for **baked beans**; and pinto, a reddish-white speckled haricot bean.

using it Beans are sold dried and canned, usually in water with salt and (occasionally) sugar. Dried beans need to be rehydrated by soaking in water before being cooked. Soaking times vary, depending on variety and how dry the beans are, but most need about 8 hours. To cook, rinse the beans, put into a pan of fresh unsalted water (if they are salted at this point they will not soften) and boil rapidly for about 10 minutes. Then cover and simmer until tender – cooking times also depend on variety and dryness and range from 1–4 hours (instructions may be given on the packet). Canned beans only need to be drained, although they benefit from a good rinse.

Occasionally beans are the main part of a dish: for refried beans (*frijoles refritos*), red or pinto beans are boiled, then mashed and fried in lard; in a cassoulet, flavoured haricot beans are layered with meats like duck, Toulouse sausages and lamb shoulder, then baked slowly; and in chilli con carne (Spanish for 'chilli with meat') they are simmered with beef, tomatoes and lots of hot chilli seasonings. But mostly beans are added to a soup such as minestrone, cooked with roast or braised lamb, added to vegetable casseroles, curries, pies or stir-fries, or used as a vegetable accompaniment. They have a special affinity with pork, sausages, sage and tomatoes.

word origin Bean comes from the Anglo-Saxon word for 'broad bean', the only type then known in Europe, and this in turn came from an ancient source meaning 'swelling'. Some individual types are identified by colour, like black and pinto (which means 'painted' or 'mottled' in Spanish), others by shape (kidney), yet others because of how they were once used. Navy beans, for instance, are so-called because they were part of US Navy rations during the 19th century. Haricot, the general name for bean in French as well as the more specific name of a white bean in English, represents an early European stab at the tongue-twisting Aztec name for the original bean, *ayacotl*.

A 'beanfeast' or 'beano' might now mean any free celebration, but can be traced back to real bean feasts of the 19th century, when employers took their employees out once a year to a free meal, which nearly always consisted of beans (the original ones were haricot) and bacon. 'Not to have a bean' means to be broke, and is based on an early 19th-century slang word for guinea. 'He's/she's full of beans' was first used to describe a spirited racehorse (it was meant to imply it was in good form) before being transferred to people.

did you know?

• Beans basically come from two continents, America and Asia. In early classical Europe only the broad bean, which originated in the nearby Middle East, was in regular use, and it was usually eaten dried and cooked into pottages of various sorts; in early China, mung beans and particularly soya beans were widely used, and the latter was being made into a remote ancestor of soy sauce by about the 2nd century BC. The major families like *Phaseolus* and *Vigna*, however, come from Central and South America, where they have been a staple part of the diet for about 7000 years; both were discovered there by early Spanish explorers and brought to Europe by the end of the 15th and beginning of the 16th centuries.

beetroot

The beetroot (*Beta vulgaris*) is a root **vegetable,** one of the four major descendants of sea beet (*Beta maritima*), a seashore plant native to the Mediterranean. (The others are mangelwurzel, yellow roots nowadays used as fodder; white-fleshed sugar beet, grown for its parsnip-like roots that are used in sugar manufacturing; and chard or spinach beet, grown for its edible stalks and leaves that taste (and can be treated) like a cross between **spinach** and spring greens.)

In appearance, beetroot is a large bulbous root with strong leaves that are similar to spring greens and used in the same way. The root is mostly a glorious deep red in colour, although some can be off-white or even yellowish. The distinctive red colour comes from the combination of a red pigment, called betacyanin, and a yellow one, betaxanthin; the more betacyanin a bulb contains, the redder it will be. In size, beetroot can be as large as an orange or as small as a lime and although it is usually round, occasional ones are oval or carrot-like in shape.

using it Most beetroot is bought ready-cooked, whole or sliced in poly-containers or bottled in vinegar. Fresh beetroot, which is available during late spring and summer, has a much more subtle taste than the preserved vegetable. Look for leafy tops that are crisp and bright, and choose smaller roots as they will be more tender than large ones. Fresh beetroot will keep for about a week in a cool dark place or double that in the refrigerator, providing the tops are taken off.

When preparing fresh beetroot, to avoid it bleeding all over you and the pot, scrub it but leave on the skin. To boil, add it whole to boiling salted water and simmer for 20–60 minutes, depending on size, then plunge into cold water to cool and loosen the skin, which can then be slipped off. Whole fresh beetroot can also be roasted, unpeeled and wrapped in foil, in a moderate oven for 45 minutes to 1¼ hours.

The classic beetroot dish is borscht, a soup served all over eastern Europe hot or cold topped with soured cream, but beetroot is also often teamed with fish: in Germany and Scandinavia it is eaten cold with rollmops or other preserved fish, and in eastern Europe it is served hot with carp. In America, it's part of a traditional New England boiled dinner, and is also sometimes served with honey or **horseradish** sauce as an accompaniment to ham, pork or beef. The pickled-in-vinegar version is used cold in sandwiches or salads, where it tends to drown out any taste it's combined with. The ready-cooked-poly-bag type is usually only dipped in vinegar, rather than stored in it, and can therefore bring a more subtle taste to the same dishes.

word origin Beetroot comes from the first half of the Latin name, *beta,* meaning beet.

did you know?

• Beetroot is an ancient vegetable, grown originally by the Greeks and Romans for both its leaves and its root, which in those days was long and narrow rather than bulbous. By the 17th century, though, the bulb had swollen to its modern proportions and major use, judging by its listing as a salad vegetable in herbals and cookery manuscripts of the time.

• As a close relative of sugar beet, it's perhaps not surprising that beetroot contains the highest natural sugar content of any vegetable (an average serving of 50g has about one teaspoonful of sugar), but it also has reasonable quantities of folate and potassium, which can help protect your heart. The main downside is its tendency to stain everything it touches, including hands, the cooking pot, and urine, if enough of it is eaten.

broad bean

The broad bean (*Vicia faba* or *Faba vulgaris*), sometimes called fava bean, is an annual **legume** native to the Mediterranean and western Asia, and one of a family of podded vegetables that also includes the green bean and the chickpea. China produces about 65 percent of the world crop, although it's grown widely throughout temperate Europe and Asia too. The plant is cultivated for its long, slightly furry green pods that fall into two basic categories, Windsors or shortpods, which contain four large seeds or beans, and longpods, which have up to eight. Colour ranges from the usual greyish-green through beige to chestnut.

using it Fresh broad beans have only a short natural season in summer, so are as often sold frozen or canned as fresh. Choose fresh beans with firm, good-coloured pods, and avoid any with discoloured skin and blackening edges. Fresh beans will keep in the refrigerator for 3–5 days.

Broad beans are always cooked before being eaten. Young thin beans, which are traditionally eaten pods and all, take only a few minutes to boil or steam; middling ones are stripped of their pods and then boiled or steamed for about five minutes. Large thicker pods indicate older, possibly tougher, beans; these are always podded before boiling or steaming for 5–8 minutes, and then need to be peeled since the skin can be hard to digest.

Broad beans are good with meat, particularly pork and bacon, when they are classically served as a purée, but could also form the basis of a summer vegetable casserole or a good salad, particularly with spinach, mushrooms and bacon. They are also sometimes combined with garlic and other herbs into a hummus-type dip, or mashed into small 'hamburger' patties with flavourings like grilled red pepper and coriander.

did you know?

• Although our neolithic ancestors ate them, broad beans had an ambivalent reputation in the ancient world and were often regarded as unclean. In classical Greece it was thought that the souls of the dead could inhabit them, possibly because the Greek word for soul, *anemos*, also meant wind, and even then broad beans were famous – or infamous – for their ability to cause flatulence. Perhaps this was why Pythagoras (the inventor of the theorem) didn't like them and forbade his disciples to touch them, although the reason could have been political rather than culinary since beans were used as voting tokens in ancient Greece. The philosopher Aristotle wasn't keen on them either, recommending that *his* followers abstain from them to keep chaste (he believed they stirred up the loins in an unsavoury manner).

broccoli

Broccoli (*Brassica oleracea* var. *botrytis*) is a subspecies of the **cabbage** family of **vegetables** and, like its close relative the cauliflower, is grown for its head, which is made up of undeveloped flower buds. There are three main types: calabrese or ordinary broccoli, which has a short, thick green stem and a large, closely packed, green flowerhead; sprouting broccoli, which has lots of thin green branches that include small leaves and loose purple (occasionally green or white) florets or mini-heads; and romanesco, a type of calabrese that looks like a smallish lime-green **cauliflower** and can be treated in the same ways.

using it Ordinary broccoli should have a tight rich headful of individual branched florets and strong green leaves; avoid any with loose florets and yellowing leaves. Sprouting broccoli should be a good colour with healthy-looking leaves. All types will keep in the refrigerator for 3–5 days.

Broccoli is usually cooked before being eaten. Both the florets and stalks of all types are edible (peel the thick stalk of ordinary broccoli, then cut into strips or coins). Boiling and steaming are the two basic cooking methods and take 2–10 minutes, depending on thickness and whether whole or broken into florets. Florets can also be added to stir-fries, **risottos** and quiche fillings; roasted and served with **vinaigrette** as a first course; and combined with other ingredients like walnuts, roasted red pepper and crème fraîche to make pasta sauces.

word origin Broccoli was reasonably common in Italy by the 17th century and cultivation had spread throughout Europe by a century later, together with the Italian name, which means 'little shoots'; calabrese is also Italian, meaning 'from Calabria', one of the country's southern provinces.

Brussels sprout

The Brussels sprout (*Brassica oleracea* var. *gemmifera*) is a subspecies of the **cabbage** family and actually looks like a tiny cabbage with its small, tight green head or bud. Unlike its parent plant, however, which has one large terminal head crowning a short stubby stalk, this **vegetable** grows in clusters up a tall thick stalk towards a terminal crown of leaves. The leaves are edible, tasting somewhere between winter cabbage and spring greens, but rarely available commercially.

using it Sprouts should be a strong green colour with tight leaves; avoid any with loose outer or yellowing leaves. They will keep in the refrigerator for about three days.

To cook, remove the outer leaves and trim the base level, then boil or steam for 6–9 minutes, depending on size. Melted butter, with or without finely chopped hard-boiled egg, is one traditional accompaniment, chestnuts another. Chopped sprouts are good stir-fried, especially with walnuts and red peppers, and make a good purée accompaniment for winter meat dishes.

word origin The vegetable was developed in Belgium, hence the Brussels part of the name; the sprout part is probably a reference to the small bud-like appearance.

• Brussels sprouts are now grown all over northern Europe, but when they evolved seems to be a mystery: some think they date back to Roman times and arrived in Belgium courtesy of the Roman army, others that they were developed in Flanders during the 13th century, while yet others believe they were the last cabbage type to develop, probably during the 18th century. First references to them in Britain occur right at the end of the 18th century.

cabbage

Sorting out the various members of this family is like tracing Old Testament genealogy. In the beginning there was the wild cabbage (*Brassica oleracea*), a non-head-forming **vegetable** native to southern Europe. This begat kale (*Brassica oleracea* var. *acephala*), also headless, with strong-tasting curly or plain leaves (the long black-leaved cavolo nero is an Italian kale), and also cultivated cabbage (*Brassica oleracea* var. *capitata*), the original headed plant from which other European brassicas like **broccoli**, **Brussels sprouts** and **cauliflower** developed. Cultivated cabbage also begat kohlrabi (*Brassica oleracea* var. *gongylodes*), which looks like an alien spaceship, tastes vaguely like **turnip** and is grown for its white or purple swollen stem base rather than its rather straggly leaves. Cultivated cabbage is the subject of this entry.

There are many varieties and several major types of cabbage. Spring greens are loose-leafed green cabbages, picked before the centres or heads have had time to form. White, green and red cabbages all have large heads. In the case of white and red cabbage, all the leaves are smooth and tightly shaped into the head, while some green cabbages have loose, usually darker, outer leaves as well. So-called 'white' cabbages are actually a very light green, and green ones can vary from light to dark and in texture from smooth to curly (the Savoy, often considered to be the best-flavoured green cabbage for cooking, has very crinkly leaves). White and red cabbages are round in shape, while green varieties vary from round to pointy.

using it Cabbages should be firm, with close unbroken heads and/or strongly coloured leaves; avoid any with discoloured, badly torn or limp leaves. They will keep for a few days in a cool dark place or up to a week in the refrigerator. Before use, outer leaves should be removed, bases and particularly thick stalk parts trimmed, and loose leaves rinsed since they often store dirt. Loose-leafed cabbage is usually torn into pieces or shredded before cooking (unless it's to be stuffed); headed cabbage is normally cut into wedges or shredded.

All cabbages contain hydrogen sulphide, which is activated as the vegetable starts to soften, creating that typical slightly rotten-egg stink of cooking cabbage. The way to avoid it is to serve the cabbage raw, or to cook it as little as possible by boiling or steaming (9–15 minutes for wedges, 3–5 minutes shredded), or to stir-fry it. Alternatively, braise it for a long time (red cabbage needs 1–1½ hours), covered. Avoiding aluminium cooking pans also helps since the metal brings out the smell.

White, green and red cabbages are sometimes served raw as salad vegetables, either by themselves or with other ingredients – coleslaw, for instance, is a mixture of shredded white cabbage, mayonnaise, grated carrot and onion, and (sometimes) caraway seeds.

White and green cabbages and spring greens all have a particular affinity with pork and bacon, taste good with beef and blend well with other vegetables like potatoes, carrots and beans, either as accompaniments to meat or fish, or in soups. Shredded cabbage fried with mashed potatoes and other flavourings makes bubble and squeak, which can be made more substantial by adding chopped leftover meat or corned beef. The large whole leaves of green cabbage can also be stuffed, then braised or steamed; white cabbage is sometimes pickled and preserved as **sauerkraut**.

Red cabbage is also pickled commercially but the fresh vegetable is usually braised or stewed slowly with ingredients like onion, apple, prunes and bacon. The red pigment in red cabbage can react to the alkalines in water, making the colour turn mauve or even blue during cooking, but this can be prevented by stirring in a little vinegar or an acidic fruit like apple or orange. Red cabbage is traditionally served with game, chicken and fatty poultry like goose or duck, and has the same affinity with pork and bacon as other cabbages.

word origin Although the first headed cabbages appeared during Roman times they didn't spread throughout Europe until around the 12th century. It was probably about a century after that that the Old English word for headless cabbage, *cole* or *colewort*, was replaced by a rough approximation of the Old French *caboce*, meaning 'head'.

did you know?

• According to Greek myth, the first cabbages were created from the sweat of Zeus, a story that may have been an early effort to explain away the cooking smell. Patrician Romans disliked it, but sometimes ate it anyway as a sort of ancient indigestion-cum-hangover cure, since they believed that it would prevent them from suffering the morning-after-the-night-before effects of too much rich food and wine. Roman peasants, and peasants everywhere else in Europe for a thousand years or more, ate it (or rather kale) as part of their staple diet in the form of 'green porrays' or pottages.

• There are oriental cabbages too, but although they belong to the large brassica genus of plants, they are from a different branch of the family. The best-known variety of pe-tsai (*Brassica pekinensis*), sometimes called Chinese cabbage or Chinese leaves, has a compact oval head with slightly crinkly light green leaves and broad whitish veins; it's used in stir-fries and soups, as a salad vegetable and is occasionally pickled. Pak choi or bok choi (*Brassica chinensis*) is the other widely available oriental cabbage, with long, loose, oval green leaves and silky broad stalks; it's mostly chopped or shredded for soups and stir-fries.

carrot

The carrot (*Daucus carota* var. *sativa*) is a biennial root **vegetable** native to Afghanistan, but now grown in temperate areas throughout the world. Originally it was tiny, with a purple skin and slightly lighter interior (a type still grown occasionally), but modern varieties are mostly orange-red in colour, slightly sausage-shaped and sweet to taste.

using it Carrots should be firm, have a good uniform colour and no cracks; if the leaves are still attached, these should be slightly moist and a good green colour. Smaller carrots on the whole will be sweeter than larger ones, which can become slightly woody. Carrots will keep for 4–6 days in a cool dark place, a little longer in the refrigerator. The greenery should be removed before storing because it leeches moisture from the roots.

Carrots are equally good raw or cooked. Grated raw, combined with a few sultanas and dressed with **vinaigrette,** they make a fresh-tasting salad; cut into sticks they are a crunchy alternative to crisps with dips, or a lunch-box snack. For cooking, cut carrots into sticks, rounds or chunks, or leave whole if small, and boil or steam until just firm, 4–12 minutes depending on size.

In savoury cooking, carrots make a perfect accompaniment to most meat and poultry dishes, and can be used in soups, in casseroles and pies, and (thinly sliced) in stir-fries. Carrots are found in sweet dishes too – traditionally used as a sugar substitute when that ingredient was too expensive or unavailable (Mrs Beeton had a recipe for fake apricot jam that used carrots to do the faking). This idea lingers on in carrot and passion cakes. Back in its home continent, carrot is an important ingredient in some halvas, a sweet dessert popular in India and Nepal.

word origin Carrot comes from the Greek for the vegetable, *karoton*. Describing someone as a 'carrot top' is straightforwardly a reference to their hair being similar to the colour of a modern carrot. The phrase 'to dangle a carrot in front of' (meaning to give an inducement) appears to have originated during Victorian times when it was a common way of encouraging reluctant donkeys to get a move on.

did you know?

• The carrots common during Greek and Roman times were probably descended from a wild type that grew around Europe and western Asia. They were cultivated for their seeds and leaves, which the Greeks used as an aphrodisiac, rather than for their tiny, bitter roots. Carrots seem to have disappeared after the fall of Rome, however, and when the vegetable re-emerged from about the 10th century on (introduced by Arabs as they spread through central Asia and southern Europe), it was as fine-tasting, large, purplish Afghani carrots or coarser yellowish roots from mutant strains of them. By the 14th century, these vegetables had reached northern Europe where the Dutch began to improve them, and it was they who eventually evolved the modern orange-coloured root.

• Carrots had rather a good Second World War. They were plentiful between 1939–45 for a start, and were known to be good suppliers of vitamin A (the beta-carotene in carrots that produces the orange colour becomes vitamin A in the body). This vitamin combines with a protein in the retina of the eye to produce rhodopsin, a substance that allows the eye to function better at night. So it was put about that fighter and bomber pilots (who often flew at night) ate vast amounts of carrots to help their night vision, an excellent way to get everybody else to eat more of them.

cauliflower

According to Mark Twain, 'A cauliflower is nothing but a cabbage with a college education.' Horticulturists describe the **vegetable** more prosaically as *Brassica oleracea* var. *botrytis*, the huge whitish bud of a type of **cabbage**, and a close relative of broccoli. Unlike cabbage, whose head is made up of close-fitting leaves, the bud or 'head' of cauliflower is made up of numerous small underdeveloped flowerbuds (called florets) that grow on stems from a central thick stalk, all protected within a frill of coarse green leaves.

using it A good cauliflower has a closely packed, light unblemished head and sturdy leaves that are a good green colour; bruised, browning heads and loose, yellowing leaves indicate that it's past its best. It will keep in the refrigerator for 4–6 days.

Cauliflower is usually cooked, although the florets are sometimes served raw with dips or in salads. Before cooking, remove the outer leaves and base of the stalk. Boil whole (10–15 minutes) or in florets (3–5 minutes); steaming will take a bit longer. The traditional British way to dress up cooked cauliflower is to serve it with a cheese or white sauce (see **béchamel sauce**), but other sauces are just as good: spicy tomato, for instance, melted butter and toasted breadcrumbs or flaked almonds, or even a classic **hollandaise**. Small florets can also be dipped in batter and deep-fried in Japanese tempura-style, and combine well with other vegetables in stews, soups, curries and stir-fries.

word origin Initially cauliflower was *cole-flory* in English before evolving into its modern name, a harking back to its origins as a flowering cabbage; the *cole* part came from the Old English word for cabbage and *flory* from the Latin *flos,* meaning 'flower'.

celeriac

Celeriac (*Apium graveolens* var. *rapaceum*) is the swollen base of the stem of certain types of **celery** (in the United States it's sometimes called celery root). It looks like a smaller, lighter, very knobbly, frankly ugly version of swede. Its flesh is creamy-white and nutty in taste. Celeriac stalks are very strong and bitter and aren't normally used in cooking.

using it Celeriac should be firm and feel heavy; avoid any with brown spots or that feel soft. It will keep in the refrigerator for 7–10 days. The flesh discolours when exposed to the air, so drop it into a bowl of water acidulated with lemon juice as soon as it is prepared.

Celeriac is peeled before being used and is normally cooked, although the flesh is occasionally grated raw and served in a rémoulade sauce (see **mayonnaise**) or added to salads. To cook, cut into chunks, then boil or steam for 8–10 minutes. It can then be puréed and served as an accompaniment (particularly good with game) or combined into a mash with potatoes; the marriage with potatoes also works well when both are cut into thin slices and baked into a *dauphinoise* (see **potato**).

word origin The name indicates its relationship to the celery plant.

did you know?

• Like modern cultivated celery, celeriac evolved from wild celery and although it was grown by early civilizations (mostly for religious and medicinal purposes), it isn't clear whether the small roots or other parts of the plant were preferred. By the 16th century, however, the whole plant, including the root, was being eaten and by a century after that, varieties with much larger roots were being developed for their roots alone.

celery

Modern celery (*Apium graveolens* var. *dulce*) is a cultivated, improved version of wild celery, a **vegetable** that grows freely all around the Mediterranean. Every part is edible: leaves, seeds, stems and even root, which can become **celeriac**. In France and Italy it is the root that is sought after; in English-speaking countries, the delicately ribbed stalk. Celery stalks vary from mid-green to pale yellow and, as a rule of thumb, the lighter they are, the less bitter they taste.

using it Stalks, also called sticks, should be firm and bright, and tightly bunched together with bright leaves. Celery will keep in the refrigerator for 7–10 days, especially if the bottoms of the stalks are immersed in water. To prepare, break off the larger outer stalks (they can be used in soups or to flavour stocks or braised meat dishes), then separate the remaining stalks (unless cooking whole). Trim the top and base of each stalk and, if you like, remove the fibrous 'strings' by peeling them off lengthways with a swivel vegetable peeler.

Celery is eaten raw and cooked. Raw, it's cut into lengths to serve with dips and pâtés, chopped and added to salads, or served with cheese at the end of a meal. Cooked celery adds flavour to soups, stews and sauces of all kinds. It can also be braised (whole or halved lengthways) with bacon, vegetables and stock covered for about an hour, to make a delicious accompaniment to winter roasts.

word origin The celery plant is related to parsley and its leaves are vaguely similar to that herb, which may be why both words come from the same root – the Greek *selinon,* meaning 'parsley'. It was used interchangeably to describe them both in the ancient world.

chickpea

The seeds of an annual **legume** native to the Middle East, chickpeas (*Cicer arietinum*) are now grown in warm dry climates around the world. Leading producers include India and Turkey (who between them produce around two-thirds of the world crop), northern Africa and southern Europe.

The short, almost rectangular pods of the chickpea bush normally contain either one or two roundish cratered beans that can be white, beige, red, brown or nearly black, depending on the variety. They are occasionally eaten young and fresh in producing countries, but most are matured and then dried or canned whole, or split to become channa dhal (see **lentil**); in the Indian subcontinent, channa dhal are also milled into a flour called besan.

using it Dried whole chickpeas need to be rehydrated and cooked in the same way as dried **beans** – soaked for at least 8 hours and then simmered for 1–3 hours. Split chickpeas don't need to be soaked and they cook much more quickly (20–25 minutes).

In cooking terms, chickpea country is a broad swathe that stretches from the Mediterranean to central Asia. In Spain and France, they are added to hearty soups and stews (especially lamb-based stews), and in northern Africa they are one of the vegetables customarily added to **couscous**. Throughout the Middle East, they are the main ingredient in falafel, the small spicy patties eaten everywhere as street snacks, and in hummus, a dip made from tahini (see **sesame seeds**), lemon juice and flavourings like garlic, cumin or cayenne that's traditionally served with pitta bread as a first course and as a sauce for fried or grilled fish and kebabs. In India, whole chickpeas are used on their own or mixed with vegetables in various savoury dishes. Split chickpeas are used in the same way as lentils, and besan flour is made into a popular noodle as well as being part of the batter for snacks like bhajis.

Elsewhere, chickpeas are added to salads, rice dishes and vegetable stews and pies. Besan flour gives an intriguing flavour to pizza dough and savoury pancakes.

word origin Chickpea comes from the French *chiche*, which is derived from the Latin for the pea, *cicer*. (The name of the Roman orator Cicero also comes from this word, apparently because one of his ancestors had a large chickpea-like wart on his face.) The American word for chickpea, garbanzo, comes from the Spanish word for the bean.

> **did you know?**
>
> • Chickpeas were first cultivated in what is now Turkey around 5500BC and were common in India by a thousand years later. They were one of the staple foods of the ancient Egyptian poor, although by 1352BC the pharaohs were obviously enjoying them too, since some were put into Tutankhamun's tomb to help feed him on his final journey.

chicory

Chicory and its close cousin endive belong to the daisy family of plants, which also includes dandelion and lettuce. The *Cichorium* branch, to which both of them belong, is one of the few edible members of the family and is native to Asia and southern Europe, although it's now cultivated in many temperate areas of the world.

There are four major types of this **vegetable**. Chicory, also called witloof or Belgian endive (*Cichorium intybus*), is a cylindrically shaped plant with oval, yellow-tipped white leaves or 'chicons' that closely hug a small central core; the leaves are

mildly bitter. Chicory is 'blanched' to achieve its shape and colour, that is, the roots are dug up in autumn and the root tips and foliage removed before being replanted in a darkened environment so that the leaves can grow white and tight; when the tips yellow, the plant is picked. Endive or frisée (*Cichorium endivia*) has narrow, crinkly leaves, the inner ones being whitish to yellow in colour, while the outer ones are green. Another *endivia*, escarole or Batavian lettuce, looks like a green, broad-leaved, tough-looking lettuce. Both of these latter plants have a bitter flavour, but escarole, and especially its inner leaves, are milder than endive. See also **radicchio**, a mottled chicory developed in Italy.

using it Chicory, endive and escarole are winter plants, and only chicory is found outside its season. All will keep in the refrigerator for 5–7 days. Chicory should have pale unblemished leaves that closely group around the core, while endive and escarole should have a good green outer colour and no soft brown spots. To prepare chicory, trim off the base and any wilting outer leaves. For endive and escarole, pull the leaves away from the base, discarding any slimy ones, and rinse thoroughly; shake or spin dry like lettuce.

These are all basically salad vegetables, although chicory can be cooked too – by braising in stock, or wrapping in ham, covering with **béchamel sauce** and baking. In salads, chicory adds a fresh, contrasting flavour to other greens and sweet fruit such as orange. Endive and escarole taste good with bacon and croutons, and also work well with peppers, mushrooms and sweetcorn.

word origin Chicory comes from the first part of the botanical name for the plant, which goes back to the Greek *kikhorion*. Witloof is Flemish for 'white leaved', appropriately, since this type of chicory was first cultivated in Belgium during the mid-19th century. Endive comes originally from the Greek *entubon* via the medieval Latin for the plant, *endivia*.

The confusion over which is called what breaks down into national preferences. In Britain, chicory is the white vegetable with yellow tips, endive the curly green lettuce with pale insides; in France and North America it's the opposite.

did you know?

• Special varieties of *Cichorium intybus*, such as Magdeburg, have been grown as coffee substitutes since about the 18th century. The thin parsnip-shaped roots are dried, roasted and ground into a powder that can either be used by itself or, since it doesn't contain caffeine, mixed with real coffee to create a lighter, more bitter blend. Chicory coffee has been popular in New Orleans since the American Civil War, when coffee was scarce.

chilli pepper

This is the 'hot' fruit of a Central and South American plant that also produces **sweet pepper**, and both belong to the same large family as the potato and the tomato. There are over 200 known varieties of chilli, most belonging to one of three species: the parent plant *Capsicum annuum*, *Capsicum frutescens*, which produces hotter varieties, or *Capsicum chinense*, a smaller species that produces the hottest types, habañero and scotch bonnet. There are huge differences from one variety to another in appearance, colour and taste or 'heat'. In shape, they can be thin and tapering, small and round, small and cylindrical or large and curved; in size they range from tiny (about 5mm in length) to large (about 20cm); and in colour they can be bright yellow through green and red to black, with many shadings in between. The heat scale differs wildly from type to type too: some are mild and almost sweet, most are fairly nippy and a few could best be described as off-with-your-head.

Small chillies are usually hotter than large ones because most of the heat is found in the pith to which the seeds are attached, and there is more pith in a small chilli than in a large one. The *reason* the pith is hot is that it contains capsaicin, an alkaloid that triggers tingling and irritation on the tongue when the chilli is eaten. As anyone who has ever eaten a really hot chilli knows, capsaicin can truly incapacitate everything it touches, so it isn't surprising to find that a synthetic version of it is now being used in some anti-mugging sprays.

Of the widely available fresh chillies, the anaheim is at the larger end in size; it is usually green in colour and generally mild. The birdseye or bird is small, tapered and red or green; it is hot and the favourite Asian chilli. The habañero is small, lethally hot, and lantern-shaped with a vivid orange or dark green colour. The red or green jalapeño is medium-sized and ranges from hottish to very hot; a smoked, dried version is called a chipotle. The poblano is broad, green and medium hot (when matured until dark red and dried it becomes an ancho, which is rich and sweet in taste). The scotch bonnet is the English-speaking West Indian version of Cuban habañero, and yellow, green or red but always scorchingly hot. The serrano is small, cylindrical and green or red in colour, and pretty hot.

Chillies are also available preserved in oil, dried (whole or in flakes) and canned; dried and ground into powders like **chilli powder** and **cayenne pepper**; or made into condiments such as **Tabasco sauce**.

using it Vivid colour and unmarked skin (some types are naturally slightly wrinkled so this isn't necessarily a quality guide) are the things to look for; avoid chillies with soft or brown spots. Chillies can be stored in the refrigerator for about a week. They can irritate the skin as well as the tongue, so it's always advisable to wear rubber gloves when dealing with them or at least to wash your hands thoroughly immediately afterwards. Within reason, any chilli can be made milder by discarding the pith and some or all of the seeds.

Chillies are an essential part of Asian curries and stir-fries, appear in practically all Mexican or Tex-Mex dishes, are the basic flavouring in harissa, the sauce served with couscous and other North African mixtures, and give a lift to kebabs and other Turkish dishes. More generally, they are combined with tomatoes and garlic in salsas to accompany plain meat or fish and used to pep up **risottos** or pasta sauces. A (very) modest amount could give a lift to salad dressings and generally cheer up most meat, seafood and vegetable dishes. Some larger, milder chillies like the Anaheim and poblano can be stuffed in the same way as sweet peppers – poblanos are filled with cheese, battered and fried to make the Mexican speciality *chiles rellenos*.

word origin Chilli comes from the Nahuatl (language of the Aztecs) for capsicum.

did you know?

• When Columbus set sail in 1492, he was hoping to find a new route to India so that Europeans would have access to regular and cheaper supplies of pepper. He didn't reach India, but when he discovered the Americas he landed another jackpot – chillies; local tribes had been cultivating them there for nearly four thousand years. He returned to Europe with a selection and from there chillies were taken to Africa, Asia, the Middle East and the Balkans, then back into Europe again. And everywhere they went, they seem to have instantly become a staple flavouring, so much so that it's now impossible to imagine the cooking of countries like India, Thailand and North Africa without them.
• In the United States the 'heat' of chillies is so established there's a special scale to measure average hotness. Invented by Wilbur Scoville in 1912, the original 'units' were crude measurements of the

amount of capsaicin a pepper contained. It's now been refined although it is still called the Scoville Scale in honour of its founder. The Scale runs from 0 units (sweet peppers) through 10,000 (jalapeño) and 60–80,000 (Tabasco) to a mind-boggling 100–300,000 for the hottest of them all, habañero and scotch bonnet.

chips

Chips are cut-up **potato** pieces that are deep-fried in hot oil or fat until brown. Technically, any potato large enough to be cut into thin or thick fingers can be used, but the best results come from floury types like Maris Piper, Desirée or King Edward. Cooking fat ranges from vegetable oils (those with a high smoke point are best, see **oils**) through to the more traditional lard or beef dripping. Other vegetables like the **sweet potato**, **Jerusalem artichoke** and **parsnip** can also be made into chips.

using them Although most chips are deep-fried once, the French method is to cook them twice, removing them before they begin to brown first time round, then frying again, this time until golden and crisp. Frozen chips, which are widely available, have their second cooking in the oven.

There's virtually nothing savoury that doesn't go with chips. The traditional British partnership is with deep-fried fish, but they are just as good with burgers, kebabs, steaks and chops. They also make a better-than-good sandwich filling, particularly on buttered white bread so that the butter melts from the heat of the chips. Accompaniments include salt and malt vinegar, or even dips like guacamole, but the heaven-made matches are with tomato ketchup and mayonnaise.

word origin They were called 'chipped potatoes' in English when they first appeared (from France) nearly 150 years ago, but this was soon shortened to the friendlier chips. In the United States

potato crisps are called chips, so when French-style thin potato fingers became popular there they were called French fries. Fries is now used interchangeably with chips around the rest of the English-speaking world.

• The words healthy and chips aren't used all that often in close proximity to each other, but chips *can* be reasonably healthy. One key is the choice of cooking fat. Traditional fats like lard and beef dripping are saturated, which can contribute to high blood cholesterol levels and increased risk of heart disease, but the vegetable oils often used nowadays are polyunsaturated and good for you in moderation. Also, if you cut big chunky chips they have less surface area exposed to the fat and so will absorb less. (Many commercial oven chips contain less than 5 percent fat, which is probably lower than any deep-fried chips.)

courgette

This **fruit** of the gourd or summer **squash** family of plants is a type of smooth-skinned baby **marrow**. The courgette (*Cucurbita pepo*) is oblong in shape, 8–12cm in length and usually green in colour, although speckled and yellow ones also appear occasionally. Its very pale green, somewhat watery insides are similar in texture and appearance to the cucumber, a distant relative. As courgettes mature, some small varieties produce orange flowers that are also edible.

using it Courgettes should feel heavy for their size, be firm and have a strong bright colour; avoid any with softening, discoloured skin. They will keep for about a week in the refrigerator.

Courgettes are normally just trimmed at both ends before use, then cut into the required lengths or pieces. If small, they can be boiled or steamed whole for 5–8 minutes; halved lengthways they can be grilled or stuffed and baked. Cut up courgettes are sautéed (5–10 minutes, depending on size and thickness), stewed gently in a sauce, or battered and deep-fried. Courgette flowers can be stuffed and deep-fried, or cooked as a pasta sauce with light saffron cream.

word origin Courgette is French and means 'little gourd'. In Italy the **vegetable** is called zucchini, and since it was probably Italian immigrants who introduced it to the United States, it is zucchini there too.

cucumber

The cucumber (*Cucumis sativus*) is the fruit of a climbing gourd from the same family as the courgette and the pumpkin, although unlike them it's an Old World **vegetable** (originating in India) rather than a New World one. It is cylindrical in shape, ranges from a tiny 4cm or so to about 25cm in length, and the skin is always green, although it can be smooth, ridged or even warty in appearance. Cucumber flesh is pale with a central core of soft seeds, and the taste is cool and refreshing – not surprising since it's made up of about 96 percent water. About two-thirds of the crop is grown to be eaten fresh (usually the longer varieties) while the rest, smaller varieties often called **gherkins**, are pickled.

using it Cucumbers should be firm (especially the ends) and have a slight sheen. Whole ones will keep in the refrigerator for about a week, but halves should be used within 3–4 days, and both should be removed from any plastic wrappings once they've been started. If the skin has been waxed it should be peeled off, but otherwise peeling is a matter of preference rather than necessity.

Although it's cooked occasionally – chopped and stewed with garlic and olive oil as an accompaniment to plain meat dishes or sliced thinly as part of stir-fries are two possibilities – normally cucumber is used raw as a salad vegetable: by itself with a delicate dressing, or as part of a mixed or Greek salad. It's also a good dip ingredient, most famously grated into Greek yoghurt with garlic to make tsatziki, and delicious as the base for a cold, creamy summer soup. As a sandwich ingredient it has a genteel Victorian image due to its association with teatime. It is also a popular garnish, especially for poached salmon and other fish dishes, and is essential in **Pimm's**.

word origin During early medieval times cucumber was called *cucumer* in English, which came from the Latin for the vegetable, *cucumis*. It gained a 'b' towards the end of the 15th century, then gradually became *cowcumber* during the 17th and 18th centuries before settling down into the word we know today.

did you know?

• Cucumbers have been cultivated for over 4000 years and were popular among ancient Egyptians, Greeks and Romans, not just as a vegetable but as an effective skin-care product. The Roman emperor Tiberius was particularly partial to cucumber and, in order to guarantee unending supplies, his were grown on wheeled raised beds so that they could be rolled out into the sun during the day and wheeled back indoors to protect them during the cool night (they hate the cold).

fennel

Most of the different parts of this plant of the **parsley** family are edible: the feathery leaves are used as a **herb**, the dried seeds as a **spice** and a special variety with a swollen base is grown as a **vegetable**.

The original plant, wild or bitter fennel (*Foeniculum vulgare*), is a native of southern Europe and still grown occasionally for its bitter-tasting seeds. Sweet fennel (*Foeniculum officinale*) was probably first developed in Italy as a less bitter alternative to the wild plant, and its slightly aniseed-flavoured seeds and feathery, frond-like green leaves are now widely used in western Europe and America. Florence fennel, or finocchio (*Foeniculum vulgare* var. *dulce*), also has feathery frond-like leaves but is grown for its bulb-like stem. Like the leek, Florence fennel is 'earthed up' (reburied from time to time while it's growing) to ensure that it remains white.

using it Fennel bulbs should be white and unblemished with good-coloured leaves. They will keep for 3–4 days in the refrigerator; the herb will last for about the same amount of time.

To prepare the bulb, cut off the base and remove the outer layer before chopping or shredding as required, to serve raw or cook. Toss shredded raw fennel with apple or celery and vinaigrette to make a crisp, fresh salad. Chop or slice the bulb, then steam for 5–8 minutes, or stew for 15–20 minutes with ingredients like onion, garlic and tomatoes, and serve with fish or red meat.

Fennel seeds are used in Asian cooking (particularly with ginger) to flavour fish dishes, vegetables and chutneys, and are also added to some western baked dishes and sauces. The herb fennel has a particular affinity with fish, and sprays are often inserted into whole fish before they are cooked.

word origin Fennel comes from the Latin name *foeniculum*, meaning 'little hay', a reference to the feathery leaves.

did you know?

• Fennel seeds were once chewed by fashion-conscious women as a slimming aid. Roasted seeds are still sometimes chewed after meals in India to help digestion and sweeten the breath, and a special type of 'tea' made from them is sometimes used to cure colic in babies.

green bean

Green beans are **legumes**, part of a vast family of podded flowering **vegetable** plants eaten either for their pods (this entry and **mangetout**) or their seeds (see **bean** and **pea**). Despite the name, green bean pods can be yellow and even occasionally purple as well as various shades of green. There are two major types, each with many different varieties. The runner bean (*Phaseolus coccineus*), also called pole bean, is a climbing plant with bright red blossoms (which is why it's also sometimes called scarlet runner) and rough, usually stringy pods. The French bean (*Phaseolus vulgaris*) is essentially the immature pod that contains what eventually become haricot beans. Varieties of French bean include snap or bobby bean, the very slim haricot vert and yellow wax bean.

using it Green beans should have good-coloured skin with a slight sheen, and no splits or blackening around the tops; French beans should also 'snap' crisply when bent in two. They will keep in the refrigerator for 4–5 days.

Green beans are always cooked before being eaten. They need to be topped and tailed first and in some cases the 'strings' have to be removed as well. To cook, boil or steam for 2–8 minutes, depending on size. Serve hot or cold (for the latter, immediately after draining, plunge into iced water to cool), on their own or with ingredients such as tomatoes and garlic. They also have an affinity with walnuts and taste good stir-fried briefly with some nuts, then drizzled with walnut oil.

word origin The botanical name *Phaseolus* comes from the Latin *phaselus*, a small sailing ship (the pods were thought to be shaped like one). Runner beans are climbers and get their name from the long thin 'runners' the plants produce so that they can attach themselves to the nearest pole while they grow.

• Green beans are native to Central and South America and were brought back to Europe by Spanish explorers and colonists. They were introduced into Britain during the 17th century but didn't become widely available until the latter half of the 20th century.

Jerusalem artichoke

The Jerusalem artichoke (*Helianthus tuberosus*) is a small **vegetable** that is native to North America, although it's now grown in temperate areas of Europe as well. It is tuberous and knobbly in appearance, anything from light to darkish beige in colour and nutty to taste.

using it This is a winter vegetable, rarely found at other times of the year. It should be firm to touch and will keep in the refrigerator for about 10 days.

Optimistic comparisons are sometimes made with the potato, and Jerusalem artichokes are occasionally offered as an alternative for that vegetable. Like potatoes they can be boiled or steamed (in their skins, preferably, and for 10–15 minutes), or roasted or baked. They even make reasonable chips.

word origin This has no connection with the globe artichoke, nor with Jerusalem or anywhere else in the Holy Land. The Jerusalem part of the name probably comes from the Italian *girasole,* meaning 'sunflower', a family member; the artichoke part can be blamed on Samuel de Champlain (see below), who once rashly described its taste as artichoke-like. It isn't.

• Jerusalem artichokes were cultivated by Native Americans, especially those who lived in what is now Massachusetts, and they introduced them to early French explorers including Samuel de Champlain, who founded Québec in the early 17th century. It was

French explorers who brought the vegetable back to northern Europe, where it enjoyed a modest vogue before its tendency to cause flatulence outweighed any novel attractions the taste might have had.

leek

A member of the **onion** family of vegetables that also includes garlic and the shallot, the leek (*Allium porrum*) is probably descended from wild leek (*Allium ampeloprasum*), which is native to the Mediterranean area. It looks different from most of its relatives, having a very small root and a thick, sheath-like 'pseudo-stem' made up of flat encircling leaves that branch into green 'flags'. The lower part of the stems, which can reach 80cm in length, are kept white by 'earthing up' (burying the plant in soil) so that only the flags are exposed during growing.

using it Leeks should have a strong fresh colour and firm dark leaves; avoid any with yellowing or drooping leaves. To prepare, remove the root and outer leaves, then rinse out the dirt from between the other leaves (it's easier to get at if you slash down the centre of the plant from the natural 'v' at the top and splay out the leaves slightly, or cut it into pieces first).

The leek is the king of the soup vegetables: cooked and puréed with potato and stock or light cream for soupe parmentier (hot) and vichyssoise (cold); chopped and teamed with chicken to become Scottish cock-a-leekie; and added to practically any other mix of ingredients. It can also be cut into lengths, then steamed or boiled for 3–5 minutes and served with meat and fish; cooked whole, then served warm or cool with **vinaigrette** as a first course; or chopped and used as a stir-fry ingredient.

word origin Leek comes from the Saxon *leauc*, their word for the vegetable.

• All the cultures of the ancient world used leeks, but they were probably first cultivated by the Egyptians. In Rome, they were considered the patrician member of the onion family, and emperor Nero was particularly partial to them – he ate leeks nearly every day, believing they would help his singing voice. It may have been the Romans who introduced leeks to Britain, where by medieval times they had become a popular ingredient in 'white porray', a soupy pottage thickened with ground almonds. This was eaten for Lent by the rich and throughout the year, adorned only by cereals and maybe pulses, by everyone else.
• There are many explanations of how the leek came to be a national symbol of Wales. One that's at least a good story has it that Welsh soldiers fighting against the Saxons on March 1, AD640 were persuaded by St David himself (presumably from heaven, since he was already dead) to wear a leek in their bonnets to identify themselves to one another in close combat (this was before military uniforms were widely worn). They won the battle, so perhaps the leek was considered to have brought good luck.

legume

This is any member of the third-largest group of flowering plants in the world (after orchids and daisies), and one of the most versatile foods we have. All legumes are podded, although only a few like **green beans** and **mangetout** are cultivated for the pods. One or two others, including **mung beans**, can be eaten as very young sprouting plants, but most are grown for the seeds contained in their pods. These seeds – **bean**, **lentil** or **pea**, depending on the family they belong to – are called pulses, and may be used fresh or dried. There are thousands of different varieties, many species and several major families including *Phaseolus* (green, kidney, haricot and **lima beans**), *Vicia* (**broad beans**), *Vigna* (mung beans), *Lens* (lentils), *Glycine* (**soya beans**) and *Pisum* (peas and mangetout). Perhaps more surprisingly **peanuts** and **tamarind** are also legumes, although the former is used as a nut and the latter as a spice.

Leguminous plants can be tall and climbing, small and bushy, or low and trailing, and pods appear only as the flowers die off. Seeds fulfil the same function as the **grains** of cereal plants and, like them, are made up of three major parts: the outer coating or skin; the large inner cotyledon, similar to the endosperm in grains, which stores the protein and energy (in the form of starch) essential to nourish the new seedling; and the tiny embryo of the new plant, which is attached to the cotyledon.

using it All legumes, except one or two sprouted plants, need to be cooked before being eaten, and only a few, such as broad beans and peas, are eaten fresh. Most dried legumes need to be rehydrated and cooked before being eaten (see **bean** and **chickpea**).

word origin Legume comes via French from the Latin *legere,* meaning 'to pick', probably because the pods were once always picked by hand. Pulse, the word for the seeds, also comes via French from the Latin *puls*, meaning a 'thick porridge', the way most dried beans and peas were eaten in the ancient and medieval worlds.

* The unfortunate consequence of enjoying legumes used to be attributed to many weird and wonderful things. St Augustine, for instance, thought that flatulence was a clear sign from God of man's fall from grace. The real reason why legumes cause 'wind', however, is more prosaic: they contain oligosaccharides (molecules consisting of up to five sugar molecules all linked together), which the human digestive tract can't process, so they pass unchanged into our lower intestines where the bacteria that live there deal with them. As they are processed, various gases are expelled as waste. About 50 percent of what emerges from the human behind is nitrogen (usually inhaled as air during eating and drinking) and the carbon dioxide expelled by the bacteria makes up most of the rest. The remainder includes two tiny ingredients called indoles and skatoles, which cause the noxious fumes.

* Pulses are the richest source of vegetable protein. Like meat, fish and poultry, the protein in soya beans contains all eight of the essential amino acids, the 'building blocks' of protein; for other pulses the amino acid balance can be improved by eating them with rice or a grain-based product like pasta. Pulses also supply fibre, a number of B vitamins, including folic acid, and iron, and they are low in fat.

lentil

An annual **legume**, the lentil (*Lens culinaris*) probably originated in the Middle East, although it's now more associated with the Indian subcontinent. Leading modern producers include India (which accounts for about half the world crop), Canada, Turkey and Egypt.

The bushy lentil plant produces small flat pods that turn yellow when they are ready to be harvested, and each one carries one or (usually) two disc-like seeds. It is these seeds that are eaten (and with **beans** and **peas** make up the family of pulses). Colours range from the most common green or brown to occasional purple and even black. Most lentils are sold by colour; only the small-seeded dusty green-blue variety grown in the Auvergne area of France known as Puy is separately identified by area of cultivation. Most lentils are husked before being sold (which can change their colour) and many are also split.

Dhal (or dal) is a staple category of food in the Indian subcontinent and is used both to describe an ingredient (strictly speaking a split lentil) and a dish made from the ingredient. In both India and elsewhere, however, it's used to describe other split pulses too, and sometimes also whole lentils or pulses (otherwise called *gram*). Popular dhals include masoor, small salmon-pink split lentils that yellow as they cook; toor (sometimes called toovar), which are larger, split, ochre-coloured pigeon peas, a near relative of lentil; moong, small yellow split **mung beans** or, occasionally, unhusked whole small green seeds; and channa, large, yellow split **chickpeas**.

using it Unlike other pulses, lentils don't need to be soaked, but they should be rinsed thoroughly in running water before boiling. Cooking times vary: unhusked lentils need about an hour, husked whole ones around 35 minutes, and Puy and split lentils about 30 minutes. They will more than double in volume when cooked.

In western countries, lentils are primarily used in soups and stews (particularly vegetable, chicken and bacon), and as an accompaniment to sausages. They can also be served cold as a salad with **vinaigrette**; or mixed with chopped vegetables and flavourings like saffron, lime juice and ginger as an unusual filling for ravioli and filo pastry or a good accompaniment to fish steaks like salmon and tuna. Puy lentils are traditionally served with roast lamb or pork.

In the subcontinent, the great dhal partnership is with rice: stirred through it, poured over it, served with it and often blended towards the end of cooking with a flavouring tarka, a mixture such as whole spices mixed with chopped onion and ginger cooked briefly in ghee. One spiced variety of dhal or a mixture can also become a separate dish, be added to vegetables (particularly okra, courgette or tomato) or to meat dishes like chicken to make dhansak.

word origin Lentil is borrowed from the French *lentille*, which comes from the Latin *lens* and in particular a diminutive form of it, *lenticula*. The modern word lens, meaning a small piece of glass with a curved surface, comes from the same source.

• Lentils were probably the first legumes to be cultivated, at least 9000 years ago and not long after barley and wheat. They are mentioned in the Bible (the mess of pottage Esau sold his birthright for was made from lentils), and were part of the staple diet of the poor in all the ancient cultures. Despite their current popularity in the Indian subcontinent, they were slow to spread there; the first records of them don't occur until about the second millennium BC.

lettuce

Lettuce (*Lactuca sativa*) is a plant of the daisy family and a relative of chicory and dandelion. It originated in Mediterranean Europe and the Near East. There are many varieties, but most lettuces belong to one of four groups. Round lettuce or butterheads are light to mid-green in colour with soft loose leaves grouped around a fairly small head (Tom Thumb is one variety). Crispheads are very light green in colour with crisp leaves closely shaped around a large cabbage-like head (iceberg and Webb's wonder are the two best-known types). Longleafs, which include cos, romaine and Little Gem, can be darker green, and are oblong in shape with crisp leaves that group loosely around a small centre. Looseleafs vary in colour (although they are always at least partly green), but are usually round in shape with no head; they include modern 'designer' leaves, such as the red-tipped Oak Leaf and frizzy-leaved red-tipped Lollo Rosso.

using it Good lettuces have fresh-looking leaves with no soft or brown spots around the base or tips. Ideally they should be eaten as soon after being picked or bought as possible; if necessary, however, they can be kept, unwashed in an airtight bag, in the refrigerator (cos types for 3–5 days, others for just 48 hours). All lettuces should be rinsed well before use.

This is *the* salad **vegetable** in the western

world, one variety by itself, several mixed together, or one or several added to other ingredients for a mixed salad. Lettuce is also cooked occasionally: with peas and small onions, or combined with stock to make what Mrs Beeton described as an 'Italian' soup. Whole leaves can even be pressed into service as wrappers, to enclose fish for steaming or to use instead of pancakes with dishes like Peking duck and South-east Asian spring rolls.

word origin Lettuce comes via Old French from the Latin *lac,* meaning milk, a reference to the liquid that oozes out when the stem is cut. Cos was developed in Turkey and neighbouring Aegean islands (including Kos), hence its name, while romaine, the American word for cos and now used in other English-speaking countries too, first became popular during Roman times, hence its name. Iceberg is so called because when it was first sold commercially, it was covered with ice to keep it fresh on the journey from producer to retailer.

did you know?

• The first lettuces were tall, spindly and probably without centres. They were revered in ancient Egypt where they were sacred to Min (the god of fertility and harvest), who was sometimes depicted in tomb paintings standing in front of them with his phallus erect and a whip in his right hand. Lettuce was popular in Greece and Rome too, as much for its medicinal qualities as its culinary ones. It was often served at the end of a meal because early varieties had opium-like soporific properties that were thought to help the diners have a good night's sleep after their (usually) excessive eating and drinking; most modern varieties have had this bred out of them.
• Wild lettuce (*Lactuca virosa*) still contains soporific properties. It was once used as an opium substitute since it is non-addictive, and as an anaesthetic. Extracts from the plant, called *lactucarium*, are still sometimes used in alternative medicine and as an ingredient in herbal cigarettes.

lima bean

The lima bean (*Phaseolus limensis* syn. *Phaseolus lunatus*) is an annual **legume** that belongs to the same family as the haricot and kidney **beans**. It originated in South America, and today is grown in tropical Africa and the United States, which produces nearly two-thirds of the world crop.

Depending on variety, the plant can be small and bushy or tall and climbing. The oval pods usually carry 2–4 kidney-shaped beans; colour ranges from the fairly common green or ivory to the more occasional red or brown, and size from mini to majestic. One of the largest varieties is the pale beige bean available dried or canned as butter bean and also sometimes known as Madagascar bean.

using it Although lima beans are sometimes available fresh in the United States, they are rarely seen in this form elsewhere. In fact, small limas are a rarity in any form outside America, the larger butter bean being preferred in Europe. Fresh limas can be treated in the same way as **broad beans**; dried ones and butter beans need to be soaked and cooked in the same way as other beans. Cooking times will vary according to size, but butter beans would take at least 1½ hours. Both lima and butter beans can be used in the same way as any other beans or **chickpeas**.

word origin The first part of the name comes from the capital of the bean's place of origin, Peru in South America; the butter bean is so-called because of its colour.

did you know?

• Most of the other important species of the *Phaseolus* family, such as French, haricot and kidney beans, originated in Central America, but this branch developed further south, around what is now Peru, and was being cultivated there by about 5000BC.

It eventually spread to Central America where it was discovered by Spanish explorers and settlers in the late 15th and early 16th centuries. They introduced it to Europe; it was taken to Africa and Madagascar by slave traders.

mangetout

The mangetout is a legume, a member of the podded pea family of **vegetables** and is native to western Asia. Most peapods have a stiff inner parchment that makes them difficult to eat; mangetout pods, however, don't contain this – the peas are tiny and unformed, the flat green pods tender and crisp, so they are eaten pods and all.

using it Good mangetout should be brightly coloured with pods tight enough to show the outline of the seeds. Those with larger seeds and curved pods, called sugar snap peas, are treated in the same way as ordinary mangetouts.

Pods need only be topped and tailed before being used raw or cooked. Raw, they add crunch and colour to salads; cooked, their delicate taste is best preserved by steaming for a few minutes or stir-frying. They go well with oriental vegetables like beansprouts and Chinese cabbage, could be added to rice or pasta dishes, or teamed with other vegetables like mushrooms, baby corn and sliced carrots as an accompaniment to chicken breast or delicate fish like sea bass or sole.

word origin Mangetout is French for 'eat all'.

marrow

In the **vegetable** world, a marrow (*Cucurbita pepo*) is a **squash**, a relative of the pumpkin and native to Central America. The word is also used to describe the delicate, jelly-like food obtained from the bone cavities of meat (see **offal**).

The marrow is a summer squash and the poor relation of a group that also includes the courgette (which is actually a tender

baby marrow). It is cylindrical in shape with soft, darkish or mottled green skin and can be very large; although the really monstrous ones tend to be grown for showing rather than eating, an average-size cooking marrow can still check in at around 1.5kg in weight. The flesh is very pale green and somewhat watery.

using it The marrow has a natural season during summer and early autumn, and is only occasionally found at other times of the year. It should be reasonably bright in colour, have no soft spots, and feel heavy for its size; it will keep for several months in a cool, dark place.

Since it's often too big to cook whole comfortably, and too watery to boil or steam successfully even in pieces, marrow is usually cubed and stewed, braised or added to curries or chillis. For this kind of cooking it is usually peeled. The most successful way of dealing with it, however, is to stuff it with a well-flavoured mixture. Depending on size, cut the marrow in half lengthways or into thick rounds and scoop out the central seeds, then blanch (boil briefly) before stuffing and baking. Stuffed halves will take 50–60 minutes in a moderate oven, thick rounds 35–40 minutes.

word origin When marrow first became popular, there was a fashion for linking unfamiliar vegetables to better-known animal foods. Therefore, marrow might have received its name because it was thought to be similar in taste or texture to meat marrow.

did you know?

•Marrow has become part of the folklore of English summer in the same way as cricket on the village green and warm beer, so it comes as a shock to realize that it was virtually unknown in Britain until about 200 years ago. It was the Victorians who popularized it. Mrs Beeton was a fan, giving eight recipes for marrow in her *Household Management*, including one for jam.

mung bean

The mung bean (*Vigna radiata*) is an annual **legume** that is native to the Indian subcontinent but now widely grown throughout Asia. The plant can reach around 1m in height. It has long, thin, slightly hairy pods, each of which contains 10–15 tiny, mostly olive-green seeds, although occasional ones can be yellowish, brown or even speckled. The seeds, or beans, are sold whole (fresh or dried), husked and split to reveal a yellowish core (when they are known as moong dhal; see **lentil**), or milled into flour. These and other beans such as soya are also sometimes germinated to produce small shoots or beansprouts.

using it Fresh or sprouted mung beans should be refrigerated, used within a day or so of buying and need no special cooking. Dried mung beans and dhal are prepared and cooked in the same way as lentils.

In China and South-east Asia, fresh mung beans and sprouts are used in many dishes including stir-fries and as fillings for spring rolls and dim sum; in India, the dried beans are more popular, especially the husked split yellow dhal, which are used in meat and vegetable dishes as well as by themselves. More generally, fresh beans and sprouts can be mixed into any stir-fry mixture, not just an oriental one, or added to salads to provide crunch; dried beans or dhal are good in soups and stews, particularly poultry ones, and in rice dishes.

Mung bean flour is used commercially to make cellophane noodles; in India it's used for poppadums as well as in batters for snack foods like bhajis. In western dishes, it would add an interesting taste to pancake batters and pizza bases, particularly if the filling had less conventional, oriental ingredients.

word origin Mung is Hindi, from the Sanskrit word for the bean, *mudga*.

• The black-eyed bean (*Vigna unguiculata*), a relative of the mung bean, originated in Africa, although it's now most commonly associated with the Caribbean and southern states of the United States. The cream-coloured beans have a black smudge at one edge (hence the name). They are a central ingredient in the American soul-food dish 'hoppin' John', where they are cooked with salt pork and spices and served with rice.

mushroom

Mushrooms are fungi, types of primitive plants closely related to **yeast** and mould that form a more or less distinct plant kingdom. Technically, the word is used to describe only the *Agaricus* and *Boletus* species, but popularly (and here), mushroom is the name given to any edible member of this kingdom.

Fungi don't grow in the sense that other plants do; they have no roots, for instance, nor do they produce flowers, and they don't contain chlorophyll, the green pigment that allows plants to absorb enough light from the sun to grow above the ground. They are therefore mostly found in cool shady places where they can live off rotting vegetation or as part of a complicated mutual feeding system with other plants – they are particularly fond of trees, and some of the best wild mushrooms can be found in deciduous forests (ceps, for example) or coniferous ones (chanterelles). They range in size from tiny to enormous and in colour from white to black and nearly all have gills or ribs under the 'cap', small spores that are part of the reproductive process. Most grow quickly (an understatement: they seem to spring up virtually overnight at certain times of the year, usually autumn). Mushrooms exist everywhere, but are marginally more prolific in the northern hemisphere than the southern.

There are around 50,000 species, about a thousand of which are poisonous. Of the rest, only relatively few actually taste good enough to eat, and these can be roughly divided into those that are now cultivated and those that are still mostly wild. Cultivated mushrooms (*Agaricus bisporus*) include the button, a smallish white mushroom with a smooth, round domed head; the chestnut, which is more or less a button mushroom with a light tan and a bit more flavour (cremini is another name for chestnut mushrooms, and portobellos are a bigger version); and open or flat mushrooms, much larger, with a firm, meaty cap and strong flavour. In general, larger mushrooms and those with open cups, which have been left to grow longer, will have more flavour than the small, closed-cup varieties. More exotic cultivated mushrooms include the Japanese shiitake (*Lentinus edodes*), which is strong-tasting, with brown and slightly wrinkled skin, and the blue-grey, pink or yellow fan-shaped oyster mushroom (*Pleurotes ostreatus*).

There are many types of wild fungi available despite problems of supply (by definition they have to be searched out and picked by hand). The **truffle**, technically a mushroom since it is an edible fungus, occupies a rarefied niche all its own (see separate entry). Of the true wild mushrooms, the cep (*Boletus edulis* and others), called porcini in Italy, is the most sought after, a brownish mushroom with a fat spongy cap and broad stalk. Other wild mushrooms include: the chanterelle (*Cantharellus cibarius*), which has a trumpet-shaped yellow cap, deep gills and a short thin stalk; the giant puffball (*Calvatia gigantea*), whose cap can reach 75cm across and is white in colour with lots of creamy flesh; and the morel (*Morchella esculenta*), unlike most mushrooms a spring fungus rather than an autumn one, which has a long, hollow cone-shaped cap made up of lots of cracks and crevices and has

virtually no stalk.

One type of fungus, *Fusarium graminearum*, is fermented until it forms a curd-like mass rather than being cultivated or eaten wild. It's then mixed with various flavourings and binders to form quorn, a myco-protein used as a meat substitute.

using it Most cultivated mushrooms should have smooth, unblemished caps and gills with a pinkish tinge; with shiitakes, look for a strong fresh colour. Poly bags make mushrooms sweat and go soggy, so keep them loose in the refrigerator or in paper bags and use within a day or so of buying. Wild mushrooms wilt quickly after being picked, so should be prepared and cooked as soon as possible. Many mushrooms like shiitake, cep and morel, dry well, and are widely available in this form.

Cultivated mushrooms can be eaten raw or cooked and are often used as a general flavouring as well as a vegetable. Some people peel as well as trim them, but this isn't really necessary: a quick wipe over with damp kitchen towel should be enough to remove any grit (soaking will make them soggy). Wild mushrooms, which are always cooked, need more preparation: for ceps, scrape away the spongy tubes under the cap; for chanterelles and morels, use a small brush, then wipe with a damp kitchen towel, to remove grit and any insects. If wild mushrooms are very dirty, they can be rinsed briefly and shaken dry.

Dried mushrooms need to be rehydrated before being used, which involves soaking them in water for 15–30 minutes, depending on the type (if they are being added to an already liquid mixture this may not be necessary, although they will need to cook for about 10 minutes to soften). Leftover mushroom soaking liquid makes a good basis for vegetarian stock and pasta sauces.

Both wild and cultivated mushrooms work well with ingredients like shallots, garlic,

Madeira and crème fraîche, and can be used in many stews, **risottos** and pasta sauces. Open mushrooms are also excellent stuffed and then baked, while the giant puffball can make a meal on its own, sliced, battered and fried like an **escalope**. Cultivated mushrooms could also be used raw in a salad (they go particularly well with spinach, bacon and red pepper).

word origin Mushroom comes from the Old French *mousseron*, a general word for edible fungus. The phenomenal speed at which they grow gives rise to the phrase 'to mushroom' (usually in size), and the domed cap shape helped christen 'mushroom cloud', the smoke and debris shape that forms in the sky after a nuclear explosion.

did you know?

• Mushrooms are probably the oldest edible plants in the world and were used by all the early cultures, sometimes in unexpected ways. Most Romans, for instance, probably considered them a great delicacy, but the emperor Claudius may not have been so enthusiasic since his wife killed him by feeding him poisoned fungi. In the Americas, ancient peoples chewed hallucinogenic mushrooms as part of religious ceremonies.

• The whole history of mushrooms reflects a certain ambivalence, perhaps not so surprising when you consider that until about 300 years ago all mushrooms were wild. So it was absolutely essential to be able to tell the edible ones from the poisonous ones – something not always that obvious to the naked eye, which meant people died every year from eating the wrong ones. This occasionally still happens, and in France where wild mushroom picking is a national sport, most mushroom hunters take their harvest to the local pharmacy before cooking to check that it won't kill them.

mustard and cress

As the name suggests, this is made up of two plants grown together, white **mustard** (*Sinapis alba*) and garden cress (*Lepidium*

sativum), both members of the cabbage family. Both have tiny roundish green leaves, those of mustard being even smaller than those of cress. Although the plants originated in the Middle East, they grow quickly anywhere and most of us will have first come across them in a school science class, trying to grow them on dampened blotting paper or saucers. Rape (*Brassica napus*) is now sometimes added to the mixture, usually at the expense of mustard seedlings although it lacks their pungency.

using it Cress leaves take a day or so longer to sprout than mustard ones, so the best punnets to buy are those containing what look like mostly mustard leaves. Mustard and cress doesn't keep well and should be bought, kept watered and used within a day or so. Rinse the leaves and shake dry before use.

Mustard and cress have two basic uses in the kitchen: as an all-purpose, slightly spicy garnish for pretty much anything, but certainly salads, eggs, vegetables and pâtés; and as a good sandwich filling, considered just as genteel in its heyday as thinly sliced cucumber, but now mostly added to other, blander, filling ingredients to give them some bite.

word origin Mustard comes from the Latin *mustum,* meaning 'must', the unfermented grape juice with which crushed mustard seeds were traditionally mixed to create the condiment; cress comes indirectly from the Latin *crescere*, 'to grow', a reference to the speed with which it matures.

okra

An annual plant related to marshmallow and cotton, okra (*Hibiscus esculentus*) is native to Africa, but now grown in tropical and subtropical areas throughout the world; major producers include India, Thailand and the southern United States. It's grown for its ridged, spear-shaped fruits, picked just before they are ripe, which are used as a **vegetable**. Okra pods range from 5–15cm long and are normally dark green in colour although occasional varieties are red. The insides are divided into sections, each of which contains edible seeds and a sticky gum that gives a unique texture to any dish to which okra is added.

using it Pods should be slightly shiny, and snap cleanly if bent; avoid any that are shrivelled or soft. They will keep in the refrigerator for 3–4 days and only need to be topped and tailed before being cooked. Whole pods can be boiled or steamed for 8–10 minutes, then deep-fried, or coated in breadcrumbs and pan-fried. Mostly, however, okra is sliced and used in soups, stews and curries to thicken and flavour them; or added to pilaffs, couscous dishes or hearty salads, especially those that are bean or rice-based. Okra goes well with tomatoes, onions and chillies and is a classic ingredient in many Creole dishes.

word origin Okra comes from a West African word for the vegetable, *nkuruma*, and had begun to be used in English by the early part of the 18th century. Gumbo, which is sometimes used to describe the vegetable as well as a soup-stew in the southern United States and the West Indies, comes from the Bantu word for the vegetable.

did you know?

• Okra was first cultivated in Ethiopia, and eventually spread to the Middle East, then further into Asia until it reached the Indian subcontinent, where it's now widely used. It was probably introduced into Europe by the Moors as they conquered and settled from the 8th century on. It reached the Americas on African slave ships, arriving in the Caribbean and South America during the 17th century and in the southern United States less than a century later.

onion

The 'truffle of the poor' is one writer's description of this family of plants, which probably originated in central Asia, although it's now grown in temperate areas throughout the world. The most important of the 500 or so species is the common onion (*Allium cepa*), grown for its bulb; it ranges in size from pearl to small melon, in colour from standard brown to yellow, white or red, and in taste from the slightly bitter (brown) to the mildly sweet (white or red). All varieties have thin, papery skin enclosing tight layers of cream or pink flesh wrapped around a small central stem bud. Near relatives include the chive, leek and spring onion, which are cultivated mainly for their stem-like leaves, and garlic and the shallot, which are prized for their bulbs.

using it Onions should be firm and unblemished, particularly around the tops; avoid any that are soft or sprouting. Most will keep happily for weeks in a cool dark place, although some small white ones need to be used within about a week of buying. Onions are odourless until cut open, when a mixture of sulphuric compounds is exposed to the air, releasing not only the pungent characteristic smell, but also a substance that causes the eye irritation that sometimes leads to tears. The smell peters out into a soft sweetness when onion is cooked.

White or red onions are best for raw dishes, sliced thinly, chopped finely or grated before being used to add crunch and bite to salads or to any mayonnaise-based sandwich or jacket potato filling like egg or tuna. In cooking, onion is primarily used as a flavouring **vegetable**, sliced or chopped and added at the beginning of cooking to just about every soup, stew, pasta sauce, rice and grain dish, Onions are also a key ingredient in many dishes: poached in stock until soft and golden to make a spectacular soup;

braised slowly to make a 'marmalade' to serve with sausages; and mixed into **béchamel sauce** to make sauce soubise. Small onions can be pickled or cooked whole to serve as a vegetable.

word origin   Onion could come from the close fitting 'unity' of onion layers or from the Latin *unio,* meaning 'large single pearl', the name ancient farmers gave the pick of their crop. (This latter may also explain the origin of 'knowing your onions', meaning to be very knowledgeable about something.)

did you know?

• Our neolithic ancestors ate onions regularly, and by early Egyptian times they were being used to decorate mummy eye sockets too. The Egyptian and Roman upper classes didn't care for the bad breath that eating onions bestowed, but for the poor, raw onions, eaten like we do apples, were part of their staple diet.
• The Romans introduced the onion to Britain where it was quickly incorporated into the peasant diet, and Christopher Columbus took it to America where it became a hit with native peoples there. So much so that the city of Chicago might be named after it: one story has it that the name comes from a local Native American word that could mean either stinky onion or skunk.

parsnip

The parsnip (*Pastinaca sativa*) is a root vegetable that comes from the same family of plants as parsley and carrot and is native to Eurasia, although it's now grown in temperate areas throughout the world. It has a tapered shape, varies from 15–30cm in length and is beige in colour with slightly spongy pale flesh and a woody core.

using it   The parsnip is a winter vegetable, by tradition dug up after the first frosts have gone because the cold converts some of its starch to sugar, thus creating its characteristic sweetness. Like most vegetables, however, it is now available

more or less all year round. Smaller parsnips are sweeter-tasting than larger ones, which can be fibrous as well as woody. The skin should be unblemished and firm. They will keep in a cool dark place for 4–5 days, a little longer in the refrigerator.

All parsnips need to be peeled, and large ones should have the woody cores cut out as well. There are three main ways to cook them: cut in rounds or chunks and boil or steam for 4–6 minutes; cut into lengths, parboil, then deep-fry to make chips; or parboil, halved or whole, toss with brown sugar or olive oil and roast for 30–40 minutes in a moderate oven. Parsnips are a good ingredient for soups, stews or casseroles, working particularly well with curry spices, ginger and nutmeg. The vegetable is also occasionally made into a country wine.

word origin   The first part of the name comes indirectly from the Latin *pastinum,* a two-pronged fork used as a sort of dibble for planting seeds and plants; the 'nip' ending came later, from the Scots word for turnip, *neep,* which parsnip was thought to resemble. It also has an unlikely literary connection: the Russian writer Boris Pasternak is actually Boris Parsnip, *pasternak* being the Russian word for the vegetable.

did you know?

• Until about the 16th century parsnips were an important part of the European diet, eaten as a savoury vegetable in the way that potatoes are now, but also used in sweet dishes as a cheap alternative to then rare and expensive sugar. After potatoes were introduced from the Americas and sugar became more available, parsnips gradually fell out of favour, and became fodder for animals rather than people. In modern times, they are making a modest comeback in northern Europe, but in southern areas they are still mainly used as fodder, classically in Italy to fatten up pigs whose flesh will eventually become prosciutto.

pea

Peas (*Pisum sativum*) are **legumes**, the seeds of a podded plant native to western Asia. There are three major types: the garden pea, usually sold in pods that contain the small, green seeds or peas; **mangetout**, a special variety with tender green pods that is eaten pods and all; and the field or grey pea, a coarser vegetable, ranging in colour from grey to yellow or green, which is now mostly used as animal fodder although it is also occasionally dried (as such it is called a pulse). Petits pois, normally available frozen rather than fresh, are a dwarf variety of garden pea. The United Kingdom and the United States are the largest suppliers of fresh and frozen peas, while most of those cultivated for drying are produced by Russia and China.

Garden peas freeze well, and since most are frozen within hours of being picked, frozen peas may actually be fresher than most bought fresh. They were among the first vegetables to be canned, although the process destroys their colour, which is usually reintroduced via dye. Almost 90 percent of cultivated peas are sold dried rather than fresh or frozen, either whole, when they will end up wizened and greyish-green in colour, or 'split' mechanically and then dried, in which case they will be yellow or green. Some are rehydrated and then canned (called processed peas) or rehydrated and puréed before canning as 'mushy' peas.

using it Fresh garden peas have a short natural season during summer, although they are occasionally available, already podded, at other times of the year. Pods should be brightly coloured with no discolouring around the tips. Shell and use the peas as quickly after buying as possible.

The basic way to cook fresh peas is in a very little water with some mint for about 5 minutes, but for a more elaborate dish they could be simmered à la française, with small onions, shredded lettuce and a little butter. Whole and split dried peas are rehydrated before being used, traditionally by being soaked overnight, although bringing them to the boil in lots of water and then leaving them for a couple of hours off the heat will do the job too. Both then require long, slow cooking, usually at least an hour, before they are ready to eat.

Peas are a traditional soup vegetable: fresh or frozen peas can be puréed into a delicate soup with milk or cream, and dried whole or split peas can be simmered with ham for a filling main-dish. In addition to being served as an accompaniment, fresh or frozen peas work well in rice, stir-fry or pasta dishes and all types of stews and casseroles.

word origin The pea has only been called pea since about the late 1600s, which was about the time that eating fresh ones first became fashionable. Before then the name was *pise* or *pease* (hence pease pudding) until it was decided (wrongly) that that was a plural word, and the 'se' was dropped. Both forms come from the Greek for the vegetable, *pison*.

potato

A round to oval **vegetable** that originated in what is now Peru in South America, the potato (*Solanum tuberosum*) is a relative of both tobacco and the tomato. Skin colours range from off-white through standard light brown and red to almost black. The flesh is normally creamy white or light yellow, although in one or two varieties it can be deep orange or even purple. In size potatoes range from tiny new Jersey Royals, where one bite and you're finished, to giants that can weigh almost a kilo each.

There are hundreds of varieties, usually divided into two rough categories: 'earlies' or 'new' potatoes (normally smaller, more delicate varieties) and 'maincrops' (larger, starchier ones). Earlies become available in late April or May in Britain and include Home Guard, Epicure and Jersey Royals. Maincrops are harvested during summer and early autumn and stored to keep us going throughout the winter; popular maincrops include King Edward, Desirée, Maris Piper, Golden Wonder, Cara and Pentland Dell. Earlies tend to be waxy in texture, while most (although not all) maincrops are floury.

using it Potatoes should be hard and reasonably unmarked; avoid any that are green-looking – at best this means they are old, at worst they could be poisonous. Earlies will keep for 4–6 days; maincrops for weeks in a cool, dark place. For both, plastic wrappings should be removed before storing, otherwise the potatoes will 'sweat' and become mouldy more quickly.

Potatoes are always cooked before being eaten. Their skin is either scrubbed or peeled off (if possible, leave the skin on as it adds to the flavour and most of the potato's nutrients are just under the skin). The standard ways of cooking are boiling, steaming, roasting, baking, deep-frying and frying, and the choice is often down to texture: floury potatoes tend to disintegrate when boiled but are good roasted, deep-fried, baked or as mash; waxy potatoes keep their shape when boiled or steamed and work well in salads, but don't mash well. All-rounders that can be used in all the basic ways include Desirée, Maris Piper, Cara and King Edward.

Boiling and steaming take 10–20 minutes, depending on size (add the potatoes to boiling water). For roasting, potatoes are usually parboiled first; the cooking time, depending on size, is 30–60 minutes in a moderate oven. Baked potatoes would take about an hour in a hot oven (prick them first to prevent them from bursting). See also **chips**.

Boiled potatoes are often mashed, one of the great comfort foods. Mash can be flavoured in many ways: with garlic (cooked first in a little milk, which should also be added), saffron threads and their soaking mixture, and grated cheese. Potatoes can be mashed with other vegetables too: celeriac, swede, carrot and sweet potato all blend in well. Baked potatoes are normally stuffed with mixtures like butter, soured cream and chives; tuna mayonnaise; grated cheese; baked beans; hummus; and Greek yoghurt and chilli sauce ... almost anything could be used.

The potato is a traditional soup ingredient, most notably with leeks in the classic vichyssoise, and makes good gratins such as gratin dauphinoise (thin potato slices layered with garlic and grated Gruyère cheese, then covered with **béchamel sauce** before being baked). Mashed potato covers fish and shepherd's pies and is a major ingredient of fishcakes. And no picnic is complete without a potato salad (small or diced cooked potatoes tossed with mayonnaise and spring onions or with cooked bacon, frankfurters and/or hard-boiled egg).

word origin Potato comes from the Haitian *batata,* meaning 'sweet potato', which was adopted as *patata* by the first Spaniards who came across them. When ordinary potatoes first arrived in England during late Elizabethan times they looked similar to the already familiar sweet version and were given the same name; 'sweet' was eventually added to orange-fleshed varieties to distinguish them from ordinary potatoes. 'Spud', a popular nickname for potato, comes from a type of spade traditionally used to dig them.

did you know?

• Potatoes were a staple food of the Incas, so Spanish conquistadors were the first Europeans to eat them. The varieties they tasted were small, brown and knobbly so they called them 'truffles', a description taken rather literally at first in Europe (the German word for potato, *kartoffel*, comes from this era and originally meant truffle). Early attempts to popularize potatoes mostly failed: they were believed to cause leprosy and were even said to be poisonous (they are related to deadly nightshade, which may have inspired this). Scottish and Irish Protestants refused to grow them because they weren't mentioned in the Bible; Irish Catholics more pragmatically blessed the seed potatoes with holy water and planted them on Good Friday.

• One thing potatoes did have going for them was that they grew well in almost any temperate climate, so once people got used to them they rapidly became a regular part of the diet wherever they were planted. They were first introduced into Ireland towards the end of the 16th century, and by a century or so later were not only part of the staple diet there, but for the great majority of people, they *were* the staple diet; they literally ate almost nothing else. Then in the 1840s potato blight wiped out the crops, not once but three times. Over a million people died from starvation and another million emigrated, since society at home had virtually broken down. Ireland lost nearly a quarter of its population.

• The potato is a good provider of starchy carbohydrate, and although it doesn't contain particularly high levels of vitamin C and iron, it is eaten so regularly that it is the highest single vegetable

provider of all of these in our diet. New potatoes have higher levels of nutrients than 'old' ones because they are normally eaten sooner after being picked. Boiling in lots of water can destroy up to 50 percent of a potato's water-soluble vitamin C. The rule of thumb to avoid this is to add them to already boiling water, or steam rather than boil, bake rather than stew or cook for a very short time.

potato crisps

An instant snack food made from **potatoes** sliced very thinly, crisps are deep-fried for only as long as it takes to become golden and hard, then preserved and packed into plastic bags. Once upon a time they were mostly flavoured with salt and malt vinegar; nowadays exotic flavourings like barbecue and prawn cocktail are just as common.

using them Crisps are usually served with drinks, particularly in pubs where they sell tons of them (probably because the salty taste combines well with beer and wine – they make you thirstier, you order more drink, so the pub owner is happy). They are also sometimes served with sandwiches or other snack lunches and make good scoops for dips.

did you know?

• During the mid-1850s at a grand hotel in Saratoga Springs in upstate New York, the mega-rich railroad magnate and gourmet Cornelius Vanderbilt kept sending back his potatoes, saying they were cut too thick. The chef, one George Crum, supposedly became so furious that he finally cut them into the thinnest, meanest rounds he could manage and deep-fried them until they were hard and crisp. Thus the potato crisp was born. It is called potato chip in the United States, and sometimes Saratoga chip.

pumpkin

The pumpkin (*Cucurbita pepo*), a giant rounded fruit of the **squash** family, is native to the Americas, but now also produced elsewhere, including various Mediterranean countries. It has thick orange, occasionally yellow or green, skin and golden-orange flesh. It weighs on average around 3kg, although special ones bred for showing have been known to reach 100kg.

using it The pumpkin is a winter squash, available from about October to Christmas. It should be firm and heavy for its size with unmarked bright skin. A whole pumpkin will keep for a couple of months in a cool dry place; halves or quarters should be kept in the refrigerator and used within 10 days.

The centre of a pumpkin contains lots of seeds and fibres or strings that should be removed before cooking (the seeds are edible – hulled, roasted and salted, they make a good snack food). To boil or steam, peel and chop the flesh; cooking time is 12–20 minutes, depending on size. For baking or roasting, leave the skin on; halves cooked in a moderately hot oven take 30–45 minutes.

In chunks, pumpkin is added to stews and curries, and it makes a superb smooth soup. Puréed, it has both sweet and savoury uses: mixed with butter and spices to serve with meat or poultry, or sweetened, spiced and mixed with cream and eggs to make pumpkin pie, the traditional dessert for American Thanksgiving dinner.

word origin Pumpkin comes indirectly from the Greek *pepon,* meaning 'large melon' (another member of the squash family).

similar to that of a pumpkin, although denser. It can be used in the same way as pumpkin.

radicchio

Radicchio (*Cichorium intybus* var. *foliosum*) is a type of small **chicory** with crisp leaves that range from pale pink to deep bronzy red in colour, always with ivory-coloured veins. It can be anything from round to oblong and slightly pointy in shape, and has a characteristic peppery, slightly bitter flavour. Radicchio was developed in northern Italy, still the major producer.

using it Radicchios will keep in the refrigerator for 5–6 days. Before use, discard outer leaves and trim the base, then separate the remaining leaves. They are normally eaten raw, usually as a salad **vegetable**: alone, with other leaves to provide contrast, or as part of a general salad. Mixing radicchio with sweeter ingredients like peppers, orange segments or even a slightly sweetened dressing creates a good sweet-sour taste. Radicchio is also sometimes cooked – grilled in wedges until slightly charred as an accompaniment to plain meats, for instance, or stewed briefly with olive oil, garlic and chilli as a sauce for pasta. It loses its colour when cooked, taking on a brownish green tinge.

word origin Although it has been around since about the 16th century, raddicchio is such a recent arrival in the English-speaking world that we have merely adopted the Italian name rather than creating our own. The Italian word is derived from the Latin *radicula*, meaning 'little root'.

radish

The radish (*Raphanus sativus*) is a small turnip-like root of the **cabbage** family and is native to the Middle East, although it's now widely grown in temperate areas around the world. In shape it can be anything from globular to egg-shaped to long and thin, with skin colour that ranges from pinkish with white tips through red to varieties that are purple or even black. The flesh is crisp, white and juicy with a spicy, peppery taste – not surprising since the radish contains a type of mustard oil just under its skin.

using it There are summer radishes and winter ones, the former being the small vegetable we are most familiar with. Winter radishes are larger, rarer types that include the dramatic-looking black varieties popular in eastern Europe. All radishes should have a good colour and healthy leaves, if they are still attached, and the bulbs should be firm. They will keep in the refrigerator for 4–5 days (remove any leaves first). To use, top and tail summer radishes; peel winter radishes.

The classic way to serve summer radish is still the best: whole, with butter and salt, as an appetite-whetter for the meal to come. Radishes are widely used in mixed salads and of course work well as a garnish. Winter radishes are sometimes cooked (like small new **turnips**) or grated into a rémoulade sauce (see **mayonnaise**).

word origin Radish comes indirectly from the Greek *raphanos,* 'something that rises quickly', a reference to the speed with which it grows.

in India, which grows much larger than western types. Oriental radish is quite mild in flavour and used in dipping sauces, soups and meat dishes.

rocket

Native to the Mediterranean area, rocket (*Eruca sativa*) is a small plant related to watercress and mustard. It is grown for its oval, dark green leaves that have a peppery taste.

using it Rocket leaves should be firm with a good colour; avoid any that are wilting or yellowing. They will keep in the refrigerator for 2–3 days. Before use, the base of the stalk can be trimmed off. Smaller, younger leaves are milder than larger, coarser ones.

Rocket is used in salads to add some bite, and works particularly well with tomatoes and goat's or feta cheese. It can also replace basil in pesto sauce or be used in a sandwich. When briefly cooked, rocket can be part of a stir-fry with other leaves and nuts, or a pasta sauce with garlic and olive oil.

word origin Rocket comes from the French for the plant, *roquette,* which is derived from the first part of the Latin name. The Italians call it *rucola,* from which the Americans get their name for it, arugula.

salad

One classic dictionary description of salad is a 'cold dish of various mixtures of raw or cooked vegetables, usually seasoned with dressing'. That's fine as far as it goes, although it doesn't admit the possibility of a warm salad (*salade tiède*) or one composed entirely of fruit.

Salads can be very simple – just one ingredient such as tomato or asparagus or only green leaves – or a mixture of different ingredients such as lettuce, tomatoes, peppers, cucumber and red onion. Many are more elaborate, substantial ones with fish, meat or beans mixed with vegetables and leaves or a grain. Warm or 'wilted' salads are usually composed of something that is briefly cooked, say goat's cheese or bacon, and added hot to the other (cold) ingredients; or the dressing is warmed before tossing with the salad components. (See also **salad dressings**.)

Classics include Caesar salad (originally cos lettuce, grated Parmesan, garlic, olive oil, Worcestershire sauce and croutons, although a modern 'authentic' one would also include 'coddled' egg); Greek salad (cucumber, tomatoes, black olives and feta cheese); salade niçoise (lettuce, tomato, anchovy, eggs, black olives plus occasionally French beans or artichoke hearts; tuna is also often added); and Waldorf salad (celery, apple, walnuts and mayonnaise).

using it Salads can be served at any point in a meal – as a first course, a main dish, an accompaniment or, in French style, after the main course and before the cheese. When fresh ingredients are used, the nearer to eating the salad is put together, the better it will be. The dressing should enhance, never overwhelm. When lettuces and other salad leaves are included, dress the salad just before serving to prevent it from becoming limp.

word origin Salad comes from the vulgar Latin *salata,* normally used with the word *herba* to mean 'salted herbs'; *salata* itself came from the Latin *sal,* meaning 'salt'.

they gave large quantities of 'saline matter' to the 'poorer inhabitants of our towns'.

sauerkraut

This is a traditional German pickled **cabbage**, made by shredding and layering white cabbage leaves with salt (and sometimes flavourings like juniper berries, caraway seeds and peppercorns), then pressing it down with heavy weights. It is allowed to ferment for up to a month in its own liquid.

using it Outside Germany sauerkraut is usually sold in cans or jars. Once opened, leftovers should be stored in the refrigerator and used within a few days. To use, rinse sauerkraut briefly, then cook for 10–20 minutes (the longer it cooks, the milder and less 'sour' it becomes).

Sauerkraut is normally served hot and goes particularly well with apple, pork, bacon and fatty poultry like goose and duck, both as an accompaniment and as part of a stuffing for the latter two. In the United States it's served with frankfurters (both introduced there by German immigrants), while in France it's teamed with potato, ham knuckle, smoked pork belly and other heavy but optional meats like sausage to make the classic Alsatian dish, choucroute garnie.

word origin Sauerkraut is German for 'sour cabbage'.

shallot

The shallot (*Allium cepa* var. *aggregatum*) originated in central Asia, although it's now produced in temperate areas throughout the world. A small member of the **onion** family of **vegetables**, it is cultivated for its bulbs which grow in small clusters, and can range from greyish to pink or light brown in colour, from round to oval in shape. Like the onion, the small shallot bulb has a papery outer skin that's removed before using. The flesh is usually white and delicate to taste. Although it has a mild version of the characteristic onion smell, the shallot doesn't irritate the eyes when cut.

using it Bulbs should be firm with unblemished skin and no sprouting shoots. They will keep in a cool dark place for 7–10 days. The shallot can be sliced and added raw to salads, but it is mostly cooked – adding subtle flavour to classic French sauces such as **béarnaise**, for example. It can also be baked as a garnish for roasts and used instead of pearl onions in recipes.

word origin The word comes (via the Old French *eschalotte*) from *Askalon*, a town in ancient Palestine; the vegetable was once thought to have originated there.

soya bean

The soya bean (*Glycine max*) is the seed of an annual **legume** native to northern China. It is now grown in warm temperate climates throughout the world, and major suppliers include the United States, which grows more than half the world crop, China and Brazil. The plant can grow to about 1m in height and has oval downy pods that usually carry 2–4 pea-sized round or oval seeds. Depending on the variety, the seeds (beans) can be yellow, green, brown, black or speckled.

Some soya beans are dried or canned, but most are made into something else. In terms of quantity, the major type of processing is solvent extraction: the seeds are cleaned and dehusked, crushed into flakes and then 'washed' with a solvent to extract a crude oil, which is further refined in various ways. The residue left after the oil is removed is soya meal, which can be heated and manufactured into various other forms like flour, grits or cream. Soya beans are also sprouted into a type of beansprout (see **mung bean**), or made into soya milk by being soaked, crushed with water and then boiled and filtered; thickened soya milk is the basis for **tofu**.

In Asia, a whole range of condiments is produced from soya beans that have been fermented by being treated with the mould *Aspergillus oryzae*. **Soy sauce** is the best known, but others include Chinese specialities like salted black beans, where the fermented beans are dried at very high temperatures, which blacken them. Fermented beans are made into several thick sauces, such as black bean sauce (flavoured with ginger, garlic and oil); hoisin sauce (a sweet-and-spicy mixture flavoured with garlic, chilli and sesame oil); and Chinese barbecue sauce (normally hoisin sauce mixed with a little tomato purée).

One of the most popular Japanese fermented soya products is miso paste, traditionally made by blending prepared beans with a *koji* or starter mould grown on a grain of some sort (usually rice or barley), then ageing the mixture for 1–3 years. *Kome-miso* is the most common rice-based miso, *mugi-miso* is barley-based, and *hatcho-miso*, a very superior (and expensive) type, is made from soya beans alone. As a rough rule of thumb, the darker the paste the stronger-tasting (and saltier) it will be.

using it The bland-tasting dried soya beans should be soaked in the same way as other dried beans, and will take 3–6 hours to cook. Sprouted soya beans can be used like mung bean sprouts. Soya flour has more protein than other flours but doesn't contain gluten and therefore needs to be mixed with wheat flour in yeasted baked goods, particularly breads, although it could be used on its own for batters or to thicken sauces. Soya milk is used in the same way as cow's milk and makes a good substitute for those who are lactose-intolerant or vegan. Refined soya oil is rich in polyunsaturated fats and has a very high 'smoke point' (see **oils**), so is widely used in cooking.

Of the various fermented soya products, miso paste is a staple flavouring in Japanese cookery, used with dashi stock to make a soup drunk more or less throughout the day (including breakfast) and as a marinade for grilled or roasted meats; more generally, it can be added to dipping sauces, especially for seafood or poultry, used (with oil or a little stock) to dress vegetables, or instead of salt. Fermented black beans on their own can be crushed and added in small quantities to Chinese-style savoury dishes, especially seafood and poultry. Black bean sauce is a common flavouring for stir-fries and Szechuan and Hunan dishes; it was once the traditional accompaniment to Peking duck, although hoisin sauce is more common now. Hoisin and barbecue sauces are also added to stir-fries as well as being used as a marinade ingredient for spareribs and other grilled and roasted meats.

Various versions of soya beans or its derivatives are used throughout the food and other industries. Soya flour, grits and cream, for instance, are used to bulk out processed meats like sausages, in baked goods, baby foods and breakfast cereals; soya milk is the basis of all sorts of vegan 'dairy foods' like yoghurt and ice-cream; and the high protein content of soya meal (it has about five times more than maize) makes it a favourite ingredient in feed for animals and pets. Various grades of soya oil are also used by the food industry to make commercial mayonnaise, ice-cream, margarine and baked goods, and by other industries to make (among other things) disinfectants, soaps, candles, cosmetics and textiles.

There is even a meat substitute that is usually made from soya beans. Called TVP (textured vegetable protein), it is made by extracting proteins from soya flour or concentrate, then chemically treating it to look and taste like meat. It had a brief vogue as a supermarket food, but is now probably more widely used in the food industry than by individual shoppers, primarily as an extender in meat-based ready-made dishes and fake 'meat' vegetarian products such as shepherd's pie.

The different soya products have differing storage requirements: milk, for instance, which is sold in cartons, should be refrigerated unless it's longlife; use fresh soya milk within 5–7 days. Most of the fermented soya products, which are available in tubes, jars or cans, will keep indefinitely, although some need to be kept in the refrigerator once opened.

word origin Soya comes from the Dutch *soja*, which is derived from the Japanese *shoyu*, meaning 'soy sauce'; the Japanese word can be traced back to *jiangyou*, the Cantonese word for 'salted beans in oil'.

did you know?

• Soya beans have been cultivated in China for at least 5000 years, and were being fermented into various condiments by the time of the Han Dynasty in about the 2nd century BC; they were taken to the rest of Asia and Japan by the Chinese, possibly by Buddhist monks. In many parts of Asia, they are still a staple food in one form or other (or several), providing protein in diets that contain no meat or relatively little, at least by western standards (soya beans contain more protein than other legumes).

• Although they were introduced into Europe during

the 17th century, soya beans didn't reach the United States until about a century later and only became an important crop after the Second World War. During the last few years, along with maize, they have been genetically modified on a large scale there, usually by being programmed to be more tolerant to herbicides (chemical weedkillers) so that they are easier to grow and provide an increased crop. A large proportion of the available agricultural land is given over to GM beans, and these beans go into most of the food (and other) products for which soya beans there are produced

spinach

Spinach (*Spinacia oleracea*) is a **vegetable** with bright to dark green oval leaves, short slender stalks and a bitter-sweet taste. It originated in Persia, but is now grown throughout the world. Spinach beet, an alternative name for chard, is actually a type of **beetroot** cultivated for its leaves rather than its bulb.

using it Leaves should be brightly coloured and crisp, and used as soon as possible after buying since they can wilt and become slimy quickly. Spinach needs a good rinse before being used.

Raw spinach, torn into pieces if the leaves are large, is very good as a salad, alone or with other ingredients like mushrooms, bacon, broad or green beans and sweet peppers. To cook, put the rinsed leaves into a pan, without extra water, and cook for 2–4 minutes or until wilted, then drain well.

Spinach is a common ingredient in Asian curries, oriental stir-fries and various Greek dishes (including the filo-pastry pie spanakopitta, where it's mixed with feta cheese as the filling). It is also used as the basis for any French or Italian dish described as 'florentine'. More generally it has a special affinity with eggs, makes a good **quiche** filling and is often teamed with ricotta cheese as a filling for pasta too. As a vegetable, it is delicious puréed, often enriched with cream or soured cream, and

seasoned with nutmeg, which brings out its sweetness.

word origin Spinach probably comes from the Old Persian for the vegetable, *aspanakh*.

• It was the Arabs who introduced spinach into Europe when they conquered southern areas of it from about the 8th century, but it seems to have been slow to catch on, only reaching England during Tudor times. Initially, spinach was used in sweet as well as savoury cooking, in particular with eggs, honey, spices and occasionally almonds to make a filling for sweet pies.
• Popeye ate spinach voluntarily, but one of the main reasons that generations of children were 'encouraged' to eat it is because it's full of iron. This isn't the whole story, however, since the iron that is in plant foods such as spinach is harder to absorb than iron from animal sources. To get the best from it nutritionally, it should either be eaten raw, or teamed with other foods rich in vitamin C like citrus fruits and peppers.

spring onion

Grown in temperate areas throughout the world, the spring onion (*Allium cepa*) is a delicately flavoured, immature **onion**, picked before the bulb has had time to develop. It is cultivated as much for its thin, hollow, green stem-like leaves as it is for its small white bulb.

using it Despite its name, the spring onion is available all year round. It should have a crisp stem with a good colour and no soft spots, particularly near the tips. It can be kept in the refrigerator for 4–6 days.

In western countries, although spring onion is occasionally cooked, it's normally served raw: chopped into summer salads, shredded over cooked dishes (or uncooked ones) as a garnish, finely chopped into mayonnaise-based fillings for sandwiches and jacket potatoes, or shredded into mashed potatoes with some milk and butter to make a classic Irish champ. It can also be substituted for **shallots** in delicate sauces or stocks, or added to fishcakes or **quiches** as part of the filling. It goes particularly well with crab, cream cheese, sweet peppers and tomatoes.

In oriental cooking, and particularly in China and Japan, a type of spring onion called Welsh onion (*Allium fistulosum*) is used in stir-fries, with ginger as part of dipping sauces, as a garnish for steamed dim sum or fish dishes, or snipped into clear broths. The varieties commonly available in the West can be substituted in these dishes.

word origin The name describes what the vegetable traditionally was: an onion harvested in spring before its bulb had had a chance to mature. Welsh onion has nothing to do with Wales and comes from the Anglo-Saxon word *welise,* meaning 'foreign'.

did you know?

• In the United States a spring onion is sometimes called a scallion, which comes from the same root as the shallot (a relative) – the ancient Middle Eastern city of Askalon, which was at one time thought to be the place where both originated. The American word was used to describe a spring onion in Britain up until the 19th century.

squash

This is a collective name for fruit of the *Cucurbitaceae* family of gourds that originated in the Americas and are used as **vegetables**. There are several species, notably *Cucurbita pepo*, *Cucurbita maxima* and *Cucurbita moshata*, and two main types: summer squash, which includes **courgettes**, **marrows** and patty pan squash, and winter squash, which includes **pumpkins**, acorn squash and butternut squash.

Most summer squash are immature versions of winter ones: they are taken off the plant earlier, and have soft seeds, thinnish skin that ranges in colour from green to yellow, and flesh that can vary from white to pale yellow. Winter squash are normally bigger and brighter, with thick skin that can be anything from yellow to glorious red-gold, and flesh that's firmer and often sweeter and more brightly coloured too. Many winter squash have large hard seeds, some of which (like pumpkin) are edible.

using it Squash should feel heavy and have bright, unblemished skin. Both summer and winter ones keep reasonably well, anywhere from about a week or so to a couple of months or more, depending on the individual type; summer squash are usually refrigerated, while winter squash can be kept in a cool dry place.

All varieties are cooked before they're eaten, with winter squash in general requiring longer, slower cooking than summer squash (see individual entries). Acorn squash are a good size to halve, stuff and bake; small patty pan squash can either be steamed whole for 5–8 minutes, or sliced and stir-fried.

word origin Squash comes from the American Algonquian word *askuta-squash*, meaning 'eaten green', i.e. before it's too mature or ripe.

did you know?

• Squash of one type or another was a staple food of many Native Americans and was also used medicinally – ground up and cooked for 'female ailments' and used generally as a diuretic. It was introduced into Europe by returning Spanish explorers, but while some squash like pumpkin became popular in a modest way quite quickly, most have only become reasonably available during the past 10–20 years.
• The shape of squashes has always lent itself to many non-cooking as well as cooking uses, of which

the Hallowe'en jack o'lantern pumpkin is probably the most famous. But at various points in history, different types of squash have been used as drinking or serving bowls, cooking utensils, musical instruments and even penis guards.

swede

The swede (*Brassica napus*) is probably a hybrid of the **cabbage** and the **turnip**, and often confused with the latter – what's called swede in southern England is known as turnip in Scotland. Swede in the English sense is a large swollen stem base rather than a true root vegetable (in fact, it's the base of the plant that provides oilseed rape). It has tough brownish-purple skin with a series of raised rings at its top end, and hard, pale yellow flesh.

using it Swede should be hard, with a good colour and will keep in a cool dark place for about a week. It's always cooked before being eaten: the basic method is to peel, cut into pieces and boil for about 15 minutes until tender. To be a vegetable accompaniment, it is then normally puréed or mashed and flavoured with butter and nutmeg, or sometimes combined with mashed potato. It can also be added to winter soups, stews and casseroles.

word origin Turnip-rooted cabbages were developed in central Europe and from there made their way to Sweden and then on to Britain during the 17th century. This is probably why they were originally called 'Swedish turnips', before settling into the friendlier swede.

sweetcorn

Sweetcorn is a type of **maize** used fresh as a **vegetable**. It grows as long seedheads or 'ears' of bright yellow or white kernels that cling to a thick central stem (the cob) and are protected by tough greenish leaves called husks. In most cases, sweetcorn should be cooked as soon as possible,

since its sugar starts to turn to starch the moment it is picked – the traditional advice to 'pick slowly, then run home and cook quickly' is still usually true. The exception to this is the new supersweet hybrids that remain sweet and non-starchy for longer. Baby corn are tiny ears picked when they are still immature.

using it Ideally buy sweetcorn still in the husk, which should look fresh and have plump kernels; avoid those with droopy, wilting husks and many missing or discoloured kernels. To boil, strip off the husks and trailing strings (the 'silk'), then cook whole for 8–10 minutes (you can check for tenderness by prodding a kernel with the tip of a knife). Serve 'corn on the cob' with butter (plain or flavoured) plus salt and pepper. Corn on the cob can also be barbecued, either cooked still in its husks or 'shucked' and wrapped in foil.

Kernels can be scraped off the cob, to be braised with peas, red peppers or mushrooms, creamed, used in soup, or added to a pancake batter to make fritters. Cooked kernels are an excellent salad or sandwich filling ingredient (they are often added to tuna mayonnaise, for instance). Baby corn is often added to stir-fries.

did you know?

• Maize was the staple grain of all the great native American cultures, including the Aztecs and Incas, and has been cultivated for several thousand years. Sweetcorn is much more recent, however, and was only developed in the United States from other types of maize after the Civil War in the mid-1800s.

sweet pepper

This is the mild-tasting hollow fruit of a plant (*Capsicum annuum*) that also produces **chilli pepper**. It originated in Central America but is now grown in warmer areas throughout the world.

Sweet peppers are usually bell-shaped

and four-lobed, but the colour can range from green through yellow, orange and red to almost black, depending on how long the individual pepper matures on the plant (the more mature the pepper is, the sweeter it will taste): if green, the pepper was picked when immature; if yellow or orange, the pepper was left to ripen a little longer; and if red, the pepper was completely ripe. Black peppers are similar in taste to green and in fact turn green if left to ripen long enough. Other varieties are occasionally available too, like the long, tapering thin-skinned romano or ramiro. Another thin-skinned type, which varies in taste from mild to pungent, is ground up to make **paprika**.

using it Sweet peppers should be firm and glossy with a good colour; avoid any that are blotchy or wrinkling. They will keep in the refrigerator for 5–7 days.

Peppers are used raw, usually to add crunch to salads, and cooked. They are often grilled or roasted until the skin is black and blistering, when it can easily be removed to leave smoky-flavoured flesh. Prepared like this, peppers make a good appetizer with olive oil and flavouring herbs, or can be puréed with olive oil, garlic and herbs into a dip or salsa. Sliced or chopped sweet pepper is added to rice and pasta dishes, and summer stews such as ratatouille. The hollow shape makes it good for stuffing, either whole (stalk end cut off) or halved lengthways, and then baking.

word origin The sweet pepper acquired the 'pepper' part of its name from Columbus and his crew. They had set off in 1492, after all, to find pepper, and they believed they had found a reasonable substitute when they came across a hotter member of the *Capsicum* family. The 'sweet' part was probably added later to distinguish these peppers from the chilli varieties. Sweet peppers weren't such an instant hit as chilli types and it's only in the last 50 years or so that they have become popular in the English-speaking world.

sweet potato

The sweet potato (*Ipomoea batatas*) is not related to the ordinary **potato**, although both originated in tropical America; major modern producers include various parts of the Americas and Australasia. Yam, another **vegetable** often confused with sweet potato, is also from a different genus of plants, and comes from another part of the world, being native to South-east Asia and Africa.

Although it's similar in general appearance to the ordinary potato, the sweet potato is usually more elongated in shape, with a skin colour that ranges from off-white to deep warm red. The flesh can be anything from light beige to bright orange, and firm or soft. The taste, although starchy, is much sweeter than ordinary potato. Yam flesh is whiter than that of sweet potato and even starchier.

using it Sweet potatoes should be firm and have a good colour; avoid any with soft patches or blemishes. They can be stored for about a week or so in a cool dry place.

Sweet potato can be used in the same ways as ordinary potato, that is, boiled, mashed, baked, roasted or deep-fried as chips. Its natural sweetness makes it particularly versatile, as it can also be puréed and sweetened to use as a dessert pie filling. Even when served as a vegetable, it is often flavoured with spices like nutmeg or cinnamon and 'candied' with brown sugar and butter. In the West Indies, where sweet potato is part of the staple diet, it is added to bean and other casseroles, but also made into a pudding with desiccated coconut, coconut milk, nutmeg and lime. Yam can be used in the same way as sweet potato.

• The sweet potato comes from what is now Peru and has been cultivated there for over 2000 years. From Peru it spread to Central America and the Caribbean, and at some point during early medieval times (and before Europeans discovered the Americas), early sailors carried it westwards to Polynesia and New Zealand. The first Europeans to come across it were Columbus and his crew in 1492 and it was the Spanish who introduced it into Europe – before the ordinary potato in fact. In Tudor England it was believed to be an aphrodisiac, and it reached the heights of chic in post-revolutionary France when the empress Josephine (a native of Martinique in the Caribbean) began to grow it in her garden at Malmaison near Paris.

tofu

Also known as bean curd, this is a very bland, white cake-like product that is high in protein and low in fat. It is made by processing **soya beans** into a thick milk, then boiling it before a curdling agent like calcium sulphate (gypsum), calcium chloride or, sometimes in Japan, nigari extract (a type of magnesium chloride) is added. The mixture is then left until it separates into curds and whey (in the same way as **cheese**), when it's drained and pressed to remove the whey. The proportion of water to beans in the initial soya milk mixture, the type and amount of curdling agent used, and the length of pressing of the curds are all variable, and help to determine the texture and firmness of the final tofu.

Tofu can be firm (similar to a cheese such as feta) or soft (more like yoghurt or crème fraîche). Silken tofu is more finely strained to create a smoother texture. Tofu is also sometimes fermented, by being inoculated with a yeast-like mould, allowed to 'rest' for a few days to allow the mould to do its work and then left in a brine solution for anything up to six months; it is then sold as white fermented bean curd (cubes submerged in ingredients like rice wine, salt, sesame oil and, optionally, chilli) and red fermented bean curd (cubes submerged in a brine that includes red rice, uncooked rice treated with a natural dye).

In Asia and in oriental supermarkets elsewhere, tofu is sold fresh in large blocks stored in water or whey, and divided up as appropriate into smaller squares at sale, or as prepared smaller blocks stored in the same solution in airtight tubs. In supermarkets and other western stores, it's normally freeze-dried before being packed, either in blocks or cubes, plain, flavoured or occasionally smoked.

using it Fresh tofu should be stored in the refrigerator and used within a day or so of purchase. Tofu in airtight tubs will keep for about a month, but should be refrigerated after opening; most other types should also be refrigerated and used within a week or so, although some long-lasting dried versions will keep for several months.

Soft and silken tofus don't just look like yoghurt and crème fraîche, they can be used like them too. Firm tofu is normally cooked by steaming, stir-frying or deep-frying. Cooking times depend on size – a 7.5cm square about 3cm thick will take 5–8 minutes to steam, 3–5 minutes to braise in a sauce.

In Japan, firm tofu is finely cubed and added to delicate soups or used to flavour noodle or rice dishes; in China it's used in stir-fries and vegetarian dishes, while softer types are used in sauces and dressings, particularly for vegetables. More generally, firm tofu could be made into vegetarian kebabs, and various types could be added to meat or vegetarian stews or casseroles, mashed into vegan scrambled 'eggs' or used instead of dairy products in pies and creamy desserts. Being so bland, tofu will go with virtually anything, but it has a particular affinity with strong flavours like chilli, ginger, curry and Worcestershire sauce. Fermented bean curd, relatively rare in the West, is used as an accompaniment to rice in China or, in the case of red bean curd, for long-cooked pork dishes.

Commercially, tofu is nearly as popular as soya meal, grits and oil with the food industry, and is used to make vegan ice-cream, dips and cheese, as well as burgers and sausages.

word origin Tofu is Japanese, and comes from the Mandarin Chinese word *doufu,* meaning 'spoiled beans'.

did you know?

- Tofu is Chinese in origin although it isn't clear when it first appeared; the popular view is that it was created during the Han Dynasty, about a hundred years or so before the birth of Christ, although there is no record of its existence until almost a thousand years later. The Chinese introduced it into Japan, where it became popular with the spread of Buddhism, which favoured vegetarianism as part of its philosophy.

tomato

The tomato (*Lycopersicon esculentum*) is technically a **fruit** – from a plant of the nightshade family (relatives include the potato and sweet pepper) – but it is used as a **vegetable**. There are over 1000 different varieties, ranging in size from tiny 'cherries' to large 'beefsteaks', and in colour from the standard red through golden yellow to green. Although most are round in shape, the popular cooking tomato, 'plum', is oval. Tomatoes grow on thick branches called vines, and the longer they are allowed to mature on them, the sweeter and richer-tasting (on average) they will be. This is why some modern tomatoes advertise themselves as 'vine-ripened', meaning they have been allowed to stay on their vines for longer than usual (most tomatoes are picked early and ripened away from them).

using it Tomatoes should be firm with a rich unblemished colour; avoid those with soft spots since it means they are too ripe. They will keep in the refrigerator for 4–6 days, although this will depend on how ripe they were when bought. If refrigerated, let them come to room temperature before eating.

Tomatoes are eaten raw and cooked. For the latter, the skins can be removed by immersing the tomatoes in boiling water for about 45 seconds; if the skin isn't already coming away from the flesh when they are removed from the water, a quick slash with a knife should release it. Both pulp and seeds are normally used, although occasional recipes call for the seeds to be removed too. Fresh raw tomatoes are the archetypal salad ingredient, by themselves, as part of a more elaborate mixed salad or with one or two other ingredients like mozzarella, avocado, red onion and basil. For cooking, plum is the variety usually recommended, and is the preferred option for stews, casseroles and especially pasta sauces. Tomato-based sauces can be plain (with only herbs and maybe garlic added) or fancy, when other ingredients like onion, white wine, ricotta, peas, bacon, mushrooms or aubergine are mixed in.

Beefsteak tomatoes cook well too, especially hollowed out and stuffed for baking. Roasting is another good way with tomatoes: halve, sprinkle with olive oil and garlic, and cook in a low oven for about 1½ hours to bring out their inherent sweetness. Prepared like this, they can be used as a pasta sauce, to flavour couscous or risotto, and as a starter with goat's cheese. Cooked or raw tomatoes can also be the basis of salsas to partner grilled fish, kebabs or steaks, and make a good snack food too: sliced and raw in sandwiches, on their own or teamed with ingredients like cheese or bacon; cooked to a thick paste, then spread like jam over toasted French bread; or (for small cherry tomatoes) hollowed out and filled with dips like taramasalata or guacamole.

Tomatoes are also canned, whole or

chopped, made into juice or purée/paste, strained and bottled as passata, or dried, particularly sun-dried, to concentrate their flavour. The most popular processed form of tomato is probably **ketchup**, a condiment that has many culinary uses.

word origin Tomato comes from *tomatl*, which in Nahuatl (the language of the Aztecs) meant 'plump fruit'. The first ones to arrive in Europe were golden in colour and round in shape, which gave rise to what is close to the word still used for tomato in Italy, *pomo d'oro*, or golden apple. In France it was originally *pomme d'or,* but somewhere along the line its membership of the nightshade family, which included aphrodisiac plants as well as poisonous ones, led to its being renamed *pomme d'amour* or love apple. And love apple was one of the early alternative names for tomato in English.

• Tomatoes originated in what is now Peru. They started out as a cornfield weed, spread northwards into what is now Mexico, and became part of the staple diet of the Aztecs, who introduced them to Spanish conquistadors. Returning Spaniards brought them to Europe where at first they were greeted with great suspicion. Red tomatoes were introduced during the 18th century.

truffle

The truffle is not only one of the most expensive foods in the world; in terms of desirability it probably outranks all the others, even gourmet treats like **caviar**. About 70 varieties grow around Europe and America, but only two are truly sought after, both of them European. The white truffle (*Tuber magnatum*) comes primarily from Piedmont in northern Italy. The black truffle (*Tuber melanosporum*), actually black with white-streaked flesh, is found in Spain and Italy, although it reaches perfection in

France, especially in the Périgord, an area in the southern part of the country that is almost synonymous with it.

Unlike most other fungi, truffles grow underground, and they grow slowly, taking several months to ripen to maturity during late autumn and winter under the sheltering branches of oak, chestnut, hazel and beech trees. Despite attempts to cultivate them, most are still found wild, and obtaining them is now closely regulated and licensed. Since they are difficult to spot on the surface of the ground, help is needed to locate them and this usually takes the form of specially trained pigs or dogs, the latter being preferred since they tend to be less keen to hang onto the prize once they find it. The idea is that they sniff out the scent, thus leading the hunter to the truffle, which he or she then digs up if it's ripe.

using it Because it's worth its weight in gold, the truffle is now used with discretion and most of us will come into contact with it canned or preserved rather than fresh. However, for the record, a fresh one should be (carefully!) wiped clean and black ones peeled (keep and use the peelings). Black truffles can be used cooked or raw. White truffles should never be cooked – it is enough to warm them just by adding them to hot food. Truffle oil, a few shavings preserved in olive oil, or peelings in tiny cans are the most affordable forms, although even they are expensive. For those who win the lottery, slightly larger cans containing a single whole black or white truffle can also be found sometimes.

The truffle has an extraordinary aroma and taste, and seems to create some sort of magic fusion with everything it's added to or served with: scrambled eggs or omelette, **risotto** or a special pâté, for instance. Shaved over pasta that has been bathed in good olive oil, it is heaven on a plate. Truffle oil might not be as good as peelings or slices, but it is better than nothing, especially sprinkled over pasta, rice, eggs and vegetables.

word origin Truffle probably comes, via French, from the Latin *tuber* meaning 'swelling', one way of describing the small knobbly, slightly slimy exterior; *tuber terrae*, literally 'swellings of the ground', was the Latin name for it.

• The ancient Egyptians and Romans ate truffles smothered in goose fat and believed them to be therapeutic. Truffles were, in fact, much more numerous in antiquity, and even up to the end of the 19th century were easier to find than they are now (they might be one of the more bizarre victims of modern deforestation). As a result they were used with gay abandon, and not just in French classic cooking: Mrs Beeton's recipe for 'Truffles au Naturel' recommends a serving of 8oz (225g) per person. Their aphrodisiac qualities have always been hinted at, and a little truffle is still believed to help love along.

turnip

The turnip (*Brassica rapa*) is a member of the **cabbage** family of **vegetables** and is closely related to the **swede**, with which it is often confused. In fact, what's called turnip in Scotland is known as swede elsewhere in the United Kingdom. Like the swede, the English turnip is a swollen stem base rather than a true root vegetable, but in this case the base in question is either a small, delicate off-white bulb (spring turnip or navet) or a larger, yellow-green one with pale flesh (winter turnip).

using it Spring turnips have a natural season in spring while, as the name suggests, larger types are available during winter; both are found occasionally at other times of the year. Store them in a cool dry place: spring turnips for 3–4 days and winter turnip for about a week.

To cook spring turnips, peel and steam whole for 5 minutes or so, and serve as a vegetable accompaniment. They can also be roasted, skin and all, and served with meat, especially duck, pork and chicken, or cooked in the French way, as part of a spring lamb stew with other new vegetables. If they are really fresh, spring turnips can be sliced thinly or grated raw into oriental-style or mixed salads. Winter turnip tastes similar to swede and can be cooked and used in the same way.

word origin In Anglo-Saxon times turnip was called *noep*, from the Latin for the vegetable, *napus*, also the origin of the Scots word *neep*. The second part of the modern word comes from the same source, but where the first part came from is uncertain although it may be a reference to its 'turned' shape.

vegetable

Vegetables are herbaceous plants or parts of herbaceous plants that are cultivated as food. They include root vegetables (e.g. **carrots** and **parsnips**), tubers (swollen underground parts of stems, such as **potatoes**), stem vegetables (**asparagus** and **celery**), green-leaved vegetables (**spinach** and **lettuce**), flowerheads (**cauliflower** and **broccoli**), berries (such as **aubergines**), and legumes (podded, such as **green beans**, or the contents of pods like **peas**). They also include **tomatoes** and **squash**, which are technically fruit, and **mushrooms**, which are edible fungi.

Most fresh vegetables are raised conventionally. This means that the soil they are grown in and the plants themselves will be treated with chemical herbicides (to control weeds) and pesticides (to get rid of pests and diseases). Those sold as organic are usually certified in the same way as **poultry**, and the most stringent accreditation body demands that vegetables are cultivated as part of a rotating crop system; herbicides are banned and usually only plant-based pesticides are permitted.

Nearly all fresh vegetables can be frozen to preserve them. Many are frozen commercially before being sold, in fact, and, since they are usually frozen quickly after being harvested, can be a good alternative to fresh. Canning is another way to preserve them and while most canned vegetables don't taste as good as their fresh counterparts, they can be convenient. Drying and pickling are older preserving methods, and a few vegetables are still popular in this form: dried **beans** and mushrooms, for instance, and pickled **gherkins** and **sauerkraut**.

using it As growing plants, all vegetables have their natural season, but thanks to global trade and refrigeration, among other things, most are now available fresh for most of the year. Storage times vary from type to type (see individual entries). Preparation is individual too, but in general vegetables should be rinsed rather than soaked before being used (to avoid losing water-soluble vitamins, especially vitamin C) and those to be peeled should be peeled as near to their surface as possible since many nutrients are located just under it. Green vegetables shouldn't be overcooked: the phrase *al dente* ('to the tooth'), usually applied to pasta, is appropriate here too – keeping them a bit firm helps to retain the basic taste as well as more of their goodness.

Vegetables are served raw or cooked, mainly as a savoury food rather than as a sweet one (there are a few exceptions, such as carrot cake and pumpkin pie). And, although this is now changing, in the western world vegetables have traditionally been used in a supporting role: as a first course, as an accompaniment to meat or fish, part of a meat, fish, pasta or rice dish, or as a salad. In some other cultures things are different, however:

many Hindus and Buddhists don't eat meat or fish for religious reasons and as a result there is a rich tradition of Asian main-dish vegetable cooking.

word origin Vegetable comes from the Latin *vegetare,* meaning 'to be active', rather ironic when you consider phrases like 'he's a vegetable' (has lost control of his mental and physical capacities) and 'she's vegetating' (living passively, and not to her full potential).

did you know?

• While Fred and the other male Flintstones were out hunting, the chances are that their womenfolk were gathering wild plants, the ancestors of today's cultivated vegetables and herbs. Grain-producing grasses were probably the first to be 'tamed' as crops, but vegetables like peas and beans followed soon after and added variety to the diet.

• Armies march on their stomachs, and soldiers are usually a conservative lot, preferring their native foods to foreign stuff. Armies of conquest and occupation throughout history, therefore, have taken seeds and plants with them to ensure a regular supply of their favourite foods. So the Romans didn't just build roads and baths in their empire, they introduced vegetables like onions and cabbage. Later, the same thing happened in Spain when North African Moors conquered and settled there, introducing previously unknown vegetables like cauliflower and spinach as they did so. Columbus didn't trust the local food either, which is how America was introduced to aubergines among other delights, although such contributions were dwarfed by the enormous range of unknown edible plants that were brought back to Europe from the New World, such as potatoes, tomatoes and beans. More recently modern transportation has done peacefully what marauding armies and colonists did previously, so vegetables like okra are shipped from one end of the planet to the other and arrive still fresh enough to eat.

• Being low in fat and rich in vitamins and minerals, vegetables are an important part of a healthy diet. Their role in preventing disease, in particular some of the modern scourges like heart disease and cancer, is also being increasingly recognized. Perhaps not surprisingly, therefore, we are urged to eat at least five portions of vegetables and fruit a day (about 400g edible weight, in total) to maintain good health and well-being.

watercress

Watercress (*Nasturtium officinale*) is a member of the mustard family of **vegetables** and is a close relative of the cress that is sold with mustard seedlings as **mustard and cress**. Native to the Middle East, it grows wild in both temperate Europe and Asia now, although with modern levels of pollution, it's not advisable to eat wild watercress unless you know something about the environment in which it has grown. The strong green, heart-shaped leaves have a distinctive peppery taste and are cultivated in fields submerged in fast-flowing, clean water.

using it Leaves should be fresh and dark-coloured; avoid any bunches with paler leaves or yellowing tips and a slightly wilted feel. Watercress will keep in the refrigerator for about a week, standing in water or, if that isn't possible, in an airtight plastic bag. Before use, trim off any thick stalks.

Although it is cooked occasionally to make a creamy soup, either by itself or with potatoes, watercress loses some of its distinctive taste when heated and so is normally eaten raw. Finely chopped, it can be used in a sandwich filling, pounded into butter to make a good accompaniment for chops and game, or added to mayonnaise to become sauce verte, a medieval favourite still sometimes served with salmon. And of course it's lavishly used with almost any kind of dish as a garnish: you name it, watercress decorates it. It's most commonly used now as a salad vegetable, giving extra zest and some welcome deep colour to a mixed leaf salad, combining well with orange or apple segments and sweet onion rings for an interesting first course, or mixed with red peppers, chopped walnuts and tomatoes into a festive Christmas salad.

word origin Cress comes from the Latin *crescere*, meaning 'to grow', a reference to the speed with which watercress matures. The Latin name for it, *nasturtium*, comes from *nasus tortus* or 'twisted nose', perhaps the description of a possible reaction to the strength of its taste.

did you know?

- The medicinal qualities of watercress have been appreciated for centuries. Both the Romans and Anglo-Saxons believed that eating it regularly could avert baldness, while in Tudor England it was used as a cure for toothache. Modern medical opinion is just as enthusiastic, and recent research suggests that the antioxidants it contains (vitamin C and beta-carotene) can also protect against cancer.

Fruit

I was never formally taught to cook, and at school I was put down for Latin instead of biology. So until I had to learn to look after myself, in my early twenties, I really knew nothing about food or nutrition.

When I did begin to piece together a few facts about eating, the biggest surprise by far was fruit. I could have guessed that sausages were high in fat and that cakes and buns piled on the pounds. But how could it be that such glorious indulgences as crunchy Cox's apples, aromatic English strawberries, juicy oranges and tangy, fresh pineapple were not sinful in any way?

Food gets ever more complex and sophisticated, and there's a tendency to forget that some of the most wonderful treats of all need no cooking and no clever

No elaborate pâtisserie confection can compete with a ripe mango in its prime.
Orlando Murrin

technical preparation – sometimes you don't even have to peel them. No mousse, gâteau or ice-cream is a match for a dish of plump, fresh raspberries. No elaborate pâtisserie confection can compete with a ripe mango in its prime.

We are so lucky in the United Kingdom to grow fresh fruit in abundance. For me, home-grown has to be best, and in summer and autumn I protest whenever I encounter imposters from abroad. (My real bugbear is 'spoiler' crops, imported a couple of weeks before the English equivalent is ready, in order to drive down the price of the real thing.) In winter and spring, however, I enjoy imported exotica from warmer climes – citrus fruit from Africa, Israel and Spain, pineapples and bananas from the West Indies and Central America. The southern hemisphere also allows us to enjoy an extra season of apples, pears and plums from New Zealand and South America – a welcome change in the darker months.

I hope this section will widen your understanding of fruit and put it where it belongs – at the heart of the food lover's experience.

Orlando Murrin

apple

The apple (*Malus pumila*) is the **fruit** of a tree of the rose family, a close relative of the pear and more distantly connected to the apricot, cherry and almond. Apple trees grow in temperate regions throughout the world, although they probably originated in Europe or western Asia; major producers include Britain, France, the United States and Australasia. Apples are pomes, fruit whose cores are divided into small compartments, each of which contains one or more seeds.

There are over 8000 varieties, although only about a hundred or so are available commercially. Fruits vary in colour from yellow through green and red to brown with various shadings in between, and in size from golf ball to baby cabbage; the flesh is usually white, although a few varieties have rosy tinges. In Great Britain, apples are categorized as cookers or eaters (also called dessert apples). This distinction isn't used anywhere else and, in fact, many eating varieties cook well too. Special types are also grown to make **cider**.

Cooking apples are green-skinned and have tart flesh that doesn't disintegrate too much during cooking. Bramley's Seedling and Grenadier are the best-known varieties. Eating apples include Braeburn, developed in New Zealand during the 1980s, with yellowish-red skin and crisp flesh; Golden Delicious, with pale yellowish-green skin and unremarkable flesh; Red Delicious, with thick, shiny red skin and sweet, very tender flesh (one of the few eating apples not also suitable for cooking); Granny Smith, with bright green skin and tart-sweet flesh; and Laxton's Superb, with green to brownish-red skin and fresh-tasting sweet flesh. Pearmain, the oldest of the British apples (they're mentioned in records dating back to the 13th century), can be green, red or various tints in between; Worcester Pearmain and Discovery are the most popular types. Pippins vary in colour from yellowish to red, but are nearly all sweet with a tart undertone; the most famous are Cox's Orange Pippin, Blenheim Orange and Gala, the last a hybrid created from Cox's Orange Pippin and Golden Delicious. Russets are brown-skinned with crisp flesh and an acidic edge; Egremont is the most widely available variety.

using it Although they are always available, eating apples *feel* like a winter fruit and many of the most popular (and best-tasting) varieties like Pearmains and Russets are only really available during autumn and winter. Of the cookers, Grenadiers are the first to arrive in August, followed by Bramley's, which stick around almost until the following summer. Apples should be firm with a bright colour and have no bruises or soft spots. They will keep for 2–3 weeks. The flesh discolours when exposed to air, so cut open just before use if possible, or sprinkle with lemon juice.

Apples are normally cooked by stewing or baking. To stew, quarter or slice the peeled fruit, then simmer with a little apple juice, sugar and spices (for a sweet dish) or with butter and seasoning (if they are to accompany meat); they will take 12–15 minutes to cook to a purée, five minutes less if they are to retain their shape as a filling for pies or tarts. Serve stewed apples (hot or cold) with custard or other milk puddings; purée for fools and mousses; or use in fritters, compotes or crumbles.

To bake, core the fruit and fill the cavity with flavourings such as brown sugar, raisins and chopped or ground nuts; cooking time is 35–40 minutes in a moderately hot oven. (Apple dumpling is made in the same way, with peeled whole fruit enclosed in sweet shortcrust pastry dough; a hole should be cut in the top to allow steam to escape.)

In savoury cooking, apples work well in dishes with veal, chicken, calf's liver, bacon, red cabbage and black pudding, and they have a real affinity with goose, duck and pork. Anything in French cookery described as *à la Normand* includes them and probably cider as well. Mixed with horseradish and/or mustard, puréed apple makes a good sauce for oily fish like mackerel.

Raw apples are a popular snack, and can be added, grated or sliced, to both fruit salads and savoury salads (they complement chicory and watercress well, for instance, and are part of a classic Waldorf salad with celery and walnuts). Apple juice can be used to soak dried fruits as well as being the liquid base for sweet and sometimes even savoury sauces.

word origin The first cultivated apples seem to have been called *abel* and variations of this, like the German *apfel*, followed the fruit as it spread around northern Europe. In England, the Anglo-Saxons called it *aeppel*, which gradually became the modern word.

Many modern apples are the result of individual labours of love. There was, for instance, a Mr Cox who invented Cox's Orange Pippin during the 1830s; a keen gardener and retired brewer, he lived near what is now Heathrow Airport outside London. There were several Mr Laxtons, a family of nurserymen who created important varieties of apple during Victorian times; and there was even a Granny Smith, Mrs Maria Ann Smith, the midwife daughter of transported convicts who developed her apple in Australia during the 1860s.

The word apple was once used to describe the pupil or central part of the eye, the probable origin of the phrase to be the 'apple of someone's eye', or favourite person, and maybe even of the nickname for New York, the 'Big Apple'.

did you know?

● The first apples were very small, very sour and had nearly as much core as flesh, more like crabapples than modern varieties, and were eaten and possibly cultivated by our neolithic ancestors. The Romans improved cultivation, may even have had one or two varieties similar to those we have today, and probably

introduced them into Britain. The Anglo-Saxons definitely grew apples, but it was the Normans – keen apple growers – who improved and expanded production after their conquest in 1066.

● Their reputation as the symbol of temptation probably hasn't done apples any harm, but in fact it's unlikely that the fruit Eve offered Adam in the Garden of Eden was an apple, and no specific fruit is named in Genesis anyway. It was probably interpreted in this way for European audiences because the apple was such a familiar fruit and because the word was sometimes used to describe fruit in general.

apricot

The apricot (*Prunus armeniaca*) is the stone fruit of a tall deciduous tree of the rose family. Native to China, it is now cultivated in warmer temperate areas throughout the world; major suppliers include the United States and Mediterranean area. The fruit is small and round to oval in shape with slightly downy skin, and can vary in colour from nearly white to deep orange, often with rosy tinges; there is even a black variety that grows in India. The flesh also varies, from almost white to orange, and the large central stone can be loose or clinging. At its best, the apricot is juicy and sweet, but the flesh can sometimes be dry, usually the result of the fruit being harvested too early (it's supposed to be picked when just under-ripe enough to reach retailers at the appropriate point of ripeness, but accidents can and do happen).

Although apricots can be canned, the most popular way to preserve them is to dry them. Most (but not all) dried apricots are stoned and treated with sulphur dioxide to preserve their typical orange colour. Sulphured, vacuum-packed fruits are normally American, Turkish or Australian; smallish unsulphured dusty brown ones usually come from Turkey or the Hunza Valley in Kashmir.

using it Apricots have a natural season during the hottest months of summer and are only occasionally available outside this time. Ripe ones should be soft and tender, but not squashy, and should be fragrant. They darken and strengthen in colour as they ripen, so pale colours, as a rule, suggest less ripe, and therefore less juicy, fruit. Depending on how ripe they are when they are bought, they will keep for about a week in the refrigerator.

Fresh apricots can be eaten raw or cooked. Before cooking, the skin is sometimes removed by immersing the fruit in boiling water for 30 seconds, then peeling. Moist dried apricots are ready to eat, whereas unsulphured types need to be rehydrated by soaking for 2–4 hours until they plump up.

Both fresh and dried fruit can be simmered to a purée with a little liquid. The purée makes a good soufflé or mousse flavouring and, mixed with thick cream, a cake or pastry filling. Fresh halves can be baked or grilled with butter and brown sugar sprinkled over, or used as a filling for tarts. Both fresh and dried fruit make excellent jam, and the flesh, or sometimes the kernels, which have a slightly almond flavour, are used to make brandy or liqueur.

Apricots are used in savoury cooking too: lamb and dried apricots is the classic combination, but they also work well in partnership with duck, chicken and ham. Both dried and fresh fruits are delicious in stuffings, particularly for pork or vegetables. Apricot jam is sometimes added to savoury sauces to create a sweet-sour taste.

word origin Apricot comes indirectly from the Latin *praecox,* meaning 'early ripening' (the tree flowers earlier than relations like the peach and plum, which may explain this). When the plant was first introduced into England from Italy, it was known as 'abrecock', a hazy anglicization of the Italian *albercocco*, which gradually evolved into the modern word.

did you know?

• Apricots were first cultivated about 4000 years ago and spread from China via Armenia and Turkey to the Middle East, often along the old silk routes set up to supply Europeans with fabrics and spices. The fruit was eventually introduced into Europe from the Middle East during the lst century AD. It didn't appear in England until the 16th century, when it was brought back from Italy by Henry VIII's gardener.

• The Hunza Valley is believed to produce the best dried apricots in the world, but it has another claim to fame: it also produces a much larger-than-usual number of people who live to a ripe and active old age – there are all sorts of wild rumours about men fathering babies at over 100 and of both men and women living until they are 150 or more. Since apricots are part of the staple diet, they're assumed to contribute to this longevity.

banana

Despite its odd appearance, the banana is a berry, the **fruit** of a giant tropical herb that originated in Malaysia and is related to ginger and turmeric. The plant grows to about 10m in height and has enormous leaves whose bases wind round the stalk to create a sort of trunk. Each plant produces a large drooping flower spike that eventually bears one bunch of fruit each year, then dies back to its roots. The bunch is made up of a series of 'hands', double rows of 12–16 'fingers' or individual bananas, which grow in half-spirals up the stem of the spike. The fruit is picked when green but full-sized, transported to its destination in refrigerated ships, and ripened when it gets there.

There are two major types that are usually assigned a species name although they aren't, in fact, separate species. The 'sweet' or eating banana (*Musa sapientum*) is normally slightly curved in shape with yellow inedible skin and pale beige, smooth, sweet pulp; there are a few red varieties with pinkish flesh. The other type is the plantain (*Musa paradisiaca*), a green or yellowish-green starchy cooking banana that tastes a little like sweet potato. It is firmer, straighter and more rigid than eating bananas.

using it Bananas should have a strong, bright colour, and feel reasonably firm and plump. They need to be stored at room temperature (the skin turns black if the fruit is refrigerated), where they will keep for about a week depending on their ripeness when bought. The flesh discolours on contact with air, so peel as near to use as possible. Plantains will probably have some brown or black areas on the skin, which won't affect their taste.

Sweet bananas make an easily digestible snack, a good addition to breakfast cereals and fruit salads, an excellent sandwich filling (especially for toasted bread) and a comforting accompaniment to custard, ice-cream, cream or yoghurt. They cook beautifully too: as fritters and in rum-and-coconut-based desserts; in teabreads, cakes and biscuits; and in savoury dishes such as curries. Bananas are also sometimes distilled into a sweet liqueur, and in Uganda and Belgium they even flavour popular beers.

Plantains are always cooked, by baking whole in their skins – in a moderate oven this will take about 45 minutes – or frying in slices or 'chips'. They are also added to Caribbean curries, and cooked and mashed to make a sort of porridge.

word origin Banana is West African, from the Guinean *banema* via a Portuguese approximation of the word. The first part of the botanical name comes from the Arabic *mouz,* meaning banana; the second part of that for sweet banana from *sapiens,* meaning wise – Indian wise men were supposed to sit under banana trees and eat the fruit.

Eating bananas doesn't make you go crazy, but the American college slang phrase of the 1960s 'going bananas' meant exactly that, and has caught on and stayed with us. Banana republic, meaning a (usually small) country that is politically unstable and overly dependent on outside capital or on one commodity, is a direct reference to the reliance of some Central American countries on their banana crop.

did you know?

• Bananas were probably first cultivated in India about 5000 years ago, but didn't arrive in Africa, where they are now a staple food in some countries, until around AD500. They were taken from West Africa to the Canaries by the Portuguese in the 15th century, and it was from there that the plant travelled to North America, then gradually worked its way down to Central America, the Caribbean and South America, the major modern producers. The first banana arrived in Britain in 1633, but it wasn't until the advent of refrigerated ships in the first years of the 20th century that they began to be available in any quantity.
• There is an Arabian myth that claims it was a banana which was offered to Adam in the Garden of Eden rather than an apple, and that after the Fall, Adam and Eve covered themselves with banana leaves rather than fig ones (if true, there would have been scarcely a glimpse of flesh since many banana leaves grow to about 4m in length).
• Despite their phallic appearance, bananas are sterile and propagated artificially from suckers cut from the root of the plant – the result is a comparative lack of genetic variety and an inability to develop resistance to common diseases and pests. Help may be at hand, however, since scientists in 11 countries are now combining to decode its genome, a project expected to last until 2006. The hope is that extra knowledge will enable growers to raise fruits more resistant to these hazards.

blackberry

Also known as the bramble, the blackberry (*Rubus fructicosus*) is the **fruit** of a wild shrub that grows in northern parts of Europe and North America. It is closely related to the raspberry and, like it, isn't botanically a berry at all, but a mound of tiny fruits called drupelets, which cling around a white centre or receptacle. As it ripens the fruit changes from green to red to black, when it's ready for picking; unlike the raspberry, the white centre stays in the fruit as it is removed from the branch. There are nearly a thousand different varieties of blackberry, including popular hybrids like loganberry and tayberry, the result of cross-breeding with raspberry.

using it There is a natural season in Britain, from roughly early August through early October, when cultivated berries are widely available, and hedgerows and heaths offer a free supply; from either source, berries should be deeply coloured and glossy; avoid any that are mouldy. They are very delicate and keep for only a day or so in the refrigerator.

At their best, blackberries need only cream or ice-cream to make a near-perfect dessert; they are also good in fools, fruit salads and mueslis and have a particular affinity with apples, with which they are often cooked as fillings for pies, tarts and crumbles. They are also a popular base for jams and jellies. Loganberries and tayberries can be treated in the same way as blackberries and all three could be used in any recipe specifying raspberries.

word origin The 'berry' part comes from the Old English *berie,* meaning 'fruit without a stone', the technical description of berry. The alternative name bramble also comes from Old English, the word *braemel* meaning 'prickly'.

did you know?

• In some country areas, eating blackberries after Michaelmas Day (September 29) used to be forbidden because Lucifer was supposed to pass by on that night and spit on every bush (presumably on his way to hell since it was on Michaelmas Day that he was expelled from heaven).

blueberry

The sweet berry fruit of several species of a wild shrub of the heather family, blueberries grow on high bushes (*Vaccinium corymbosum*) and on low ones (*Vaccinium angustifolium*); both types originated in northern parts of North America and are now widely cultivated there. The cranberry is a relative, as is the smaller wild bilberry (*Vaccinium myrtillus*) which is native to northern parts of central Europe.

using it Blueberries should be a good colour, plump, smooth and firm. The faint white coating, or 'bloom', on the skin preserves their moisture and keeps them fresh; they will keep for a week or more in the refrigerator. They make a good instant dessert with cream, ice-cream or yoghurt; can be used in a berry salad or fruit salad; and are excellent with muesli or waffles. They are also used to flavour ice-cream and jam and in baking they are used as fillings for pies and cheesecakes, muffins and teabreads. Although not as sweet as blueberries, bilberries can be used in much the same way; in northern Europe, they are sometimes used to flavour a sauce served with game.

word origin See **blackberry**.

did you know?

• Native Americans ate blueberries fresh but, also dried them in the sun and used them in cooking. In particular, they were added to a type of jerky called pemmican, a ground mixture of dried meat and fat that was part of several northern tribes' staple diet. Pemmican was light and kept well so was particularly useful for long journeys, facts later exploited by Arctic explorers and mountaineers.

cherry

This is the small, heart-shaped stone **fruit** of a member of the rose family, which probably originated somewhere in western Asia. It is now widely cultivated throughout the world, especially in Europe and the United States. Cherries range in colour from pale yellow through red to almost black, with many shadings in between, and in size from roughly raspberry to smallish strawberry.

There are upwards of a thousand varieties altogether, and three main types: sweet cherries (*Prunus avium*), which are now usually classified according to whether they are harvested early, middle or late in the season rather than (as they were until recently) on whether their flesh is firm and dry (*bigarreaux*) or moist and juicy (*geans*); sour cherries (*Prunus cerasus*), which are normally subdivided into pale-coloured amarelles and morellos or griottes that vary in colour from mid-red to almost black; and hybrid cherries, called dukes or royals, which are a mixture of sweet and sour varieties.

using it Despite modern transportation, sweet cherries have remained a seasonal treat and just as their arrival in June heralds the start of true summer, their departure around the end of August probably signals that it's coming to an end – although they do now sometimes re-appear later as a hugely expensive Christmas treat. Cherries should have firm, brightly coloured, glossy skin and be plump; avoid any with brown spots. They don't keep particularly well and are best bought on an as needs (or wants!) basis. Sour cherries are rarely sold fresh in the United Kingdom, but are available in cans or jars. Sweet cherries can be eaten raw, but sour ones should be cooked before being used; most hybrids are cooked too.

Raw sweet cherries make wonderful desserts: halve, stone and stir into plain yoghurt, add to other fruits or serve with ice-cream. Or cook them: poach and flambé with kirsch (a liqueur made from the kernels and flesh of morello cherries) to make cherries jubilee; bake in a sweet pancake batter to become clafoutis; or use as a filling for a pie. Cherries have a special affinity with chocolate, as seen in many cakes and confectionery.

In savoury dishes, cherries are often served with meat, particularly game or duck – in French cookery, any game, poultry or sweet dish called montmorency has a sauce of sour cherries (montmorency is a variety of amarelle) – and they are blended with wine, brandy and soured cream to make a fabulous cold Hungarian soup. A special type of sour cherry called marasca, grown in Croatia and northern Italy, is made into maraschino liqueur.

Cherries make good jam. Glacé or candied cherries often decorate baked goods, especially cakes, or are chopped and stirred into fruit cake, and a type of maraschino-flavoured cherry is also used to garnish drinks.

word origin The Greek word for the cherry tree was *kerasos*, which eventually led to the medieval Latin word for the fruit, *ceresia*, which became *cerise* in French. Our word cherry is taken from the French, the 'se' being dropped because the medieval English thought that such an ending meant it was plural.

The need to make the most of what was an occasional treat has given rise to having 'another bite of the cherry' (keep trying to succeed at something) and 'cherry picking' (choosing only the best). Its use to denote giving up virginity ('losing your cherry') is less clear, but may refer to the general drinking, merriment and mayhem (and their consequences) that went on during the medieval fairs held to celebrate the picking of the fruit.

did you know?

- The *Cherry Tree Carol* tells the story of Mary and Joseph and the cherry tree. They were walking by one while Mary was pregnant, but when she asked Joseph to pick her a cherry, he refused, saying that whoever had made her pregnant could do it. The unborn Jesus commanded the tree to bow down and give his mother some fruit – which it did.

cranberry

This is the **fruit** of various species of a wild heathery shrub and is closely related to the blueberry. There are two main types of cranberry: *Vaccinium macrocarpon*, which produces large berries and is native to America, where it's now widely cultivated, and *Vaccinium oxycoccus*, a species native to the northern parts of Europe, which has small berries and mostly grows wild. The United States, and in particular Massachusetts, supplies more than half the world crop of cranberries.

Cranberries are very small, very hard and very red, with tough, waxy thick skin and a sharp, tart taste. They grow in bogs where the water level is artificially controlled so that it's low during the growing season and flooded during harvesting. Then the water is agitated mechanically to detach the berries from their bushes and float them in islands to collection areas along the water's edge.

using it Their natural season is late October to January, although dried or frozen cranberries are available throughout the year. Fresh ones should be brightly coloured, hard and unwrinkled, and bounce when dropped; they will keep happily for several weeks in the refrigerator.

Cranberries are almost always cooked – they are too sour-tasting to be eaten raw. The most popular way to use them is in a relish for poultry or game, especially turkey, made by simmering the berries with sugar and a little liquid (often orange juice) until they 'pop'. They are also used as a stuffing ingredient, usually for poultry. Despite their tartness, cranberries work well in desserts and baking too, suitably sweetened. Cranberry juice is an invigorating cold drink.

word origin Cranberry comes from the German *kranbeere*, meaning 'craneberry', an old name for the fruit. Depending on what you believe, it was called this because the flowers of the plant looked like a crane's head, because the stamen looked like a crane's neck, or because the birds ate the berries.

> ***did you know?***
>
> • Native Americans used cranberries fresh and dried in much the same way as they used blueberries, long before white settlers arrived in America, and they introduced the Pilgrim Fathers to them. Despite legend, however, cranberries probably weren't part of the first Thanksgiving celebration (a feast that went on for three days) – the fruit was available, but in 1621 sugar wasn't, and cranberries without sugar would have been a penance rather than a pleasure. The partnership with turkey is more likely to have developed when German and Scandinavian immigrants used to eating the European version of the fruit with goose and game arrived in the United States.

currant

Grown primarily in northern parts of Europe, currants are the small round berry fruits of a family of Eurasian shrubs that includes the gooseberry. They are not the fresh version of dried currants, which are produced from grapes (see **raisin**, **sultana** & **currant**).

There are three types of fresh currant, and many varieties. The blackcurrant (*Ribes nigrum*), the largest, juiciest and sweetest of the three, is the one grown most widely in the United Kingdom. The redcurrant (*Ribes rubrum* and others), with smaller, sharper fruit, is cultivated more widely than the blackcurrant elsewhere in Europe, particularly in Scandinavia and eastern Europe. The white currant (*Ribes rubrum*) is actually a type of redcurrant, and in sweetness and taste is somewhere between the other two.

using it Currants are seasonal, available between June and September, with the black varieties appearing first. They are rarely seen fresh at other times of the year, but both blackcurrants and redcurrants freeze well and can be used from frozen out of season. They should be firm, plump and glossy; avoid any with soft spots. Currants are delicate and spoil easily, although they will keep in the refrigerator for a day or so. The fruits can be removed from their stalks by drawing the prongs of a fork down the length.

Blackcurrants are sweet enough to eat raw, and are used in fruit salads, served with ice-cream or yoghurt, puréed as a flavouring for fools, mousses and sorbets, and are an essential ingredient in summer pudding. Apple and blackcurrant is a classic combination, often used in pies and crumbles. Blackcurrants also make good jelly, and in France are made into the liqueur crème de cassis, which is mixed with white wine or champagne to make kir.

Redcurrants can also be used raw or cooked, but need more sweetening than blackcurrants. As a dessert fruit, they flavour creams, provide the filling for tarts (particularly in Scandinavia) and are sometimes also added to summer puddings. In Britain, however, they are primarily made into a jelly that is served with lamb. Redcurrant jelly is also a basic ingredient (with port, orange zest and mustard) in Cumberland sauce, a traditional accompaniment for cold ham.

White currants are neither as available nor as popular as the other two, but can be used, suitably sweetened, in desserts instead of either.

word origin Although they aren't related to dried currants, these fruits owe their name to them: when fresh currants were first introduced into Britain, they were believed to be the fresh fruits of the dried berries that had been popular for centuries, and were given their name – which stuck. Currant itself is a shortened version of the original name for the dried fruit, '*raisons of Corauntz*', an old name for Corinth in Greece, where they came from.

• Redcurrants were the first currants to be cultivated, probably in the Netherlands and in the late 15th century; blackcurrants followed about a hundred years later and both had reached Britain by the end of the 16th century. Originally they were grown for medicinal rather than culinary reasons – blackcurrant, in particular, was used both as a laxative and to make a healing 'tea' for coughs and sore throats.

• There was a wild American species of currant known to native tribes long before European settlers arrived (they were used in the same way as blueberries and cranberries), but it seems never to have been cultivated. European species, however, were brought to the United States and *were* cultivated – with disastrous consequences, because in the 19th century these imported bushes hosted a virulent tree fungus called blister rust that killed off millions of pine trees. As a result blackcurrants are no longer grown in many states.

date

This is the **fruit** of the date palm (*Phoenix dactylifera*), an ancient tree native to the Middle East and India. It prefers desert conditions of high heat and low humidity and when it gets them it just keeps on growing (it can reach heights of 30m), adding a new leaf crown each year, which flowers and eventually fruits. The fruit grows in 'strands', each one containing about 30 dates; there are about 40 strands in a 'bunch' or cluster and each tree produces about five bunches a year, or an average yield of around 6000 dates. They vary slightly in appearance depending on the variety (there are hundreds of them), but almost all are oblong in shape and start out green, gradually ripening to golden or dark brown in colour; the flesh is pulpy with a long stone in the centre, and tastes rich, almost fudgy.

There are three major types: fresh dates, soft, plump and light brown in colour, which come from the Middle East, especially Israel;

semi-dried dessert dates, normally the Deglet Noor variety from North Africa or the Middle East, which are usually dried artificially first to preserve them, then partially rehydrated and coated with glucose or other syrups to keep them soft and sticky; and dried cooking dates, only rarely seen nowadays, and available as blocks. Medjool, a semi-dried dessert date marketed under its variety name, has a deep reddish-brown colour and rich taste, and usually comes from California.

using it Fresh dates are available for a few months each autumn; those around at other times have probably been frozen. Fresh dates should be firm and plump, with a good colour and sheen; avoid any with dull, slightly wrinkled skin or light spots. They will keep in the refrigerator for 5–7 days. Dessert and block dates can be kept for several months in a cool dry place, although dessert dates will harden slightly after a month or so.

The papery skin is edible, but easily removed by taking off the stalk at the top of the fruit and carefully squeezing the other end; the flesh should just slip out. To remove the stone, either use a skewer to push the stone through from one end to the other, or halve the fruit and lift it out. Dried cooking dates usually need to be rehydrated before being used; soaking for 2–4 hours is normally sufficient.

Fresh and dessert dates are eaten uncooked as snacks, as part of an exotic fruit salad or chopped into cream cheese, yoghurt, ice-cream or breakfast cereal. They can be stuffed too, particularly with cream cheese, chopped **candied fruit** or marzipan. In the West, dates are added to sweet cooked dishes or used in baking, particularly steamed puddings, pastries, cakes or biscuits, but in the Middle East and India they are just as popular in savoury stews, curries, couscous- and rice-based dishes or in chutney.

word origin Date is from the Greek *daktulos*, meaning finger or toe, probably a reference to the shape of the fruit.

• Dates have been eaten since prehistoric times and cultivated for at least 6000 years. They were part of the staple diet in ancient Egypt, where among other things they were made into wine. In ancient Rome, the cookery writer Apicius added Jericho dates (the city is still producing them) to an elaborate dressing for lettuce and chicory salad, and also used them in his sauce for boiled ostrich.

fig

The fig (*Ficus carica*) grows on a tree that originated in western Asia, and is a relative of the mulberry, the tree that provides food for silkworms. It is unique in that the small bulbous 'fruit' is not, technically speaking, a **fruit** at all, only a container or receptacle for the pulp that contains over a thousand of the real fruits – tiny individual seed-like blobs called achenes, which flower and ripen inside the receptacle.

There are many varieties, ranging in colour from light yellow-green through red and purple to nearly black. The pulp varies in colour too, from pale green through pink to deep red, and at its best is rich and sweet to taste. Most figs are now grown around the Mediterranean (Turkey is a major producer and Smyrna figs, grown around Izmir in Turkey, are considered to be the best dried ones) or in California, where the major variety is an American version of Smyrna called Calimyrna.

Fresh figs are fragile, so it's only recently that they have been able to travel much beyond their producing countries, one reason they were often dried. The best-quality dried figs are dried in the sun before being sterilized and packed for selling: the heat bakes a layer of sugar onto the surface of the fruit as it dries, which helps to preserve it naturally and also preserves its taste. Figs destined solely for cooking are normally preserved artificially, often in blocks.

using it Fresh figs are available from September to November; at other times the choice is between canned (usually in cloying syrup) or dried, which can vary from luscious and rich to the frankly medicinal. Fresh fruits have a 'bloom' on the skin; avoid any with soft spots or that are too squashy. When ripe, figs are soft but with a bit of resistance, and can be kept in the refrigerator for a day or two. Dried figs are eaten as they are or rehydrated, depending on the type; any liquid can be used for soaking – red wine, port or fruit juice will all add to their flavour.

Ripe fresh figs are a treat eaten by themselves as a snack, or as a dessert. They are occasionally served with rice pudding or custard, made into jam or used as a filling for tarts. The classic savoury pairing is with **prosciutto**, but figs also work well with smoked salmon and with cheese, either as part of a special course or as a dessert with mascarpone or sweetened ricotta. Dried figs can be stuffed with nuts, but are usually cooked as part of compotes, fruit cakes, biscuits or jams. They are also occasionally used in savoury dishes, as a substitute for prunes with pork, rabbit or game birds, or with duck, and are also sometimes made into chutney.

word origin Adam and Eve might have preserved their modesty with fig leaves after the Fall, but the fruit itself has a racier reputation and its appearance has only helped, resembling as it does the female sexual organs (the Greek *sukon* reflected this, being not only the word for these, but also for fig). Somehow *sukon* became *ficus* in Latin and perhaps predictably modern Italian *fica* still has the alternative meaning of female private parts. *Ficus* became *figue* in Old French, and English borrowed from this. The carol *We Wish You a Merry Christmas* might still extol the virtues of figgy pudding,

but few of us eat it any more. In its day it was a sort of plum pudding (more often eaten on Palm Sunday than at Christmas), and sometimes may not even have contained dried figs, since the word fig could be used to describe any dried fruit, especially raisins.

did you know?

- Figs were being cultivated in Mesopotamia and Egypt by 3000BC, and were popular in Rome, where the delicate, expensive fresh fruits were the food of the rich, while common folk and slaves subsisted on dried ones. The Romans probably introduced them into England. The 'fruit of Heaven', as the fig is sometimes called, is sacred both to Muslims and Buddhists (Buddha is believed to have found wisdom under a fig tree).
- In various forms, figs are believed to be health-giving: a syrup made from unripe fruit or leaves used to be widely fed to anyone suspected of having a cold, cough or sore throat; the milky sap that oozes from the tree is still sometimes used to cure toothache; and the fruit itself is known as a fail-safe cure for even the most stubborn constipation.

fruit

This is the term commonly used to describe the fleshy product of a plant that can be eaten raw or cooked, usually as a dessert or baked item. Technically, however, it's actually the fertilized ovary of a flowering plant that contains the seed or seeds from which the next generation of plants can develop. The technical definition means that many foods we normally eat as vegetables, such as **tomatoes** and **avocados**, are actually fruits.

Fruits are divided into several broad groups based on their physical characteristics. Berries are single fruits with seeds scattered throughout their flesh and include some unexpected members like the **banana**, although normally when we describe something as a berry we mean a small 'soft' fruit like a **blackcurrant**. **Raspberries** and **blackberries** are popularly assigned to this category too, although in fact they aren't a single fruit at all, but what are called aggregate fruits, fused mounds of individual tiny fruits called drupelets, each enclosing a minute edible stone. The **strawberry** isn't technically a berry either, but a 'false' fruit – what we think of as the fruit is actually a sort of placenta for the true fruits, those tiny 'seeds' that can be seen on the outside of the skin. Berry fruits on the whole are small and round to oval in shape, and their seeds can be edible or inedible; most grow in temperate to warm climates.

The citrus group includes any fruit from a family of trees or shrubs native to an area stretching from north-eastern to south-western Asia. Citrus fruits are technically berries, with a pitted rind, white pith and flesh made up of a number of separate segments called carpels, each one containing many little tubes of juice. Seeds are scattered throughout the segments rather than being contained in a central cavity. Citrus fruits are grown in tropical or subtropical climates, and are more or less acidic to taste. Popular ones include **oranges**, **lemons** and **grapefruits**.

Gourds are fruits of the *Cucumis* family, which includes cucumber and marrow, and come from America, Asia and Africa. They have a thick rind and watery, refreshing flesh. The only gourds used as fruit are **melons** and **watermelons**. Pome is the word used to describe fruits with edible skin and a central core that is divided into sections, each one containing at least one seed. Although it's one of the most important categories, it only contains three fruits: the **apple**, **pear** and quince, all of them temperate-climate plants.

Stone fruits are united by the fact that each member of the group has a large inedible central stone called a drupe that encloses and protects its seed, and which can be loose or cling to the flesh surrounding it. These fruits grow in tropical, subtropical or temperate climates and often

have edible skin. The **plum**, **peach** and **cherry** are good examples.

Most fruit is grown conventionally, which means that the soil they are grown in and the plants themselves will be treated with chemical herbicides (to control weeds), fungicides (to treat mildew and scab) and insecticides. Fruit sold as organic is not treated with chemical herbicides, fungicides and insecticides.

Drying was used to preserve all foods before canning and freezing were invented, and many fruits like grapes, apples, apricots and mangoes are still popular in their dried form. Nearly all fruits freeze well, either by being dry-frozen in airtight freezer bags or in dry sugar or sugar syrup. Canning is another modern way of prolonging shelf life. Fruit canned in its own or other fruit juice usually tastes more 'fruity' than fruit in a sugary syrup. Fruit is also made into jams, jellies and chutneys.

using it All fruit to be eaten without peeling needs to be washed before use; delicate berries, which can soften if soaked, can usually be given just a quick rinse. Like vegetables, many of the vitamins and minerals contained in fruit are found just under the skin, so if peel is edible, it should be eaten; when it has to be removed, use a peeler to take it off thinly.

Most fruits are at their best eaten raw, as a snack or dessert, although most are also used in baking and in savoury salads and cooked dishes too (see individual entries). They are also made into classic preparations such as compote (a mixture of fresh or dried fruits simmered in a flavoured liquid); coulis (a sauce usually made by puréeing or sieving fruit); or fool (puréed sweetened fruit mixed with stiffly whipped cream and sometimes custard). Many are also pulped or squeezed for juice, and a few, such as grapes, apples and oranges, also provide the flavouring for popular alcoholic drinks.

word origin Fruit is from the Latin *fruit* 'to enjoy', and was used initially to describe any plant used as a food. The derivation from 'enjoying' may have been the origin of some fruits being described in the Bible as tempting or forbidden, and when information or news is described as 'fruity' it has the idea of being enjoyable in a slightly salacious or forbidden sort of way.

• The very first fruits were eaten wild and were probably very sour. They must have had something, though, because people persevered and gradually began to cultivate and improve them.

• Fruits were spread from one part of the world to another in much the same way as vegetables: the Romans brought apples and peaches into Britain when they invaded, then settled; later Moorish conquests of southern Europe introduced oranges and lemons to that part of the world and they gradually made their way northwards; and Christopher Columbus took melons and citrus fruit with him when he set off on his voyages, and brought back delights like the pineapple. More recently international trade and refrigerated ships have introduced us to such exotica as carambola or star fruit (*Averrhoa carambola*), a waxy yellowish-green ridged fruit that, when sliced crossways, is shaped like a star, and sharon fruit (*Diospyros kaki*), a round or oval tomato-like fruit related to the persimmon, first developed in Israel.

• Fruits contain lots of vitamins, and their role in maintaining our health and well-being is now widely appreciated. They are low in fat and calories and, along with vegetables, are our main source of antioxidants, which help protect the body from some of the modern scourges like heart disease and cancer. Perhaps not surprisingly, therefore, health experts urge us all to eat at least five portions of a variety of fruit and vegetables a day, a portion being one medium fruit (e.g. apple, orange, banana), a large slice of melon, two small fruit (e.g. plums, apricots), 2–3 tablespoons of fresh, stewed or canned fruit salad, a glass (150ml) of fruit juice, a cupful (80g) of summer berries and about 100g of smaller or cut-up fruit.

gooseberry

The gooseberry (*Ribes grossularia*) is the berry **fruit** of a thorny shrub that grows best in northern climates and is closely related to the currant. It is popular in Britain and reasonably popular in the Netherlands, but only rarely cultivated anywhere else. The berries are round to oval in shape, yellowish through green to red in colour, and the pulpy flesh contains lots of tiny edible seeds. Gooseberries are divided into two main types according to their taste, each with many varieties: sour gooseberries, always green in colour, are hard-skinned and hairy; and sweet or dessert gooseberries, which can be any colour, are larger and softer, and vary from smooth-skinned to hairy.

using it Sour gooseberries start to become available towards the end of May; sweet ones come a little later, from mid-June to mid- or late August. The former should feel very hard, but the latter ought to be softer, almost translucent; avoid any that are too squashy or have discoloured patches. Sour fruit will keep for about a week in the refrigerator, sweeter varieties 3–4 days.

Sweet gooseberries are best raw (they lose some taste if they're cooked), while sour ones must be cooked. To prepare, 'top and tail' with scissors (this isn't essential for sweet gooseberries), then pulp quickly over a low heat, with sugar and a little liquid, for about five minutes.

Add sweet gooseberries to fruit salads, serve with ice-cream or yoghurt, or purée to make a classic dessert fool. Cooked gooseberries are normally used as a filling for pies, tarts or crumbles, or made into jam. Being tart, sour gooseberries are sometimes served with savoury dishes, particularly fatty ones: as a sauce for oily fish (see **mackerel**), for instance, and as a stuffing ingredient for poultry like duck or goose. Flavoured with elderflowers, gooseberries also make a good honey-coloured wine.

word origin Is there a connection with goose? Some say yes, some say no. The 'yeses' think the association with fatty poultry led to the name (gooseberries *were* a common stuffing ingredient for goose in Tudor England); the 'noes' think that the word comes from the French for currant, *groseille*, a case strengthened by the fact that one of the colloquial names for gooseberry in Scotland, *grosart*, is probably derived from the same word.

did you know?

• The fruit known as cape gooseberry or physalis (*Physalis peruviana*) has no connection at all with ordinary gooseberry (it's actually a member of the same family of plants as potato). The cape gooseberry is a sweet, cherry-sized orange fruit protected inside a beige papery husk. It is a good addition to berry or mixed fruit salads, and being so decorative is often used as a garnish.

grape

The grape (*Vitis vinifera*) is the berry **fruit** of a climbing vine and is probably native to western Asia, although it is now grown in warm to temperate areas as far apart as France and New Zealand. Grapes grow in bunches, each one containing anything from a few to a few hundred fruits. They range in skin colour from pale greenish-yellow through green and light red to black, and can have pale or reddish pulp, with or without seeds, be large or small, sweet or quite tart. There are thousands of varieties. About 70 percent of the world crop is used to make **wine** or **vinegar**, and 10 percent is processed into **raisin**, **sultana** & **currant**. The remainder is grown for eating (table grapes).

Table grapes, which tend to be thinner-skinned than other types, are usually described as white (actually yellow or green) or black (anything from light red to black). Popular varieties include Alicante, seeded black grapes now grown mostly in California; Chasselas, a sweet-tasting group of seeded French varieties that range in colour from yellowish to pink; Muscat, the name used to describe several varieties of large, very sweet seeded grapes used for wine-making and drying as well as eating, and which range in colour from pale yellow to black; and Thompson Seedless, an American variety used for both eating and drying, which, as the name suggests, has no seeds.

using it Grapes are supposed to be picked ripe (they do not ripen off the vine). Look for those that are firm and plump, and still on their bunch; avoid any that have fallen off or have slight discolouring around the top. A 'bloom' is an indication of freshness. Green grapes with a yellowish tinge will probably be sweeter than those that are darker green. Most grapes will keep in the refrigerator for 5–7 days. To be used in cooked dishes, they may need to be skinned and deseeded: the former is done by immersing the fruits in boiling water for a few seconds, then peeling back the skin; for the latter the grapes are halved so that the seeds can be dug out with the tip of a knife.

Used raw, grapes work well in both sweet fruit salads and savoury leaf or chicory salads. They are also good in stuffings for game or poultry, and are the basis of the French sauce called Véronique, with stock, wine and cream, which accompanies chicken or white fish. Grapes complement cheese so well that it is traditional to offer some with a cheese course.

The fruit is pressed for its juice, and a cooking oil (grapeseed) is extracted from the seeds. The edible leaves of the vine are popular in Greek cuisine, where they act as the wrapper for stuffed dishes like dolmades.

word origin At first, in English, the fruit was called 'wineberry' after what was its main use, but in later Norman times, *grape* was borrowed from the French and has been used ever since. The original French word simply meant a bunch of grapes.

• According to the Bible, one of the first things Noah did after the Flood waters receded was to plant a vineyard, and grapes were definitely being cultivated by 2500BC in Egypt, around the time the first pyramids were being built. By Roman times cultivation was sophisticated and grapes were being grown for wine-making, drying and eating. In cooking, the unfermented juice of fresh grapes called must was an important ingredient in many Roman sauces, and was mixed with honey to make *mulsum*, occasionally used in cooking, but mostly offered as a refreshing drink with the first course of a Roman meal. Verjuice, the juice of unripe grapes, was also used in cooking, added to dishes more or less in the way that vinegar is now.

• The Romans introduced grapes to all the countries they conquered, including England, and although only the southern part of the country was warm enough to grow them, cultivation was quite widespread. After the Romans left, responsibility for England's vineyards was shouldered by the monasteries, and 38 survived long enough to be recorded in the Domesday Book in 1086. (It took Henry VIII and his dissolution of the monasteries to wipe them out, at least until the second half of the 20th century.)

• Although the *Vitis vinifera* species has spread all over the world and accounts for about 95 percent of all grapes grown, there are different types in other parts of the world, especially in North America. There are several varieties of the major American species (*Vitis labrusca*), the most important being Concord, which produces blue-black eating and wine grapes. *Vitis labrusca* used to grow prolifically all over north-eastern North America and it was presumably the endless vines of this species that led the 11th-century Viking Leif Ericsson to call the place he had just reached Vinland, or land of vines.

grapefruit

The grapefruit (*Citrus paradisi*) is most probably a hybrid of sweet **orange** and pomelo, the largest member of the citrus family. Jamaica, the United States, Israel and South Africa are the major producers.

There are three main types, each with many varieties: Duncans have seeds and pale pitted yellow skin with pale flesh; Marshes are seedless, less flavourful than Duncans, with pale yellow or pinkish skin and pale flesh; and Rubys are a type of Marsh, with skin and flesh that ranges from pale to deep pink. Yellow grapefruits vary in tartness from mouth-puckering to sour-sweet, but pink varieties are genuinely sweet. Well over half the world's supply is made into juice, which is sold freshly squeezed, as a reconstituted concentrate or canned; the fruit itself is also sometimes canned in segments, although pink varieties discolour and aren't available in this form.

using it Fresh **fruit** should be heavy for its size and look shiny and firm. It will keep for up to two weeks in a cool place. Refrigeration hardens the flesh, so if a grapefruit is to be squeezed it should remain at room temperature.

Grapefruit juice or the halved fruit are widely enjoyed for breakfast; halves can also be served as a first course, plain or grilled with a topping like butter, brown sugar and sherry. Like most citrus fruits, grapefruit also makes a good **sorbet** and an excellent marmalade.

Both tart and sweet grapefruit are sometimes used in savoury dishes: sweet pink grapefruit peeled and cut into pieces, then mixed with watercress and chicory for a winter salad; or either type mixed with leftover lean poultry, red onion and avocado. Tart grapefruit can also be substituted for gooseberries with oily fish like mackerel or herring, and sweeter varieties could replace orange in duck or goose recipes.

word origin Grapefruit grows in clusters, like grapes – not an overwhelming reason to call them after grapes, but probably better than the alternative explanation, that someone thought they tasted like them.

• Its parent plant pomelo was known about for many centuries, but grapefruit was only developed during the 18th century in the West Indies; first reports to Britain at that time described it as 'forbidden fruit'. Despite this promising start, it didn't become reasonably available until the end of the 19th century.

• The grapefruit's modern popularity rests in part on its alleged ability to burn up calories, which has led to its prominent inclusion in several slimming diets. If only. What is indisputable is that it is *low* in calories, as long as sugar isn't added to it. And since it also contains a high supply of vitamin C, among other good things, it is well worth eating, whether it's part of a slimming regime or not.

guava

The berry **fruit** of a small bushy tree that originated in Central America, the guava (*Psidium guajava* and others) is now grown in other tropical and subtropical areas of the world like India, Egypt and Hawaii. Several closely related species produce fruits that range in size from small to large, and in shape from the usual oval or pear to the occasional sphere; skin colour varies too, from the common yellowish, orange or even cream to the reddish-green of the highly regarded strawberry guava (*Psidium littorale*). This latter type has deep pink flesh, but the slightly astringent flesh of other varieties can be white, yellow or light pink. In all types of guava, the flesh surrounds a central pulpy area containing many small, dark hard seeds; these are technically edible, though rarely eaten. The green-skinned, creamy-fleshed pineapple guava from South America, sometimes called feijoa (*Feijoa sellowiana*), is a member of the same family, although it isn't closely related.

using it Ripe guavas should be soft; avoid those with soft spots or blemishes. They can be kept 4–5 days in the refrigerator, depending on how ripe they were when bought; under-ripe ones will mature within a few days stored in a paper bag in a warm kitchen. Although the skin is edible, the fruit is often peeled; the pulp and seeds (especially in larger ones) are normally scraped out too.

The best way to eat guava is raw and halved as a dessert, by itself, possibly with mascarpone or yoghurt, or cut up as part of a fruit salad. It can also be pressed to make a refreshing drink, used as a flavouring for ice-cream, or made into jelly or chutney.

word origin Guava comes via Spanish from the Arawak Indian for the plant, *guayavu*.

kiwi fruit

Also called Chinese gooseberry, the kiwi (*Actinidia chinensis*) is the berry fruit of a climbing plant that looks like a vine. It originated in China, although the major producers are now New Zealand, France and California. The kiwi fruit is about the size and shape of a large egg, with brown hairy skin. The vivid green, translucent flesh contains lots of tiny, dark edible seeds arranged around a yellowish centre.

using it One of the great things about kiwi fruit is that it keeps well, and since it comes from various parts of the globe this guarantees year-round availability. It can be bought hard and under-ripe, when it will keep in the refrigerator for a month or so, or with a little 'give', in which case it will keep for 2–3 weeks. When ripe it will be as soft and tender as a ripe peach. It's nearly always used raw, either halved so the flesh can be scooped out with a spoon, or peeled and then sliced or cut into chunks.

Kiwi fruit is added to fruit salads and breakfast cereals, used to make ice-cream or other creamy desserts like mousse or fool, and is a key ingredient (along with passionfruit) in Pavlova, a spectacular meringue cake with a rich cream and fruit filling. Raw kiwi fruit shouldn't be used in gelatine-based desserts, since acid in the fruit will prevent them from setting (cooking the fruit first will solve this problem).

When kiwi fruit first became popular it was used everywhere as a garnish, and its colour and sweet acidity still make a good foil for fish pâtés, cream cheese dips and cold meats. The acid enzyme can also help to tenderize steak and other meats: pulp the fruit and rub over both sides of the meat, then leave for 30 minutes or so, depending on the thickness; scrape off before the meat is cooked.

word origin Chinese gooseberry was the original name and was probably given to the fruit because of its origin and because it had a slightly hairy skin and green flesh − it (very) vaguely resembled gooseberry. The name change occurred during the 1960s, when the Americans decided to rechristen it after the national emblem of the chief producer, New Zealand.

did you know?

• Unlikely though it now seems, virtually no one in New Zealand had even heard of kiwi fruit until about 1904, when someone imported a few seedlings from China and began to grow it. The fruit didn't become a commercial crop there until the 1940s and only began to be exported on any scale during the 1970s, when it became a worldwide symbol of *nouvelle cuisine*.

kumquat

This is the **fruit** of a small ornamental shrub native to China, part of the same family of plants as the orange and the lime, although it isn't a true citrus fruit. The kumquat is grown in subtropical to warm temperate climates throughout the world, and major producers include China, Japan and the United States.

There are two main types: the common oval-shaped species (*Fortunella margarita*) and a larger, round one (*Fortunella japonica*). Both are dainty, rarely more than 5cm long, with thin, soft pitted orange rind and sectioned juicy flesh that contains scattered seeds.

using it The kumquat is available in late autumn or early winter. It will keep for 5–7 days at room temperature and for about two weeks in the refrigerator. The whole thing is eaten, rind, flesh and all – the rind tastes quite sweet, the flesh slightly bitter. To get the most from it, roll between the fingers to release the scented oils from the zest.

It can be sliced raw into fruit or savoury salads, or used as a garnish, particularly for exotic rice and couscous dishes, but normally kumquat is cooked, chopped up and used in baked goods, and in stuffings or sauces for poultry or game, especially duck and pigeon. It can also be made into marmalade, sliced and candied, or poached whole in brandy or orange liqueur as a dessert.

word origin Kumquat is from the Cantonese *kam kwat,* meaning 'golden orange'.

did you know?

• Kumquats have been cultivated in China for several millennia and in Japan for nearly as long. They were introduced into Europe in 1846 by the British plant collector Robert Fortune, whose surname is the basis of their botanical name.

lemon

The lemon (*Citrus limon*) is the **fruit** of a smallish subtropical evergreen tree of the citrus family and probably native to India, although most of the world's modern supply comes from the Mediterranean area and California. There are many varieties, some with thick skin, some with thin, but basically all lemons are shaped like largish eggs with a pimple at one end. They all have yellow, finely grained skin and the familiar 'sectioned' flesh of all citrus fruit. Most have seeds and are tart to taste, although some hybrids are seedless and a few even have a sweetish rather than sour taste.

using it Fruits should be firm and heavy for their weight, with skin that is closely rather than loosely grained; those with a greenish tinge will probably be more acidic than those that are yellow all over. Brittle, dull skins are signs that the fruit is past its best and should be avoided. Uncut lemons keep for 7–10 days at room temperature and for about two weeks in the refrigerator. Most have waxed skin (although unwaxed fruits are available); and if the zest is to be used, the fruit should first be scrubbed with soapy water. Immersing the fruit in hot water for a few minutes before squeezing will provide more juice.

All the different parts of this fruit are used in sweet and savoury cooking, in baking and preserving, and to make drinks. For desserts, the juice brings out the flavour of exotic fruits like mango and papaya, can be made into sorbet, or become the basis of soufflés, mousses, syllabubs and custards, preferably with some grated zest to intensify the flavour. In baking, the juice, zest and often the candied peel are added to cakes, cheesecakes, biscuits and steamed puddings, as well as being made into a filling for lemon meringue pie. The juice, grated zest and thin slices that have been cooked in a sugar syrup make the filling for a classic French tarte au citron.

In savoury cooking, lemon juice can be substituted for or added with vinegar to **vinaigrette**, and is often beaten into mayonnaise to give a sharper, fresher taste. Lemon juice is also sprinkled over avocados and other vegetables and fruits to prevent them from discolouring. Grated zest gives intense flavour to stuffings and sauces. Lemon slices or wedges are the universal garnish for grilled or fried seafood, and preserved lemon, a North African speciality, is added to many local stews. They can be preserved in other ways too: as lemon curd, an old-fashioned spread for bread that's still sometimes used in baking, and as marmalade, chutney and pickles. Lemon is also the basic flavouring in many sweet fizzy drinks and can be made into one of the best hot-weather drinks in the world (home-made **lemonade**); slices of lemon are often added to hot or iced tea.

word origin Lemon is from the Arabic *limah,* meaning 'citrus fruit', also the root of the English word 'lime', via the Old French *limon.* The sourness of the taste and smallness of the size probably account for the origin of 'it's a lemon', something that performs poorly and fails to meet expectations.

• There is some dispute about when exactly lemons arrived in Europe – it could have been during classical Roman times, but if they did reach Rome then, they disappeared with its downfall in AD410. The Arabs, however, cultivated lemon trees and took them with them as they spread through the southern parts of Europe from about the 8th century, although lemons only really surfaced in northern areas during the 12th century, brought back from the Middle East by returning Crusaders. At first they were used as ornamental plants, then healing ones, but gradually lemon juice began to replace verjuice (the juice of unripe grapes) as a sharp flavouring for savoury dishes.
• Lemon is a natural antiseptic: Casanova reported in his memoirs that the juice and zest were used as a contraceptive and to detect venereal disease.

lime

Sometimes called West Indian or Key lime (*Citrus aurantifolia*), the lime is the **fruit** of a thorny tropical evergreen tree of the citrus family. It originated in Malaysia; today's major producers include the West Indies, Central America and the southern United States. In addition to the main species, which still accounts for much of the world's crop, there are two widely cultivated hybrids: *Citrus latifolia*, sometimes called Tahitian lime, developed from *Citrus aurantifolia* and the citron fruit, the only lime now grown in the United States and the only seedless lime; and *Citrus limettoides*, less acid than other limes and therefore described as 'sweet', although where lime is concerned, this is relative rather than absolute.

Limes are smaller and rounder than lemons, and the flesh is divided into segments like all citrus fruit. Almost all types have thin, vivid green skins because they are picked when immature; if they stayed on the tree long enough they would turn yellow like lemons.

using it Fruits should feel heavy for their size, and be a good deep colour with a slightly oily skin; avoid any with dried, brittle skin and brown patches. They will keep in a cool place for about two weeks, nearly double that in the refrigerator.

As a fellow sour citrus fruit, lime can be used in much the same way as **lemon**. Strips of zest can also be dried, then stored in caster sugar, and the resulting flavoured sugar added to desserts and cakes, or zest can be candied and used as a colourful decoration for baked dishes. In savoury cooking, lime has an affinity with pork and oily fish. The juice, zest and occasionally the sliced fruit are stirred into some West Indian and Thai curries, while the juice and zest are also added to salsas for plainly cooked food (popular partners include chilli, garlic, coriander and tomato, and chilli, garlic and avocado). Lime juice is the preserving/cooking agent in ceviche, a classic Latin American dish where pieces of white fish like snapper are immersed in lime juice flavoured with chilli and herbs until opaque.

Lime juice is used to make drinks too: as a regular ingredient in rum punch (a definite affinity) and the tequila-based Margarita cocktail. A wedge of lime traditionally accompanies Mexican beer (it's supposed to be sucked dry before the beer is drunk).

word origin Lime has the same root as lemon, the Arabic *limah,* meaning 'citrus fruit', but in this case it reached English via the Spanish *lima*.

did you know?

Citrus fruits were unknown in the New World before Spanish explorers and settlers took them there, but the climate in the West Indies and Central America was just right for limes in particular and they have flourished there ever since. And it was in the West Indies during the late 18th century that lime juice was first added to navy rations (instead of lemons, since limes were cheaper) to help prevent scurvy. For Americans, lime became so associated with the British Navy and its sailors throughout the world that they and any British settlers who travelled after them became known as 'lime-juicers', eventually shortened to just 'limeys'.

lychee

The stone **fruit** of an evergreen tree that originated in southern China, the lychee (*Litchi chinensis*) is now also grown in various other tropical and subtropical areas. Major producers include India, South Africa, Thailand and Australia as well as China. The tree is enormous, occasionally reaching nearly 30m in height, and each one produces about 60–100kg of fruit per year. The fruits themselves grow in clusters and are endearingly dainty compared with what they come from, rarely larger than about 3cm in diameter and always either oval or round in shape. They have a slightly rubbery, pockmarked pinkish skin that encloses almost translucent, soft white musky flesh and a large central brown stone.

using it A ripe lychee is heavy with firm skin of a good 'blush' colour; avoid any that are cracked or brown (the latter means the fruit is older). Lychees will keep for about a week in the refrigerator. They are also widely available canned.

The rubbery skin peels off easily if the fruit is nicked at one end, either with a knife or a finger. The refreshing, perfumed taste of the flesh is unique and best appreciated by eating the fruit raw, on its own, or with ice-cream, yoghurt or something similar.

Stoned, lychee can be added to a fruit or mixed savoury-sweet salad. It is (briefly) cooked occasionally, too, usually with savoury ingredients: added to exotic pilaffs or couscous dishes, for instance, or to vegetable and poultry stir-fries.

word origin Lychee is from the Cantonese for the fruit, *lai ji*. When it was first recorded in English in Tudor times, it was as *lechia*; later variations included *leechee* and *litchi,* before the word settled into its current spelling.

did you know?

• The rambutan (*Naphelium lapaceum*) is a hairy version of the lychee (it looks more like a pet than a fruit), which originated in Malaysia. The flesh resembles that of the lychee although the taste is not as fine.

mandarin

The mandarin (*Citrus reticulata*) is the **orange**-like **fruit** of a dwarf species of citrus tree and is native to South-east Asia. Although it used to be called tangerine, that description is now more usually given to particular varieties of mandarin with deep reddish skin, especially in the United States. Mandarins are small, about half the size of standard oranges, are slightly flatter in shape, and range in colour from pale to deep reddish-orange. They are less acidic than oranges, but the main difference is that they have thin skin that encases the flesh very loosely, which makes them easier to peel. Like all citrus fruits, mandarin flesh is arranged in separate segments.

There are several major types: the mandarin itself, which is mostly produced in Asia and the United States, and has varieties that range from quite heavily seeded to virtually seedless; the satsuma, a small fruit with a bright colour, usually seedless, which originated in Japan although it's now cultivated both there and in Spain; and the Mediterranean mandarin, which is slightly paler than other mandarins

and usually has a tiny knob-like protuberance on its top (this contains a baby fruit). The clementine, a cross between mandarin and bitter (Seville) orange, has sweet flesh with a hint of sharpness; most varieties are seedless or virtually so. Clementines are mainly grown around the Mediterranean and in the United States.

using it We associate mandarins with autumn and winter, since they start to appear towards the end of October and stay more or less until spring. Fruits should be reasonably soft and have clear, shiny skin. They will keep for about two weeks.

Mandarins are so sweet and easy to peel that they are normally eaten as they are, as a healthy snack, instant dessert or perfect lunch-box treat. They are one of the real delights of Christmas (especially clementines): pushed into stockings, decorating the tree or table with their warm colour and delicious scent, or handed round after the festive dinner. In the kitchen, they can be used in much the same way as oranges, particularly in desserts, or as a decoration or filling for cakes and cheesecakes.

word origin Mandarin is from the French *mandarine*, after the officials in imperial China who wore robes similar in colour to the fruit. The tangerine is named after the port of Tangiers in Morocco, once a centre for exporting mandarin oranges; satsuma was developed in Japan and is named after a former province of that country; and clementine is named after the French priest who bred it (in Algeria) at the beginning of the 20th century, Father Clément Dozier.

did you know?

• Mandarins aren't just crossbred with oranges – they are also mixed with other fruit, most notably grapefruit to produce the large thick-skinned ugli fruit, which originated in Jamaica and combines the taste of both with the peelability of mandarins.

mango

The mango (*Mangifera indica*) is the stone **fruit** of an evergreen tree related to pistachio and probably originated in India; the Indian subcontinent, Thailand, Mexico and South Africa are the major suppliers today. A mango is usually oval or kidney-shaped, like an extra-large pear in size, and has a tough green outer skin which, depending on the variety, sometimes blushes red or turns yellowish-red as it ripens. The aromatic, juicy flesh, which varies from glowing orange to mellow yellow, can be slightly fibrous, and clings determinedly to a central flat stone.

using it A ripe mango will give a little when pressed and will have a good perfume; avoid any with soft spots or shrivelling. They will keep for 4–6 days in the refrigerator; under-ripe ones (but not those that are completely green) will mature if they are left at warm room temperature for a few days.

Mangoes are usually eaten raw, but getting access to the flesh can be messy. The idea is to separate it from both the stone and the skin (which isn't eaten), something easier said than done. Hold the mango upright and slice down on either side of the stone to make three separate pieces, the middle one containing the stone. You can then just eat the flesh from the outside pieces, using a spoon. Or cut the flesh halves into lengthways slices and slip a knife under the flesh of each one to free it from the skin, then cut the flesh into thinner slices or into chunks. The middle slice, with the stone, has flesh that can be cut away, or you can enjoy it as a cook's perk. It's always a good idea to prepare mango on a plate so that the juice that comes out can be saved. The best way to enjoy a ripe mango is to eat it raw, sprinkled with a little lime juice and possibly grated nutmeg; or serve it with ice-cream, yoghurt, coconut-flavoured cream or crème fraîche. Mango purée can be the basis of a delicate ice-cream, an exotic fool, or mousse or, with whipped cream, a good filling for cakes and meringues.

In savoury cooking, mango is added to rice-based or salad dishes, served with prosciutto in the same way as melon slices, and puréed with coriander, lime and chilli to make a salsa for grilled fish or meat. Sharper-tasting green, unripe mangoes have always been widely used in Asian, especially Indian, savoury cooking, added to curries or used as a basis for chutneys, pickles and raitas.

word origin Mango probably comes from the Tamil *mankay,* meaning mango tree fruit, via the Portuguese *manga*.

Mangoes have been cultivated in India for about 4000 years and have always had a special place in its history; they are mentioned in the *Veda* (the Hindu holy books) and for a long time only nawabs and rajahs were allowed to own mango orchards. The Portuguese found them there in the 16th century, and took them to Africa, Latin America and the West Indies, where they are still cultivated. Their first appearance in Britain was as a pickle, exported from India by the East India Company towards the end of the 17th century.

melon

The melon (*Cucumis melo*) is the **fruit** of a member of the gourd family of plants that also includes the cucumber and the marrow, and probably originated in Africa.

Sweet melons have a hard rind, succulent flesh (which is mostly water) and a cavity containing lots of seeds. There are three main types, each with many varieties and hybrids. Cantaloupes tend to be small and round and often have a sectioned rind. Popular varieties include Charentais, which has greenish rind and rich-tasting orange-coloured flesh, and Ogen, with greenish-yellow striped rind and well-flavoured green flesh. Musk or netted melons are round in shape and vary in colour from yellow to green, although they always have a raised, beige 'netted' pattern on their rind; the flesh is normally orange and well-flavoured. (Confusingly musk melons are called cantaloupes in the United States.) The third main type are winter melons, which are oval and usually have ribbed skins. The most popular variety is honeydew, with yellowish rind and pale green, translucent, slightly insipid flesh.

Tart cooking melons are grown all over Asia where they are used like a vegetable or in pickling; they are rarely found elsewhere. The **watermelon** belongs to a different family of gourds.

using it Ripe melons are heavy for their size, with a little 'give' at the stem end, and should have a sweet fragrance; avoid any that are softish all over or have bruises. They will keep for a few days at room temperature; once cut, they should be wrapped in cling film, stored in the refrigerator and used within a day. They need no real preparation before being eaten: cutting into sections and scooping out the seeds is all it takes.

The light, refreshing quality of melon flesh means that it tastes good at the beginning or end of a meal. For an appetizer, small melons can be halved and sprinkled with ginger or lime juice; larger ones can be cut in sections and served with **prosciutto** or smoked meat or fish. As a dessert, melon can be served with ice-cream or yoghurt in its cavity, or the flesh can be scooped into small balls and served in a melon salad or mixed with other fruits. Melon makes a delicate **sorbet** too, and is occasionally also made into a refreshing summer soup.

word origin Melon is from the Greek *melopepon*, *melo* meaning 'apple' and *pepon* 'gourd'. Cantaloupes are named after the former papal estate near Rome, Cantalupo, where they were first cultivated during the 15th century; Ogen comes from the name of the kibbutz in Israel that first developed the variety. Galia, an increasingly popular green-fleshed hybrid related to

Ogen, was also developed in Israel, and is named after the daughter of the man who first created it. The variety Charentais is cultivated mostly in the Charente region of France, hence *its* name.

• Although the early civilizations in the Indus Valley were eating melons around 2500BC, and they were known and appreciated early on in other parts of Asia and China, they probably spread there from northern Africa and the Middle East. They didn't reach Europe until after the fall of the Roman Empire, probably being introduced by the Moors who conquered and settled in southern Europe from the 8th century on; they finally arrived in Britain around the 16th century.

• When the town council of Cavaillon in southern France was setting up a town library, it wrote to Alexandre Dumas (author of *The Three Musketeers*) asking him for the donation of 'two or three of his best novels'. Dumas was a big fan of the melons grown around the town, so he offered a complete set of all his published works (according to him around 400–500 volumes) if the Council would vote him a lifetime supply of 12 melons a year. It did – and got its books.

orange

This is the **fruit** of an evergreen shrub of the citrus family that originated in the Far East, probably in China. Most oranges are round, about the size of an apple, and have the familiar segmented flesh common to all citrus fruit. Rind can be thick or thin, heavily or lightly pitted and always has a white pith that usually fits closely to the flesh. There are two major species: the bitter orange (*Citrus aurantium*), sometimes known as Seville, grown mostly in Spain and primarily used for making marmalade; and the sweet orange (*Citrus sinensis*), which has closely clinging rind and includes the various types of dessert oranges around today. The **mandarin**, an orange-like citrus fruit, is described separately.

Popular sweet oranges include the common orange, the standard fruit with pitted rind sometimes sold by varietal names like Valencia (chief producers include California and Florida), and Jaffa, which originated in Palestine although it's now also grown around the Mediterranean; the blood orange, a special Italian type with red-flushed skin and flesh (it gets its unique colour from red pigments called anthocyanins, which are triggered by extreme temperature changes that occur while the fruits are still on the tree); and the navel orange, which has a small knob-like protuberance at the top end (this contains an embryonic 'baby' orange) and fewer seeds than most other types. Navel oranges are grown around the Mediterranean, and in South America and the United States.

Oranges are picked when ripe but still greenish and are then treated with ethylene gas to improve their colour to the traditional orange. All oranges except Sevilles are also coated with wax to make their skin shinier.

using it Although individual types have seasons (navels, for instance, are usually more plentiful during autumn and winter, bloods arrive in early spring, Sevilles appear only between January and February), there are oranges available all year round. Fruit should be heavy for its weight and feel firm. Oranges will keep for up to two weeks. If the zest is to be used, it should be scrubbed with soapy water first. Immersing the fruit in hot water for a few minutes before squeezing will provide more juice, and segmenting is easier if the orange is refrigerated for 30 minutes or so first.

An orange is a good snack food as well as being used in sweet and savoury cooking and for making drinks and juice. In pieces or sections, it's mixed with other citrus fruits (or other fruits) to make a salad, or used as the basis for mousses, **sorbets**, **soufflés**, custards and other creamy desserts. In baking, the juice, grated zest and candied peel are added to cakes, icings, biscuits, pastries and chocolates. In savoury dishes,

slices or pieces provide an interesting contrast in salads, particularly those containing chicory, watercress and radicchio (a little juice could be added to the dressing too), and they are also good in main-dish salads based on rice, bulghur wheat and pasta. The orange has a real affinity with poultry, especially chicken and duck, and goes well with pork, veal and fish too, especially white fish and seafood such as scallops. Classic sauces are Maltaise (**hollandaise** with blood orange) and Bigarade (traditionally made with bitter orange, and served with wild duck or game).

Over 75 percent of Florida oranges eventually end up as juice, and orange juice in one form or another makes a refreshing and healthy start to the day, as well as brightening it later as a mix for drinks like vodka and gin. Orange is a favourite flavouring for fizzy soft drinks too and could make a form of home-made orangeade similar to **lemonade,** except that very little (if any) extra sugar would be needed. Oil from the rind of bitter oranges flavours liqueurs like Cointreau and Grand Marnier.

word origin Orange comes from the Dravidian *narayam,* meaning 'perfume within', via the Arabic *naranj*, the medieval Latin *aurantium* and Italian *arancia*. An orangery is a conservatory-like building originally constructed to give oranges protection against frost and cold weather – the first one was built in France at the Tuileries palace in Paris and is now an art gallery, but the biggest one was constructed for Louis XIV at Versailles so that he could have a year-round supply of fruit.

The description orangeman, meaning a militantly Protestant person in Northern Ireland, comes from the Orange Order set up in 1795 to 'protect' that country from Catholicism. It got its name from the orange badges original members wore, to indicate their allegiance to the Protestant king William III, who came from Holland but whose family belonged to the House of Orange (still the ruling family of the Netherlands), which had its origins in the city of Orange in France.

• Oranges made their way from China to India, then through Asia to the Middle East where they became popular in the Arab cultures of the Mediterranean. They were probably introduced into Europe through Arab conquest, although they may have arrived earlier, via Arab trade. The first ones were bitter, similar to modern Sevilles; sweet oranges didn't arrive until very late in the 15th century, brought to Portugal via India and China, which is why they were initially known as 'China' oranges to distinguish them from bitter ones. Columbus took oranges to the New World where they flourished, and the first orange groves were in operation in Florida by 1580.

• A few first sweet oranges seem to have arrived in Britain by the late 16th century, but they reached the height of their popularity around the middle of the 17th century when they became a popular theatre snack, sold by young girls like Nell Gwyn, who later found fame and fortune as the mistress of king Charles II.

• The flowers of the orange tree are nearly as useful as the fruit: the blossoms of bitter oranges are distilled into neroli, an important aromatherapy oil, and a combination of neroli and water makes orange-flower water, a popular ingredient in baking and sweets. Orange blossoms, of course, are also associated with purity and eternal love, and therefore often feature at weddings. They should be discarded before the end of the first month of the marriage, however, because according to one old tale, if they are kept for longer the marriage will be childless.

papaya

The papaya (*Carica papaya*) is the berry **fruit** of a tree-like herb that is native to Central America, but now produced in tropical areas around the world, including Brazil, the West Indies, Hawaii and South-east Asia. It is occasionally (and confusingly) called pawpaw, although this fruit has no connection with the knobbly, soft-fleshed tropical fruit of the *Annonaceae* family

called pawpaw, which is actually a type of custard apple.

The papaya plant is tall with a frill of star-shaped leaves at the top. Under this the fruits grow in clusters around the trunk-like stalk, anything from 50–150 per plant. Papayas are similar in shape and size to large pears, with inedible skin that starts off green and becomes blotchy yellow-orange as it ripens. Their flesh is buttery in consistency, melon-like in taste and orange or salmon pink in colour, and there are lots of tiny black seeds encased in a sort of jelly in the central cavity. The plant has one oddity: some varieties have different male and female trees, with the female ones only fruiting when pollinated by a male, but others are hermaphroditic, having both male and female characteristics in the one plant, and so are self-pollinating.

using it Papayas should be firm, but with some 'give' when pressed; avoid very soft fruit or any with soft spots. They will keep in the refrigerator for 4–6 days depending on how ripe they were when bought; an under-ripe papaya will mature in a few days at warm room temperature.

Papayas can be eaten like avocados: halve, discard the seeds and spoon out the flesh, preferably with some lime juice sprinkled over. Or peel, cut up and mix with yoghurt, mascarpone or sweetened coconut cream, or add to fruit salads. Puréed flesh can be used to flavour ice-creams, fools, **soufflés** and other desserts; papaya shouldn't, however, be used with gelatine-based ones since it contains an enzyme that prevents them from setting. Papaya is occasionally used in savoury dishes, working well with prosciutto, cooked ham or smoked chicken, or can be used to make chutney or jam.

word origin Spanish explorers found papaya in Central America and introduced it to Europe. Their name for it has been borrowed into English, and comes from the Carib name for the fruit, *ababai*.

• Unripe papaya, papaya leaves and papaya stalks contain a milky residue called papain, which can tenderize meat so effectively that the leaves are ground into a powder used in commercial meat tenderizers. In countries where the fruit is produced, the leaves are simply wrapped around meat and left for a time to do the same thing; in the United Kingdom since the leaves aren't available, unripe green papaya might do the trick, sliced or pulped and spread over both sides, in the same way as **kiwi fruit**.

passionfruit

This is the name given to the **fruit** of several related climbing vines native to Brazil, but now grown in tropical areas around the world, including Latin America, Australia, Hawaii and Malaysia. The most important species of passionfruit, sometimes called purple granadilla, is *Passiflora edulis*, which is golf ball-sized. It starts off with a smooth green shell when immature, turning brittle, purple-brown then slightly dimpled as it becomes ripe; inside, the pink-tinged shell contains greenish-orange pulpy flesh with many tiny edible black seeds. The only other species occasionally available in Europe is the giant granadilla (*Passiflora quadrangularis*), which is larger with an orange-brown shell. Both types have a unique sweet-sharp taste and rich perfume, the giant granadilla being less flavourful than the smaller purple fruit.

using it Fruits should be shiny and look slightly moist; if they are still smooth they are unripe. Unripe passionfruit will mature in a few days at warm room temperature; ripe fruit will keep in a cool place for 3–4 days.

To eat most simply, cut in half and spoon out the pulp and seeds, which can be served with cream, ice-cream or yoghurt, or added to fruit salads. When passionfruit is used as the flavouring base for mousses, **soufflés**, jellies, fools or **sorbets**, the seeds are usually removed by pushing the pulp through a sieve; warming the pulp slightly first will make it separate more easily from the seeds. Passionfruit pulp is a traditional filling for cheesecake and Pavlova.

word origin The fruit is named after its flower, the passionflower (see below).

• The name of the fruit and flower doesn't mean they are aphrodisiacs – the 'passion' they refer to is the Passion or suffering and death of Christ. The flower was given its name by early Spanish missionaries in South America because they believed it had been created to enable them to teach native peoples about the Crucifixion: different parts of the flower represented the nails that pinned Christ to the Cross, his wounds, the crown of thorns put on his head, and the sponge soaked in vinegar offered to him as he hung there. The 10 petals also had significance, standing in for the 12 disciples, minus Judas and Peter.

peach

Native to China, the peach (*Prunus persica*) is the stone **fruit** of a deciduous tree of the rose family, and is related to the apricot, plum and almond. It grows best in warm temperate climates and major producers include the Mediterranean area, the United States and South Africa.

There are three main types, each with many varieties. Freestone and clingstone peaches both have downy skin, and range in colour from nearly white to red-flushed yellow; their main point of difference, as their names suggest, is that in freestone peaches the stones are loosely positioned inside the fruits, while in clingstones, they adhere to the surrounding flesh. Nectarines (*Prunus persica* var. *nectarina*) are not, as is commonly believed, a cross between peach and plum, but smooth-skinned peaches. They are often a deeper reddish-yellow colour than downy-skinned varieties, and can have free or clinging stones. Their flesh is a little firmer than that of peaches, and there is a hint of tartness under the sweet taste.

Most peaches and nectarines are picked just before ripe, then refrigerated so that they finish ripening at their destination. Those allowed to ripen on the tree before being harvested have a better flavour.

using it These fruits are relatively rare and expensive outside their natural summer season. They should be heavy for their weight, have clear unblemished skin and just a little 'give' when pressed; avoid any with greenish tinges since it could mean that they were picked too early and are dry and rather tasteless. White-fleshed peaches are more perfumed than darker-fleshed ones. Peaches will keep in the refrigerator for a few days. The skin is edible, but if it needs to be removed, immerse the fruit in boiling water for 30–45 seconds, after which it should peel off easily.

Ripe fruits can be enjoyed as they are. Puréed flesh can flavour fools, ice-creams and **soufflés**, as well as being used as a filling for pancakes, cakes and tarts; halves or slices can be spiced and grilled with a layer of brown sugar and butter, and combined with almonds to make crumbles or pies. The French chef Escoffier created the classic peach dish, peach Melba (poached halves filled with vanilla ice-cream and topped with raspberry coulis), in honour of the early 20th-century Australian soprano Nellie Melba, a lady who liked her food. By stirring a little kirsch into the coulis, and sprinkling over some chopped almonds, this became peach cardinal.

Peaches are occasionally used in savoury dishes too: they have an affinity with chicken, pork and ham, and also give a sweet taste to otherwise savoury rice- or pasta-based salads. Nectarines can be substituted for peaches in recipes.

word origin Peach is from the Latin *Malum persicum*, meaning 'Persian apple' (peaches first came to Europe from Persia, and early Greeks and Romans thought the fruit originated there). This was later shortened to just *persica*, which became *peche* in medieval French, and the English word was borrowed from the French. Nectarines first appeared in England in the 17th century and were so juicy and sweet they were described as being 'nectar-like', hence the name.

did you know?

• Peaches were cultivated in China over 3000 years ago and spread west to Persia (modern-day Iran). It was there, so the legends say, that they were found by Alexander the Great, who brought them back to Europe in the 3rd century BC. The Romans probably introduced them to Britain where they remained exotic and rare, only really grown in the odd rich gentleman's hothouse until refrigerated transport brought fresh ones within the reach of most people in the early years of the 20th century.

• The Chinese have many legends about the peach tree. There is, for instance, the miraculous Peachtree of the Gods that took a thousand years to grow, a further thousand to flower and a final thousand to produce ripe fruit, but which bestowed on anyone who ate even one of its fruit a lifespan of 3000 years. The enthusiastic (or the greedy) who ate several more became immortal.

pear

The common pear (*Pyrus communis*) is the pome **fruit** of a temperate tree of the rose family, native to Europe and western Asia. It is closely related to the apple, and more distantly to stone fruits like the apricot and cherry. It is probably descended from original wild ancestors that include the Asian pear (*Pyrus pyrifolia*), a crisp, apple-shaped fruit still cultivated in China and Japan, among other places. But it isn't related at all to the prickly pear, the fruit of various cactus plants, which has thick warty skin that can be anything from green to red depending on the variety, and fragrant green, orange or red flesh.

There are thousands of varieties of ordinary pear, although only about a hundred or so are cultivated commercially; major producers include Italy, France and the United States. Fruits range from yellowish through various greens to reddish-brown in colour, from squat and almost round to thin, elongated and teardrop in shape, and are usually about the same size as an avocado. The flesh varies a little in colour too, from off-white to greenish or even pink-tinged. Pears spoil very quickly after they mature and so are picked before they are ripe and ripened off the tree.

The most popular varieties include Comice, plump and squat with mottled green-brownish-yellow skin and juicy flesh – probably the best-tasting variety and one of the most versatile, being equally good for cooking and eating; Conference, thinner and smaller than most other varieties, with greenish-brown skin and fairly hard flesh that can be crisp and refreshing; Williams', which comes in several varieties, and can be yellowish-green to brownish-yellow in colour, good for cooking, and the type normally used in canning; and Beurré, which also comes in several varieties, all of which have sweet, soft juicy flesh.

using it Although there's usually some sort of pear around, most of the better varieties like Comice and Conference have an autumn/winter season, while Williams' become available in late summer. It's quite difficult to tell when a pear is ripe (one clue is that the stem area should have a little 'give'), so it's probably better to buy it slightly hard for eating and let it ripen at room temperature for a few days. The skin is edible and adds to the crispness of taste, but the fruit is often peeled. The flesh discolours quite quickly when exposed to air, so cut as near to using as possible.

Pear is a popular ingredient in desserts and baking: poached and puréed to flavour soufflés, sorbets and creams; halved and poached in flavoured sweetened wine to make one of the easiest of puddings; and halved, poached and combined with chocolate sauce and vanilla ice-cream to make poires Belle Hélène, the French dessert named after an Offenbach operetta about Helen of Troy. Poached pear halves or slices make a good filling for tarts too.

Pears can also be used with savoury ingredients: as part of a salad, particularly with more bitter leaves like radicchio and rocket; with avocado as a 'two pear' salad with a nutty **vinaigrette** or light blue-cheese dressing; instead of fig or melon with **prosciutto**; and, perhaps best of all, with blue or Brie cheese as a first course. Williams' pears are the ones used to make the French liqueur Poire William, and other varieties are specially grown to make perry, a drink similar to **cider**.

word origin Pear comes from the Latin for the fruit, *pirum*. The full name of the Comice variety, which originated in Angers in France in the 19th century, is Doyenné du Comice, meaning 'the society's best' (it was developed in the gardens of the local *comice horticole* or horticultural society). The British Conference variety is named after an International Pear Conference, where it won first prize in 1885. The appearance of the fruit is the origin for 'pear-shaped' when it refers to someone's (usually female) body, indicating that the bottom half is more than somewhat larger than the top bit; and 'to go pear-shaped' is probably based on much the same idea, being originally Air Force slang for something that 'went wrong'.

did you know?

• By medieval times, pear cultivation in England was sophisticated, and there were distinct varieties for eating and cooking, the latter being called 'wardens' and often treated almost like a separate fruit. Williams' pears were created in Britain, by a Mr Stair, schoolmaster in Berkshire in the late 18th century, and were called Stair's Pears at first (there *was* a Mr Williams, however; he was the nurseryman who popularized the variety). Williams' pears were taken to the United States by a man called Enoch Bartlett and renamed Bartletts there, the name by which they are still known in North America.

• The pear gives its name to a well-known medieval instrument of torture, the 'pear of confession'. It was a fiendish pear-shaped metal device that was inserted into the mouth of its victims, then expanded. Slowly.

pineapple

The **fruit** of a small herbaceous plant, pineapple (*Ananas comosus*) is probably native to Brazil, but now cultivated in tropical areas around the world, including the West Indies, Hawaii and parts of Africa and Southeast Asia. It isn't, in fact, one fruit, but a collection of about 150 lozenge-like fruitlets that grow on a short stem, fused together in a mound around a central woody core, and topped by a plume of thick, sharp, narrow green leaves. Although the knobbly skin is thick and tough (it's made from the modified leaves or bracts and sepals of the plant), inside the flesh is sweet, fragrant and very juicy. There are many varieties, ranging in colour from pale yellowy brown to deep orange-brown, and in weight from dwarf (about 500g) to a fairly monstrous 3–4kg. Pineapples are picked as near to being ripe as possible since they stop maturing once removed from the plant (they will become softer but not sweeter). Luckily they keep quite well, which means they can be transported across the world and still be in good condition when they arrive.

A great deal of the crop is canned, still one of the most popular ways to eat the fruit, and trimmings from canning are pressed to create pineapple juice.

using it The best pineapples are uniformly coloured and plump with crisp, green leaves. The most reliable test for ripeness is a sweet fragrance. Ripe fruits will usually keep in the refrigerator for a day or so after purchase. Canned pineapple isn't a patch on the fresh fruit; that canned in juice is less cloying than fruit preserved in syrup.

Getting at the flesh isn't as complicated as it's sometimes made out to be. Cut off the base and the crown of leaves, then stand the fruit upright and slice down the sides to cut off the skin, taking as many of the 'eyes' (the little brown discs) as possible. For wedges or chunks, cut the fruit lengthways into quarters and remove the core; for rings, cut across the fruit, then cut out the core from each slice.

Pineapple can be served on its own, with rum or kirsch, ginger and coconut-flavoured cream (there is a real affinity with all of these), or with other fruit in a salad. Pineapple is also used in baking, as a filling for tarts, cakes and cheesecakes. With savoury foods, it complements ham, pork and chicken, and is often added to Chinese-style sweet-and-sour dishes. Pineapple juice can be used in punches, and is one of the ingredients (along with tequila and coconut cream) in a classic piña colada.

Pineapple contains an enzyme (see below) that breaks down protein, so the fresh fruit cannot be used in puddings set with gelatine. For the same reason, if mixing it with yoghurt or soft cheese, it should be added just before serving. (Cooking the fruit deactivates the enzyme.)

word origin Pineapple comes from the Spanish *piña*, a reference to the fruit's resemblance to a pine cone. In fact, when the unknown, odd-looking fruit first turned up in England in the 17th century it was known simply as 'pine'. The 'apple' ending was added later, probably in an attempt to make it seem less strange by linking it with a familiar fruit, rather than for any supposed resemblance in taste to apple.

• It was in the West Indies that Spanish explorers first came across pineapple during Columbus's second voyage in 1493. They introduced it into Europe where it became fashionable, even in cool rainy Britain. In the 18th and 19th centuries, the rich English gentry not only cultivated pineapples at vast expense in their hothouses, but also sculpted them in stone to stick on their gates and over their doors as a symbol of harmony and prosperity.

• Pineapple contains the enzyme bromelin, which is similar to the enzymes in **kiwi fruit** and **papaya** that tenderize meat. The pineapple enzyme is particularly fierce, however, so much so that those who pick the fruit or work in the canneries need to wear special gloves to protect the flesh on their hands.

plum

A relative of the peach, apricot and cherry, the plum is the fruit of a temperate tree of the rose family that probably originated in western Asia. It is usually oval to round in shape, and skin colour varies from yellow through green, red and purple to bluish-black. The flesh varies in colour too, from yellow through dark red, and in taste it can be anything from very sweet and juicy to mouth-puckeringly sour. Plums always contain a central stone, sometimes clinging to the flesh, sometimes loose.

There are several types. The common plum (*Prunus domestica*) deserves its name since most cultivated plums belong to this species. Depending on variety, it can be large or small and almost any colour, but it is always sweet. Common plums include favourites like Victoria and Laxton, both with yellowish-red skins and sweet flesh. The Japanese plum (*Prunus salicina*) actually originated in China, but is so called because Europeans first came across it there. It can vary in colour from yellowish-green to deep red and is widely grown in California. Popular varieties include Santa Rosa, which is usually dark red in colour. The American plum (*Prunus americana* and others) is native to America and still grown there, especially along the east coast of the United States; it is now often crossbred with the Japanese plum to create hybrid varieties. The damson (*Prunus insititia*), native to eastern Europe, nearly always has dark skin and is small and hard, with a sour taste. The greengage (*Prunus insititia italica*), which probably originated in Armenia, is round, with skin and flesh that can vary from yellowish to mid-green; it tastes very sweet. The sloe (*Prunus spinosa*), the wild fruit of the blackthorn tree and native to Britain, is small, with bluish skin and green flesh. It is the sourest of them all, and is always used cooked or fermented. See also **prune**, which is a dried plum.

using it Many plums are available throughout the year, but greengages (July–August), Victorias (September–October), and damsons and sloes (October–November) are still seasonal. Sweet plums should be firm with some 'give' when pressed; avoid any with soft spots. Most will keep for 3–4 days in a cool place, about double that in the refrigerator. Some sweet plums and most cooking ones have tough skin; this can be removed by immersing the fruit in boiling water for 30 seconds, then peeling.

Sweet plums (including greengages) can be eaten raw or cooked. Slice them raw into fruit salads or halve and serve with ice-cream or yoghurt. Cooked plums are very versatile: poach into a compote by themselves or with other fruit, or use as a filling for tarts, pies or crumbles, especially with almonds. They are also occasionally made into ice-cream, and sweet ripe plums can be used in some recipes instead of cherries or peaches.

In savoury cooking, plums are made into a dipping sauce widely used in Chinese cooking, occasionally baked with pork or made into a soup (in the same way as sour cherries). All plums make good jam (damsons are rarely used for anything else), and many are used in chutneys and pickles as well. They add a good flavour to alcohol too; plums and damsons make good wine and brandy, while sloes are now used mostly to make wine and a type of gin.

word origin Plum comes from the Latin for the fruit, *prunum*. Damsons originally reached Europe from the Middle East via Damascus in present-day Syria and during medieval times were known as damascenes, gradually shortened to the modern word. The romantic French name for greengage, *Reine Claude* (Queen Claude), comes from the wife of the 16th-century French king François I, who helped introduce the fruit to France; it got its English name from Sir William Gage, who introduced the fruit into Britain in the early part of the 18th century.

A 'plum' was the slang expression for £100,000, which may be why the phrase 'it's a plum', meaning wonderful or very desirable, came about. Plum puddings or cakes probably did contain dried plums (prunes) at one point, but by medieval times these had been replaced by raisins; the names of the dishes, however, continued as they were, and in fact the word 'plum' was sometimes used to describe dried fruit generally.

pomegranate

This is the **fruit** of a shrub (*Punica granatum*) that is native to Iran, but now grown in tropical and subtropical areas around the world; major modern producers include Iran, India, Israel and Spain. The pomegranate tree can reach 2–4m in height and is deciduous in Europe, but evergreen in tropical areas. The fruit is harvested mature (it doesn't ripen off the tree) and is roughly the same shape and size as an orange, with inedible, tough leathery skin that ranges in colour from yellowish-brown through to bright rich red. A thick, equally inedible pith lies under the skin, protecting the bits that *are* edible – sections of small, individual, juicy pink-red sacs, each containing a tiny

seed, which look like jewels and have a refreshingly tart-sweet flavour.

using it Pomegranates are normally available in larger supermarkets during autumn and the run-up to Christmas. The best ones are plump and bright in colour and feel heavy for their size; it is best to avoid any that look dull or are starting to wrinkle slightly. If stored in the refrigerator they will keep for three weeks or more, but they dry out at room temperature.

One of the reasons for the pomegranate's lukewarm popularity is that it's time-consuming and messy to prepare: cut the top off, score the skin lengthways into quarters and gently break open the fruit, then separate the pulp from the pith and membranes (this will make a lot of juice that can stain work surfaces and clothes). Preparing the fruit in a bowl of cold water makes the job neater and easier, as the pulp sinks to the bottom, leaving the skin and pith floating on top to be scooped off. The flesh can be used in an exotic fruit salad or as a beautiful garnish for puddings. The seeds are sometimes dried and served separately as a condiment or garnish, particularly in India and China.

Pomegranates are used in savoury cooking too, either as flesh or juice (there is a commercial juice concentrate available). In the national dish of Iran, fesenjoon, browned pieces of duck or lamb are simmered in a sauce made from stock, sugar, onions, ground walnuts and pomegranate juice. The combination with walnuts is common in Georgia and other countries of the Caucasus too, featuring in soups and meat and game casseroles. In the West, pomegranate juice is sweetened and concentrated commercially to make the syrup grenadine, a popular ingredient in cocktails.

word origin Pomegranate comes via Old French from the medieval Latin *pomum granatum,* meaning 'apple with many seeds'. It first arrived in English as *poumgarnet* during the 14th century.

• The many seeds of the pomegranate didn't go unnoticed in the ancient world, so the fruit became a fertility symbol. It also has its own Greek myth, the one that explains how winter and summer came to be. The story involves a nymph (Persephone), a god (of the underworld, Pluto), and lust (he captured her and carried her off to his kingdom). Pluto chose the wrong nymph – this one had a mother and she happened to be the goddess of fruit and fertility. In an attempt to get her daughter back, Demeter (the mother) decreed that no plant should bear fruit while she was in the underworld. Persephone knew that if she swallowed food during her captivity she couldn't return to the world, but eventually succumbed and ate a pomegranate. She then tried to pretend that she hadn't by spitting out the seeds – all except six, which she swallowed. She did eventually return to the world, of course, but ever after had to spend a month in the underworld every year for each seed she had eaten. And plants were only allowed to blossom when she re-emerged.

prune

A prune is a dried **plum**, always one of the firm-fleshed, dark-skinned, sugary varieties with loose stones. Traditionally, the best-quality prunes were dried in the sun, but nowadays they are normally harvested ripe, washed and put into special ovens until they lose about four-fifths of their moisture (larger, moister vacuum-packed fruits have some of this moisture restored before packing). Sometimes the stone is removed before this procedure, sometimes not. Although several varieties of plum are used to produce prunes, only those made from prune d'Agen, a type named after the town of Agen in France, are sold under their varietal name.

using it Most prunes are stoneless and don't require rehydrating before being used, but those that do should be steeped in a liquid like water, tea, wine or fruit juice for 4–8 hours until they plump up. If they are to be added to a moist stew or compote to be cooked for a long time, they won't need to be rehydrated.

Prunes used to have a bad press: all those nursery-type meals where they were teamed with watery milk puddings or custard put generations of people off for life. This is a shame, because poached or soaked prunes served with a creamy custard or rice pudding can be delicious and they are equally good with yoghurt or as part of a fruit compote or salad. The French traditionally steep them in Armagnac (made just up the road from Agen, where the best prunes come from), and serve them as is or make the mixture into an ice-cream, **soufflé** or mousse. Prunes are also used in baking: as a filling for tarts and pastries, with apples in crumbles or pies, or stirred into cake and muffin mixtures.

The sweetness of prunes can be used to particularly good effect in savoury dishes too: rabbit, chicken and pork are the classic partners, but prunes can also be part of a stuffing for turkey, goose or even firm-fleshed fish, or as part of a sauce for game. They can be stirred into cabbage dishes too, particularly red cabbage, or into butter- or kidney-bean stews.

word origin Prune comes from the Latin for plum, *prunum*.

• Plums were probably first commercially dried into prunes in the area around Turkey and Persia (modern-day Iran), and reached France in the 12th or 13th century. Agen near Bordeaux became the centre of the trade. Agen prunes reached America courtesy of the 1848 California Gold Rush and a French nurseryman called Louis Pellier, who went there to seek his fortune. He didn't find gold, but bought some orchards instead and a few years later sent home for cuttings of his favourite plum tree. These trees became the foundation of the prune industry in California, which now accounts for about 80 percent of the world market.

raisin, sultana & currant

These are the dried **fruits** of various varieties of **grape**. Most are dried naturally in bunches in the sun, in the vineyards where they are grown, until they lose roughly four-fifths of their moisture, when they are stripped from the branches, cleaned and packed. It takes about 1.8kg of fresh grapes to create 450g of dried fruit. The practice of drying grapes probably originates in the Mediterranean area, still an important producer, although California is the world's largest supplier of raisins.

Raisins are dried white (green) grapes, normally Thompson Seedless in California and seeded Valencias and Muscatels in Spain (their seeds are mechanically removed after drying). Valencias and golden raisins (similar to sultanas and produced in California) are treated with sulphur dioxide to keep their colour light. In size, raisins are usually smaller than sultanas, but larger and less wrinkled than currants.

Sultanas are produced from several varieties of white seedless grapes, notably in Turkey, Greece and Australia. Most are treated with sulphur dioxide to help keep their colour light, and those from the Mediterranean are often moistened with mineral oil to keep their skin shiny as well. Currants are dried small, hard black grapes of various varieties. They are produced mainly in Greece, although Australia and the United States also produce some. Currants are the darkest and most shrivelled of the three types, and should not be confused with the berry fruits of the same name (see **currants**).

using them Nearly all the raisins and sultanas sold now are moist enough not to require rehydrating, although steeping them in liquid (anything from tea or fruit juice to wine or brandy) will enhance their flavour.

A handful of raisins or sultanas makes a good snack, or an addition to fruit salads or breakfast cereals. These fruits are also cooked and are versatile enough to be used in sweet dishes, baked ones or with savoury ingredients. In desserts they are added to other fruits like apple or rhubarb as part of a filling for pies, crumbles or steamed puddings; and in savoury cooking they can be stirred into lamb, chicken or pork curries, tagines, pilaffs, or stuffings for poultry, fish or vegetables. All three types are used in baking to flavour cakes, cheesecakes, biscuits, tarts, teabreads, muffins and scones.

word origin Raisin means grape in French, probably the origin of the English word. 'Raisons of Corauntz', or grapes from Corinth, was the name given to small dried fruit in England during medieval times (the Greek city of Corinth was one of the centres of production at that time), but gradually this mouthful was shortened to 'currants'. Sultanas originally came from Turkey; sultana is also the name of one of the varieties of grape used to make the dried fruit.

did you know?

• 'Raisons of Corauntz' were introduced into England during the early 14th century and became more popular and fashionable than fresh fruit (which was regarded with suspicion and thought to cause plague, among other things). They were used with abandon by the rich since they were expensive, but even the poor managed a few on high days and holy days, serving them with fish, as purées with meat and as an ingredient in cameline sauce, a medieval cinnamon-flavoured ketchup served with meat dishes.

raspberry

This is the small, slightly hairy, oval **fruit** of a bush of the rose family that originated in Eurasia and is a distant relative of the peach and the almond. Like its close relative the **blackberry**, the raspberry isn't botanically a berry at all, but a mound of tiny fruits called drupelets, which cling around a white core or receptacle; when a raspberry is ready for picking, the fruit comes away easily from the receptacle, leaving it on the bush. Although nearly all the fruits we come across are red, raspberries can vary in colour from pale yellow through red to black (a wild American species, *Rubus occidentalis*); in taste they range from quite tart to sweet.

Most modern raspberries are descended from the European wild raspberry (*Rubus idaeus*) and crossed with other species like the American *Rubus strigosus* to make them hardier and more resistant to disease. Raspberry bushes grow in cool temperate zones all around the world – even in Alaska and the Himalayas. The bulk of the British crop is grown in Scotland, which claims to cultivate the best raspberries in the world. The close relationship with the blackberry has led to cross-breeding during recent years, to create popular hybrids like the loganberry and tayberry.

using it There is a natural season during summer between late June and late August, but in reality raspberries are now available for most of the year – at a price. Fruits should be plump, firm and without their receptacles (unripe ones may still have them); avoid any that are losing their shape and colour and any punnets with profuse staining on the bottom. Raspberries can be stored in the refrigerator, unwashed and with plenty of room in a dish or punnet, for about 48 hours.

Raspberries are always a treat, and cream, yoghurt or crème fraîche plus perhaps a little sugar is all that is needed to make the perfect dessert. They are also used to flavour jellies, **sorbets**, fools, mousses or **soufflés**, are the basis of a classic coulis, and make a popular filling for cakes, pastries and tarts and one of the best fruit jams. They are an essential ingredient in summer pudding, a sweetened mixture of berry fruits, including black or red currants, blackberries and strawberries,

encased in bread and weighted overnight until cold and solid. Loganberries and tayberries can be substituted for raspberries, and all three can be used in any recipe for blackberries.

Raspberries are used occasionally with savoury ingredients – for example, in a salad or as part of a sauce for game, especially the feathered variety popular in Scotland, like grouse – and they make a good-flavoured vinegar.

word origin The first part is a shortened version of the original English word for raspberry, *raspis*, although where that came from isn't known. The Latin name *idaeus* can be traced back to Mount Ida in Crete, where many wild raspberries grew. 'To blow a raspberry at', meaning to make a rude noise indicating disapproval, we owe to rhyming slang: raspberry tart meaning 'fart'.

rhubarb

Technically a vegetable grown for its stalk, rhubarb (*Rheum rhaponticum* and others) is now always used as a fruit. It is a perennial plant distantly related to dock and **sorrel** which, depending on the species (there are several), originated in China, the Himalayas or Siberia. Stalks are 2.5–7cm in width and 10–18cm in length, and may be yellowish-green to red in colour. In taste rhubarb ranges from quite sour to very sour. It contains oxalic acid, large quantities of which can be poisonous; the large, thick green leaves contain much more of this and so shouldn't be eaten.

using it Rhubarb is a late winter/early spring plant. The first forced stalks come into shops towards the end of January, with unforced ones being available from the middle of March; they are more or less gone by June, although they can be found from time to time out of season. Stalks should be crisp, firm and unblemished and as red as possible (forced rhubarb is pink or pale red;

later rhubarb is deep red); avoid any that are floppy or split. Both types will keep in the refrigerator for a few days.

Rhubarb is too tart to be eaten raw and is therefore always cooked. To prepare, trim off the ends; if the stalks are stringy, peel them too. Cut into 5cm lengths and stew for 10–15 minutes with as much sugar as personal taste dictates, plus flavourings like ginger, cinnamon and allspice (no liquid is needed). Hot or cold, the traditional accompaniment is custard, but yoghurt, ice-cream and cream taste just as good. Rhubarb can also be made into ice-cream or jam (the latter with the flavourings suggested above), and used as a basis for fools, crumbles or pies, often with apples.

Rhubarb is occasionally used in savoury dishes – it goes quite well with pork (as part of the flavouring for a stew perhaps) and can be substituted for gooseberries in sauces for oily fish like mackerel and herring.

word origin Rhubarb is from the Greek *rha barbaron,* meaning 'foreign rhubarb': *rha* was the word the Greeks used for the River Volga in Russia and may have been used as a definition of foreignness, although in this case it could also have been literal, since early medicinal rhubarb (see below) was transported to Europe from China, and the Volga was en route.

did you know?

• Dried rhubarb root was imported into ancient Greece and Rome as a laxative (a property also attributed to fresh rhubarb), but the fresh stalks don't seem to have been used at all. It was introduced into England during the 16th century, again as a medicinal or ornamental plant, and it wasn't until the early 1800s that anybody thought to cook it. Queen Victoria was partial to rhubarb, and both she and her husband, Prince Albert, had varieties named after them.

strawberry

The strawberry (*Fragaria ananassa* and others) is one of several trailing plants of the rose family, native to cooler climates in Europe, Asia and the Americas, depending on the species. Technically it is a 'false' **fruit**, and is actually a receptacle for the little dry specks on the outside of the strawberry which are, in fact, tiny individual fruits, each containing a seed. Strawberries vary considerably in size and shape, although they are normally round or conical, and can be bright to mottled red in colour. At their best, they are very sweet and juicy, but can be tough and quite tasteless if picked too early.

using it Traditionally this was the fruit that meant summer had arrived, appearing as it did on shop shelves about the middle of June and disappearing from them around the end of August. Now, however, strawberries are grown all around the world and are available for most of the year. Berries should be firm and a good bright colour with unblemished skin; avoid any with soft spots. They should be used as soon after picking (or buying) as possible, but will keep for a day or so in the refrigerator.

If ripe and sweet, strawberries need only to be hulled before serving with cream, crème fraîche, yoghurt or ice-cream. Red wine, liqueurs and orange juice work well with strawberries (in the classic French dessert strawberries Romanov, they are sliced and steeped in a mixture of orange juice and orange liqueur before being served with whipped cream); new ideas include a sprinkling of black pepper or a drip or two of rich balsamic vinegar. Strawberries are a popular ingredient in baking, particularly as a filling for tarts, cheesecakes and shortcakes, and the purée can flavour **soufflés**, ice-creams, fools, mousses and milkshakes. The fruit makes wonderful jam too.

word origin Strawberry probably comes from the Anglo-Saxon for the wild strawberry plant, *streawberige*, literally berries with runners (the plant is notorious for spreading itself by growing runners with plantlets on them).

did you know?

• The small, fragrant fruits we know as wild strawberries were grown in classical Rome and in gardens in both France and England during medieval times. However, during the 17th century a new species, *Fragaria virginiana*, was brought from North America to Europe, to be joined in the early years of the 18th century by another new type, *Fragaria chiloensis*, this time sent from South America by a French naval officer called Amédée Frezier. The two American species eventually hybridized naturally to produce the ancestor of most of the 500-plus cultivated varieties of strawberry we know today.

watermelon

The watermelon (*Citrullus lanatus*) is the **fruit** of a member of the gourd family and a relative therefore of the cucumber, marrow, and New World squashes like the pumpkin. It is only distantly related to the melon. It is native to Africa, but grows in hot climates elsewhere; Israel, North and South America and Africa are the main producers.

Watermelons are round or oval in shape and vary from light yellowish-green to dark green in colour, with some striped or spotted varieties in between. They can grow to an enormous size: specimens of up to 25kg aren't that uncommon, although one of the most popular varieties, called Sugar Baby, usually weighs in at a more modest 4–5kg. The flesh is normally red, although pink or yellow are seen occasionally. The flesh is actually a sort of placenta for the edible, mostly black seeds that, unlike melons, are distributed throughout the fruit rather than being contained in a central cavity.

using it Although it's available all year round, the watermelon is associated with hot summer days and is therefore mainly available then. It should be heavy for its size (an awesome thought) and sound dull when tapped. Given the size, most shops sell it whole, halved or even quartered; when cut, look for flesh with a good strong colour and no white streaks. Whole watermelons will keep for about two weeks in a cool place; cut ones can be stored in the refrigerator for 2–4 days.

Being almost 95 percent water, a slice of chilled watermelon is very refreshing. Cut into chunks, it can be added to fruit salads, or used to make a type of water-ice. The rind is occasionally pickled.

word origin The first part of the name is an acknowledgment that this particular melon is about 10 percent more watery than any other type; the second comes from the Greek *melopepon*, meaning 'apple gourd'.

did you know?

• Watermelons were cultivated in ancient Egypt and India, but don't seem to have reached classical Greece or Rome, and were probably introduced into Europe through the Moorish conquest of Spain. They reached Britain around the end of the 16th century. They were carried on slave ships from Africa to America, where they have been cultivated ever since, especially in the southern United States and in Brazil.
• There is now a square watermelon, invented by the Japanese to fit better into refrigerators and made by growing the plant inside a glass mold. Prices are gratifyingly square-shaped too, at about £60 per melon.

Bread, Cakes & Baking

Baking is one of the oldest food traditions in a world that has become a global village, and where we British now regularly eat foods from every continent. This has added even more excitement and pleasure to baking and eating bread, cakes and biscuits, as we can now extend our repertoire to include baked goods from a variety of countries. Home baking has always been strongest in the north and west of the United Kingdom, where traditional recipes and techniques have been preserved and high tea, with its wonderful selection of baked goods, is still an institution.

We are renowned for our traditional enriched breads, cakes and biscuits. I'm not sure why this is, but it might have something to do with our national sweet tooth!

Take advantage of what is available to discover and enjoy a veritable bakery cornucopia.
Gary Rhodes

It is rumoured that the institution of afternoon tea was invented by the gentry purely in order to have an extra meal at which to enjoy cakes and other dainties.

Bringing back and taking forward the best of British cookery has long been a passion of mine, and I am delighted that people today are once again choosing, cooking and eating traditional foods that had lost popularity over the years. Nowhere is this more evident than with the choice of bread, cakes and biscuits that we can buy or bake today. Take advantage of what is available to discover and enjoy a veritable bakery cornucopia.

bagel

This is a small, Jewish, ring-shaped **bread** made from an enriched yeast-raised dough. Traditional bagels have a glossy chewy crust and dense texture, thanks to the unusual cooking method – after the shaped dough has risen for the second time, the rings are boiled for a minute or so before being glazed and baked until golden. Many commercial bagels aren't made in this way any more, however, but instead are cooked in steam-injected ovens. Bagels are available plain or flavoured (garlic, caraway and cinnamon and/or raisins are popular), or with toppings like onion flakes and poppy or sesame seeds.

using it Fresh bagels should be eaten as close to baking as possible; packaged ones will keep for a few days or can be frozen. Bagels are usually split in half, toasted and buttered, to be eaten at breakfast or brunch, often with scrambled or poached eggs or, the popular classic, with smoked salmon and cream cheese. They can also be served with fillings – roast beef with horseradish, fish pâté, cold salmon and cucumber, and tuna mayonnaise are all good.

word origin Bagel probably comes from the German *bügel,* meaning 'stirrup', or *beigel,* 'ring', via the Yiddish *beygel,* and could be an indication of its shape, or a reference to the story below.

did you know?

• The first printed reference to 'beygel' seems to have been in Cracow, Poland, in 1610, when it was recommended as a food for pregnant women (not just Jewish ones, *any* pregnant women). The favourite theory about the origin of the bagel, however, is that it was created by Jewish bakers in Vienna in 1683 and shaped like a stirrup to honour the King of Poland's prowess as a horseman and to thank him for helping Austria repel the Turks. However it came to be, its popularity spread around eastern Europe and from there reached the United States, probably around the beginning of the 20th century. From there it has spread out from its original ethnic base to become a national bread, and its current popularity elsewhere is probably due to American influence rather than any other.

baking powder

This is a flavourless commercial mixture used as a raising agent in baking. It's made up of an alkali (**bicarbonate of soda**), an acid (traditionally cream of tartar, but now often a mix of this plus another slower-acting acid like sodium pyrophosphate, or the latter alone) and a starchy filler, such as cornflour or arrowroot. The filler is included because a mixture containing only an alkali and an acid could spontaneously activate and give off carbon dioxide gas if it comes into contact with liquid, even moisture from its surroundings; the filler's job is to 'soak up' any environmental dampness and prevent this.

using it Baking powder does eventually lose its strength, but will keep for several months stored somewhere cool and dry. The amount needed depends on the quantity and type of flour and other ingredients being used, but is based on about a teaspoon per 100g of flour. To use, it is sifted with flour, which is then blended with liquid to make a batter or dough. The addition of the liquid activates the baking powder, the carbon dioxide gas produced as a result becoming trapped in the dough as air bubbles. When the dough is later cooked, the heat of the oven causes the mixture to rise.

Baking powder is normally used in recipes for cakes, biscuits and teabreads that include non-acidic liquids like water or milk: bicarbonate of soda can be used on its own to raise breads like **soda bread,** but only when combined with an acidic liquid like soured milk.

• Baking powder is an American creation and older than you might think: a crude alkali-only version based on potassium carbonate (called pearl ash) was around by the end of the 18th century. Unlike modern baking powder, however, pearl ash gave an unpleasant taste to whatever it was raising and, being an alkali-only mixture, it needed to be mixed with acidic liquids like soured milk or vinegar in order to work. Modern baking powder was invented (by horror actor Vincent Price's grandfather) about the middle of the 19th century.

bicarbonate of soda

Also known as baking soda or $NaHCO_3$, bicarbonate of soda is a powdered raising agent used in baking. It is an alkali, so needs to be combined with an acid in order to produce the carbon dioxide that causes mixtures to rise. This is done in one of three ways: by adding an acidic liquid like lemon juice, buttermilk or molasses to the dry mixture that contains the soda; by mixing it with a powdered acid (normally cream of tartar) and later activating the mixture by adding a non-acidic liquid such as water or ordinary milk; or by using it as part of commercial **baking powder**.

using it Bicarbonate of soda keeps for months in a cool dry place. When used by itself, it takes about ½ teaspoon per 100g of flour to raise an average dough, although this depends to some extent on the flour and other ingredients being used; with cream of tartar the ratio would be about ½ teaspoon cream of tartar, to ¼ teaspoon soda for the same amount. Baking powder, which contains a starchy filler as well as bicarbonate of soda and an acid, is weaker and a teaspoonful would be needed to activate 100g of flour. By itself or as part of a mixture, bicarbonate of soda is normally sifted with the flour and other dry ingredients before being blended with liquid.

This is the traditional raising agent in **soda bread** and biscuits like ginger nuts and digestives, but it can also be used to raise scones, muffins and cakes, providing it's mixed with an acidic liquid.

word origin The chemical compound is sodium bicarbonate, an alkaline salt; the alternative name of baking soda suggests one of its main uses.

• Various types of bicarbonate of soda go back a long way, to Roman times at least. The Roman cookery author, Apicius, recommended boiling green vegetables in water containing a pinch of *nitrum* (a Roman form of soda) to keep the colour bright, something that was still being done in 19th-century Britain despite the fact that it turned the vegetables mushy and soft.

biscuits

A biscuit is a small, thin cake that can be sweet or savoury and hard and crisp or soft and chewy. It is usually made from flour, with other ingredients such as sugar, fat, egg, ground nuts or oatmeal, and raising agents (normally **baking powder** or **bicarbonate of soda**) are added as appropriate and required. Most also contain flavourings like ginger, chocolate, dried fruit, golden syrup, icing or even grated cheese.

Biscuits are made in a variety of ways. The simplest are produced by mixing dry ingredients and flavourings together, then adding melted or solid fat and/or liquid and combining everything together into a thick dough. The dough is shaped by hand, or rolled out and cut into shapes (normally fingers or rounds), before being baked.

There are hundreds of popular biscuits. Sweet types include bourbons (crisp chocolate-flavoured fingers sandwiched together with chocolate filling), chocolate chip cookies (buttery discs containing small pieces of chocolate and sometimes nuts), digestives (semi-sweet crunchy rounds, sometimes topped with chocolate) and macaroons (based on ground almonds and egg whites). See also **shortbread**. Savoury favourites include Bath olivers (yeast-based rounds enriched with butter), cream crackers (crisp squares), oatcakes (made from oatmeal and classically raised with baking soda), and cheese straws (thin sticks flavoured with grated hard cheese and cayenne pepper).

using them Packaged biscuits will keep indefinitely, but once opened store them in an airtight tin and eat within a week or so. Home-made biscuits are best eaten within a day or so of being baked.

Most biscuits are enjoyed for themselves, but some are used in other dishes: finely crushed digestives, for instance, can be mixed with melted butter to make a base for a cheesecake and coarsely crushed macaroons or ginger nuts can be sprinkled on top of ice-cream (particularly vanilla or chocolate), fools or other creamy desserts. Sponge fingers, or boudoir biscuits, are sometimes used in trifles instead of trifle sponges; make a container for classic fruit and cream charlottes; and, moistened with Tia Maria and coffee, are layered with mascarpone in the Italian tiramisu.

word origin Biscuit comes from the Old French *bis* ('twice') and *cuit* ('cooked'), because traditionally biscuits were baked once to cook the dough, then again to dry them out and improve their keeping properties. At first, the English word was *bisket* or even *bisket bread*, but at some point during the 18th century this changed to the modern spelling. In the United States, the word biscuit is only used for a savoury scone-like bread; sweet biscuits are called cookies and savoury ones crackers.

Some individual biscuits have intriguing names. Digestives, for instance, are so called because they contain bicarbonate of soda, which helps to control flatulence;

hence they were originally marketed as being good for the digestion. Bath Olivers were created in the city of Bath by a Dr Oliver in the 18th century and have a stamp of their inventor in the middle. Boudoir biscuits actually started out life as funeral biscuits, but acquired their name because they became a favourite snack food at ladies' teas, presumably in their boudoirs.

did you know?

• A form of savoury biscuit was known in classical times: the Roman army appears not so much to have marched on its stomach as on a supply of what was called Parthian bread, a kind of heavy, dry biscuit. Navies relied on savoury biscuits as much as armies, and ship's biscuits, or hardtack as they were called, were an important part of sailors' diets during the days of sailing ships. On long voyages they were easy and light to store and kept for years without going off; there the good news ended – on a stormy voyage they rarely stayed dry and were often infested by weevils. Those biscuits that escaped this fate were often so hard that a hammer was needed to break them up.

• Sweet biscuits are equally ancient (the Romans had fried ones). By medieval times, slices of leftover enriched bread slices were being sprinkled with sugar and spices and baked again to make them into a type of hardened rusk. Gradually over the centuries they became a delicacy in themselves, and by the 18th century new varieties had developed that didn't need to be cooked twice. The real breakthrough came in the 19th century, when new cutting machines and ovens heralded the launch of cheap mass-produced commercially made biscuits. The industry has never looked back; currently in the United Kingdom we spend about £1.6 billion per year on biscuits and wafers, or about £27.50 for every man, woman and child in the country.

bread

This is a cooked shaped dough made from **flour** and liquid. Virtually any flour can be used – in western societies milled **wheat** and **rye** are the most popular, while in other parts of the world **maize** and **chickpea** flours are widely used. Breads are either 'raised' (leavened), that is they are puffed up and have an airy texture, or they are unleavened and flat. Most traditional European breads are raised, but elsewhere, particularly in Asia and Latin America, unleavened types are more popular. **Yeast**, a sourdough starter, **baking powder** and **bicarbonate of soda** are all used as raising agents. Bread dough can also be 'enriched' to improve its appearance or sweeten it, and egg, butter, oil, sugar, spices and dried fruit, among others, are added for this purpose. Finally, although most raised dough is baked at some point during its making process, some individual breads are boiled before baking or they may be deep-fried. Most unleavened bread is cooked on a griddle or something similar.

Broadly speaking, bread is categorized according to the method of leavening and/or by whether it is enriched or not. Yeast breads include loaves and buns, as well as flatter types like **pitta** and **naan**; sourdough breads are raised by a 'starter' mixture containing wild yeasts; sweet breads are made from an enriched dough (**croissants** are one example) that is usually (but not always) raised with commercial yeast; quick breads (e.g. **soda bread**) are raised with bicarbonate of soda; and unleavened breads (e.g. **chapatti** and **tortilla**) are made without any raising agent at all.

A home-made yeast bread dough is kneaded for 10–15 minutes by hand (less if using the dough hook on an electric mixer) to develop and distribute the gluten present in the flour (the strands of gluten trap the carbon dioxide bubbles that are released as the dough ferments). Then the dough is left to ferment, or rise, until doubled in size (the time this takes depends on the dough and the temperature, but is usually between 45 and 90 minutes). After shaping, some doughs are ready to be baked, while others are given a second rise. To test if a yeast bread is cooked, tip it out of its tin and tap the base; it should sound hollow like a drum.

Store-bought bread is produced in a more streamlined way. Nearly all of it is now made by one of two methods: the Bulk Fermentation Process (BFP), which is based on traditional methods and used when a classic loaf is required, and the Chorleywood Bread Process (CBP), the one used for mass-produced loaves. In BFP, all the ingredients are mixed together to form a dough, which is allowed to ferment for two hours or more before being baked. CBP produces yeast-based bread without the need to ferment the dough at length in bulk; instead it's worked intensively by machines at high speed for a few minutes, then allowed a very brief first 'resting' period before being shaped and moulded, then risen and baked. In addition to the normal ingredients, commercial bread also contains improvers, usually ascorbic acid (vitamin C) and preservatives like acetic acid (vinegar) to help prevent it from becoming too stale too quickly.

There is a huge variety of commercial bread available today, including the baguette, the archetypal French white yeast bread, a long thin stick with a particularly light texture and chewy, flaky crust; bap, a floury, soft yeast roll made from white flour and (sometimes) lard; bara brith, a Welsh yeast- or soda-raised sweet bread containing spices and tea-soaked dried fruit; ciabatta, an oval-shaped, flattish Italian yeast bread with an open texture, flavoured with olive oil; focaccia, a Mediterranean flat yeast bread often topped with coarse salt, herbs, garlic, chilli or cheese; granary, a yeast bread made from a special flour containing wheatmeal and malted wheatflakes; and pumpernickel, a dark, dense German sourdough bread made from rye flour.

using it Commercially produced bread made by the CBP method keeps reasonably well for a few days; most other breads, including home-made, are best eaten on the day of purchase or baking, although many can be 'refreshed' on day two or even three by being warmed in the oven for 5–10 minutes. Toasting is another option.

Bread is one of the staple foods of the world, served at most meals and often forming the basis of the meal itself. In western countries at the beginning of the day, sliced toasted bread or small breads like bagels or muffins, spread with butter, sometimes with jam, marmalade or honey, are eaten; in the middle of the day, sandwiches made from virtually any type of bread have taken over lunchtime; and in the evening, bread slices or rolls can be served before the meal (sometimes with a dip of olive oil) as well as with first courses like soup or pâté. Other societies are just as dedicated to their breads, and tortillas and chapattis, to name two, also feature in most meals in their home countries.

Bread is also used in cooking. In savoury dishes, sliced French bread is sprinkled with grated cheese, floated on top of onion soup, then grilled or baked until the cheese has melted; or rubbed with garlic and added to the beef and beer stew called carbonnade. Baguettes and ciabatta can be sliced into rounds and grilled or toasted for bruschetta. Crustless sliced bread can be moistened in milk or water and added to minced meat for meatballs and meat-loaves, or made into the eggless Greek mayonnaise skordalia. For Melba toast, extra-thin slices are toasted twice to dry them to a crisp. Other breads like pitta, naan and tortilla are also used in savoury cooking (see separate entries).

In sweet cookery, buttered white bread slices are layered with raisins and sultanas and moistened with a custard mixture, then baked to become bread-and-butter pudding. Sliced white bread is also soaked in fruit juice, brandy or sherry to make the casing for summer pudding.

Slightly stale bread can be cut into cubes and cooked in butter or oil to make crunchy croûtons, traditionally added to soups, but nowadays also used in salads. Plain or toasted, stale bread can also be processed into breadcrumbs, one of the handiest ingredients in the kitchen: they coat fish fillets before they're cooked, are added to many stuffings and dumplings, and are used as the basis of a bread sauce to accompany roast pheasant. Brown breadcrumbs are also used to flavour ice-cream, are stirred into batters for steamed puddings, or made into Queen of Puddings, a traditional baked custard and breadcrumb mixture topped with glazed jam and meringue.

word origin Bread is derived from *breadru*, an Old English word meaning 'pieces', or *breotan*, meaning 'to break'; loaf also comes from Old English, this time from *hlaf,* meaning 'bread'. The most common method of creating commercial bread is called after Chorleywood in Hertfordshire, where the Flour Milling and Baking Research Association, which invented it, was based.

Bread is so common and perceived to be so necessary to life that it has almost become a metaphor for sustaining life itself. It is at the heart of both Christianity and Judaism, for example, and is used (as is dough) as a slang word for money (another essential of life). Unsurprisingly, there are also many phrases linked to its production. 'A baker's dozen' is actually 13, and usually describes an overzealous estimate of something; originally it was straightforward – most bakers were so terrified of being prosecuted for supplying underweight bread or rolls that they supplied a 13th to their dozen to make sure they weren't. 'Upper crust' is medieval in origin.

Commercial bread ovens were grubby affairs (they were heated by bundles of faggots and when the ashes were swept out, the bread dough was put in), so the rich and powerful cut off the bottom crust of the baked bread and offloaded it onto their servants while they nibbled the soft insides and a bit of the 'upper' crust themselves.

did you know?

- Early breads were crude, unleavened porridge-like mixtures of ground barley and water. It is the Egyptians who are generally credited with improving them: first by the discovery, probably by accident, of leavening, then by introducing the idea of using wheat, although it was the Greeks who popularized this, believing that wheat bread was more digestible than barley. The Romans adopted wheat too and helped to introduce the idea of leavened wheat bread throughout their empire. Other societies used the grain that was handiest and cheapest, so maize (corn) became the staple used to make bread in Latin America.
- There were commercial bakers in Egypt by 2000BC, and a street of bakeries was found in Pompeii, the city near Naples buried in volcanic ash in AD79. By medieval times in Europe, bakers had formed themselves into powerful guilds and by the 13th century in England a special 'Assize of Bread' had convened to regulate price and weight. The type of loaf you ate depended on your station in life: the rich ate refined white bread called pandemain or manchet, the middle classes either coarser unrefined wheat bread or maslin, a mixture of wheat and rye, and the poor, very coarse loaves made from barley, oats or bran. Special large coarse-grain breads called trenchers were left to harden for a few days, then cut in half horizontally to be used as plates (which were often eaten by the poor once the meal had finished).
- Bread was made in traditional crude ovens for millennia – larger and better-regulated ovens were not invented until the 18th century, and it was a century after that before the dough could be at least partly prepared mechanically. Sliced bread was even longer in coming: the American baker Otto Rohwedder began trying to invent a machine that would slice and pack bread in 1912, but only presented the finished article at a bakery fair in 1928.

bun

In England, a bun is a small, sweet roll made from enriched, yeast-raised **bread** dough. In most other English-speaking countries, most particularly in the United States, the word can also be used to describe an unsweetened, round flat roll. In Scotland additionally, a bun is a rich fruit and spice cake.

There are many traditional English buns, including the Chelsea bun, a square spiral of sweetened dough filled with spices, brown sugar and dried fruits and topped with a sticky sugar glaze, which was first made in the Chelsea Bun House in the late 18th century by a member of the Hand family, unsurprisingly nicknamed Captain Bun. Other English buns include the Devonshire split, a soft round roll with a scattering of icing sugar on top, split open before serving, often with clotted cream and jam; and the hot cross bun, a round roll containing dried fruit and spices with a shortcrust pastry cross on top.

using it English-style buns should be eaten on the day they are made or bought. Some are eaten as they are, but others need to be warmed or toasted. American-style buns, which are normally used as containers for savoury fillings like sausages and hamburgers, can be toasted or warmed. The Scottish version is usually allowed to mature for a few weeks before being served in the same way as fruit cake.

word origin Although bun goes back to medieval times (when it started out as a small, flat ordinary loaf, probably not all that dissimilar from the modern-day bap), the origins are unknown. Some people believe it may come from the Old French *bugne*, which means 'swelling', or *bugnete,* meaning 'fritter'.

• The cross on hot cross buns predates Christianity – early Saxons offered similar breads to their goddess of spring, Eostre, to symbolize the rebirth of the year, the 'cross' at that point representing the four seasons. By the 16th century, when dried fruit and spices began to be added, it was officially decreed that spiced buns be reserved for serving at Easter, Christmas and funerals; the crossed buns had an obvious link with the death of Christ on the Cross and therefore began to be associated with Good Friday.

• The most famous Scottish bun is black bun, a dense rich cake filled almost to overflowing with dried fruit and encased in shortcrust pastry. It is traditionally served at Hogmanay to help the New Year whisky go down.

cake

This is a baked batter, normally made from a mixture of flour, eggs, sugar and fat (usually butter or margarine) plus often a raising agent. Various flavourings, such as chocolate, coffee, spices, dried fruit and nuts, are also added. A cake can be any shape or size, decorated or plain, filled or not.

There are five ways to make a cake mixture. The all-in-one method is the quickest and produces a light-textured cake simply by beating the ingredients together all at once. For the creaming method, the fat and sugar are beaten together until light, then eggs are beaten in, followed by flour and other dry ingredients. The melting method gives a moist, slightly sticky finish by warming together sugar, fat and any liquid before beating in the other ingredients together with any eggs. For the rubbing-in method, fat and flour are rubbed together first (as when making pastry dough) before the other ingredients are added. The whisking method produces very light, airy cakes by whisking sugar and eggs together until pale, before folding in flour and other dry ingredients. The first two methods, with some variations, are the ones most commonly used in modern kitchens; commercial cakes are made by industrial versions of these classic methods.

Cakes can be grouped into broad categories: **sponge cake**, for instance, is baked from a light-textured mixture, normally made by the whisking, creaming or all-in-one method; **fruit cake**, heavier and denser with dried fruit, candied peel and often nuts, is made by a variation of the creaming method or melting method; and gâteau (the French word for cake) in English implies a fancy, elaborately decorated concoction with a sponge base. **Cheesecake**, although called a cake, is actually a filled pie.

There are hundreds of individual cakes – most western countries have their own tradition and their own extensive repertoire – but some popular representative ones are: angel cake, an extra-light American sponge made by the whisking method; cup cake or fairy cake, a tiny sponge traditionally cooked in a frilly paper case; **gingerbread**, a spicy, moist and often sticky cake made by the melting method; Madeira cake, a loaf cake made by the creaming method, flavoured with lemon zest and juice and topped with candied citron; and rock cake, a small, fairly solid cake full of dried fruit and candied peel, made by the rubbing-in method. In addition, some firmer cake mixtures are baked in a tin and cut into small squares or bars for serving. Of these, rich, moist and chocolaty brownies, made by the creaming method, and flapjacks (chewy bars made by the melting method with rolled oats and golden syrup) are the most popular.

using it With the exception of richer fruit cakes, cakes are usually served within a day or so of being made. Most are eaten as snacks or desserts, although plainer ones are occasionally used as the basis of other desserts (see **sponge cake**).

word origin Cake comes from the Old Norse *kaka*, meaning 'cook'. The ease (and speed) with which cakes can be eaten probably inspired the phrase 'it's a piece of cake', meaning it's very easy and requires little effort.

did you know?

• The boundary lines between cakes, breads and biscuits are often indistinct even today, not surprising since both sweet biscuits and cakes started out as sweetened enriched breads. Perhaps because they were more expensive and time-consuming to make, however, cakes always seem to have had an air of celebration about them and tended to be 'saved' for special occasions. Many countries and regions, in fact, evolved special cakes for high days and holy days, some of which are still with us. Birthday and Christmas cakes are the most obvious, but in Britain, simnel cake continues to be associated with Easter, and both here and in other European countries, special cakes are still baked to celebrate Twelfth Night, the last day of the Christmas celebrations.

• Royal connections with cake make colourful reading. In England there is the tale of how the 9th-century king of Wessex, Alfred the Great, allowed some cakes to burn (in between fighting off Danish invaders) and was robustly rebuked for it by one of his humbler subjects. Unfortunately, there is no real evidence that he (or the peasant) did anything of the sort, and in fact the story doesn't seem to have surfaced until two or three centuries after his death. And in France in 1789, there was Marie Antoinette and 'let them eat cake' (*qu'ils mangent de la brioche* in French), allegedly her response to the news that peasants were storming Versailles because they were starving and couldn't afford to buy bread. There's no evidence of this one either, although the French philosopher Jean Jacques Rousseau records an earlier queen of France (Marie-Thérèse, wife of Louis XIV) saying something similar a hundred years before. The memoirs of various mid-18th century French courtiers attribute the phrase to two of Marie Antoinette's aunts-in-law.

chapatti

This round unleavened Indian **bread** is simply a mixture of plain wholemeal flour and water. It's made by beating these ingredients into a stiff dough, kneading it, 'resting' it, then dividing it and rolling out to an appropriate thinness and size (roughly similar to a small crêpe). Traditionally, chapatti is dipped in flour and dry-fried on a cast-iron griddle called a *tava* until it's slightly puffed up and has brown spots on the surface.

using it Commercial chapattis should be used within a day or so of opening (any left over can be frozen). They need to be warmed under the grill for about 30 seconds per side or in a moderate oven for 2–3 minutes before being served. Freshly cooked home-made chapattis can be wrapped in buttered foil and kept in a warm place for 20–30 minutes before serving. Chapatti is similar to a wheat **tortilla**, and can be used in the same way.

word origin Chapatti is an anglicization of the Hindi *capati*, meaning 'flat cake'.

cheesecake

Despite the name, a cheesecake is actually a flan or **pie** with a rich filling based on **cheese**. It can be sweet or savoury, and filled with one type of cheese, a mixture, or cheese mixed with other ingredients like cream, soured cream, crème fraîche or Greek yoghurt. Sweet cheese fillings include cream cheese, mascarpone, ricotta, curd or quark, while savoury ones are usually based on Cheddar, curd, ricotta, fromage frais or Parmesan. Toppings and other flavourings depend on whether the pie is sweet or savoury too, but include chopped nuts, fresh fruit (e.g. berries, kiwi fruit, pineapple), chocolate and spices for sweet versions, and seafood, tomatoes and basil, spinach, olives and mushrooms for savoury ones.

There are two main types. Baked cheesecake, as the name suggests, is always cooked and nearly always has a pastry case or base. The cheese filling is normally 'set' by beating in eggs and flour. Chilled cheesecake is uncooked and although it sometimes has a (baked blind) pastry case (see **shortcrust pastry**), most have a base made from biscuit crumbs and/or crushed nuts. The filling is normally set with gelatine.

using it Sweet cheesecakes are normally served as desserts, savoury ones as a starter or main dish. Small savoury cheesecakes could also be used as drinks snacks.

word origin The first half of the word comes from the Latin *caseus,* meaning 'cheese', via the German *käse*, and the second part from the Old Norse *kaka*, meaning 'cook'. Cheesecakes have probably always been nice to look at and rather a treat, the only even vaguely logical reason for the word cheesecake being applied to saucy portrayals of women.

did you know?

• Something akin to cheesecake was served to athletes at the Olympic Games in 776 BC, and the Romans, being great cheesemakers, made them too. They may have introduced the idea into Britain, but the first English recipes for both sweet and savoury cheesecakes appear in a 14th-century cookery book from the court of king Richard II. Cheesecakes have always been particularly popular in eastern Europe and it was probably eastern European immigrants who took them to the United States. The 20th-century escalation in popularity – and the invention of the no-cook version – took place in America and spread to other parts of the world from there.

choux pastry

This unique **pastry** is the only major type whose preparation includes cooking. The ingredients are simple (plain flour, salt, butter, eggs and either milk or water or a mixture of the two, plus a little sugar if the baked pastry is to have a sweet filling) and making it is too: the butter and liquid are boiled together, and the flour and salt are beaten in all at once until smooth; the mixture is then beaten over a low heat until it leaves the sides of the pan, when eggs are beaten in one at a time until the dough is shiny and has a consistency that drops from the spoon. To use, choux is either piped into the desired shape or (especially for smaller pastries) shaped between two spoons before being baked.

using it Although many individual items made from choux are available ready-made, the pastry itself isn't, so if you want to use it you have to make it yourself. It's best made on the day it's to be eaten, although cooked pastry freezes quite well.

Choux is the basis of rich cakes such as profiteroles (small buns filled with whipped cream, ice-cream or pastry cream, then drizzled with chocolate sauce), éclairs (finger-shaped profiteroles topped with chocolate or coffee icing) and choux puffs (larger individual buns filled with flavoured whipped cream and dredged with icing sugar). It is also an integral part of gâteau St Honoré (a shortcrust pastry base topped with a ring of choux, then little choux balls glazed with caramel, the centre filled with whipped flavoured cream). Choux can be used to make savoury pastries too: gougère is a large ring of choux flavoured with Gruyère or Emmenthal cheese. Bite-sized choux buns filled with flavoured cream cheese and prawn mayonnaise are good cocktail snacks.

word origin Choux is the French word for cabbage and the name was originally given to small round cakes made from the pastry because they were shaped like little cabbages. The pastry itself was called *pâte* *à choux* (pastry for these small round cakes), gradually shortened to just choux, regardless of what the finished dish was.

• One of the most famous choux pastry cakes is the wheel-shaped Paris-Brest, which is named after a bicycle race, a mini-Tour de France between Paris and Brittany. The cake, two choux rings sandwiched together with praline-flavoured cream and with 'spokes' made from eclairs, was created in 1891 by an enterprising pâtissier whose shop lay along the race route.

Christmas pudding

Ingredients for this traditional dish vary from cook to cook, but most include flour, breadcrumbs, suet, sugar, eggs, lots of dried fruit (including raisins, sultanas, currants and mixed peel), spices (cinnamon, nutmeg and allspice) and alcohol (anything from stout to brandy). Extra flavourings like citrus zest, nuts, golden syrup, grated apple or even carrot are also sometimes included. The mixture is made by combining the dry ingredients, stirring in the fruit and then beating in the liquids. It is spooned into a heatproof basin – or, more traditionally, a pudding cloth and shaped into a ball – and good-luck tokens are often pushed in. Then it is steamed or boiled for several hours.

using it Home-cooked puddings are usually made at least 6 weeks (or up to a year) before Christmas, to allow them time to mature. Before serving they are steamed or boiled again for about 2 hours. Bought puddings are reheated in the same way, for 30–90 minutes. Puddings are turned out (or unwrapped) for serving.

Serving has its rituals: a sprig of holly is often set on the top and sometimes warmed brandy or rum is poured over the pudding and set alight. The pudding is nearly always accompanied by one (or more) classic sauces like custard, flavoured whipped cream or brandy butter, a 'sauce' made by beating butter and sugar together with a flavouring of brandy to make a stiff paste.

word origin This type of pudding is very old, but the idea of serving it more or less exclusively at Christmas is comparatively recent, and probably dates from early Victorian times. The word 'pudding' itself was used in medieval times at first to describe a type of sausage (hence black pudding), but gradually came to mean anything cooked in a casing or cloth.

• The earliest ancestor of Christmas pudding was a medieval porridge made from wheat called frumenty, which probably contained meat. Later it was made a bit more special by stirring in spices and dried fruit like raisins and prunes, and the meat gradually disappeared (the suet in modern Christmas puddings is a relic of it). It began to be called 'plum' pudding, because when prunes first arrived in the United Kingdom they were called plums (they are dried plums) and gradually the word came to mean any kind of dried fruit. The invention of the pudding cloth in the 17th century meant that plum pudding could be firmer-textured and steamed until set, rather than boiled and served as porridge.

croissant

A croissant is a light, flaky crescent-shaped roll traditionally made from an enriched yeast-raised dough. The dough is mixed and kneaded in the same way as **bread**; after the first rising, however, the dough is rolled out and dotted with diced fat (usually butter when home-made; either butter or a mixture of butter and margarine if commercially made), then folded, turned and rolled out again several times in the same way as **puff pastry**. It is then cut into thin triangles, which are shaped into crescents by being rolled up from the wide end and curved inwards slightly at the points. Baking is done in a hot oven for about 10–15 minutes.

These buttery pastries are sometimes further enriched with a filling of almond paste plus flaked almonds on top, and the same dough is also shaped into oblongs and filled with chocolate for pains au chocolate.

using it Croissants should be eaten as soon after being made or bought as possible, although most packaged ones will last for a day or so. Before eating, heat croissants in the oven for a few minutes, then serve with butter or butter and jam for a breakfast treat. Larger croissants can be halved, filled and served as a sandwich; Brie, ham and Gruyère cheese are among the most popular fillings.

word origin Croissant is French and means 'crescent', a reference to the shape.

did you know?

• The most popular explanation of how croissants came to be is almost certainly untrue, but a good story nevertheless. When the Turkish army was besieging Vienna in 1683 (or it could have been Budapest in 1686, according to some versions) bakers working at night heard the attackers digging a tunnel under their premises to get into the city. They raised the alarm, the Turks were fought off and as a reward the heroic bakers were allowed to shape their breads into crescents, the Turkish emblem.

crumpet

In appearance part thick **pancake** and part **muffin**, a crumpet is a small, flat, round British cake with a holed top and smooth bottom. It is made from a yeast-raised batter, which is cooked in metal rings on a griddle (or heavy frying pan). During cooking bubbles on the surface of the batter swell and burst to give the familiar holes.

using it Bought crumpets will keep for a day or so but, like those that are home-made, they are best eaten as fresh as possible. Traditionally they are toasted and served with butter, preferably melting into the holes – and dripping onto the chin – and perhaps jam or honey as well.

word origin Crumpet comes from the Old English *crump,* meaning 'crooked', perhaps a reference to the holes that dot the surface – or maybe even to their shape in the days when people cooked them by eye and hand rather than by using a metal ring. The use of 'crumpet' to describe fanciable people of either sex is fairly recent and fairly inexplicable, unless it's a reference to its perceived desirability, freshly toasted and dripping with butter.

did you know?

• There are vague references to something called *crompid cake* in a late 14th-century document (actually an early English translation of the Bible), but it wasn't until the middle of the 18th century that a recognizable recipe for 'tea crumpets' was published. The great heyday of crumpets was the Victorian era when, together with muffins, they regularly appeared on the groaning afternoon tea tables of the time.

doughnut

A small, sweet ball or ring-shaped raised **bread**, the doughnut gets its unique soft texture and crust by being deep-fried rather than baked. The dough is often sweetened and enriched with butter, eggs and milk or buttermilk, and the raising agent can be yeast or **baking powder**. Spices like nutmeg and allspice are also often added. Ball-shaped doughnuts may be filled (jam and thick fruit purée are popular) and are usually dredged with sugar or icing sugar; ring doughnuts are sometimes topped with a glaze or icing.

using it Doughnuts can be enjoyed for breakfast or as a comfort-food snack at any time of the day.

word origin When they first appeared in the United States in the early part of the 19th century, doughnuts were called either 'oly-koks', from the Dutch *oile-koek*, meaning 'oilcake' (a reference to the way they were cooked and the part of the world they probably came from), or dough nuts, a description of what was probably their original shape and content. Oly-kok, being neither attractive nor easy to pronounce, lost out to what was thought to be the more appropriate 'American' name of doughnut.

filo pastry

This is a wafer-thin **pastry** made from plain flour and water and, sometimes, egg. The ingredients are beaten into a soft dough, which is kneaded and 'rested' for about 20 minutes, then rolled out as thinly as possible. To make it even thinner it is pulled and stretched (by hand if home-made). The finished dough should be wafer thin – it is said you should be able to read a newspaper through it.

Filo pastry probably originated in Turkey, but is now a feature of Greek and Cypriot cuisine too. The most famous of their sweet pastries is baklava: butter-brushed sheets of filo (10 or more) are arranged in layers in a greased tin, with the filling (sugar and ground nuts such as almonds, pistachios and walnuts) usually in a layer in the middle. After baking, the pastry is dredged with a sweet syrup flavoured with rosewater.

using it Being so laborious to prepare, filo pastry is usually bought frozen, as a roll of large square or rectangular sheets. It needs to be thawed before use. Home-made filo should be used immediately after rolling out. Both bought and home-made filo dry out quickly, so should be kept covered, usually with a damp cloth, while being used,

removing each sheet as it is needed.

Filo pastry is layered, each sheet being first brushed with melted butter or oil. A filling, which can be savoury or sweet, is normally layered with the pastry or the layered pastry is rolled around the filling. Small squares of filo are also layered and shaped into delicate cups, moneybag shapes and other individual pastries.

Popular savoury fillings for filo pastries include cooked or smoked salmon; crumbled feta cheese, spinach and onion (the classic Greek spanakopitta); and cooked vegetable and lentil mixtures. Sweet fillings include apple, rhubarb and mincemeat.

word origin Filo comes from the Greek *phyllon,* meaning 'leaf'.

did you know?

• Paper-thin German strudel pastry, which is widely used in Austrian and central European cookery, is very similar to filo. It is the basis for mainly sweet pastries, although savoury strudels are made too. The best known is apple strudel, made by rolling the layered sheets around a filling of apples, dried fruit and spices.

fruit cake

A rich heavy cake, this is packed with dried fruit – normally raisins, sultanas, currants, glacé cherries and candied peel, although other fruits such as prunes, dates and figs are also sometimes used. Some fruit cakes are 'raised' by **baking powder**, but heavier, denser ones are leavened only with eggs. Flavourings like spices (e.g. nutmeg, cinnamon, mixed spice), syrup or treacle, and even brandy are also sometimes added, as are ground or chopped nuts.

Simpler fruit cakes are made by a variation of the creaming method (see **cake**) and the various dried fruits and any nuts are beaten in after the other ingredients are blended. The mixture is baked in a greased cake tin in a low oven for 2–4 hours, depending on size and density; the cake is cooked when a skewer inserted into the centre comes out clean. Richer, more solid cakes are normally baked 4–6 weeks before they are needed so that they have time to 'mature'.

using it Fruit cakes are quintessentially British, associated with Victorian (and later) teatimes. Nowadays, they are normally used as the basis for birthday or Christmas cakes and for this they are traditionally covered with **marzipan**, then **icing** and other decorations.

word origin The current name is fairly modern: when the first cakes were made from dried fruits, probably in medieval times, they were called 'plum' cakes, since all dried fruits were known as plums.

did you know?

• Dundee cake, a rich fruit cake decorated on top with a circle of whole almonds, was first made around the end of the 19th century by James Keiller, a company noted for its marmalade, which happened to have a factory in Dundee in Scotland. In addition to the usual raisins and sultanas, the cake also contains candied orange and lemon peel, and so probably helped to use up any fruits left over from marmalade-making.

gingerbread

Gingerbread is a moist, dark spicy cake usually raised with **bicarbonate of soda**. It is sweetened with treacle or syrup in addition to sugar, and spiced generously with ginger. Occasionally cinnamon, other spices, dried fruit and nuts are also added. Texture varies from soft and cake-like, when it's traditionally made by the melting method (see **cake**) and baked in a tin, to crisp and biscuit-like, when the creaming method is used and the resulting dough is rolled out and cut into shapes.

using it Bought cake-style gingerbread will keep for a few days; a home-made cake should be eaten within a day or so, preferably warm, sliced and spread with butter. Biscuit-style gingerbread is usually made at home and can be any shape you want. For gingerbread people, currants, Smarties or other sweets and even icing can be pressed into service for the eyes, nose, mouth and any indications of clothing down the front.

word origin Gingerbread comes from the Old French *gingebras*, meaning 'preserved ginger'. It got its inappropriate ending because '*-bras*' was an unfamiliar sound to the 13th-century English, who therefore replaced it with the more familiar 'bread'. During the 17th century, some light gingerbreads were made more eye-catching (and expensive) by being decorated with gold foil, and from this came to 'take the gilt (i.e. gold) off the gingerbread', meaning to make something less attractive and valuable than it was originally.

did you know?

• Gingerbread began life as a medieval boiled honey and breadcrumb mixture that may or may not have included preserved ginger. It was particularly associated with fairs, sometimes being stamped or embossed with the image of the fair's patron saint (if there was one), and it was often made in special shapes that could include animals and flowers as well as 'men', the latter being traditionally eaten by unmarried women in some areas to improve their chances of finding a husband. By the 15th century, it definitely included ginger and often other spices as well, and by a century later, flour had replaced the breadcrumbs.

muffin

In Britain, a muffin is a small, soft yeast-raised **bread**. It is similar to a **crumpet** in appearance, but without the large holes, and is made from a dough rather than a batter. The dough is cut into rounds and then cooked, either on top of the stove on a greased griddle until the top and bottom are browned, or baked in a hot oven.

In the United States, and now elsewhere too, a muffin is a small, light-textured sweet cake raised with baking powder and often flavoured with ingredients like blueberry and chocolate.

using it Muffins are traditional teacakes in Great Britain, split with the fingers and toasted to eat with butter and preserves. American-style muffins are a traditional breakfast or snack food.

word origin Muffin comes from *muffen*, plural of the German *muffe,* meaning 'cake'.

did you know?

• Muffins have been around since the beginning of the 18th century, but were most popular during Victorian times when special muffin men used to tour the streets of large cities selling their wares just in time for tea. They attracted custom by ringing their bells, loudly apparently, since an Act of Parliament of the 1840s banned them from using the bells.

naan

This is a flattish, teardrop-shaped **bread**, usually raised with yeast and enriched with yoghurt. The dough may be flavoured (garlic, poppy seeds and coriander are popular), and some naans are 'filled' before being cooked – with mixtures such as lentil-based curries or vegetable purées. Naans are traditionally baked in a tandoor, which is a clay oven sunk into the ground, but they can also be successfully cooked under a hot grill for a few minutes on each side until they puff up and are speckled brown.

using it Home-made naan should be served straight after being cooked, or at least the same day; commercial naan can be kept for months. Traditionally they are served warm,

heated either in the oven or under the grill, with Indian-style food, especially tandoori and balti dishes. Packaged mini-naans can be used as a base for lunch-style toppings like hummus, seafood mayonnaise, mini-kebabs or meatballs.

word origin Naan is borrowed from the Hindi word for the bread.

did you know?

• Many countries like Iran, Afghanistan and even China make versions of naan, but in the United Kingdom it's most associated with the Indian subcontinent and especially the Punjab. There (and in good Indian restaurants elsewhere), naan is stuck onto the walls of the tandoor and baked while the tandoori meats and fish, such as chicken and prawns, are cooking on the floor of the oven.

pancake

A pancake is a very thin cake made from a batter; when particularly thin it is often called a crêpe. The batter consists of plain flour, egg and liquid (usually milk or a combination of milk and water) and a little sugar is stirred in if the filling is to be sweet, while melted butter or oil are also sometimes added. The batter is spooned into a special pancake pan with curved sides, or a frying pan, which is tilted so the batter spreads out evenly, and then cooked briefly on both sides. A fish slice or palette knife will help with turning it; the more confident (or rash) can try tossing it. Pancakes are served hot from the pan, or stacked up interleaved with greaseproof paper for serving later.

Pancakes are nearly always used as a base or container for other ingredients, either savoury or sweet – rolled or folded round them or layered with the filling into a sort of 'cake'.

using it Bought pancakes will keep for anything between a few days and a few months. Both home-made and bought pancakes freeze well and since they don't take long to thaw, this is a good way to store them.

Popular savoury fillings include chopped mushrooms, spinach, grated cheese and seafood mixtures. Sweet fillings can be cooked or uncooked: sugar with lemon juice, and jam are traditional favourites; others are grated chocolate, fruit compote, and crushed nuts and cream.

Many countries have their own versions: smaller and thicker American pancakes (or griddle cakes) are served at breakfast or brunch with bacon and maple syrup; thin Chinese pancakes (*bao bing*) are used as a wrapper for dishes such as Peking duck and dim sum; Hungarian pancakes (palacsinta) are thin crêpes normally served as a dessert with soured cream and cherries; Italian pancakes (crespelle) are used in much the same way as pasta – layered with a filling and sauce like lasagne or rolled up around a filling and baked like cannelloni; thick Irish pancakes (boxty), made from grated raw potato, mashed potato and flour, are eaten as a snack meal with toppings or fillings; and Russian pancakes (blini), made from a yeast-raised **buckwheat** flour batter, are served topped with caviar or smoked salmon and soured cream. Scotch pancakes, called drop scones in England, are similar in appearance to American pancakes.

word origin Pancake is a literal description of what it is, a 'cake' cooked in a pan, and has been around since about the 15th century. Crêpe is French and means 'thin pancake'.

• Pancakes or an approximation of them may go back to Roman times. They've been made in Britain since the early Middle Ages, although they were probably inherited from the northern French (Brittany in particular is still famous for its crêpes). Pancakes have always been associated with the run-up to Easter, and especially with Shrove Tuesday, the day before the start of Lent when many carnivals were held to compensate for the austerity to come. Part of the celebrations in many villages was a special pancake race for the women of the community (some still survive, in fact), where they were required to take part in a short sprint, tossing their home-made pancakes as they ran.

• The most famous French pancake dish is crêpes Suzette, for which pancakes are filled with sugar and orange zest and juice, folded into triangles and warmed (usually flambéed) in orange liqueur. It was supposed to have been invented in Monte Carlo in 1896 for the then Prince of Wales and his lady companion (Suzette), but since the chef who claimed to have created it was only a young boy at the time, the story seems to be wishful thinking. The first written references to it were made in a cookery book published about 15 years after that date.

pastry

Pastry is both a cooked dough made from flour and (most of the time) fat, to which other ingredients like eggs and sugar may be added, depending on the type being made, and an item *made* from the dough. Pastry is used to enclose, cover or support fillings or toppings of one sort or another, each different type bringing a separate texture and taste to specific types of pies, tarts and similar dishes.

There are many different types of pastry, such as **choux**, which is more like a sticky paste and puffs up during baking; **filo**, which is stretched into ultra-thin sheets that become crisp when baked; **puff**, which bakes into delicate, buttery layers; and **shortcrust**, which holds its shape well and bakes to a tender crumbly texture. Others still used occasionally include flaky or rough puff, a simpler version of puff pastry; suetcrust, made in the same way as shortcrust but with suet, and traditionally used for savoury steamed puddings; and hot-water crust, made by melting fat in boiling water and beating in flour, and used as the case for cold game and other meat pies.

using it Filo, puff and shortcrust pastries can be bought ready-made, usually frozen.

When pastry is made at home, the standard ingredients, especially the fat, can be varied to suit the dish: soured cream or crème fraîche, for instance, is sometimes added to shortcrust or puff doughs for fish or chicken pies, and ground nuts like almonds, hazelnuts and walnuts are often used in cheesecake or other sweet pie doughs.

word origin Pastry comes from the Greek *paste,* meaning 'barley porridge', via Latin *pasta* and Old French *paste* which both meant 'dough'. When dough was first used as a pie container in Britain during medieval times, English borrowed the French word, and in fact continued to use it until the end of the 18th century. Pastry in its second meaning, as a baked item made from dough, had meanwhile evolved around the 16th century and it was this form that gradually expanded its meaning to take over when *paste* fell out of fashion.

did you know?

• People have been making pastry since ancient times – the Romans, for instance, made a dough from flour, water and olive oil that they used as a crust to cover and preserve fillings, although they didn't eat it. By medieval times, northern Europeans, including the British, were successfully making similar mixtures, but using butter, lard or suet rather than oil, which created a stiffer crust that kept its shape well. In England these doughs were often made into what were called 'coffins' – coarse protective crusts for choice fillings – which were sometimes eaten, although admittedly only by the poor who did not normally have much choice. Some doughs *were* meant to be eaten, however, and were made from more refined ingredients and baked as edible shells for delicate tarts and flans. By the 17th century,

recognizable modern pastries, including rich shortcrust and puff, were being made.

pie

A pie is a large or small baked dish, made up of a filling mixture encased in or covered by **pastry** or another mixture such as mashed potato, crushed biscuits or meringue. Fillings can be sweet or savoury, and range from fruit-based (e.g. blackberry and apple, blueberry, lemon or mincemeat) to meat, poultry or fish (e.g. steak and kidney, chicken and ham or seafood).

using it Most savoury pies are served hot as a main dish; sweet pies can be eaten hot, warm or cold, as snacks or desserts, often with cream, custard or ice-cream.

word origin Pie has been used in Britain since about the 14th century and comes from the name for the bird magpie (which was sometimes called pye). Magpies had the reputation of taking different things from various places and bringing them back to be enclosed in their nests – so with pies, which were a mixture of various ingredients in a 'nest' of pastry. In North America, pie also means a filled pastry case. The word was once used in this way in British English too, but that type of dish is now called a tart or flan.

did you know?

• It might sound unlikely that four-and-twenty blackbirds baked in a pie would begin to sing when the pie was opened, but it's not impossible. The birds could have been put into an empty pie dish and covered briefly with an already baked pastry crust before being set before the king; they would still have been alive when the pie was cut open, although whether they would have felt like singing is another matter. There is, apparently, a real historical precedent for the nursery rhyme, a 16th-century Italian recipe that suggests ways of making pies that birds could fly out of when the crusts were opened up (the idea was that they would fly to the candles lighting the room and put them out, to the merriment of those assembled to witness it).

pitta

This is a flat, round or oval-shaped, yeast-raised **bread** made with white or wholemeal flour; the dough is occasionally flavoured with garlic, chilli, sesame seeds and so on. Although pitta is leavened, slightly less than the normal amount of yeast is used so that the finished bread is flat and chewy. The shaped breads are baked quickly in a hot oven until they have puffed up to create the familiar hollow pocket.

using it Bought pittas, which can be large or small, will keep for a few days. They freeze well and since they thaw quickly, or can be toasted or grilled from frozen, this is probably the best way to store them. Home-made pittas should be eaten as soon as possible after being made, or frozen. Pittas are always served warm, so heat under a grill or in the oven or a toaster for a few minutes.

Pitta quarters or fingers make good scoops for dips such as taramasalata, hummus and guacamole (see **avocado**); smaller toasted pieces can be added to salads, (such as the Middle Eastern salad fattoush, with tomatoes, cucumber and red onion). Mostly, however, pittas are cut open and the pockets stuffed; typical fillings include doner kebab, often with salad; falafel (see **chickpea**) with salad; chopped sausages and baked beans; and spicy mince or lentils.

word origin Pitta is Greek and means 'cake' or 'pie'.

did you know?

• Although we tend to think of pitta as being Cypriot, it's actually Arabic in origin and versions are found all over the Middle East and North Africa. Large round pittas called khoubz are particularly popular, and sometimes have 'filling' mixtures beaten in and cooked with the dough.

pizza

Pizza is Italian in origin and traditionally consists of a round, flat yeast-raised **bread** base covered with (usually) tomatoes plus a variety of other savoury ingredients. The base may be very thin and crisp or thicker and more chewy. A simple tomato-based sauce is normally spread over the shaped dough and topped with whatever takes your fancy: popular toppings include shredded or sliced mozzarella, mushrooms, peperoni or other sausage, sliced peppers, black olives, ham, smoked salmon and prawns. A traditional Italian pizza is baked quickly on a hot cooking stone in a very hot oven; a deep-pan pizza, which has a much thicker dough base, is baked in a special tin.

'Instant' pizzas can be made using **scone** or **soda bread** dough for the base, or slices or pieces of bread such as focaccia, ciabatta and French bread, even halved **muffins**.

using it Most pizzas are bought ready-made or as prepared bases. Popular versions include American hot (peperoni slices and crushed chillies on a tomato base); bianca (shredded mozzarella, olive oil, anchovies and either oregano or basil, but without tomatoes or tomato sauce); margherita (named after a pizza-loving queen of Italy and incorporating the colours of the Italian flag, basically tomato sauce plus shredded mozzarella and chopped basil); marinara (tomato sauce topped with garlic, oregano and olive oil); napoletana (the original classic, consisting of tomatoes or tomato sauce sprinkled with oregano – outside Naples anchovy fillets are also often added); and quattrostagione (the tomato base is divided into quarters, each one topped with different ingredients, typically cheese such as mozzarella, garlic and basil, mushrooms and sliced sausage or ham). Pizza dough can also be made into calzone ('trouser leg' in Italian), by being folded over a filling to enclose it completely, like a turnover.

word origin Pizza is very old and, although the origin is unclear, it may come from the Latin *pix,* meaning 'pitch', a reference to the flatness of the base (pine pitch forms itself into flat layers). A place where pizzas are sold and eaten is a *pizzeria*, and good ones will insert and remove their pizza stones from a wood-fired oven with the traditional long paddle.

did you know?

• Modern pizzas are particularly associated with Naples, although nearly all the regions of Italy have made approximations of it for a thousand years or more. Italian immigrants took the dish to the United States (the first American *pizzeria* opened in New York in 1905), but it wasn't until American GIs returned from Italy after the Second World War with a taste for it that its popularity really began to take off.

pretzel

A pretzel is a shiny, dense biscuit-bread, traditionally shaped like a loose knot or a stick. Flavourings like caraway seeds and coarse salt are often added. There are two main types. A 'soft' pretzel is made with a yeast-raised **bread** dough. After shaping, it is first cooked in boiling water with a little **bicarbonate of soda**, then glazed and baked in a fairly hot oven until golden and solid. A 'hard' pretzel is made without yeast. The shaped dough is sprayed with a heated alkaline solution and then salt, before being baked in a very hot oven to make the surface hard and shiny; it's then baked again, this time in a fairly hot oven, until it has completely dried out.

using it Both types are served as a savoury snack with beer or other drinks; soft pretzels

are sometimes smeared with mustard before being eaten or used as a scoop for spicy dips.

word origin Pretzel is German, derived from the medieval Latin *brachitum,* meaning 'bracelet'.

did you know?

• Pretzels seem to have first been made by monks in the Mediterranean area about 1200 years ago, and the unique shape is supposed to represent Christians praying. They gradually spread throughout Europe, becoming particularly popular in what are now Germany and Austria (where there's even a variation on the **croissant** story involving pretzels and invading Turks). They were probably taken to America by Austrian and German immigrants during the 19th century.

puff pastry

This is a crisp, rich but delicate, multi-layered pastry made from roughly equal quantities of flour and fat (usually butter if home-made; a mixture of butter and other fats if commercial). Making puff pastry is time-consuming: first some of the fat is mixed with the flour to make a dough, which is then wrapped around the remaining fat. After at least six 'turns' (rolling out and folding into thirds), with 'resting' times in between, the pastry is ready to be shaped and baked in a hot oven.

using it Since it can take half a day to create, not surprisingly puff pastry is usually bought; some brands are even already rolled.

One of the major uses for puff pastry is as a container or cover for savoury, and especially meat-based, pies. Puff pastry dough is also cut into smaller squares or circles, filled with sweet or savoury mixtures like apple and then folded over into turnovers; used as a container for small individual pies, like mince pies; or shaped into large or small vol-au-vents, deep, round cases with a lid. Puff is also made into millefeuilles, which is French for 'a thousand leaves': layers of baked puff pastry sandwiched together by sweet fillings (for example, jam and whipped cream, usually topped with decorative icing); or savoury (creamed salmon or other fish or vegetables).

word origin Puff pastry is a literal description of what it is, a dough that 'puffs up' when baked. Vol-au-vents were invented by the 18th-century French chef Carême, who also named them; he claimed the pastry was so light and delicate when it emerged from the oven that it '*s'envola au vent*', flew away in the wind.

did you know?

• Puff pastry as we know it is French in origin, and was perfected into its modern form during the 17th century. There are two separate theories about who did this: the romantic version has it that it was the brainchild of the landscape painter Claude Lorrain, who is thought to have been an apprentice pastry cook at one time; the other that it was created by a chef named Feuillet who was in the employ of the powerful Condé family in France.

quiche

A quiche is a savoury tart with a **shortcrust pastry** case and custard-based filling. The classic is quiche Lorraine, originally made only with a custard of eggs and cream, but which now usually includes grilled bacon and Gruyère cheese as well. Other filling flavourings include caramelized onion, sliced tomatoes with herbs, smoked salmon and goat's cheese, broccoli and Stilton, and roasted Mediterranean vegetables.

using it Quiche can be eaten warm or cold but is best on the day it's made, since the pastry becomes less crisp with storing.

word origin This dish goes back to late medieval times in Europe, when open savoury flans were served with fillings 'set' in a heavy egg and cream custard; quiche itself was a speciality of Lorraine in eastern France, an area that was shuffled between France and Germany for centuries, a fate echoed in the word, which is French but from the German *küchen,* meaning 'cake'.

sandwich

At its most basic a sandwich is two slices of (usually buttered) **bread** with a filling in between, but this is just the beginning. The bread can be white, brown or granary, a bread roll, bap or bagel, a 'new' bread like ciabatta or baguette, and it can be toasted or plain. Most sandwiches are double-deckers (that is, with one filling between two slices of bread), but some are triple (two fillings and three bread slices) or open (a slice of bread, toasted or untoasted, with a topping).

About 50 percent of the bread sold in the United Kingdom is made into sandwiches, now the standard workday lunch.

using it Sandwiches are known by their fillings and two American classics are BLT, a combination of crumbled cooked bacon, lettuce, sliced tomato and mayonnaise on toasted bread; and club, a toasted triple decker, basically a BLT plus cooked chicken or turkey. Other favourite fillings include tuna, egg or prawn mayonnaise, roast beef, ham and cheese, chicken tikka, crumbled bacon and guacamole (see **avocado**), pastrami and sliced gherkin (preferably smeared with mustard rather than butter), smoked salmon, Brie and redcurrant jelly, and so on. The ploughman's lunch, while not a sandwich, comprises the elements of a sandwich: cheese (usually Cheddar) and pickle, served with a wedge of bread.

• People have probably been eating combinations of filling and bread more or less since they started making bread, but what we now call a sandwich only got its name in the 18th century, from John Montagu, the 4th Earl of Sandwich. The earl was so addicted to gambling that he couldn't bear to leave the gaming tables even to eat. At some point he decided that if he wouldn't go to the food, the food could come to him, and ordered a 'portable' meal of meat and bread to be brought to him at his table. For the record, that first 'sandwich' was toasted and contained roast beef.

scone

This British teacake is made from a soft dough that usually contains buttermilk; egg is also sometimes added to enrich the mixture and it is usually risen with **baking powder** (in the form of self-raising flour) or a mixture of **bicarbonate of soda** and cream of tartar. The dough is cut into small round shapes, or formed into a larger round scored into triangles before being cooked – traditionally on a griddle, but more usually now in a hot oven.

Scones can be sweet or savoury. For sweet scones, sugar, dried fruit and spices are often added, while savoury ones are made with grated cheese, herbs and potato. A drop scone isn't actually a scone at all, but a type of small thick pancake.

using it Scones are best eaten warm, the day they are baked or bought. The classic accompaniments for sweet scones are butter, clotted cream and jam; savoury ones are usually toasted and served with butter.

Unsweetened scone dough has occasional other uses: it can be rolled out and used as a base for home-made pizza or, as a sheet or cut into small rounds or triangles, instead of pastry as a topping for savoury pies.

word origin Scone comes indirectly from the Middle Dutch *schoonbroot,* meaning 'fine bread'.

• Scones are particularly associated with Scotland and northern England. In Scotland, where scones have been popular for hundreds of years, they traditionally include oatmeal and are shaped into large rounds to cook on the griddle. In the north of England a favourite is a large plain scone with currants, called singin' hinny.

shortbread

Despite the name, this is a crumbly butter-rich **biscuit**, usually made from plain flour and rice flour, although wholemeal flour or fine semolina is sometimes substituted for the latter. Flavourings like grated orange zest and cinnamon can also be added. The shortbread dough is rolled out and cut into shapes – traditionally either fingers or large rounds scored into triangles. Rounds may be pressed into special moulds or baked flat on a baking tray. After baking, the biscuits are often sprinkled with sugar, or they can be topped with caramel and a chocolate icing to make millionaire's shortbread.

using it Most shortbreads are eaten as a sweet snack, although larger rounds can also be topped with strawberries or other berries, glazed with melted jam, and served as a dessert.

word origin Shortbread comes from the method of preparation: the fat is 'shortened' into a dough by being rubbed or beaten with sugar and flour.

• Shortbread has always been associated with Scotland and various types have been baked there for hundreds of years. One of the most popular is petticoat tail, a thin triangular biscuit flavoured with almonds. There are several different explanations of its origins, and most of them lead back to Mary, Queen of Scots, who lived in France for most of her youth and loved all things French, including the food. The French chefs she brought with her when she returned to her native Scotland enabled her to indulge her passion for *petites gatelles* (little cakes), and one of these could be the ancestor of today's biscuit. A simpler explanation is that petticoat tails have always been baked in special moulds, possibly shaped like the hooped dresses of her court ladies.

shortcrust pastry

The easiest to make and most versatile **pastry**, shortcrust has a light crumbly texture. It is made from plain flour (white or wholemeal) and fat (traditionally butter, which gives the best flavour, but also sometimes margarine or lard or a mixture of fats – butter and lard are the classic combination). The pastry dough is made by rubbing the cold fat into the flour until the mixture looks like breadcrumbs, then binding with a little liquid.

A basic shortcrust is usually made with one part fat to two parts flour, and is bound with cold water. Rich shortcrust pastry uses one and a half parts fat (usually butter) to two parts flour and is bound with egg or egg yolk; if used for a sweet pie or tart, sugar is added. An even sweeter rich shortcrust is French pâte sucrée. There are also shortcrust pastries that include ground almonds or other nuts, grated cheese and chopped herbs.

using it Basic shortcrust can be bought ready-made; both it and home-made shortcrust can be kept in the refrigerator for a day or two or frozen.

Shortcrust pastry is used primarily as a container for flans and tarts, pies and quiche, and as a topping for deep pies; it is also occasionally used as a base for fancy cakes and pastry confections. Pastry cases are either filled before being baked or

baked blind, that is without a filling. For this, the case is lined with greaseproof paper or foil and weighted down with baking beans to prevent it from shrinking and puffing up during baking. Pastry cases are either partially baked blind (if they will be filled and baked further) or completely baked.

word origin Shortcrust gets its name from its texture, which comes from the fat being 'shortened' into a dough by being rubbed with flour.

soda bread

This is a quick and easy **bread** made by combining plain flour (white, wholemeal or a mixture), **bicarbonate of soda** and an acidic liquid (such as buttermilk, soured cream or yoghurt) into a smooth dough. When the liquid isn't acidic (i.e. if ordinary milk or water is used), cream of tartar is included to activate the soda. Butter is also occasionally added to create a richer mixture. The dough is shaped into a round ball and a deep cross cut into the top (essentially sectioning the bread into quarters) before it's baked in a hot oven.

using it Both home-made and bought soda bread are best eaten on the day they are made or purchased. Serve warm, with butter and jam or cheese, or use in the same way as ordinary bread.

word origin Soda bread is named after its raising agent, bicarbonate of soda.

did you know?

• Soda bread has been associated with Ireland for nearly 200 years, and was traditionally baked there in a small pot oven over the dying fire. The cross was cut into the top, partly to ensure even baking, but also (according to tradition) to 'let the devil out'.

sponge cake

A sponge is a light airy cake that can be made from any number of ingredients, but always includes flour (usually white, but sometimes wholemeal or a mixture of the two), sugar (normally caster) and eggs. Fat (butter or margarine) is added to most sponges, as is baking powder to help them rise, and flavourings such as spices, cocoa and coffee powder and vanilla essence are also common.

There are three methods used to make a sponge cake: all-in-one, creaming and whisking (see **cake**). The whisking method produces the lightest sponge of all, and the classic is made just with eggs, sugar and flour, no fat. A moister version, which contains melted butter, is the Genoese sponge.

using it Sponge cake should be eaten fresh. A classic whisked sponge will not keep, so bake it the day you are going to serve it.

Most sponges are eaten as a dessert or at teatime. Favourite British ones include the Swiss roll, where a thin rectangular cake is spread with a filling, such as whipped cream and jam, then rolled up; and the Victoria sponge, where two sponge cakes are sandwiched together with jam (traditionally raspberry) and the top is dusted with sugar. A sponge mixture can also be baked into sponge finger biscuits and flan cases, or, flavoured with almond, it can be the filling for a Bakewell tart. Sponge cake can be used as part of other desserts, such as classic trifle, where slices of sponge are doused with sherry (or brandy, Grand Marnier, Tia Maria or even rum), then topped with thick custard, fruit and whipped cream.

word origin The name comes from the texture of the finished cake, and has been around for about 200 years.

tortilla

A tortilla is a traditional Mexican unleavened bread made from flour – **maize** (corn) or **wheat** – and water. The dough is patted out into thin rounds and then 'baked' briefly on a griddle or pan until mottled brown on both sides.

Tortilla is also the word for a flat Spanish omelette traditionally made with potatoes and onions (see **omelette**).

using it Most commercial tortillas keep well, up to several months in some cases, but home-made ones should be eaten as soon as possible after cooking. They are usually served warm. Corn tortillas are normally fried or deep-fried until they have just softened or become crisp, while those made with wheat can be warmed in the oven or under the grill.

Tortillas are Mexico's everyday bread, served as an accompaniment to all meals, as sandwich wraps or as a container or base for other mixtures. Classic tortilla-based dishes include burritos (wheat tortillas folded and rolled to enclose a savoury filling, typically refried beans or chilli con carne); enchiladas (softened corn tortillas rolled around a filling, then covered with a tomato salsa and served hot); nachos (tortilla chips – deep-fried corn tortilla pieces – topped with melted cheese and chillies); and tacos (folded, usually deep-fried, corn tortillas with fillings such as browned mince or chorizo, refried beans, soured cream, shredded lettuce, cheese, guacamole and salsa).

word origin Tortilla is Spanish and means 'little tart' or 'cake'. Spanish conquistadors were the first Europeans to eat the Mexican breads, and probably gave them a comfortingly familiar name because they had difficulty pronouncing the Aztec word for them (*tlaxcalli*).

did you know?

• Central Americans had been eating corn tortillas for millennia before the Spanish arrived in Mexico in the early 16th century. Making them was an everyday task always done by the women: first they would cook maize kernels with water and a little unslaked lime (this loosened the husks, which were then removed by hand). Then the huskless kernels were ground into a flour on a *metlatl* or special stone roller, water being added if necessary to make it into a paste. And finally this paste was kneaded and shaped into flat rounds, which were cooked on a *comalli*, a shallow earthenware dish perched on hearthstones over the fire.

yeast

Yeast is a living organism used as a raising agent in baking and to ferment **beer** and **wine**. When yeast comes into contact with sugar or starch, in the ideal warm and moist conditions, it multiplies rapidly and produces alcohol and carbon dioxide. In breadmaking, the carbon dioxide produced by the yeast is what causes doughs to rise.

There are millions of microscopic yeast spores in the air. These airborne 'wild' yeasts, once the only means of raising doughs, are today still used to make 'starter' doughs for sourdough breads. Commercial yeast for baking, cultured from the *Saccharomyces* yeast strain, is available fresh (in small, moist cakes) or dried (as granules or powder).

Adding yeast to a flour mixture introduces the yeast cells to their 'food', and as they start eating (and multiplying), they ferment and convert the food to carbon dioxide. Most yeast doughs are kneaded, (that is, manipulated, folded and stretched), so that the carbon dioxide bubbles are distributed throughout and the gluten present in the flour is developed to make a framework to hold them in place. Then the dough is set aside to rise (the equivalent of fermentation in beer), the time depending on the ingredients used and the warmth of the environment – the dough should double in size. Many doughs are given a second rising. The heat of the oven finally stops the fermenting process by killing off the yeast.

using it Fresh yeast is perishable, so should be bought when needed; it can be kept in the refrigerator for a few days (or the freezer for about two months). Avoid any that looks dry or has dark patches since this means it's probably stale and won't raise dough. Dried yeast will keep for up to a year in a cool dry place or in the refrigerator.

Both fresh yeast and standard dried yeast granules need to be mixed with lukewarm liquid before being blended with flour and other dry ingredients. (Yeast is inactive in cold temperatures and destroyed by excessively high ones; liquid at about 25°C is considered ideal.) With fresh yeast, cream it with the liquid until smooth, then add to the flour. With dried yeast, stir with the liquid until dissolved, then set aside in a warm place to give it time to come to life, normally 10–15 minutes; the mixture should be foamy. Fast-action or easy-blend dried yeast doesn't need to be reactivated first and so can be added directly to the flour, before the liquid is blended in. About 30g fresh yeast would be needed to raise 1kg of flour, half that amount for standard dried and half again for fast-action yeast, although this would also depend on the amount of salt and sugar the dough contained.

Although theoretically yeast can be used to raise any kind of baked item, in practice it is normally used to make bread, where its characteristic taste becomes an asset to the finished product. Of the other major raising agents, **baking powder** is used in conjunction with non-acidic liquids like water for cakes and teacakes, and **bicarbonate of soda** on its own helps to raise breads such as soda bread, but only when combined with an acidic liquid like buttermilk.

word origin People have been using yeast to create both raised bread and beer since ancient Egyptian times. Up until about two centuries ago, the yeast used to leaven bread came from the foam, called barm, that is created by newly brewed beer. The word itself reflects this, and comes from the Old German *Gischt,* meaning 'to froth' or 'create sediment'.

did you know?

* Although yeast has been used every day for at least 6000 years, no one knew how it worked, although most were grateful that it did. The man who changed this was the French scientist Louis Pasteur. In 1857, he discovered that yeasts were 'live' microscopic organisms; until then the rising and fermenting processes had been assumed to be chemical reactions.

Sugars, Sweets & Sweet Preserves

Some of you may have seen me strapped to a bed, tubes coming out of my arms, being tested for my insulin resistance level on the BBC programme *Food Junkies*. We all know that we shouldn't eat too much sugar, and I believe that sugar can have a negative effect on our health if we consume too much of it. In a way, we are our own worst enemies: sugar consumption at the beginning of the 20th century was about 1.8kg per person per year, but it is now up to an incredible 63kg.

While we should all be trying to reduce our consumption of sugar, especially refined sugar, there is absolutely nothing wrong with

...there is absolutely nothing wrong with enjoying sweet things from time to time...
Antony Worrall Thompson

enjoying sweet things from time to time – as the saying goes, everything is fine in moderation. I believe it is far preferable to eat a little sugar, which is a natural product, than to replace it with artificial sweeteners. I personally try to use organic sugar wherever possible.

In this section you will find a wealth of information about all sorts of foods that appeal to the many among us with a sweet tooth. As well as discussing sugar itself, it includes facts and anecdotes about a variety of preserves and sweets. After reading this, you will be able to make the best possible choices when you shop and cook.

candy

This is both a process used to preserve and sweeten fruits, herbs and strips of citrus peel (the subject of this entry) and boiled **sweets** glazed with sugar. Most reasonably firm fruits can be candied, although softer berries like raspberries are unsuitable since they would probably disintegrate during the steeping process. Smaller fruits like plums tend to be preserved whole, while larger ones such as pineapple are normally sliced or chopped first. The only herb regularly candied now is angelica, although technically other similar herbs could be treated in the same way; oranges and lemons are the most popular types of candied peel.

Most fruits are softened before being candied, usually by being boiled until just tender (angelica is soaked and blanched), then stirred into a thick **sugar** and water syrup. They remain there until they are semi-transparent (usually several days), with the syrup being drained off two or three times during this period and replaced by a stronger one – proportions vary from item to item, but on average a mixture would start out as equal quantities of sugar and water and gradually increase to three parts sugar to one part water (this progressive strengthening means that the items being candied will retain their shape and texture and not shrivel up). After this period, the candied pieces are removed from the syrup and left to dry out completely in a warm place, which takes at least a day or so.

All candied foods can be used as is, but most candied fruits are also crystallized, that is rolled in white sugar, or coated in a sugar-based syrup to give them a shiny finish (see **glacé fruit).**

using it Candied angelica and peel are primarily used in baking and in desserts: as part of fruit cake mixtures and as decoration for cakes and tarts, for instance, or mixed with whipped cream to make a filling for cakes, a

layer in trifles or a rich addition to cold baked rice. Candied whole fruit or fruit pieces tend either to decorate fancier cakes or gâteaux, or to be eaten as after-dinner sweets.

Both commercial and home-made candied foods keep for months.

word origin When fruit was first preserved in sugar syrup during the Middle Ages it was called sugar candy in English, which came, via French, from the Arabic *sukkar qandi*, meaning 'sugar in crystalline pieces'. Gradually this was shortened to just candy, and for a time came to mean any kind of sweet or sweetmeat, the way the word is still used in the United States.

> **did you know?**
>
> • The favourite seaside and fairground treat candyfloss isn't really 'candy' as described above, despite the name – this fluffy pink concoction on a stick is made by cooking dyed granulated sugar in a revolving drum, which first melts it and then spins it into threads that are extruded through special holes in the machine onto the stick.

caramel

At its simplest, caramel is **sugar** boiled in water until it becomes a sticky brown mass (usually reached above 160°C on a sugar thermometer). It's also the name given to a soft brown **toffee** made from sugar, cream and butter, plus occasional other ingredients like golden syrup, condensed milk, honey, chocolate and vanilla.

using it Caramel syrup is used commercially as a coating or filling for sweets, and to colour and flavour items as diverse as sweet pickles, stock cubes, soft drinks and spirits. Home-made caramel syrup can be used as a sauce for ice-cream, a coating for choux pastry, or as a flavouring for mousse and other creamy desserts. Caramel sweets are made in the same way as **toffee** (see entry).

word origin Caramel is French and first appeared in English during the 18th century. The French word comes from the Spanish *caramelo* and both are probably derived from the medieval Latin *calamellus,* meaning 'little tube', a reference to sugar cane, at that time the only source of refined sugar.

did you know?

• Crème caramel and crème brûlée are 'caramelized' in slightly different ways. For the former, sugar is heated until it becomes a rich brown syrup, then poured into an empty baking mould and tipped around to coat it. The 'crème', or custard, is then spooned in and the mixture baked until the custard has set. It's turned out to serve so that the caramel coats the top and sides. For crème brûlée, a thick layer of sugar is sprinkled over the surface of a baked custard and grilled until melted, then left to cool until it has formed a hard shiny shell.

carob

Carob (*Ceratonia siliqua*) is the podded fruit of an evergreen tree related to tamarind and native to the Mediterranean area. Modern suppliers include Spain, Portugal, Italy, Mexico and Australia. Young pods look similar to those of broad beans, but they become shiny and brown as they mature. Each one contains a sweet pulp and up to 15 seeds. To turn them into food, the pods are first cleaned, then 'kibbled' – coarsely ground to separate the seeds from the pulp – before being used as animal fodder or roasted and milled into a powder. The seeds are processed separately to produce a type of gum.

Carob tastes similar to **chocolate,** but is sweeter and it does not contain the stimulants caffeine and theobromine that are found in chocolate. Although carob itself has less fat than cacao, from which chocolate is made, carob bars have the same amount of calories and fat as similar-size chocolate bars, as they are usually made with coconut oil or a hydrogenated vegetable oil.

using it All carob products keep indefinitely. The powder is primarily a cocoa or chocolate substitute used especially in baking and confectionery – about one and a half parts carob to one part cocoa powder is the usual proportion and, since it is considerably sweeter than cocoa, less sugar is needed. Carob powder has a tendency to lump, so is usually mixed with a little hot liquid before being added to other ingredients. Commercially, carob powder is also used as a food colouring.

Carob gum is used commercially too, as a setting agent and stabilizer, particularly in ice-creams, fruit desserts and pet foods. It's also occasionally mixed with tragacanth gum (a resin extracted from certain other leguminous plants) in confectionery.

word origin Carob comes, via Old French, from the Arabic word for the pod, *kharrub*. In the ancient world the seeds, known in Greek as *keration*, were also sometimes used as units of weight, from which we get the modern word carat.

did you know?

• Carob has been cultivated for about 5000 years and the adhesive properties were known early – in Egypt it was used to bind mummy dressings and both the pods and seeds have been found in tombs there. There are Biblical connections too: alternative names for carob are locust bean and St John's bread, the former leading to the latter and a great deal of confusion – John the Baptist was said to have lived on 'locusts and wild honey' as he wandered in the wilderness. Whether this was the pods of the carob tree or the insects of the same name no one knows.

chewing gum

Chewing gum was originally made from sugar, flavourings such as liquorice and peppermint, and chicle, the coagulated form of a milky liquid that exudes from the sapodilla tree – it was chicle that gave the gum its elasticity and 'pulling' power. Nowadays demand far outstrips supply, so although chicle or other natural latexes like jelutong are still sometimes used, most chewing gums are produced with synthetic substitutes. Sweeteners can now include corn syrup and aspartame (see **sweeteners**) as well as sugar.

Modern gum is made in several stages: first the gum base is ground, melted and purified in a centrifuge; then, while it's still hot, the refined base is transferred to mixers where other ingredients like sweeteners, flavourings and glycerine or hydrogenated vegetable oils (added to soften the finished gum) are blended in and the mixture beaten until it resembles a stiff bread dough; finally, the 'dough' goes through a series of rollers that flatten it out into a thin ribbon, which is lightly coated with powdered sugar to prevent it from sticking, then marked into single sticks. The finished gum is set aside to cool before being packaged.

using it Gum is chewed by about half the population of the western world, and the chewing action is supposed to help people relax and stay mentally alert. Once there is absolutely no flavouring left, the gum is discarded, not swallowed.

word origin The 'gum' part comes from the Latin *gummi* via the Old French *gomme*.

did you know?

• The sapodilla tree comes from Central America and chicle was a favourite snack of the Aztecs, among others, although similar gums from various other types of tree were chewed for millennia all around the world. The idea of mixing them with sugar came from the Middle East, but the first commercial gum was actually made in the United States during the 1850s – from spruce tree resin. Its flavour was an acquired taste, however, and was soon dropped in favour of chicle. By the beginning of the 20th century, the finished gum was sometimes being coated with sugar syrup that was then allowed to harden around it, and 30 years after that, bubble gum made its first appearance.

• One of the first men to make his fortune from chewing gum was William Wrigley, who set up business in Chicago towards the end of the 19th century. He started out selling soap and the way he encouraged business was to give away free gifts with the merchandise. The first gift was a fairly new substance called baking powder. It was such a success he switched to selling it. Later his **baking powder** freebie was packs of another new product, chewing gum, and this was hugely popular too. He began to manufacture gum, and both the classic Wrigley brands, Juicy Fruit and Spearmint, had appeared by 1893.

chocolate

Like cocoa and drinking chocolate, chocolate comes from the podded fruit of a tropical tree (*Theobroma cacao*), which is native to Central and South America, but now widely grown in many other countries such as the Ivory Coast, Nigeria and Indonesia. Mexico, once the home of chocolate, contributes only about 1.5 percent of modern world production.

Each cacao pod contains 20–60 fatty beans. During the manufacturing process that turns these beans into various cocoa and chocolate products (see **cocoa**), they are ground into a pulpy liquid called the chocolate mass, the basis of all of them. Most of the fat, called cocoa butter, is removed from this mass and what remains (the cocoa solids) is then treated in various ways, depending on what is being made: some is pressed again to release more cocoa butter, then formed into cakes and ground to create cocoa powder, the basis not only of cocoa but of drinking chocolate powder; some is allowed to harden into a bitter-tasting solid chocolate used by commercial confectioners and bakers; and the rest is further processed into different types of eating chocolate.

To make eating chocolate, sugar is usually mixed into the cocoa solids and normally some cocoa butter is also added back into the mixture; milk solids are blended in too if milk chocolate is being made. This enriched mixture is heated and pressed through rollers again to make it smooth. Finally, it is 'conched', that is, subjected to a rapid to-and-fro agitation by granite rollers to make it even smoother and to bring out the taste (this can take anywhere from a few hours to several days, depending on the quality of the final chocolate). If the chocolate is to be flavoured with, say, mint or vanilla, this is added towards the end of the conching process.

The chocolate is now 'tempered' (heated, cooled and then warmed slightly) so that it can be moulded or shaped to create sweets. For mass-produced individual sweets and bars, the chosen filling is mechanically 'enrobed' by a coating of thick liquid chocolate. For more expensive confectionery, moulds are mechanically coated with molten chocolate, the fillings are added and the whole thing topped by a final coating of chocolate. For hand-made chocolates, the centres are individually dipped into thick liquid chocolate to coat them. Moulds vary in size and in shape, from standard small squares, rounds and ovals to 'fun' shapes like bunnies, mice or fruits.

There are three main types of chocolate. Dark or plain chocolate is made essentially from cocoa solids, reintroduced cocoa butter and, normally, sugar and a little lecithin (a vegetable-based emulsifier), which will bind it; the best dark chocolate, often called continental or bittersweet chocolate, contains about 70 percent cocoa solids and either no sugar or a relatively small amount. Milk chocolate combines cocoa solids with dried milk solids, more sugar than dark chocolate, vegetable fats like soya and palm oil, emulsifier and a relatively small amount of cocoa butter. White chocolate contains no cocoa solids at all, and is made from cocoa butter, sugar, dried milk solids and emulsifier.

using it Chocolate bars and sweets keep well, although this is something that's rarely put to the test. Any type of unflavoured commercial chocolate can be used in cooking, although the richest flavour will come from bars containing 70 percent cocoa solids, also often identified on the label as 'cocoa mass'.

When used in desserts, puddings and baking, chocolate is usually first melted in a bowl set over simmering water (or over direct heat if being melted with butter or cream). It can then be added to the basic mixture for custard and ice-cream; used as a sauce (with or without cream) for ice-cream, fruit or profiteroles (see **choux pastry**); mixed with rum or brandy and then folded into whipped sweetened cream and stiffly whisked egg whites to make a simple mousse; and used as a flavouring in icings to decorate or fill cakes or biscuits. Melted chocolate combined with some sugar and brandy or Grand Marnier becomes a dessert fondue, the perfect dipping sauce for cut-up fresh fruit.

Chocolate is also used occasionally in savoury cooking, most famously as the basis of Mexican mole sauce, where it's mixed with chillies, ground almonds and sesame seeds among other ingredients, and traditionally served with turkey.

word origin Chocolate drinks were part of the native cultures of Central America, and Spanish conquistadors first came across them at the court of the Aztec king, Montezuma, during the early 1500s. At some point later in the same century they started calling this drink *chocolate*, an adaptation of the Mayan *chocol,* meaning 'hot' or 'bitter', and the Aztec *atl,* meaning 'water' – probably a literal translation since the original Aztec drink contained chilli. Drinking chocolate was popular for centuries before modern solid chocolate came along in the early to mid-19th century, so the latter retained the same name as the familiar drink.

did you know?

• Solid 'lozenges' were around in Spain and her colonies by the end of the 17th century, but were simply gritty little versions of chocolate mass, full of fat, unpleasant to eat and difficult to digest. Then in 1828 a Dutchman named Conrad van Houten invented a machine that allowed cocoa butter to be extracted from this mass, resulting in a chocolate that was smoother, better-tasting and easier to digest. The first new 'eating' chocolate was made in 1847 by J S Fry and Sons, but it was Cadbury's who introduced the first box of chocolates in 1868. As this was the age of Victorian sentimentality, the cover had a painting of John Cadbury's daughter Jessica holding a kitten in her arms. It was a wild success.

• Some of the early chocolate manufacturers came from strong religious backgrounds: the Frys, Cadburys and Rowntrees were all Quakers, who believed in pacifism and good works, and all three were teetotal (one of the reasons they were enthusiastic about chocolate is that they wanted to promote it as an alternative to gin); in the United States, Milton Snavely Hershey, whose Bars and Kisses dominate the American market, was a member of the Pennsylvania Mennonites. The Cadburys created a model town for their workers at Bournville near Birmingham, and Joseph Rowntree built a similar one near York. Milton Hershey's town, Hershey ('the Chocolate Town'), in Pennsylvania, has 12,000 inhabitants, and main streets called Chocolate and Cocoa Avenues. At the Hershey Hotel, the spa offers some unique treatments, including chocolate mud hydrotherapy and a whipped cocoa bath.

• Chocolate in whatever form is a compelling mix of compounds that flavour, relax and stimulate: it contains theobromine, which resembles caffeine, as well as caffeine itself. See also **coffee**.

fondant

This is both a **sweet** and an **icing**, made from sugar, water and either glucose or cream of tartar. The resulting mixture can be very sweet, which is why tart or strong flavourings such as lemon, peppermint, coffee or spice are often added in. Fondant is created by boiling the ingredients together until they reach the 'soft ball' stage (see **sugar**), then working the mixture to and fro with a spatula on a cold surface until it's cool enough to be kneaded by hand – the idea is to turn the clear thick liquid into a stiff but pliable white dough.

using it Fondant can be used warm or cold. To use warm, the mixture is melted or softened with any flavourings or colouring in a bowl set over a pan of simmering water. The fondant can then be poured or spooned into moulds in the same way as **chocolate** to provide shells or fillings for sweets, or used as a coating for small fruits. Softened to a spreading consistency, the mixture can also be used to ice or decorate cakes and pastries. To make sweets from cold fondant, flavourings and colourings are kneaded in, then the mixture is rolled out, cut into shapes and dusted with icing sugar.

word origin Fondant first appeared in English during the late 19th century and comes from the French *fondre,* meaning 'to melt' – the idea was probably that fondants would 'melt in the mouth'. In the confectionary trade, the word is used to describe creamy fillings for chocolates.

fudge

Fudge is a soft-textured **sweet** made from sugar, butter and milk (or cream, or golden or maple syrup); flavourings like vanilla, chocolate and desiccated coconut, and ingredients like chopped nuts and raisins, are also often added. To make fudge, the sugar, butter and milk are boiled together until they reach the 'soft ball' stage (see **sugar**), then the flavouring and other ingredients are added and the mixture is beaten until it is creamy and starting to thicken. It's poured into shallow tins or moulds to cool and firm up.

using it Home-made fudge mixtures can be used warm as a thick dessert sauce (particularly with ice-cream), and make a good topping for brownies and other biscuits or a great filling for cakes. Once set, fudge is a sweet snack.

word origin When the word initially appeared in the 17th century (see below) it meant 'to make something up', to 'cover up' or 'nonsense'. It was only two centuries later, in the United States, that it was given to an easy-to-make sweet especially popular among college students. The connection between the two isn't clear, unless the sweet was so called because it was easy to make (up).

did you know?

• The original meaning of the word is said to come from a 17th-century ship's captain named Fudge; in fact he was called 'Lying Fudge' because he always lied about the cargoes he brought back for his owners. Eventually whenever sailors thought somebody was lying, they would shout, 'You fudge it!'

glacé fruit

This is fruit (and occasionally nuts) coated in a shiny, sugar-based syrup. In theory, any fruit can be used, but in practice it is primarily cherries, pineapple and grapes that are treated in this way. The fruit is first candied (see **candy**), then dipped into a dense sugar syrup that has been boiled to the 'hard crack' stage (see **sugar**) and set aside to dry. (The candying process can be omitted, but uncandied fruit needs to be as dry as possible before being dipped into the dense syrup, otherwise it won't adhere properly.)

The only nut regularly glacéed is **chestnut**, which is shelled and cooked, then poached in a flavoured sugar syrup for about 48 hours to make marrons glacés. It's given a final coating of melted sugar and allowed to dry to a clear gloss before being packaged for sale.

using it Commercially made glacé cherries are widely available and keep indefinitely; glacé fruit made without being candied first

doesn't keep well and should be used within a day or so. Glacé fruits, chopped or whole, are added to fruit cake mixtures and biscuit doughs, and can also be used to decorate cakes and cocktails. Marrons glacés are eaten as an after-dinner sweet, or used to decorate fancy gâteaux or chestnut-purée desserts.

word origin Glacé is French, the past participle of *glacer,* meaning 'to ice' or 'give a shine to'. It was first associated with fruit in the late 19th century, but was also used to describe highly polished or shiny materials such as silk.

honey

The natural sweet nectar produced by flowers, honey is collected and processed by certain types of bee (most notably *Apis mellifera*) in spring and summer, then stored by them in honeycombs to use as food during winter.

Most honey is produced in hives, and modern ones are arranged in sections: the lower part houses the nursery where the large queen bee lives and produces larvae destined mostly to become worker bees or drones, while the upper part is divided into removable slatted frames imprinted with hexagonal beeswax cells (honeycombs) that are used to store the honey. The queen bee is confined to the lower part of the hive by a perforated metal excluder, which has holes large enough to permit the smaller worker bees to store the honey in the upper part. A typical hive at its peak will contain one queen, several hundred drones and about 30,000 workers; a queen bee can produce more than 200,000 eggs during a season and will survive for two or more years.

Drones have only one function in life, to mate with the queen. Worker bees, on the other hand, deserve their name: at various points in their brief lives (the average span is about six weeks during spring/summer, about double this during winter), they look after the queen and nursery, help to build new wax cells on which to store the honey, guard the entrance to the hive and clean out any rubbish, and help to process and store the honey itself. Most importantly of all, they fly up to several kilometres away to collect nectar and pollen (the powdery yellow grains that fertilize flowers and are fed to the developing larvae for the first part of their lives, before they begin to live on honey). They swallow the nectar into special sacs in their bodies and carry the pollen on their back legs to get it back to the hive. Up to 100,000 journeys are required to bring back five litres of nectar, about enough to make one litre of honey.

Processing the nectar into honey starts in the hive, when worker bees regurgitate and then evaporate it by fanning their wings so that what is left is a sticky concentrated liquid. Honey is removed from the hive by taking out the vertical slats (beekeepers use smoke to make the bees sleepy and less likely to sting so that they can do this, and also wear protective clothing), then extracting it from the honeycombs, usually by vacuum or centrifuge. The resulting honey is then normally warmed and filtered to remove debris and any remaining pollen before being packaged for sale; the honeycomb cells themselves are also sometimes removed, crushed and added in chunks to the honey containers.

In its normal state, honey is a clear runny liquid, but it can be further treated to remove more moisture to make a solid, opaque mixture that's easier to spread on bread. In colour, it can vary from pale yellow through to dark brown and, in some rare cases, almost black. The reason for these variations, and also differences in scent and flavour, is that individual flowers produce differently flavoured and coloured nectar; by carefully positioning hives near to appropriate flowers, in fact, beekeepers can produce honeys with predominating flavours of heather, lavender, thyme, orange or lime blossom, to name just

a few. In addition, some regions of the world produce highly scented honeys simply because of the wealth of different flowers that grow there – Greek mountain honey is one good example.

using it Honey keeps indefinitely in a cool, dry place and is used in virtually all types of cooking. Most simply it's spread over bread or toast, or used as a substitute for sugar in tea or coffee, although it's sweeter than sugar so if it is being used instead of it, less will be needed: about one part honey to one and a half parts sugar. But this is just the start: it's also mixed into bread, cake, biscuit and **nougat** doughs, poured over desserts such as pancakes, ice-cream and yoghurt, and used as a glaze for lamb, duck or ham. Honey is used to make drinks too, or added to them as a flavouring: honey, hot water and yeast are brewed together to make mead, and it's also used to flavour beer and liqueurs like Drambuie. And the drinks don't have to be alcoholic: honey mixed with freshly squeezed lemon juice, hot water or milk makes a soothing nightcap.

word origin Honey is Old English in origin and dates back to the 9th century as *hunig*, *huny* and even *honi*; it probably came from the Early German *khunagom*, which may have described its colour.

Before sugar became affordable, honey wasn't just the main sweetening ingredient for most people; it was the only one, unless you counted fruit or the odd sweet vegetable. The Biblical Promised Land was described in terms designed to maximize its appeal to a sweet-toothed population as a 'land flowing with milk and honey', and the general high regard also led to its use as a term of endearment ('Honey, I shrunk the kids'). And of course there's 'honeymoon', the newly married couple's holiday after the wedding, which may just mean the 'sweet month' after the marriage ('moon' having its old meaning of 'month'), but is also interpreted as a short period when everything is fine, but that things may go downhill after it's over. Bees' lifestyle has contributed phrases too. After the workers collect nectar and pollen they return to the hive as quickly as possible by the most direct route, hence to 'make a beeline for'.

• A 15,000-year-old cave painting in eastern Spain shows someone up what looks like a ladder with a bag disturbing a bees' nest in a tree, the first recorded instance of honey being collected. It's always been popular in Britain – early Druid priests described this country as the 'Isle of Honey', and when the Romans arrived they noted that the natives drank extremely large amounts of a honey brew that sounds similar to mead. The Romans were also fond of honey, and used it to preserve meat and fruit and to spice dishes, among other things.

• Honey is nearly as popular an ingredient in medicines and cosmetics as it is in the kitchen. In some parts of the world, for instance, it's still spread over wounds and burns, although its most common medicinal use is as a soother of sore throats. Royal jelly, taken from the bees that nurse the larvae and used to stimulate the growth of new queen bees (hence the name), has become a popular health and anti-ageing supplement. Even propolis, the gluey substance bees collect from sticky buds and use to fill cracks in the hive, is believed to have medicinal virtues and is added to some toothpastes and soaps.

icing

At its simplest, icing is a thick paste made from sugar and liquid, usually water. The sugar used is normally powdered 'icing' sugar, although caster and granulated are occasionally preferred; other ingredients such as egg, cream, chocolate and food colouring, and flavourings like vanilla essence can also be beaten in.

There are four major types. Smooth, flowing glacé icing is made by mixing icing sugar with just enough warm water (or fruit juice, liqueur and so on) to make a mixture that will coat the back of a spoon. Rich and spreadable buttercream is almost as easy – usually one part soft unsalted butter is beaten with two parts icing sugar; classic French buttercream (or crème au beurre) is made by beating a hot sugar syrup into egg yolks and then beating this into creamed butter. Thick, sweet fondant icing is made from a kneaded sugar syrup (see **fondant**). For fluffy, white royal icing, egg whites are whisked with icing sugar until the mixture stands up in peaks.

Icing mixtures that are cooked are usually called frosting.

using it Icings are primarily used to decorate cakes, biscuits and pastries. Glacé icing, a favourite coating for biscuits, individual small cakes like fairy cakes and simple sponges, only needs to be smoothed over quickly with a palette knife. Buttercream fills sandwich cakes and can be swirled thickly over the tops and sides too. Fondant icing makes a glossy coating for cakes and pastries, especially choux. Royal icing is the hard smooth covering for wedding, Christmas and birthday cakes, usually over a coating of **marzipan**. Royal icing is also often piped onto these cakes in decorative features like rosettes and flowers.

word origin The word comes from icing's resemblance to ice, and was first recorded around the middle of the 18th century.

• During the Middle Ages, 'icing' was simply a thick dusting of sugar sprinkled over savoury as well as sweet foods. The modern paste appeared during the 17th century and was made by beating sugar with egg whites. It was 'set' by being cooked in a very low oven for a few minutes, something Mrs Beeton was still doing in the 19th century.

jam

This is a thick sweet conserve normally

made from fruit cooked with sugar. Any type of fruit can be used: some of the most popular are soft fruits such as strawberries and blackcurrants, exotic types such as passionfruit and guava, and stone fruits like apricot and cherry. Some fruits (e.g. apple and redcurrant) are more likely to be made into jelly, where only the juice drained from the fruit pulp is cooked with the sugar, while others (e.g. citrus fruits) are used to make a type of jam called **marmalade**. Vegetables such as marrow are also occasionally used to make jam.

Three things are needed to make jam: sugar, pectin (a substance found in the cell walls of many fruits and vegetables) and acid, and fruits contain all three, but in varying strengths and proportions. Refined sugar, or another sweetener, is always added both to sweeten and to help preserve the jam. Pectin in combination with acid causes the mixture to jell or set. Some fruits are low in pectin (strawberries for instance) and to boost this, commercial pectin or high-pectin fruit or juice (such as that from sour or crab apples) can be added, as can an acid such as lemon juice.

Jam is made in two main stages: first the fruit is poached until just tender, then it's boiled with the sugar until setting point is reached. An alternative method is to sprinkle the fruit with the sugar, leave overnight (this helps the fruit to keep its shape) and then simmer to setting point. The most accurate way to check that the jam is at setting point is to use a sugar thermometer; it should register 105°C. An alternative is the saucer test: spoon a tiny amount onto a cold saucer, cool and then push gently with a finger; the surface of the jam should wrinkle. When setting point is reached, jams are cooled for 15–20 minutes before being poured into warmed sterilized jars, topped with wax discs and sealed.

To make jelly rather than jam, the fruit is cooked until soft, then left to drain in a jelly bag. The resulting juice is boiled with sugar (and lemon juice if the fruit is low in pectin) to setting point, then potted and covered.

using it Fruit cooked in this way is preserved for a long period – at least a year in a cool, dry dark place. Both bought and home-made jams should be stored in the refrigerator once the jar has been opened.

Jams and jellies are first and foremost an instant spread with bread and butter – or with clotted cream for scones. They are used extensively in baking and desserts too: as a filling for biscuits, tarts, doughnuts and simple sponges like Victoria; dolloped over custard or ice-cream; or melted as an instant 'sauce' for steamed puddings, fruit or pies. Melted apricot jam is brushed over the cake base for sachertorte and other fancy cakes before the icing is layered on, as well as glazing fruit fillings in tarts; and a good soft fruit jam is the classic 'sandwich' filling between cooked custard and meringue in a traditional Queen of Puddings.

Jams and jellies are also used in savoury cooking. For example, a spoonful or two of apricot jam added to curried mayonnaise makes a sweet-sour dressing for chicken and potato salads. Redcurrant jelly is traditionally served with pork, lamb and duck, and mint jelly is popular with lamb.

word origin The word jam first appeared in this sense in the 18th century, probably because the process of turning fruit into jam involved crushing and squeezing things together, the original meaning of the word.

jelly

Jelly is a flavoured savoury or sweet liquid usually mixed with some sort of setting agent, then allowed to cool until it has solidified. There are two types of jelly set with gelatine, a substance extracted from the bones, skin and feet of animals that is either ground into a powder or processed into thin sheets or 'leaves'. One of these is a wobbly semi-transparent pudding, the other a 'set' springy **sweet**. In addition, a naturally setting meat jelly can be created simply by boiling and then cooling the parts of animals that contain gelatine. Clear jelly preserve, which is made from strained fruit juice and sugar, is set with pectin rather than gelatine (see **jam**).

Jelly puddings can be prepared from scratch, using gelatine and sweetened fruit juice, or from a commerical jelly base, which is a block made from sugar, glucose syrup, gelatine, citric and acetic acids, fruit juice flavourings and colourings.

Jelly sweets vary in texture from soft and spongy (e.g. Jelly Babies, Turkish Delight) to quite hard and chewy (wine gums). They are made by combining liquids (e.g. water, fruit juice) and sugars, then stirring in a setting agent (traditionally gelatine, but now sometimes gelatine and gum arabic) plus flavourings (crushed fruit, citric acid, spices, orange-flower water or rosewater and so on) and starch. Once firm and 'set', the jelly is shaped and coated either with sugar or a mixture of icing sugar and cornflour.

using it Making a jelly pudding from scratch is easy. If using powdered gelatine, sprinkle it over cold water and leave it to soak and swell, then stir into hot (but not boiling) liquid, such as sweetened fruit juice, until completely dissolved (if adding to cool liquid, dissolve the gelatine first by setting the bowl over simmering water). For leaf gelatine, soak it in a little cold liquid for about 10 minutes to soften it, then squeeze out excess water before adding to hot liquid and stirring to dissolve. Pour into a mould and chill until firm. About 11g (one envelope) of powdered gelatine, or 4 sheets of leaf gelatine, will set 600ml of liquid.

The commercial block jelly base needs to be melted in boiling water, then topped up with cold water before being poured into a mould to set. Water is the most usual liquid used, but this can be partly or wholly replaced with milk, single cream, yoghurt, evaporated milk or even wine (port is particularly good),

and chopped fresh or canned fruit can also be tipped in, to ring the changes.

Savoury liquids set with gelatine, usually known as aspics, are made for moulds of cooked fish such as salmon or cooked meat pieces like chicken or turkey. Vegetarian substitutes include agar-agar and carrageen, both of which are gums extracted from **seaweed**.

word origin Jelly first surfaced in English in the 14th century and spellings ranged through *geli*, *gele* and *chely* before being standardized into the modern word. It comes, via French, from the Latin *gelata*, meaning 'frozen, congealed', probably a reference to the fact that jelly dishes were basically 'set' liquids. In the beginning, the name was only used to describe the jelly made from animal parts, but by the 17th century it had expanded to include moulded dessert mixtures as well. Jelly sweets came later, around the beginning of the 20th century.

did you know?

* Modern jelly desserts are direct descendants of a medieval savoury pudding called blancmange. Blancmanges today are sweet desserts made from milk and cornflour and set with gelatine, but initially they were made from ingredients like cooked shredded chicken meat, sugar and rice cooked in almond milk, and thickened with rice flour or ground almonds.

liquorice

Liquorice (*Glycyrrhiza glabra*) is a small member of the **pea** family of plants, and grows wild in Asia and parts of southern Europe. The root of the plant contains glycyrrhizin, a compound 50 times sweeter than sugar, and juice extracted from it is used to flavour a range of **sweets**. To extract the juice (and the glycyrrhizin), the root is boiled in water, then evaporated until it forms a thick black mass.

Sweets made from liquorice juice are normally soft, pliable and chewy. They are produced by combining the boiled juice mass with flour, water, sweetener and gelatine, then flavouring it before extruding it into typical shapes. Occasionally the juice is used to make harder sweets, which are normally sold as sticks; these contain gum arabic to enable the mixture to set more firmly, as well as sweeteners and flavourings like mint.

The range of liquorice sweets includes 'laces', long thin black strips that look like shoe laces; small flat discs called Pontefract cakes; and Liquorice Allsorts, squares or rounds with differently coloured **fondant** coatings or fillings, which were first manufactured in 1928. Before soft drinks became widely available, sticks of liquorice were also sometimes boiled and steeped in water to make a refreshing drink.

Commercially, liquorice juice is used by the brewing industry to colour beers and by the tobacco industry to sweeten its product.

using it Liquorice sweets are eaten as a treat.

word origin Liquorice has nothing to do with *liquor* in the sense of a liquid, but is based on the first part of the botanical name for the plant, which comes from the Greek *glykys,* meaning 'sweet', and *rhiza,* 'root'. It first appeared in English in the early 13th century, around the time the plant itself first appeared. Pontefract cakes are called after the town in Yorkshire where the plant was grown, and sweets have been produced there since the 17th century.

did you know?

• Liquorice root was used both as a medicine and as a sweetener in ancient India and China; the *Kama Sutra* even recommended it as an aphrodisiac (mixed with milk and sugar, it was supposed to improve sexual prowess). When it spread to Europe in medieval times, liquorice was normally ground up as a sweet flavouring for cakes and puddings, or as a remedy for constipation and sore throats.

marmalade

A clear preserve made from water, sugar and citrus fruit, marmalade is set by pectin, which is mainly contained in the fruit pith and pips. The bitter Seville-type orange is considered to make the best marmalade; sweet oranges are usually combined with other citrus fruit like lemons and grapefruit, or these are used alone.

Marmalade is made by simmering the fruit juice, chopped flesh and shredded peel with the pith and pips until the peel is completely soft. Then the pips and pith are discarded, sugar is stirred in and the mixture boiled until setting point is reached (see **jam**).

using it Marmalade is traditionally made at home during early spring when Seville oranges are available, although nowadays most is store-bought. It will keep for a year or two in a cool dry place, but should be stored in the refrigerator once the jar has been opened.

This is the classic accompaniment for toast as part of a proper British breakfast, but is good on buttered fresh bread at any time of the day. It's also used occasionally in other ways. In savoury cooking, for instance, melted marmalade makes a good glaze for duck or ham, and a little is also sometimes mixed into stuffings or gravies for game or poultry generally. In baking, marmalade can be substituted for jam in fillings for cakes or biscuits, or melted and used as a glaze in the same way as apricot jam.

word origin Marmalade comes via French from the Portuguese for quince, *marmelo,* and first appeared in English during the early 16th century. For the following hundred years or so it was used only to describe a thick solid paste made from quinces, but the meaning eventually expanded to include other fruits like plums and dates that were made into similar pastes. It wasn't until Victorian times that marmalade began to be used exclusively for preserves made from citrus fruits and peel.

• Although the earliest marmalades were made from quince, when citrus fruits and especially oranges began to be more widely available during the 17th century in Great Britain they were sometimes mixed into similar thick 'marmalades' with fruits like apple. All of these pastes were arranged in decorative boxes and served as part of the dessert table, where they were cut into pieces and eaten like cakes.

• Scotland is credited with inventing the first thinner, spreadable marmalades, probably in the 18th century, but they could still be made from any kind of fruit then. It wasn't until a hundred years later that a distinction began to be made in the United Kingdom between citrus-based jams and ordinary types (other European countries never did differentiate in this way). The word marmalade is now protected by European law and can only be applied to jams made from oranges, lemons and grapefruit.

marshmallow

Marshmallow is a shrub-like herb (*Althaea officinalis*) that grows near salty marshland. Originally the roots of the plant were used to make the springy, sticky white or pink **sweet** also called marshmallow, but today commercial sweets that carry this name are made from sugars, water, starch, gelatine or gum arabic and egg whites. They are produced in the same way as **jelly** sweets, but have a unique texture as stiffly whisked egg whites are beaten into the cooling mixture before it is 'set'. They are coated with a mixture of icing sugar and cornflour.

using it Although marshmallows can be eaten as they are, they are traditionally lightly toasted, often on a long fork, on a winter's day, in front of a roaring fire. They can also be sprinkled over hot chocolate or cappuccino and allowed to melt into the liquid, or spread over brownies or other biscuits before baking.

• During medieval times both the roots and leaves of marshmallow were thought to be aids to digestion and health – one 17th-century book of medicines reckoned they could cure nearly 50 diseases. The sweets came later, dating from the late 19th century.

nougat

Nougat is a chewy, dense **sweet** made from nuts, honey, sugar syrup and, usually, egg whites. Most modern nougats include chopped hazelnuts or almonds, whereas early ones were made from walnuts. Other ingredients like chocolate, glacé cherries and angelica are also sometimes added. Nougat is made by heating a sugar syrup to the 'soft crack' stage (see **sugar**), then adding honey and boiling until it returns to the same stage. The mixture is gradually beaten into stiffly whisked egg whites before nuts and flavourings are stirred in. It's firmed in shallow frames or weighted down and usually cut into squares before being sold.

using it Nougat is normally eaten as a snack or an after-dinner sweet, but is also occasionally used to flavour ice-creams or to make toppings for biscuits.

word origin Nougat comes, via French, from the Latin *nux,* meaning 'walnut' or simply 'nut', and first appeared in English during the early part of the 19th century.

• The Romans made sweetmeats from honey, walnuts and egg white, which they served as special treats or as offerings to the gods. Six or seven centuries later the Arabs introduced something similar into Spain, this time made from almonds. France, however, claims the credit for inventing modern nougat during the 16th century. The town of Montélimar in Provence in southern France is the centre of French nougat manufacturing, and a special almond-based variety is called montelimar after it.

peppermints

This is a range of **sweets** flavoured with oil or essence processed from peppermint (*Mentha* x *piperita*), a herb belonging to the **mint** family. There are many different types, ranging from brittle boiled 'sucking' sweets, like striped humbugs, to softer white or coloured **fondants** and even softer peppermint creams, which are made from a stiff flavoured icing sugar and egg white dough, which is cut into individual shapes and hardened for about a day.

using them The refreshing taste means that these sweets aren't just used in the normal way as a snack, but as a sort of mouth-freshener too. Peppermint creams, sometimes with a chocolate coating, are also often served with coffee after a meal as a digestive aid (mint is believed to be good for the digestion).

word origin Peppermint is a direct reference to the main flavouring, which got its name from its hot spicy taste. Peppermint sweets first appeared at the end of the 18th century.

praline

This hard, sweet, golden brown confection is made from sugar and (nearly always) **almonds**, normally in equal quantities. The sugar and almonds are warmed together until the sugar has melted, then boiled to the 'caramel' stage (see **sugar**). The mixture is then poured onto a cold oiled surface and left to set until hard before being crushed into very small pieces or a rough powder.

using it Praline is nearly always added to other ingredients rather than served or eaten alone. Commercially, it's used as a filling or flavouring for individual chocolates and chocolate bars, and added to ice-creams and biscuits. At home, a hot praline mixture could be used as an alternative topping for crème brûlée (see **caramel**), while small pieces or powder could be stirred through softened vanilla ice-cream or creamy yoghurt, or mixed with whipped cream as a filling for cakes and pastries.

word origin Praline comes from a 17th-century French nobleman, the Maréchal César du Plessis-Praslin, who commanded Louis XIV's army and whose cook invented a method of coating whole almonds in hot sugar syrup (still the main meaning of praline in French). The word first appeared in English during the 18th century as *prawlin* or *prawling* before settling into the modern version.

sherbet

This word has several meanings, all logical extensions of the original: a refreshing Middle Eastern drink made from fruit juice (especially lemon), water and sugar or honey that was cooled with ice or snow. An instant version of this drink was invented in Britain, a powdered mixture of **bicarbonate of soda**, tartaric acid, sugar and flavouring (usually lemon) that became fizzy when mixed with water. The powder (still called sherbet) was good to eat by itself and so began to be used as a sort of dip, something to suck up through special liquorice 'tubes' (which were also eaten) or to coat lollipops. The powder has now gone out of fashion and instead we have hard-boiled **sweets** called sherbet lemons, which contain a filling made from a similar mixture. When you bite through to it you get the same effervescent 'kick'.

using it The original drink, which is basically a Middle Eastern version of lemonade, makes a refreshing hot-weather cooler.

word origin Sherbet comes, via Turkish and Persian, from the Arabic *sharba,* meaning 'drink', the same root as **sorbet**.

did you know?

• The Middle Eastern drink first arrived in Britain during the early part of the 17th century, while the fizzy drink appeared about two centuries later. Sherbet sweets were later still, only becoming really popular after the Second World War.

sorbet

Also called water ice, sorbet is a frozen dish made from sugar and liquid, normally a combination of water and fruit juice or purée. Almost any fruit can be used, although the most popular are tangy citrus ones like lemon and lime; occasionally vegetables, herbs and wine are substituted for the fruit. Whisked egg white is often added to smooth and lighten the texture; adding gelatine has the same effect.

A basic sorbet is made by adding fruit purée or juice to a sugar syrup, then freezing. The best texture is achieved by using an ice-cream maker (see **ice-cream**).

The same basic mixture is used for granita, but is stirred during freezing to achieve the requisite coarse, snow-like texture. While a sorbet can be kept in the freezer, a granita must be eaten as soon as it is ready.

using it The range of commercial sorbet flavours is limited, but at home many different ingredients can be blended to create something special: champagne (white or rosé), crème de menthe and Campari are all good for savoury or semi-sweet sorbets, as are cucumber and mint, or tomato and basil. Fruits like pear, passionfruit and redcurrant make good sweet sorbets, as do exotic mixtures like pineapple with rum, and ginger with whisky.

Sweet sorbets are served as a dessert, while tarter-tasting ones usually appear between courses during more formal meals, especially before the main or meat course, to cleanse the palate.

word origin Sorbet is French. When the Middle Eastern fruit juice drink called **sherbet** in English first arrived in Europe during the 17th century, it was called *sorbetto* in Italy and *sorbet* in France, names it kept as the drink became a frozen confection during the 19th century. Both are derived from *sharba*, the Arabic word for 'drink'.

did you know?

• The original *sharba* was cooling and refreshing, part of daily life in the Middle East. It was often drunk at celebrations and special dinners, sometimes between courses to refresh the palate for the next dish down the line, one of the ways it was served when first introduced into Europe. As time went on, however, it became thicker, often contained some alcohol and was eaten rather than drunk. It was also served at the end of the meal rather than during it, although the practice of serving savoury or tart sorbets in the middle of a meal was revived during the 20th century.

sugar

As most of us recognize it, sugar is a refined, sweet crystalline substance usually extracted from one of two plants: sugar cane (*Saccharum officinarum*), a bamboo-like grass that grows only in tropical or subtropical areas of the world, and sugar beet (*Beta vulgaris*), part of the same family as beetroot and grown in temperate climates.

Sugar also has a broader scientific meaning, however, as a natural substance that exists in all living things, including plants like sugar cane and sugar beet. The most basic natural sugars are monosaccharides ('single' sugars), simple molecules that can dissolve in water and turn into alcohol if mixed with a fermenting agent like **yeast**, and disaccharides ('double' sugars), which consist of two bound-together single sugar molecules and are also soluble in water. The commonest single sugar is dextrose, or glucose as it's normally called (found in fruits, vegetables, cereals and nuts among others), but there are others too, such as fructose (found in fruit and especially in **honey**) and galactose, which is part of **milk**.

Double sugars include sucrose (a mixture of glucose and fructose found in nearly all plants, but particularly abundant in sugar cane and sugar beet) and lactose (a mixture of glucose and galactose contained in milk). Refined sugar consists of about 99 percent sucrose.

Creating refined sugar from the natural sugars in cane and beet is complicated. Cane sugar processing takes place partly in the producing country (major suppliers include India and Brazil) and partly at a refinery, usually thousands of kilometres away. In the producing country, the canes are crushed to extract their sugary juice, which is heated, clarified by being boiled with lime and then evaporated to become raw sugar – coarse crystals covered with a liquid coating known as molasses (see **treacle**).

The raw sugar is now refined. This complicated process begins by boiling it to loosen the molasses coating, then centrifuging to separate the sugar crystals from the molasses; the molasses remaining from this stage are then centrifuged twice more to extract more crystals. The crystals are now washed, dissolved into liquid form and clarified or filtered to remove more molasses and any other insoluble non-sucrose material they contain, and the resulting brownish liquid is de-colourized. The now white liquid is evaporated and 'seeded' with fine sugar crystals to recrystallize it, and the final stage of processing (a spin in the centrifuge machine to remove any remaining syrup followed by washing and drying) takes place. The crystals are now refined white sugar and ready for sale, usually as granulated sugar. The size of the crystals can be controlled and adapted to produce larger crystals for preserving sugar and smaller ones for caster sugar, or they can be powdered and mixed with a small amount of calcium phosphate or cornflour to produce icing sugar. Some granulated sugar is also moistened with syrup, then compressed into lumps as cube sugar. To produce sugar from sugar beet, the white roots are washed, cut into strips and then 'diffused', that is steeped in hot water in the same way as tea. This process draws out a bluish-black sugar juice, which is then refined in the same way as cane sugar.

White refined sugar from either cane or beet can be turned into brown sugar by adding back cane molasses or caramel, but this is not true brown sugar. The real thing is cane sugar crystals that have been only lightly refined and still retain a fair proportion of molasses. The amount of molasses that the crystals contain defines what the brown sugar is called: a small amount produces a light brown sugar known as demerara (although some demerara is now just white refined sugar with molasses or caramel added back); a greater amount produces a mid-brown sugar called light muscovado; and the greatest amount produces a dark brown sugar, dark muscovado.

About 99 percent of commercial sugars come from cane or beet (and cane accounts for nearly two-thirds of this), but there are a few other sources too. In North America, especially New England and Canada, for example, maple sugar is obtained by processing the sap of maple trees, although most of this is sold as maple **syrup**. In the Indian subcontinent, palm trees produce a sugar called jaggery or gur.

using it Sugar is probably eaten far more often than most people realize. It is used extensively in food processing and preserving, for instance, and even unlikely savoury items like canned soups and baked beans contain a fair amount; jams and marmalades are full of it (they're simply fruits boiled to a spread consistency with sugar) and so are more savoury-sounding pickles and chutneys. Many soft and fizzy drinks contain large quantities of pure or industrially treated sugar to make them attractively sweet and palatable, as do many liqueurs and other alcoholic drinks – rum, in fact, started out more or less as a byproduct of sugar refining.

Boiled sugar or syrup is one of the main ingredients in confectionery, and is also sometimes used in baking and desserts. When sugar is heated in water it dissolves to form a syrup, and as the temperature increases (when more water has evaporated) there will be greater concentrations of sugar. While commercial manufacturers employ sophisticated controls, home-made sweetmaking requires only a sugar thermometer. There are seven temperature ranges for sugar boiling:

106–110°C: the 'thread' stage – a small amount of syrup dropped from a spoon will form a thin thread.

112–116°C: the 'soft ball' stage – a small amount of syrup dropped into very cold or iced water will form a soft ball. (This stage produces sweets like fudge.)

118–121°C: the 'firm ball' stage – a small amount of syrup dropped into very cold or iced water will form a firm but pliable ball. (This stage produces slightly firmer but still soft sweets like soft caramels.)

121–130°C: the 'hard ball' stage – a small amount of syrup dropped into very cold or iced water will form a ball that holds its shape under pressure and will also be quite sticky. (This stage produces sweets like marshmallows.)

132–143°C: the 'soft crack' stage – a small amount of syrup dropped into very cold or iced water will be able to be stretched into threads that will be hard but bendable – that is, not brittle. (This stage produces sweets like butterscotch and seaside rock.)

144–155°C: the 'hard crack' stage – a small amount of syrup dropped into very cold or iced water will be hard and brittle, and will snap when bent. (This stage produces sweets such as hard toffee.)

160–175°C: the 'caramel' stage – a small

spoonful of syrup poured onto a white plate will be the required colour, from golden to darkish amber, depending on what the caramel is required for. (This stage produces **praline**.) If the syrup is cooked beyond this point, it will burn, go black and be quite bitter.

In addition to confectionery, sugar is used extensively at home: it can be stirred into tea, coffee and other hot drinks, and is also added to more or less every dessert. It's widely used in baking too, and added in small quantities to some savoury dishes: sweet-and-sour sauces, for instance, can get the 'sweet' part of their taste from sugar, particularly brown sugar. Sugar is mixed with other ingredients like mustard to make a glaze for ham or beef, and a small amount is also sometimes added to salad dressings, particularly **vinaigrettes**.

word origin Sugar first appeared in English towards the end of the 13th century as *zuker,* then *zuccary*, *sucere*, *sewger* and even *sogyr* before settling into its modern form during the 17th and 18th centuries. Ultimately, it comes from the ancient Sanskrit *sarkara,* meaning 'ground, candied sugar', which became *saccharon* in Greek, *zuccarum* or *succarum* in medieval Latin, and *sucre* in French. Demerera is named after the city in Guyana, South America, where the sugar was first produced; muscovado comes from the Portuguese *mascabado,* meaning 'of the lowest quality'. Caster sugar is so called because it was (and sometimes still is) put into a sugar caster (a pot with a finely perforated top) and 'cast' or sprinkled over food.

did you know?

• Our earliest ancestors relied on fruit, some vegetables and an unreliable and difficult-to-get source – honey – to add sweetness to their food. About 4000 years ago, however, sugar cane began to be cultivated and crudely refined, probably in India, and from there it spread to China, the Far East and the Arab world. Europeans first came across it in 325BC when troops of Alexander the Great arrived in northern India and described it as 'honey not from bees'. Later, it was grown briefly in Spain and Sicily during the Arab occupation of southern Europe, but sugar only really began coming into other parts of Europe in small, expensive quantities during the 12th and 13th centuries.

• Most of Europe is unsuitable for growing sugar cane, but many of the 'new' countries of the Caribbean and Latin America are suitable, so canes were exported to them as part of a general European expansion from the 16th century on. Large plantations were set up and worked by slaves, most of them captured in Africa and transported to the Americas. Cane has been refined in Britain since then; beet refining is more recent, however: the German chemist Andreas Marggraf discovered in 1747 that sugar could be extracted from the plant (which *could* be grown in Europe), and refineries were set up in Britain and France.

• Refined sugar consists almost entirely of sucrose, which has no nutritional value although it does provide energy (calories). Eating excessive amounts of it can lead to tooth decay, not a modern phenomenon despite propaganda: Elizabeth I of England and many other members of the Tudor nobility were famous (or infamous) for their black teeth in the 16th century.

sweeteners

The simple culinary definition of a sweetener is that it is a substance that imparts a sweet flavour, usually to other food. It can be more or less natural (see **honey**); or the refined food of plants like sugar cane and beet (see **sugar**); or it can be an artificial substitute for any of these.

There are several different types of artificial sweetener, ranging in strength from saccharin (400 times sweeter than sugar) through acesulfame-K and aspartame (200 and about 160 times sweeter than sugar respectively) to cyclamate (30 times sweeter). Some commercial sweeteners on the market are a mixture of these substances, while others are made from only one.

Unlike sugar and honey, artificial

sweeteners are classified as 'non-caloric', because they aren't absorbed when they are eaten or drunk – they simply pass through the kidneys and exit the body. They are therefore popular with people who are concerned about their weight, but who still like a sweet taste.

using them Sweeteners are sold in packets of powder or (much more common nowadays) in small plastic dispensers as tiny tablets. Commercially, artificial sweeteners are added to diet foods, processed foods and, especially, soft diet drinks; at home they are normally used in tea or coffee.

word origin Sweet comes originally from the ancient Sanskrit *suadus,* meaning 'pleasant' or 'having a pleasant taste', via the Latin *suavis*. Sweetener has been used in its current commercial sense for the last 50 years or so.

did you know?

• Saccharin was discovered accidentally in 1879. A young chemistry student working on coal-tar research in a laboratory at Johns Hopkins University in the United States ate some bread one day and noticed that it was unexpectedly sweet. He traced the taste back to a compound he had been working on, later isolated and named saccharin. It began to be manufactured in 1894.

sweets

This is the general name given to a whole range of confectionery products made from sugar. Almost all contain other ingredients such as butter, cream, fruit concentrate, nuts, spices or herbs and chocolate. They are nearly always small, but can be virtually any shape, from the conventional round or oval to animal-shaped or even something that resembles favourite TV characters. Colours vary too, and all the hues of the rainbow are represented, sometimes several of them in one small sweet.

Most western sweets can be grouped into

categories by texture: those that are chewy but still reasonably soft, such as **fondant** and **fudge**; those that are more brittle, such as **praline** and **toffee**; and those 'set' with gelatine, such as wine gums (see **jelly**). In addition, there are of course sweets made with **chocolate**. Other parts of the world have sweets too, especially Asia, and these tend to be either gelatine-based, such as Turkish Delight, or milk or grain-based like Indian halvas.

There are hundreds of different types of sweets, and new ones appear virtually every month or so. Some popular ones include coconut ice (pink and white squares traditionally made from sugar, milk and desiccated coconut boiled to the 'thread' or 'soft ball' stage; see **sugar**); fruit pastilles (soft, flattish, sugar-coated squares or rounds made from sugar, fruit flavourings, spices and colourings, usually set with gelatine); lollipops (flavoured sugar-based mixtures boiled to the 'hard-crack' stage, then shaped around thin sticks before they harden too much); and seaside rock (long 'pulled' candy sticks, usually pink on the outside and white on the inside, made from sugar boiled to the 'soft crack' stage).

using them All sweets are eaten as a snack, but a few, depending on type, are also served after meals with coffee, and some are even occasionally used in cooking (see individual entries).

word origin The idea of something being described as 'sweet' goes back to the 9th century, although the word had a variety of spellings like *swoete*, *swete*, *swiete* before settling down into the modern version. It comes, via Latin, from the Sanskrit *suadus*, meaning 'pleasant' or 'having a pleasant taste'. The current use as a noun for small pieces of confectionery is much more recent, appearing during the 19th century, although 'sweetie' meaning sweet was common in Scotland a century before this. Sweet has occasional other meanings too: as an old-fashioned description of the dessert or pudding course of a meal, and as a term of endearment, both harking back in their different ways to something or someone pleasant.

• Early European sweets were made mostly from fruits, nuts or honey, and included coloured and shaped marzipan, and small fruits and nuts coated in the then rare and expensive sugar or sugar syrup. By Tudor times, sugar was more available although still expensive, and sweets were being eaten by the nobility, usually at the end of banquets along with other sweet dishes like the dry quince pastes called marmalades. A century or so later they were filtering down the social system and being eaten by themselves, and more elaborate ones like marrons glacés (see **glacé fruit**) and even lollipops had been invented. By the 19th century sugar had become relatively inexpensive and industrialization meant that there were machines that could make sweets quickly and cheaply, so they became a mass-market product. They've never looked back. Today every man, woman and child in the United Kingdom eats the equivalent of about 5.3kg of sweets a year.

• When sugar first became available in Europe it was sold by apothecaries, who sometimes added it to bitter-tasting medicines to make them more palatable – pastilles and lozenges began life in this way, and the latter word at least is still used mostly to describe sweets taken to relieve sore throats.

syrup

A syrup is a thick sweet liquid that can be manufactured from refined sugar, processed from natural plant sugars or produced by boiling sugar with liquid, usually water (see **sugar**).

Commercial syrup, which is yellow to light brown in colour, was originally a byproduct of the process that created sugar from sugar cane liquid. The idea was to make a sweet liquid product that didn't crystallize, and nowadays this is done by heating and treating the already refined sugar crystals with acid so that most of the sucrose will 'invert' or change back into the liquid 'single sugars', glucose and fructose (single sugars are much less likely to crystallize than double sugars like sucrose). The most common commercially produced syrup is golden syrup. **Treacle** is a dark, dense, slightly bitter syrup (see entry).

Fruits, trees and cereals (among others) contain natural sugars, and syrups are also sometimes processed from them. The most famous is maple syrup, made from the sap of several types of maple tree, most importantly the sugar maple (*Acer saccharum*). The trees are drilled to release the sap, which is carried in tubes to holding tanks and concentrated by boiling; maple sugar is made from the syrup, by boiling it further to the point where it solidifies and forms crystals when it cools. Another syrup produced from natural plant sugar is corn syrup, which is made from starch granules extracted from **maize** kernels. These are treated with acid or cultured moulds to create a thick sweet liquid.

using it Golden syrup lasts more or less indefinitely, although it can generate small crystals as it ages; other commercial syrups like maple are usually sold in small quantities since they can be quite expensive. All commercial syrups should be stored in a cool dry place.

Syrups are used as a spread for bread and toast, and spooned onto porridge and other breakfast cereals or pancakes (maple syrup is a traditional topping for American breakfast pancakes). For desserts, a spoonful stirred into or over yoghurt, ice-cream or even custard gives it a delicious lift, and they are an essential part of many steamed puddings. In savoury cooking syrups are used as a coating for ham and bacon joints, or generally as a substitute for honey. Mostly, however, syrups are used in baking and sweetmaking: golden syrup (and sometimes treacle) are favourite

ingredients in gingerbread, chocolate and other cakes and biscuits, and most syrups can be used to flavour sweets like toffee and fudge.

Syrups are also widely used in the food industry: corn syrup, for instance, sweetens soft drinks, alcohol such as whisky, and ketchup and pickles among other things, while other types are used in fruit canning, ice-cream and sorbet-making, and in most types of confectionery.

word origin When syrup first appeared in English in the 14th century it was spelled *sirop*, and often used to describe the melted cane sugar that was added to medicines to make them taste better. It was borrowed from Old French, which in turn came from the medieval Latin *siropus,* meaning 'medicinal drink'; both were derived from the Arabic *sharba*, which gave us, among other words, **sherbet** and **sorbet**.

● Until Europeans began to colonize North America, maple syrup was the only sweetener other than fruits known on the continent (honey bees came with the settlers and sugar cane hadn't yet been planted in the Caribbean). Native Americans, however, knew how to tap maple trees to extract the liquid, which they mixed with everything – including bear fat to make a type of dip.

● There are non-culinary syrups too. Modern cough syrups can be traced back to the original meaning of the word as a medicinal drink, being thick sweet liquids with healing flavourings like menthol and eucalyptus that are still used as remedies for coughs, sore throats and colds. Some fruits become syrups by themselves if they are boiled for long enough, most notably figs, which produce the very medicinal-tasting syrup of figs, well known as a laxative.

toffee

This is a small sticky **sweet** made from sugar, butter, syrup or treacle, milk or cream and vinegar; other ingredients and flavourings such as chopped nuts, honey, vanilla or mint are also often added. Toffees can vary in colour from light to dark brown depending on their ingredients, and range in texture from softish (caramels, for instance) to hard (butterscotch) or very hard (known as brittle).

The texture of toffee is achieved by boiling all the basic ingredients together to the 'firm ball', 'soft' or 'hard crack' stages (see **sugar**), depending on the finished texture of the sweet being made, then stirring in flavourings and allowing it to set. Softer toffee slabs are marked out as individual shapes before they set too much, whereas hard types are cooled first and then smashed into rough individual pieces.

using it In addition to being used as a sweet snack, smashed-up hard toffee pieces can also be used to flavour desserts: stirred through softened vanilla ice-cream or scattered over mousses or creams to add some crunch. Medium toffees – butterscotch in particular – can be kept liquid and mixed with some extra cream, then used as a sauce for ice-cream, steamed puddings or plain cakes or as a topping for home-made biscuits.

word origin Toffee first appeared in English during the early part of the 19th century as *tuffy*, *toughy* or *toffy* as well as the current version, and a related word, *taffy*, is still used in northern Britain and the United States.

did you know?

* Toffee apples are made differently to ordinary toffee. A fresh apple is impaled on a thin stick, then dipped in a thick sugar syrup coloured with a red food dye; the syrup hardens as it cools around the apple. During the First World War, toffee apple was a slang expression for a type of bomb, one that was smallish, reddish and shiny, and presumably resembled the real thing.

treacle

A thick, heavy **syrup** with a strong, almost bitter taste, treacle is a byproduct of sugar refining. It ranges in colour from deep golden (when it is more often called molasses) to almost black (when it is called black treacle). During the process that turns sugar cane into refined sugar crystals (see **sugar**), the raw sugar and its liquid coating (known as molasses) are centrifuged several times to separate out the molasses from the crystals. Most molasses is processed from the residue of the first or second centrifuge extraction; residue left after the third and last one is considered to be too bitter to be sold for direct consumption and is normally used as animal feed and to make rum or industrial alcohol.

using it Treacle and molasses are occasionally spread over bread or toast or spooned over porridge, but mostly they are used in baking and confectionery: in gingerbread, fruit cakes and steamed puddings, for example, and to flavour toffee. Despite its name, treacle tart is now sweetened with golden syrup rather than treacle.

did you know?

* From about the 14th century on, treacle was the word used to describe a medicine reputed to cure a whole range of ailments including venereal disease and snake bites. It came, via the Old French *triacle* and the Spanish *triaca,* from the Greek *theriake antidotos,* meaning 'antidote against venomous bites'. Even after it began to be used in its modern sense in the 17th century, it was still often associated with medicine – as in brimstone (sulphur) and treacle, a sort of all-purpose medicine given to anyone who complained of anything; the treacle was there to sweeten or otherwise disguise the wincingly bitter taste of the brimstone.

Nuts, Seeds & Oils

My Italian roots mean that I have always seen cooking and eating as sociable and adventurous activities. The family dinner table provided a relaxed setting for my early culinary education, and I began to learn how the diverse flavours of nuts, seeds and oils could transform a dish into something truly magical.

When I was growing up, olive oil was a staple part of every meal, and at an early age I was told how the olive tree has been an integral part of Italian life for generations. Basic olive oil was to be used for sauces, cooking and frying, whereas the 'king' of olive oils, extra virgin, was always used sparingly for dressing salads and on cold dishes. Historically, wood from the olive tree was used to stoke the fire, and the lowest-quality oil left after the harvest was used in

I began to learn how the diverse flavours of nuts, seeds and oils could transform a dish into something truly magical.
Antonio Carluccio

oil lamps. Since then, the health benefits of olive oil, particularly its cholesterol-lowering properties, have been recognized, and its popularity means that good-quality oil is now readily available at a reasonable price.

Flavoured oils are also becoming increasingly commonplace and many of them use another often misunderstood ingredient – nuts. Almond, hazelnut and walnut oil, among others, are used in many types of cuisine and provide an excellent flavour and good value for money. Education is a priority for future generations if we are to counteract recent health scares about nuts and demystify the use of seeds in cooking. For those who are able to enjoy these wonderful treats, there are countless ways to transform basic ingredients such as nuts and seeds into tasty dishes with very little preparation.

The following section gives a comprehensive account of how nuts, seeds and oils fit into our daily lives. I hope this will encourage everyone to explore these fantastic ingredients and discover just how many mouth-watering creations are possible using them. *Buon appetito*!

almond

This is a nut obtained from the fruit of the almond tree (*Prunus amygdalus*), a relative of the peach and plum, and probably native to India. Almond trees flourish in warm temperate climates and major suppliers include California (which produces about half the world's supply), Spain and Italy.

Almond kernels mature inside protective layers, rather like the smallest doll in a set of Russian dolls. The outermost part is an inedible **fruit** with a leathery green 'husk' that corresponds to the fleshy part of peaches, although the ratio of flesh to stone is much less. The husk splits when the nut is fully grown, to reveal the stone (normally called the shell), and the shell in turn is opened to reveal the brittle brown-skinned creamy seed or kernel. Occasionally almonds are sold 'green' – fresh in their shells – but normally they are dried out in the sun before being processed and sold.

There are two types, each with many varieties that vary in size, shape, oiliness and thickness of shell. Bitter almonds (*Prunus amygdalus* var. *amara*) contain prussic acid and are heated to remove the poisons before being processed to produce oil or flavouring essence. Sweet almonds (*Prunus amygdalus* var. *dulcis*) are the ones we eat, and are available in supermarkets in various forms, such as whole, blanched and skinned, flaked, split and nibbed. Some sweet almonds are marketed under their varietal name; Jordans, a medium-shell nut considered to be particularly good tasting, is an example.

using it Almonds can be bought blanched and skinned, and flaked and toasted, but it is easy to do this at home (see **nuts** and **seeds**). Split, flaked or nibbed almonds are a universal decoration for desserts such as ice-creams, mousses and other creamy mixtures. In confectionery, whole almonds are coated in chocolate to make sweets, covered with boiled caramelized sugar to make **praline** or chopped and blended with honey, sugar and egg whites to make **nougat**. Ground almonds are a basic ingredient in baking: used instead of flour or with it in cakes to give extra moistness; combined with sugar and egg whites to make macaroons; and mixed with sugar to become **marzipan**, the classic covering for formal cakes. Flaked almonds are also used in savoury dishes: as a classic garnish for kormas and pulaos, stir-fried with duck, chicken and prawns, and combined with butter as a sauce for fish or chicken.

The oil extracted from bitter almonds is used mainly in commercial confectionery. Almond essence is distilled from the residue remaining after oil extraction, and is used as a flavouring for cakes, desserts and liqueurs like Amaretto.

word origin Almond is borrowed from the Old French *alemande*, which comes indirectly from the Greek *amugdale*. The variety Jordans has no connection with the country of the same name and is, in fact, a corruption of the Spanish word for garden, *jardín*.

did you know?

• Almonds were eaten by our prehistoric ancestors and have been cultivated since early Biblical times (Aaron's rod was made from almond wood), but it was the Greeks who introduced them to Europe and the ancient Romans called them 'Greek nuts' in tribute. The Romans probably brought them to Britain, where some trees continued to grow wild in the warmer southern parts of the country at least until medieval times.
• There were many holy days in the medieval Christian calendar, when meat and dairy produce were not allowed. Almond 'milk' (at its simplest, ground almonds boiled in water, allowed to soak for 10–15 minutes and then strained) therefore became *the* cooking ingredient for pretty much everything from soups and blancmanges (in those days a savoury dish) to early cakes and puddings.

brazil nut

Brazil **nuts** come from the *Bertholletia excelsa* tree, a giant plant that can grow to about 50m in height and which has a 1–2m diameter trunk. Nearly all the world's supply comes from the Amazon basin in South America where the tree mostly grows wild in managed forests. The 'fruit' of the tree looks rather like a hairless coconut, but is actually a large pod containing 12–25 individual semi-circular nuts that are arranged like segments inside an orange. The nuts themselves have thick, woody, reddish-brown shells; when opened, the shells reveal brown-skinned, creamy, oblong kernels that taste a little like coconut.

Harvesting the nuts is a haphazard business. Like many jungle trees, the branches of this one grow as near to its top as they can, making it impossible to climb up to get the fruit. Since individual pods can weigh up to 2kg, and become deadly missiles if they fall on an unsuspecting body from a great height, they are only collected after they are already on the ground. To get at the precious contents, the pods are opened with machetes and the nuts cleaned, then dried before being sold.

using it Shelled brazils should have creamy flesh; avoid yellowing ones since this suggests they are old. The shells are particularly tough to crack, but steaming for a few minutes before tackling them with nutcrackers makes them easier to handle.

Brazils are often simply eaten as they are or with fruit. The shape and size are one of the attractions so whole nuts make a good decoration for fruit and other larger cakes, and can also be added to fruit or savoury salads. Roughly chopped brazils could be mixed with other nuts as part of a roast or added as a 'meaty' taste to sweet-and-sour vegetarian rice dishes. Ground brazils can be blended with other nuts, biscuit crumbs and melted butter to make a base for cheesecakes and creamy tarts.

word origin Although it looks as if the word comes from the tree's home – Brazil is still one of the major producers – in fact, both nut and country are named after a South American hardwood called brasilwood, which produces a reddish-brown dye. Brasilwood itself gets its name from the Spanish *brasa,* meaning 'glowing coals'.

cashew nut

Cashews come from the **fruit** of *Anacardium occidentale*, an evergreen tree native to Brazil and the Amazon basin, and a relative of pistachio and poison ivy. The tree was taken to India and eastern Africa by the Portuguese in the 16th century, and these areas are now the largest producers, with India providing more than three-quarters of the world's supply.

Anacardium occidentale produces a green bean-shaped fruitlet that houses the **nut**, which is attached to a yellow or red fruit similar in shape and size to a pear, called cashew 'apple'. (The bean-shaped fruitlet is the true fruit of the plant; the apple is actually a receptacle that grows after it develops.) After harvesting, the fruitlet is separated from the apple and the job of processing it to obtain the nuts begins. Each nut has a two-layered shell with a membrane between the layers containing an irritant oil designed to protect the nuts from insects (it can burn human skin too, which is why cashews are never sold in their shells). The oil is removed by roasting the cashews in large drums, which also separately collect it for other uses (see below). After this initial roasting, the nuts are sprayed with water, dried, shelled and skinned, then roasted and sprayed again, before being sold.

using it Cashews should be pale and creamy in colour and have a good shape, if whole. Both salted and unsalted nuts are primarily used as they are, as drinks snacks, but unsalted cashews are also used in cooking: added to savoury salads to provide crunch; included in stir-fries, particularly with chicken, duck or prawns; stirred into rice dishes, meat or vegetable stews or curries; or used to garnish all of these. Crushed and mixed with other nuts they make a good roast, and crushed and mixed with a tablespoon or two of oil, a milder alternative to peanut butter.

word origin Cashew comes from the Tupi name for the nut, *acaju*, via the Portuguese *caju*.

did you know?

• The oil extracted from cashew nuts is used in insecticides, brake linings, and in resins and varnishes that protect wood against termites, among other things.

chestnut

This is the **nut** of a large tree related to oak that is probably native to Asia; major producers include China, Italy, Spain and Japan. There are several major species including the sweet or Spanish chestnut (*Castanea sativa*), the type most widely grown in Europe; the Chinese chestnut (*Castanea mollissima*), still widely cultivated in China and also now in the United States; and the Japanese chestnut (*Castanea crenata*), which has larger nuts than any of the others and, as the name suggests, is the principal species in Japan. The sweet chestnut tree isn't related to the horse chestnut tree, whose nuts are called conkers.

The chestnut tree produces green spiky husks called burrs that split open when ripe to reveal usually three round nuts with reddish-brown, shiny shells. Inside the shells, the creamy-coloured kernels are covered with a protective pale brown, furry skin. The trees grow wild but are also cultivated, especially in southern Europe, and when the nuts are gathered commercially in these warmer climates, they are left in the sun for a few days or dried artificially before being sold.

Chestnuts are sometimes ground into a flour used to make pancakes, or even cakes and biscuits.

using it There are still chestnut trees growing wild in the United Kingdom, mostly in southern England, and their nuts are ready to eat in October or November. Normally, however, they are imported and bought still in their shell, shelled and dried, or whole or puréed in cans. Those still in the shell should be heavy for their size and have a good rich, shiny colour; avoid any that are greyish or wrinkling. Chestnuts will keep in the refrigerator for about two weeks; canned ones keep for months, but should be used up reasonably quickly once opened.

To shell, slit the round tops into a cross, then boil for 10 minutes or microwave for a minute or so. When cool enough to handle, peel off the shells and bitter-tasting skin. To make a purée, simmer the peeled flesh with a little liquid for about 40 minutes until it softens, then mash or purée in a food processor. Dried chestnuts need to be rehydrated by soaking in water for 1–2 hours, then simmering for 45–50 minutes. Roasting chestnuts over an open fire is easy to do – provided you use a proper long-handled perforated roaster – but it's simpler, if less romantic, to slit them and then roast in a hot oven for 15 minutes.

Unlike other nuts, chestnuts aren't eaten raw, but their starchy taste (they have more carbohydrate by weight than potatoes) means they're useful in most types of cooking. For sweet dishes, purée can be mixed with cream to make a fool; with brown sugar, chopped walnuts and cream to make Peking dust; and flavoured with vanilla, topped with stiffly whipped cream and decorated with marrons glacés to become a classic French Mont Blanc. In savoury cooking, whole nuts can be added to duck casseroles, tossed with Brussels sprouts, and braised or roasted to accompany meat, poultry or game. Puréed chestnut is a good stuffing ingredient for poultry and can be made into a rich soup. Any savoury or sweet dish called Nesselrode contains chestnuts.

word origin Chestnut comes from the Greek *kastanea*, literally the 'nut from Castanea' (a city in ancient Asia Minor), which initially became *chesten* in Old English. Medieval English borrowed the French word *chesteine* (which came from the same root), tucked a 'nut' on the end and eventually arrived at the current word.

In modern French there are two words for chestnut: *châtaigne*, based on the original word and now usually meaning a small ordinary chestnut, and *marron*, finer, larger and cultivated, usually the fruit of a husk that contains only one nut instead of the more usual three. *Marrons* are normally sold as marrons glacés (see **glacé fruit**).

• It was the Greeks who introduced the sweet chestnut tree into Europe and both they and the Romans cultivated it; it was the Romans who brought the tree to England. In medieval southern Europe, wild chestnuts were a staple food of the poor, and even as far north as southern England, hot-chestnut sellers were a common feature of street life, as they still are today.
• Early Romans ground chestnuts into a sort of meal, and Italians have been doing this ever since. Before maize became available in Europe (it was brought back by Spanish explorers from the New World during the late 15th and early 16th centuries), chestnut flour was used to make *polenta*, a staple of northern Italian cooking.

coconut

The coconut is the **fruit** of a tall palm tree (*Cocos nucifera*), which is probably native to Malaysia and the western Pacific, but now grows in moist tropical climates around the world, often near seashores since it likes sandy soil. Major producers include the Philippines, Indonesia, Africa, Central America and the West Indies.

The coconut fruit is a stone fruit and the familiar nuts are the stone part. The outer husk is smooth and tough, and turns from green to yellowish or brown as it ripens. When the husk is opened, the familiar coarsely matted brown shell with its three 'eyes' at one end appears. When this shell is removed in its turn, it exposes a thin brittle skin called the testa; inside this is the hollow kernel itself, with its thin coating of white flesh and 'milk' (not to be confused with commercial coconut milk which is made from the flesh). The milk is sweet and refreshing, and can be consumed as a drink. The flesh is shredded or flaked and then dried to become desiccated coconut; processed into blocks as creamed coconut; squeezed through strainers to become commercial coconut milk; or dried to become copra, which is pressed to make oil.

using it Whole coconuts are available throughout the year; all the foods produced from coconut are sold packaged or canned. Whole nuts should be heavy for their size and sound full of liquid, a good indication of sweetness. They can be kept for about a month at room temperature; once opened, the flesh should be stored in water in the refrigerator to prevent it from drying out, or frozen. To get at the flesh, first pierce two of the eyes with a skewer and hold the coconut over a bowl to drain out the milk. After this, bake the coconut in a hot oven for about 20 minutes (this makes it crack more easily), then hit it with a hammer and prize the flesh from the shell. The brown protective testa should come off easily from the flesh with the help of a knife or peeler.

Coconut milk is available in cans, but can also be made at home. Pour boiling water over grated fresh or desiccated coconut, leave for 45–60 minutes and then strain through a sieve, pressing down well. Pieces of creamed coconut can also be dissolved in boiling water to make coconut milk.

In Europe and the English-speaking world, desiccated coconut is more widely used than any other type, particularly in baking and confectionery where it is used as a flavouring and a decoration for cakes, biscuits, pies or sweets. It also flavours desserts, particularly fruit salads, dishes containing pineapple and mango, and creamy dishes or ice-cream. In Asia and the West Indies, grated fresh coconut and coconut milk or cream are added to curries and other savoury dishes, particularly those made with rice.

Coconut oil, which is high in saturated fats, solidifies at cool temperatures, but it keeps well and is popular for frying and other cooking, particularly in Asia. It is also used commercially to make confectionery and margarines.

word origin It was the Spanish and Portuguese who supplied the name. They thought that the three small eyes at the end of the nut looked like a face, and in particular the grinning face of a monkey – *coco* meant 'monkey' or 'goblin' in Spanish. Along the line somewhere, the 'nut' ending was added to make the modern word.

did you know?

• There are references to both the coconut and its palm in early Sanskrit writings, but it doesn't appear to have been known to Europeans until the 13th century when Marco Polo came across it in Indonesia during his travels. The Spanish and Portuguese introduced it to Central and South America during the 16th century.
• Practically every part of the coconut palm is useful. The wood is used to make furniture, the leaves as thatch to make shelters, the ribs of the leaves to make brooms, and the sugary sap is brewed into a drink. From the nut itself, the fibrous matting inside the husk (called coir) is used to make floor coverings, among other things, the shells are burned to make a type of charcoal, and fat or 'butter' extracted from copra isn't just used as oil in cooking, but also to make soaps, shampoos and candles.

hazelnut
This is the **fruit** of the hazel tree, which grows wild in Europe, America and Asia and is found in hedgerows in Britain; Spain, Italy and Turkey are the major suppliers. There are several species and many varieties, including the wild Eurasian hazel (*Corylus avellana*), the most common species, which produces small round nuts and whose cultivated nuts are called cobnuts; and the filbert (*Corylus maxima*), which is cultivated and produces larger, oval-shaped nuts.

Hazelnuts grow in small bunches of one to four nuts, each inside a protective shaggy, green, hood-like 'husk' or covering, which can be short and semi-enclosing in the case of cultivated cobs, or long and completely enclosing in the case of filberts. After harvesting, the husk splits to reveal a shiny brown shell, which can be thick or thin depending on the variety. Within this shell is the kernel itself, covered with a thin, brittle, brown skin. A few nuts are sold fresh and still in their husks, but most are dried and processed first.

using it Fresh nuts in their husks have a brief season between late August and mid-October, but otherwise hazels are available dried, whole, chopped or ground. Whole nuts should be shiny and feel slightly heavy for their size; they will keep for about two months in a cool dry place. They can be bought blanched and skinned, although this is easy to do at home (as is toasting) to bring out their flavour (see **nuts** and **seeds**).

Hazelnuts are eaten as snacks as well as used in most types of cooking. In sweet dishes, they have a particular affinity with chocolate so are added to sauces, mousses and **soufflés** containing it. Chopped nuts can also be used as a garnish for fruit salads and creamy desserts. In savoury cooking, hazelnuts are added whole to breakfast cereals and savoury salads; ground and beaten into butter to serve with white fish fillets or chicken breasts (they can be used to coat and garnish them too); and crushed or chopped with other nuts to make a nut roast or poultry stuffing. In baking and confectionery, ground hazelnuts are a popular flavouring for meringues, cakes and biscuits; are beaten into pastry doughs for pies or tarts; and used as part of a crumble topping (sweet or savoury). Commercially, whole hazelnuts are coated with chocolate to make bars or sweets.

A delicate-tasting **oil** is cold-pressed from hazelnuts; it can be used instead of olive oil in **vinaigrettes**, or sprinkled over steamed vegetables or rice dishes just before serving.

word origin Hazelnut comes from the Anglo-Saxon *haesil*, a headdress (a reference to the shape of the husk); the first part of the botanical name is also based on the husk's appearance and comes from the Greek *korys*, meaning 'helmet'. Filberts get their name, so it's said, because they ripen around August 22, the feast day of the 7th-century St Philibert.

did you know?

• Wild hazels probably provided food for dinosaurs on several continents before people evolved, but they were first cultivated only in classical Roman times. Although species of the tree grew in North America, the nuts they produced were small, so early settlers imported European varieties. Most cultivated hazelnuts there now are descended from these varieties or are hybrids of them and a native species.
• Hazel trees have always grown wild in Britain, but they have also been cultivated for many centuries, traditionally in Kent. Confusingly, however, the fresh hazelnuts that arrive in greengrocers and supermarkets in October called Kentish cobs aren't

cobnuts at all, but the longer, larger filberts and of a variety created by a Mr Lambert about 150 years ago – hence their alternative name of Lambert's filberts.

margarine

Margarine is a fat made from vegetable oils and, sometimes, rendered animal fats that remains solid at room temperature. By law, 'margarine' must contain a minimum of 80 percent fat, which is why a margarine with a lower fat content is now called a 'spread'. The remaining 20 percent or so is made up of liquid (usually water) and various other substances like milk solids, emulsifiers, beta-carotene or annatto (to give the desired buttery yellow colour), modified starch and salt. Margarine is also fortified with vitamins A and D to bring levels to those of **butter**. Margarine can be made from a mixture of oils and fats or from a single oil, and in the latter case, the basic flavouring usually becomes part of the description, like sunflower or soya spread.

There are three major types: table spreads or margarines, soft mixtures sold in tubs that can be used straight from the refrigerator, which tend to be made mostly from polyunsaturated vegetable oils and water; hard margarines, sold in firm slabs, which are made from vegetable, animal or fish oils and skimmed milk; and low-fat spread substitutes, which contain extra water and air to reduce the amount of fat in the usually vegetable-oil mixture.

Making margarine involves a series of procedures that often includes hydrogenation, a method of adding hydrogen to polyunsaturated oil to make it keep better and to become solid (and therefore spreadable) at room temperature. Hydrogenation unfortunately converts some of the polyunsaturated fats from the normal configuration to trans fatty acids. Because 'trans fats' may raise blood cholesterol levels in the same way that saturated fat does, many modern table spreads either hydrogenate only lightly or avoid it by using emulsifiers or a little coconut or palm oil to bind and solidify the mixture instead. Usually, the harder the margarine, the more saturated fat and possibly trans fat it contains. (See **oils** for more information on unsaturated and saturated fats.)

using it Most margarines and spreads contain preservatives and will keep for 1–2 months in the refrigerator. Hard margarines are intended for cooking (particularly baking) rather than spreading. Table spreads are used as a butter substitute, especially with bread, toast and sandwiches, and many can also be used for cooking; however, they aren't recommended for deep-frying. Low-fat spreads are not suitable for cooking.

word origin When margarine first arrived in Britain it was called 'butterine', a description that didn't particularly please the dairy industry. This was later changed (by Act of Parliament!) to margarine, a name that came originally from the Greek *margaron,* meaning 'pearl', from the shiny appearance of the first margarine.

• During the 1860s there was a shortage of butter in France and emperor Napoleon III sponsored a competition in 1869 to find a cheap synthetic substitute. It was won by a chemist called Hippolyte Mège-Mouriès, who invented a white spread based on rendered beef fat, chopped cow's udders, water and milk: the first margarine.

marzipan

Also commonly called almond paste, this is a sweet, yellow or white, cooked or uncooked paste made from ground almonds and sugar, usually bound with eggs or egg whites. For the cooked version a sugar syrup is boiled to the 'hard ball' stage (see **sugar**) and then beaten into ground almonds; the uncooked version is made simply by beating together the sugar, ground almonds and egg. The resulting paste is kneaded lightly until smooth, then rolled out like pastry dough for a cake covering or moulded into decorative shapes.

using it Marzipan is used primarily in baking and to make sweets. In baking, its main role is as a smooth base for icing on festive fruit cakes, such as those for weddings and Christmas. Occasionally, marzipan is used *instead* of icing, as in, for example, a traditional simnel cake (still associated with Easter in Britain), where a rich fruit cake is sandwiched and topped with marzipan, then decorated with 11 small marzipan balls, one for each of the disciples minus Judas.

In Italy, and especially Sicily, marzipan is dyed and sculpted into artificial fruit; in central Europe, Christmas tree ornaments are sometimes made from it; and it can be coloured and shaped into sweets like marzipan mice. It's also occasionally covered in chocolate or **praline** and cut into sweetmeats (petits fours) to serve with coffee.

word origin There have been several versions of marzipan, all of them British attempts at anglicizing what was either medieval French or Italian (*marcepain* or *marzapane*, respectively). Initially in English it became *martspane*, which turned into *marchpane*, the word used to describe marzipan until the 19th century.

• Almonds were popular during medieval times and marzipan has been made since then. It was used to make sweetmeats, probably not all that far removed from today's petits fours, and many feasts ended with the serving of *marchpane*, a whole cake made of marzipan with a biscuit base, which may be the ancestor of modern wedding and birthday cakes.

nuts and seeds

To most of us, nuts are edible kernels or seeds protected by hard outer shells. To botanists, however, they are single-stone fruits with a tough outer layer (the shell) that corresponds to the fleshy part of edible fruits. The popular meaning is used here since the botanical one would exclude **almond** (which is basically the same as the stone in fruit relatives like peach) and **peanut**, which is a **legume** and related to beans.

Seeds are contained in flowers or fruit and are the reproductive part of the plant, protected by a thin hull roughly equivalent to the skin around a nut rather than its shell. Common edible seeds include **sesame**, which comes from a herbaceous plant, and **pine nuts** which, despite the name, are the seeds of several species of pine tree.

using them   Both nuts and seeds are available throughout the year, although nuts in the shell tend to be most visible in the run-up to Christmas. Nuts are occasionally eaten fresh, but most are dried and processed before being sold whole, skinned or unskinned, halved, split, flaked, chopped or ground, toasted or plain, salted or unsalted. Seeds are available hulled or unhulled, and sometimes toasted or not, salted or not. Both nuts and seeds contain fat, which means they become rancid quite quickly. So buy them in small quantities from shops with a fast turnover, and store in airtight containers in a cool dry place. Most unshelled nuts will keep for about six months and are best opened with nutcrackers; packaged nuts and seeds will stay fresher longer if they are kept in airtight containers in the refrigerator after opening. Nearly all shelled nuts and seeds freeze well, so extra supplies can be stored in this way.

Although many nuts are sold already blanched and skinned, this is easy to do at home. For nuts such as almonds and pistachios, pour over boiling water and leave for 2–3 minutes; the skin should then be loose enough to pinch or rub off easily. For hazelnuts, spread them in a single layer in a baking tray and bake in a moderate oven for 5–7 minutes, then rub the nuts in a tea towel to remove the skins.

Toasting nuts enhances their flavour. To toast nuts such as almonds, hazelnuts, pine nuts and walnuts, spread them out in a frying pan and cook over a low heat, turning frequently, until they are lightly browned or, in the case of walnuts, smell 'nutty'. Alternatively, spread in a baking tray and toast in the oven or under the grill. Watch carefully to prevent them from scorching.

Most nuts and seeds are eaten as snacks or used as garnishes, but many are also used in cooking (see individual entries for specific information). Some nuts and seeds are also processed into butters or oils.

word origin   Both nut and seed come from Old English, nut from *hnutu* (probably via the Latin *nux*) and seed from *saed*, which may be derived from the Old German *Saat*. The phrase 'it's a tough nut to crack' comes directly from the practical difficulties of getting at a nut, as does 'hard nut' meaning a difficult, rather brittle person. The 'seeds' in a tennis tournament are the stronger competitors expected to survive until later, not all that far removed from the function of seeds as the guardian of a plant's future survival.

did you know?

● Many nuts and seeds predate the breakup of the world into continents, so different members of the same family of plants are often found in several separate areas of the world. The only nut indigenous to Australia didn't spread anywhere else by itself, however. It is the macadamia (processed from various species of the *Macadamia* tree), which has a fleshy green husk that splits open when ripe to reveal the white-fleshed kernel in its hard brown shell. It was only introduced to other parts of the world like Hawaii (now a major producer) at the end of the 19th century.

• Although most nuts and seeds are high in fat, it is primarily monounsaturated or polyunsaturated (the good guys of the fat world). With the exception of chestnuts, nuts are also a good source of protein, and they contain fibre and a range of B vitamins. Nuts and seeds are a particularly valuable source of protein and iron in vegan diets.

oils

Oils are fats extracted from many substances; those used for cooking come mainly from vegetable sources (plants, nuts, seeds and so on). They often have a single plant base such as fruit (**olive**), cereal (**maize**) and seed (**sunflower**), and this will usually be part of the name; those sold as 'vegetable' oil are a mixture of plant oils, usually with a rapeseed-oil base. Most edible oils are high in either monounsaturated fats (e.g. olive oil) or polyunsaturated fats (most of the rest), the main exceptions being **coconut** and palm oils, which are high in saturated fats (see below). Most oils remain liquid at room temperature and all are insoluble in water.

Mass-market oils are produced chemically or mechanically, or by a combination of the two. Solvent extraction is the chemical method: the base materials (seeds, cereals etc.) are ground, cooked and then mixed with a solvent (usually hexane, a type of petroleum), which 'extracts' their oil (the solvent is later removed). Mechanical extraction or hot-pressing doesn't involve chemicals: the cooked base materials are fed into one end of a continuous press, subjected to great heat and spun at high speed to separate the oil from everything else so that it can be expressed out the other end. A few oils, mainly olive and **sesame**, are cold-pressed industrially in the same way, but at lower temperatures (although these are still around 30–60°C, roughly quarter of the heat applied during hot pressing).

Most industrially produced oils are refined before being bottled and sold, and this usually involves chemical treatment at high temperatures, then filtering, bleaching and 'deodorizing' – steam distilling to remove anything that could affect smell and taste. The end product is cleansed not just of impurities and plant substances, but often of taste, colour and nutrients as well, so that what is left is a light, neutral oil. Cold-pressing allows more of the intrinsic taste and aroma of the plant to remain, but is slower and less efficient to manufacture, so oils produced in this way tend to be more expensive. They tend to be less efficient as a cooking medium too, or at least their 'smoke point' is lower, which makes them less useful. (An oil's smoke point is the stage below its boiling point when it begins to decompose. The higher the smoke point, the more efficiently the oil can be used over direct heat.)

using them Oils are sold in bottles or cans and should be kept sealed. Hot-pressed oils will keep for several months; the more delicate cold-pressed oils can become rancid quite quickly so will not keep as long and should be stored in a cool dark place.

Oils are used primarily to cook or flavour food. Hot-pressed oils like safflower, groundnut and **soya** have a high smoke point, so can be used very successfully for frying or deep-frying at high temperatures. Cold-pressed oils, such as virgin olive oil, **walnut**, **hazelnut** and sesame, retain more of the original flavour of their basic ingredient and are the best ones to use in **vinaigrettes**, marinades, mayonnaise or as condiments at the table.

word origin Oil comes indirectly from the Latin *oleum,* meaning 'olive oil'. Oil and water don't blend, so when people talk about two people or things being like 'oil and water', they mean that they don't agree or get on with each other; being 'well oiled', on the other hand, refers to another quality of oil; it lubricates – in this case, alcoholically.

• The first 'oil' was probably the melted fat of animals, but the pressed juice of early fruits and seeds, particularly olive and sesame, wasn't far behind, and oil was almost certainly being pressed from olives around the Mediterranean 5000 years ago.

• All fats and oils contain a mixture of fatty acids, linked or 'bonded' molecules that can be saturated, monounsaturated or polyunsaturated. Saturated fatty acids are molecules where all the 'bonds' or links are saturated with hydrogen; monounsaturated fatty acids have one unsaturated bond, and polyunsaturated fatty acids contain more than one unsaturated bond. Saturated fats tend to remain solid at room temperature, but most oils, which contain less than 15 percent saturated fat, do not (the exceptions that prove the rule being coconut and palm oils, which check in at 85 and 45 percent saturated fat respectively). Monounsaturated oils like olive are liquid at room temperature, but thicken and cloud at refrigerator temperatures.

olive oil

About 90 percent of the fruit of the olive tree (*Olea europaea*) is used to create olive oil, one of the most coveted cooking ingredients in the world (the other 10 percent is processed to become table **olives**). The tree itself is native to the Mediterranean, and most olive oil is produced in that area of southern Europe, particularly in Italy, Spain, France and Greece.

Most olive oil is now made industrially by hot or cold-pressing (see **oils**), but a small amount is still traditionally milled. This usually begins with the olives being picked by hand (to avoid using damaged fruit) and washed before being crushed. The resulting paste is then sandwiched in layers between filtering mats and pressed to extract the liquid (a mixture of oil and water), after which a centrifuge separates out the oil from the water. The oil is decanted into storage containers before being (mostly) filtered and bottled. The first pressing doesn't release all the oil from the olives, so they are sometimes pressed a second time, and hot-pressed after that to release all of it.

To be called 'virgin', the oil must come from the first cold pressing (industrial or traditional) and be produced without chemical treatments and anything else that would lead to a change in the oil (too much heat during pressing, for instance, would alter the taste); it is allowed to be washed, centrifuged and filtered. Virgin oil is graded by acidity level (the rule of thumb being that the lower in acid it is, the better quality the oil): extra virgin olive oil has no more than 1 percent acidity (many of the best ones have half that); fine virgin olive oil has 1.5 percent acidity; and virgin olive oil up to 3 percent acidity. Any virgin oil that doesn't meet these standards (called virgin olive oil lampante) is further processed to produce refined olive oil, or used to make olive oil, which is basically refined oil with the addition of a small quantity of virgin or extra virgin oil to provide flavour. Light olive oil is an industrial oil that is lighter in colour and flavour than other types.

The colour of olive oil, which ranges from pale gold to green, is usually more of an indication of the variety of olives used and their ripeness when picked than of quality or taste. The best green oils come from the first cold pressing of early-gathered fruit, but some manufacturers now create the colour artificially by adding ground olive leaves to the olives during processing. Although most olive oils are clear, some unfiltered ones are cloudy and have small amounts of residue in the bottle; neither is harmful and the taste isn't affected.

using it Olive oils are sold in bottles and cans and will keep in a cool dark place for several months. Extra virgin oils are more delicate than other types, so are best decanted into dark sealed bottles and stored away from the heat of the kitchen if possible.

Refined, ordinary olive oil and virgin oil are good for most types of cooking. Cold-pressed extra virgin oils lose some of their delicate flavour when exposed to direct heat, so are better sprinkled over pasta, vegetable dishes and salads just before serving or used as a dip for bread. Fine or less expensive extra virgin oils make a good base for **vinaigrette** and pesto sauce. Commercially, olive oil is sometimes made into a table spread.

word origin Olive oil comes from the Latin *oliva,* meaning 'olive', and *oleum*, 'olive oil'.

did you know?

• Olive oil has been processed (by methods similar to the traditional one described above) for over 5000 years and has always been an essential part of the lives of Mediterranean people. It was used to anoint kings, bishops and popes and confirm their authority and status; to comfort the dead and consecrate holy places; to massage athletes, wrestlers and dancers; to bathe the heads and feet of honoured guests; and as a cleansing oil – the Greeks even used it to make the first cosmetic cold cream invented in the 2nd century AD.

peanut

The peanut (*Arachis hypogaea*) isn't technically a nut at all, but the seed of a **legume**, the podded fruit of a small tropical or semitropical bush or trailing plant that originated in South America and is related to the pea and bean. Major producers include India, the United States and West Africa.

After the peanut plant flowers and withers, the flower stems lengthen, bend and burrow into the ground where the pods grow and ripen (hence one of the peanut's alternative names, groundnut). The pods, which are inedible and correspond to those of peas, contain 2–6 nuts depending on the variety, each protected by a thin, reddish-brown or streaked skin that is usually removed before eating. To harvest the nuts, the whole plant is pulled up and dried before removing the pods. The seeds (or nuts) are then either left in the shell or processed into dried nuts, peanut butter and groundnut oil.

using it Peanuts in the shell (called monkey nuts) don't keep as well as most other nuts and should be used within two months. Peanuts bought shelled and skinned, roasted or unroasted, salted or unsalted have a longer shelf life.

Most peanuts are eaten as a snack, but unsalted ones can also be used in savoury cooking and baking, either as they are or toasted and roughly ground. The most popular byproduct is peanut butter, made by roasting the nuts, rubbing off the skins and then grinding them with a little salt and, if necessary, groundnut oil to create a thick paste. Peanut butter is used as a sandwich filling, either on its own or with other ingredients such as jam, banana or chopped dates, and is a key ingredient in satay sauce, a spicy accompaniment to Indonesian kebabs.

In other savoury dishes, whole or chopped unsalted nuts can be added to salads or stir-fries, or used as a garnish for curries and other meat, fish or rice dishes. Ground peanuts are sometimes added to African meat or vegetable stews to thicken them and they can also be combined with other ground nuts into a 'roast'. In baking, ground nuts are occasionally added to pastry doughs and used to flavour biscuits and cakes.

Groundnut oil has a neutral flavour and is widely used both commercially and domestically. Commercially it's used in canning and ready-made dishes and to make margarine; domestically, since it is polyunsaturated and has a high 'smoke point' (see **oils**), it's a popular oil for frying and deep-frying. It is blander than olive oil, but can be substituted for or mixed with it to make mayonnaise or **vinaigrette**.

word origin Because of the pod's habit of burying itself in the ground to ripen, the nut was first known as groundnut, then ground pea in English, and became peanut only around the beginning of the 19th century. Monkey nut appears to be fairly recent too, and to have come about because it was a popular nut for feeding to monkeys in zoos.

did you know?

• Peanuts were being eaten in Peru over 3000 years ago, long before the Incas came to power there. Portuguese explorers spread the peanut to Asia and Africa, where it is now part of the staple diet in some countries, and from there it was taken to North America on slave ships.

• Unlikely as it now seems, modern peanut butter was invented in 1890 as a health food aimed at the elderly and infirm, and in particular as an easy-to-chew protein food for patients who had lost their teeth or whose teeth were too fragile to allow them to eat meat. About 50 percent of the US crop now goes to make peanut butter.

pecan nut

This is the **fruit** of any of 300 or so varieties of a species of tall hickory tree (*Carya illinoensis*), a relative of the walnut. It is native to North America, where most of the world crop comes from.

The outer covering or flesh of the pecan 'fruit' is greenish and tough, and encloses a smooth, reddish-brown shell or stone. Inside the shell is the **nut** or kernel itself, which has two halves or lobes like a walnut, and is creamy with a thin brown skin. When the fruits are ripe, the outer covering splits into four to reveal the nut, and trees are shaken mechanically to release the fruits onto canvas sheets on the ground. They are then semi-dried, the outer covering removed if necessary and the nuts 'improved' by being sanded, dyed to give them their familiar rich colour, and polished.

using it Pecan nuts in the shell should be heavy for their size and shouldn't rattle when shaken; they will keep for about three months. Once shelled, the nuts will keep for about two months in the refrigerator.

Pecans are used in both sweet and savoury dishes. They can be chopped and sprinkled over fruit salads or creamy desserts, stirred into a vanilla ice-cream mixture before freezing, or added to biscuits or teabreads. Whole pecan nuts are a classic American pie filling, and they make a good decoration for larger cakes. They are usually ground or chopped for savoury dishes, as part of stuffings for turkey and game, as a coating for fillets of fish like red snapper or mixed with vegetable oil to make a butter similar to peanut butter. They can be used in any recipe as a substitute for **walnuts**.

word origin Pecan comes from the American Algonquian *paccan*, their word for hickory nut.

did you know?

• Although wild pecans were eaten, their shells were thick and difficult to crack. When they began to be cultivated, therefore, one of the aims was to create thin-skinned varieties that would be easier to shell, but just as good to eat. The hero who first managed to produce this was a slave named Antoine – working during the 1840s on a nut plantation in Louisiana, he created the variety called Centennial, the ancestor of all modern thin-skinned pecans.

pine nut

The pine nut, sometimes called pine kernel or pignolia, is the sweet-tasting seed of many different species of pine tree, including the southern European stone or umbrella pine (*Pinus pinea*), and *Pinus cembroides* and *Pinus edulis* from Central and North America respectively. Italy, Spain and China are among the leading producers.

Up to a hundred nuts can be lodged in the scales of one pine cone, and as it matures the cone opens to reveal them, still in their brittle, reddish-brown hulls. The cones are collected (usually by hand) and left to dry and open so that the nuts become accessible; they are then extricated and the hulls removed to reveal the tiny, thin, creamy kernels themselves.

using it Once a packet is opened, pine nuts should be stored in the refrigerator and used within a month. To enhance their flavour, they are often toasted (see **nuts** and **seeds**).

Pine nuts are widely used in Italy, for example in *agrodolce* (sweet-and-sour) dishes and meatballs, to garnish fish, **risottos** and sauces, and in pesto sauce. In North Africa, they are tossed into couscous, and in Spain they're served with fish or put into stuffing mixtures. More generally, pine nuts can be scattered over vegetables, stews, salads and pasta to add texture and taste.

word origin Pine nut is a simple description of what it is and where it's from. The alternative name *pignolia*, is Italian for 'pine nuts'.

did you know?

• Pine nuts were popular in ancient Rome – remains of them preserved in honey were found at Pompeii, and the cookery writer Apicius used them in practically everything from little meatballs and sausages to fish and meat sauces. The Romans brought them to Britain, and empty pine cone shells have been found in excavated Roman sites around the country.

pistachio

This nut comes from the stone fruit of a deciduous tree (*Pistacia vera*), which is native to western Asia and the Middle East where it is still grown, especially in Iran. The fruit, which is small, dry and olive-like, grows in clusters. As it ripens, it yellows, shrinks and then splits open to reveal the outer, light brown shell of the nut. This opens too, so that the thin brownish-red skin that protects the unique bright green kernel can be seen.

To harvest cultivated varieties, the tree is shaken so that the fruits are dislodged. After they are gathered, they are soaked to remove the outer fleshy covering and then dried, when the shells can take on a pink tinge; some are dyed a reddish colour before being sold on.

using it Pistachios are sold whole, in the shell or shelled, salted or natural. Removing the shells is simple: they are slightly open anyway, so need only be prized apart a little more to access the nut itself. The skin is edible but it can be removed easily (see **nuts** and **seeds**).

The luxurious look and taste of pistachios mean that they're in demand as a garnish for both sweet and savoury food, but they also make an excellent flavouring ingredient. In desserts, they are used in ice-creams and **soufflés**; in baking, they are chopped or ground for biscuits, cakes and pastries. In savoury cooking, they are often used whole in pâtés as well as ground to mix into stuffings, especially for fish and poultry.

word origin Pistachio comes, via French, from the Persian *pistah*.

did you know?

• Pistachios were being cultivated in Egypt 3500 years ago, and not just as food – they were an ingredient in what might be the world's first anti-wrinkle cream (along with wax, grass and poppy seed oil). The Romans introduced pistachios into Europe about 1500 years later and they spread all around the Mediterranean, where they are still widely cultivated. They reached America only at the end of the 19th century, but they are now cultivated there too.

sesame

Both sesame seeds and oil come from the tropical or subtropical flowering plant

Sesamum indicum, which is native to Indonesia and East Africa; major producers include China, India, the southern United States and Central America. The tiny oval seeds, which grow inside long oval pods, have creamy, red, brown or black hulls depending on the variety, although the insides are always white. Sesame oil is extracted from the seeds and is polyunsaturated; most of the better-quality ones are roasted before being cold-pressed, and therefore have a low 'smoke point' (see **oils**).

using it Hulled sesame seeds become rancid quite quickly so should be stored in the refrigerator and used within a month, or frozen. Roasting, or as it's often called, toasting, brings out the nutty flavour: spread them out in a heavy frying pan and cook until they start to 'jump' and are lightly browned.

The seeds are used to decorate breads, buns and biscuits, and are occasionally scattered over salads. Roasted sesame seeds can be ground to coat fish like snapper or tuna or aubergine slices to be fried or grilled. In the Middle East, crushed sesame seeds are used to make a type of halva, and are also the basis of tahini, a paste made from soaked and grilled seeds that is a key ingredient in the chickpea dip hummus, as well as other dips and sauces. Sesame seeds are particularly popular in Asian cooking: in Japan the roasted seeds are mixed with salt and used as a condiment or added to dressings, dipping sauces, vegetable and **tofu** dishes; in China, they are sprinkled over deep-fried dishes, especially fruit fritters; and in India they garnish raitas, curries and rice dishes.

Roasted sesame oil keeps well and is used mostly as a condiment, dressing oil or dipping sauce. A mix of sesame and other, more neutral oils with a higher smoke point, such as sunflower, is sold as 'stir-fry' oil in Europe. It gives the unique flavour of sesame without the smoking problems of the pure oil for dishes that require cooking over high heat.

word origin The word sesame comes from the ancient Egyptian *sesemt*, via the Greek *sesamon*. 'Open, sesame!', the phrase that opened the robbers' cave in *Ali Baba and the Forty Thieves* and which is now used to mean something that gives free access, comes from the sesame pod's habit of breaking open and scattering its seeds as it dries.

did you know?

• Sesame was cultivated at least 5000 years ago in Asia and Egypt, probably for both its seeds and oil, and ancient Egyptians and classical Romans both sprinkled the seeds over bread doughs in much the same way as we do today. The plant had spread to China via Persia by the 5th century AD, and reached the Americas on board slave ships from West Africa.

sunflower

A plant of the daisy family that originated in North America, sunflower (*Helianthus annuus*) can reach enormous heights. It is grown primarily for the polyunsaturated oil extracted from its seeds, which are botanically achenes – tiny fruits similar to those found on the exterior of **strawberries**. Each large flower disc can contain anything from several hundred to well over a thousand greyish seeds with grey, grey-black or striped husks, depending on the variety. Although there are over a hundred varieties growing around the world in temperate climates, only two are cultivated as food plants: a variety grown mostly in Russia and central Europe for its oil and one grown primarily in the United States for use as edible sunflower seeds or birdseed.

using it Removing the hulls from unhulled sunflower seeds is fiddly, so it's easier to buy them already hulled if you prefer not to eat the outer covering. Seeds make a good snack or can be sprinkled over virtually any food, including salads, cakes, buns, breakfast cereals and rice dishes.

Sunflower oil is a versatile cooking medium since it has a neutral flavour and a high 'smoke point' (see **oils**), and it can also be substituted for olive oil to make lighter-tasting mayonnaise and **vinaigrette**.

word origin The botanical name *Helianthus* means the same as the common one, coming from the Greek *helios*, 'the sun', and *anthos*, 'flower', either because the flowerhead looks like the sun or because of the plant's supposed habit of turning the flowerhead so that it always faces it.

did you know?

• Sunflowers were cultivated as food crops in the Americas over 5000 years ago. Native Americans ground the seeds into flour which they used to make bread, among other things. The Spaniards introduced them into Europe during the 16th century.

walnut

This **nut** comes from the stone fruit of a tall deciduous tree that grows in warm temperate areas throughout the world and is related to pecan; major producers include the United States, France, Italy, China and Turkey. The green, thin-fleshed fruit, called the husk or 'shuck', is tough and sour, although it's still more or less edible when immature, before the shells protecting the nut have had time to develop. The shuck splits open when ripe to reveal the shell which, depending on species and variety, can be anything from pale beige to brownish-black in colour. Inside the shell lies the two-part nut itself, a creamy-coloured kernel protected by an edible, brittle, beige to light brown skin.

There are about 15 species of walnut and many varieties, including the Persian or 'English' walnut (*Juglans regia*), which is native to an area stretching from the Mediterranean to central Asia, and has a thin, light brown shell; the black walnut (*Juglans nigra*), which is native to North America and has a thick, brownish-black shell and a strong flavour; and the butternut or 'white' walnut (*Juglans cinerea*), which is native to the eastern part of the United States, and has a light, thick shell and oily flesh. The dominant eating variety throughout the world is the English walnut.

'Green' walnuts are picked before the shell has formed, while others are selected half-ripe, but most are harvested mechanically when fully ripe (the tree is shaken so that the fruit falls to the ground). After they have been gathered, the nuts are dried in the sun or artificially, then usually bleached before being graded for selling. Walnuts destined for oil are stored for two to three months before they are cold-pressed (see **oils**).

using it Next to the almond, the walnut is the most popular nut in Europe, and is used in all types of cooking. 'Green' nuts are normally immersed in brine until they become dark green, then dried and pickled as a traditional accompaniment to cheese or cold meats, or made into ketchups and jams. Half-ripe walnuts (those just ripe enough to be extricated from their shuck) are preserved in syrup.

Dried ripe walnuts are the ones we come across most frequently. Still in their shell, they are sometimes served as a special course at the end of a meal or with cheese. In desserts, half or whole nuts are used to decorate fruit salads and creamy mousses and fools, while chopped ones flavour ice-creams and are folded into steamed puddings. In baking, walnuts are used more or less all the time: whole or half nuts can be substituted for pecans to make walnut pie; and ground or chopped nuts are mixed into pastry doughs, crumble toppings, teabreads, biscuits and cakes, with half kernels decorating the latter too. In savoury cooking, walnuts are ground to make a creamy, unusual-tasting soup; added to sauces and stuffings (especially for poultry and oily fish like salmon); chopped or ground as a substitute for (or as well as) pine nuts in pesto sauce; and tossed into salads, particulary with carrots, celery and apples.

The delicate, nutty taste of walnut oil is used occasionally in cooking (it goes particularly well with green beans, especially if some chopped nuts are added to the pan as well), but its primary function is as a dressing oil, in **vinaigrette** or to sprinkle over already-cooked pasta, rice and vegetable dishes.

word origin Walnut comes from the Anglo-Saxon *walh hnutu,* meaning 'foreign nut' (the first part comes from the same root as the word Wales).

did you know?

• Wild walnuts have been eaten since neolithic times and were probably first cultivated by the Greeks, who made them sacred to the goddess Diana. The Romans made them a symbol of fertility and marriage (they were traditionally thrown at weddings). The vague resemblance to the human brain didn't go unnoticed either – both the Greeks and Romans thought this meant that eating walnuts could cure headaches.
• Artists once used walnut oil as a medium for mixing white and delicate colours, and a brown dye made from the shell is used as a furniture stain.

Herbs & Spices

Herbs and spices are an integral part of every cuisine, adding flavour and balance to dishes all over the world. Their versatility is demonstrated perfectly by Chinese cuisine. Over the centuries, the Chinese have developed a unique approach to food that amounts almost to a philosophy. Most apparent is an emphasis on the freshness of ingredients and the balance of tastes. The Chinese use spices and herbs but never to the extent that they overwhelm the main ingredients. Ginger, spring onions, five-spice powder, star anise, fresh coriander, garlic, soy sauce, chilli bean sauce and other seasonings are clearly but never obtrusively present. They are always

combined with fresh ingredients in the most appropriate way. One would think there might be a limit to the number of dishes resulting

It is herbs and spices that define a particular cuisine.
Ken Hom

from these masterful combinations, yet I always find surprises when I visit different places, whether in markets, restaurants or private homes.

It is herbs and spices that define a particular cuisine. Whenever I travel to Chinatowns throughout the world, I encounter Chinese cooking in all its variety and pungency. In China, Hong Kong, Taiwan, Australia, Europe and America, I have observed the wide variety of readily available Chinese foods. Yet despite regional variations, there is a unity of style that comes from shared techniques and seasonings.

Almost all the spices and herbs called for in cookbooks can now be obtained from ordinary supermarkets. In this book you will find advice on what to look for when shopping for these exotic ingredients, how to use them, and how to store them. It is my hope that, armed with information about good spices and herbs, you will understand how to bring the best out of your cooking with them, just as the Chinese do.

balti

This is the name given to a range of savoury dishes flavoured with Asian spices, similar to **curry**. Balti dishes are made from virtually any ingredient – meat, fish or vegetables – but are dryish rather than liquid, aromatic rather than fiercely hot. The word is also sometimes used to describe the two-handled wok-like pan or karahi in which the dish is cooked.

using it Traditionally, balti dishes are cooked in the karahi and served in it as well, and with **naan** bread rather than rice; the food is scooped up with the bread.

word origin Balti is short for Baltistan, the northernmost state in Pakistan where the type of food originated.

basil

There are many varieties of this aromatic **herb** of the **mint** family, which originated in India and South-east Asia. They include sweet basil (*Ocimum basilicum*), the green oval-leaved plant with the peppery scent that you are most likely to see in supermarkets; purple basil (*Ocimum basilicum* var. *purpurascens*), a hybrid of sweet basil with purple leaves; bush basil (*Ocimum minimum*), a miniature plant with smaller leaves and a weaker flavour than sweet basil; and holy basil (*Ocimum sanctum*), the type most commonly used in South-east Asia, which has a clove-like fragrance.

using it Basil is available fresh as well as dried. Fresh leaves are torn, shredded or used whole, preferably added at the end of cooking to make the most of their unique flavour.

This is one of the most versatile herbs in the kitchen, equally good as a flavouring for Mediterranean stews and sauces, Thai quick-fry dishes, and summer vegetable or salad combinations. A magic partnership is basil with tomatoes: stir the herb into any tomato-based sauce for pasta, and scatter over both roasted and raw tomato salads.

Basil pounded with olive oil, pine nuts, garlic and Parmesan makes versatile pesto sauce – superb not just as a dressing for pasta, but also as a salsa for tuna steaks, a flavouring for minestrone, a partner with sliced tomatoes in a sandwich, and a final addition to a vegetable or fish **risotto**.

word origin Basil was known as the 'royal' herb in ancient Greece, and the name reflects it, from the same root as the word for king, *basileus*. Holy basil, called *tulsi* in India, is associated with the Hindu god Vishnu and considered sacred, hence its name.

did you know?

● Although it has been cultivated in Asia for thousands of years, basil has only been used in western Europe since medieval times. It was a herb you loved or loathed, and some thought it poisonous. The 14th-century Florentine writer Boccaccio immortalized this ambivalence in his macabre tale of *Isabella and the Pot of Basil*. Poor Isabella's unsuitable lover was murdered by her brothers and she was so grief-stricken when she found his body that she cut off his head and planted it in a large pot. She then planted sweet basil on top of it, which thereafter she watered with her tears (it flourished; she didn't).

bay leaf

This is the oval, waxy, vanilla-scented leaf of the bay laurel tree (*Laurus nobilis*), an evergreen shrub related to **cinnamon** and avocado. The tree, which can occasionally reach 15m in height, is native to the Mediterranean, but now grown widely in cool to warm climates around the world. The leaves are used as a **herb**.

using it Bay leaf is nearly always available fresh, although newly picked leaves can be slightly bitter and are best kept for a day or so before being used. It dries well; in fact dried bay leaf is almost as good as fresh. Bay leaf is best added near the beginning of cooking, whole or torn into pieces if fresh, so that its flavour has time to permeate.

This herb is added as a matter of course to nearly all stocks, soups and marinades, both on its own or as part of a **bouquet garni.** It makes a good flavouring for meat stews and casseroles, can be tucked inside the cavity of more or less any bird or whole fish before cooking, and tastes just as good in sweet sauces like custard as it does in savoury ones, although it needs to be removed before the sauce is served. It's also occasionally used to decorate food, particularly meat pâtés.

word origin Bay is derived from the Old French for the berry of the tree, *baie*, which came from the Latin *baca*.

• According to Greek myth, the nymph Daphne, who was sworn to perpetual celibacy, was pursued by the god Apollo and turned into a bay laurel by the other gods to protect her virginity. As a result, Apollo declared the bay laurel to be sacred to himself, and his priestesses nibbled the leaves before they chanted oracles at Delphi (bay is a mild narcotic, so they probably looked as if they were in a trance). Later, in classical Greece and Rome, heroes, athletes and poets were crowned with bay laurel leaves as a mark of their excellence, something which survives today, metaphorically at least, in 'poet laureate'.

bouquet garni

A bouquet garni is a small bunch of flavouring ingredients (nearly always herbs) which is added to a dish at the beginning of cooking and removed before serving. The mixture can vary depending on the dish, but the classic is a **bay leaf**, two or three **parsley** sprigs and a sprig or two of **thyme**. Other flavourings sometimes added include: a curl or two of bitter orange peel, a piece of celery stalk or leek, chervil or chives, and whole spices such as peppercorns or allspice berries.

using it For a fresh bouquet garni, tie the herbs and vegetables together with string (preferably with a loop at one end so that the bundle can be easily removed from the pot); or if whole spices are included, pack into a small muslin pouch. Ready-made dried bouquet garnis are usually sold in small muslin bags or mini-teabags.

A bouquet garni can be used to flavour virtually anything savoury, including soups, stocks, sauces, stews, casseroles and pies.

word origin Bouquet garni is French and means 'garnished bouquet'.

caraway

Caraway (*Carum carvi*) is a biennial plant related to carrot, **fennel** and parsley, which is native to northern Europe and Asia; major producers include Russia, Germany and the Netherlands. The plant can reach 60cm in height and is cultivated mainly for its long, thin, grey-brown 'seeds' that taste like a slightly bitter version of **cumin**. The seeds (despite the name) are actually the halved dried fruits of the plant. The leaves, which look like those of carrot and taste like parsley, are also used occasionally.

using it Caraway is available ground into a powder or as dried seeds, the latter being the better- and stronger-tasting of the two. Both ground caraway and caraway seeds are used as a **spice**. Crush the seeds slightly before using to release their warm aromatic flavour, and add to dishes 10–15 minutes before the end of cooking to allow the flavour to develop.

The distinctive taste is particularly associated with German and central European cooking, and is used in both savoury and sweet dishes. In savoury cooking, caraway is a standard ingredient in goulash and other central European meat stews as well as cabbage-based dishes like **sauerkraut**, and it tastes good with sausages, pork, potatoes and apple.

It is mixed into some cheeses (e.g. Liptauer, cream cheese) and served with others (Münster), and is a favourite bread flavouring, particularly for rye breads. In the United Kingdom, it's the classic seed in seed cake. Commercially, oil pressed from caraway makes one alcoholic drink (kümmel) and flavours others, like schnapps.

word origin Caraway comes from the Arabic for the plant, *alkarawiya*, via the Spanish version of this, *alcarahueya*.

did you know?

• This may have been the first cultivated spice in Europe – at any rate, seeds have been found in archaeological sites dating back about 8000 years. Caraway was particularly popular during medieval times, when the seeds were dipped in syrup, then rolled in sugar and chewed as comfits, and it was as comfits that they were originally baked into seed cakes and buns. They are still occasionally chewed, plain or sugared, before meals to help digest food properly or afterwards to help sweeten the breath (they're especially good at disguising the smell of garlic).

cardamom

A perennial plant of the **ginger** family, cardamom (*Elettaria cardamomum*) is native to India and Sri Lanka, and these two countries, together with Guatemala, are the major producers. The cardamom plant can grow to over 5m in height, and what appear to be pods are, in fact, the dried fruits, each of which contains many tiny, aromatic black seeds. 'True' cardamom produces smallish green pods, which are harvested before they are ripe and then dried slowly in the sun; other closely related species produce larger brownish pods sold occasionally as cardamom, which are dried artificially. White cardamom pods are bleached that colour before being sold.

using it Cardamom is available as pods, seeds or ground into a powder. Most pods

sold in Europe are green and have a more delicate taste than brown ones. Pods keep better than seeds or powder. Before use, crush the pods to open them, then add whole or extricate the seeds and discard the husk. Cardamom is usually added to dishes towards the beginning of cooking so that the peppery sweet taste has time to permeate.

In the Indian subcontinent, cardamom is part of **spice** mixtures like **garam masala** as well as being used by itself in many meat, fish and rice dishes; in the Middle East, it's a favourite flavouring for Turkish-style coffee; and in Europe, particularly in Scandinavia where it's more popular than elsewhere, it's added to mulled wines and liqueurs, baked dishes such as fruit pies, biscuits and cakes, and fruit desserts. More generally, it can be used as an unusual flavouring for home-made ice-cream and custard, or added to savoury marinades and stuffings, especially for poultry and pork.

word origin Cardamom comes via Latin from the Greek *kardamomon*, a mixture of *kardamon*, 'peppergrass', and *amomon*, a spice produced from a relative of cardamom.

cayenne pepper

A ground **spice** made from dried birdseye **chilli peppers** (*Capsicum frutescens*), cayenne pepper is lightish red in colour and hot to taste, thanks to the presence of ground seeds as well as flesh in the powder. *Capsicum frutescens* is native to South and Central America, although nowadays cayenne pepper is just as likely to come from Africa or Asia.

using it Cayenne has an affinity with seafood, especially crab, and is also sometimes used to cheer up blander cheese dishes like Welsh rarebit and cheese straws. The original version of **Tabasco sauce** is made from a similar variety of *Capsicum frutescens,* as is pure chilli powder, and cayenne pepper can be substituted for both of these in recipes.

word origin The capital city of French Guiana in the north-eastern part of South America is called Cayenne. The name of both the spice and the city is probably a corruption of a local South American word for the *Capsicum* plant, *kyinha*.

chilli powder

This is both a brown-red **spice** mixture based on **chilli peppers**, which is used primarily to flavour Mexican and Tex-Mex dishes, and a paler red powder made from dried chilli peppers and seeds. The 'Mexican' powder (sometimes called chile powder) is sold in various strengths from mild to hot and usually contains other flavourings like cumin, oregano and garlic powder in addition to chillies.

using it The mixed powder is the classic flavouring for dishes such as chilli con carne, although it can also add warmth to other meat dishes like stews, burgers, sausages and pasta sauces. A small amount can also spice up mayonnaise dressings, particularly for substantial salads like mixed bean, potato or chicken. Pure chilli pepper powder is used commercially as part of spice mixtures such as curry powder or instead of chillies themselves and, since it's similar to **cayenne pepper,** can be substituted for this in recipes.

word origin The chilli part of the name comes from the Nahuatl (Aztec) word for *Capsicum*.

chive

This smallest and mildest member of the **onion** family is native to central Europe, but grows profusely in temperate climates around the world. The chive (*Allium schoenoprasum*) is cultivated for its green, tubular, stem-like leaves, which can reach about 35cm in height and are used as a **herb**.

using it Chives have a natural season from spring to autumn although they are usually available throughout the year. They should be cut with scissors rather than cut or torn.

Snipped leaves are used to flavour omelettes and dips, either by themselves or as part of *fines herbes* (a classic mixture of chives, chervil, parsley and tarragon). They can also be mixed with softened butter to make an accompaniment to fish or steak, or with soured cream as a filling for baked potatoes. As a garnish they can decorate soups, sauces and salads, particularly those made with potato and tomato, to add extra colour as well as flavour.

word origin Chive comes, via Old French, from the Latin *cepa,* meaning 'onion'.

did you know?

● Chinese chives (*Allium tuberosum*), which have been grown in China for over 5000 years, are bigger and coarser than ordinary chives, with a pronounced garlic flavour. Larger Chinese chives are cooked as a leaf vegetable while smaller ones are used as a garnish.

cinnamon

Cinnamon (*Cinnamomum verum* or *zeylanicum*) is a **spice** made from the bark of an evergreen member of the laurel family. It originated in Sri Lanka which, along with the Seychelles and the Malagasy Republic, is still one of the major modern suppliers. The bark is harvested in long strips and the outer parts peeled off, then the inner barks are carefully packed in layers, one inside another, and rolled into tight cylinders or quills. The cylinders are cured briefly, then dried and trimmed; some are also bleached. A closely related plant, cassia (*Cinnamomum cassia*), is treated in the same way to produce a spice sold in some parts of the world as cinnamon.

using it Cinnamon is available as sticks or ground into a powder, and each has its own uses. Sticks are a popular flavouring for mulled wine and punch, and in parts of the Middle East and India are added to couscous, pilaffs and other savoury rice dishes to flavour and garnish them. Ground cinnamon is an ingredient in commercial mixed spice (see **spices**) and **garam masala**, and is sometimes also used as a condiment on toast, fresh melon and coffee, particularly cappuccino. In European cooking, cinnamon is mostly added to sweet dishes now, particularly pies, cakes and desserts (it tastes especially good with apples and chocolate), although in the Middle Ages it was often used, as it still is in Asia, to flavour beef and other savoury dishes.

word origin Cinnamon probably comes from the Hebrew *qinnamon*. An alternative name in medieval England, *canel*, comes via Old French from the Latin *canna*, meaning 'cane', a reference to the shape of the sticks.

did you know?

• This was one of the spices supplied to Europe via the Silk Road, and its cost and scarcity were two of the reasons that Columbus set sail in 1492. Cinnamon was also the essential ingredient in cameline sauce, a medieval ketchup so popular that ready-made versions were sold by professional sauce-makers on the streets of large cities such as Paris.

clove

This is the dried unopened flowerbud of the evergreen tree *Syzygium aromaticum*, a member of the myrtle family. The tree originated in the Moluccas in Indonesia, but the main supplier of cloves now is Zanzibar, where the best plantations are situated close to the sea. Cloves are harvested as soon as the buds turn from green to pink and before the petals appear; they turn brown as they dry out.

using it Cloves are sold either whole, as dark 'nails' or sticks, or ground into a powder. Whole cloves keep their flavour for longer than ground, which becomes musty quite quickly. Nails are difficult to grind at home, however, so if the ground spice is required, it's best bought as such.

Cloves are used as a spice in both savoury and sweet dishes. Whole, they are stuck into gammon joints to be roasted and into whole onions too, especially when the latter are being used as a flavouring for other dishes, such as the milk for **béchamel** or bread sauce. They are also added to pickles, to the sousing mixture that creates rollmops, and to mulled wine, punch and fruit-based sauces. Ground cloves are essential in commercial mixtures like mixed spice, Chinese five-spice powder (see **spices**) and **garam masala**, and are also widely used in baking to flavour pies, breads, cakes, biscuits and puddings.

word origin Clove comes from the Latin *clavus,* meaning 'nail', a reference to the appearance of the dried bud.

did you know?

• In the Middle Ages cloves weren't just used in cooking — an orange stuck with whole cloves, from which people then sucked the juice, was believed to help ward off plague, and in southern Italy special sweets made from cloves were believed to be aphrodisiacs. In India they were mixed with *bhang*, a plant similar to cannabis, which was chewed in cuds like tobacco; in Indonesia they still flavour the tobacco used to make *kretek*, a type of local cigarette.
• Oil of cloves, made from the buds, leaves and flower stalks of the tree, is still sometimes used as a mouthwash and cure for toothache.

coriander

An annual or biennial plant of the **parsley** family, coriander (*Coriandrum sativum*) is grown both for its scalloped-edged, pungent green leaves, which are used as a **herb**, and for its small, round aromatic berries, called seeds, which are dried and used as a **spice**. Coriander is native to southern Europe and the Middle East, although it's now more associated with the cooking of India and South-east Asia, and Central and South America. In the United States and Latin America the fresh herb is called cilantro.

using it Fresh coriander is widely available, and can be frozen or preserved in oil, if only to avoid using the rather musty dried version. Seeds can be bought whole or ground into a powder; the former keep better than the latter and are easy to grind up when needed. To get the most from the warming, fresh taste, add the fresh leaves, whole or chopped, to a cooked dish just before serving; add seeds and powder at the beginning of cooking.

Fresh leaves are primarily used to flavour or garnish ethnic food like curries, stir-fries, fresh chutneys, pilaffs, couscous and chillies, but they are also used more generally now as a flavouring for salads; in puréed dips with garlic and aubergine or red pepper; and with seafood, especially prawns, crab and squid.

Seeds or powder are part of commercial spice mixtures like mixed spice (see **spices**), curry powder, **garam masala** and harissa sauce, and in northern Europe they are used to flavour pickles and chutneys, cabbage-based dishes, game casseroles and baked goods, especially cakes.

word origin Coriander comes indirectly from the Greek *koris*, meaning 'bedbug'. The leaves and unripe seeds do have an unpleasant smell until the seeds ripen, which may explain this.

did you know?

• Coriander has been cultivated for over 3500 years. Ancient Egyptians knew it and used it, and in the Bible, manna, the food from heaven that saved the Israelites in the wilderness, was described in Exodus as being 'like coriander seed'. It had arrived in Britain by the Bronze Age and was particularly popular during medieval and Tudor times, when it was used in medicines and love potions as well as in cooking. Spanish conquistadors took the plant with them to Central and South America where it was discovered to have a real affinity with the local food.

cumin

This is the dried fruit of *Cuminum cyminum*, an annual plant belonging to the same family as parsley and **caraway**, which is native to the eastern Mediterranean, but is also now grown in Iran, India, China and Russia. The cumin fruit is about 5mm long and greyish-green when fresh, but dries into a thin, spindly, grey-brown seed. Black cumin can either be a rare variety of 'true' cumin or *Nigella sativa*, a plant belonging to the buttercup family; the latter isn't related to *Cuminum cyminum* and doesn't particularly taste like it either, but like ordinary cumin it's used as a **spice**, particularly in Arabic and Indian cooking.

using it Cumin can be bought as seeds or ground into a powder; the seeds keep better than the powder and have a better flavour too. To bring out their full flavour, toast the seeds in a small pan, then crush slightly. They are usually added at the beginning of cooking.

Cumin is part of commercial spice mixtures such as curry powder, **garam masala** and chilli powder, but it also tastes good on its own in North African stews and couscous, Mexican dishes like chilli con carne (in addition to the obligatory chilli powder) and most Indian savoury dishes. More generally, it has an affinity with chicken and vegetables like courgette and aubergine, and (in small quantities) could also be stirred into mince dishes like shepherd's pie to give them added flavour. Cumin is the traditional seed in some eastern European breads and cakes.

word origin Cumin comes, via Old French, from the Latin for the spice, *cuminum*.

did you know?

• Cumin was used as a preservative in the ancient world: the Egyptians used it to mummify their pharaohs, while the Romans mixed it with coriander and vinegar and used it to preserve meat. They also used it as a cosmetic and, if the Roman writer Pliny is to be believed, the seeds were smoked to give the face a fashionable, scholarly pallor.

curry

Outside the Indian subcontinent, this is a blanket term for just about any cooked savoury dish flavoured with mixtures of Asian spices called masalas (see **garam masala**). A 'curry' can therefore describe anything from a delicate aromatic Moghul dish to an off-with-your-head Madras one, and include a hot and sour vinegar-based vindaloo as well as a mildly flavoured tandoori. Although this type of food originated in the subcontinent, similar dishes are also part of the cooking tradition in Thailand, Malaysia, Indonesia and the West Indies.

using it Asian curries are normally served with rice, bread like **naan** or, occasionally, (especially in South-east Asia) noodles. In India, a selection of 'curry' dishes is traditionally served in small individual bowls (*katoris*) grouped around a central pile of rice or bread on a large metal tray (*thali*).

word origin Curry comes from the Tamil *kari*, meaning 'spiced sauce'.

did you know?

• Karis were slightly sloppy spice mixtures made fresh each day from varying ingredients and served with plainer rice and lentil dishes to add flavour and interest – a long way from modern commercial curry powder and from the dishes now called curries. Those first karis probably weren't very hot, since before the discovery of the Americas, chillies were unknown and most mixtures would have contained nothing more lethal than black pepper.

curry powder

This is a commercial mixture of about eight or more **spices** ground together to approximate the traditional blends used to flavour savoury dishes in the Indian subcontinent and parts of South-east Asia. Classic Indian ingredients include coriander, cumin, fenugreek and mustard seeds, chilli powder and/or dried chillies, black pepper, garlic and turmeric; other flavourings such as bay leaves, cardamom, cinnamon, cloves, ginger and poppy seeds are also added as appropriate, depending on the type being made.

Most Indian curry powders are sold by strength – hot, medium and mild – or style (e.g. Madras, tikka, tandoori). Thai mixtures are usually made into pastes, and nearly always contain lemon grass as well as a selection of the ingredients listed above.

using it Commercial powders keep reasonably well, but there's no real need for them. All the individual spices they contain are readily available as seeds or powder, and food processors or coffee grinders remove the hassle and time it once took to blend them together. So a fresh home-made 'curry powder' can be made in an instant – and varied to suit the dish it's to spice.

For the best flavour toast the seeds in a small pan or in a low oven before grinding. Curry mixtures are normally added at the beginning of cooking to allow the flavours to permeate, preferably directly after any flavouring vegetables and fresh ginger.

The main use, commercial or home-made, is still as a flavouring for Indian, South-east Asian, West Indian or Anglo-Indian food, but curry powder can also be mixed with flour to create a spicy batter for oily fish like herring; blended with browned onions and garlic, then white wine to steam mussels; or beaten with yoghurt and/or mayonnaise to make a spicy dressing for cold seafood salad or chicken.

did you know?

• When the British were in India they acquired a taste for '*karis*' (see **curry**) and wanted to continue eating them when they returned home. Somewhere on the journey, the original spiced sauce mixtures became stews ,initially usually containing meat, and flavoured by a standard spice mixture. The first commercial powders were around by the end of the 18th century. although they weren't widely available until about a century later.

dill

An annual plant of the **parsley** family and closely related to fennel (which it resembles), dill (*Anethum graveolens*) is native to southern Europe and the Middle East, although it is now cultivated in temperate areas elsewhere. It's grown both for its delicate feathery leaves (which are used as a **herb**) and for its brownish, ridged seeds, actually the fruits of the plant, which are used as a **spice**.

using it Fresh dill is fragile, so store in the refrigerator with the stems in water and use within a day or so of purchase; it doesn't dry particularly well. Dill seeds are added to a dish during cooking, whereas the leaves are usually stirred in either before cooking or just after.

Fresh dill is used widely with fish: tucked into cavities before cooking and used to garnish after, and as the major flavouring in gravadlax, the Scandinavian cured salmon speciality (dill is particularly popular in northern Europe); it is also added to salads, particularly potato-, cucumber- and beetroot-based ones. Seeds are widely used in pickling, classically with gherkins but also with fish, and occasionally in baking.

word origin Dill comes from the Old Norse *dilla,* 'to lull', probably in recognition of the plant's calming properties – a water made from dill was traditionally used to soothe babies and it is still an ingredient in gripe water.

garam masala

This is a spice mixture used to flavour Indian-style savoury dishes. Ingredients can vary slightly, but most mixtures contain 'warming' spices, such as black **pepper**, **cinnamon** and **cloves**, and 'cooling' ones like **cardamom**,

coriander and **cumin**. Occasionally other flavourings such as **bay leaf**, **ginger**, **nutmeg** or mace are added too.

using it Ready-made commercial garam masala keeps quite well, but a fresher-tasting, more pungent version can easily be made at home by grinding the selected spices in a food processor or coffee grinder. For the best flavour, toast the seeds in a small pan or low oven before grinding.

Garam masala is usually added at the end of cooking, as a final flavouring for meat, poultry and rice dishes. The warm spiciness can also be mixed with plain yoghurt as a basting sauce for kebabs and chops or as an accompanying sauce for plainly grilled meat.

word origin Garam masala means 'hot mixture' in Urdu.

did you know?

• There are many *masalas* or spice mixtures in India – in fact, they are the basis of the cuisine – and different regions have different *masalas*. Those from the north, like garam masala, tend to be dry mixtures of pounded seeds or powders, while those from the south can be pastes, made from a mixture of fresh herbs and liquids such as lime juice or coconut milk.

garlic

This pungent member of the **onion** family originated in central Asia, but now grows in temperate climates around the world. Garlic (*Allium sativum*) is a perennial plant with long flat leaves and flowering stalks that can reach 50cm in height. It is cultivated for its underground bulb or 'head', although its leaves are also sometimes used as a **herb**. Each bulb is covered with layers of thick, papery, off-white to rosy membrane; this membrane also separates and encloses the 10–15 individual segments, or 'cloves', within the bulb. The flesh of the cloves is normally light cream in colour.

using it Garlic is usually bought semi-fresh, and in this form keeps for several months, especially stored away from the moisture of the kitchen. The bulb is sometimes roasted whole, but most often the cloves are separated and peeled, then used whole, crushed or chopped. To crush, use a special press or a mortar and pestle, or simply press down on the clove with the flat side of a large knife. The more finely garlic is crushed or chopped, the stronger it will taste (especially when used raw), but it sweetens and becomes milder with long cooking. Raw garlic can be added to uncooked dishes, and at the beginning of cooking or at the end, depending on the dish and whether it's to be strongly or more subtly flavoured.

Garlic was traditionally associated with Mediterranean and Asian cooking, but is now increasingly popular everywhere else since it seems to go with practically everything. Raw garlic is an essential part of pesto sauce (see **basil**); beaten with butter, it can provide an accompaniment for steaks or chops and a spread for bread that's then baked; it can be beaten into mayonnaise to make aioli; and mixed with chopped parsley and grated lemon zest to make gremolada (see **parsley**). It's also often added to salad dressings like **vinaigrette** or (for a more subtle taste), a cut clove can be rubbed around the inside of the salad bowl.

In cooking, garlic is added more or less automatically to most pasta sauces, especially tomato- and meat-based ones; stir-fried with herbs and seafood, especially squid and prawns; and added to meat and vegetable stews or to stuffings for the same ingredients. Cloves are sometimes cut into slivers and inserted into lamb before it's roasted, or they can be left whole, with or without their skins, and cooked underneath it. Unskinned cloves can also be simmered in milk, then squeezed out of their skins and into mashed potatoes, or puréed with **béchamel sauce** to serve with plainly cooked meat.

word origin Garlic comes from the Anglo-Saxon *gar,* meaning 'spear', and *leac*, 'leek'.

• Garlic has been cultivated for about 5000 years, for healing as well as for eating. It was considered to be a strengthening food, so was fed to the workers who built the pyramids and to both Greek and Roman soldiers to keep them healthy and protect them from disease. Later, during the Middle Ages, it was believed to ward off the plague and of course it has always protected against Satan, ill luck and vampires. No one quite knows why people believed it would repulse Dracula's little 'love bites', but it's possible that it was because it was known to repel mosquitoes and prevent *their* bites.
• Modern science is discovering that many of the medicinal properties claimed for garlic throughout history could be true. Spagnum moss soaked in garlic juice was found to be an effective antibiotic during the First World War, for instance, and more recent research suggests anti-fungal claims could be true too and that eating garlic regularly could reduce cholesterol levels, and thus help to prevent heart disease and strokes.

ginger

Ginger (*Zingiber officinale*) is a tall, broad-leaved perennial plant native to tropical South-east Asia. It is cultivated for its knobbly, beige, underground thickened stem system or rhizome, which is used as a **spice**. Major modern suppliers include India, which produces half the world crop of ginger, and Jamaica, which produces the best. Rhizomes are either harvested young and used fresh (root or 'green' ginger), crystallized in sugar, or preserved in syrup as stem ginger; or they are dug up two or three months later, when they are normally dried and ground into a powder.

using it Fresh root ginger will keep for several weeks unpeeled, but once it has been peeled it should be wrapped in foil, stored in the refrigerator and used within 7–10 days, otherwise it will shrivel and lose its juiciness. If it's to be used only for grating, peeled root ginger can be kept in the freezer and grated straight from frozen. Root ginger is always peeled and any woody bits cut away before the flesh is sliced, chopped or grated to use.

In Asian cooking, the fresh root is used to flavour practically all savoury dishes, cooked and uncooked: finely chopped and added at the beginning of stir-fries to flavour the oil in which the other ingredients are cooked; sliced and tucked into whole fish or vegetables to be steamed; chopped or grated into cooking oil with other flavourings like garlic and chilli to spice up Indian stews; and grated raw into dipping sauces for Japanese deep-fried or other plainly cooked foods.

In the western world, the fresh root is still mostly used in various types of ethnic savoury cooking or the occasional salsa, often with tomato. Ground ginger can be added to preserved foods such as chutney and jam, but mostly it's used in desserts, especially those including pineapple, melon, rhubarb and apple, and in baking – classically to make gingerbread or ginger biscuits, but also as a general flavouring for cakes, biscuits and buns. Crystallized ginger makes a good decoration for cakes, gingerbreads and desserts, but can be chopped into fruit compotes and vanilla ice-cream to give them extra taste too. Stem ginger is also used in baking and to flavour ice-cream or other creamy desserts.

Oil processed from ginger is the traditional basis of mildly alcoholic drinks like ginger wine and ginger beer.

word origin Ginger comes from the Sanskrit *srnga-veram*, meaning 'horn root', which eventually ended up as the Latin *zingiber,* then the Old English *gingifer*. The bracing taste accounts for 'to ginger it up', meaning to make something more exciting, usually by exaggerating a bit. When we talk of hair being 'ginger', we are comparing it to the red-orange colour of the preserved root rather than the beige of the fresh one.

did you know?

• Ginger has been cultivated in Asia for over 4000 years and spread to Europe quite early – both the Greeks and especially the Romans knew of it, although they seem to have used it as a medicine rather than as a flavouring. The Romans spread it throughout Europe, and by medieval times it had become one of the most popular spices in England, more or less on a par with black pepper.

• Medicinally, ginger was used to relieve muscle aches, prevent flatulence and to aid digestion (it's still used in this latter way in some parts of the world), and it was also known to encourage sweating, which was probably why it was used to treat plague victims when the Black Death swept Europe in the 14th century (the idea was to sweat it out of them). By Tudor times in England, it was believed to be an aphrodisiac.

herbs

These are mostly temperate plants whose leaves and occasionally bulbs and flowers are used in healing and to flavour food; **spices**, with which herbs are often used and confused, tend to come from the flowerbuds, fruits and even bark of tropical plants. Most herbs are small and oval-leaved (**basil**, **oregano**, **mint**), but some are long, narrow and stem-like (**chives**, **lemon grass**), and a few are cultivated for their flowers (nasturtium) or bulbs (**garlic**). Some plants do double duty, yielding herbs from their leaves and spices from their fruit (**coriander**), or vegetables from their roots and herbs and seeds from the rest of the plant (**fennel**).

using them Fresh herbs are widely available, either home-grown or bought in growing pots or poly bags. Nearly all are also available dried, although quality varies from herb to herb; some are now also commercially freeze-dried or preserved in oil. Bought growing herbs will keep for 3–7 days depending on the herb and should be watered occasionally to keep them going; bought fresh packaged herbs should be stored in their containers in the refrigerator and used within 3–5 days. Dried herbs should be bought in small quantities and stored in jars large enough to give them some ventilation in a cool dark place; they will last for about six months. Those preserved in oil need to be refrigerated once the jar has been opened.

Fresh herbs can be frozen either by storing them in airtight freezer bags or by chopping them into ice-cube trays and filling up with water; the cubes can be used straight from frozen. Herbs can be dried at home too, either in the microwave (most manufacturers give instructions) or by laying them out in a single layer on a rack in a warm, dark, dry place such as an airing cupboard. They will take 5–8 days to dry out to a proper crispness, when they should be stripped from their stalks and stored. To keep the individual flavour, dry each herb separately.

For individual preparation and cooking information, see separate entries. Many herbs can be used in less conventional ways too: some, such as **tarragon** and **thyme**, are submerged in bottles of salad oils or vinegars to add extra flavour; others, like mint and **sage**, are made into special teas or *tisanes*, which are drunk for their soothing properties as well as their flavour; and the leaves of yet others such as basil are crushed to extract their essential oils, which are then used in aromatherapy, cosmetics and herbal medicine.

word origin Herb comes from the Latin *herba,* meaning 'green plant' or 'grass'. When the adjective 'herbal' is used as a noun, the old association with healing resurfaces – it means a book that describes herbs, and in particular their healing powers. 'Herbalism', another noun from this adjective, is a type of medicine based on herbal remedies. The American pronunciation of the word (without the 'h' so that it sounds like 'erb') was actually the standard way of saying herb in British English until the 19th century.

● Herbs have been used as medicines for thousands of years. The first herbal was Chinese and was written almost 5000 years ago, although only part of it is known, but the earliest one to survive was written by the Greek physician Dioscorides in the 1st century AD. It described over 500 herbs and their properties so accurately that it became the foundation of most medical practice for the next 1700 years. Many others followed, with later writers gradually adding information on cooking and gardening as well as healing.

● In the smelly rooms that were part and parcel of medieval life, herbs like rosemary and thyme were strewn on the floor to sweeten the air; and many homes would also have had small pomanders or bouquets of fresh or dried herbs imparting their scent to clothes and furniture, forerunners of today's potpourris.

juniper berry

The juniper berry is the small dried fruit of an evergreen shrub (*Juniperus communis*), a member of the cypress family. Unusually for a **spice**, it is native to northern Europe and still grows wild there. The shrub reaches heights of 5m or more, and its fruits, which are actually small cones, vary in colour and shape depending on whether they are male (yellow and catkin-like) or female (blue-green and berry-like). Only the female 'berries' are used, ripened from their original colour over a period of 2–3 years until they become purple-blue; they darken to blue-black as they are dried.

using it Juniper berries are often crushed before use, to release their pungent, slightly sour flavour. They are one of the main flavourings in gin and are occasionally used to flavour beer and schnapps too. In cooking, juniper is used mostly in Scandinavian and German dishes like **sauerkraut**, but a few berries would also add flavour to marinades, sousing liquids for fish like herring, red cabbage dishes, and stuffings and sauces for game, especially partridge. It also goes particularly well with pork.

word origin   Juniper comes from the Latin for the shrub, *Juniperus*.

did you know?

• Both the tree and its berries were believed to have supernatural powers in the ancient world, and these feature in *The Juniper Tree*, a tale collected by the Grimm Brothers. A wicked stepmother kills her stepson and bakes him in a pie, which she then feeds to the boy's father and his daughter. The daughter collects the bones and places them in the juniper tree, where they turn into a bird. The bird passes on the news of the boy's death to various neighbours including the miller, who gives it a millstone, which it uses to kill the stepmother. At this point the bird magically turns back into the little boy, alive and safe.

lemon grass

This is a perennial plant native to South-east Asia that is used as a **herb**. Lemon grass (*Cymbopogon citratus*) can reach about 60cm in height and is cultivated for its long thin stem, which is actually the base of the plant and made up of layers of long, thin, sharp-edged leaves.

using it   Most of the taste is in the lower part of the plant, the first 15cm or so from the bottom of the base. To use lemon grass, therefore, strip off the outer brittle layers and top part of the plant, then bash or bruise the remainder to release the flavour. Depending on the dish, lemon grass is used whole or chopped into thin rounds and is normally added towards the beginning of cooking. It is also available dried in stalks or ground into a powder, neither of which has the true taste of the fresh plant.

Lemon grass is used all over South-east Asia, but is particularly associated with the cooking of Thailand. The whole stalk is added to fish like sea bass, and seafood such as crab, prawns and scallops, either as part of a marinade before they're cooked, or as part of the flavouring when they're baked or steamed. Chopped lemon grass is added

to stir-fries, curries and similar mixtures, but also tastes good with chicken, as part of the stuffing or sauce for a whole roasted bird, or as a fresh flavouring for stews and risottos.

word origin   The English name indicates the fresh citrus flavour.

did you know?

• **Lime** leaf, sometimes called kaffir lime (*Citrus hystrix*), is another Asian flavouring with a citrus base. The beautiful green, figure-of-eight-shaped leaves are widely used in Thai and South-east Asian cooking, added to soups, marinades and stews in much the same way as bay leaf is in western cooking.

marjoram

This 'herb of grace', as Shakespeare called it, belongs to the **mint** family and is closely related to **oregano**, with which it's often confused – in fact, in some countries the two names are interchangeable. There are many types of both **herbs**; only those most widely available and known as marjoram in the United Kingdom are listed here.

Sweet marjoram (*Origanum majorana*), the most delicately flavoured type, originates in the Mediterranean region, but is found all over Europe and western Asia; it can reach 45cm in height, and has small, greyish-green, oval leaves and tiny purple or white flowers borne in knotted clusters along the stems (hence its alternative name of knotted marjoram). Pot or French marjoram (*Origanum onites*), which comes from the eastern Mediterranean, is smaller than sweet marjoram with more strongly flavoured leaves; winter marjoram (*Origanum heracleoticum*), which is native to Greece and the smallest of the three (it rarely grows to more than 25cm), has small leaves that are very strongly flavoured.

using it   Fresh marjoram is usually available, although the dried version is an acceptable substitute. To use fresh, strip the leaves from the stalks and tear, chop or add whole to dishes towards the end of cooking.

Marjoram is used in soups, sauces, stuffings (particularly for poultry) and sausages and with vegetables like carrots and peas.

word origin Marjoram comes from the medieval Latin *majorana*, which may be derived from the classical Latin *maior*, meaning 'larger', 'more important'.

did you know?

● In the ancient world marjoram was a symbol of happiness, and wreaths made from it were used to crown lovers. The Romans introduced it to northern Europe, including Britain, and by medieval times it wasn't just being used to flavour food but to protect against witchcraft; nosegays of sweet marjoram were also believed to ward off plague.

mint

There are several thousand species of plants in the *Labiatae* or mint family, including **herbs** such as **marjoram**, **oregano**, **sage** and **thyme**, in addition to the perennial *Menthe* genus, the subject of this entry. The genus is native to the Mediterranean area, although most species have naturalized themselves all over the world.

The most popular species include garden mint or spearmint (*Mentha spicata*), which gets the latter name from its oval grey-green leaves with their slightly pointy serrated edges; it is the tallest of the readily available varieties, reaching 80cm in height, and the classic cooking mint. Peppermint (*Mentha* x *piperita*), which is probably a hybrid of spearmint and water mint (*Menthe aquatica*), has darkish green leaves with a red tinge to their veins; its flavour is slightly hot and warm like pepper, hence its name. Peppermint is grown all over Europe and especially in North America, as much for its essential oil as its spicy leaves. Moroccan mint (*Mentha spicata* 'Moroccan') is a slightly milder version of spearmint; ginger mint (*Mentha* x *gracilis*) has

greenish-gold serrated leaves with a warm flavour; and apple mint (*Mentha suaveolens*) is a fresh-tasting variety with downy leaves.

using it Fresh mint is available all year round; it doesn't dry well. To use, strip the leaves from their stalks and chop, tear or leave whole. Add during cooking or after.

Spearmint is used as a garnish with more or less anything, but most successfully with new potatoes and peas, and made into a jelly or sauce to serve with roast lamb. It's also chopped and mixed with chillies or cucumber, garlic and Greek yoghurt to make a refreshing raita or chutney to accompany Indian foods; combined with parsley to flavour **bulghur wheat** for tabbouleh; and used as a flavouring for pickles, couscous and pilaffs. Whole sprigs are also sometimes used to decorate drinks like **Pimm's**, juleps and punches, and to make a refreshing tea.

Peppermint is added to food as much for its medicinal qualities as for flavouring. Chewing it is supposed to increase concentration, as good a reason as any to add it to chewing gum, and the fresh antiseptic taste plus its digestive properties make it a popular ingredient in sweets like peppermints, liqueurs like crème de menthe and herbal teas or *tisanes*. An essential oil obtained from the leaves contains menthol, a substance that is both antiseptic and anaesthetic and used widely in various industries to flavour products from cigarettes and toothpaste to herbal remedies. Both ginger and apple mint give their own flavour to salads and boiled vegetables.

word origin Mint comes from *menta*, the Latin version of the name of the Greek nymph, *Minthe*.

did you know?

● In mythical Greece, Pluto (the god of the underworld) took a fancy to Minthe, daughter of the river god. Unfortunately for him, his wife Persephone's reaction was predictable rather than acquiescent and so, depending on which version of the story is being told, either Pluto changed Minthe into a plant to protect her from his wife's vengeance, or Persephone tried to crush her to death with her foot; but Minthe, instead of dying, became an aromatic plant, one that smelled even sweeter after it had been crushed.

nutmeg

This is the kernel of the yellow plum-like fruit of the tropical nutmeg tree (*Myristica fragrans*), a native of the Moluccas in Indonesia, still a major producer along with Grenada in the West Indies. The evergreen tree can reach 10m or more in height and its fruit (which is edible) splits open when ripe to reveal a large seed or nut surrounded by a lacy red outer covering or aril. The aril is removed and dried until it becomes gingery brown, and the lacy strips (called mace) are either flattened into 'blades' or powdered. The nut, meanwhile, is also dried until it darkens, then cracked open to extract the wizened dark brown kernel or nutmeg.

using it Although nutmeg is available ground into a powder, it should be bought whole if possible and grated as needed – it keeps its taste better when stored whole and gives a sharp, warm flavour to food when freshly grated. Mace is occasionally available as blades, but is normally bought ground; its taste is similar to nutmeg, but stronger, so should be used in very small quantities. Both nutmeg and mace can be added at the beginning or end of cooking or as a garnish.

Nutmeg is an ingredient in commercial **spice** mixtures such as mixed spice and **garam masala**, and on its own flavours both savoury and sweet dishes. In savoury cooking, it's stirred into sauces such as **béchamel** or cheese, grated over vegetables like broccoli, mushrooms or petits pois, and occasionally added to pot roasts and stews. In sweet cooking, it's sprinkled over puddings, custards, fruit (especially apple, pineapple and peach), and added to

cakes and biscuits too. Used in moderation, it also brings out the flavour of alcoholic punches and non-alcoholic drinks like warm milk or chocolate. Mace is mostly used to flavour pâtés, in baking or occasionally to flavour drinks, especially mulled wine.

word origin Nutmeg comes from the Latin *nux muscata*, meaning 'musky nut'. The word is also used on a football pitch occasionally – when a player passes the ball between the legs of another player, he or she is said to be 'nutmegging', an imaginative extension of an old use of the word, as slang for 'nuts' or testicles. Mace comes from the Greek *makir*, the name of a type of bark once used as a spice.

did you know?

• There are no recorded sightings of nutmeg in Europe much before the 8th century AD, but it had become fashionable if expensive by medieval times, a popularity that led to a series of invasions of the Moluccas by European countries eager to seize control of the valuable trade in it and other spices. In fairly swift order the islands were occupied first by the Portuguese, then the Dutch and finally the British, who had the foresight to plant *Myristica* seedlings everywhere they went in the world that looked remotely suitable. Most didn't amount to much, but they struck lucky in the volcanic soil of Grenada.

oregano

A **herb** of the **mint** family, oregano is so closely related to and confused with **marjoram** that the word is sometimes used for stronger flavours of either plant; in the United States, in fact, all members of the family (and a few other herbs besides) are known as oregano.

Common oregano (*Origanum vulgare*), which is, confusingly, often called wild marjoram, reaches about 45cm in height; it has tiny mauve flowers and dark green, slightly hairy leaves whose flavour varies from pungent to merely aromatic depending on where it's grown – the nearer it is to its native

Mediterranean climate, the stronger-tasting it becomes. Greek oregano (*Origanum vulgare* ssp. *hirtum*), which is eastern Mediterranean in origin, grows to about the same size as common oregano, but has white flowers and pungent, lighter grey-green leaves. What is called Mexican oregano (*Lippia graveolens*) comes from another branch of the mint family, although its flavour is similar to true oregano.

using it Oregano is widely available fresh, even if the taste is milder in northern regions than in southern ones, and is one of the few herbs where the dried version rivals the fresh. To use fresh in cooking, strip the leaves from the stalks and add whole or chopped, preferably towards the end of cooking.

Oregano is particularly associated with the cooking of southern Europe, especially Italy and Greece. Leaves are often added to tomato-based dishes or mixed into lamb or pork stews, roasts or casseroles; whole sprigs are tucked into barbecued fish and meat, or used as a garnish for pizzas and salads.

word origin Oregano comes from the Greek *oros* (mountain) and *ganos* (joy), and entered the English language in medieval times as *organ*; it went through various adaptations before adopting the modern, American Spanish version of the word during the 18th century.

did you know?

• Historically, it's difficult to untangle marjoram and oregano. The major varieties of both have been known and popular since classical times and were used medicinally and cosmetically as well as in cooking. In Greece, common oregano was thought to be a good antidote to poison, and since both oregano and marjoram were known to have cleansing properties, they were used as bath oils and disinfectants in both Greece and Rome.

paprika

Paprika is the powdered flesh of special varieties of **sweet peppers** (*Capsicum annuum*). The thin-fleshed peppers are mechanically washed, dried, crushed (and if necessary stripped of pith and seeds), then ground; the end result can range from mild and sweet to semi-hot, depending on the specific variety or combination of varieties used in manufacture.

using it At its best (and freshest), paprika is a vibrant deep red in colour; avoid brownish paprika as it is probably stale.

This **spice** is practically synonymous with Hungarian cooking and most savoury dishes from there seem to be flavoured with generous quantities of it, including the archetypal Hungarian goulash, a spicy stew usually made from cubed meat or poultry and vegetables. Spain also has a type of paprika, called pimentón, for which another variety of sweet pepper is smoke-dried before grinding. Slightly paler in colour than Hungarian paprika, pimentón is used to colour and flavour food such as chorizo and paella. Both paprika and pimentón have a particular affinity with pork, veal and chicken and work well in dishes containing them. A little of either added to flour would make a good coating for **escalopes**, and a sprinkling of either would be an attractive garnish for vegetables, egg-based dishes, and pale dips and pâtés.

word origin Paprika comes from the Hungarian *paprikas*, which is derived from the Serbo-Croat *papar*, 'pepper'.

parsley

A member of the same family as the carrot, parsley (*Petroselinum crispum*) is native to southern Europe, although it's now naturalized and grown widely in temperate climates throughout the world. There are three main types: common parsley, a tall biennial **herb** with vibrant green, curly leaves and a mild flavour; flat-leaved or French parsley, a taller, hardier plant with strongly-flavoured flat leaves that look similar to those of its relative, coriander; and the much rarer Hamburg parsley, a flat-leaved plant cultivated for its roots, which are used in the same way as **parsnip**.

using it Fresh parsley is almost always available; it doesn't dry well. It is used as whole sprigs, or the leaves are separated and torn or chopped. Parsley can be added at any point in the cooking process.

Curly-leaved parsley was once more popular than flat-leaved in the United Kingdom, with the reverse being true in other parts of Europe and in the Middle East, but now flat-leaved parsley is just as widely used here. This is the commonest flavouring in the kitchen, added everywhere to stocks, sauces, stews, stuffings, salads, fish, meat, vegetables – you name it, parsley will flavour it – and also used ubiquitously as a garnish, either as is or deep-fried to make it crisper and darker.

Parsley combines well with other herbs (whole sprigs are part of **bouquet garni**; chopped leaves part of *fines herbes*). It also has a natural partnership with garlic: chopped leaves and crushed cloves become persillade, one of the commonest French garnishes; the same two ingredients plus moistened breadcrumbs make a good coating for lamb or pork joints; and parsley, garlic and lemon zest form gremolada, which is traditionally stirred into osso buco at the end of cooking, but could also be used to flavour steamed mussels and stir-fried squid, prawn and mushroom dishes. In Great Britain, chopped parsley is stirred into **béchamel sauce** and served with fish, especially cod, and in the Middle East copious amounts of it are mixed with **bulghur wheat** and lots of fresh mint to make tabbouleh.

word origin Parsley was introduced into Britain by the Romans, vanished during the Dark Ages and reappeared during the Middle Ages as *petersilie*, from the Greek *petroselinon,* which could mean either 'rock parsley' or 'celery', yet another member of the family.

• The Greeks were ambivalent about parsley. It was dedicated to Persephone, the part-time queen of the underworld (see **pomegranate**) because it was supposed to 'visit' her there nine times before sprouting, but it was also believed to have sprung from the blood of heroes and so was used to crown victors at the games and to decorate deserving tombs. The Roman view was simpler: they served parsley at banquets, not just on plates to eat, but as wreaths for guests to wear, since it was believed to maintain sobriety.

pepper

The pepper tree (*Piper nigrum*), a climbing vine native to the Malabar coast of India, is grown for its fruits – small berries (peppercorns) – which are used as a **spice**. India and Indonesia are the major modern suppliers. Peppercorns can be green, black or white, depending on when the berries are harvested during their ripening process. Green peppercorns are berries picked before they ripen; they are either freeze-dried or pickled in brine or vinegar. Black peppercorns are berries picked as they begin to ripen and turn red; they are dried in the sun until they are black and wizened. White peppercorns are berries that remain on the vine until ripe and red; they are processed to remove the outer husk before being dried.

Pink peppercorns, which look and taste like green peppercorns, come from an unrelated plant, *Schinus terebinthifolius*, which is native to Brazil. **Cayenne pepper**, **paprika** and **chilli powder** are all also described as 'pepper', and they too come from unrelated plants, in this case various species of the *Capsicum* family.

using it Black and white peppercorns are available whole, cracked or ready-ground, white being milder in taste than black; green peppercorns, which are fruity in flavour, are only available whole. Peppercorns keep better than already-ground pepper, and are best when freshly milled from a grinder as needed.

Pepper, normally black, is used to flavour practically every food, and the major use is in savoury dishes, during cooking or before serving or eating. Whole peppercorns are a good addition to marinades, pickling mixtures, salamis and stocks, and can be used as decoration for pâtés; cracked or crushed black peppercorns are the traditional coating for steak au poivre, but taste just as good with calves' liver and lamb chops; and ground pepper is added to pretty much everything else. Green peppercorns have an affinity with pork and can be mixed with soured cream to make a sauce for plainly cooked chops; this sauce also tastes good with strong fish like tuna.

More unexpectedly, ground pepper is also used occasionally in baking and to flavour sweet dishes. It lends a lift to spicy sweet biscuits called *pfeffernüsse* (literally, pepper nuts) in Germany and *pepperkaker* in Norway and, tasting a lot better than it sounds, it can be sprinkled over sliced strawberries to make a simple dessert.

word origin Pepper is a corruption of the Latin name for the tree. 'Corn' tagged onto it is a reference to the size of the individual berries and comes from an Indo-European root meaning 'worn-down particle' or 'grain'. Not surprisingly for such a widely used ingredient, it appears in several phrases that either relate to the hotness of its taste or the way it's used, such as 'he's a peppery character' (quick to lose his temper) or 'she peppered the conversation with...' (sprinkled in references throughout).

• Pepper was being cultivated in India by about 2000BC and reached Europe early: first the Phoenicians, then Alexander the Great introduced it to southern Europe, and the Romans eventually controlled its entry and kept both demand and prices up. It was used so abundantly to flavour food in ancient Rome, in fact, that its fame spread far enough to reach the ears of Alaric the Visigoth. And when Alaric besieged Rome in AD408 he demanded nearly 1400 kilos of peppercorns as part of his price for lifting the blockade. The Romans paid up, but two years later he sacked the city anyway.

• By the 11th century pepper was the most popular spice in England and a special (and powerful) guild of pepperers was set up, later to be called *grossarii* after the heavy beam or *peso grosso* used to weigh spices, and from which we probably get the word grocer.

rosemary

Rosemary (*Rosmarinus officinalis*) is an evergreen shrub that is native to the Mediterranean, but now grows widely in temperate areas throughout the world. The bush can reach nearly 2m in height, and is cultivated for its slender spiky leaves, dark green on the upper side and silvery white on the lower, which are used as a **herb**.

using it Fresh rosemary is always available and dries reasonably well. The needle-like leaves can be slightly indigestible whole, so fresh rosemary is better chopped finely before being used, either added during or towards the end of cooking.

The classic partnership is with roast lamb, placed under it as sprigs, poked into it as small leaf clusters or chopped and added to its gravy. But rosemary tastes equally good with chicken, turkey and sausages, is an excellent flavouring for stronger-tasting fish like red mullet and snapper, makes a good herb vinegar and goes just as well with root vegetables, particularly roast potatoes. Branches from the bush also add a good fragrance to barbecue coals, and the stripped woody branches can be pressed into service as emergency skewers as well.

word origin Rosemary comes from the Latin *ros marinus*, meaning 'dew of the sea', perhaps because the shrub grows particularly well close to the sea and often has dew-like bubbles on its branches. To Ophelia it meant remembrance, but in Shakespeare's time rosemary also symbolized faithfulness – Elizabethan wedding parties often sported a sprig of it in much the same way that modern ones wear white carnations.

did you know?

• Rosemary has always been grown as much for its healing powers as for its taste. It was believed to keep you young, rumoured to stimulate the scalp (it is found in many modern shampoos) and thought to be able to kick-start the brain – medieval students used to wear rosemary wreaths in their hair when taking exams. Rosemary oil is still used in aromatherapy.

saffron

This is the most expensive **spice** in the world and it's not hard to see why. First of all it comes from a special type of crocus (*Crocus sativus*) – it is the dried orange-red stigmas of the plant (the three rather lewd-looking slender stalks that wave about attracting pollen into the flower); secondly, the stigmas are so small and delicate they can only be picked by hand; and thirdly (the clincher) it takes about 250,000 stigmas to yield half a kilo of the stuff. The best saffron is reckoned to come from Spain, but it probably originated in Persia; and modern-day Iran, along with India, is still an important supplier.

using it Saffron is available as slender, dark red-gold 'threads' or as a powder. The threads are generally better – apart from anything else you know what you're getting since some powders are adulterated with other, cheaper plants like safflower, marigold or even **turmeric** (occasionally optimistically described as Indian saffron, which it isn't). To use the threads, infuse them in a little warm liquid for about five minutes to extract flavour and colour, then add the whole lot to the dish, preferably towards the end of cooking. For a garnish, heat the saffron threads briefly in a low oven until they crumble slightly, then scatter over the chosen food.

The haunting, warm-bitter flavour of saffron is particularly associated with Mediterranean and Indian cooking, but is used all over the world to add colour and taste to special dishes: it's an ingredient in paella and other rice-based classics like pilaff and biriani, several French fish soups including bouillabaisse, and Italian risotto milanese. In England, saffron was traditionally associated with West Country cooking and was used to flavour and colour cakes and breads. More generally it can be combined with toasted almonds and cream to make a delicate sauce for chicken breasts or white fish; poured with its infusing liquid into cooked potatoes to make a gorgeous-looking as well as -tasting mash; and added to the cooking liquid for rice salads.

word origin Saffron comes, via Old French, from the Arabic *za'faran,* meaning 'yellow'.

did you know?

• The first recorded references to saffron are in an Egyptian scroll of 1550BC. It was used then and later in the ancient world not only in cooking but as a scented oil and as a dye, particularly for clothing; the special association with Buddhism began shortly after the Buddha died, when it was made the official colour for the robes of his monks.
• Although saffron comes from a warm-weather plant, it seems to have taken rather well in England: saffron plantations have existed in the Home Counties for over 300 years, particularly in Essex. Cultivation was so important to one town that it added Saffron to its existing name of Walden.

sage

A hardy evergreen **herb** of the **mint** family, sage is native to the northern Mediterranean, but widely cultivated in temperate areas around the world. There are hundreds of species, including common sage (*Salvia officinalis*), which grows into a 50cm bush with purple-blue flowers and soft, slightly furry oval green leaves; purple sage (*Salvia officinalis purpurascens*), a purple-leaved version of common sage; and clary sage (*Salvia sclarea*), a slightly different, larger species with longer, narrower leaves.

using it Fresh sage is available all year round, but doesn't keep well so should be used within a day or two of buying. Sage is also available dried, either rubbed or ground, but neither has the taste of the fresh herb. Whether fresh or dried, it has a strong flavour, so is best used in small quantities and at the beginning of cooking rather than towards the end.

The traditional partnership is with fatty meat like duck, goose and sausage, where the herb helps digest the richness, but sage is equally good in stuffings for chicken, turkey and pork and adds flavour to the cooking juices for calves' liver and veal escalope. It also goes well with stronger-tasting vegetables like broad beans and tastes good in cheese dishes such as Welsh rarebit. The juices pressed from sage are mixed into cheeses like sage Derby during the production process.

Clary sage occasionally flavours liqueurs and wines such as vermouth, but is mostly grown for its oil, which is used in aromatherapy and as a flavouring for perfumes and soap.

word origin Sage comes from the Latin *salvia,* meaning 'healing plant'.

menstrual periods and to cure a whole range of ailments from diarrhoea to amnesia. And it's always had a special role in dental care – the leaves were used to clean teeth during medieval times, and until relatively recently infusions made from it were used as a mouthwash and to treat bleeding gums.

• *Salvia divinorum*, a type of Mexican sage, has been used there for centuries as a sacred hallucinogenic drug. Since it's legal, it is now being adopted as a recreational smoke in other parts of the Americas too, despite the fact that it's harsh-tasting and expensive.

salt

Salt is a compound made up of the minerals sodium and chloride (NaCl), and sea salt and rock salt are the two basic types. Sea salt, which comes from the sea or from salt springs, is either dried artificially or naturally by the heat of the sun so that only the salt elements remain. The coast of Brittany in France and the town of Maldon in Essex are both centres of sea salt production. Rock salt, which is obtained from the dried-out underground remains of prehistoric seas, is still occasionally mined in the traditional way: brought to the surface in blocks, which are later processed to the desired degree of fineness. More usually now, however, water is pumped into prepared areas of deposit to dissolve it, and the resulting brine is brought to the surface to be heated until the water has evaporated and only salt is left. In Europe there are famous salt quarries at Nantwich in Cheshire and Hallstätt in Austria.

Table salt is rock salt refined into small crystals or fine powder, then usually treated with starch or substances like magnesium carbonate so that it pours easily; some salts also contain small amounts of iodine, which was initially added as a health measure since lack of it in the diet can lead to diseases such as goitre. Saltpetre (potassium or sodium nitrate) is a related compound processed from soil containing decaying animal and plant refuse. It is often used in modern preserving.

When we sweat excessively we lose sodium, a mineral essential to life, and it has to be replaced via the food we eat. Salt is one of the best food sources for sodium and therefore an important ingredient in every cuisine in the world.

Salt is fundamental to the preservation of food. Before canning and freezing were invented, salting food was the most effective way to preserve it because immersing or covering something in salt or a salt solution helps to destroy or slow down the actions of the micro-organisms and enzymes that help to spoil it. And although the necessity for protecting food in this way has passed, our taste for it hasn't, hence the continuing popularity of certain sausages and cured herring. Reducing the water content to a point where the micro-organisms that cause spoilage can't operate (drying) also preserves food, but it takes time to reach this level and the food continues to decay in the meantime; salting something to be dried speeds up the drying process as well as arresting decay, so most food to be dried, such as **prosciutto** and salami, is salted beforehand. Salt is also added to most canned products, and instant snacks and ready meals contain substantial amounts too.

using it In the preparation of food, raw ingredients like aubergines are sometimes lightly salted (*dégorgé*), because by being less moist they will absorb less liquid or fat during cooking. Salt's inhibiting qualities are also used in baking, when it's added to uncooked dough to help control and guide the actions of yeast and other raising agents, as well as contributing flavour to the finished product.

Salt is a good flavour enhancer, and adding it to dishes in moderate quantities during cooking helps to bring out the individual tastes of the other ingredients. If the dish contains salty ingredients such as soy sauce or previously salted products like anchovy, however, extra salt at this stage

shouldn't be necessary and any balancing of flavour is probably best done at the table.

word origin Salt comes from the Indo-European *sal*, which, in one form or another, has been adopted by most European languages: not just English salt, but French *sel*, German *salz* and Italian *sale* too. It appears in many phrases and sayings, most of them reflecting its necessity and value: 'salt of the earth' (unpretentious but admired); 'to salt away' (to save or hoard); and 'an old salt' (usually an experienced sailor, who will have been well 'salted' by the sea).

did you know?

• Salt has been mined and used as a preservative since prehistory, and by Egyptian times it didn't just help food to last longer; it was used in the mummification process to help dead pharaohs last longer as well. The Romans gave their soldiers a *salarium* or salt ration as part of their entitlement, then later a money allowance to buy it (and *salarium* became salary in English). In 13th-century France, the French kings, not slow to climb on a good bandwagon, acknowledged the everyday necessity of salt by taxing it, and the *gabelle*, as the salt tax was called, was one of the bitterly resented injustices that led to the French Revolution. In Africa, the Vakaranga tribe who built Great Zimbabwe, abandoned it to trek hundreds of kilometres when the local supply of salt ran out.

• In the Middle Ages in England, salt had a more unexpected use. When villains and other unfortunates were hung, drawn and quartered, their heads were often exhibited in public as a warning of potential retribution to future wrongdoers. To avoid the embarrassment of putrefaction during this period, the heads were first boiled in lots of salt and cumin seed to help preserve them.

• The average adult intake of salt in the United Kingdom is about 9g a day, which considerably exceeds our requirements (Government recommendations are 6g per day). Most people aren't affected by excess salt intake – the body just gets rid of what isn't needed – but to those who are susceptible it can cause high blood pressure, which is a major risk factor for heart disease and stroke. Reducing salt intake can be difficult, because up to 85 percent of the salt in our diet is hidden in processed foods – a 34.5g packet of crisps contains about 1g, for example, while a 400g can of cream of tomato soup has about 4g.

sorrel

This is a member of the dock family whose leaves are normally used as a **herb,** but also sometimes as a vegetable. There are two types: common sorrel (*Rumex acetosa*), a spinach-like perennial plant with arrowhead-shaped green leaves and thick stalks, and French or buckler leaf sorrel (*Rumex scutatus*), which has smaller, shield-like leaves and a more delicate stalk. Both have become naturalized around the world, although they are native to Europe and Asia. French sorrel is milder and more subtle than common sorrel, but both contain oxalic acid and are therefore fairly sour to taste.

using it The thick stalks can be quite tough and are usually removed before the leaves are used. Sorrel is occasionally cooked in the same way as **spinach** as a vegetable, but needs to be blanched beforehand to remove some of the acidity. It forms the basis of hot and cold summer soups (with potato and cream), and a classic sauce for eggs or fish, especially salmon. Small young leaves can be torn into mixed salads (and the dressing will need less vinegar or lemon juice as a result).

word origin Sorrel comes from the Old French *sorele*, meaning 'sour' or 'acid'.

spices

These are mostly tropical or semi-tropical plants whose dried fruits, flowerbuds, bark or roots are used to flavour food; **herbs,** which are used in much the same way, are (usually) the fresh leaves, stalks or bulbs of temperate plants. Spices include flavourings like **caraway, cumin** and **cardamom** 'seeds' (actually the dried fruits of the plant), **cloves** (the

flowerbuds), **cinnamon** (the inner bark of a tree) and **ginger** and **turmeric** (rhizomes or swollen stems). Some plants yield spices from their fruits and herbs from their leaves (**coriander**), or vegetables from the roots and spices and herbs from the rest of the plant (**fennel**).

using them Spices are normally available dried, whole or ground and, in any of these forms, they are best bought in small quantities since they lose flavour quite quickly. To help prolong their shelf life, store them in a jar large enough to give them some ventilation and keep out of direct sunlight. See separate entries for specific information on individual spices.

    Like herbs, spices are occasionally blended together to create special mixtures. Some of these are now commercially available, although the ingredients used can vary from manufacturer to manufacturer. Mixed spice is a traditional British mixture primarily used in baking, and usually consists of allspice, cinnamon, cloves, coriander, mace and nutmeg. Five-spice powder is Chinese in origin and, confusingly, can sometimes contain six or more individual spices – cassia (see **cinnamon**), cloves, fennel, star anise, Szechuan pepper and/or ginger are usually there somewhere, and cardamom is an occasional addition; five-spice powder is normally used in marinades and stir-fries. See also **chilli powder, curry powder** and **garam masala**.

word origin Spice is probably a variation of the Old French *éspice*, which in turn is related to the Latin *species*, meaning 'goods', a reference to spice's origins as a trade. Initially the meaning was broader than it is today, and included sweeteners like honey and sugar as well as some plants now regarded as herbs. The place where many of the most coveted spices came from (the Moluccas in the Indian Ocean) once supplied so many of Europe's favourites that it was called the Spice Islands.

did you know?

• Although most spices originated in Asia, Europeans discovered them early and there was a brisk trade in pepper and cinnamon by about 1500BC. Overland trails often at least partly followed what was called the Silk Road, designated routes from China and other parts of Asia to Europe, created to satisfy rich Europeans' cravings for silk. Indian and Arab traders controlled the first part of the journey with, in the ancient world, first the Phoenicians, then the Greeks and finally the Romans keeping a stranglehold on both quantity and price as they reached the Mediterranean; later, it was the turn of Italian city states like Genoa and Venice to get rich on the back of the trade.

• Spices were very, very expensive in medieval Europe, so of course they became fashion items in rich kitchens. The more that were added to a dish, the better – many recipes of the age included four or five of them. This probably led to the idea that spices were used to disguise food that was going off, but in fact it's just as likely to have been a display of conspicuous consumption plus an attempt to make dull food more interesting.

• It was the need to find alternative ways to guarantee supplies and reduce the cost of spices that inspired several of the great sea explorations of the 15th and 16th centuries, and in particular attempts to find a new route to India where many came from. Christopher Columbus didn't find India in 1492 (although he thought he had at first, hence the name West Indies), but he did discover (or rediscover) America, and unknown spices like chilli pepper. Four years later, Vasco da Gama *did* make it to India and after this spices gradually became more available and a bit cheaper.

tamarind

Although it is normally used as a **spice**, tamarind is actually a **legume**, part of the same family of podded plants as the bean and the peanut. The curved, slightly hairy brown pods come from a tall evergreen tree, *Tamarindus indica*, which is native to tropical Africa, but now cultivated also in South-east Asia, India and the West Indies. The pods are harvested ripe and the outer part discarded; the tart, reddish-brown, fibrous pulp inside, which contains anything

from 1–10 large seeds, is then either semi-dried (usually seeds and all) and pressed into 'cakes', or processed into a purée.

using it To use tamarind cake, break off the amount needed, just cover with hot water and soak for about 30 minutes. Then remove any seeds before pressing the softened pulp through a sieve with the soaking liquid. Tamarind purée is easier to use as it simply needs to be thinned out with a little hot water or added as is to recipes.

Tamarind is primarily used in Indian and South-east Asian cooking to flavour meat and vegetable dishes and as an occasional basis for chutney. In the West Indies it flavours a refreshing drink made by soaking the pulp in water overnight, then straining it and adding sugar to taste. Commercially, it's an ingredient in Worcestershire sauce.

word origin Tamarind comes via Latin from the Arabic *tamar hindi*, meaning 'Indian date'.

tarragon

There are two main types of this **herb** of the daisy family. The Rolls-Royce version is French tarragon (*Artemisia dracunculus*), a perennial plant native to southern Europe and western Asia that can reach 75cm in height. Its long, floppy, thin green leaves have a warming peppery, aniseed taste. The other type is the similar-looking but coarser-tasting Russian tarragon (*Artemisia dracunculoides*), which is native to Siberia.

using it Fresh tarragon is widely available. Leaves are usually stripped from the stalks and added whole or chopped into dishes towards the end of cooking. Dried tarragon retains much of the flavour of the fresh herb.

Tarragon is one of the herbs that make up *fines herbes* (see **chive**), and is a classic flavouring in **béarnaise sauce** and some mayonnaise-based sauces. The traditional partnership, however, is with chicken: chopped into cream as a sauce for poached or fried breasts; a few sprigs tucked inside the cavity of a whole bird to be roasted; or chopped leaves added to the stuffing and gravy that are to be served with it. Tarragon is also a good salad herb, especially for green, tomato and potato salads, and makes an excellent filling for omelettes. Commercially it is used to flavour mustard and wine vinegar.

word origin Tarragon probably comes indirectly from the medieval Greek *tarkhon* or the classical *drakon*, both meaning 'dragon', although whether this is because of the shape of the root, the heat of the leaf or its supposed ability to cure snake bites isn't known.

thyme

There are many species of this small, slightly resinous perennial **herb** of the **mint** family, which is native to the Mediterranean, but now found all over the world in cool areas like Greenland as well as temperate ones such as Europe and northern America. Common thyme (*Thymus vulgaris*) is the one with the neat, pungent green leaves; golden thyme (*Thymus vulgaris aureus*) has green leaves that turn gold in summer. Others include wild thyme (*Thymus praecox* spp. *arcticus*), a creeping plant with small leaves and a milder taste than common thyme; and lemon thyme (*Thymus* x *citriodorus*), which has fairly large green leaves by thyme standards and (not surprisingly) a lemon flavour.

using it Fresh thyme, which isn't as aromatic in northern areas as it is in southern ones, is widely available fresh; the dried version is an acceptable substitute. Fresh leaves are usually stripped from the stalks and added whole to dishes towards the end of cooking or scattered over before serving.

Thyme is a part of a classic **bouquet garni**; a popular flavouring for honey as well as for barbecued meat and fish (it can be put into marinades for them, scattered on the coals, or spread over them whilst they are being cooked); and is used to garnish pizzas and flavour tomato-based dishes. In Britain, thyme is also traditionally stirred into sauces and soups, is a classic herb for stuffings, added to fish and chicken dishes, and is a good flavouring for beef stews and casseroles. The distinctive taste of lemon thyme can be used in the same way as **tarragon** in chicken dishes, or added to fish or even sweet custards.

word origin Thyme comes from the Greek *thuein,* meaning to 'burn sacrificially'.

turmeric

This is the rhizome (swollen underground stem system) of *Curcuma longa*, a perennial tropical plant related to ginger, which is native to India and South-east Asia. These areas, as well as the West Indies and Peru, are the major producers.

The turmeric plant, which grows to about a metre in height, has a short stalk and large, green oval leaves. The rhizome is smaller than that of ginger, but with a similar knotted woody rind; the flesh inside is much brighter in colour, normally a vibrant orange. After harvesting, turmeric rhizomes are sometimes used fresh in producing areas; usually, however, they are cleaned, boiled and dried, then either left whole or ground into a powder. After drying, the colour fades to a brightish yellow.

using it Although it's much more widely available as a powder in the United Kingdom, turmeric 'root' can occasionally be found in larger supermarkets or Asian stores. The root can be treated in the same way as ginger, although it's much harder to peel and grate. The powder keeps its colour well, but loses its flavour quite quickly.

Commercially, turmeric is used both for its earthy warming flavour and its colour in curry powder, in most made mustards and in pickles such as piccalilli. The similarity in colour to **saffron** (although it doesn't have nearly such a subtle taste) and dissimilarity in price (it's a fraction of saffron's cost) mean that turmeric is also sometimes used as a substitute for it. On its own, it gives a good, slightly sharp taste to rice and seafood dishes, stir-fries, and lentil and vegetable stews.

word origin Turmeric comes from the Old French *terre mérite*, meaning 'deserving earth', although why isn't clear.

• Not surprisingly, given its distinctive colour, turmeric has been used as a dye for many centuries. Less well known is its reputation as a cosmetic: in India a cream made of turmeric is used as a depilatory to ensure smooth skin, and many traditional Hindu brides put some turmeric on their face on their wedding day.

vanilla

Vanilla is the pod-like seeded fruit of a tall climbing orchid, *Vanilla planifolia*, which is native to Central America. It is still grown there and in other tropical areas such as the Malagasy Republic (previously Madagascar) and the Comoros and Reunion islands in the Indian Ocean. The pods are harvested before they are totally ripe and cured to bring out their flavour by being steamed, then left to ferment and dry for anything up to three months. At the end of this period, the once yellow-green pods will have become blackened and leathery, and covered with tiny frosty crystals of vanillin, the substance that gives vanilla its unique flavour.

Chopped vanilla pods are soaked in alcohol and water to produce 'pure' vanilla essence or extract. A synthetic form of vanillin, obtained from a variety of sources including wood pulp, is used to make vanilla flavouring.

using it Both pods and pure essence or extract are expensive, but keep indefinitely; vanilla flavouring keeps well too and is cheaper, although it lacks the subtlety and fragrance of the real thing. Pods can be added whole to dishes during cooking,or they can be slit open (the seeds may be scraped out and used separately). Afterwards, the pods can be rinsed and dried, then used again or stored in a container of caster sugar to flavour it and make vanilla sugar.

The unique rich flavour is nearly always used in sweet cooking or baking. Pods, parts of pods or seeds infuse custard, particularly that used as a base for ice-cream, as well as chocolate dishes and fruit compotes. Vanilla essence and vanilla sugar flavour many cakes, biscuits and desserts.

word origin Vanilla comes from the Spanish *vainilla*, meaning 'little sheath' or 'pod'.

• In its homeland, vanilla was primarily used to flavour drinking chocolate, and it was probably the Aztec king Montezuma who introduced the drink and its flavouring to Spanish conquistadors. The Spanish brought both vanilla and chocolate to Europe during the 16th century, and from there they spread around the globe.
• The vanilla orchid could pollinate itself in its native area, but it wasn't capable of doing this anywhere else. So although the plant was taken to Madagascar and Réunion by the French early in the 19th century, it wasn't until 1841 that commercial growing could begin there. This was made possible by a 12-year-old slave on Réunion named Edmond Albius, who came up with a simple method of artificial pollination.

Sauces & Condiments

What better way to add a bit of sparkle to your meal than with the judicious use of sauces and condiments? A sauce can turn ordinary food into truly fab food, and this doesn't necessarily mean spending hours in the kitchen. Follow a few basic rules and you can come up with something simple that will lift and complement a dish rather than overpower it. The sauce-making course at my cookery school is one of the most popular. People are fascinated by sauces and we aim to take the mystery out of them, so that they become second nature to make.

I find that the classic combinations work best: steak with béarnaise,

seared cod with beurre blanc, lamb with tomato and basil sauce, big chips with ketchup. These are not just accidental partnerships,

...reach into the larder and add new inspiration to your cooking!
Nick Nairn

but all-time winners. They have been tried and tested over many years and, quite simply, work really well together.

If making a béarnaise sauce is not for you, then there are limitless possibilities open to us nowadays with the ever-increasing number of sauces and condiments arriving in our shops from all over the world. Experiment with them to your heart's content, but always remember to think about which flavours go with what. Fusion cooking in the wrong hands can be a disaster, so forget about adding a dash of Thai fish sauce to your boiled eggs in the morning – it just won't work. Instead, try contrasts of sweet and salt, sweet and sour, hot and cold, hot and sour, remembering all the time exactly what you are trying to bring out in a dish.

In this section you will find the fascinating stories that lie behind both familiar and more obscure sauces and condiments. Enjoy reading them, then get into the kitchen, reach into the larder and add new inspiration to your cooking!

Nick Nairn

béarnaise sauce

This creamy **sauce** is made from egg yolks, butter, wine vinegar and herbs. The egg yolks are beaten with a reduction of vinegar, tarragon and shallots (boiled together to evaporate and concentrate the flavour), then the butter is slowly whisked in, either in small knobs or melted, until the mixture is the consistency of mayonnaise. The sauce is finished by stirring in fresh herbs such as tarragon, chervil or *fines herbes* (see **chive**), and is served warm.

using it Béarnaise should be made as near to serving as possible. It is traditionally spooned onto grilled steak and fish, especially salmon or salmon trout, but is also delicious with eggs, boiled new potatoes and other vegetables. To make it into sauce choron, stir in a tablespoon or two of tomato purée with the herbs; for sauce paloise, flavour with chopped mint instead of tarragon.

word origin Béarnaise means 'something that comes from Béarn', a region in south-western France.

did you know?

• The link between the sauce and the area is tenuous and revolves around the 16th-century French king Henri IV, who came from Béarn (he was the one who promised to put a 'chicken in every pot'). He did not, of course, invent the sauce himself; it was created during the 1830s by the chef at a restaurant in St-Germain-en-Laye near Paris called the Pavillon Henri IV.

béchamel sauce

A savoury mixture of milk, flour and butter, béchamel is *the* classic French white **sauce**. It's made by stirring equal quantities of flour and melted butter together to make a smooth paste or roux, then mixing in milk and simmering until thickened and smooth. The milk is often flavoured by warming it with an onion, a bay leaf and some peppercorns and then leaving it for at least 10 minutes to infuse; the flavourings are strained out before adding the milk to the roux. Alternatively, the sauce can be flavoured with salt, pepper and grated nutmeg at the end of cooking.

Béchamel can be thin (when it is the base for soups and other sauces), medium (to coat cooked food) or thick (as the base for mixtures that need to be bound together). The proportions of roux to milk govern the consistency: about 250ml milk and 20g each of flour and butter will make a medium sauce.

using it This is the 'mother' of many other sauces, including: sauce aurore (flavoured with tomato purée), sauce mornay (flavoured with grated Gruyère or Parmesan cheese and enriched with egg yolk), parsley sauce (with chopped parsley) and sauce soubise (with cooked onions).

Béchamel is added to dishes during cooking or served hot as an accompaniment. Used during cooking, it combines other ingredients like sliced potatoes or fish into classic moist *gratins* or pie fillings, and poured between layers or on top of pasta like lasagne, it adds richness and contrast to the finished dish. A basic béchamel can be served as an accompaniment to cooked vegetables, eggs, fish or meat. Mornay sauce is traditionally served with cauliflower or used to make macaroni cheese; parsley sauce traditionally accompanies white fish fillets such as cod and sole; and soubise is a classic partner for steak, sausages and chops.

word origin Béchamel is named for a 17th-century French nobleman, the Marquis Louis de Béchamel, a member of the court of king Louis XIV. Mornay was either the 17th-century Huguenot writer Philippe de Mornay or a famous chef of that name.

caper

The caper is the pickled or preserved green flowerbud of a straggling bushy shrub (*Capparis spinosa*), which is native to the Mediterranean area; major producers include southern France, Italy, Spain and northern Africa.

During the growing season raw caper buds are picked every 10 days or so and graded by size, the smallest being the most desirable. In France there are several different categories, from the best and smallest called *nonpareille,* progressing in size and diminishing desirability through *surfine*, *capucine*, *fine* and *commune*. The fresh buds are bland to taste and are either pickled in brine or layered in salt to develop their characteristic, slightly bitter taste. Semi-mature fruits of the plant, called caperberries, are also sometimes pickled and used in the same way or as a condiment.

using it Capers sold in jars will keep indefinitely; once opened, however, they should be stored in the refrigerator. Those preserved in salt need to be rinsed under cold running water or soaked for 30–60 minutes to remove the salt before being added to recipes. As they are pungent, capers are normally used in small quantities.

Not surprisingly, given their origin, capers are particularly associated with Mediterranean cooking. In France they are an ingredient in the traditional butter sauce served with skate, part of the spicy dip called tapenade (see **olive**) and added to mayonnaise to create tartare sauce, while in Italy they are sprinkled over pizza or blended with anchovy to make a sauce for swordfish or veal escalopes. In the United Kingdom the classic dish is caper sauce, a traditional accompaniment to mutton, lamb, veal or fish, which is made by blending flour and melted butter to a paste, then adding meat cooking juices, stock, drained mashed capers and a dash of vinegar, and stirring until thick.

word origin Caper comes from the Latin for the plant, *capparis*.

did you know?

• Caper buds have been pickled for thousands of years, since at least classical Greek and Roman times, and have been used in Britain since the 15th century. Medicinally, they are alleged to reduce flatulence, and infusions made from the root of the plant were once used to treat arthritis and gout.

chutney

A chutney is a preserved or fresh relish similar to **pickle**, made from herbs, spices, fruit or vegetables. There are two main types: a traditional British-style chutney is preserved by being cooked, and is usually quite sweet, whereas an Indian-style chutney can be preserved or fresh, and is normally hotter and more sour-tasting. Preserved chutneys are made by cooking fruit or vegetables slowly with herbs, spices, sugar and vinegar until they reach the consistency of chunky jam. A fresh chutney is usually uncooked and consists of various herbs, spices and/or fruits pounded or processed to a paste, often with yoghurt.

using it Outside the Indian subcontinent, most chutneys are commercially made preserves that will keep more or less indefinitely, although some need to be refrigerated after they are opened. Home-made preserved chutney should be stored for at least 2–3 months before being used, so it has time to 'mature' in flavour. Fresh chutney is perishable, best eaten on the day it's made, although most will keep for a day or so in the refrigerator.

A chutney is basically a flavour-enhancer for other food. British-style ones are served with cold meats, meat pies or cheese and occasionally with hot food like sausages and barbecued meat. Outside the subcontinent, Indian-style chutneys, fresh or preserved, are served as appetizers with poppadoms and more generally as accompaniments to plainer meat or vegetable dishes.

Chutney is used occasionally in cooking too: mango chutney and curry powder mixed with mayonnaise makes a good dressing for egg, potato and poultry salads; tomato chutney can give extra piquancy to a sauce or baste for grilled meats; and a spoonful of herb-based chutney such as mint or coriander will add extra flavour to stuffings for vegetables and dishes like Scotch egg.

word origin Chutney comes from the Hindi *chatni,* meaning 'strong spices'.

did you know?

• Chutneys originated in India as mixtures of spices and herbs ground to a paste with ingredients like lime, tamarind or mango and were made fresh for each meal, normally as an accompaniment to plainer dishes like rice and lentils. The British found them during their occupation of the country and brought back their taste for them when they returned home. The first anglicized commercial chutneys appeared during the early 19th century.

condiment

Condiments are flavourings or mixtures of flavourings added to dishes at the table to complement the taste of the food and to help digest it. They include single ingredients like **pepper**, **salt**, **mustard** and **vinegar**, **herbs** and **spices**, and prepared products such as bottled sauces, **pickles**, **chutneys** and **ketchups**.

using it Habits vary from country to country and from dish to dish, but most people sprinkle, spread or shake something over some of their cooked or uncooked food before they eat it. In the English-speaking world bottled sauces like **Worcestershire**, **Tabasco** and especially ketchup are popular; the French prefer 'created' sauces like **béarnaise** and **mayonnaise**; and the Italians

use **olives** and spicy pickled fruit mostardas. Other parts of the world are equally addicted: India has a whole range of popular chutneys and pickles; the Chinese and Japanese add **soy sauce** to their food; many South-east Asians use **fish sauce** instead; and in northern Africa, fiery harissa sauce is a necessary accompaniment to many dishes.

word origin Condiment comes from the Latin *condire,* meaning 'to preserve or pickle'.

did you know?

• One of the initial purposes of a condiment (as the origin of the name suggests) was to help prolong the life of fresh food before the invention of freezing or canning. Both salt and vinegar have preservative qualities so, although they can be used as condiments in themselves, they have also always been added to almost all pickles, chutneys and bottled sauces as part of the preservation process.

custard

Custard can be any of three things: a classic French sweet **sauce** (called crème anglaise) made from eggs, sugar and flavoured milk or cream; an approximation of this made from a commercial cornflour and sugar powder that is mixed with milk; and any sweet or savoury mixture containing milk or cream and eggs that is 'set' by baking.

Custard sauce is made by beating egg yolks with sugar in a heatproof bowl set over simmering water, then gradually adding warm milk (usually flavoured with vanilla) and stirring until slightly thickened. When ready, the custard will coat the back of the spoon and a finger drawn across will leave a clear trail. Proportions vary depending on how thick the custard is to be, but 4–5 egg yolks to 500ml milk is standard. Occasionally fewer egg yolks are used and cornflour is added to help with the thickening; the cornflour also makes the sauce less likely to curdle if overheated.

Commercial custard powder is made into a sauce by mixing it to a paste with a little cold milk, then gradually stirring this into hot milk and simmering briefly until smooth and thickened.

A set custard is usually baked in a dish, or it may be the sweet or savoury filling for a pastry case (see **quiche**). Whole eggs are used, or whole eggs with extra egg yolks to make a richer mixture. To prevent overcooking and to maintain the required even heat, dishes containing custards are set in a bain-marie (a shallow tin half-filled with hot water) for baking.

using it Vanilla is the basic flavouring for sweet custard (when using a pod, add it to the milk before warming and leave to infuse for 10–15 minutes; stir in vanilla essence at the end of cooking), but grated orange zest, chocolate, coffee, liqueurs such as Cointreau and spices like nutmeg or cinnamon can also be used.

Custard sauce is served hot or cold as an accompaniment to stewed fruit, pies, tarts, crumbles and steamed puddings. It's also the basis of other sweet dishes such as traditional ice-cream and is layered into trifle. A very thick version of custard sauce, called crème pâtissière or pastry cream, is used to fill choux pastries such as éclairs, as well as French fruit tarts. Sweet baked custards include crème caramel and Spanish flan.

word origin Custard comes from the Middle English *crustade*, meaning tart with a filling. There are literal custard pies and metaphorical ones – the latter describes a type of slapstick humour and can be blamed on early Hollywood, where in the era of silent films there was great emphasis (not surprisingly) on broad, visual gags. Throwing custard pies became so popular in early movies, in fact, that special ones were made for the film studios with extra-thick pastry

and extra runny custard that would 'splat' satisfactorily.

did you know?

* During their first heyday in the Middle Ages, custards were open savoury tarts with a meat or fish filling 'set' in a heavy egg and cream mixture, a direct forerunner of modern quiche. Over time, however, the name became associated with the setting mixture itself, which gradually became a separate dish.
* Custard powder was invented in England in the mid-19th century by a chemist named Alfred Bird. His wife was allergic to eggs, so he experimented with various ingredients until he produced the cornflour and sugar mixture that is still the basis of the modern powder. The bright yellow colour is created artificially, by adding annatto.

fish sauce

Called nam pla in Thailand and nuoc-mam in Vietnam, this is a flavouring used all over South-east Asia, both in cooking and as a **condiment**. It's made from liquid drawn off from fish fermented in vats of salt and water brine, then matured in the sun before being bottled. It smells terrible, but blends well with other ingredients when cooked.

using it In most western countries, fish **sauce** is used almost exclusively in South-east Asian cooking, but since it resembles anchovy essence it could be substituted for that flavouring in other recipes.

word origin Both the Thai and Vietnamese names mean 'fish water'.

did you know?

* Fish sauce is probably the nearest modern equivalent to garum or liquamen, a seasoning used to flavour just about everything from salad dressings to pies in ancient Greece and Rome. It was made from the fermented entrails of various fish, including anchovy and tuna.

gherkin

The gherkin is a small pickled **cucumber**, made from either dwarf, usually ridged, varieties of the common cucumber (*Cucumis sativus*), which ranges in length from 4–10cm, or a West Indian gherkin (*Cucumis anguria*), a rough-skinned type that rarely exceeds 5cm in size. Pickled gherkins can be fermented or unfermented. Fermented gherkins are cured in flavoured brine for several weeks, then cleaned, cooked briefly and bottled in vinegar with flavourings like dill, bay leaf, peppercorns and coriander seeds. Unfermented gherkins can be steeped briefly in brine, but are usually cooked in a vinegar solution, then drained and bottled. Gherkins are particularly popular in eastern Europe and North America.

using it The classic use for gherkins is as a garnish for meat pâtés, chopped liver and spiced or salted beef, or with these or similar ingredients as a sandwich filling. Midget gherkins, called cornichons, are the traditional accompaniment to French charcuterie (pork-based cured meat like salami and garlic sausage, often served as a first course). Finely chopped gherkin is also added to mayonnaise to make sauces like tartare.

word origin Gherkin comes from the Dutch *gurkkijn*, which is derived indirectly from the Middle Greek for little cucumber, *angourion*. *Cornichon* is French and means 'little horn'.

did you know?

• Dwarf cucumbers and gherkins are part of the large *Cucurbitaceae* family of plants whose members come from several continents. The cucumber itself is Asian; the West Indian gherkin, along with relatives such as watermelon, originated in Africa and was introduced into the Americas through the slave trade, while yet other members of the family like the pumpkin are actually native to the Americas.

gravy

Gravy is slightly thickened liquid traditionally made from the caramelized cooking juices of (usually) roasted meat, in the tin vacated by it. To make traditional meat gravy, seasonings and liquid (usually stock, occasionally wine or water) are stirred into the pan 'juices' (the liquid drippings and brown sediment that come from the meat while it's cooking), then boiled over a high heat until they concentrate and thicken a little; a separate thickening agent like flour is sometimes stirred into the juices and browned before the stock is added. Although most gravy is meat- or poultry-based, technically one could also be made from fried or roasted fish and fish stock, or even from braised vegetables and their cooking liquid.

using it Classic gravy is made on the day from (preferably) home-made stock and served immediately with the food it has been created to accompany. In real life, however, various shortcuts are usually employed: the stock is made from diluted stock cubes or bouillon powder, or the whole thing is made from commercial gravy powder or granules that need only to be dissolved in boiling water and left to 'set' before being served.

Gravy lends itself to all sorts of additions. A tablespoon or two of wine is one of the most obvious – red or Madeira adds depth to red meat gravies, while white wine works similar miracles for white meat like chicken; a teaspoon of redcurrant jelly stirred into lamb or game gravy improves its colour and adds sweetness, while a similar amount of horseradish relish spices up a beef gravy. More substantial ingredients like shallots, caramelized onions or sliced mushrooms can also be added, particularly to gravy for red meat.

word origin Gravy comes from either the Old French *graine,* meaning 'meat', or grané, 'grain' (early sauces for stews were called granés and normally included 'grains' of spice).

• *Granés* were popular all over Europe during medieval times and were basically boiled white meat or fish served in a thick sauce. The cooking broth was the basis of the sauce, spices like ginger and cinnamon were popular additions and it was usually thickened with ground almonds or even eggs and cheese. During the 17th century roasted meats were popular and the idea of serving them with a version of the early sauce made from roasting-tin drippings gradually evolved.

hollandaise sauce

This is a classic savoury **sauce** based on egg yolks and butter. There are several ways to make it, but the traditional method is to whisk egg yolks with a little water over heat (usually in a bowl set over a pan of simmering water) until very thick and light, then to gradually add warm, melted butter and whisk to the consistency of thick cream. Lemon juice is added to flavour the sauce. Standard proportions are about 3 egg yolks to 175g unsalted butter.

using it Hollandaise is traditionally served warm with poached salmon, turbot, steak and asparagus. It also forms the basis of several other sauces, including sauce maltaise (flavoured with blood-orange juice and grated zest) for poached white fish and vegetables; sauce mousseline (enriched with whipped cream), good with poached or baked chicken breast, eggs and vegetables like cauliflower; and sauce moutarde (with Dijon mustard), excellent with steak and chops.

word origin The modern name is French, although the translation ('Dutch sauce') was used in English from about the 16th century. The sauce may have been invented by French Huguenots exiled in Holland, hence the name.

• Making a thickened sauce from butter and egg yolks is a relatively modern idea; in the Middle Ages, breadcrumbs or ground almonds were used as thickeners, succeeded by flour around the 16th century. The first egg and butter emulsion was a 'fragrant' sauce for asparagus, given in 1651 by the great French chef and writer La Varenne in his book *Le Cuisinier François*.

horseradish

The horseradish (*Armoracia rusticana*) is the tapering root of a leafy weed that belongs to the same family of plants as the cabbage and is native to south-eastern Europe and western Asia. Despite the name, it is only distantly related to radish. Horseradish root, which can reach lengths of up to 50cm, has a brownish-yellow skin and white flesh. Its distinctive hot taste is caused by sinigrin, a substance also found in some types of mustard (another distant relative). Horseradish is popular in eastern and northern Europe, particularly in Scandinavia, Germany and Britain.

using it Although horseradish is normally sold ready prepared as a **sauce** or cream, the fresh root is sometimes available during late spring and summer, its natural season. It should be firm and will keep for about a week; once cut, however, it deteriorates quickly, and leftovers need to be preserved in some way – drying or mixing with vinegar will both work. To use, peel off the skin and remove the woody core.

An averagely hot horseradish sauce can be made by stirring 2 tablespoons of grated fresh root into 200ml of cream (whipped double or whipping cream or crème fraîche), or a mixture of cream and Greek yoghurt, with a little wine vinegar, seasoning and sugar to taste. Other ingredients like mustard, grated cooked beetroot or even grated apple can be added for extra flavour.

Horseradish cream or sauce is traditionally served with roast beef and hot-smoked fish, especially mackerel or trout, but a spoonful or two can also be stirred into fish mousse or pâté mixtures, into softened butter (to serve with steaks or pork chops) and into mayonnaise to dress hearty potato, beetroot or egg salads. It will also give some bite to beef or game stews, preferably adding it just before serving since its heat disappears with cooking.

word origin Horseradish comes from the Old English *hoarse,* meaning 'large and coarse', and the Latin *radix,* 'root'.

did you know?

• Grated horseradish is sometimes served as part of *maror,* the bitter herbs served at a Jewish Passover feast to symbolize the bitterness of slavery. It's pungent rather than bitter, however, and probably wasn't one of the original five Biblical bitter herbs (the most likely candidates are bitter lettuce, endive, knapweed, sea holly and sow thistle).

ketchup

A salty-sweet preserved **condiment**, ketchup is made in roughly the same way as **chutney**. Although technically it could be created from any ingredient, in reality only mushroom and tomato ketchups are now produced commercially and only tomato, a thick, smooth pouring sauce made from concentrated tomato pulp, salt, sugars and vinegar, is widely popular.

using it Ketchup keeps indefinitely, although this is rarely put to the test. Almost every home has its bottle of the tomato version somewhere in the kitchen since it's the standard accompaniment to many of the staple fast foods of the English-speaking world, such as burgers, fish and chips, sausages and scrambled eggs. It's occasionally mixed into dishes before cooking too: home-made hamburgers, shepherd's pie and meat loaf, for example. Many smoked fish pâtés and

dips could also benefit from a tablespoon or two.

word origin Ketchup comes from the Chinese *koetsiap,* meaning 'pickled fish sauce' – although modern ketchup is a western phenomenon, it's descended from oriental fish sauces.

did you know?

• When ketchups first arrived in Britain in the 17th century, they were thinner, darker and more pungent than they are now and made from ingredients like walnuts, oysters and fermented mushrooms – more like Worcestershire sauce (which also has oriental ancestors) than the modern-day relish. It was the Americans who first came up with the idea of making a ketchup from tomatoes towards the end of the 18th century, and about a hundred years after that, Heinz first began to make its classic version.

Marmite™

Marmite is a thick, dark brown, slightly sticky paste made by concentrating spent brewer's **yeast**, then mixing it either with vegetable extract, salt, vitamins and spices (the UK version) or sugar, wheatgerm extract, caramel, mineral salt plus vitamins and spices (the New Zealand version).

using it Spread over toast or bread, Marmite is one of the great comfort foods, and the addition of a boiled egg or two makes the cosy snack into a meal. It can be used in cooking too, and is particularly useful in vegetarian cooking: a spoonful or two stirred into vegetable stocks, soups or stews gives them colour and richness, and it can add extra taste and 'bite' to otherwise bland bean dishes as well.

word origin The word marmite is French and describes a cooking pot with two handles; it may come from an older French word meaning 'hypocrite' (because you couldn't tell what was cooking from looking at the pot).

• Marmite was the brainchild of Justus von Liebig, a 19th-century German chemist who discovered that spent yeast could be processed into something that tasted meaty. It has been manufactured for just over a hundred years in Burton-on-Trent in England; most of the yeast comes from Bass's Brewery nearby, and the brewery pays the company to remove it! As a yeast extract, Marmite is particularly useful for vegans and vegetarians since it contains a number of B vitamins, including B12, which is normally only obtained from animal sources and can be lacking in a meatless, fishless diet.

mayonnaise

This is a thick, cold **sauce** or dressing made from egg yolks, oil and flavourings like vinegar, lemon juice, mustard and seasonings. Classically, the oil used is olive, but good-quality vegetable, groundnut, corn or sunflower oil are sometimes substituted (or mixed with olive oil) to give a more neutral taste. Standard proportions are 1 egg yolk to 175ml oil.

The 'tricks' to making mayonnaise by hand are that the ingredients should be at room temperature, that the yolks should be beaten until thick before the oil is added, and that the oil should be whisked in drop by drop at first, gradually increasing the amount as the sauce thickens. Some flavourings such as mustard are mixed with the yolks at the beginning of the process, but most, like lemon juice and vinegar, are beaten in towards the end, alternating with the oil. Making mayonnaise in a food processor is a bit easier and faster.

If the oil is added too quickly at the beginning, the mayonnaise can curdle, or separate into its component parts. It can be rescued by whisking the curdled mixture, drop by drop, into another egg yolk, then continuing with the gradual addition of the rest of the oil.

The FSA advise that raw eggs (uncooked) and dishes made from them may pose a health risk. Some vulnerable groups should avoid raw eggs completely (see **egg**).

using it Ready-made mayonnaise, in jars, tubs and tubes, is now widely available and keeps indefinitely, although once opened it should be stored in the refrigerator. Home-made mayonnaise will keep for about a week in the refrigerator.

Classic mayonnaise is rich, and is often mixed with other ingredients that have a similar consistency but a lighter taste, like Greek yoghurt, before being used in dishes. It is also the basis of other sauces and dressings, including aioli (flavoured with lots of crushed garlic); blue-cheese dressing (mashed with softened blue cheese); sauce rémoulade (with Dijon mustard, capers, gherkins, anchovies and herbs); tartare sauce (with chopped hard-boiled egg, onion or chives, gherkins, capers and herbs); and thousand island dressing (with tomato ketchup, chopped pimiento-stuffed green olives, chilli and sweet peppers, and spring onions).

Mayonnaise can be used to dress green and mixed salads, but is more usually mixed with seafood, poultry, eggs and vegetables to create luxurious cold dishes that can be served as first courses, main dishes or even as part of other dishes (like avocado stuffed with seafood mayonnaise), depending on the ingredient(s). The Belgians and Dutch use mayonnaise as a **condiment** with chips, and it's essential in sandwiches like BLT.

word origin There are almost as many guesses about this as there are variations of the dish. Pole position is usually given to *mahonnaise*, meaning 'of Mahon', the name of the capital of Minorca in the Mediterranean. (Mayonnaise could have been invented to celebrate the capture of Port Mahon by the French Duc de Richelieu in 1756.) Other possibilities include being a corruption of *bayonnaise*, something that comes from the city of Bayonne in south-western France, or the Old French *moyeu,* meaning 'egg yolk'.

• Not all mayonnaise contains eggs. Greek skordalia, for instance, is made by pounding generous amounts of garlic in a mortar, then adding oil in the same way as for mayonnaise until the mixture is thick, at which point ground nuts (usually almonds) and soaked breadcrumbs are stirred in; lemon juice or vinegar and chopped herbs to taste are also often added. Skordalia is served with grilled or fried fish or fried sliced aubergine, but could also be substituted for conventional mayonnaise in many dishes.

mustard

This is a **condiment** made from the seeds of any of three plants of the **cabbage** family: white or yellow mustard (*Sinapis alba*), which is native to Mediterranean Europe, has large, mild yellow seeds and is the mustard part of **mustard and cress**; brown or Indian mustard (*Brassica juncea*), which is native to western Asia, has small, mild, reddish-brown or yellow seeds; and black mustard (*Brassica nigra*), which is also native to Mediterranean Europe, and has small, spicy, brown-black seeds.

Making mustard is straightforward. The chosen seeds are crushed and the hull and bran (see **grains**) sifted out (or not, depending on the type being made); the crushed seeds are then steeped in liquid – water, wine, vinegar, must (the unfermented juice of grapes) and verjuice (the juice of unripe grapes) are all used – before being mashed and occasionally simmered into a paste with stabilizing agents, colourings, preservatives and flavourings. The sharp heat comes from the plants' 'oils', substances that only develop when the seeds are broken and mixed with a liquid, which is why most mustards are sold as pastes and why those sold as powder need to be mixed with liquid before they are effective.

National preferences to some degree dictate different types. British mustards are stronger than most others, nearly always made from a mixture of white and brown seeds (the vivid yellow colour comes from added turmeric), and can be bought as a paste or powder. American mustards vary from light to dark yellow in colour (depending on the amount of turmeric added), but are usually made from white seeds only; they are always pastes and are nearly always quite mild in flavour. French mustards vary in colour too, but are normally pastes made from brown seeds. They are usually aromatic and spicy rather than very hot.

using it Mustard is available in jars, cans and tubes and keeps indefinitely, although most pastes need to be stored in the refrigerator once opened. Basic commercial pastes often have other flavourings added, such as green peppercorns, honey and garlic, but it would be easy to add these and other flavourings such as grated horseradish and chopped tarragon (or other herbs) to plain mustard at home to achieve a similar effect.

Next to pepper and salt, mustard used to be the traditional condiment of choice in Britain, until recently dabbed over most meats and many vegetable and fish dishes too, with a particular affinity for steaks, sausages, ham, root vegetables and smoked oily fish. It's still sometimes used as a spread for sandwiches (with ham and beef in particular) and is added to **vinaigrettes** and most mayonnaise. In cooking, mustard can be mixed with crème fraîche or cream, then stirred into meat or poultry stews or pie fillings to add some 'bite'; whisked into white sauce to make a more piquant accompaniment for vegetables like cauliflower or beetroot; and used as a classic coating or sauce for rabbit, pork or oily fish like mackerel or herring.

In India, the seeds of both black and white mustard are used as a spice, added whole at the beginning of cooking with other seeds like poppy and coriander and cooked until they 'pop', or ground into a spice mixture with ingredients like chillies, coriander and cumin; whole brown mustard seeds are also a popular flavouring in pickles and relishes.

word origin Mustard comes via Old French from the Latin *mustum*, meaning 'must', the juice with which mustard seeds were traditionally mixed to make a paste. The phrase 'as keen as mustard' (meaning very eager to succeed) comes from the name of one of the first British commercial producers of mustard, Messrs Keen & Sons.

did you know?

• Mustard seeds have been enjoyed since Biblical times, and in a form similar to their modern one. All the ancient cultures valued mustard as a condiment (the seeds were crushed and used in the same way that black pepper is today) and also for its medicinal qualities: the Romans ground it into smelling salts and chewed the seeds to relieve toothache. It was the Romans who introduced white and black mustard into Britain, where both plants still grow in the wild.
• In medieval France, the king and the pope (who was temporarily based in Avignon) appointed special *mustardii* to oversee the quality of the mustard they ate, but much of what was generally offered was so adulterated that laws were eventually passed to improve quality and to confine manufacture to recognized makers. By the middle of the 17th century the right to produce it was given exclusively to the mustard-makers of Dijon. The city's status as mustard capital of France was underscored in 1856 when a local producer substituted verjuice for vinegar in his mustard and created the modern 'Dijon' taste.
• In Britain, Tewkesbury in Gloucestershire was initially the centre of the mustard industry, thanks to a local resident, Mrs Clements, who devised a way of grinding the greasy oily seeds into dry powder. But mustard eating only really took off in the early part of the 19th century when Jeremiah Colman & Co. of Norwich first began to mass-produce both mustard powder and made mustard, something they still do today.

olive

The olive (*Olea europaea*) is the small stone fruit of an evergreen tree native to the eastern Mediterranean; leading producers include Spain, Italy, Greece and California. The tree grows to an average of 4–10m high and is very long-lived – there are many around the Mediterranean area (where 95 percent of the world's olives are still grown) that are 200–300 years old. About 90 percent of the crop is used to make oil (see **olive oil**); this entry describes the remainder, table olives.

There are many varieties, some large, some small, but all olives can be grouped according to colour. Green olives are picked while they are still unripe but have reached their mature size, when the flesh is firm and relatively dry, while black olives ripen to purple or black before they are harvested, when their flesh is soft and quite oily.

Olives taste bitter when they are removed from the tree, and are therefore 'cured' or pickled before being sold, a process that usually takes several months and which varies from producing country to producing country. Spanish olives tend to be harvested green, are washed with a lye solution to remove bitterness, then rinsed and allowed to ferment in a flavoured salt and water brine for a period of time, before being stored in fresh brine or oil for selling. Californian olives are picked half-ripe, when their colour is changing from green to purple, and are chemically blackened; they aren't allowed to ferment and are simply washed in a lye solution, then rinsed, stoned, canned in brine and sterilized before being sold. Greek olives are usually harvested black and ripe, and aren't washed in lye but go straight to fermenting, either in a dry salt-only brine or a salt-and-water one. Other producing countries either process their olives by the Spanish or Greek methods or employ yet other forms of curing, such as soaking in oil for several months or dry-curing in salt and then rubbing with oil before selling on.

Although most olives are sold by size or colour, there are a few that are unique enough to be known by their variety name or place of origin: Greek Kalamata olives are one, medium-sized and black, they are usually sold ready-flavoured with garlic and herbs; Manzanillas are green Spanish olives normally available stoned and stuffed with pimiento, anchovy paste or almond; and mild-tasting Gaetas are small, black wrinkled olives from Italy.

using it Olives are sold in cans and jars and from delicatessen barrels. Cans and jars will keep for about a year, although they should be refrigerated once opened and used within a week or so. Delicatessen olives are more perishable, but will still keep for 5–7 days in the refrigerator.

A bowl of olives is often put on the table in restaurants for diners to eat as they choose their meal, and in bars to eat with drinks. Olives can also be served as a snack meal with bread and cheese. Black olives are added to many salads (Greek salad for instance) and are used as an all-purpose garnish, especially with Mediterranean fish dishes or dips like taramasalata. They can also be mashed with other ingredients into dips like Provençal tapenade, a thick paste of black olives, capers and anchovies that also makes a good pasta sauce.

In cooking, olives have a real affinity with tomatoes, and any French dish called niçoise or provençale contains both. They are a popular pizza topping and can be used to flavour classic duck, chicken and rabbit casseroles.

word origin Olive comes from the Latin *oliva*, the name for the fruit.

In Genesis, when the dove returned to the Ark bringing Noah an olive twig with a leaf in its beak, it was a sign that the Flood waters were abating, that the worst was over. The olive branch has been a symbol of hope and peace ever since. The modern phrase to 'extend an olive branch', meaning to offer the possibility of reconciliation or peace, harks back to this.

did you know?

- Our neolithic ancestors were eating wild olives 10,000 years ago, and by 3000BC the tree was being cultivated in Crete and probably in early Egypt and the Middle East as well. In classical Greece, leaves from the sacred olive trees that grew around the Temple of Zeus were woven into a wreath to crown victors in the ancient Olympic Games, although the branches had first to be cut down by a 'pure boy' with living parents, using a golden sickle, before they could be used. The first recorded sports physio, Hippocrates, believed in using olives to benefit athletes too, and advocated that Olympic contestants be 'scientifically' massaged with olive oil.

pickle

This is both an ingredient or mixture of ingredients preserved in an acidic liquid or salt to prolong shelf life, and (as a verb) the process by which the preserving is done. Virtually any solid ingredient can be pickled: vegetables are the most popular, often a mixture of them, but fruits such as lime or mango are pickled too, as are eggs. Fish (especially oily ones such as herring) and meat like pork can also be preserved in this way. The choice liquid for pickling is **vinegar**, normally malt, cider or spirit, but brine (a salt and water mixture), salt, or even lime or lemon juice is used occasionally too. In Korea and Japan, where pickle consumption is enthusiastic, rice-wine vinegar is the preferred pickling medium.

Some, usually commercial sweet, pickles have a jam-like consistency and are virtually **chutneys** by another name. In more classic pickles, the ingredients retain shape and crispness and remain more separate from their preserving liquid. Most classic fruit-based pickles are cooked to the required texture in sweetened flavoured vinegar, then cooled and potted up in jars with the boiled-down concentrated pickling liquid. A few pickles are made by cooking the fruit or vegetables in the usual way until crisp, then combining them with a flavoured vinegar solution that has been prepared separately. Another method, for vegetable pickles, is to layer the ingredients with salt or immerse them in brine for varying periods of time before draining and combining with the pickling liquid in the usual way.

using it   Pickles keep well, although some need to be stored in the refrigerator after opening. Home-made pickles need to be 'matured' for a few months before being eaten, and kept in the refrigerator after they are opened.

Sweet pickles and traditional ones like piccalilli are primarily used as a condiment with cold meats and salads or in sandwiches (sweet pickles are often part of a 'ploughman's' lunch, for instance); traditional Indian pickles like lime are used in the same way as Indian chutneys, as an appetizer with poppadoms or to accompany grilled or baked meat, vegetable or fish dishes. Pickled eggs are usually eaten on their own as a snack food or as a sandwich filling, and pickled onions are a classic accompaniment to fish and chips. See also **gherkin**, **ham**, **herring**, **olive** and **sauerkraut**.

word origin   Pickle comes from the Middle German *pekel*, meaning 'food preserved in brine'. It was originally used in English to describe a spicy sauce or relish served with meat, not far from its modern meaning.

did you know?

* Food has been pickled since ancient times (a type of cabbage preserved in rice vinegar was eaten by the workers who built the early part of the Great Wall of China between the 4th and 3rd centuries BC), and probably began as a way of using up gluts so that they could provide food when fresh food was scarce. Pickling as we know it now dates from early medieval times, when the spiciness may also have helped make dried food such as beans and salted food like fish – the staple diet for a good part of the year – more palatable.

salad dressings

These are liquid sauce-like mixtures, usually containing herbs and seasonings, that are tossed through or poured over (usually cold) raw or cooked ingredients to add flavour and texture and to bring out their natural taste.

Dressings can vary as much as individual **salads**, but can be grouped into four categories: **vinaigrettes**, those based on a mixture of oil and vinegar, to which virtually anything (or nothing else) is added; **mayonnaise**, a thick egg-and-oil emulsion to which, again, almost anything can be added; creamy dressings, mostly built around soured cream, crème fraîche or plain yoghurt and used for more substantial salad mixtures; and oriental dressings, normally based on seasoned soy sauce, and used for exotic rice and vegetable mixtures.

using them   Most dressings are easy to make or you can buy them ready-made. With the latter, you can add flavourings such as chopped fresh herbs, crushed garlic, crumbled dried chillies and finely chopped anchovy to give extra taste and interest.

Dressings should be chosen to complement the salad ingredients and only just enough should be added – the idea is to bathe rather than drown. Toss leafy salads with their dressing just before eating, as they become limp and soggy if they're dressed too early.

did you know?

* We'll never know who first had the brilliant idea of adding a dressing to some otherwise glum vegetable and leaf mixture, nor will we ever know what that first dressing was. What we do know is that they have always ranged from the simple to the more or less absurd. The Roman cookery writer Apicius, for instance, had recipes for modern-sounding vinaigrettes that were spooned over lettuce or chicory leaves, but he also used an all-purpose reeking fish sauce called

liquamen or garum as the basis for others that sound more doubtful, including one which he claimed would prevent flatulence. It was made from a mixture of dates, cumin, ginger, honey, pepper and vinegar.

• The late 18th century saw the rise of the first celebrity chef in Britain. Predictably he was a Frenchman, an émigré nobleman called the Chevalier d'Albignac, who went round the great houses of London to dress their salads. The Chevalier was very grand, however, so although he concocted himself what he considered to be the appropriate dressing for each salad from his travelling hoard of suitable ingredients, his servant did the actual tossing of the mixture.

sauce

A sauce is a seasoned thickened liquid used to enhance the flavour of other foods or to bind them together. There are two basic types: 'made' sauces (those that were traditionally made at home or by chefs in restaurants, although they are now often bought) and ready-made sauces (those which have always been commercially manufactured). A salsa is a sauce by another name – in this case the Mexican and Spanish word for it. Salsas may be fresh or cooked, bought or made at home.

Made sauces are an integral part of most cuisines, and can be hot or cold, sweet or savoury, simple or complicated. Hot savoury sauces include French classics like **béchamel** and **béarnaise** (both of which also form the basis of other sauces); homelier Italian mixtures like Bolognese (see **pasta sauces**); mole, a chocolate and chilli mixture from Mexico; and various Indian combinations. Cold savoury sauces include western classics such as **mayonnaise**, **vinaigrette** and the relish-like pesto (see **basil**), as well as oriental dipping sauces and thick spicy mixtures like hoisin and black bean sauce (see **soya bean**). **Custard** is the most famous classic sweet sauce. Ready-made sauces in the English-speaking world are usually spicy-sweet like tomato **ketchup** and brown sauce, but Asian ones are often salty and thin, like **fish sauce** and **soy sauce**.

using it How sauces are used depends on what they are. Classic French savoury sauces that are served hot are normally accompaniments to meat and fish dishes; a little may be poured over before serving, the rest passed around at the table. Pasta sauces are mixed into bland starchy pasta to liven up the taste, while most Chinese and Indian sauces are mixed into casseroles, stews and stir-fries to provide moisture during cooking and extra taste at the end of it. Cold savoury sauces are mixed into or poured over salads or other cold cooked or uncooked ingredients (mayonnaise and vinaigrette); used to provide contrast and flavour to hot bland ingredients such as pasta and potatoes (pesto for example); or served separately as a dipping condiment to (usually) hot food (Japanese and South-east Asian dipping sauces). Sweet sauces are normally served as an accompaniment to desserts and puddings such as fruit pies and crumbles.

Ready-made sauces like ketchup and soy sauce are **condiments**, sprinkled or poured over cooked food at the table, in order to season it or add extra flavour.

word origin Sauce comes from the Latin *sal*, meaning 'salt'.

did you know?

• Ancient 'made' sauces were fairly crude affairs, often based on vinegar and containing so many spices and flavourings that they may have overwhelmed rather than enhanced the taste of the food they were served with. They were thickened with bread or (the more refined ones) ground almonds.
• Ready-made sauces aren't a modern phenomenon. Medieval housewives used to buy spicy-sweet sauces like cameline (cinnamon, ginger and raisins were the major flavouring ingredients) from travelling sauce-makers who sold their wares on the streets of cities like Paris and London.

soy sauce

This salty liquid flavouring is made from **soya beans** and is more or less the universal **condiment** in China, Japan and parts of South-east Asia. There are two styles, Chinese and Japanese, and three types. Both countries produce light soy **sauce** (thinner and more salty than other types) and dark soy sauce (thicker and stronger-tasting); Japan, in addition, produces tamari, a thick, rich soy sauce made without wheat.

To make traditional soy sauce, steamed soya beans and (usually) roasted crushed wheat are mashed together, then fermented for a few days with a starter 'culture' made from a mixture of *Aspergillus oryzae* and *Aspergillus soyae* moulds. Further fermenting agents and a salt and water brine are then added and the mixture is left to ferment again for 3–18 months before being filtered, pasteurized and bottled. Light soy sauces are fermented for about three months, dark ones and tamari for 6–18 months. Cheaper soy sauces are not fermented at all, but simply hydrolized briefly in huge vats before being bottled.

using it Soy sauce keeps indefinitely. Chinese and Japanese versions can be used more or less interchangeably, although Japanese sauces tend to be slightly sweeter. Mass-produced soy sauces are pale imitations of properly fermented ones, so where possible – especially when they are to be used uncooked – traditionally made sauces are better.

This sauce more or less replaces salt in oriental food, especially in plainer rice and noodle dishes, but is also often mixed with other ingredients into a sauce or dressing: with grated ginger and/or wasabi (the Japanese version of horseradish) as a basic dipping sauce for grilled or deep-fried foods; with mirin (a sweet Japanese rice wine used for cooking), rice vinegar and ginger as a marinade for fish, **tofu** and meat (it tastes good served with them afterwards too); and with rice vinegar or citrus juice and grated zest as an oriental **vinaigrette**. It can also be used *during* cooking – to add moisture to stir-fries, colour and taste to long-cooked dishes (western as well as eastern), and as a basting liquid for oriental kebabs and other grilled foods.

word origin The first part of the name comes from the Dutch *soja*, which in turn is derived from the Japanese *shoyu*, meaning 'soy sauce'; the Japanese word can be traced back to *jiangyou*, the Cantonese Chinese for 'salted beans in oil'.

stock

Also called bouillon and broth, stock is a clear, flavoured liquid usually created from meat or fish bones, water and seasonings. A classic stock can be 'white' (really golden brown) when it is made by simmering bones or a carcass in water – or it can be 'brown', when the bones (of meat only) are browned first by frying or roasting them. Nowadays, of course, many people create stock instantly by dissolving a cube or powder in boiling water.

The best meat stock is made by simmering the bones of roast beef, lamb or veal, or the carcass or **giblets** of lean poultry like chicken and turkey, in plenty of water with flavourings like herbs, peppercorns, onions, carrots and celery; cooking time can be as long as 4–5 hours. Fish stock is made in the same way, using the head, bones and (in the case of shellfish) shells, but cooking for a shorter time (20–30 minutes only). For vegetable stock, a good variety of vegetables such as onions, celery, carrots, parsnip, leeks and cabbage replaces the bones; colour is improved if the vegetables are browned first or if tomatoes are included. Dashi, a Japanese stock, is made by cooking kombu (a type of dried seaweed) in plenty of water for a few minutes, then removing it and stirring in katsuobushi (dried bonito flakes); the mixture is left to infuse for a few minutes before straining.

using it Stock cubes and bouillon powder keep well, although cubes soften eventually so should be used within about a year. Home-made stock will keep for a few days in the refrigerator and freezes very well. To make it less bulky to freeze, boil down until very concentrated, then freeze in ice-cube trays; these home-made stock 'cubes' can be used straight from frozen.

Stock is one of the basic staples of savoury cooking, used as the basis of soups, sauces, stews, casseroles, gravies and much else besides. Although it isn't absolutely essential, chicken stock is better than other meat stocks with chicken or other poultry dishes, while meat stock will give more flavour to meat dishes. Dashi is the basis of most Japanese soups and many dipping sauces.

word origin Stock comes from the Dutch *stok,* meaning to 'have a store of'.

Tabasco™

This is the trade name of a range of bottled sauces made from **chilli peppers** in the southern United States. The best known and most widely available is the original Tabasco pepper sauce, made from a type of small, very hot red chilli, which is steeped in distilled grain vinegar and local salt before being matured in oak barrels for three years. This sauce is so well known around the

world that 'tabasco' has become the generic term for a hot chilli sauce. Others in the range include: green pepper sauce, made from jalapeño peppers and green peppers and described as 'mild', although in this range that is relative; hot and spicy garlic pepper sauce, which is a mixture of cayenne, tabasco and jalapeño peppers; and the hottest of them all, habañero pepper sauce, a knock-your-socks-off blend of exotic fruit, ginger and habañero chillies.

using it All of these sauces will keep indefinitely and are normally used in very small quantities – since even the 'mild' green one is hot by most standards, a few drops are usually enough to add zest to a pizza, pasta sauce, stir-fry, dip, bean dish or fish soup. Tabasco sauces are widely used in Tex-Mex cookery and the original red sauce is a classic ingredient in a Bloody Mary cocktail (see **vodka**).

word origin Tabasco is the name of a state in south-eastern Mexico and also the name of the chilli pepper used to make the original red sauce (it comes from the state). In Spanish the word means 'damp earth'.

did you know?

• The name Tabasco is the registered trademark of the McIlhenny Co., which is based in Louisiana in the southern United States. They have been making red pepper sauce there since 1868, from peppers grown from seeds brought back from Mexico by the founder of the company, Edmund McIlhenny.

vinaigrette

Vinaigrette is a slightly thickened salad dressing usually made from oil, vinegar and seasonings. Traditionally olive oil is used, but others like sunflower, walnut or groundnut oil are sometimes substituted or mixed with it. The vinegar is normally wine-based – red, white or balsamic; lemon juice is occasionally used instead. It takes only a few seconds to make vinaigrette: put the ingredients into a jar, cover and shake until mixed. Proportions of oil to vinegar vary from cook to cook (and from salad to salad), but the standard ratio is three or four parts oil to one part vinegar.

using it Ready-made vinaigrettes should be stored in the refrigerator once opened and used within about a week. Home-made vinaigrette can be kept in an airtight container in the fridge for a few days.

Vinaigrette can be flavoured to make other dressings such as Italian (add crushed garlic and herbs to taste), mustard and honey, and chilli (add finely chopped chillies or a dash or two of **Tabasco sauce**). Other possible additions and flavourings include chopped herbs such as tarragon, parsley or chives, shallots, sun-dried tomatoes and crumbled hard-boiled egg.

The classic partnership is with leafy green salad, but vinaigrette of one kind or another can be used with virtually any combination of raw or cooked salad ingredients. It's also used as a cold sauce, mostly for first-course dishes like avocado (halved or sliced), asparagus or globe artichoke. Vinaigrette is occasionally cooked too: warmed to create a 'wilted' salad; and simmered with vegetables such as leeks, then cooled to serve à la grecque.

word origin Vinaigrette is French and means 'little vinegar'.

• There have been vinaigrettes around for over 2000 years – the Roman cookery writer Apicius recommended dressing lettuce with oil, vinegar and salt in the 1st century AD, and although by the 14th century lettuce was out of favour, according to a court recipe book from his reign, Richard II of England was eating salads of herbs, sorrel leaves and onions flavoured by 'rawe oile, vynegar and salt'. When the diarist John Evelyn wrote the first book on salads in 1699, lettuce was

once again a popular ingredient, and being dressed by much the same mixture as Apicius had used 1600 years before.

vinegar

This is a bottled **condiment** made by converting fermented alcohol into sour-tasting acetic acid. Theoretically vinegar can be made from any ingredient capable of fermenting into alcohol – dates, coconut and cane sugar will all do this – but in reality most commercial vinegars are made from wine (red, white, champagne and sherry), cider, unhopped beer (malt) or distilled malt (spirit). In Japan and China a mild sweetish vinegar is brewed from rice wine.

If wine (or any other alcohol) is exposed to air and airborne bacteria, it will oxidize or ferment naturally and although in vinegar-making fermentation is controlled, it is based on this fact. To make classic wine vinegar, wine is poured into wooden barrels with air holes and mixed with a 'vinegar mother' (a thick skin of special bacteria). The mixture is allowed to ferment and turn into weak acetic acid (which is vinegar) that sinks to the bottom of the barrel, where some of it can be drawn off, filtered and bottled. And as vinegar is drawn off, new wine is added to the top of the barrel. Fermentation can take several months, and topping up and drawing off go on virtually non-stop.

Cheaper vinegars, including some wine and most cider, malt and spirit vinegars, are made by putting the alcohol base into large heated vats and then 'brewing' it with vinegar-soaked shavings until it has become acetic acid. It is then matured in vats for varying amounts of time (cider for a month, malt for six) before being clarified and bottled. Light malt vinegars contain less malt extract than ordinary ones, and caramel is added to ordinary malt vinegars to deepen the colour. Malt vinegar is also sometimes distilled after brewing, to become clear spirit vinegar.

Balsamic vinegar, which is made only around Modena in central Italy, is produced in yet another way. To begin with, it's made from must, the unfermented juice of grapes, in this case sweet white Trebbiano and sometimes Lambrusco grapes, rather than from wine itself. The must is simmered to concentrate its flavour, then fermented for a year before being matured in a series of ever smaller barrels, each made from a different wood. Traditional balsamic (*aceto balsamico tradizionale di Modena*), which is tightly regulated by what amounts to *appellation contrôlée* laws, is aged for a minimum of 12 years before being bottled and sold; a *tradizionale extra vecchio* spends at least 25 years in cask. Ordinary balsamic vinegar isn't governed by these laws and can sometimes contain wine vinegar or grape juice to balance its taste; it is aged for a minimum of 1–2 years, although many are matured for longer.

using it Vinegars keep well, although they need to be kept tightly stoppered to prevent a spontaneous fermentation (this causes the slight mould that sometimes appears on the top of the vinegar in an opened bottle; it isn't harmful and can just be strained off). Most vinegars are plain, but some have added flavourings: herbs like tarragon and rosemary are the most common, but chilli and garlic are also popular and occasional fruits like raspberry find their way into them as well.

Different types of vinegar tend to have different uses. Wine vinegars are used most in cooking: white wine vinegar is added to sauces like mayonnaise and **hollandaise** to flavour them; any type (or a mixture) is a basic ingredient in **vinaigrette**; and balsamic or sherry vinegar is sometimes added towards the end of cooking calves' liver, steak or veal escalope to enrich the pan juices. Cider and wine vinegars can be added to marinades or stirred into stews and casseroles to create a sour-sweet taste, and malt and cider vinegars are also sometimes used as a condiment, especially with chips. Acetic acid acts as a preservative, which is why spirit or malt vinegar is an important ingredient in both commercial and home-made pickles and chutneys. A really exceptional, mellow balsamic vinegar can even be served as an after-dinner liqueur.

word origin Vinegar comes from the Medieval French *vyn eger,* meaning 'soured wine', which is basically what vinegar is. Balsamic vinegar was once believed to have powerful healing qualities, hence its name, from the Italian *balsamico*, meaning 'balm'.

did you know?

• Vinegar has probably been around for as long as wine has been made. It was popular in Egypt, both as a condiment and as an early male contraceptive (it was believed to kill off sperm and thus prevent fertilization). The Greeks used vinegar as a dipping sauce for bread, and the Romans diluted it with water and consumed it as a refreshing drink. The Romans also introduced vinegar into Britain. The northerly climate here meant that wine wasn't always available however, so gradually people improvized by allowing local ale and cider to ferment into vinegar too.
• Vinegar production around the city of Orléans in France was so important in medieval times that a special vinegar-makers' guild was set up to regulate quality and price. The city is still the centre of French vinegar production, and the traditional method of making good-quality wine vinegar is called the Orléans process.

Worcestershire sauce™

This is a proprietary bottled **condiment** made from vinegar, tamarind, onions, garlic, molasses, anchovies, sugar and spices.

using it In western cooking, Worcestershire sauce is served as a pouring sauce with steak and chops, while in Japan and China it is used as an alternative to soy sauce in some dipping sauces, particularly for spring rolls and deep-fried seafood and meat. In cooking, its spicy sweetness adds flavour to mince mixtures such as those for hamburgers and cottage or shepherd's pie, as well as for beef or game stews and grilled cheese dishes like Welsh rarebit. It's also one of the classic ingredients in a Bloody Mary cocktail (see **vodka**).

word origin The 'Worcestershire' part of the name indicates its geographical origin; the manufacturer, Lea & Perrins, is based in the county.

• During the 19th century, Lord Marcus Sandys from (naturally) Worcestershire brought home with him his own notion of an Indian sauce he had enjoyed while serving his country as governor of Bengal, and persuaded his local grocers, Messrs Lea & Perrins, to make up a batch for him. For one reason or another a good part of the batch lay forgotten in their cellars for several years before being found again, when it was discovered that the accidental 'maturing' period had done it a power of good, creating a richer, more mellow taste. It has been manufactured commercially since 1838.

Drinks

They say that a little knowledge is a dangerous thing, but they are quite wrong as far as drink is concerned. To drink without knowing a little bit about what you're drinking is to miss out on a lot of the pleasure that a drink can offer. Where alcohol is concerned, it is also potentially dangerous.

The thing that distinguishes alcoholic drinks from the rest is, of course, alcohol. Consumed sensibly, alcohol can be a hugely positive thing, making you and the world seem a much better place. Consumed ignorantly, it can do all sorts of damage to you, your friends and even strangers. So I would strongly urge you to read this section, if only so that when you drink it is you who is in charge of the drink rather than the other way round.

The single most important thing

Knowing the story behind what you eat and drink makes eating and drinking so much more interesting and rewarding.
Jancis Robinson

to grasp is the different alcoholic strengths of the various drinks on offer, so that you can pace your consumption. Do always read the label of whatever you are drinking, to check how strong it is.

My favourite drink happens to be wine – partly because I love the many varied tastes of it, partly because it goes so well with food (it is far better for your body to consume alcohol with food than on an empty stomach), and partly because I know that behind every single bottle there's a fascinating human story. Knowing the story behind what you eat and drink makes eating and drinking so much more interesting and rewarding.

As you'll see in this section, there is now a wider choice of drinks than ever before. You can choose between grape juice fermented in Uruguay, a whisky that uniquely expresses a particular glen in Scotland, beers from all over the world, and all manner of concoctions dreamed up by busy marketing departments and creative bartenders.

May you enjoy whichever is your favourite, keep on experimenting, and remember that the healthiest drink in the world is the one described on page 354 – water. For the sake of my health, I always try to drink at least as much water as I do wine.

alcohol

Alcohol is the word commonly used to describe liquids produced as a result of fermentation or distillation, or both combined – those drinks that intoxicate us, like **beer**, **wine** and **spirits**. Technically, however, alcohol is defined as a variety of compounds made from carbon, hydrogen and oxygen, particularly ethyl alcohol, or ethanol (C_2H_5OH), a colourless liquid with a slight but pleasant smell that's present in varying strengths in all alcoholic drinks. In Europe the amount of alcohol contained in a bottle of beer, wine or spirits is expressed by volume and shown on the label. The higher it is, the more alcoholic the drink: spirits, for instance, are high (normally 28–45 percent), while beer is low (usually 3–9 percent).

using it Alcohol can be stimulating or relaxing, complement food or help digest it. It can be used in cooking, although the alcohol itself burns off when heated, so that only the flavour is left. See individual entries for further information.

word origin Alcohol comes from the Arabic *al-koh'l* – *al* being the definite article, the Arabic equivalent of 'the', while *koh'l* started off as a refined cosmetic powder for eyelids and eyebrows, but was later also used to describe a refined chemical powder. It settled into its modern meaning in about the 16th century.

did you know?

• Alcoholic strength used to be referred to as 'proof' because in the early days of distilling, spirits were mixed with equal amounts of gunpowder and then lit to test whether they were safe to drink. If the mixture didn't ignite, it was too weak; if it burned too much (or exploded!), it was too strong. But if the flame was mild and blue, it was 'proved' to be suitable.

alcopops

This is the name given to a range of commercial fruit-based drinks that have a low alcohol content (about 4–5 percent) and contain large amounts of sugar.

using it Alcopops are primarily pub or party drinks.

word origin Alcopops combine the idea of a trendy alcoholic 'fixer' with the innocuous but appealing 'pop' (as in popular or something that goes pop).

did you know?

• Alcopops were created in the early 1990s and probably reached the height of their popularity in the middle of the decade. They have now more or less morphed into FABs (flavoured alcoholic beverages), such as breezers (Bacardi rum mixed with various fruit juices) and Red Square (vodka and cranberry juice).

beer

Beer is an alcoholic drink made from **barley**, hops, sugar, **yeast** and water and brewed in stages. First the barley is malted by being steeped in water to allow it to germinate, then it is dried out in kilns. Next, the resulting malt is crushed into a coarse powder called grist, which is mixed with hot water to become mash, and the natural sugars in the mash are dissolved to create a dark, sweet liquid called wort. Now hops and sugar are introduced into the wort, boiled with it and strained off. After the liquid has cooled, yeast is added to the wort and the mixture is allowed to ferment until the desired alcohol level is reached. Finally, the beer is conditioned, either by being refined and left to 'come into condition' in casks in pub cellars or (in the case of most keg, canned and bottled beers) by being filtered, pasteurized and sometimes sterilized at the brewery.

During the brewing process, the quantity

and proportions of ingredients and flavourings used and the amount of time spent in the kiln are varied to create beers of differing type, strength and colour. Lager, for instance, is a pale beer made by using special 'bottom-fermenting' yeasts that operate at cold temperatures (traditionally 5–12°C) to produce a light, crisp-tasting drink that is stored at around 0°C for at least a month. Bitter or ale is created from 'top-fermenting' yeasts that operate at warm temperatures (traditionally 15–25°C). Top-fermenting yeast liquids are matured at warm temperatures for anything between a few days and a few weeks to produce beer with a fuller taste. Stout, a dark, heavy beer, is made with top-fermenting yeast and barley that has been dried in the kiln for a long time to create a darker, roasted flavour. Barley wine is a type of extra-strong bitter – the second part of the name is meant to imply that it is as strong as most wines.

Lighter beers, such as lager and bitter, have an alcoholic strength of about 3–5 percent, while stout can be as strong as 8–9 percent; barley wine varies from 6–11 percent (see **alcohol**).

Almost every country in the world creates its own unique beers. Belgium, for instance, flavours some with fruit such as orange and banana, as well as brewing an enormous range of more conventional ones – which might account for it having one of the highest consumptions of beer per capita in the world. Many brewers would argue that what makes *their* beer special is the water they use, and it's true that in the 18th and 19th centuries several areas with good sources of pure water – Pilsen in the Czech Republic, Burton-on-Trent in England and Bavaria in Germany – did become great brewing centres.

using it Beer is drunk at home, in pubs or bars, with food, or by itself. Lagers are usually served cold, bitters and stouts at room temperature. The best are drawn from the keg on request, although most are also available in bottles and cans. Beer is often mixed with other drinks, too: bitter added to lemonade makes shandy; lager can be drunk with a splash of lemonade (lager top) or lime; and stout, unlikely though it sounds, can be combined with vodka to create black Russian or with champagne to make black velvet – reputedly an efficient hangover cure as well as a good-tasting drink.

In cooking, beer can be the liquid component of pot roasts and casseroles or the moistening ingredient for slowly stewed sliced onions. It can be beaten into batters for deep-fried fish and is also used occasionally as a soaking liquid for dried fruit (and could be added to cake or pudding batters with the fruit). Stout gives a sweeter, richer taste, and is sometimes stirred into Christmas cakes and puddings.

word origin Beer probably originated in the Middle East, but the English word for it comes from the Old German *bior*. During the Middle Ages it was used to describe hopped beer (as opposed to the Anglo-Saxon *ale*, which became the word for unhopped beer). The process of storing light beer at cold temperatures before bottling is called 'lagering', hence the word lager; both come from the German *lagern*, meaning 'to store'. The mixture of beer and lemonade called shandy comes from *shandygaff*, an old English dialect word meaning 'wild' or 'boisterous'.

• A recent excavation in Syria found what could be the world's oldest brewery, dating back to 6000BC. Other evidence from Mesopotamia (present-day Iraq) and Egypt shows that our ancestors were just as fond of a pint as we are today, although their beer was probably flavoured with date juice rather than hops. Early inhabitants of Britain drank beer too, and brewing was well established by the time the Romans arrived in AD43.

• Hops, which are now used to give beer its rather bitter flavour, were first added to barley by monks in Germany in the 13th century – and the result was usually drunk warm. Hopped beer finally made its way to Britain in the 15th century.

• Every brewery uses its own special yeasts to ferment its various beers and keeps a stock of them on site. But should disaster strike, all would not be lost: the National Yeast Collection in Norwich holds a sample of every yeast used in the UK, so new batches could be cultivated from them if necessary.

brandy

Brandy is an alcoholic drink normally made from grape-based **wine**, which is then distilled and aged, usually in oak barrels, before being bottled. Most countries that produce wine also produce brandy, and distillation can take place in either traditional pot stills or more modern continuous ones (see **spirits**). Brandy has an alcoholic strength of 40 percent (see **alcohol**).

The most famous brandies are French, made from white grape varieties. Cognac, produced in the Charente area of western France, is distilled twice in copper pot stills before being aged, while armagnac, from Gascony in south-western France, is distilled either once in specially modified continuous stills or twice in pot stills. Most cognacs have three stars, VS, VSOP, and XO or Napoleon on their labels. The stars and VS mean the same thing – that the bottle contains brandy that is at least three years old. VSOP stands for 'Very Special or Superior Old Pale' and means that the brandy is at least five years old, while XO or Napoleon indicates that it has been aged for a minimum of six years. Three-star armagnacs are aged for at least two years; otherwise descriptions such as VSOP, XO or Napoleon mean the same as for cognacs. Armagnacs may also have the year of bottling on their label and it is possible (but very expensive) to buy one

that dates back a hundred years. Other French brandies include *marc*, which is made from lees – the sediment or dregs left after wine has been pressed.

Other countries that distil brandy include Greece, where the best ones have seven stars and are made from a mixture of brandy and ouzo (an aniseed-flavoured alcoholic drink); Spain, where it is made in both sherry- and wine-producing areas; and Italy, where grappa (made, like *marc*, from the lees of wine) is the most popular type.

There are also brandies made from fruits other than grapes: apple brandy is probably the best example, especially the famous calvados, from Normandy in northern France. Grape brandies are sometimes flavoured with other fruits and/ or fruit kernels soaked in spirits, or fruit oils: apricot brandy is a good example of the former, while Grand Marnier, a mixture of brandy and bitter orange oils, is typical of the latter.

using it By itself, brandy is served as an after-dinner drink, traditionally in a large, tapering bulb of a glass so that the flavours can 'breathe' as the drink is being consumed. Mixed with other ingredients, it becomes a pre-dinner drink: with soda water or ginger ale as a standard mixed drink, or as part of cocktails such as brandy Alexander (equal quantities of brandy, crème de cacao and cream). It is also often added to punches.

Brandy is very useful in the kitchen. In savoury cooking, it flambés meat, is added to sauces and is occasionally included in marinades, while in baking it is a frequent ingredient in festive cakes and puddings. In desserts, brandy of one sort or another can set things alight literally (think of Christmas pudding) or metaphorically (think of anything from trifles, mousses and soufflés to fruit salads, compotes and ice-cream). Armagnac makes the perfect partner for prunes, while dried apricots are transformed by being steeped in plain or flavoured brandy before use.

word origin Brandy comes from the Old Dutch *brandewijn*, meaning 'burnt wine' – a fairly literal description of the first attempts at making it. It eventually became *brandwine* or *brandewine* in English before settling into the modern word.

did you know?

• During the 15th and 16th centuries, according to one story, Dutch, English and Scandinavian sailors used to bring back wine from the Charente, in France. In order to save valuable cargo space, they boiled the wine down to reduce its volume (this also saved on tax back home, as it was charged on bulk). The idea was to add water later to return it to wine but this didn't work, so what they drank was a kind of early brandy. By the 17th century the Dutch especially had grown to like it, and for convenience set up early stills around the town of Cognac so that the wine could be distilled on the spot.

champagne

Champagne is a sparkling **wine**, usually made from a blend of black and white grapes (particularly pinot noir and chardonnay). It is fermented once in barrels and once in the bottle; it gets its 'bubbles' from this second fermentation.

There are several complex stages to go through before fresh grapes become champagne, but the process begins in the classic way by pressing them and storing the resulting mixture in barrels to ferment into wine. Wines from various barrels are then blended, put into thick bottles with sugar and (usually) special yeasts, and sealed with very strong corks, which are pushed in and wired down. Over a period of about three months a second fermentation takes place in the bottle and a 'sediment', or residue forms, after which the wine is left to mature. Now comes the delicate process of removing the sediment: the bottles are shaken occasionally and gradually tipped from a slightly sloping horizontal angle into an upside-down vertical position in order to force the sediment to settle near the corks (a process called *remuage*, or riddling; the bottles can be moved up to 200 times during *remuage*). After *remuage* comes *dégorgement*, when the necks of the bottles are frozen, then uncorked, and the sediment shoots out. Finally, the bottles are topped up, re-corked and overlaid with the protective wire cages that remain there until they are opened for drinking.

Champagne ranges from very dry (*brut*) through varying degrees of dryness (*extra-sec*, *sec* or *demi-sec*) to sweet (*doux*). A bottle marked vintage is a champagne made in a specific year (most are blends of wine from different years), while one marked *blanc de blanc* is made only from white chardonnay grapes. *Rosé* champagne is made in the same way as ordinary champagne except that either the black grapes are allowed to remain in the grape mixture for a little longer to impart some colour, or some still red wine is added to the mixture. The average alcoholic strength of champagne is 12 percent (see **alcohol**).

using it Champagne is usually served lightly chilled in tall, slender glasses. The safest way to open the bottle is to remove the wire cage and then, keeping a thumb over the top of the cork, carefully twist the bottle off the cork (rather than the other way round), until you can gently ease out the cork, making sure your thumb stays in place. Hold the bottle at an angle and point it away from you and from anyone else – flying champagne corks can cause severe eye injuries. Once opened, the wine gradually loses its fizz (a good excuse to drink the bottle quickly), but a special stopper or a spoon handle inserted into the top of the bottle delays the process.

This is the drink chosen above all others to celebrate special occasions, from weddings to Grand Prix victories. It can be drunk before, during or after a meal, and mixes well with other soft or alcoholic drinks – with orange juice to make buck's fizz, with stout to make black velvet, with crème de cassis for kir royale. Champagne can be used in the kitchen too, although since the bubbles disappear when it is cooked, it seems rather wasteful. It does, however, moisten a fruit salad well and could also be used to flavour a jelly or **sorbet**.

word origin Champagne is the name of an area around the towns of Reims and Epernay, north-east of Paris, where champagne is made. Similar sparkling wines are produced in other areas of France and other parts of the world too but, by law, only sparkling wine made in this area by the method described above (known as *méthode champenoise*) can be called champagne. Producers of good-quality sparkling wine elsewhere, who use the same grape varieties and the same method, try to get round this by putting the words *méthode champenoise* on their labels.

did you know?

• The 17th-century Benedictine monk, Dom Pierre Pérignon, didn't invent sparkling wine (in fact, he spent most of his life trying to take the slight natural fizziness out of his wine), but he did introduce the idea of using a black grape variety to create white wine, and of blending different grapes from different vineyards to create better-quality wine. He may also have recommended using cork stoppers to seal bottles instead of the oil-soaked hemp wads that were normally employed, although this probably wasn't adopted during his lifetime. Bottle fermentation came later, too, but created serious problems, since pressure from fermentation often made the thin bottles of the day explode. Workers would go into areas where wine was fermenting with wire masks over their faces, and over half of production could be lost to flying glass. Thicker bottles were the answer, and this was the English contribution to champagne, since the technique for making them was invented in England at the end of the 17th century.
• Nicole-Barbe Clicquot-Ponsardin, known as the 'Widow' (Veuve), whose champagne with its famous yellow label is still known as Veuve Clicquot, is another hero of the champagne story. It was the Widow's champagne house that invented the *remuage* and *dégorgement* processes described above, thus solving the problem of how to get rid of the sediment remaining in the bottle after the second fermentation without losing bubbles and a lot of the wine.

cider

Cider is an alcoholic drink made from fermented **apples**. About 350 varieties of apple are grown for cider-making, many blessed with quirky names such as brown snout and slack-my-girdle. They tend to have a higher tannin content than other apples, and consequently a more bitter taste, although individual types range from sweet to sharp, with many bitter-sweet combinations in between. Most ciders are a blend of several apple varieties. British cider has an alcoholic strength of 4–8 percent (see **alcohol**).

Making cider is straightforward. The ripe apples are cleaned and pulped to produce pomace. This is pressed to squeeze out the juice, which is then put into barrels or vats to ferment for at least a month. After fermenting, the liquid is matured for varying lengths of time, then filtered and stored in tanks before being blended and bottled or kegged.

Cider can be sweet or dry, depending on the blend of apple varieties. It is naturally still, but fizzy varieties are usually produced by adding carbonated gas to the mixture before bottling or kegging, although some (like **champagne**) are fermented in the cask or bottle. 'Clear' cider is clarified to get rid of cloudiness before bottling.

using it Cider is drunk in much the same way as **beer**, and can also be combined with other drinks and spices to make punch. Its fresh flavour works well in cooking: as the liquid in a pork dish that includes apples, for instance; or with chicken or rabbit, or even red cabbage, where it will not only enhance the taste, but prevent the cabbage turning blue during cooking. Still cider goes well with dried fruits such as prunes and can be used to poach them.

word origin Cider probably comes, via French and Greek, from the Hebrew *shekar*, meaning 'strong drink'.

did you know?

• Cider has been made for thousands of years and was already around in England when the Romans arrived. The earliest written records, however, go back only as far as the 8th or 9th century, when emperor Charlemagne of France passed laws governing its production. By the 11th century, Normandy and Brittany were the main production centres so it was only natural that the Normans should bring their apple trees and cider-making techniques with them when they arrived in Britain in 1066. Today, British cider is produced mostly in the West Country – notably Somerset, Devon and Herefordshire.

cocktails

Cocktails are mixed drinks based on **alcohol** (particularly champagne, brandies or spirits), usually with added fruit juices, flavourings (anything from Angostura bitters to mint) and crushed ice. There are hundreds of combinations, each with its own, sometimes bizarre, name, and new ones are invented on a regular basis. Classics include daiquiri, dry martini, Manhattan and Bloody Mary (see **rum**, **gin**, **whisky** and **vodka** respectively).

using them Some cocktails are shaken (and memorably not stirred), most are poured into special glasses that differ in shape and size depending on the cocktail chosen, and nearly all contain garnishes that can range from the sublime (an olive in a martini) to the ridiculous (paper umbrellas and tired fruit that interfere with access to the drink). Cocktails are now mostly enjoyed as a pre-dinner drink, but during their heyday in the 1920s they were used as an excuse to give elaborate early-evening parties.

word origin There are almost as many versions of how the cocktail got its name as there are mixed drinks, and most are colourful, to say the least. One of the more plausible stories starts with racecourse slang: during the 19th century, mixed-breed horses had their tails docked to distinguish them from thoroughbreds, a procedure described as 'cocktailing'. The leap to the modern meaning is a long one, but presumably based on the idea of 'mixing' something rather than leaving it 'pure'. Nowadays the word is also used to describe other mixtures of ingredients, such as seafood or fruit.

did you know?

• Mixed drinks are probably as old as unmixed drinks, but the first book to contain recipes for them was published during the 17th century by the Distillers Company of London, which described them as medicinal. The honour of creating the first 'named' cocktail, however, goes to a Frenchman called Antoine Amadée Peychaud, who created something called the Sazerac – a heady combination of cognac, absinthe (later replaced by Pernod), sugar and bitters – in his pharmacy in New Orleans during the mid-19th century.

cocoa

This is a hot drink made from cocoa powder. All cocoa and chocolate products come from the podded fruit of a tropical tree (*Theobroma cacao*), which although native to Central and South America is now widely grown in many other countries. West Africa accounts for over 50 percent of world production, followed by Indonesia, Brazil, Ecuador and Colombia. Mexico, the home of the cocoa bean, now contributes only about 1.5 percent.

Each *cacao* pod contains 20–60 beans, which are extracted and fermented with the fleshy pulp from the pods for 5–6 days in the producing country, then dried and sent to manufacturers around the world for their final processing. This involves roasting them and removing their husks to reveal the kernels or 'nibs'. The nibs are ground to make a brown, pulpy liquid called the chocolate mass or liquor. This mass is refined, then pressed to remove most of the fat, which is called cocoa butter; nibs are more than 50 percent fat. The mass that remains is treated in various ways depending on which product is being made: most is processed further to create solid chocolate; much of the rest is pressed to release more cocoa butter, then formed into cakes and ground to create cocoa powder. The brown powder sold as drinking chocolate is made from cocoa powder plus sugar and (sometimes) flavourings; it should contain at least 25 percent cocoa powder.

using it To make hot cocoa, the powder is mixed with a little cold milk until smooth, then hot milk or water is poured in and sugar added to taste. It is normally enjoyed as a soothing drink. Hot chocolate is made in much the same way, except that it is usually mixed initially with a little hot water or milk and doesn't need additional sweetening. Cocoa powder is also used in cooking, especially baking. It adds a good, rich chocolate flavour to cakes, biscuits, icings and desserts, and can be sifted over the tops of creamy puddings or cakes as a decoration.

word origin When the cocoa bean was first brought back to Europe by Spanish conquistadors in the 16th century, it was called *cacao*, a word adapted from the Mayan *kakaw(a)*, meaning 'cocoa seed'. At some point, however, the Spaniards began to call the drink made from it *chocolate* (allegedly because cacao was uncomfortably similar to *caca*, the Spanish word for excrement), so when the drink became popular in Britain during the 17th century it was under this name. By the end of the 18th century, things had changed again, however, and the name of the drink became cocoa, a rough anglicization of the original name for the bean.

did you know?

• Drinks made from cocoa beans were an important part of all the native cultures of Central America, although some believed them to be sacred and reserved them for rulers and the armies that kept them in power. The Mayans and Aztecs made the sacred drink in much the same way: the beans were roasted and pounded to a powder, then blended with water and flavourings such as vanilla, chilli, maize or seeds from the silk-cotton tree. The resulting mixture was poured from a height, from one cup or pot to another a number of times, in order to create a foamy top, considered to be one of the pleasures of the drink. It could be drunk hot or cold, depending on preference.

• Cocoa beans were used as a currency throughout Central America. One early 16th-century writer described how the Nicarao people used them to buy things: a rabbit cost 10 beans, a slave 100 and a prostitute about 8–10, and that last price was negotiable. When the Spanish conquistadors arrived, the Aztec king, Montezuma, had more than a million cocoa beans in his warehouses, only a small number of them destined to be made into the drink.

• At first the Spaniards didn't like the rather bitter drink, and it only became popular when they 'Europeanized' it by adding sugar and spices. It was eventually taken back to Europe and reached Britain during the early part of the 17th century, where it was considered an exotic, expensive concoction. Special 'chocolate houses' (like early coffee houses) were set up to cater for those who wished to experience it, two of which (the Garrick and White's) subsequently became gentlemen's clubs. By the 18th and 19th centuries the modern version, now called cocoa, was being promoted by temperance groups campaigning against alcohol, and less than a century later it was a favourite drink during the First and Second World Wars.

coffee

This is a drink made from the roasted ground seeds (called beans) of the *Coffea* bush, a member of the same family of plants as quinine, and native to the Horn of Africa around Ethiopia. There are about 25 different species, but only two are commonly used to produce coffee: *Coffea arabica*, known as arabica, and *Coffea canephora* or *robusta*, called robusta. Arabica is the more sought after of the two. It has large beans, accounts for about 80 percent of world production and is grown primarily in East Africa, India and Central and Latin America (especially Brazil, the world's largest producer). Robusta has smaller beans and is grown mostly in Central and West Africa and South-east Asia. Robusta beans contain more caffeine than arabica and are normally used as a blend with arabica or other coffees.

Coffee bushes grow in high equatorial regions and bear clusters of berries, which are known as cherries, since they turn red when mature. Each berry usually contains two flattish oval beans. To turn 'cherries' into coffee, the beans are removed and dried in the producing country and, now known as 'green beans', packed into sacks and sent to coffee manufacturers around the world. The manufacturers roast the beans to develop their flavour and aroma – a process that changes their colour from greenish-grey to the familiar brown. The hotter the roasting temperature and the longer they are roasted, the darker and stronger-flavoured the beans will be. The roasted beans are either ground or left whole before being vacuum-packed ready for sale.

Instant coffee undergoes further processing, and is made by brewing up water and ground beans, then evaporating the water either in a vacuum or by freeze-drying it. Decaffeinated coffee is made by steaming the beans, then washing them with solvents, which flush away the caffeine. The solvents themselves are then washed away before the beans are dried, roasted and, usually, ground.

using it Coffee is available as roasted whole or ground beans, or as an instant powder or granules – about 80 percent of coffee drunk in the UK is instant. Roasted or ground beans are usually the better arabica types, whereas instant coffee is normally made from robusta beans or a blend of robusta and arabica. Whole beans keep better than ready-ground ones, but both should be stored in an airtight container in the refrigerator once opened, the former used within a month and the latter within a couple of weeks. Instant coffee deteriorates slightly once its seal has been broken but is less sensitive to spoilage, and will be fine for a month or so.

Coffee enthusiasts buy the best roasted beans, grind them just before use, then add almost-boiling water and percolate or filter them. Ready-ground coffee is percolated or filtered in the same way, while instant coffee needs only hot water to reconstitute it. Coffee can be served black (i.e. with no additions), with milk or cream, and/or sugar or sweeteners. Decaffeinated coffee is now widely drunk, particularly in the evening, since caffeine (see below) can keep you awake.

There are other, more elaborate, ways of making coffee, of course. Espresso, for instance, is a strong black coffee produced in a machine or special pot in which boiling water and steam are forced or 'expressed' through about double the normal quantity of finely ground beans. Cappuccino is espresso with a topping of hot frothy milk or whipped cream and sometimes grated chocolate or ground cinnamon. Turkish coffee is made from roughly equal quantities of coffee grounds and sugar topped up with a relatively small amount of water, then brewed three times. Recently, other mixtures have become almost as popular: caffè latte (coffee with steamed milk), caffè mocha (a mixture of coffee, chocolate and hot milk), and caffè americano (espresso diluted with extra hot water).

Coffee can be used in cooking, especially in desserts, confectionery and baking. It flavours ice-creams, water ices such as the Italian granita, and **soufflés**, mousses or other creamy mixtures. It also goes particularly well with chocolate; any dish described as mocha includes both. In confectionery, the combination with chocolate is common in truffles, while in baking, coffee is used to add colour and flavour to icings, biscuits and cakes. It is also occasionally mixed with alcohol to make a spectacular ending to a meal: with rum to become Jamaican coffee, with whiskey and cream for Irish coffee.

word origin The coffee bush originated in Ethiopia, so coffee could have been named after Kaffa, a province there. Or it might have come from *qahwa*, an Arab word for wine and the name given to it by early Arab growers and traders. When it arrived in Britain, coffee was variously called *chaoua*, *cahve* and *kauhi* – all quite close to the original Arabic word – but settled into *coffee* from the Dutch *koffie* (the Dutch were among the first Europeans to cultivate the beans).

Espresso and cappuccino coffees were created in Italy during the early 20th century and both words have been borrowed directly from their original language: espresso meaning 'pressed out' and cappuccino the Italian name for a Christian order of monks (the Capuchins) who wear brown cloaks and hoods similar to the colour of the coffee.

• An Ethiopian legend has it that coffee was invented when a goatherd noticed that his goats got livelier after eating berries from the *coffea* plant and told the local monastery about it. The monks tried the berries, too, and found that they kept them awake during night-long prayers. By some means or other, the berries found their way to the Arab trading port of Aln-Makkha (Mocha) in Yemen, almost certainly by the end of the 11th century. A few centuries later, the beans were being cultivated, ground and infused with hot water into more or less the drink we know today.

• In the Arab world, coffee houses sprang up to cater for the new brew and became centres not only for drinking coffee but also for meeting friends, gossiping and even singing and dancing. By the 17th century, Venetian traders had brought coffee to Europe and soon there were coffee houses everywhere, including England. The one founded by Edward Lloyd in London in 1688 later became the largest insurance company in the world, because marine insurers used to meet there and the proprietor would keep lists of the ships they were insuring.

• An average cup of coffee contains 75–100mg of caffeine, depending on the type and strength of coffee used to make it (this compares with about 50mg of caffeine in black tea, around 40mg in a can of cola and about 75mg in energy drinks). Caffeine acts like a drug on the central nervous system: in moderation, it stimulates, keeps us alert and awake and makes our muscles less tired, but too much of it can blunt our perceptions and cause irregular heartbeats and muscle tremors. It also has a diuretic effect. Coffee can be addictive, and people who drink many cups a day can get withdrawal symptoms if they stop suddenly.

cola

In its various proprietary brands, cola is the world's most popular non-alcoholic fizzy drink. Although each company jealously guards its secret formula, essentially all colas contain carbonated water and probably ground extracts of dried cola or kola nuts, as well as other ingredients such as caramel colouring, spice oils, citric or phosphoric acid and sweeteners. Cola nuts are the seeds of a tropical tree related to *Theobroma cacao*, the tree that produces cocoa beans, the basis of cocoa and chocolate. Like cocoa beans, cola nuts contain caffeine, as well as a similar stimulant called theobromine. These are the substances that give colas their 'kick' (see **coffee** and **chocolate**). 'Diet' colas contain artificial sweeteners such as aspartame and acesulfame-K, rather than sugar.

using it Cola is mostly drunk cold and 'straight', perhaps with ice cubes. It's also sometimes used as a mixer with spirits, especially rum and bourbon whiskey.

word origin The drink is named after the nut, but is more likely to be known under the two world-dominating brand names, Coca-Cola (Coke) and Pepsi-Cola (Pepsi). The name Coca-Cola was apparently chosen by a bookkeeper working for the drink's inventor (see below), who also contributed the flowing script that is still the company logo. The 'coca' part (despite urban myths) doesn't necessarily indicate that the coca plant was once used in manufacturing it, and was probably simply an attempt to link the drink to the stimulating powers of the plant, which did not, at that time, have its current sinister connections with cocaine. Pepsi's first name comes from 'pep' as in 'something that peps you up'.

did you know?

● Coca-Cola was invented in 1886 by a pharmacist from Atlanta, Georgia, called John S. Pemberton. He and his company (which was founded in 1892) sold it as a syrup to local soda fountains for them to make up into drinks, and even today the corporation produces only the syrup and licenses other companies to bottle it worldwide. An early advertisement promoted the drink as a 'brain tonic and intellectual soda fountain beverage'. In his first year of business Dr Pemberton grossed $50, sold an average of nine syrups a day and, not surprisingly, made a loss.

● Pepsi-Cola appeared in 1898, invented by another pharmacist, Caleb D. Bradham, in New Bern, North Carolina. It was also originally a syrup flavouring for soda fountains and was at first advertised as 'aiding digestion'. The company had an up-and-down career until the 1950s, when it began to establish itself as a rival to Coca-Cola.

cordial

This is the name given to a range of concentrated plant-based drinks that, in addition to their basic flavouring (which makes up anything from 10–30 percent of the concentrate), also contain citric acid, sugar, and sometimes preservatives and colouring. Commercial cordials include lime, cranberry, ginger and lemon grass, and elderflower.

using it Most cordials are served diluted with water and, depending on type and strength, proportions can be anything from one part cordial to four parts water (traditional ones like lime), to one part cordial to ten or more of water (others like elderflower).

word origin Cordial comes from the medieval Latin word, *cordialis*, meaning 'comforting' or 'stimulating', which is related to the Latin *cor*, meaning 'heart'.

did you know?

● Cordials date from medieval times, when the word was used as a medical term and could be applied to drinks, food and ointments that stimulated the heart and circulation. Early cordial drinks usually contained fruit, flowers or herbs, but were often alcoholic.

curaçao

This is a general name for any **liqueur** made from sweet or bitter oranges and **brandy** or a similar spirit. Depending on the maker, curaçao can be colourless, orange, green or even blue. Although alcoholic strength varies slightly depending on type, its strength is usually 40 percent (see **alcohol**). Curaçaos are sometimes sold simply as curaçao, but better-known ones are marketed under brand names such as Cointreau and Grand Marnier.

using it By themselves, curaçaos are served as an after-dinner drink, but they can also be mixed with other ingredients to make cocktails such as white lady (orange liqueur, lemon juice and gin).

Curaçaos are quite sweet and some (especially Grand Marnier) are therefore used occasionally in desserts: as the basic flavouring in a classic sweet **soufflé**; in strawberries Romanov, when it is poured over strawberries and sometimes whipped into the cream that accompanies them; or as the traditional flambé ingredient in *crêpes Suzette* (see **pancake**).

word origin The name comes from the West Indian island of Curaçao, which once supplied the bitter oranges used to make the liqueur.

• Both classic branded curaçaos come from France. Cointreau was invented in 1849 by two confectioners called Cointreau in the town of Angers, and is now made from a blend of natural colourless spirits and sweet and bitter oranges. Grand Marnier was launched in 1880 and is now made just outside Paris from cognac, wild West Indian oranges, orange peel and various secret flavourings.

energy drinks

When sportsmen and women drink mysterious concoctions from plastic bottles during their game, they are trying to replace the sugar, salts and minerals they have lost through their sweaty exertions with (usually) a liquid combination of sugars, such as glucose and sucrose, and caffeine (see **coffee**). The idea behind these 'sports' drinks, of essentially replacing lost energy, has now been transferred to a more ordinary market that might want extra stimulation without an alcoholic boost (and without the sweaty exertion).

Many proprietary brands have been developed to cater for this market and, although ingredients vary from brand to brand, almost all are based on a mixture of sugars (particularly glucose) and caffeine, and are usually carbonated. Other flavourings include fruit, herbs such as ginseng, and berries such as the South American guarana, which contains caffeine. One popular energy drink from Austria even contains taurine, an amino acid originally obtained from ox bile, but now manufactured chemically; it helps to metabolize fats, and there is perhaps just the merest suggestion that drinking it will give you the strength of an ox.

using it Most energy drinks are drunk straight, but some are also used as mixers with alcohol such as tequila, vodka and even champagne.

word origin Many sports drinks use terms like isotonic, hypertonic and hypotonic to emphasize that their main aim is to replace essential salts and minerals lost through sweating when exercising. Isotonic means replacing the same amount, hypertonic drinks are for people with high muscle tone, and hypotonic ones for people with low muscle tone.

• The idea of energy drinks goes back many centuries, and most cultures have mixed herbs, spices and fruit juices together at some point to ward off disease or give themselves a pick-me-up. However, the first modern energy drink was invented in 1927, when a Newcastle chemist concocted a drink containing glucose to help sick children overcome blood sugar deficiency. The drink was called Glucozade, later changed to Lucozade, which was marketed commercially and gradually became of one of Britain's biggest-selling soft drinks.

fruit drinks

These are non-sparkling drinks that get their flavouring and at least part of their liquid from fruit or a combination of fruits. There are three major types: pure fruit juice is made only from freshly squeezed fruit or frozen fruit concentrate and is sometimes pasteurized; fruit drink is usually ready-diluted and made from water, sweeteners, vitamin C, preservatives and colouring, with a fruit-juice base; and fruit squash is a concentrated cloudy drink made from ingredients similar to those that make up fruit drink.

There is no minimum legal requirement for the amount of fruit juice in fruit drinks or squashes, but most of the former contain 6–10 percent and most of the latter between 10–20 percent, although once they are diluted at home the amount will be considerably less, of course. Popular pure juices often have a citrus base; squashes and juice drinks can be made from a single juice or a mixture – one of the most popular, Ribena, is made from blackcurrants.

using it Commercial or home-made freshly squeezed pure fruit juices don't keep well and should be bought or made more or less as needed. Pure juices made from concentrates should be stored in the refrigerator and used within 3–4 days of opening. Long-life pure juices keep well, but should also be stored in the refrigerator after being opened, and used within 4–6 days. Ready-diluted juice drinks and concentrated squashes keep indefinitely; concentrates are normally diluted in proportions of about one part concentrate to four parts water.

Pure citrus and apple juices and their longer-life versions are normally served at breakfast, although there's nothing to stop people drinking them at any point during the day, or with meals.

Freshly crushed berry juices are sometimes made into smoothies or milkshakes. Citrus and apple juices can be used in cooking, too: they go well with chicken, pork and rabbit and can be added to sauces accompanying these meats or used as the liquid part of stews containing them.

did you know?

● Modern barley water is a concentrated fruit squash containing about 17 percent fruit juice (the most popular are lemon and orange) and just about justifies its name with 2 percent barley flour. The original drink was made at home by boiling pearl barley in water with sugar and lemon rind, then straining it and sometimes diluting it with milk. It was supposed to be particularly good for kidney problems.

gin

This strong, colourless, almost flavourless, alcoholic drink is usually made by distilling fermented grain with **juniper berries** and different secret mixtures of various natural flavourings such as herbs and spices. These are called botanicals in the trade, and gins can contain any number from about four to 15. Alcoholic strength is usually 35–42 percent (see **alcohol**).

There are three types of gin. The original Dutch drink, called genever, or Hollands, is made from fermented malt barley, rye and sometimes maize, and distilled at least twice in pot stills, then distilled again with juniper berries and other botanicals. Genever can be *oude* (old), when it is light golden in colour and sweetish to taste, or *yonge* (young), when it is drier and paler in colour. The other two types are 'English' or dry gins, and are usually made from fermented barley and maize or molasses (see **treacle**). They are distilled initially in a continuous still, then in a pot still, before being redistilled with juniper and other botanicals. (See **spirits** for information on stills.) London Dry, the more common English gin, is light and lends itself to mixing, while Plymouth, made only in the town of Plymouth in Devon, is fuller-bodied and more aromatic. English gins aren't aged, but some genevers are, for anything from one to three years.

using it Traditional genever is sold in crocks and drunk cold and neat. Other gins are normally used with mixers such as tonic water or bitter lemon, or as the basis for cocktails like pink gin (Plymouth gin with a few drops of Angostura bitters and water to taste) and dry martini (see below). The branded drink, **Pimm's**, is also based on gin.

word origin The Dutch word for gin comes from the Old French *genèvre*, meaning 'juniper', an important ingredient in the drink. The British started calling it *geneva* because they related the name (mistakenly) to the city in Switzerland, soon shortening it to *gin*.

• Gin was invented in the Netherlands in the 17th century as a cure for kidney and stomach problems. British soldiers came across it while fighting there, discovered that drinking it helped get them through battles, and eventually brought their 'Dutch Courage' back to Britain with them. At first it was sold from apothecary shops as a medicine, but it became so popular, especially among the urban poor, that by the early 18th century it was said that roughly one house in four in London sold gin under some guise or another (gripe water was one favourite). Quality was usually horrible, but it was very cheap – 'Drunk for a penny, dead drunk for tuppence' was the promise – and evocative brand names like Mother's Milk and Cuckold's Comfort began to appear. The Government of the day feared for the moral fibre of the nation and passed laws, first of all banning it (this didn't work), then controlling its use by taxing it and improving production (this did).
• The most famous gin-based cocktail is dry martini, classically made from gin and dry **vermouth**, although James Bond popularized a version using vodka. The proportions of gin and vermouth have varied wildly over the years. Originally it was about

two parts gin to one of vermouth but nowadays it can be as high as ten to one – effectively gin with a few drops of vermouth – making it much drier in taste and far more potent to drink. Winston Churchill apparently thought that even this was too much, and recommended that passing the vermouth cork over the gin in the glass was enough.

lemonade

Originally, lemonade was a non-fizzy home-made drink of lemon juice, water and, more often than not, sugar. Many supermarkets now sell fresh lemonade similar to this in their chiller cabinets. However, the most commonly available type of modern commercial lemonade is different – usually a colourless carbonated water containing about 2 percent lemon juice, sugars such as fructose, glucose and sucrose, citric acid, flavourings and preservatives. A yellowish version is described as 'original' or 'traditional', and diet lemonades replace the sugar in them with artificial **sweeteners**. Although '-ades' started off as citrus-based drinks, popular ones now include cherryade and gingerade.

using it On a hot day, traditional lemonade is one of the most refreshing drinks in the world – a simple mixture of freshly squeezed lemon juice topped up with water, sugar and ice to taste. Commercial fizzy lemonades are aimed mostly at children, who drink them neat. They also make a good addition to a summer punch, **Pimm's** and mixed drinks based on brandy and whisky.

word origin Lemonade first appeared in English during the 17th century, borrowed from the French *limonade* (*limon* was then the French word for lemon).

• Home-made lemonade was particularly popular during Victorian times. Mrs Beeton gave several recipes for it in her book, *Household Management*, including one for invalids, which included lemon zest as well as juice and boiling water; the mixture was cooled and strained before being drunk. Her classic version included a little bicarbonate of soda to give the drink some effervescence – the idea was to drink it while it was still fizzing.

liqueurs

Liqueur is the name given to a range of strong, usually sweet, alcoholic drinks that have a **spirit** base and are flavoured with herbs, spices, fruits, plants or roots in various combinations. The spirit can be one of any number, including **brandy**, **gin**, **rum** or **whisky**. Alcoholic strength varies from drink to drink, but is usually 28–40 percent (see **alcohol**).

Proprietary liqueurs are produced to a variety of secret formulas. Popular ones include Amaretto, a slightly bittersweet drink from northern Italy, flavoured with almonds and apricot kernels; Benedictine, which is French in origin, a greenish-amber mixture of brandy and over 25 herbs and plants; Drambuie, the Scottish contribution, which has a malt whisky, honey and herb base; and Jamaican Tia Maria, made from local Blue Mountain coffee and dark rum.

using them Most liqueurs are drunk on their own after a meal or combined with other types of alcohol, soft drinks and flavourings to make cocktails or punches.

In cooking, liqueurs are used most frequently in sweet dishes, and can be flambéd – a more than good enough excuse to make them into sauces for desserts like *crêpes Suzette* (where Grand Marnier is a classic ingredient). They are also occasionally used as a flavouring for sweet **soufflés**, mousses or trifles (see **sponge cake**).

word origin Liqueur comes from the Latin *liquor*, meaning 'liquid'. Benedictine takes its name from the order of monks because it was first made in a Benedictine monastery in Normandy in the 16th century, although the modern drink has no connection with the order. Drambuie comes from the Gaelic *an dram buidheach* – 'the satisfying drink' – and the secret recipe for it is alleged to have been provided by Bonnie Prince Charlie in gratitude for helping him to escape to France after the failure of the Jacobite Rebellion in 1745.

did you know?

● Medieval liqueurs may have been developed initially to hide the taste of the first distilled spirits, which could be crude, or just to give them some extra flavour. Many were invented by monks and, since herbs, spices and plants were known to have medicinal properties, and it was hoped that spirits were beneficial too, they were used to dress wounds and protect against disease, besides being enjoyed as a restorative drink.

Madeira

This is a fortified **wine** made on the island of Madeira by a unique process called *estufagem*. The grapes are picked, pressed and fermented in the usual way, and most are fortified with brandy or a spirit made from sugar cane either during fermentation or just after (cheaper wines, however, are fortified later). The resulting mixture is transferred to special tanks or casks, which are artificially heated over a period of 3–6 months or more. It is then either stored in bulk for 18 months before being shipped and bottled (cheaper ones) or aged for 3–15 years or more before being blended and bottled (better ones); a special vintage Madeira stays in casks for a minimum of 20 years.

Different grape varieties are used to create four main types, ranging from very dry (*sercial*), through dryish (*verdelho*) and sweetish (*bual*), to very sweet (*malmsey* or *malvasia*). The alcoholic strength is around 17.5 percent (see **alcohol**).

using it Madeira lasts almost indefinitely, even once it has been opened. The sweeter types are still sometimes served as an after-dinner drink in much the same way as port and, like port, are decanted to remove any sediment. Dry Madeira is mainly used for cooking now, and can be added in small quantities to stocks and sauces, particularly those for beef or game, or used as part of the liquid for red meat casseroles. It also has a real affinity with mushrooms.

word origin Madeira is still the only producer of this type of wine, so the drink is named after the island.

did you know?

• Madeira was invented by accident. The island was settled in 1419 by the Portuguese and, because of its strategic position, became the port of call for European sailing ships going to Africa, Asia and the Americas. The Portuguese had brought vines with them, so naturally the sailors stocked up with wine when they reached port. It was not very good wine, but the sailors noticed that after some months of being rolled about in their ships in the hot tropics, the strength and taste improved. So for the next few hundred years the wine was sent on long sea voyages to turn it into what we now know as Madeira. When this became too expensive, the process was reproduced on land.

mineral water

This is water from underground sources that is extracted and bottled for sale – either 'still' or with carbon dioxide or natural gases from the water's source added to make it fizzy. Unlike other drinking waters, mineral water must emerge at source pure and drinkable in its natural state and can't be treated before being bottled. Under EU law, bottled spring water should conform to the same criteria as mineral water except that it doesn't have to contain a consistent mineral content, but in the UK it is permissible to treat it before bottling. Tap **water** is always purified before use.

'Mineral' water is an accurate description because the water has generally filtered down from the earth's surface through rocks to form large underground lakes, rivers or aquifers (bodies of rock containing or transmitting groundwater), and in the process absorbs a number of minerals from its surroundings. The best tend to come from mountainous areas such as the French Alps or Scottish Highlands, where there is a large amount of snow in winter (when it melts, some of the water runs off into rivers, but a lot is absorbed deep into the ground).

The presence of these minerals, though in small quantities, gives the water additional qualities that may have a beneficial effect on the body. Typical mineral waters contain traces of calcium, magnesium, sodium, potassium, iron, chlorides, nitrates and sulphides.

using it Some fanatics use mineral water for everything – cooking, brushing their teeth, diluting drinks – but most of us drink it cold with, between and after meals. Carbonated mineral water is sometimes substituted for soda water and mixed with white wine to make a spritzer.

Pimm's

Pimm's is the brand name of a bottled red-coloured **cocktail** containing **gin** and various secret ingredients and spices. It has an alcoholic strength of 25 percent (see **alcohol**).

using it The label on the bottle reads 'Pimm's Original No. 1 Cup' and that remains one of the most popular ways to serve it: mixed with lemonade or ginger ale and ice cubes in a large jug or 'cup'. Fruit such as sliced apple, strawberry and peach, slices of cucumber and sprigs of mint are all used as garnishes, occasionally at the same time. The proportion of Pimm's to lemonade is down to personal taste, but about three parts lemonade to one part Pimm's would be averagely alcoholic and two parts lemonade to one part Pimm's probably even better.

word origin There was a Mr Pimm, although it's unlikely that he invented his 'cup'. James Pimm owned Pimm's Oyster Warehouse in the City of London during the 1840s, which later developed into Pimm's Restaurant. Along with its food, the restaurant provided various 'cups' or punches for its clientele.

did you know?

• It isn't clear exactly when Pimm's most popular offering was first bottled and sold outside the restaurant. However, by the end of the 19th century it was being exported in large quantities to keep up the morale of British regiments (almost certainly officer class only) in various parts of the Empire – it went with Kitchener to Khartoum, for instance – as well as being consumed by a widening public at home.
• The reason Pimm's is called 'No. 1 Cup' is that for some time there were others: No. 2 was made with whisky, No. 3 was brandy-based and No. 4 contained rum. However, they were less successful than the gin-based drink and have now been phased out.

port

A fortified **wine** from Portugal, port is made in several stages. In the autumn, grapes are pressed at farms called *quintas*, then allowed to ferment for a day or so before being piped into vats containing about 20 percent spirit (a type of brandy called *aguardente*), which stops the fermentation. The following spring the treated wine is sent down to the city of Oporto, to 'lodges' where it is matured in wooden casks or tanks for at least 18 months and usually much longer. At this point, the wine is blended (most ports are a mixture of wine made from several types of grapes in several different years), then filtered and bottled. A few

special ports are bottled relatively early and matured in the bottle rather than in casks. Port has an alcoholic strength of about 20 percent (see **alcohol**).

Most port is red and sweet and there are several types. Ruby is matured for up to three years and sold ready to drink. Traditional tawny is matured in wooden casks for at least six years, usually much longer (good ones will have the number of years on the label), and shouldn't be confused with cheap tawny, a brown-tinged wine usually made by blending ruby port with white port; both are bottled ready to drink. Vintage port is made from a blend of the best grapes from a single year (which will be marked on the bottle), thought to be so good it is declared a 'vintage'. It is matured in wooden casks for 2–3 years, then bottled and sold, with the knowledge that it needs to mature in the bottle for a minimum of 15 years before being ready to drink, and will be at its best several years after that. Crusted port, named after the 'crust', or sediment, that forms in the bottle, is matured in the cask for three years before being bottled, but is a blend of wines from several years. Like vintage port, it continues to age in the bottle for several more years before it is ready for drinking. A small amount of port is also made from white grapes to produce white port, a blend of young wines matured for at least 18 months, which is mostly medium-dry.

using it Once opened, ruby, tawny and white ports will keep for three weeks or more; vintage and crusted ones should be drunk within a few days. Crusted and vintage ports are bottled without being filtered and need to be decanted before serving to get rid of the crust or sediment in the bottle.

Red ports are normally served at room temperature as an after-dinner drink, often with cheese. They have a particular affinity with blue cheese and 'port and Stilton' is one of those traditional combinations that appear regularly, especially around Christmas. White port is lighter than red and is usually served chilled as an apéritif. Ruby port used to be mixed with non-alcoholic drinks such as lemonade, although this is less popular now.

Ruby port is occasionally used in cooking – perhaps to make a rich ice-cream or jelly. In small quantities, it can also add flavour and colour to stocks, particularly for beef or game, and to relishes like the cranberry one that accompanies Christmas turkey. It is a traditional ingredient in Cumberland sauce, the classic English accompaniment to game and ham.

word origin Port is named after the city of Oporto where the blending, maturing and shipping of the wine take place.

did you know?

• Port was once called 'the Englishman's wine'. This stems from some local difficulties between the French and English that started in the 17th century and didn't really finish until the early 19th century. A few wars and a lot of banning of imports or heavy taxation made English wine merchants look for other sources of supply. Some enterprising ones came up with the red wine produced around the River Douro in Portugal, but unfortunately it didn't travel well. To help keep it in good condition, brandy began to be added before the journey. An 18th-century treaty gave Portugal 'favoured nation' treatment on wine, and a market was born that lasted until the 20th century.

punch

Punch is a mixed drink that is usually combined in large quantities in a bowl or pitcher. It can be hot or cold and based on almost anything alcoholic, such as rum, vodka, brandy, liqueur, and fortified, sparkling still wine. Other ingredients such as sugar, fruit, spices, water and even tea or milk are also added according to taste or whim. Sangria, a mixture of red wine,

sliced fruit, sugar, soda water and (optionally) brandy, is probably the best-known cold punch, while glögg, a potent blend of brandy, spices, raisins, almonds, sugar and medium sherry, is a typical hot one.

using it Normally punch is prepared for a party or celebration, or at least a gathering of people. Once in its bowl, it is ladled into appropriate glasses and handed round until it is finished (or the people drinking it are).

word origin Punch may come from the Hindi *panch*, meaning 'five', to indicate the five ingredients used initially to make it: spirits, sugar, lemons, water and either spices or tea. Another possibility is that it comes from 'puncheon', a large cask used in the West Indies to store rum, and from which punch may have been served.

did you know?

• Punch could be one of the better legacies of Britain's imperial past, since it seems to have first appeared in India in the 17th century, probably as a British spin on something local and more innocent. The tradition of serving what was at that time a cooling mixture spread to any hot country where Englishmen toiled for the greater glory of the Empire, including the West Indies, where punches based on rum are still popular.

rum

Rum is a **spirit**, distilled sometimes from fermented sugar-cane juice but more usually from fermented blackstrap molasses (see **treacle**), a residue of sugar processing. How it is produced depends on the type being made: light rums are fermented quickly, normally for 1–2 days, before being distilled in a continuous still (see **spirits**); heavy rums are fermented for about 12 days, then distilled twice in a pot still. Light rums are aged for about a year or so, but heavier ones spend a minimum of three years in oak casks and some stay there for as long as six.

Although rum is made in many countries, the best-known sources are the Caribbean islands, each one creating its own unique type. The main producer is Puerto Rico, with most of its supply going to the United States; other notable producers include Barbados, Jamaica, Martinique and Trinidad. Rums have an alcoholic strength of about 37.5–40 percent (see **alcohol**).

using it As well as being drunk neat or with water, rum is mixed with various soft drinks (classically cola) and also forms the basis of many breezers, punches and classic cocktails, such as daiquiri, which is made from white rum, lime juice and sugar.

Rum is used in cooking, too, especially in desserts – pineapple and bananas are the most popular partners (particularly with desiccated or creamed coconut), but chocolate runs a close third. Dried fruit is often rehydrated in rum before being added to cakes or puddings, and since it flambés well, rum is also occasionally substituted for brandy in flamed desserts.

word origin The earliest written mention of rum dates back to 1651, to something called rumbullion that was drunk on sugar plantations in the West Indies. It was also sometimes called rumbustion, and both words were associated with making a loud noise, possibly as a result of drinking too much of it. More prosaically, the word could have come from the Malay *brum*, meaning 'fermented drink', or from the last part of each of the Latin names for sugar cane, *Saccharum officinarum*. The cocktail daiquiri, gets its name from a tin mine in Cuba, where it was allegedly served to keep visitors cool.

From the beginning of the 18th century until 1970, rum was served to crews on board British Navy ships – first to keep the sailors warm in icy waters, then just by tradition and to keep them happy. Initially it was drunk neat but, not surprisingly, this led to a lot of drunkenness, so in 1740 Admiral Vernon ordered that the daily ration be diluted with water. It so happened that he had a nickname, 'Old Grog', from the cloak made of grogram that he always wore. From this came 'grog', meaning a mixture of spirits (usually rum) and water, and 'groggy', which originally meant to feel unsteady or ill because of too much drink.

did you know?

* The Spaniards took sugar cane to the Caribbean and Latin America in the late 15th and early 16th centuries, and crude rum was probably produced from it shortly after. In the hot West Indian climate, rum was thought to have virtues as a stimulant and also medicinal value – as, in fact, it did, since it was used as an anaesthetic until the 19th century.
* By the 18th century, rum was an established drink in Britain and France and, equally importantly, in the American colonies. The career of George Washington was launched on rum, since he was elected to the Virginia House of Burgesses not by campaigning but by providing 75 gallons (340 litres) of free rum to the voters. It was also sometimes used as barter to get slaves in Africa, or to buy or exchange them in the early slave markets of the New World.

sherry

Sherry is a fortified **wine** produced in south-western Spain around the city of Jerez de la Frontera. It is made mainly from Palomino grapes, which are pressed and then fermented in *bodegas*, or cellars. When fermentation is complete, the wine is drawn off, fortified by the addition of brandy and left to develop in small groups of casks called *criaderas*. It remains in the casks for about six months, until a *flor*, or yeast, forms on top. Those that develop *flor* are separated out to become dry sherry, while those that don't develop it become sweet. Both eventually enter the complex *solera* system, which blends and matures the new wine. There the *criaderas* are grouped according to age, and wine for bottling is drawn from the oldest casks, which are then topped up with wine from the next oldest and so on, down the line to the newest wine. Thousands of casks can be involved and the wine can mature for many years.

The style of the sherry depends on whether it contained *flor* or not, the amount of brandy used and the length of time it was matured. Alcoholic strength ranges from 15–18 percent (see **alcohol**), colour from yellow to dark brown, and taste from very dry to very sweet. Because of the nature of the *solera* system, there are no named vineyards or any vintage years, and each bottle is identified by type. Fino is the palest and driest sherry, made from *flor* wine and considered to be the finest; manzanilla is a type of fino, produced near the sea at Sanlucar de Barrameda, and has a salty tang; amontillado is a stronger, medium-dry fino; and oloroso is darker, richer and stronger than any fino, made from wine without *flor*. Cream sherry is usually a blend of oloroso (and sometimes other types) and ordinary wine made from sweet Pedro Ximenez grapes.

using it Drier sherries should be stored in the refrigerator and served ice-cold; sweeter ones are normally drunk at room temperature or with ice. Once opened, dry sherries should be used within a week or so but sweeter ones last a little longer – perhaps 2–3 weeks. Sherry is usually served as an apéritif, traditionally in schooners, long, narrow glasses that flare slightly at the top. Most sherries make a good addition to punch and are occasionally mixed with soft drinks such as lemonade.

In cooking, medium or sweet sherries moisten trifles (see **sponge cake**) and compotes, and are used to flavour ice-cream, dessert sauces and cakes. Dry or medium ones can also be used in savoury cooking to provide a sauce for calf's liver, pork or veal escalopes. A spoonful or two added to mushrooms or meat stock gives extra richness.

word origin Sherry comes from the name of the city at the centre of the sherry trade, Jerez de la Frontera, whose original Moorish name was Seris. The English used to call the strong wine from the area 'sack', which became 'Sherris sack' to identify its place of origin, then eventually 'sherry'.

did you know?

• Wine may have been made by the Phoenicians in the Jerez region in around 1000BC and was definitely being produced there by the Romans until about AD400. From the 8th to the 14th centuries the area was occupied by the Moors, and Jerez was a frontier town – hence its name. After the Christians regained possession, the wine trade redeveloped (although it hadn't stopped under the Moors) and the export trade with England became important.

soda water

This is a slightly bitter fizzy drink made from sodium bicarbonate and carbonated water. To be called soda water, it must contain a minimum of 550mg of sodium bicarbonate per litre.

using it Soda water can be drunk on its own, but is normally used as a mixer with spirits such as whisky and brandy, or added to wine to create a spritzer.

word origin The name is borrowed from the medieval Latin, *soda*, but where that came from is unknown. In the United States, soda is used more broadly to mean a sweet fizzy drink. This was originally bought at a soda fountain, usually the soft drinks and ice-cream counter of neighbourhood pharmacies.

spirits

This is the name given to fermented drinks that are then distilled, a process based on the fact that **alcohol** has a lower boiling point than water. Spirits include **brandy** (made from wine), **rum** (made from molasses) and **vodka**, **gin** and **whisky** (made from what is essentially unhopped beer, although sometimes vodka is made from molasses, too).

During distillation, weak fermented liquids such as beer and wine are heated in machines called stills until the alcohol in them forms a vapour. This is drawn off from the remaining liquid, cooled down and converted back into a concentrated alcoholic liquid, the principal component of which is ethyl alcohol (ethanol). There are two different types of still: continuous, also known as patent, where essentially the fermented liquid is fed into the machine and, after a complicated process, emerges as a drinkable spirit; and pot, the older and simpler of the two, where the spirits that emerge after the first distillation are undrinkable and therefore distilled a second time to purify and improve them. Pot-stilled spirits retain more flavour and character than continuous-stilled ones, but the pot needs to be cooled, cleaned and refilled after each distillation, so it is more expensive to run. Brandy and malt whisky are usually made in pot stills, while more neutral-tasting spirits such as vodka tend to be made in continuous ones.

using it Most spirits are served by themselves with ice, mixed with soft drinks such as soda or tonic water, or added to cocktails and punches. Some, especially brandy, are also used in cooking.

word origin Spirit comes from the Latin *spirare*, meaning 'to breathe'.

• Crude spirits were being made in parts of Asia by about 750BC, but it was probably the Arabs who invented what would now be regarded as distillation. By the 15th century, stills were being developed in Italy to produce a spirit from wine called *aqua vitae* (Latin for 'water of life'), although this was initially regarded as a medicine and only later as a pleasurable drink. It was the Dutch who took things a stage further in the 17th century. As a great seafaring nation, they wanted something that could be kept in reasonable condition to drink on long voyages and then traded at their final destinations. Distilled wine (which by this time had become brandy) and distilled grain (which had become gin) were ideal for the purpose.

• In an earlier development, monks in Ireland and Scotland created their own water of life from barley grains, which soon became what we now know as whisky. And by the 17th century, after the earlier introduction of sugar cane into the West Indies, rum began to be made from the molasses it produces.

tea

This is (usually) the drink that results when boiling water is poured over the leaves of an evergreen bush, *Camellia sinensis*, which is native to both China and India and the subject of this entry. The word is also used to describe a drink made in a similar way from herbs, spices and flowers such as camomile and peppermint.

At the last count, there were over 3000 varieties of *Camellia sinensis*, growing in mostly tropical or subtropical hilly regions of the world that have plenty of rain and some sunshine. Harvesting takes place frequently and by hand – about 25–50 times a year – and only the top two young leaves and the unopened bud are taken from each branch.

Tea is categorized according to whether it has been fermented or not. Black tea is fermented. The leaves are spread out to dry on large trays, called withering, then crushed either in a rolling machine or by putting them through a cutting and tearing machine. All the leaves are then fermented and after that they are dried (called firing), when they turn dark brown or black. Green tea is unfermented. The leaves are steam-heated to prevent fermentation before being rolled and dried like black tea. Oolong tea is made in the same way as black tea, except that it is fermented for only half the amount of time. Northern India, Sri Lanka, Kenya, Malawi and China are the major producers of black tea. China and Japan are the leading suppliers of green tea, while Taiwan produces the most oolong.

Black teas are graded by leaf size (it's important that leaves in a packet are similar in size, since small leaves brew more quickly than larger ones). A black tea described as pekoe will be high in quality, with very young, full leaves. Orange pekoe means that the tea includes not only immature leaves but unopened leaf buds as well, and broken pekoe that the leaves have been broken into pieces by the more desirable method of rolling. The Chinese black tea, Lapsang souchong, is wood-smoked to achieve its unique flavour. Locality names are a good indication of quality and type: tea from Assam, for instance, will be dark and full-bodied, those labelled Darjeeling more delicate and fragrant. Blending is an integral part of tea production and some blends, like Earl Grey, a black tea flavoured with bergamot oil, have become famous in their own right.

using it Tea can be bought as teabags (invented by a New York tea merchant about a hundred years ago as a way of sending samples to his clients) or in packets of loose leaves, and both keep indefinitely. Only about 15 percent of consumption worldwide is in the form of teabags, although they account for roughly 80 percent of tea sold in the UK. It is 'brewed' by infusing loose leaves or teabags in a pot of boiling water for a few minutes or by pouring the water over a teabag in a cup

and dunking it for a few minutes until it imparts its colour and flavour. Milk and sugar or sweeteners are optional extras in tea, and it can also be served with a slice of lemon, the traditional Russian way. Chinese and Japanese green teas and oolongs are drunk without any additions, although in some North African and Middle Eastern countries mint and even pine nuts can be added to green tea. In hot weather, tea is often served iced.

In Western countries, tea is drunk with, between or after meals, while green tea is drunk throughout Chinese meals and after Japanese ones. Tea is occasionally used in cooking – for example, to rehydrate dried fruit, such as raisins and prunes, for making cakes and tea breads. It is sometimes stirred into punches. Earl Grey tea is occasionally used as a flavouring for ice-cream.

In its heyday during the 19th and early 20th centuries, tea was such an important staple that two meals were named after it. High tea was a working-class meal, eaten after work in the early evening, and included meat or fish and bread and butter, all washed down with tea. Afternoon tea involved a degree of leisure, nicely bridging the gap between a light lunch and a not-so-light dinner, and revolved around not only tea but also a selection of delicate sandwiches, warm scones and as many cakes as could be decently stuffed down. A whole repertoire of breads and buns have become known as 'tea' breads and cakes because they were served either with one of these meals or as a snack with tea at other times of day.

word origin Tea comes from the Chinese Amoy word, *t'e*. Amoy, now Xiamen, was a port from which Dutch traders took the leaves (which they called *thee*) to Europe. By the time the leaves arrived in Britain in the 17th century they were being called *tee*, or *tay*, from which the modern name evolved. Earl Grey gets its name from a British prime minister in the 1830s, who was supposed to have been given the recipe by a grateful Chinese mandarin. Chinese gunpowder tea isn't so called because it blows your head off when you drink it, but because the young green leaves are made into little balls that look like gunpowder pellets.

did you know?

• During 2737BC in China, so the story goes, the emperor, Shen Nung, was sitting under a wild tea bush boiling up some water when a few leaves floated down into his bowl. When he drank the resulting 'brew', he found it refreshed him and made him much more active. Strangely, though, he doesn't appear to have passed on the good news to anyone; the first written references to tea in China occur only around the 4th century AD.

• In China and Japan, tea was originally considered a medicine or tonic. Gradually, however, along with the development of Zen Buddhism in both countries, it came to be seen as a contribution to a particular life pattern – so much so that by the 13th and 14th centuries an elaborate tea ceremony, called *Cha-no-yu*, had developed in Japan, in which four ideals – harmony, respect, purity and tranquillity – are embodied. The tea ceremony can last for two hours or more and involves not only the drinking of tea itself, but also its careful preparation in special pots from which the tea is poured into exquisite small bowls.

• Tea has played its part in Western history too, in particular during the Boston Tea Party in 1773 and the 19th-century Opium Wars. The Boston Tea Party took place when Britain imposed taxes on the import of goods, including tea, into its North American colonies. The Americans refused to accept this and, in a show of defiance, a group disguised as Native Americans boarded ships in Boston harbour and threw chests of tea overboard; from this and other incidents, the American War of Independence began. The Opium Wars resulted after Britain began to pay for its growing imports of tea from China by exporting opium from India to China. The Chinese didn't like this, tried to ban opium and, when this didn't succeed, banned tea

exports instead. This led to war between the two countries, and also to the British developing their own tea plantations in India.

• Tea can be good for you, according to modern research. It contains flavonoids (which can help to prevent heart disease, various cancers and strokes), potassium (helps maintain a healthy heartbeat and tones up nerves and muscles), manganese (good for bone growth), fluoride (helps prevent tooth and gum decay) and various vitamins. However, it also contains caffeine (see **coffee**), although at around 50mg for an average cup of black tea, this works out at about two-thirds of the amount in a cup of instant coffee and half that in brewed coffee.

tequila

Tequila is a Mexican spirit made from blue agave, a perennial plant native to Central America and related to the lily. The blue agave is matured for about 8–10 years before being harvested to be made into tequila, a process that includes steam-cooking it to extract the sugary sap and fermenting the sap with yeast before the resulting liquid is distilled twice in pot stills (see **spirits**). Tequila is aged in barrels for anything from a week or so to over a year, depending on type. Ordinary white tequila is scarcely aged at all, but a tequila described as *reposado* will have been matured for between a few months and a year, while an *añejo* will have been stored for over a year. Most have an alcoholic strength of 38 percent (see **alcohol**).

Production is strictly regulated and, to be called tequila, the drink must contain at least 51 percent fermented sugars obtained from blue agave, be pot stilled twice and produced in specially designated areas, mostly the state of Jalisco. Mezcal is a similar spirit made from other species of the agave plant. It is distilled only once and is produced throughout Mexico.

using it In Mexico, neat tequila is sometimes served with a chaser called *sangrita*, a fiery combination of orange and tomato juice, chilli and spices. Elsewhere it is mostly mixed into cocktails, like margarita, which was invented by an American socialite (called Margarita!) for a poolside party in Acapulco, Mexico, in 1948 and consists of tequila, Cointreau and lime juice. Before serving, the rim of the glass (V-shaped for preference) is traditionally rubbed with lime juice and then dipped in salt.

word origin The drink was first made in central Mexico around the town of Tequila, near Guadalajara, which is still the centre of production.

did you know?

• The idea behind tequila – boiling and fermenting agave to produce alcohol – is very old, going back to Aztec times and perhaps even before. It was called *tepemexcal* then, used in religious rituals and for healing, and may have been similar to *pulque*, a beer-like drink that is still made in Mexico. The Spaniards introduced distilling techniques when they settled in Mexico in the 16th century, and the first records of distilled tequila date back to about 1600.

tonic water

A bittersweet fizzy drink made from sweetened carbonated water, tonic water is flavoured with quinine (see below). In order to be called tonic water, it must contain a minimum of 57mg of quinine per litre.

using it Tonic water is sometimes drunk on its own (usually with ice), but its most popular role is as a mixer with alcohol, particularly gin and vodka.

word origin Tonic comes from the Greek *tonikos*, meaning 'helping to maintain or restore physical well-being' – an indication of at least one of the original aims of the drink (although there are those who would argue that it's the addition of gin and vodka that helps it truly achieve this aim).

did you know?

• Quinine comes from the bark of the South American cinchona tree, and was sometimes called Jesuit's bark because it was Catholic priests who first learned about 'the fever tree' and its special properties from local tribes. For hundreds of years it was the only effective treatment for malaria, and therefore became a popular addition to soda water on 'medicinal' grounds, particularly in Raj India. When commercial 'tonic water' first appeared, one brand added the word 'Indian' to the name to stress its restorative powers. Modern medicinal imbibers should know, however, that the average quinine content of a gin and tonic is about 20mg – less than a tenth of the strength of most quinine tablets.

vermouth

Vermouth is a drink made from **wine**, sugar, various flavourings and spirits, usually a colourless brandy. Most is produced around Turin in Italy and Marseilles in France, although other wine-producing countries make similar drinks.

Wormwood (*Artemisia absinthium*), a bitter-tasting herb of the daisy family, is one of the major flavourings, but others such as coriander, orange peel, cloves and quinine are also used. Each manufacturer has its own closely guarded secret recipe. Flavourings are added in a variety of ways: steeped or macerated in water or spirits, then mixed into the sweetened fortified wine; infused or passed through water or spirits; distilled into a concentrated liquid with them before being added; or a combination of these. The resulting mixture is clarified, pasteurized, filtered, then 'rested' for a few months before being bottled.

Vermouth can be dry or sweet, and red, white or rosé in colour. Almost all are sold as commercial brands, such as Martini & Rossi and Cinzano (Italian); Noilly Prat and Chambéry (French). The alcoholic strength varies from 15–18 percent (see **alcohol**).

using it Dry vermouth should be kept in the refrigerator after opening and drunk within 10–14 days; sweeter types keep for 3–4 weeks.

Branded vermouths were traditionally served chilled as apéritifs, although they are probably now more popular as ingredients in cocktails such as dry martini or Manhattan (see **gin** and **whisky**). They are occasionally used in cooking: Noilly Prat is sometimes added to sauces for fish, while the Italian vermouths can enrich sauces for fried or grilled meat.

word origin Vermouth comes, via French, from the German *wermut*, meaning wormwood.

did you know?

● If vermouth is considered as just a 'herbal' drink, it has been around for thousands of years. Our ancient ancestors were constantly mixing herbs with their wine, often to disguise wine that had gone off, but also for its supposed medicinal benefits. The Greeks believed that adding herbs to wine could cure hangovers, and rmperor Nero's physician (a Greek) prescribed wormwood wine as an aphrodisiac as far back as AD60. Later, doctors used wormwood wine to induce vomiting and as part of a poultice mixture for wounds.
● By the end of the 18th century, Antonio Benedetto Carpano had his own 'wine bar' in Turin, where you could go and order a 'vermouth', specify which concoction of herbs you wanted and have it made up for you on the spot. The idea was so successful that he had to stay open round the clock to satisfy demand. Carpano also made the first commercially bottled vermouth; other modern manufacturers were in business by the middle of the 19th century.

vodka

Nowadays this colourless, tasteless, slightly oily spirit is usually distilled from **grain**, although in theory it can be made from almost anything, like potatoes, molasses or fruit – as it traditionally was when there was a surplus. The main centres of production are in Russi[a] countr[y] to produc[e] in a continu[ous] diluted with disti[lled] strength, then filtere[d] charcoal to get rid of rem[aining]. The result is a strong alcoho[l]. 35–45 percent (see **alcohol**).

using it In Russia and Poland the usual practice is to drink vodka neat, straight from the freezer and in small glasses. It has become a standard accompaniment there to delicacies such as caviar. Elsewhere it is normally served with mixers such as tonic water or orange juice, or used as the basis for cocktails such as Bloody Mary, which was first concocted in Harry's Bar in Paris from a mixture of vodka, tomato juice, Worcestershire sauce, lemon and (optionally) Tabasco sauce. There's even a version of dry martini that uses vodka instead of gin.

word origin Vodka is Russian and means 'little water'. The Bloody Mary cocktail is allegedly named after the 16th-century Catholic Queen Mary of England, who was so called because of the enthusiastic way she executed Protestants.

did you know?

● You could probably start a war by claiming in Russia that Poland invented vodka, and vice versa. What is indisputable is that a kind of *aqua vitae* had developed in the monasteries of both countries by the 12th century and, as in other countries with similar spirits, it was initially drunk as a herbal remedy rather than for pleasure. It was being produced commercially in both countries by the 17th century.
● Although the basic spirit is flavourless, other ingredients are sometimes added to give vodka extra taste – favourites include lemon, honey and cherries. Peter the Great of Russia was said to prefer his vodka flavoured with a dose of pepper, while Polish

...a is infused with zubrowka grass,
...ing for the country's wild bison. A blade
...nside each bottle.

...er

...ancient Sumerians called water *a*,
...ch also meant sperm, since they realized
...at both were life-giving forces. More
prosaically it is a colourless, odourless liquid
made up of two parts hydrogen and one
part oxygen (H_2O). It combines easily with
other substances, so even 'pure' water
holds traces of isotopes like deuterium
and tritium, while 'ordinary' water (the stuff
in rainfall and rivers) always contains
dissolved gases and solids absorbed from
its surroundings. As for 'drinking' water
(the water that emerges from cold taps and
comes from springs, lakes, rivers and
reservoirs), it almost always has to go
through some degree of purification and
sterilization before it can be drunk. The most
common practice is to add chlorine to
destroy harmful bacteria and, if the water is
'hard' (because it has absorbed minerals
such as calcium from surrounding rocks),
treat it with lime and sometimes soda to
make it 'soft'. Sodium fluoride is also usually
added to help prevent tooth decay. The
result is 'cleaner' water, but often the taste
leaves a lot to be desired, probably one
reason for the recent growth in sales of
bottled **mineral water**.

using it All living creatures and plants
contain water and need it in order to stay
alive. More than 70 percent of human body
weight is water and this needs constant
replenishing, since we lose a lot through
perspiration, transpiration (breathing) and
excretion. The general consensus is that
under normal circumstances we need
about 1.5–2 litres of fluid a day. We get
around 0.75–1.25 litres from the food we
eat – salad vegetables, for instance, are
about 90 percent water, fruit about 85
percent and even raw meat contains about

70 percent. Some of our liquid intake can
be tea and coffee, but we should also drink
plenty of water.

Water is used extensively in cooking:
as a medium for cooking other food (for
example, by boiling or steaming), as an
ingredient in sauces, casseroles, bread and
many other dishes, and also to dilute or
rehydrate foods. And, of course, most
drinks like tea, coffee, soft drinks and
alcohol are made with water.

word origin Water comes from the Old
English *waeter*, which was Germanic in
origin.

did you know?

• There might be 'Water, water, everywhere', but the
poet got it right when he went on to say, 'Nor any drop
to drink'. About 71 percent of the earth's surface is
covered by water, but unfortunately more than 98
percent of it is salty seawater that is unfit to drink
without expensive desalination. The remainder is
'fresh' – i.e. without salt – but most of this is frozen as
icecaps in the Arctic and Antarctic and a lot of the rest
is held in clouds and vapour in the atmosphere, some
of which comes to us as rain. Accessible fresh water
on the ground or under it amounts to roughly 500,000
cubic kilometres. This may sound adequate but, with
increasing populations and more and more demands
on the water supply, there are real worries that there
won't be enough to go around in the future.
• In medieval times, the scientists of the day
(alchemists) spent a lot of energy searching for the
'water of life' (*aqua vitae* in Latin), a mysterious
substance they thought would give them eternal
youth. A Spanish explorer, Ponce de Leon, spent many
years in the New World looking for its source, the
fountain of youth. But even though they failed to find
eternal youth, alchemists did, in the course of their
experiments, eventually come up with an eternal
substitute for it, the alcoholic spirits industry.

whisky

This is a strong alcoholic **spirit** made from
distilled grains such as **barley**, **maize** and

rye. Although a number of countries produce whisky, the four main centres are Scotland, Ireland, the United States and Canada, Scotland being pre-eminent. Whiskies usually have an alcoholic strength of about 40 percent (see **alcohol**).

Scottish malt whisky is made from malted barley, which is steeped in water, then allowed to germinate before being dried over peat fires. The resulting grain is ground and 'mashed' to produce wort – this is put into a large vat with hot water, then agitated to dissolve the sugars in the grain. The wort is fermented into wash (a sort of unhopped beer) before being distilled twice in pot stills (see **spirits**). It acquires its colour from the wooden casks in which it is matured for anything from 3–15 years before being bottled ready for sale. Most Scottish malt is single – the product of one distillery, but different casks and ages – although occasional bottles of single cask are available. These are malt from a single distillation and cask in one distillery, the finest that money (a lot of it) can buy.

Scottish grain whiskies are made in continuous stills, from a mixture of malted barley and unmalted cereals that can include maize or **wheat**. Like malt whisky, they are matured in wooden casks. Blended Scotch whiskies are usually a mix of 15–50 different malt and grain whiskies, which are brought together after the initial maturing period, then 'married' in casks for a further 6–8 months before being bottled and sold. The more malt whisky a blend contains, the better it's considered to be: standard blends have about 20–30 percent, premium up to 45 percent and deluxe over 50 percent.

Irish malt whiskey has its own unique, mild flavour, and is usually made from malted barley or a blend of malted and unmalted barley. While Scottish malt has a double distillation, Irish has triple, and in Ireland the barley is dried over coal rather than by the peat smoke or 'reek' preferred

in Scotland. It is matured for the same length of time.

American whiskeys are made from malted barley and maize or rye (sometimes both) and are distilled in continuous stills. They are fermented as a sweet mash or sour: for sweet mash, fresh yeast is used and fermentation lasts no more than two days; for sour, residue from a previous batch is used again in addition to fresh yeast, and fermentation continues for about four days. The resulting liquor is normally aged in charred wooden casks for a minimum of two years. Straight American whiskey is unblended, made from only one type of grain (normally rye or maize). Bourbon, one of the most popular, is a sour mash that contains at least 51 percent maize, as does Tennessee's favourite son, Jack Daniels. Canadian whisky is made from a blend of grains, including rye, barley, maize and wheat, often with rye predominating, and is distilled in continuous stills, then matured for at least three years.

using it A good malt whisky should be treasured, preferably by itself after a meal. Blended or other grain whiskies are usually served as pre-dinner drinks, sometimes 'neat' (i.e. with no additions), sometimes over ice, or with water or soft drinks such as soda water, ginger ale, and even cola in the case of bourbons. These whiskies are also used in cocktails like the Manhattan, named after the Manhattan district of New York where the drink was first invented, and made from a blend of rye whiskey, dry or sweet vermouth and Angostura bitters.

Whisky is also used in cooking occasionally, mostly in Scotland: there are tales of it being stirred into porridge, and it's one of the ingredients in the classic raspberry dessert, cranachan (the others being cream, honey and toasted oats).

word origin Whisky comes from the Gaelic *uisgebeathe*, meaning 'water of life' – an indication of how both the Scots and Irish regarded it. In the 18th and 19th centuries the drink could be spelt with or without an 'e', regardless of where it came from. Nowadays, however, 'whisky' is reserved for Scottish and Canadian whiskies and 'whiskey' for Irish and American ones.

did you know?

• Whisky almost certainly originated in Ireland and, as is often the case with alcohol, it was monks who played the major role in developing it. And it was probably Irish monks who, when they were trying to convert the Scots to Christianity, brought their 'water of life' with them to help the process along.

wine

Wine is an alcoholic drink made from fermented **grapes**. This entry describes still, unfortified table wines. Other types, such as **champagne**, wines that have been fortified with brandy (for example, **Madeira**, **port** and **sherry**) and fortified wines that have been flavoured with herbs, such as **vermouth** are described elsewhere. Other fruits, vegetables and flowers are sometimes used instead of grapes to make what are known as country wines.

There are three main steps in wine-making. First, the grapes are crushed to create a juice called must, to which sulphur dioxide and sometimes a little sugar are added. Then the must mixture is transferred to fermentation vats where yeast is added and the mixture left until it turns into alcohol. Finally, the resulting wine is run off and usually 'racked' several times (that is, transferred into fresh casks or vats, leaving the sediment, or lees, behind), before being fined (clarified) and/or filtered and bottled for maturing or drinking.

Of course, if it were that simple, all wine would probably taste the same. However, there are many variables – the climate and soil in which the grapes are grown, the grape varieties used, the fermentation

processes, the different winemakers – all of which contribute to the style of individual wines. Wines have an alcoholic strength of 8–14 percent (see **alcohol**).

Table wines come in three colours. Red wine is made from black grapes and gets its colour because the grape skins are kept on until the fermenting process is almost complete. Most are allowed to 'age', usually in oak barrels, for 1–2 years before being bottled. Some fine wines will continue to age in their bottles and only be ready for drinking after a further 5–10 years. There are a large number of red grape varieties used to make wine, including cabernet sauvignon, merlot, pinot noir and shiraz.

White wine is actually pale green or yellow in colour and is usually made from white grapes. The process is similar to that for red wine except that the grape skins are removed after crushing. Unlike red wine, white wines can be sweet, medium or dry. Sweeter grapes are used to make sweet and medium wines and fermentation is usually stopped before all the sugar has converted to alcohol, while for dry white wine, tarter grape must continues to ferment until all the sugar has gone. White wines are normally aged for less time than reds and some are aged *sur lie* (on the lees), which means they aren't racked before being bottled – this should produce a fresher, more flavoursome wine. Common white wine grape varieties include chardonnay, sauvignon blanc, riesling and sémillon.

Rosé wine is classically made from black grapes but the skins are allowed to remain on for only a day or so during fermentation; it is also now sometimes made by blending red and white wines to the correct colour.

Wines are made in warm to temperate climates around the world. France, Italy, Germany and Spain are the best and most prolific European producers, but it could be argued that New World countries such as the United States, Chile, Argentina,

Australia, New Zealand and South Africa are now overtaking them in both quality and availability. Most New World wines rely on the reputation of the winemaker or blender to identify them, but many European countries protect their better wines by law. In France, the highest general rating is *appellation contrôlée*, an accreditation that defines the area of origin of both the grapes and wine and confirms its quality. Italy, Spain and Germany have similar gradings called *Denominazione di origine controllata e garantita*, *Denominacion de origen* and *Qualitätswein* respectively.

using it Wine is normally served with food, although it can be drunk on its own, too. Whites and rosés are usually chilled for a few hours before serving, but red wines are nearly always served at room temperature. Very good red wines and some old ones will have sediment at the bottom of the bottle and the wine should be decanted to keep it there. All wines are better served in reasonably small quantities in largish glasses that will allow the flavours to 'breathe' and develop.

Wine doesn't just taste wonderful *with* food, it tastes good *in* food too. In savoury cooking, stocks, marinades and sauces are given depth and body by the addition of a glug or two of wine, and poultry, meat and fish can all benefit from being cooked with wine – think of the classic French *coq au vin*. In desserts, dry or sweet white wine or rosé are often used for macerating or poaching fruit. Both red and white wine can also be used to make punch and are sometimes mixed with other drinks such as *crème de cassis* (to make kir) and soda water (to make a spritzer).

word origin Wine comes from the Latin word *vinum*, meaning wine.

did you know?

• Vines have been cultivated for winemaking around the shores of the Mediterranean and Black Sea for thousands of years. The first real evidence comes from Georgia, where cuttings from vines have been found in a burial tomb that dates back to 3000BC. By New Kingdom Egypt, around 1352BC, the tomb of Tutankhamun was furnished with wine jars that not only showed how old the wine was (the earliest evidence of a vintage!), but also gave the names of the winemakers and sometimes specified the quality (two were rated 'very good quality').